Marketing:
Essentials

5e

Kenneth E. Clow

University of Louisiana, Monroe

Dana-Nicoleta Lascu

University of Richmond

▦ *Textbook Media Press*

The Quality Instructors Expect
At Prices Students Can Afford

Replacing Oligarch Textbooks Since 2004

For more information, contact

Textbook Media Press
1808 Dayton Avenue
Saint Paul, MN 55104

Or you can visit our Internet site at

http://www.textbookmedia.com

or write

info@textbookmedia.com

For permission to use material from this text
or product, submit a request online at
info@textbookmedia.com

Marketing: Essentials 5e

Kenneth E. Clow / Dana-Nicoleta Lascu

ISBN 978-0-9960954-4-0

Textbook Media Press is a Minnesota-based educational publisher.

We deliver textbooks and supplements with the quality instructors expect,
while providing students with media options at uniquely affordable prices.

All our publications are made in the U.S.A.

Dedication

This book is dedicated to my sons—Dallas, Wes, Tim, and Roy—who always provide

me with the encouragement to do another project, and especially to my wife, Susan, who was

patient and understanding of the long hours it took to complete this project.

—Kenneth E. Clow

This book is dedicated to the memory of Valeria and Doru Lupse,
and to my parents, Lucia and Damian Lascu.

—Dana-Nicoleta Lascu

About the Publisher

Here's the picture: textbooks cost too much. 65% of student consumers opted out of buying a college textbook due to high prices and 94% were concerned their decision to forgo purchasing the textbook would hurt their grade in the course.*

College textbooks often cost $200 or more. Sky-high prices from the oligarch publishing houses can undercut student performance and inflict long-term difficulty. They contribute to the student loan debt that's swamping so many of today's students, and, in some cases, they deter some students from buying a book at all.

Textbook Media offers an alternative path.

We specialize in acquiring the rights to under-served textbooks from the big publishers, and then revising them for our textbook media model. That means a quality textbook from proven authors—a textbook that was *developed by the oligarchs via peer reviews*, and includes a competitive instructor support package. So instructors get the quality they expect, while knowing they're helping to keep course costs reasonable.

Textbook *Renovation...*

- Proven, popular, and previously published (by one of the oligarchs).

- Business & Econ textbooks revised for our *textbook media model.*

- Harnessing technology to *deliver affordable student options.*

- Most student textbook options start at $24.95.

Since 2004, Textbook Media Press has been quietly contributing towards *making college more affordable.*

No bells. No whistles. Just practical publishing **with proven results**. With one million students served, our affordable textbooks have freed up significant education dollars to be invested towards tuition and/or fees.

Our typical line-up of textbook media options include:

- Online textbook
- Online textbook + PDF chapters
- Online textbook + loose-leaf (3-hole punched)
- Online textbook + one-color paperback
- Online textbook + color paperback

"This is incredible! Finally a fair way for students to get textbooks without spending a fortune!"
–Jocelyn, Student; Towson University

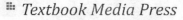

Textbook Media Press

The Quality Instructors Expect
At Prices Students Can Afford

Replacing Oligarch Textbooks Since 2004

"In the fall semester I had 177 students using your book. The experience was very good-- for me as an instructor and for my students. Their feedback was all positive—including the "online" and the book's content. I will have 500 students using Textbook Media this spring. Keep up the great work!
– Dave Johnson – U of Arkansas

*The U.S. PIRG Education Fund's 2014 Survey on Textbook Affordability

Brief Table of Contents

Detailed Table of Contents

Part Two: Foundations of Marketing Page 54

Chapter Three: Marketing Ethics, Regulations, and Social Responsibility Page 55

Chapter Four: Consumer Behavior Page 84

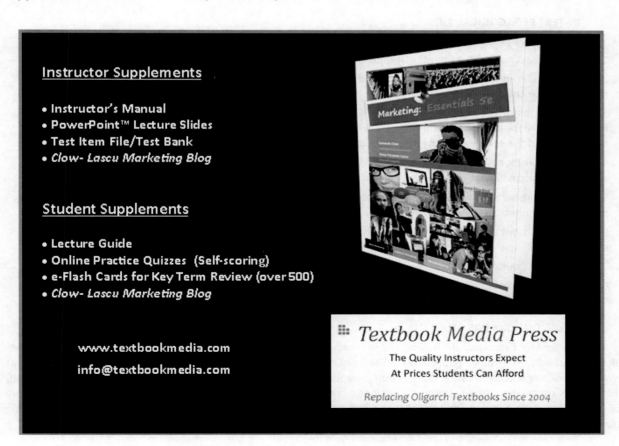

Preface

Through marketing, customers are identified and contacted using a variety of means. Everyone in an organization needs a basic understanding of marketing. *Marketing: Essentials 5e* was written to offer a basic understanding of and appreciation for marketing.

This text has a number of unique characteristics that set it apart. First, this is a condensed version of marketing principles. The authors have provided a concise, yet thorough, introduction to the field of marketing, presenting basic concepts and current theory along with memorable and up-to-date marketing practice examples.

Second, Dr. Lascu's international heritage and experience provide a higher level of understanding of marketing within the global environment. The international environment affects all companies, regardless of size, that often either sell to or purchase materials from international firms. As the world continues to shrink through advances in telecommunication technology and infrastructure, an understanding of marketing within a global context becomes even more critical.

Third, Dr. Clow's extensive business experience provides compelling examples, added understanding, and valuable perspectives of business-to-business marketing principles. With the majority of marketing dollars spent on trade promotions and business-to-business activities, it is essential that students understand the business-to-business marketing environment. Numerous examples and references aid students in their understanding of this sector of the market, as well as of marketing through channel structures from the producer to the end consumer.

Marketing: Essentials 5e reveals to students that marketing is both a science built on a complex theoretical framework and an art that engages marketing practitioners and consumers alike, while creating value for each. In the process of illustrating these two aspects of marketing, the text provides extensive and engaging applications and illustrations that together create an integrated marketing experience for students. The text examines current developments in marketing and other functional areas that have a profound impact on marketing and offers current examples from an operating environment that the Internet has redefined and profoundly affected.

IN-TEXT PEDAGOGICAL AIDS

Marketing: Essentials 5e enhances learning with the following pedagogical devices:

1. Each chapter opens with a Chapter Outline and a list of Chapter Objectives.

2. Smartly rendered four-color illustrations and photos throughout the online and PDF textbook versions clarify and enhance chapter concepts.

3. In all versions of the textbook (online, PDF and paperback), key terms are highlighted and defined. Key terms are also defined in the text margins and listed in alphabetical order at the end of each chapter. A glossary at the end of the each version of the textbook presents all the definitions alphabetically.

4. Links to an author-written blog are provided. The blog contains links to videos and articles that are relevant and current. Discussion questions are provided that can be used for class discussion or assignments.

5. A comprehensive Summary at the end of each chapter reviews the Chapter Objectives, and content appropriate to each objective is summarized.

6. Review Questions at the end of each chapter allow students to check their comprehension of the chapter's major concepts.

7. End-of-chapter Discussion Questions suggest possible essay topics or in-class discussion issues.

8. Cases at the end of each chapter provide a wide range of scenarios and real-life situations, along with questions to help guide student analysis.

MEDIA OPTIONS FOR STUDENTS

Marketing: Essentials 5e is available in multiple media versions; online, PDF, and in print (loose-leaf, one-color paperback, full-color paperback). The online version is bundled with all student purchases at www.textbookmedia.com because the publisher wants each student to have access to the online search function, which allows students to quickly locate discussions of specific topics throughout the text, as well as the option to buy the inexpensive, interactive quizzing tool that's embedded into the student's online version. It features self-scoring quizzes, and over 500 e-Flash cards with all the glossary terms.

ANCILLARY MATERIALS

Textbook Media is pleased to offer a competitive suite of supplemental materials for instructors using its textbooks. These ancillaries include a Test Bank, PowerPoint Slides, and an Instructor's Manual.

The Test Item Files have been created by the authors and includes 100-200 questions per chapter in a wide range of difficulty levels. They offer not only the correct answer for each question but also a rationale or explanation for the correct answer. The Test Item Files are available in computerized Test Banks that use Diploma Software from Wimba (part of Blackboard, Inc.) The software allows the instructor to easily create customized or multiple versions of a test and includes the option of editing or adding to the existing question bank.

A full set of PowerPoint Slides, written by the authors, is available for this text. This is designed to provide instructors with comprehensive visual aids for each chapter in the book. These slides include outlines of each chapter, highlighting important terms, concepts, and discussion points.

The Instructor's Manual for this book has also been written by the authors and offers suggested syllabi for 10- and 14-week terms; lecture outlines and notes; in-class and take-home assignments; recommendations for multimedia resources such as films and websites; and long and short essay questions and their answers, appropriate for use on tests. The 5th edition of the Instructor's Manual offers a case for each chapter that can be used for testing, review, discussion, or a writing assignment.

ACKNOWLEDGMENTS

We would like to express our gratitude to the staff at Textbook Media Press, who were the editorial team at Atomic Dog Publishing—our original publisher— for having the vision to put us together for this project. Even though we had never met or written together, these editors believed that we each had unique abilities that would allow us to be successful with this project.

Ken would like to thank his wife, Susan, for all of her devotion, faith, and patience. She was especially understanding of the short deadlines and the multiple projects Ken had to accomplish while working on this textbook. Dana would like to thank her family and students for their tolerance and inspiration.

About the Authors

Kenneth E. Clow is Professor of Marketing at the University of Louisiana at Monroe, where he holds the Biedenharn Endowed Chair in Business. He has a Ph.D. in marketing from the University of Arkansas and has spent time at Pittsburg State University and the University of North Carolina at Pembroke. Dr. Clow's primary research activities are in the areas of services marketing and advertising. He has published more than 200 articles and six textbooks, including a second edition of *Services Marketing* and a sixth edition of *Integrated Advertising, Promotion, and Marketing Communications*. His articles have been published in many journals, such as *Journal of Services Marketing, Journal of Professional Services Marketing, Marketing Health Services, Journal of Business Research, Journal of Marketing Education, Journal of Restaurant and Foodservices Marketing, Journal of Hospitality and Leisure Marketing*, and *Journal of Marketing Management*. Dr. Clow also operated and owned a contract cleaning service for over a decade.

Dana-Nicoleta Lascu is Professor of Marketing at the University of Richmond. She has a Ph.D. in marketing from the University of South Carolina, a master's in international management from Thunderbird, and a B.A. in English and French from the University of Arizona. She was a Fulbright Distinguished Chair in International Business at the Johannes Kepler University of Linz, Austria. She has published in *International Marketing Review, International Business Review, European Journal of Marketing, Journal of Business Research, Journal of Business Ethics,* and *Multinational Business Review*, among others and is the author of *International Marketing 4e* (with a fifth edition scheduled for a 2016 copyright). Dr. Lascu was a simultaneous and consecutive translator in English, French, and Romanian in Romania and Rwanda, and she worked as an international training coordinator in the United States, teaching managerial skills to civil servants from developing countries.

Part 1

Introduction

to

Marketing

Chapter 1

Scope and Concepts of Marketing

Learning Objectives

After studying
this chapter,
you should be able to:

1. Address the central role of marketing in the twenty-first century.

2. Define marketing and identify its key concepts.

3. Address the different marketing philosophies and explain them in view of the historical development of marketing.

4. Discuss the key elements of the societal marketing concept and the importance of these elements in meeting the needs of consumers, society, and the organization.

Chapter Outline

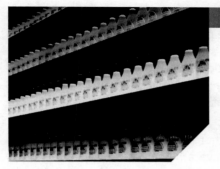

Figure 1-1: Sleek, colorful and super-clean displays with just the right lighting announce a shopping experience masterfully created through well-thought-out marketing strategies.

1-1 CHAPTER OVERVIEW

Successful companies, such as Procter & Gamble, Kraft, Microsoft, Siemens, and Apple, rely on marketing to ensure the success of their products and services in the marketplace. What is marketing? Many people—including some management professionals—think of marketing simply as advertising or selling. Indeed, promotion in the form of selling and advertising is omnipresent, arriving in neat packages in our mailboxes at home and at the office, resonating on our television screens and radios, popping up in our e-mails and Web sites, calling for our attention from billboards on the side of the road, and enchanting us with memorable slogans, such as *"I'm Lovin' It"* for McDonald's and *"Das Auto"* for Volkswagen. Promotion is part of marketing: it is an important marketing function.

Yet marketing is much more. It is an integral part of contemporary life. Marketing is pervasive, permeating many aspects of our daily existence, from our selection of the neighborhoods where we live, to the brands we purchase, to our choice of retailers and service providers, and to our selection of television and radio programs (see Figure 1-1). Marketing profoundly affects our decisions and features prominently in our lives.

This chapter presents marketing as an engine of the modern economy and as an important determinant of our high standard of living. Section 1-2 addresses the importance of marketing in the twenty-first-century economy, as a driver of economic growth and development, and as a vehicle for enhancing buyers' well-being and quality of life. Section 1-3 offers a definition of marketing and describes the important concepts of marketing. Section 1-4 examines the different marketing philosophies, and section 1-5 addresses the key elements of the societal marketing concept that focus on consumer and society needs.

1-2 THE IMPORTANCE OF MARKETING IN THE 21st CENTURY ECONOMY

Marketing constitutes an ever-growing, important driving force of today's modern society. In the United States there are more than 308 million consumers living in 110 million households, spending over $5 trillion on products and services, or two-thirds of the national **gross domestic product (GDP).** According to data published by the U.S. Bureau of Labor Statistics, retail salespeople and cashiers were occupations that combined make up nearly 6 percent of total U.S. employment, at 7.8 million. A significant number of all Americans are employed entirely or in part in assisting the marketing system to perform its functions. More than 30 million Americans work directly within the aggregate marketing system, with salespeople accounting for the largest segment.[1] There are almost 20 million business-to-business buyers, 3 million of which

> **Gross Domestic Product (GDP):** The sum of all goods and services produced within the boundaries of a country.

are retailers that resell to consumers and another half-million are wholesalers. Firms in general spend more than $200 billion per year on advertising; all these figures do not account for the marketing expenditures of professional practice, such as doctors, lawyers, and other service providers who must engage in marketing to attract and maintain their clients (see Figure 1-2).[2]

Figure 1-2: This advertisement for Ouachita Independent Bank points out that individuals should have confidence in their bank.

Source: Courtesy of Newcomer, Morris & Young.

The broad marketing system is integral to a society's economic system, offering employment and income for millions working in the marketing field, enabling them to be productive and earn money needed for consumption. In this process, private investments for the marketing system further assist in the development of the national infrastructure, in such areas as transportation, telecommunication, medical care, and finance. In turn, companies engaged in marketing pay taxes that further fund public programs. The system's mass-market efficiencies allow for lower costs, lower prices, and increased overall consumer access, fostering innovation that ultimately benefits consumption.[3]

Marketing enhances economic development. Nations with higher proportions of their populations involved in marketing and with a developed marketing system also have a higher GDP. It is important to note, however, that the roles of the marketing system differ by stage of economic development.[4] In the least developed countries, the focus of production is to satisfy basic needs, such as hunger and shelter; here, the limited excess production is traded in local markets. In developed, high-income countries, marketing is manifest in all aspects of production and consumption, and all marketing functions are essential for a company to survive—accounting for 50 cents of every dollar spent on consumer products.

Marketing also enhances consumers' well-being and quality of life. In many organizations, marketing practitioners represent consumers' interests, influencing the decisions of which products and services will be offered. The marketing system then informs consumers about the offerings through advertising campaigns and supports the delivery of goods and services in a manner that is convenient to consumers. Competition leads to a broader spectrum of product choices and to an improved distribution system that reduces product costs. These efforts further help improve the overall national infrastructure, such as telecommunications and transportation.[5]

As an important aspect of the daily life of a consumer, marketing informs the consumer about new products, their benefits, and their side effects. It offers choices of products, prices, and retailers. It entertains with well-executed commercials, it irritates with intrusive sounds that demand attention, and it attempts to satisfy many consumer needs and desires. What, then, is marketing?

1-3 DEFINING MARKETING

Marketing is described by management guru Peter Drucker as "the most effective engine of economic development, particularly in its ability to develop entrepreneurs and managers."[6] He defines marketing as a systematic business discipline that teaches us in an orderly, purposeful, and planned way to go about finding and creating customers; identifying and defining **markets**; and integrating customers' needs, wants, and preferences. Marketing is also the intellectual and creative capacity and skills of an industrial society to facilitate the design of new and better products and new distribution concepts and processes.[7]

> **Markets:**
> All of the actual and potential consumers of a company's products.

In this textbook, we will adhere to the definition of marketing developed by the American Marketing Association:[8]

> *"Marketing is the activity, set of institutions, and processes for creating, communicating, delivering, and exchanging offerings that have value for customers, clients, partners, and society at large."*
>
> -*American Marketing Association*

In the following sections, the definition of marketing is explained in more detail.

1-3a: Needs, Wants, and Demands

Successful marketers must be able to identify target consumers and their needs, wants, and demands. **Needs** are defined as basic human requirements: physiological needs, such as food, water and shelter; safety needs; social needs, such as affection and acceptance; self-esteem needs, such as the need for recognition; and self-actualization needs, such as the need for self-improvement. (A hierarchy of these needs will be addressed in Chapter 5.) Marketers attempt to address consumer needs with the different goods and services they offer.

Needs become wants when they are directed to a particular product. Wants are shaped by one's culture. Shelter in the United States typically consists of frame housing with Tyvek (synthetic) insulation. In much of Europe, it consists of brick or cement block homes, whereas in sub-Saharan Africa, it consists of round huts made out of straw and/or mud. In each format, the home meets the consumers' need for shelter. Self-esteem needs can be addressed in the United States and Europe through education or through luxury possessions, such as a home in the right neighborhood with the right furnishings (see Figure 1-3) or an automobile that qualifies as appropriate for the individual's aspirations. In sub-Saharan Africa, self-esteem needs are addressed by the number of cattle owned, and in many low-income countries, self-esteem is addressed by the number of servants helping with housework.

Figure 1-3: Inside an uptown home in Minneapolis where simple but upscale furnishings are selected for their fit to the room's purpose.

Wants become **demands** when they are backed by the ability to buy a respective good or service. Discerning adults with deep pockets can buy San Pelegrino mineral water, drive a BMW M-class, or take the Queen Mary 2 ultramodern gigantic cruise ship, self-touted as the grandest, most magnificent ocean liner ever built, on a transatlantic voyage. Health conscious moms who are pressed for time can purchase Amy's organic ready-made frozen food to feed their family.

1-3b: Value, Quality, and Satisfaction

Companies are successful because they provide products of value. That **value**, defined as the overall price given the quality of the product, is especially important to consumers when they first purchase the product. Consumers vary in how they define value. To one consumer, a good value may be a cheap price. To another consumer, the value may be a quality product at a moderate price. To a third consumer, value may be an expensive product that conveys an image of prestige. Although consumers define value differently, each consumer makes a purchase because, in the exchange process, he or she anticipates obtaining something of value.

Importantly, consumers monitor the price that other consumers pay for the same product and service and will readily switch to pay the lower price. In the past few years, deal websites such as Groupon, have been offering half-price deals to attract new buyers. In the process, some services using deal sites have alienated loyal consumers who have been paying full price.

> **Needs:**
> Basic human requirements:
> such as food and water.
>
> **Wants:**
> Needs that are directed at a
> particular product—for
> example, to meet the need for
> transportation, consumers
> may purchase an automobile
> or a bus ride.
>
> **Demands:**
> Wants backed by the ability to buy
> a respective good or service.
>
> **Value:**
> The overall price given the quality
> of the product; perceived as
> important for the first
> purchase decision.

Closely tied with the concept of value is quality, which is the overall product value, reliability, and the extent to which it meets consumers' needs. Perceived quality has the greatest impact on satisfaction. As noted, successful companies sell products that are perceived to be of high quality relative to the price being charged. The quality of food served at a four-star restaurant is higher than that in a value meal at McDonald's. But for the amount a consumer pays at McDonald's, it is perceived to be a quality meal. Indeed, fast-food restaurants are quickly bridging the quality gap by providing healthier food. For example, Hardee's sells a line of premium Thickburgers made from Angus beef, and Arby's is offering quality entrée salads and a line of low-carb wraps, all for a reasonable price of around $5.

Companies that do not provide quality that is reflective of the price may get someone to try the product once, but more than likely that consumer will not come back. Word about poor quality offerings travels fast through websites such as Yelp, TripAdvisor, and service and product specific sites such as Healthgrades for physicians. Products and service providers with low ratings tend to not fare well. Product recall and the manner in which companies handle recalls have a direct impact on the companies' bottom line. Frequent recalls for many of Ford's speed control–equipped super duty trucks, Excursions, E-450 vans, Explorers, and Mountaineers from the late 1990s until 2002, and the steering issues of the Ford Focus in 2014 have cast a doubt in the minds of the consumers as to the quality of the Ford brand.

Satisfaction is the key to whether consumers or businesses purchase again. If someone is satisfied with the taste and quality of a new flavor of potato chips, he or she will purchase them again. If not, that consumer will purchase another brand. The same is true for a business that is purchasing raw materials or components to manufacture a vacuum cleaner. The level of satisfaction is a function of the quality and perceived value and whether it adequately meets the need or want for which it was purchased.

> **Satisfaction:**
> A match between consumer expectations and good or service performance.

1-3c: Goods, Services, Ideas or Experience

As the definition of marketing states, the primary focus of marketing is on the creation and distribution of goods, services, ideas, and experiences that satisfy consumer needs and wants. **Goods** generally refer to tangible goods, such as cereals, automobiles, and clothing. In industrial marketing, equipment, component parts, and hospital uniforms are examples of goods. **Services** refer to intangible activities or benefits that individuals acquire but do not result in ownership. Airplane trips, a massage, a meal at a restaurant, and the preparation of a will are examples of services. **Ideas** and **experiences** refer to concepts and experiences that consumers perceive as valuable because they fulfill consumer needs and wants: Watching a movie, riding Dumbo at Disneyland, and going on a kayak trip in the heart of the Grand Canyon fulfill consumers' needs for adventure and exploration. See Table 1-1 for more examples of goods, services, ideas, and experiences.

> **Goods:**
> Tangible products, such as cereals, automobiles, and clothing.
>
> **Services:**
> Intangible activities or benefits that individuals acquire but that do not result in ownership, such as an airplane trip, a massage, or the preparation of a will.
>
> **Ideas:**
> Concepts that can be used to fulfill consumer needs and wants.
>
> **Experiences:**
> Personal experiences that consumers perceive as valuable because they fulfill consumer needs and wants.
>
> **Products:**
> Any offering that can satisfy consumer needs and wants.

Table 1-1: Goods, Services, Ideas or Experience?	
1.	A tennis racquet is a... **good.**
2.	A beauty salon provides a... **service.**
3.	A political candidate is an example of... **idea.**
4.	A dentist provides a... **service.**
5.	A trip to the beach is an... **experience.**
6.	Toothpaste is a... **good.**
7.	A college textbook is a... **good.**
8.	A college education is an example of an... **idea.**
9.	A haircut is a... **service.**
10.	Bungee jumping is an... **experience.**

A restaurant is a service—or is it? Take for example the Twin Peaks restaurant chain. It claims to be a man cave, serving beer at cold temperatures and showing local sports, including boxing matches, on crisp, high definition screens. The wait staff – the Twin Peaks Girls, marketed as the playful but barely clad girl next door – are trained to make sure everyone feels special. Twin Peaks follows in the style of Hooters, a similar restaurant chain whose primary distinction rests with its equally minimally dressed wait staff, the Hooters Girls.

In this text, goods, services, ideas, and experiences will be collectively referred to as **products**. Products represent the first P of marketing. Marketing has four Ps that jointly shape the marketing strategy for a particular brand, as the chapters that follow illustrate.

1-3d: Exchanges and Transactions, Relationships and Markets

Exchanges and transactions refer to obtaining a desired good or service in exchange for something else of value. Exchanges involve at least two parties that mutually agree on the desirability of the traded items. Shelter in New York City can be obtained by renting a tiny one-bedroom apartment in one of the city's expensive condos in exchange for about $4,000 a month, renting a room at a hotel in Times Square in exchange for about $250 per night, renting a room at a hotel in Queens for about $150 per night, or going to a homeless shelter. Other examples of exchanges involve voting for a particular political candidate for a promise of lower taxes or offering donations to charity in exchange for the comfort of knowing that others will be better off as a result. All of these are examples of transactions in which an exchange of something of value was given in return for something else of perceived equal value.

> **Exchanges and Transactions:** Obtaining a desired good or service in exchange for some-thing else of value; involving at least two parties that mutually agree on the desirability of the traded items.

The exchange process is central to marketing. Ultimately, an exchange takes place between consumers and manufacturers or service providers. Consumers pay money for the goods and services produced by manufacturers or service providers. In reality, the exchange is more complicated because it usually involves a complex distribution process and middlemen:

- The first level of the exchange takes place between the manufacturer and a wholesaler: The wholesaler buys the product from the manufacturer.
- A second exchange takes place between that wholesaler and another wholesaler who is closer to the consumer; there could be several levels of wholesalers in the distribution chain, and at each level, an exchange will take place.
- Yet another exchange takes place between the wholesaler and the retailer where the target consumer will purchase the product.
- The final exchange takes place between the consumer and the retailer when the consumer pays the retailer for the product.

At each level, **products** (goods, services, ideas, or experiences) are exchanged for a monetary sum. Each product has a price (cost) at each level of distribution, with the consumer paying the final price for the good or service at the end of the distribution channel. **Price** is the second P of marketing.

At all these levels, important relationships of mutual benefit develop. Consumers develop loyalty or preference for the brand or the retailer. The retailer develops relationships with wholesalers, and wholesalers develop relationships with manufacturers. The manufacturer nurtures a relationship with all the parties involved in marketing its products and with the final consumer. This is known as **relationship marketing**, which is defined as the process of developing and nurturing relationships with the parties participating in the transactions involving a company's products. The parties involved in the exchange are part of the distribution process; distribution is referred to as **place**—the third P of marketing.

> **Relationship Marketing:** The process of developing and nurturing relationships with all the parties participating in the transactions involving a company's products; the development of marketing strategies aimed at enhancing relationships in the channel.

The manufacturer develops these relationships by communicating with the wholesalers, retailers, and especially, with its market. A market is the set of all the actual and potential buyers of the company's products whose needs can be satisfied with the respective products. The company needs to understand its markets to produce goods that address the markets' needs and wants and to communicate with them effectively about their products. Communication with the market is accomplished through promotion in the form of advertising, personal selling, sales promotion, or public relations. Promotion is the fourth P of marketing (see Figure 1-4).

Figure 1-4: Banks today are advertising heavily. In Europe, it is not unusual for banks to advertise their services on the side of buses.

Hence, product, place, price, and promotion—the four Ps of marketing—are used to address the needs and wants of the final consumer. The four Ps of marketing are described in Figure 1-5.

Figure 1–5: The 4 *Ps* of Marketing

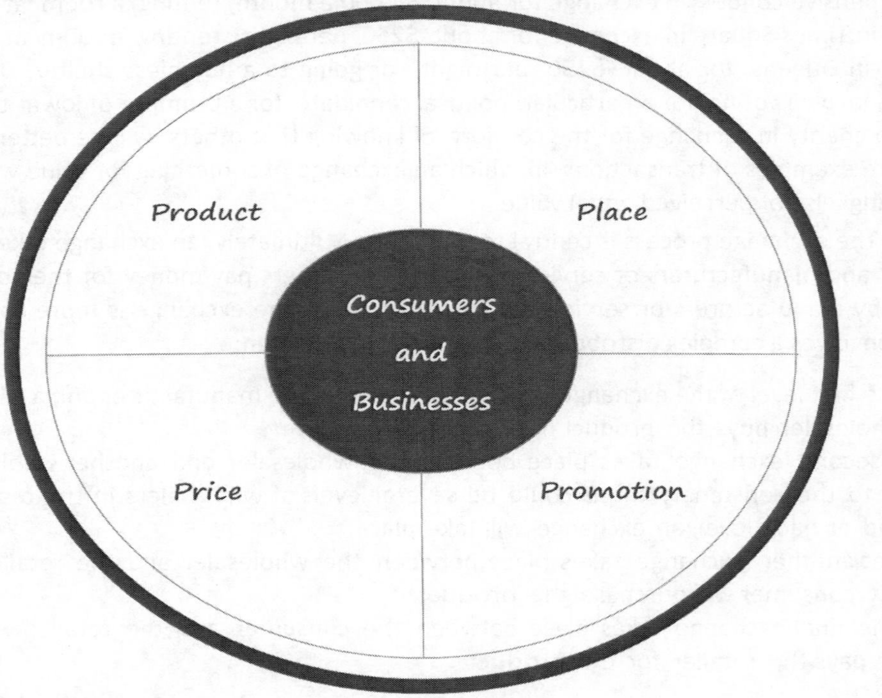

Product:
Any offering that can satisfy consumer needs and wants; products include goods (tangible products), services, ideas, and experiences; the first P of marketing

Price:
The amount of money necessary to purchase a product.; the second P of marketing.

Place:
The physical movement of products from the producer to individual or organizational consumers and the transfer of ownership and risk; the third P of marketing.

Promotion:
All forms of external communications directed toward consumers and businesses with an ultimate goal of developing customers; the forth P of marketing.

1-4 MARKETING PHILOSOPHIES

Firms can opt for one of five different approaches to marketing. The company could either:

1. Place a heavy emphasis on producing the best product it can, hoping someone will buy it.

2. Reduce costs through improved manufacturing processes and technological development, thus selling its products at a lower cost than its competition.

3. Put a heavy emphasis on selling its products to consumers and businesses, striving to convince customers of the superiority of its product.

4. Find out what customers want first and then develop a product that meets that want.

5. Produce and market the product in the way that will best benefit society.

1-4a: The Product/Production Concepts

Production Concept:
A marketing philosophy that assumes consumers prefer products that are easily accessible and inexpensive.

Product Concept:
A marketing philosophy that assumes consumers prefer products that are of the highest quality and optimal performance.

The **production concept** assumes that consumers prefer products that are easily accessible and inexpensive. The **product concept** assumes that consumers prefer products that are of the highest quality and optimal performance. For the company, product and production concepts both focus strategies on the production process and delivery, devoting significant resources to research, product development, manufacturing, and engineering. Artesyn Technologies is a manufacturer of power supplies. The firm's focus is on both the product and production concepts. In terms of the product concept, Artesyn's goal is to manufacture better-quality products. In terms of the production concept, Artesyn is concerned with faster production time and lower production costs, with just-in-time technology.

Certainly, there are trade-offs between a production orientation where the goal is to cut costs and a product orientation where the goal is to provide a high-quality product. The production orientation works well for mass-market service organizations, such as fast-food providers and retailers; for people-processing government agencies; and in developing countries in general, as consumers in low-income countries cannot afford high-priced products.

Other organizations, such as medical and dental practices and law firms, may also attempt to optimize their use of resources. However, their primary goal is to provide the highest-quality service using the latest techniques based on the latest information available in the industry itself. Given this goal, they are more likely to focus on the product first and production second. As such, they are guided primarily by the product concept but still are cognizant of the production process and costs.

Firms at the forefront of technology introducing new products to the market are most likely to adopt the product concept. Pharmaceutical firms developing drugs that revolutionize the treatment of formerly incurable illnesses and manufacturers developing the latest communication and computing technology tend to have a product focus.

However, even these firms have to fend off competition and broaden their customer base when patents expire and competitors appropriate their new technology and know-how. At that point, firms with a product orientation are likely to shift to a production orientation. For example, patent expiration presented challenges to Claritin, a popular allergy medicine. Competitors were allowed to offer generic allergy medicine using its identical formula at significantly lower cost. As a result, Claritin had to adapt its entire marketing strategy by obtaining approvals for the brand's over-the-counter distribution and offering it to the mass market for a lower price.

The main disadvantage of the product and production orientations is that the focus is on the product and production processes, rather than the consumer. It is manufacturing, engineering, research, and development that dictate what products should be made, rather than the preferences and interests of the final consumer.

1-4b: The Selling Concept

The **selling concept** assumes that when left alone, consumers will not normally purchase the products the firm is selling or will not purchase enough products. Consumers, according to the selling concept, need to be aggressively targeted and approached with personal selling and advertising to be persuaded to purchase the company's products. Although firms may focus on aggressive selling when they have excess inventories at the end of the year or when new models must replace the old on the retail floor, companies are more likely to embrace the selling concept when their products are unsought goods, such as time-shares and insurance services.

In the process of selling time-shares, companies such as Fairfield Resorts identify prospective buyers, approach them with an offer of two nights close to the resort location, and then require those who choose to take advantage of the offer to spend about two hours in a hard-sell environment. Similarly, Hilton Grand Vacations Company is aggressively targeting gay travelers offering attractive vacation packages to bring in high-traveling and high-spending gay tourists to their resorts to then sell them on timeshares.[9]

Even mainstream department store retailers, such as Macy's and Lord and Taylor's, adopt the selling concept toward the end of the year, just before the Thanksgiving holiday. At that time, they aggressively promote their merchandise, increasing their advertising in local newspapers and sending direct mail to their target consumers. Mailers advertise the ''Biggest SALE of the year, look for our lowest prices of the season'' in large white letters against a bright red background. These communications also offer different types of promotions, such as coupons worth 15 percent off total purchase price, an all-day shopping pass, a zero percent finance charge, and other attractive deals. In their deluge of communications, retailers are often assisted by manufacturers, who offer additional promotional incentives to consumers, which reinforces the selling strategy (see Figure 1-6).

Market Pantry

Screenshot

family favorites, without the big brand price.

Figure 1-6: Retailers often promote their own brands. Here, Target promotes its own Market Pantry brand.

In both the time-share and the retailer examples, the focus is on persuading consumers to want products, rather than offering them the products that best fit their needs and interests. In the case of the time-shares, consumers might respond to the offer only to obtain the subsidized stay at the hotel or the loyalty points. In the case of the retailers' holiday blitz, consumer response will be short term and most likely focused on the promotions offered.

1-4c: The Marketing Concept

The **marketing concept** assumes that a company can compete more effectively if it first researches consumers' generic needs, wants, and preferences, as well as product- or service-related attitudes and personal interests. With this knowledge of the consumer, the firm is able to deliver the goods and services that consumers want more efficiently and effectively than the competition. This marketing philosophy entails a company-wide consumer focus across all functional areas.

At Arby's, adopting the marketing concept is not limited to the product offering or the restaurant ambience. Arby's restaurants are located conveniently to target consumers, typically close to shopping centers that are frequented by its target market. Its prices are somewhat higher than those at a McDonald's or Burger King. Sandwiches, for example, cost more, but they are marketed as being of superior quality and match the taste desires of older Americans. Convenient locations, appropriate pricing, and well-targeted promotions are indicative of a consumer focus, hence reflecting a marketing concept philosophy. Following in its footsteps, McDonald's is now offering a McCafé line of smoothies and coffee-based beverages, and KFC (Yum! Brands) is testing a new fast-casual concept. KFC Eleven, in Louisville, Kentucky, is offering better value to its customers through offering a more urban look to its customers facility, high-ceiling roofs, limited seating, and higher quality food served in real dishes.[10]

The marketing concept has five principal components that are essential to a company's performance. They are: a market orientation, an integrated marketing approach, a focus on consumer needs, a value-based philosophy, and an organizational goal orientation—as illustrated in Figure 1-7. Each will be discussed in detail in Section 1-5.

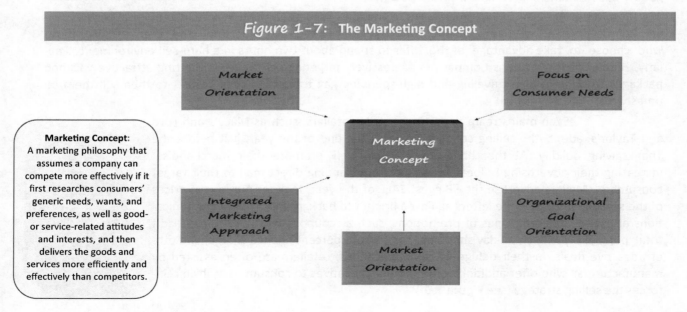

Figure 1-7: The Marketing Concept

Market Orientation

Focus on Consumer Needs

Marketing Concept

Integrated Marketing Approach

Organizational Goal Orientation

Market Orientation

Marketing Concept: A marketing philosophy that assumes a company can compete more effectively if it first researches consumers' generic needs, wants, and preferences, as well as good- or service-related attitudes and interests, and then delivers the goods and services more efficiently and effectively than competitors.

The marketing concept is superior to the selling concept in two primary ways. The outcome of a focus on aggressive selling leads to short-term results (sales), whereas adopting the marketing concept leads to a long-term relationship with the customer. Selling has as its primary goal increasing sales volume, whereas the marketing concept has as its primary goal addressing customer needs and wants. **Figure 1-8** illustrates the differences between a selling philosophy and a marketing philosophy.

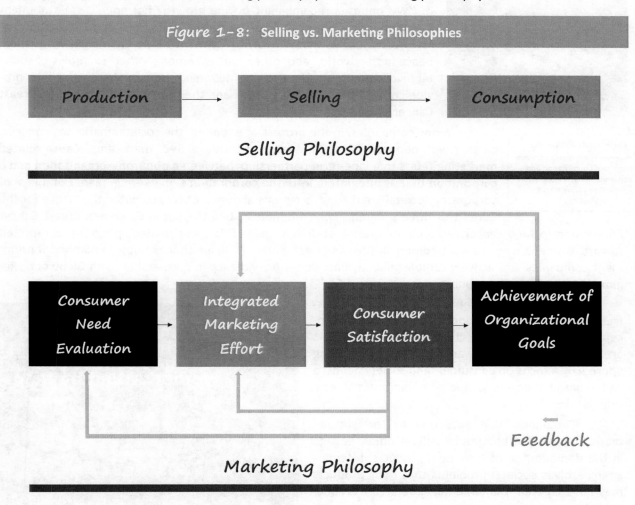

Figure 1-8: Selling vs. Marketing Philosophies

1-4d: The Societal Marketing Concept

The **societal marketing concept** assumes that the company will have an advantage over competi-tors if it applies the marketing concept in a manner that maximizes society's well-being. Presently compa-nies are expected to be good citizens of society and to build societal considerations into their marketing endeavors while they pursue organizational profit goals. Thus, the societal marketing concept assumes that a company can compete more effectively if it first researches consumers' generic needs, wants, and preferences and product- or service-related attitudes and personal interests and then delivers the products and services more efficiently and effectively than com-petitors in a manner that maximizes society's well-being.

> **Societal Marketing Concept:** A marketing philosophy that assumes the company will have an advantage over competitors if it applies the marketing concept in a manner that maximizes society's well-being.

Arby's has established an exemplary record of following the societal mar-keting concept through its social involvement. The Arby's Foundation supports Big Brothers and Big Sisters of America, the Boys & Girls Clubs of America, and various other causes through donations from franchisees, suppliers, employees, customers, and sponsors. It also sponsors initiatives such as the Arby's Charity Tour, a series of

amateur golf tournaments benefiting its national charities, and local youth mentoring organizations in cities where the tournaments take place. Ben & Jerry's, a Unilever subsidiary, positions itself as a supporter of social causes. The company ensures that none of its ice cream products are made with milk from hormone-fed cows and takes a strong stand against it. "We oppose recombinant bovine growth hormone" is a statement found on most of the Ben & Jerry's packages. It also supports environmental efforts, such as those involving Vermont's Lake Champlain Watershed, peace in the world, and other causes. Among other examples of societal involvement are the Ronald McDonald House Charities, which provide comfort to children in need and their families, and the Avon Breast Cancer Crusade.

> **Cause-Related Marketing:**
> A long-term partnership between a non-profit organization and a corporation that is integrated into the corporation's marketing plan.

Many companies, in the process of adopting the societal marketing concept, partner with nonprofit firms to engage in cause-related marketing. **Cause-related marketing** refers to a long-term partnership between a nonprofit organization and a corporation that is integrated into the corporation's marketing plan. Examples of corporate societal marketing programs abound. BMW promoted the "Drive for the Cure" test drive program, which donates $1 to the Susan G. Komen Breast Cancer Foundation to fund cancer research for every test-driven mile. This cause-related program is targeted toward women, who are not traditionally BMW's target market.[11] In another example, a number of prominent companies are actively campaigning against domestic violence in partnership with Glenwood Regional Medical Center in Louisiana (see Figure 1-9).

The societal marketing concept can be illustrated as a modified version of the marketing concept (refer to Figure 1-7). Its principal components are a market orientation, an integrated marketing approach, a focus on consumer and society needs, a value-based philosophy, and an organizational goal orientation.

Companies that subscribe to the societal marketing concept philosophy will, at times, engage in the **demarketing** of their own products if demarketing solves societal problems that their products may have created. Demarketing is defined as reducing the demand for a company's own products if that is in the interest of society. Philip Morris, for example, uses an expensive, sleek newspaper insert that directs consumers to its Web site to find information on the serious effects of smoking, quitting smoking, cigarette ingredients, and talking to children about not smoking. The insert has articles such as "Women and Smoking: A Report of the Surgeon General" and "National Cancer Institute—Low-Tar Cigarettes: Evidence Does Not Indicate a Benefit to Public Health." In one of the articles, the pamphlet states: "Philip Morris U.S.A. believes that the conclusions of public health officials concerning environmental tobacco smoke, also known as secondhand smoke, are sufficient to warrant measures that regulate

> **Demarketing:**
> A company strategy aimed at reducing demand for its own products to benefit society.

Figure 1-9: This advertisement, created by French Creative Group, highlights the problems with domestic violence. The ad was sponsored by French Creative, the News-Star, TV8, Glenwood Regional Medical Center, Philip Morris Company, and the YMCA.

Source: Courtesy of French Creative Group, Monroe, LA.

smoking in public spaces'' (p. 13).[12] In effect, through this brochure, Philip Morris is instructing its own target market to reduce demand for its product or to quit smoking.

Demarketing for vice products, such as cigarettes and alcohol, although focusing the messages on vulnerable populations, such as children, the elderly, and the poor, demonstrates social concern on the part of the company and may diffuse public scrutiny of the sponsor's products and practices.

1-4e: The History of Marketing Philosophies

The product/production concept, the selling concept, and the marketing concept can be traced historically to the **production era**, the **sales era**, and the **marketing era**—the periods when the respective philosophies were dominant. The production era, between 1870 and 1930, was characterized by firms focusing their attention on physical production and the production process. Firms attempted to fit products within their production capabilities, rather than focusing on customer needs. Output consisted of limited product lines, and because demand exceeded supply, competition was minimal. Retailers and wholesalers were only of peripheral concern because the products practically sold themselves.[13]

> **Production Era:**
> Period between 1870 and 1930, when the primary focus of marketing was on producing the best products possible at the lowest price.
>
> **Sales Era:**
> Period between 1930 and 1950, when the primary focus of marketing was on selling.
>
> **Marketing Era:**
> Period from 1950 until the present, when the primary focus of marketing shifted to the needs of consumers and society.

Production efficiency led to a new phenomenon: overproduction. Companies turned to marketing professionals to sell their products during the sales era, between 1930 and 1950. The sales era was characterized by a focus on selling, which was based on the assumption that if the customer were left alone, he or she would not purchase the product or would not purchase enough products. Also supply exceeded demand. With excess supply, companies had to persuade consumers and other businesses to buy their brand instead of the competitors'.

In the 1950s, scholars were concerned that marketers were not paying enough attention to the customers' needs and wants. Thus the marketing concept emerged as the dominant marketing paradigm. It was then agreed that the main task of the marketing function should not be ''to be skillful in making the customer do what suits the interests of the business ... but to be skillful in conceiving and then making the business do what suits the interests of the customer.''[14]

The marketing concept is the dominant philosophy for today's successful companies, such as Unilever, McDonald's, and Apple (see Figure 1-10).

Figure 1-10: Apple's success is attributed to its use of the marketing philosophy.

1-4f: Beyond the Marketing Philosophies: Avoiding Marketing Myopia

The danger of the product, production, and selling concepts is that they may lead to marketing myopia.[15] This term is attributed to Theodore Levitt, one of the most notable early marketing theorists, who noticed that marketers at the time (in the 1950s) were ignoring an important market—seniors. The term marketing myopia is defined here as the tendency of marketing efforts to focus on products, production, or sales and ignore specific consumer needs or important markets.

Even companies that embrace the societal marketing concept could experience marketing myopia. A case in point is the limited attention, relative to potential, that certain ethnic markets receive in the United States. Ethnic Americans—African Americans, Hispanic Americans, and Asian Americans—have a spending power of more than \$1 trillion; the projected growth of these three ethnic populations is 115.2 million by the year 2020.[16] And yet for mainstream marketing, they primarily represent little more than an afterthought.[17] Marketers need to redefine their target markets with a more precise focus, strengthening their advertising presence in ethnic media vehicles, such as cable channels like Telemundo and Black Entertainment Television and magazines such as *Latin*, *Vibe*, and *A*, to gain both the recognition and loyalty of these markets. Indeed, even in the general media, a full racial palette and representation is still rare.

These examples illustrate that even if companies do focus on consumers and society, they need to follow developments in the marketplace and give due focus to traditionally overlooked consumer segments, such as the elderly and ethnic markets.

1-5 KEY ELEMENTS OF THE SOCIETAL MARKETING CONCEPT

Marketing managers today understand that their firms can no longer afford to limit their focus on the needs of their consumers and the needs of their organizations. The marketing concept alone cannot lead to optimal firm performance in the marketplace. As corporate citizens of society and as employers, companies must meet the needs of their consumers and society, as well as those of their employees and other relevant stakeholders, and achieve their own organizational goals in the process.

1-5a: A Market Orientation and an Integrated Marketing Approach

Today, marketing managers agree on the importance of a firm-wide focus on customer needs and on delivering high quality to consumers and other businesses in the process of achieving company objectives (i.e., on the importance of adopting a market orientation). A **market orientation** should be part of the company culture. The company should systematically seek marketing information at the organization level; disseminate that information to the other departments, such as finance, research and development, engineering, manufacturing, and purchasing; and ensure that the entire organization can respond to this information in a manner that best meets customers' needs.[18] A market orientation is defined as a company wide culture creating the necessary behaviors for delivering superior value to buyers.[19] It is a systematic quest for and dissemination of information across departments and subsequent organization-wide response in a manner that best addresses customers' needs and preferences. A market orientation also requires that the marketing function has considerable prominence in company-wide decision making, with the marketing vice president occupying a senior position in the firm.[20] In other words, a marketing orientation calls for an integrated marketing approach.

> **Market Orientation:**
> A firm-wide focus on customer needs and on delivering high quality to consumers in the process of achieving company objectives.

Adopting a marketing orientation necessitates top management commitment. Without the involvement and commitment of top management, it would be difficult to create an environment in which information is openly and systematically disseminated across departments, where organizational response is aimed at delivering quality goods and services to customers, thereby increasing customer satisfaction.

Like manufacturers, retailers also have to adapt to meet the needs of consumers and to adopt a market orientation to succeed. Especially today, in the Information Age, consumers want to find the merchandise they need in stock quickly and at an attractive price. To meet this need, retailers are learning more about their consumers' needs and desires by using a tactic called **data mining**, which is the systematic data analysis procedure of compiling personal, pertinent, and actionable information about the purchasing habits of current and potential consumers.[21] Through data mining, retailers hope to:

> **Data Mining:**
> The process of compiling personal, pertinent, actionable information about the purchasing habits of current and potential consumers.

- Increase sales from their existing customers and hence solidify and increase market share.
- Determine purchase habits of consumers with regard to price preferences, sale or regular prices, fashion, and size.
- Find out who customers are and what, where, and how often they buy (see Figure 1-11).
- Obtain information about products, services, and marketing practices of Competition.

Figure 1-11: This sign for the Eastern Shore Pottery is placed just one mile before the store, on the main highway that leads to it, so that consumers who drive by can quickly decide to take a break and look at the merchandise. Courtesy of Sting-Ray's.

1-5b A Focus on Consumer Needs and the Needs of Society

For optimal performance in the marketplace, marketers need to address consumer needs and wants more effectively than competitors. That is, they have to employ a marketing strategy using the four Ps of marketing in a manner that optimally addresses consumer needs. This requires that a company:

- Offers the goods or services that best satisfy consumer needs.
- Offers a price the consumer perceives as fair in return for the value received.
- Makes the product available at retailers that are conveniently located close to the consumer.
- Promotes its marketing efforts through vehicles that effectively reach the target consumer.

For example, the Gap is successful in its marketing campaign. The company has undertaken substantial research of its target market, younger consumers, and provides fashions that appeal to them, being careful to follow the trends that are popular with this market. The Gap combines a relaxed shopping environment with bold brand expressions, which enhances sales associates' ability to provide outstanding service. Its goal is to make every customer's experience the best of any retailer.[22]

The Gap advertises using lively, bold ads in fashion magazines and on television during prime time. Gap stores are conveniently located in regional malls, within easy access of target consumers. And Gap brand prices are in line with consumers' ability to pay—for example, about $30 for a sweater and $50 for a pair of jeans. The Gap website also serves as a venue for promoting the store to consumers and a retail venue that offers convenience at a fair price. For orders over $100, the Gap offers free shipping.

The Gap's social marketing endeavors resonates well with its target market. Its donations focus on the Boys & Girls Clubs of America and the Lorraine Monroe Leadership Institute, both of which aim to help students to develop self-esteem, stay in school, and succeed academically so that they can lead rewarding and fulfilling lives. The Gap emphasizes the importance of a code of conduct that it requires of its vendors and other distributors, such as compliance with local labor laws, working conditions, and the environment; and expectations regarding wages, child labor, safety, and respect of the right of workers to unionize. Finally, it communicates to employees the importance of reducing waste in its packaging materials and of recycling and purchasing products that contain high percentages of recycled material.[23]

1-5c: A Value-Based Philosophy

> **Value-based Philosophy:**
> A philosophy that focuses on customers, ensuring that their needs are addressed in a manner that delivers a product of high quality and value, leading to consumer satisfaction.

A **value-based philosophy** is essential to organizational success. Companies with a value-based philosophy ensure that their consumers' needs are addressed in a manner that delivers a good or service of high quality and value that ultimately leads to consumer satisfaction, and it does so while also enhancing consumers' and society's quality of life. In fact, successful companies that adopt a value-based philosophy are also likely to invest in society, primarily for altruistic reasons that benefit society, not the company—even if, ultimately, there is an expectation of commercial return.[24]

Product quality, product value, and consumer satisfaction are interrelated. One measure that addresses both quality and consumer satisfaction is the American Consumer Satisfaction Index, a national economic indicator of the quality of goods and services from companies producing about one-third of the national GDP. The following are the dimensions related to consumer satisfaction,[25] and they will be further addressed in Chapter 9, which discusses the gap theory related to the discrepancy between expectations and performance:

1. Customer expectations occur when consumers anticipate product performance based on their experiences, on information received from the media, and on information from other consumers. Expectations influence the evaluation of good or service quality and predict how the good or service will perform on the market.

2. Quality refers to overall product quality, reliability, and the extent to which it meets consumers' needs. Perceived quality has the greatest impact on satisfaction (see Figure 1-12).

3. Value refers to the overall price given the quality of the product; perceived value is important in the purchase decision.

4. Consumer complaints are measured as the percentage of consumers that report a problem with a good or service; complaints are related to dissatisfaction.

5. Consumer retention refers to the likelihood to purchase the product in the future.

lasers to preserve lifestyles

Figure 1-12:
This newspaper advertisement by Haik Humble Eye Center highlights the importance of quality in terms of using the "most advanced eye surgery" techniques.

Source: Sartor Associates, Inc., for Haik Humble Eye Center.

The new Haik Humble Eye Center has added the area's most advanced eye surgery center. Our ophthalmologists use three different lasers to treat diabetic retinopathy, macular degeneration, and clouding after cataract surgery. Plus, LASIK continues to be a reliable option to reduce or eliminate dependence on contacts and glasses!
Call 325-2610 today to get your free booklet: "What You Need to Know About Cataracts." Hurry! Supplies are limited.

1804 N. 7th Street • West Monroe • 325-2610

Over time, the American Consumer Satisfaction Index has demonstrated that companies rating highly are more profitable and have greater shareholder value. These companies are in a better position to reach their organizational goals.

Goods manufacturers, service providers, retailers, and wholesalers frequently conduct consumer satisfaction surveys to assess their own performance. Historically, consumer satisfaction has been defined as a match between consumer expectations and good or service performance:

- If a product or service performs better than expected, then consumers are likely to be satisfied with it. If satisfied, consumers are likely to purchase the good or service in the future.

- If performance matches expectations, consumers are somewhat satisfied.

- Psychologists refer to this as "satisficing" or "neutrality"—meaning that the consumer is satis-fied but would switch to another good or service without much persuasion.

- If expectations are greater than performance—that is, product performance is not up to consum-er expectations—then consumers are likely to be dissatisfied with the good or service and may never purchase it again. These consumers are expected to engage in negative word-of-mouth communications about the good or service and brand or firm switching behavior.

To understand these concepts, take the test in Table 1-2 (next page) to evaluate your recent experi-ence with a retail website.

Table 1-2: Web Site Satisfaction Self-Test

How would you rate the retailer Web site you have used most recently? Take the following test.
Indicate the extent to which you agree or disagree with the following statements by circling one of the following numbers:

5 = you strongly agree, 4 = you agree, 3 = you neither agree nor disagree, 2 = you disagree, 1 = you strongly disagree
Please answer EVERY question!

Expectations		Performance The most recent retailer Web site you visited:	
Have an attractive design and other visuals.	5 4 3 2 1	Have an attractive design and other visuals.	5 4 3 2 1
Have little clutter.	5 4 3 2 1	Have little clutter.	5 4 3 2 1
Have few or no banners.	5 4 3 2 1	Have few or no banners.	5 4 3 2 1
Are easy to navigate and allow rapid access to the different pages and links.	5 4 3 2 1	Are easy to navigate and allow rapid access to the different pages and links.	5 4 3 2 1
Are easy to access day or night.	5 4 3 2 1	Are easy to access day or night.	5 4 3 2 1
Require customers to fill in only a minimum of necessary information.	5 4 3 2 1	Require customers to fill in only a minimum of necessary information.	5 4 3 2 1
Allow customers to reach a customer service center at all times.	5 4 3 2 1	Allow customers to reach a customer service center at all times.	5 4 3 2 1
Have a customer service center that is always willing to help clients.	5 4 3 2 1	Have a customer service center that is always willing to help clients.	5 4 3 2 1
Have a customer service center that will promptly respond to customer inquiries.	5 4 3 2 1	Have a customer service center that will promptly respond to customer inquiries.	5 4 3 2 1
Have a customer service center that is consistently courteous.	5 4 3 2 1	Have a customer service center that is consistently courteous.	5 4 3 2 1
Have a knowledgeable customer service center that can address client questions.	5 4 3 2 1	Have a knowledgeable customer service center that can address client questions.	5 4 3 2 1
Let consumers know exactly when they will receive their products.	5 4 3 2 1	Let consumers know exactly when they will receive their products.	5 4 3 2 1
Deliver their products when they promise to do so.	5 4 3 2 1	Deliver their products when they promise to do so.	5 4 3 2 1
Deliver the quality products that are accurately described on the Web site.	5 4 3 2 1	Deliver the quality products that are accurately described on the Web site.	5 4 3 2 1
Sell products at a fair price.	5 4 3 2 1	Sell products at a fair price.	5 4 3 2 1
Allow you to compare prices with other sites.	5 4 3 2 1	Allow you to compare prices with other sites.	5 4 3 2 1
Show a sincere interest in solving customers' problems.	5 4 3 2 1	Show a sincere interest in solving customers' problems.	5 4 3 2 1
Protect customers' personal information.	5 4 3 2 1	Protect customers' personal information.	5 4 3 2 1
Offer safe transactions.	5 4 3 2 1	Offer safe transactions.	5 4 3 2 1
Offer customers personal attention when needed.	5 4 3 2 1	Offer customers personal attention when needed.	5 4 3 2 1
Have the customers' interests at heart.	5 4 3 2 1	Have the customers' interests at heart.	5 4 3 2 1
Tailor their offering based on customer preferences and/or purchase history.	5 4 3 2 1	Tailor their offering based on customer preferences and/or purchase history.	5 4 3 2 1
Add the circled numbers in the expectations column: _____		Add the circled numbers in the expectations column: _____	

Subtract the expectations score from the performance score. If the number is positive, you are satisfied with the Web site and will continue to use it. If the number is zero, you are sort of satisfied (psychologists refer to this as satisficing—meaning that you are satisfied but could switch to another site without extensive persuasion). If the number is negative, expectations are greater than performance; you are somewhat dissatisfied with the Web site and may not use it again.

Source: Adapted from Dana-Nicoleta Lascu and Kenneth Clow, *"The Website Interaction Satisfaction Scale,"* working paper.

1-5d: An Organizational Goal Orientation

The ultimate organizational goal is creating profit for the company and wealth for its shareholders. In that sense, increasing productivity and production volume, maximizing consumption, and as a result, increasing sales constitute primary objectives. In the process of achieving organizational goals, companies offer quality and value to consumers and businesses, leading to a higher level of consumer satisfaction. They compete to offer a wide variety of goods and services and a maximum of choices for consumers. As they compete, they lower prices that consumers pay for their products to gain market share. Ultimately, the marketing system creates a higher standard of living for consumers while improving their quality of life.

1-5e: The Next Level of Marketing: Integrating Societal Marketing Practices through Customer Relationship Management (CRM)

Societal marketing practices are formally integrated into a process known as **customer relationship management (CRM).** CRM is defined as a database application program designed to build long-term loyalty with customers through the use of a personal touch. Its eight building blocks are vision, strategy, customer experience, organizational collaboration, CRM processes, CRM information, CRM technology, and CRM metrics.[26]

> **Customer Relationship Management (CRM):**
> A database application program designed to build long-term loyalty with customers through the use of a personal touch.

As a direct outgrowth of the marketing concept, CRM:[27]

- Incorporates an organizational focus on the behavior of, and communication with, the customer.

- Uses technology for mining data related to customer preferences and behaviors; that is, the company codes or grades customers based on these data.

- Shares the collected data across the entire enterprise.

- Uses the technology to design business processes that enhance efficiency and effectiveness.

- Boosts customer satisfaction by providing consistent, seamless, quality experiences.

The customer database is particularly valuable. It provides a unified customer view across the enterprise, tying together all the interaction between the company and a particular customer. For example, the call center can find out about Web transactions or direct mail pieces sent to a particular customer, and the customer thus does not have to repeat or reenter information to engage in a new transaction.

CRM allows for multichannel marketing so that customers can deal with the firm when they want to. The customer can go to the retail store during store hours to purchase a product, he or she can go to the website, or he or she can order the product by phone. Ultimately, CRM leads to more efficient customer targeting and retention, improving cost management and increasing profitability and thus shareholder equity. However, the Gartner Group, which specializes in CRM applications, predicts that most companies will use CRM to increase revenue or customer loyalty, rather than use them to save money.[28]

> **Customer Lifetime Value (LTV):**
> The estimated profitability of the customer over the course of his or her entire relationship with a company.

For CRM to be profitable, companies must retain their customers for long periods. At the heart of customer relationship management is the concept of **customer lifetime value (LTV)**, defined as the estimated profitability of the customer over the course of his or her entire relationship with a company. Companies that understand customer value have been shown to be 60 percent more profitable than those that do not.[29]

CRM has proven itself as a vital ingredient in the value creation strategy. Yet even though CRM technologies have matured in the past decade, their implementation failure rates are high, ranging from 55 to 75 percent.[30] Some of the reasons behind their failure are: implementing CRM before creating an adequate customer-focused strategy or before making the appropriate organizational transformation; assuming that more CRM technology is better, rather than focusing on the appropriate technology; and stalking; rather than wooing customers.[31]

The keys to CRM success are:[32]

- Getting executive buy-in.
- Determining why and where CRM is needed.
- Defining objectives.
- Setting measurable goals.
- Taking an incremental approach.
- Building and training the right teams.
- Managing and selling change internally.
- Having an outside marketing specialist monitor the program.
- Developing effective feedback mechanisms.
- And conducting ongoing systematic customer research.

Summary

1. *Address the central role of marketing in the twenty-first century.* Marketing constitutes an ever-growing, important driving force of today's modern society. In the United States alone, there are more than 275 million consumers living in 100 million households, spending $5 trillion on products and services—equal to two- thirds of the national GDP. A significant portion of all Americans are employed entirely or in part in assisting the marketing system to perform its functions. Thus the broad marketing system is integral to a society's economic system, offering employment and income for millions working in the marketing field, enabling them to be productive and earn money needed for consumption, and leading to an improved national infrastructure in such areas as transportation, telecommunication, medical care, and finance. Companies engaged in marketing pay taxes that further fund public programs. The system's mass-market efficiencies allow for lower costs, lower prices, and increased overall consumer access, fostering innovation that ultimately benefits consumption. Marketing enhances economic development, buyers' well-being, and general quality of life.

2. *Define marketing and identify its key concepts.* Marketing is defined as the process of planning and executing the conception, pricing, promotion, and distribution of ideas, goods, and services to create exchanges that satisfy individual and organizational objectives. Important concepts in marketing are needs (basic human requirements), wants (directed to a particular product), and demands (wants backed by the ability to buy the respective product or service brand). The four P s of marketing are products (goods, services, ideas, and experiences), price, place (distribution), and promotion. At each level of distribution between the manufacturer, wholesaler, retailer, and consumer, an exchange takes place: A desired good or service is obtained in exchange for something else. Exchanges involve at least two parties that mutually agree on the desirability of the exchange.

3. Address the different marketing philosophies and explain them in view of the historical development of marketing. The different philosophies are the production concept, which assumes that consumers prefer products that are easily accessible and inexpensive; the product concept, which assumes that consumers prefer products that are of the highest quality and optimal performance; the selling concept, which assumes that consumers left alone will not buy or not buy enough (they need to be aggressively sold to purchase); the marketing concept, which focuses on consumers' needs and works to create a good or service that matches those needs; and the societal marketing concept, a philosophy that applies the marketing concept in a manner that maximizes society's well-being. Historically, the product/ production concept can be traced back to the product era (1870–1930), when the focus was on products and production; the selling concept to the sales era (1930–1950), when the focus was on selling overproduction to consumers; and the marketing concept to the marketing era (1950–present), when the focus shifted to the needs of the consumer, and later, to the needs of society.

4. Discuss the key elements of the societal marketing concept and the importance of these elements in meeting the needs of consumers, society, and the organization. The first key element is a market orientation and an integrated marketing approach, which is a firm-wide focus on customer needs and on delivering high-quality products to consumers. The second key concept is the achievement of company objectives. The third key element is the dissemination of marketing information across departments using an integrated marketing approach. The fourth key element is a focus on consumer and societal needs. The fifth key element is a value-based philosophy that puts value, quality, and consumer satisfaction first. This is accomplished through the last key element, which is an organizational goal orientation that creates profit and shareholder wealth, while offering goods or services that are desirable, competitively priced, and delivered within easy consumer access.

Key Terms

customer lifetime value (LTV)
customer relationship management (CRM)
data mining demands
demarketing
exchanges and transactions
experiences
goods
gross domestic product (GDP)
ideas marketing
marketing

concept marketing
era marketing
marketing myopia
market orientation
markets
needs
place (or distribution)
price
product
product concept
production concept
production era products
promotion

relationship marketing
sales era
satisfaction
selling concept
services
societal marketing concept
value
value-based philosophy
wants

Discussion Questions

1. You take an aspirin and you feel better. You take Claritin, an allergy medicine, and you have fewer allergy symptoms. When you purchase these drugs, do you buy the products or the reaction to the products? In that sense, are they goods, services, ideas, or experiences?

2. Are the aspirin and the Claritin in the previous question wants or demands? What need do they address?

3. Examine the marketing philosophies presented in Section 1.4. For each of the companies or brands below, which of the marketing philosophies do you think the company (or brand) is using? Justify your answer.

    a. AT&T cell phone service
    b. Dish satellite TV service
    c. Exxon gas
    d. Apple (electronics)
    e. Nabisco (cookies and crackers)
    f. Reebok (shoes)

4. What marketing philosophy is likely to be embraced in general by the manufacturer of Claritin, the allergy medicine mentioned in question 1? Explain. Now that Claritin's patent has expired, and the brand is available over the counter, along with countless generic copies, how should the company philosophy change?

5. As described in the chapter, Philip Morris USA, the manufacturer of Marlboro and the creator of the legendary Marlboro Man, is attempting to reach consumers with pamphlets of information on the dangers of smoking. Does Philip Morris subscribe to the social marketing concept? Explain.

6. Is it important to you for a company to be involved in societal issues and concerns? Why or why not? Does it impact the brands you purchase? Explain. Are there brands you will not purchase because you feel they do not care about the environment and society? Explain.

7. Identify five brands that you believe provide good value to you. Explain why you consider the brands to be good values. Discuss the relationship of quality to price.

8. How important is customer service to you at a restaurant? Which is more important, good service or good food? Explain.

9. Develop an exercise that helps you calculate your degree of satisfaction with a prime-time television program. Use the website satisfaction survey in Section 1-5c as a model.

Review Questions
(Answers are on Last Page of the Chapter)

True or False

1. Marketing is a process of exchange at different levels.

2. The production concept assumes that consumers prefer products of the highest quality and performance.

3. The societal marketing concept assumes that the company will have an advantage over competitors if it is applied in a manner that maximizes society's well-being.

4. The selling concept assumes that, if consumers are left alone, they will normally purchase the product.

5. Overall product quality is a set of norms used by the manufacturer to meet the production specification.

6. The marketing concept emerged in the 1950s as a dominant marketing paradigm.

7. Either product or production orientation constitute the best approaches to satisfying consumers.

8. The selling concept is superior to the marketing concept.

9. A market orientation is defined as a company-wide culture creating the necessary behaviors for delivering superior value to buyers.

10. Companies that adopt a value-based philosophy offer high-priced products.

Multiple Choice

11. Which of the following refers to demands?
> a. Basic human requirements
> b. Needs directed at a particular product
> c. Wants backed by customer ability to buy a product
> d. Obtaining a product in exchange for something else

12. A haircut is an example of a(n)
> a. good.
> b. service.
> c. idea.
> d. none of the above.

13. Demarketing is defined as a
> a. decline in retail distribution.
> b. reduction in demand for the company's own product for the well-being of society.
> c. a process of changing advertisements in the media.
> d. none of the above.

14. The production era corresponds to
> a. 1850 to 1870
> b. 1870–1930.
> c. 1930–1950.
> d. 1950–present.

15. Companies provide products of value. Value is defined as
    - a. a low price guarantee.
    - b. product quality at moderate price.
    - c. an expensive product that conveys prestige.
    - d. a product's overall price given its quality.

16. The marketing mix consists of the following four main components:
    - a. product, people, place, and price.
    - b. product, perception, price, and place.
    - c. product, price, place, and promotion.
    - d. prosperity, product, potential, and price.

17. Marketing myopia is defined as
    - a. considering an important market segment.
    - b. selling a new brand product within a short period.
    - c. a marketing philosophy that is rooted in price and promotion.
    - d. a tendency of marketing efforts to focus on product, production, and sales.

18. Components of consumer satisfaction are
    - a. customer expectations and product quality.
    - b. value and consumer retention.
    - c. consumer complaints.
    - d. all of the above.

19. To gain a competitive advantage in the marketplace, a company should
    - a. offer products that satisfy consumers at a perceived fair price.
    - b. make products available to consumers.
    - c. use effective promotion to reach a target consumer.
    - d. all of the above.

20. The ultimate organizational goal is to
    - a. provide high-quality products at low prices.
    - b. create profit for the company and wealth for its shareholders.
    - c. offer products that consumers deem as satisfactory.
    - d. increase marketing efforts.

Blog

Clow-Lascu: *Marketing: Essentials 5e Blog*

What is Happening Today?

Learn More! For videos and articles that relate to Chapter 1:

blogclowlascu.net/category/chapter01

Includes Discussion Questions with each Post!

Screenshot of YouTube Video highlighted in Clow-Lascu *Marketing Essentials 5e* blog.

Notes

1. William L. Wilkie and Elizabeth S. Moore, "Marketing's Contribution to Society," *Journal of Marketing* 63, no.1 (1999): 198–218. Consumer Expenditure Survey, U.S. Bureau of Labor Statistics, September, 2013: http://www.bls.gov/cex/2012/combined/cusize.pdf
2. Ibid.
3. Ibid.
4. Ibid.
5. Ibid.
6. Ibid.
7. Peter Drucker, "Marketing and Economic Development," *Journal of Marketing* 22, no. 1 (July 1957–April 1958): 252–259.
8. American Marketing Association, Definition of Marketing, July 2013. Accessed at https://www.ama.org/AboutAMA/Pages/Definition-of-Marketing.aspx on November 16, 2014.
9. http://www.nytimes.com/2014/06/01/travel/the-evolving-world-of-gay-travel.html?_r=0
10. http://www.thedailybeast.com/articles/2013/08/13/fast-food-goes-upscale.html
11. Steve Hoeffler and Kevin Lane Keller, "Building Brand Equity through Corporate Societal Marketing," *Journal of Public Policy & Marketing* 21, no. 1 (Spring 2002): 78–89.
12. "Where Can You Find Information On ... ?" Philip Morris Newspaper Insert (November 2002): 13.
13. Robert A. Fullerton, "How Modern Is Modern Marketing?" *Journal of Marketing*, 52, no. 1 (January 1988): 108–126.
14. J. B. McKitterick, "What Is the Marketing Management Concept?" in *Frontiers of Marketing Thought and Action*, ed. F. Bass (Chicago: American Marketing Association, 1957): 71–82.
15. Term coined by Theodore Levitt, "Marketing Myopia," *Harvard Business Review* (July–August 1960): 45–56.
16. Cultural Access Group, U.S. Ethnic Markets, www.accesscag.com/hispanic.htm, accessed on April 20, 2005.
17. "Media Matters," *Adweek* 42, no. 9 (February 26, 2001): 44–50.
18. Ajay K. Kohli and Bernard J. Jaworski, "Market Orientation: The Construct, Research Propositions, and Managerial Implications," *Journal of Marketing* 54 (April 1990): 1–18.
19. J. C. Narver and S. F. Slater, "The Effect of a Market Orientation on Business Profitability," *Journal of Marketing* 54 (October 1990): 20–35.
20. Dana-Nicoleta Lascu, Lalita Manrai, Ajay Manrai, and Ryszard Kleczek, "Interfunctional Dynamics and Firm Performance: A Comparison between Firms in Poland and the United States," *International Business Review* 15, no. 6 (2006): 641–659.
21. Tom Hicks, "Data Mining Offers Mother Lode of Information," *Sporting Goods Business* 33, no. 13 (August 23, 2000): 16–17.
22. See www.gap.com.
23. Ibid.
24. Marylyn Collins, "Global Corporate Philanthropy: Marketing beyond the Call of Duty?" *European Journal of Marketing* 27, no. 2 (1993): 46–55.
25. Adapted from www.theacsi.org.
26. Sudhir H. Khale, "CRM in Gaming: It's No Crapshoot!" *UNLV Gaming Research & Review Journal* 7, no. 2 (2003): 43–54.
27. Ibid.
28. Ed Thompson and Michael Maoz, "Grow Revenue Again," Gartner Research, www.gartner.com, accessed on January 7, 2005.
29. Khale, "CRM in Gaming."
30. Joseph O. Chan, "Toward a Unified View of Customer Relationship Management," *Journal of the American Academy of Business* 6, no. 1 (March 2005): 32–38.
31. Khale, "CRM in Gaming."
32. Ibid.

Cases

Case 1-1 Customer Relationship

Demarketing at Mama's Pizza

Karen Jensen and her family own and manage Mama's Pizza in Scottsdale, Arizona. This has been a successful family business for many years, but recently, they have been running into trouble. They send coupons to their customers regularly in hopes that they return often and bring their families along. However, they have always had their share of customers who are problematic: they complain about the size of their drink or the temperature of the pizza and expect, in return, to receive a free drink or a free pizza in addition to the discount. These customers are the exception, but they are quite a nuisance and Karen is seriously thinking about eliminating them from the mailing list because, even though they come to Mama's relatively often, they tend to be trouble. But somehow she is having difficulty reconciling this situation with the ingrained idea that the customer is always right.

She tried to find out how other businesses deal with this type of problematic customer. Karen found out that many other companies have problem customers. At Best Buy, an electronics retailer, they are known as "devils." Best Buy classifies customers as "angels"—customers who are less demanding and spend money on expensive and new technologies—and devils—customers who seemingly buy products, apply for rebates, return the purchases, and then buy them back at returned merchandise discounts. And they request that the company honors their lowest-price pledge by finding low-price deals on the Internet. The devils, according to the company, can wreak havoc on the company, and they should be discarded.

A marketing consultant informed Karen that, just as companies are taught to manage their products much like investments, by using a product portfolio, customers should be managed in a similar way. If customers are the most important assets of the business, then it makes sense to manage customers and allocate firm resources to those who are the most profitable. That made sense to her. Many articles Karen read suggest that only the right customer is always right. These customers are satisfied, they derive value from the company and its offerings, they provide referrals, and they make money for the company. Karen has many of those customers. They are always happy, friendly, love Mama's Pizza, and bring their families over often.

According to an article in *Business Week*, customer supremacy can be destructive, especially when a customer's demand for low prices destroys profitability but also when the customer demands a different product, creating extra work for staff, and also when a customer disrespects employees. Clearly, for Karen, the problematic customers are seriously eroding her business' profitability. One thing that she can do first is to eliminate these customers from her marketing list so that she does not waste money on advertising to them, on special offers, or other communications. Best Buy established that 20 percent of their customers are wrong for the firm. Karen is wondering: what percentage of her customers are problem customers?

Questions:

1. You have learned, throughout you experience as a customer, that the customer is always right. Did you ever do something that would lead one to conclude that you, as a customer, were wrong? Explain.

2. What are some problematic, but ubiquitous, consumer behaviors?

3. When is it appropriate for a business to terminate a relationship? Discuss Mama's Pizza's situation, and suggest to Karen how to handle these problem customers, beyond taking them off her mailing list.

Sources: Ian Gordon, "Relationship Demarketing: Managing Wasteful or Worthless Customer Relationships," *Ivey Business Journal Online* (March/April 2006): 1; Jack Suzy Welch, "That's Management!" *Business Week* (February 19, 2007): 94.

Case 1-2: Kraft Foods: Changing the Focus from Yummy to Healthy

It is hard to be the manufacturer of yummy food nowadays, and Kraft knows that only too well: Its Oreo and Nila cookies, its Tobler chocolate, and its Oscar Mayer hot dogs have been washed down with Kool-Aid to create a profitable bottom line for the company. Kraft further bet on the cookie business in 2000 with its $15 billion acquisition of Nabisco. However, a few years later, the nation's largest food manufacturer is cutting back on its indulgence food. Its Oreos in particular have become the bad poster child for trans fats; Atkins and the South Beach diet, the growing obesity epidemic, and the popularity of low-carbohydrate diets have severely eaten into the company's profits.

As a reaction to the falling profits, the company cut 6,000 jobs and closed 20 plants in 2004 in an effort to reduce operating costs and placed the savings into marketing. In addition, Kraft decided to change its marketing strategy to focus on social responsibility as its main theme. Kraft Chief Executive Officer, Roger Deromedi, admitted that the company has been hurt lately, particularly in four businesses: cereal, cookies, frozen pizza, and candy. He hosted analysts and reporters for a daylong presentation at the company's headquarters north of Chicago to inform them about changes in its offerings: healthier, better-for-you food choices. In a radical move toward socially responsible marketing, the company decided to help fight obesity around the world by instituting limits on portion sizes, offering nutritional guidelines for its products, and ending all in-school marketing efforts aimed at boosting consumption.

Today, social responsibility efforts at Kraft go beyond its partnership with Save the Children USA: Kraft boasts a broad Sensible Solution program as part of a strategy to improve its customers' health. Sensible Solution is a labeling program to help consumers easily identify better-for-you choices from the company's product mix. The company has formed a global council of advisers to develop policies, standards, measures, and timetables to address the obesity issue. The council boasts experts, mostly academic, in obesity, nutrition, physical activity, behavior, lifestyle education, and intervention programs. The council developed standards in line with the 2005 U.S. Dietary Guidelines, authoritative statements from the U.S. Food and Drug Administration, National Academy of Sciences, and other public health authorities. Kraft then labeled its food with Sensible Solution flags.

To qualify for bearing a flag, the product must provide beneficial nutrients, such as protein, calcium, or fiber/whole grain, at nutritionally meaningful levels or deliver a functional benefit, such as hearth health or hydration. At the same time, it must meet specific limits in terms of calories, fat, sodium, and sugar. Alternatively, the product must meet specifications for reduced, low, or free in calories, fat, saturated fat, sugar, or sodium. Among the products bearing the flag are Crystal Light ready-to-drink beverages, Kraft 2% Milk Mild Cheddar Reduced Fat cheese shreds, Minute Rice Instant whole grain brown rice, Post Shredded Wheat cereal, and Triscuit Original baked whole grain wheat crackers.

In other efforts to be socially responsible, Kraft had already reduced the fat content in 200 of its products. In its current health drive, it has stocked shelves with new snacks that cater to diet-conscious consumers pursuing a healthy lifestyle. Among Kraft's new offerings are 100-calorie packages of Chips Ahoy, Cheese Nips, and Wheat Thins Minis. The company also introduced its CarbWell line of cereals, salad dressing, and barbecue and steak sauce.

The company also reformulated products to meet the U.S. Food and Drug Administration standard of zero grams of trans fat per serving. Among the products that have been reformulated are reduced fat Oreo cookies, Golden Oreo cookies, Triscuit crackers, Back to Nature organic and natural products, and the Boca line of meat alternatives. In 2012, Kraft spun off the Kraft Foods division, comprised primarily of confectionery and snacks, to its shareholders under a new name, Mondelēz International.

Its pursuit of a healthy lifestyle reaches far beyond U.S. borders and into Canada. There, Kraft partnered with the Boys and Girls Clubs of Canada, launching Cool Moves, a program director's guide for a health and fitness program, creating and testing recipes in Kraft Kitchens. The program has two parts: Eat Smart, which encourages children to eat healthy, and Play Cool, which encourages physical activity. Among others, children record their progress in a journal daily, they create grocery lists at the club and purchase the products later, with their parents. The program was a great success, with more than 80,000 children participating.

Questions:

1. Kraft eliminated a number of jobs and closed its plants, thus cutting costs and improving the stockholders' bottom line. It also used some of its profits to enhance its marketing communications. Is Kraft endorsing the societal marketing concept?

2. How is Kraft demonstrating social responsibility in its new health-oriented strategy? Or is the company simply jumping on the current health fad?

3. Will the current new health focus bring long- term success for Kraft? Justify your response.

4. Suggest how Kraft could incorporate the concepts of CRM in its new health drive.

Sources: "Diets Force Kraft to Change Marketing Approach" *Marketing News* (September 15, 2004): 37; www.kraft.com; "Kraft Launches Initiatives to Fight Obesity," *Nation's Restaurant News* 37, no. 28 (July 14, 2003): 46; Natalia Williams, "The Skinny on Obesity—Kraft," *Strategy* (August 2006): 50.

Answers to Review Questions

Answers: 1) True, 2) False, 3) True, 4) False, 5) False, 6) True, 7) False, 80 False, 9) True, 10) False, 11) c, 12) b, 13) b, 14) b, 15) d, 16) c, 17) d, 18) d, 19) d, 20) b

Chapter 2

The Environment of Marketing in the 21st Century

Learning Objectives

After studying this chapter, you should be able to:

1. Provide an overview of the marketing microenvironment and all of its components.

2. Provide an overview of the sociodemographic and cultural environment components of the macroenvironment and related trends.

3. Address the economic and natural environment components of the macroenvironment and the topic of economic development.

4. Examine changes in the technological environment component of the macroenvironment.

5. Address the political environment component of the macroenvironment and discuss indicators of political risk and company approaches to political risk management.

Figure 2-1: Understanding what young women enjoy reading is part of the microenvironment that must be analyzed by marketers n order to reach them effectively.

2-1 CHAPTER OVERVIEW

Marketing managers need to constantly monitor the environment, which is the **microenvironment.** Management must also constantly monitor the **macroenvironment** in order to be able to react to the threats and take advantage of the opportunities in the sociodemographic and cultural environment, the economic and natural environment, the technological environment, and the political and legal environment. Section 2-2 addresses each of the elements in the microenvironment: consumers, suppliers, wholesalers, other facilitators of marketing functions, and competition.

Section 2-3 addresses the macroenvironment components. The sociodemographic and cultural environment, discussed in Section 2-3a, focuses on important demographic changes among key demographic market segments and on cultural change. The economic and natural environment, discussed in Section 2-4, focuses on the phenomenon of interdependence in the world economy, on economic development, and on the impact of the economy on the consumer. The technological environment, discussed in Section 2-5, focuses on the fast pace of technological change and the impact of technology on competition and consumers. The political environment, discussed in Section 2-6, addresses the risks related to economic performance, government economic policy, labor and political action groups, and terrorism. The legal environment, which is a component of the macroenvironment, is addressed in Chapter 3.

2-2 THE MICROENVIRONMENT

A major function of marketing is to develop a company's customer base. Potential customers must be identified, targeted with appropriate marketing strategies, and persuaded to purchase a company's goods or services. Although this task may appear to be rather simple, it becomes daunting when the company's microenvironment is considered. Strengths and weaknesses of internal company dynamics, current and potential customers, suppliers, and competing firms can influence how successfully the marketing function is performed. It is the responsibility of the marketing department to manage these various components of the microenvironment, addressing their weaknesses and focusing on their strengths in a manner that is congruent with the company's marketing and organizational goals.

2-2a: The Company

Within the company itself, the marketing manager or marketing department will be involved in three arenas: battling for limited resources, seeking a voice in company strategies, and developing a marketing mind-set. To succeed, the mar-

Microenvironment: Environment of the firm, which includes the company, its consumers, suppliers, distributors, and other facilitators of the marketing function and competition.

Macroenvironment: Environment of the firm, which includes the sociodemographic and cultural environment, the economic and natural environment, the political environment, and the technological environment.

keting manager must successfully interact with the various departmental representatives in the company to ensure the marketing function is appropriately stressed and promoted.

First is the battle for limited resources. Every department within a firm is seeking resources to carry out its role within the company. Most departments feel they do not have enough money or people to accomplish the work assigned to them. Marketing departments reflect the same sentiment. Seldom are there enough funds to satisfy everyone. On the average, most firms spend around 10 percent of their sales revenue on the marketing function. **Figure 2-2** provides an idea of how the marketing budget relates to a firm's overall revenue.[1]

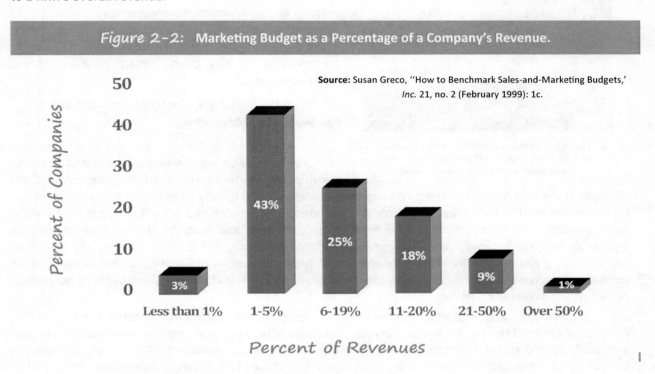

Figure 2-2: Marketing Budget as a Percentage of a Company's Revenue.

Source: Susan Greco, "How to Benchmark Sales-and-Marketing Budgets," *Inc.* 21, no. 2 (February 1999): 1c.

The second internal factor affecting the marketing function is gaining a share of the voice in developing corporate strategies. Because marketing strategies are derived from corporate goals and objectives, it is important that the marketing department be involved in developing corporate strategies—even in the development of the company's mission statement. By having a voice at the corporate level, marketing managers can ensure that top-level executives understand the marketing function and the importance of marketing in developing plans for the corporation. For example, a decision to expand into another region or country will involve understanding the market potential and the capability of the firm to gain sufficient market share to make the expansion profitable. Marketing influences decisions about production and product modifications based on understanding customer needs and wants.

The third internal company force the marketing department has to address is developing a marketing mindset. Creating a company-wide culture that emphasizes delivering superior value to consumers—that is, creating a market orientation—is essential. In firms where marketing plays a prominent role-- the marketing information is broadly disseminated--the marketing department has access to information from other functional areas of the company. This information can be used to deliver high value to customers, resulting in a better performance record and higher customer retention rates.[2]

It is important for every employee in the organization to understand who the firm's customers are and what is being promised to them (see **Figure 2-3**, which illustrates a promise of expertise and care by Glenwood Regional Medical Center). Although product quality is important, so is the manner in which customers are handled. A bad experience with a company worker can send a customer to a competitor as quickly as a defective product. It costs approximately six times more to gain new customers as it does to

You have a lot to live for.
That is why we have
expanded our heart program.

Glenwood's Cardiology Services is focused on bringing you the treatment and experience you need
to stay in the best possible health. Services like cardiac catheterization.
We offer Northeast Louisiana's only fully equipped, dedicated
cardiac catheterization labs. We provide the labs
to allow our experienced cardiologists to perform
the following procedures on a regular basis:

Peripheral Vascular Studies   *Cardiac Catheterization*
Coronary Stents   *Electrophysiology*
Balloon Angioplasty   *Arhrectomy*

all ♡ heart

When it comes to heart care, Glenwood
provides a level of experience few
communities can attain, for a level of
reassurance few communities can match.

318-329-8590
or visit us on-line at
www.grmc.com

Glenwood
REGIONAL MEDICAL CENTER
CARDIOLOGY SERVICES

Figure 2-3: Glenwood Regional Medical Hospital
advertises they provide a high level of heart care.
Source: Courtesy of Newcomer, Morris & Young.

keep current customers, so it is imperative that company employees understand the marketing goals of the organization.

Sharing information and promoting interaction between the functional areas of the firm is essential for company success. Companies that rate highly on inter-departmental connectedness -- sharing marketing information with all the other functional areas, such as research and development, engineering, finance and accounting, and purchasing, and sharing nonmarketing information with the marketing department -- are more successful in reaching overall organizational sales and profit objectives.[3]

2-2b: Suppliers, Distributors, and Other Facilitators of Marketing

Although it is the purchasing department that primarily deals with suppliers, the outcome of this relationship is important to the marketing department. For example, if the cost of raw materials and supplies increases, it will usually reverberate into price increases for the company. The marketing department has to decide how much of a price increase is necessary to cover the additional costs, what the impact will be on customers, and how it will affect competition. The marketing department may even be responsible for communicating the price increase to the customer and providing justification for why it is necessary. Any disruptions in the supply, such as a labor strike, currency exchange factors that may increase the price, or a natural disaster (e.g., a drought or hurricane), can affect the marketing function.

Similarly, a delay in product delivery can lead consumers to switch to competitors. Recently, Cisco's delays for key Ethernet switches, firewalls, and other network gear created unhappy customers who eventually turned to the competition. Angry customers quickly cancelled orders and many defected to competitors Juniper and HP, as well as other suppliers that offered free shipping to encourage the switch.[4]

Although the marketing area is primarily looking toward customers, it must keep an eye on suppliers, distributors, and other factors to ensure that customers will always have the product when and where they want it and at the price they are willing to pay.

Distributors are middlemen whose task is to ensure the convenient, timely, and safe distribution of the product to consumers. Manufacturers rely on distributors to deliver their products, to advertise and promote the products, and, often, to offer financing to other distributors down the channel or to the consumer, and thus facilitate purchase. Often they use the services of physical distribution firms, such as warehousing firms, transportation firms, and other facilitators of the marketing function, such as banks, insurance companies, advertising firms, and market research firms.

> **Distributors:**
> Intermediaries whose task is to
> ensure the convenient, timely,
> and safe distribution of the
> product to consumers.

2-2c: Customers

Not all customers are alike. Not only are there individual differences among customers, but there are also different types of customers, and each requires a different marketing plan. The primary customer groups are consumers, manufacturers, governments, institutions, other businesses, and retailers.

Because of differences in these customer groups, companies have to be diligent in developing their marketing plan. They must make sure that their marketing plan meets customer needs and, if more than one group is targeted, that additional marketing plans are developed. To understand these differences, think about the marketing of office supplies, such as pens, notebooks, paper, folders, and

staplers. For consumers, a firm would need to advertise the location of its stores and the attributes of its products. If these companies were selling the office supplies over the Internet, then the site would be designed to be attractive and easy to use for consumers. If the company were selling office supplies to a manufacturer or another business, then it would require a salesperson calling on the customer. Once a relationship has been established, the business may then purchase the products online or by phone.

Selling office supplies to the federal, state, or local government would require the office supply company to submit a bid. To make the sale, it would have to outbid its competitors either on price or some other designated criterion. Most institutions, such as schools and hospitals, also use a bidding process.

The marketing method used to sell to retailers depends on whether the office supplies are for resale or would be used by the retailer's employees. If the office supplies are for resale by the retail store, then the office supply business would have to compete with other firms on the basis of price and marketing deals it would offer the retailer to stock its brand. If the office supplies are just being used by the retailer and not resold, as would be the case with a florist or bakery, then the office supply firm may use salespeople for large retailers but would use a catalog, the Internet, and direct mail for the smaller firms.

For the international market, all of these scenarios are repeated, but they become more complex because of potential language and cultural differences. For each country, the office supply business would have to identify the marketing strategies that would work best in the respective market. Whereas advertising may work in one country, sending direct-mail pieces or offering coupons may not be an option there if the mail system is unreliable and couponing is illegal.

Figure 2-4: This advertisement by Ol'Man highlights the superiority of its tree stand for deer hunting over the competition. It is more comfortable, easier to use, the highest quality, and the safety leader.

Source: Courtesy of Newcomer, Morris and Young.

2-2d: Competition

In developing a marketing strategy, a company must take into consideration its competitors. The task of marketing is to meet the needs and wants of consumers more effectively and efficiently than competitors. Marketers must ask the question, "What do we offer customers that the competition does not?" When making a brand selection, consumers often have many choices and will readily compare one brand to another. The brand chosen will be the one the consumer feels is superior in some way or offers the best value (companies stress the superiority of their product over that of the competition—see Figure 2-4).

In evaluating competitive forces, it is important to understand there are several layers of competition. Consider the case of Burger King (see Figure 2-5). Burger King's primary competitors are those fast-food operations that sell hamburgers, such as McDonald's, Wendy's, and Hardee's. At a second level are fast-food franchises, such as Kentucky Fried Chicken, Taco Bell, and Subway. These businesses sell products other than hamburgers but are still fast-food outlets. At a third level are all of the dine-in restaurants. Although they are not shown in Figure 2-5, you could argue for other layers, such as grocery stores that have a café serving hot lunch or dinner food or convenience stores, such as 7-Eleven, which offer sandwiches and wraps to go. Yet another layer could consist of various types of food stores that do not have a sit-down café and do not offer sandwiches to go.

The key to understanding the impact of competition on marketing is to examine it from the consumer's point of view. As a consumer, you are hungry. For Burger King to be considered as an option, you would think about it in terms of the competition. Do I want to eat at Burger King, McDonald's, Hardee's, or another fast-food outlet that sells hamburgers? Is there one close to me? If you decide you want chicken or Mexican food, then you may consider Burger King, but you would also consider all of the other options in the second layer. If you are not particular whether it is fast food or dine-in, then all of the options in layer three come into play. Consequently, in developing a marketing plan, Burger King would have to consider all of the options that you, as a consumer, would.

Figure 2-5: Burger King's Competitors

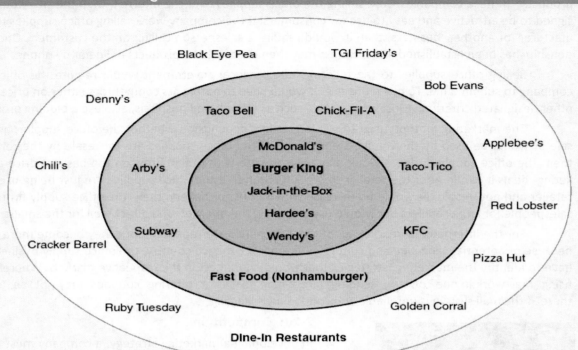

Sociodemographic and Cultural Environment:

A component of the macroenvironment that comprises elements such as demographics, subcultures, cultural values, and all other elements in the environment related to consumers' backgrounds, values, attitudes, interests, and behaviors.

2-3 THE MACROENVIRONMENT

The macroenvironment encompasses the elements of the broader environment that affect the firm. Marketing managers have no control over the macroenvironment but must continually monitor it to identify changing threats and opportunities that might impact the firm. The elements of the macroenvironment include the sociodemographic and cultural environment, the economic and natural environment, the technological environment, the political environment, and the legal environment.

2-3a: The Sociodemographic and Cultural Environment

The **sociodemographic and cultural environment** comprises many different elements, such as demographics, subcultures and cultures, and all other elements in the environment related to consumers' backgrounds, values, attitudes, interests, and behaviors. These variables constitute an important part of a marketing plan. Consider how many products are marketed based on the target consumer's gender, age, social class, or subculture. Even the same product may be marketed differently based on sociodemographic and cultural characteristics. For example, common products, such as deodorant, shampoo, and razors, are marketed differently to males than they are to females (see Figure 2-6).

Figure 2.6: This convenience store in Poland is marketing primarily to men, selling tobacco products, beverages, and alcohol.

Demographics are the statistics that describe the population, such as gender, age, ethnicity, education, and income. Demographic trends that will affect marketing in the future include a slower population growth rate, an aging population, and a more diverse population.[5] Because individuals are waiting longer to get married and having smaller families than in the past, the U.S. population is not expected to grow as fast during the twenty-first century as it did during the twentieth century.

> **Demographics:** Statistics that describe the population, such as age, gender, education, occupation, and income.

Although the growth is slower, the average age of the American population will increase. This is primarily a result of advances in medical knowledge. In addition, the diversity of the U.S. population will increase as a result of higher birth rates among minorities than among the Caucasian population. Immigration is also a factor in this increase in diversity, as the United States will continue to draw immigrants from around the world.

For many marketers, age is an important characteristic in examining the U.S. population. Spending habits, media preferences, and interests vary among the different age categories. Figure 2-7 divides the population into six different age groups based on the spending power of each group. Table 2-1 provides some additional comparative statistics for each of the demographic groups.

Figure 2-7: Spending Power of U.S. Demographic Age Groups

Generation Y 5%
Empty Nester 13%
Younger Boomer 26%
Senior 14%
Older Boomer 24%
Generation X 18%

Demographic	Total Number of Households (millions)	Average Number in Household	Spending Power (billions)	Annual Average Household Income	Annual Group Average Spending per Household
Generation Y	8.3	1.9	$187	$19,744	$22,563
Generation X	18.9	2.9	$736	$45,498	$38,945
Younger Boomer	23.9	3.3	$1,100	$56,500	$45,149
Older Boomer	21.9	2.7	$1,000	$58,889	$46,160
Empty Nester	14.1	2.1	$557	$48,108	$39,340
Senior	22.1	1.7	$588	$25,220	$26,533

Table 2-1: Spending Power of U.S. Demographic Age Groups

2-3b: An Age Categorization of Sociodemographic Groups

Generation Y

Generation Y is the fastest-growing segment in the workplace. There is debate about the composition of this category; however, for the purpose of this text, we are going to identify it as consisting of individuals born between 1977 and 2002. Some publications indicate Generation Y as being born between 1978 and 1995. (The younger generation in this sequence has yet to be clearly defined; currently, it is referred to as Generation Z, but this categorization is not definitive, as it shares many traits with Generation Y.) There are many terms used to label Generation Y, some referring to subgroups: Echo-Boomers, Millennials, the Net Generation, Digital Natives, the MyPod Generation (merging MySpace and iPod), and the Next Generation, or GenNext.

Generation Y:
A segment of individuals born between 1978 and 2002; they spend substantial amounts on clothing, automobiles, and college education; they live in rental apartments or with parents.

Generation Y is comparable in size to Boomers, making up 24 percent of the U.S. population. Few are married (only 21 percent, compared with 42 percent for Boomers), and they make up 20 percent of the same-sex couples. It is the most educated generation, with 23 percent with a Bachelor's degree or higher, and the most racially and ethnically diverse — 19 percent Hispanic, 14 percent African American, and 5 percent Asian. They adhere to a speak-your-mind philosophy: They are smart, brash, wear flip-flops to the office; they have been pampered, nurtured, and programmed with many activities since childhood; and they are both high performance and high maintenance. They have financial smarts and have already started saving for retirement, and they want jobs with flexibility, allowing them to accommodate family and personal lives. As consumers, they are multitaskers, juggling e-mail while talking on cell phones, texting and working online. They are also open to different cultures and international experiences.[6]

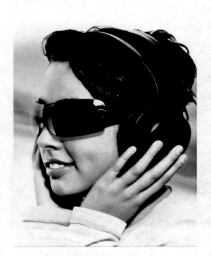

Figure 2-8: Generation Y consumers are more interested in stereos and music equipment than in home furnishings.

Clothes, automobiles, and college are the big-ticket items for this group, which spends 3.3 times more on education than the average person and 1.5 times more on vehicles and apparel than the average person. Nearly 90 percent of this group is either living in a rental or living with parents; spending on homes and home furnishings is a low priority for this market. Generation Y spends substantial amounts on television sets and stereo systems, rather than on refrigerators (the representatives of Generation Y in Figure 2-8 have invested in musical instruments). The collective spending priorities of Generation Y revolve around personal appearance and fun.[7]

Although Generation Y alludes to that cohort's successional relationship to Generation X, the term Echo Boomers is used to allude to the generation's close tie to the primary childbearing years of Baby Boomers; the term Second Baby Boom is also used in this way and to denote the population expansion that Generation Y represents. The terms Millennials, Net Generation, MyPod Generation, and Next Generation are attempts to give the Generation Y cohort more independent names that are tied with key events and cultural trends that are strongly associated with the generation. No single term is the "correct" term to describe members of this generation.

Generation X:
A segment of individuals born between 1965 and 1977, whose focus is on family and children, striving to balance family with work, and outsourcing household chores and babysitting.

Generation X

Contributing 18 percent of the total spending power of consumers in the United States, **Generation X** (individuals born between 1965 and 1976) focuses on the family and children. Food, housing, transportation, and personal services are the important categories for this market segment. Generation X-ers spend 78 percent more on personal services than the average consumer. Time is at a premium as they strive to balance work and family, so they outsource daily tasks, such as house cleaning, lawn mowing, babysitting, and other domestic chores. (Figure 2-9 illustrates Generation X-ers with children at a park.) Dan Bishop, founder and CEO of The Maids, stated, "Customers are asking us to do more things. They want the laundry done, the carpet cleaned, the light bulb changed that's 20 feet in the air, the patio furniture cleaned, and the furnace filters changed."[8]

Figure 2-9: Generation X consumers focus on family life, such as time with children on the weekend.

Younger Boomers

Baby boomers, born between 1946 and 1964, represent 42 percent of the population in the United States, but they account for 50 percent of the total spending. Because of the size of this group, it has been divided into younger boomers, born between 1954 and 1964, and older boomers, born between 1946 and 1953. The estimated spending power of the **younger boomers** is $1.1 trillion. The home and family are the focus of younger boomers' spending. Since the majority, 60 percent, own their own home, consequently, a considerable amount of their income is allocated to mortgage expenditures, home furnishings and renovation. The remaining disposable income is spent on family purchases, such as pets, toys, playground equipment, and large recreational items, such as a boat or four-wheel-drive vehicle.[9]

> **Younger Boomers:**
> A segment of individuals born between 1954 and 1964, whose focus is on family and home, who pay a large proportion of their income for mortgages, furnishings, pets, and children's toys.

Older Boomers

Older boomers account for 24 percent of the total spending—or an estimated $1 trillion. Among priorities of this demographic group are upgrading their homes, ensuring education and independence of their children, obtaining luxury items such as boats, and going on vacation. Despite the higher cost of children's education, this group can afford to remodel their home, purchase better furniture, and buy higher-quality clothing for themselves. Insurance and investments are high-ticket items as they begin to think about their later years and retirement. With fewer responsibilities at home, older boomers spend considerably more on vacation and recreation (see Figure 2-10) than any of the other demographic groups.[10]

Figure 2-10: Boats, recreation, and vacations are major expenditures for the older baby boomers and zoomers.

Zoomers are a special subcategory of boomers whose lifestyles resemble those of individuals who are 20 years younger and who plan to continue living this way. These are the yuppies of the 1980s, those who made *Sex and the City* a success, consumers who are adamantly refusing to acknowledge their senior status.

According to Dr. David J. Demko, a professor of gerontology who originally coined the term, a zoomer is a boomer who performs daily exercise, calculates daily nutritional and caloric needs, orchestrates a social support system, has a positive self-concept and a passion for living to the fullest, and acquires the resources necessary to live an adventurous life.[11] Zoomers refuse to retire and want to continue to look good physically; consequently, they are spending large amounts of money on cosmetic surgery, clothing, and sports automobiles. In marketing to zoomers, firms must be aware that they will not respond well if they are portrayed as older consumers. Any reference to seniors is outright rejected by this demographic group.

> **Older Boomers:**
> A segment of individuals born between 1946 and 1953, that spends money on upgrading the family home, on taking vacations, and on ensuring children's education and independence.
>
> **Zoomers:**
> A special subcategory of boomers whose lifestyles resemble those of individuals who are 20 years younger, who perform daily exercise, calculate daily nutritional and caloric needs, orchestrate a social support system, have a positive self-concept and a passion for living to the fullest, and acquire the resources necessary to live an adventurous life.

Empty Nesters

Empty nesters are a market identified to be between the ages of 55 and 64. It should be noted that, at this moment in time, empty nesters are a subsegment of the baby boom generation. Their children have left home, and they have already paid the college bills. Home mortgages, new furniture, new automobiles, and personal indulgence items represent priorities for this segment. More than 80 percent own their home, and many have paid their mortgage in full. Investments and insurance are high-ticket items, and their attention is now focused on fancy, nice automobiles they could not afford before. New furniture, appliances, and china are purchased to enhance the appearance of their home.[12] Many of the boomers are currently in the empty nest stage.

Seniors

Seniors, individuals older than age 65, are also partially a subsegment of the baby boom generation and account for 14 percent of all spending in the United States—that is, approximately $588 million a year. Seniors primarily live on fixed incomes, which also mean tighter budgets; for the senior market, household income and spending decline sharply. Health care becomes the number one priority, as seniors spend six times more than the average person (see Figure 2-11). Drugs, health insurance, and health care constitute the top three categories of spending for this group, followed closely by medical supplies and medical expenses. This group tends to reside at home more and spend large amounts on home-related expenses and groceries. Seniors spend 50 percent more than the average consumer on fruits, vegetables, and other food items.[13]

Baby boomers are rapidly entering the senior category; however, many of them refuse to be referred to as seniors, or retirees for that matter.

2-3c Ethnic Diversity and Subcultures

The United States is often described as a melting pot. It is indeed a country where many subcultures are maintaining their old traditions but also building common new traditions—a national culture. Culture, a society's personality, is defined as a continually evolving totality of learned and shared meanings, rituals, norms, and traditions among the members of an organization or society. The elements of culture are language, religion, **cultural values** (beliefs about a specific mode of conduct or desirable end state that guide the selection or evaluation of behavior),[14] and norms (which are derived from values and are rules that dictate what is right or wrong, acceptable or unacceptable). These elements will be addressed at length in Chapter 4.

Culture is continually changing: Individualism and materialism were dominant values in the United States. However, after the September 11, 2001, terrorist attacks, and after the Great Recession, individuals are turning their attention more

Figure 2-11: This advertisement by Lincoln General Hospital is directed at seniors, who spend six times more on health care than the average person.
Source: Courtesy of Newcomer, Morris and Young.

Cultural Values:
Beliefs about a specific mode of conduct or desirable end state that guide the selection or evaluation of behavior.

and more to family and nurturing relationships in general. The message that resonated well during the 1980s' quest for material possessions, "greed is good," sounds shallow today. Family values, the home, and religion have made a strong comeback in the past decade.

The cultural landscape has also changed radically with the increase in multiculturalism—an important cultural trend in the United States. Ethnic subcultures have shaped and continue to shape culture in the United States. Bagels and tacos, sushi and filet mignon are part of the daily American fare. Hispanic music, hip-hop, and rap have wide appeal beyond the Hispanic American and African American subcultures. Marketing managers study the different subcultures to provide goods and services that meet their needs most effectively. They advertise to Hispanic American consumers on Spanish-language cable television programs. Using ethnic newspapers, companies offer cosmetic product lines that are specifically designed to address the needs of African American women. Sensitized to the religious needs of consumers, companies have identified products as Kosher or Halel and inform consumers that a product might contain beef or pork by-products or alcohol.

2-4 THE ECONOMIC AND NATURAL ENVIRONMENT

The economic environment encompasses all the factors in the environment that affect the use of resources, including natural resources, production of goods and services, and their allocation to individual and organizational consumers. Marketing is an important driver of the economy; in turn, the economy has a profound impact on marketing decisions and on consumers, determining consumer income and spending, borrowing decisions, and savings—which, in turn, affect the economy.

2-4a: Interdependence in the World Economy

The United States is an important participant in the world economy, but its dominant position is unstable. It was common to hear that when the United States sneezes, Europe and Asia catch a cold. Indeed, when the United States is experiencing a downturn in the economy, reverberations echo throughout the world. Central and South American countries need International Monetary Fund (IMF) intervention, Asian economies flounder, and banks in developing countries default on their debt. The world economy is increasingly affected by market blocs, such as the European Union (EU), and even by developments in important emerging markets, such as China. The United States is equally affected by the world economy. The war between Russia and the Ukraine resulted in a rapid rise in oil prices everywhere in the world. The 8.8 percent fall of China's Shanghai Composite Index in 2007 quickly spread to Asia, Europe, and the United States, where major stock averages suffered their worst one-day percentage losses in many years.

The tsunamis and earthquakes in Southeast Asia directly affected numerous U.S. business interests. Indirectly, the resulting political instability in the region affects the security of U.S. businesses in the area and the viability of small and medium enterprises in the United States that have substantial dealings with businesses in the affected countries.

Countries are becoming more and more connected by trade, by capital markets, by the flow of technology and ideas across national borders, and by psychology. Rather than rising and falling separately, national economies increasingly respond to the same forces.[15] Interdependence has become the leading principle of globalization, with crises in one part of the world instantly affecting other areas.

Although economies and markets worldwide are interdependent, some markets and economies are more advanced than others and tend to grow more rapidly. There are many competing classifications of countries from an economic development perspective. Historically, the informal and frequently used classification in the West has referred to highly industrialized, developed countries as the First World, to socialist countries as the Second World, and to developing countries as the Third World. Of this classification, only the term Third World has been used widely, and it is still being used. A United Nations (UN) classification contrasts least-developed, lowest-income countries (LLDCs) and less-developed, lower-income countries (LDCs) to developed countries.

Yet other classifications bring in other dimensions, such as newly industrialized countries (NICs), in reference to what used to be known in the 1980s and 1990s as the Asian Tigers (Taiwan, Singapore, South Korea, and Hong Kong [now part of China]) and **emerging markets** (such as Brazil, Argentina, Chile, Peru, and the transitional economies of Central and Eastern Europe). In this textbook, we will refer to categories of countries based on the classification used by the World Bank. This classification takes gross national income (GNI) per capita into consideration in identifying different country categories. This section will also discuss the previous categorization system because many current publications continue to use these terms.

High-income countries (also known as developed countries in the previous classification)—These highly industrialized countries have well-developed industrial and service sectors. NICs and countries that have had a developed status for many years fall into this category (see Figure 2-12). Although these countries present great potential because they have consumers with the highest per capita income, they also present challenges to international firms because their markets are in a mature stage, consumers have established preferences, and competition is intense. The World Bank counts in this category countries with a GNI per capita of $12,746 (U.S. dollars) and above.

Emerging Markets:
Markets that are developing rapidly and have great potential.

High-Income Countries:
Highly industrialized countries that have well-developed industrial and service sectors and have a gross national income per capita of $12,676 and above.

Middle-Income Countries:
Countries that are developing rapidly and have great potential.

Big Emerging Markets (BEMs):
Large countries with emerging markets that present the greatest protection for international trade and expansion.

Figure 2-12: This photo shows infrastructure-related advances made by high-income countries; modern buildings and bridges that appear to defy gravity are the norm in large cities.

Middle-Income countries (also known as countries with emerging markets in the previous classification)—Countries considered as emerging markets both are developing rapidly and have great potential. They are countries in Latin America, such as Argentina, Brazil, Uruguay, Paraguay, Chile, Peru, and Bolivia; countries in Asia, such as China, with its immense market, and India, with its substantial middle class; and the transition economies of Central and Eastern Europe, which are rapidly privatizing state-owned industries and adopting market reforms. Important in this category are **big emerging markets (BEMs)** such as Brazil and China, which present the greatest potential for international trade and expansion. The middle-income country category is further divided into two income groups, as follows:

♦ **Upper-Middle-Income Countries**—These countries have rapidly developing economies, and they have an infrastructure that is on par with that of developed countries, especially in urban areas. They are countries in Latin America, such as Argentina, Chile, and Mexico. Among the transition economies of Central and Eastern Europe, new EU member countries that have rapidly privatized state-owned industries and adopted market reforms, such as the Czech Republic, Estonia, Hungary, Latvia, Lithuania, and Poland, are in this category. The Russian Federation is also in the category. According to the World Bank, countries considered upper-middle-income countries have a GNI per capita of $4,126 to $12,745 (U.S. dollars).

♦ **Lower-Middle-Income Countries**—This is a diverse group of countries that includes China, much of North Africa and the Middle East, and many of the former Soviet Socialist Republics, such as Armenia, Azerbaijan, Belarus, Georgia, Kazakhstan, Moldova, Turkmenistan, and the Ukraine. According to the World Bank, countries in this category have a GNI per capita of $1,046 to $4,125 (U.S. dollars).

Low-Income Countries (also known as developing countries, in the previous classification)—Countries in this category are primarily agrarian, have low per capita income levels, and are located in different regions in Asia and in Sub-Saharan Africa. Developing countries are often neglected or underserved by large multinationals and consequently present great potential as niche markets. However, even the countries with the lowest per capita income have a stratum of society that can afford global products. Furthermore, because they are primary recipients of international development aid, they present important opportunities for firms operating in the areas of infrastructure development and industrial sector development and for related consultancies. According to the World Bank, countries in this category have a GNI per capita of less than $1,045 (U.S. dollars).

Throughout the textbook, there are examples of marketing challenges and opportunities in emerging markets, in middle-income countries, and in low-income countries.

The discrepancy between the countries in these categories is evident. With regard to the gross national product (GNP) distribution worldwide, high-income, highly industrialized countries account for close to 80 percent of the world's GNP, while accounting for less than 15 percent of the population.

To illustrate this discrepancy, the United Nations Development Program monitors human development worldwide, publishing the Human Development Report. The report compares countries based on life expectancy, literacy, and gross national income per capita, among other criteria. Table 2-2 compares countries in the low human development category on those dimensions.

> **Upper-Middle-Income Countries:**
> Countries with rapidly developing economies, and especially in urban areas, an infrastructure that is on par with that of developed countries. According to the World Bank, countries considered upper-middle-income countries have a gross national income per capita of $3,466 to $12,615 (U.S. dollars).
>
> **Lower-Middle-Income Countries**
> Countries in this diverse group have a gross national income per capita of $1036 to $4,085 (U.S. dollars).
>
> **Low-Income Countries:**
> Countries that are primarily agrarian and have low per capita income.

Table 2-2:
An Illustration of Human Development in Select Low Human Development Countries

Rank	Country	Life Expectancy at Birth	Mean Years of Schooling	Gross National Income per Capita
167	Rwanda	55.7	3.3	1,147
171	Sudan	61.8	3.1	1,848
175	Afghanistan	49.1	3.1	1,000
182	Mali	51.9	2.0	853
184	Chad	49.9	1.5	1,258
186	Niger	55.1	1.4	701

Source: Human Development Report, United Nations Development Programme, 2013,
http://hdr.undp.org/sites/default/files/reports/14/hdr2013_en_complete.pdf

2-4b: Economic Development: The Rostow Modernization Model

Economic development can be explained in terms of productivity, economic exchange, technological improvements, and income. Economic growth requires advancing from one stage to another. According to the Rostow model of economic development,[16] the modernization stages are:

- Traditional society
- Transitional society
- Takeoff
- The drive to maturity
- High mass consumption

Traditional Society

Countries in the traditional society stage are characterized by an economic structure that is dominated by agriculture. Minimal productivity occurs, and only a few exchange transactions take place. Economic change and technological improvements are not sufficient to sustain any growth in per capita output, which is low.

Transitional Society (Preconditions for Takeoff)

The transitional society stage is characterized by increased productivity in agriculture, and modern manufacturing begins to emerge. In manufacturing, low productivity remains the norm.

Takeoff

During takeoff, growth becomes the norm and improvements in production lead to the emergence of leading sectors. Income rises across the board, and a new class of entrepreneurs emerges.

The Drive to Maturity

In the drive to maturity stage, modern technology is fully adopted in all economic activity, and new leading sectors emerge. The economy demonstrates the technological and entrepreneurial skill to produce anything it chooses to. The economy looks beyond the country's border for development.

High Mass Consumption

In the age of high mass consumption leading sectors shift toward durable goods. A surge occurs in per capita income, and there is increased allocation to social welfare programs. The masses can afford goods beyond food, clothing, and shelter.

In the United States and most other industrialized, high-income countries, the focus of the economy is shifting toward services, which currently account for most of the output. All companies, however small, are affected by changes in the international economic environment, by the availability of raw materials in developing countries, by disruptions in important labor markets, and by the stability of international and local financial institutions. The local bakery and the mom-and-pop hardware store are affected by national and international economic cycles, by prices of raw materials from developing countries, by the local labor market, and by consumer income. Large multinational companies are also affected by developments in the economy, in the international labor markets, and in consumer spending in the different markets where they operate. The next section addresses the impact of the economy on consumer income and spending.

Rostow Model of Economic Development: A model of economic development in which each stage of development is a function of productivity, economic exchange, technological improvements, and income.

Traditional Society: Economic development stage in which the economy is dominated by agriculture, minimal productivity, and low growth in per capita output.

Transitional Society: Economic development stage in which there is increased productivity in agriculture; manufacturing begins to emerge.

Takeoff: Economic development stage in which growth becomes the norm, income rises, and leading sectors emerge.

Drive to Maturity: Stage of economic development in which modern technology is applied in all areas of the economy.

High Mass Consumption: Stage of economic development in which leading sectors shift toward durable goods and an increased allocation to social welfare programs.

2-4c: The Economy and the Consumer

The economy affects consumer income and spending patterns. In periods of economic growth, consumers give in to their materialistic drive, purchasing products they may or may not need.

In a slow economy, when companies reduce their workers' hours and the nation's payrolls shrink by thousands of jobs monthly, consumers tend to be more cautious with their expenditures. They "deliberate over a purchase for weeks and then decide against it."[17] Retailers, who are already offering blanket sales all year long for their products, need to cut prices even further because customers do not respond to their promotions unless they perceive that they are truly getting a great deal.

The distribution of income across social class categories has important implications for marketing decisions. Upper-class consumers are less likely to be affected by economic cycles; their purchase patterns remain constant because they continue to purchase products and services, such as high-fashion clothing, gourmet food, cleaning services for their large homes, exotic vacations, and country club memberships. Middle-class consumers are more vulnerable during economic downturns and could experience job loss or the threat of job loss; consequently, they are more likely to reduce consumption, limiting purchases to necessities. The lower-class consumers are most likely to be affected by economic slowdown because part-time jobs or jobs requiring a lower skill level are likely to be cut.

Table 2-3 illustrates annual expenditures of consumers for different household income levels. Housing is by far the greatest expense for all income levels. Expenses for necessities such as food and personal care products and services decrease as a proportion of income as household income increases, allowing households with higher income to spend more on entertainment, education, and vacations, and to save for the future.

Figure 2-3: Average Annual Expenditures of Consumers: A Comparison for Different Household Income Level Expenditures

	Average Household Income:				
	Lowest 20%	Second 20%	Third 20%	Forth 20%	Highest 20%
	$10,174	$27,094	$47,017	$71,426	$164,647
Food	$3,570	$4,683	$5,854	$7,525	$11,348
Housing	$8,843	$12,134	$14,674	$19,021	$30,504
Transportation	$3,605	$5,687	$8,029	$11,034	$16,630

Source: From Consumer Expenditure Survey, 2013; U.S. Department of Labor, Bureau of Labor Statistics (September 2013)

Figure 2-13: Protecting natural resources is an important societal concern.

2-4d: The Economy and Natural Resources

As mentioned in Section 2-4, the economic environment encompasses all the factors in the environment that affect the use of resources. Although many resources are renewable or recyclable (e.g., timber), important natural resources, such as minerals, natural gas, and petroleum, are finite (protecting natural resources, such as the Smokey Mountains (see Figure 2-13), is an important priority). Increased control over these limited resources by national governments has led to higher prices for oil and the need to evaluate alternative energy sources and technologies.

Other aspects of the natural environment have important repercussions on the economy and on the overall quality of life of consumers. Pollution in the form of greenhouse gases has led to global warming, dying coral reefs, and an overall change in the ecological equilibrium of oceans. Chemical spills and nuclear waste are compromising the water supply and landfills are overflowing with packaging material, much of which is not biodegradable (see Figure 2-14, which highlights the importance of purchasing energy-efficient office equipment). Some of these environmental concerns are directly attributable to marketing efforts to create products that are convenient or attractive for consumers, such as excessive packaging that helps products stand out on supermarket shelves, the use of nonbiodegradable Styrofoam in packaging to protect products or for cups used to hold hot beverages, and convenient, disposable diapers, among others. Marketing is also attempting to demarket (slow down or reduce) the use of environmentally harmful products. For example, fast-food companies have decided to limit the use of Styrofoam cups and containers, replacing them with paper bags and cardboard. Many products are now offered in environmentally friendly, recyclable packaging; in fact, many companies provide incentives for consumers who recycle their packages.

Figure 2-14: Appliances often have information on energy consumption. Energy Star appliances not only save money on energy, but they are also less harmful for the environment.

Topography, hydrology, climate, population, and environmental quality determine the status of a particular country as a viable trade partner. Topography is important because it determines access to the market and affects distribution decisions. For example, Holland has a flat terrain, allowing for efficient transportation. On the other hand, a mountainous terrain restricts access to markets. The Andes only allow minimal access to local consumers, which can be accomplished only at great company expense. Hydrology determines access to local markets as well. Ocean access allows for the affordable shipping of goods to the local target market. Rivers and lakes offer access and potential for the development of agriculture and manufacturing. Hydroelectric power is essential for local development. In general, economic development is related to hydrology. In the Netherlands, the topography was altered to increase access by creating an effective network of human-made canals that cross the country in every direction, allowing for easy access to markets (see Figure 2-15). Climate is also an essential determinant of economic development. Arid lands, such as the desert lands of the Sahara and the Southwestern United States, are inhabitable only at a very high cost. In Eastern and Southeastern United States, excessive rain often leads to flooding and the destruction of the local infrastructure.

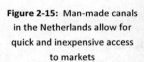

Figure 2-15: Man-made canals in the Netherlands allow for quick and inexpensive access to markets

One relevant aspect of the natural environment is the scarcity of natural resources, and especially raw materials, in light of today's high population growth. High population growth, despite limited natural resources, has led to famine and precipitated conflict in Ethiopia, Somalia, Rwanda, and Burundi in Sub-Saharan Africa. In these markets, the overall infrastructure is insufficient and cannot meet the basic needs of the population. Elsewhere in the world, the concentration in large cities of millions of inhabitants, such as Mumbai (Bombay), Shanghai, Mexico City, and Cairo, has taxed the infrastructure and impeded the optimal functioning of business. The world's population exceeds six billion and is growing rapidly, especially in developing countries. Table 2-4 illustrates the less developed regions, compared to more developed regions. The population growth rate is highest for the developing countries of South Asia and Sub-Saharan Africa.

Table 2–4: Population Growth Trends		
Year		
2000	2013	2025
World Population (in billions)		
6,102.00	7,124.50	8,036.40
Age		
0-14	15-65	65+
(in millions)		

Source: World Development Indicators, World Development Report 2014, World Bank Group, available at: http://wdi.worldbank.org/table/2.1

	0-14	15-65	65+
Low income countries	636.7	848.7	1091
Middle income countries	4254.6	4969.7	5589.7
Lower middle income	2089.4	2561.1	2993
Upper middle income	2165.2	2408.7	2596.6
Low & middle income countries	4891.3	5818.4	6680.6
East Asia & Pacific	1812.2	2005.8	2151.3
Europe & Central Asia	256.3	272.2	283.4
Latin America & Caribbean	500.3	588	660.2
Middle East & North Africa	276.6	345.4	413.3
South Asia	1382.2	1670.8	1909.8
Sub-Saharan Africa	663.7	936.1	1262.7
High income countries	1210.7	1306.1	1355.7

2-5 THE TECHNOLOGICAL ENVIRONMENT

Technology is the primary driver of change in the environment. Our lives are changing dramatically and at a faster pace as a result of technological change. Just in the past decade, the pharmaceutical industry has created numerous miracle drugs: For example, Celebrex has greatly improved the quality of life of people with arthritis despite its greatly debated health side effects, and Viagra has revolutionized the sex life of older men. Magnetic resonance imaging (MRI), laser, and endoscopic instruments have revolutionized diagnostics and treatment in medicine (see Figure 2-16). The Internet has become an important venue for communication with a company's target market and an effective retailing venue. The computer has changed our daily lives, from the manner in which we communicate in our work and home environment, to the manner in which we distribute documents, obtain approvals, and share the latest photographs of our loved ones. Handheld computers are allowing us to handle such communication without having to physically access our desktops. And cellular phones allow us to communicate from anywhere on the planet.

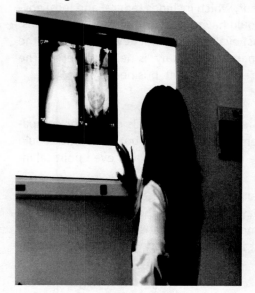

Figure 2-16: Advances in pharmaceutical knowledge and medical procedures are critical to saving lives.

Technological change is taking place rapidly in all domains of human endeavor. Companies are under pressure to develop new and better products, with new technologies, to gain advantage over competitors, or simply to keep up. Table 2-5 illustrates the amount spent by corporations in research and development. The continued growth of research and development spending is largely attributed to industry's realization that structural and operational changes are not the only road to profitability. Continued investment in research and especially in development is required for long-term survival.[18]

	Gross Expenditures on Research and Development	
	(in Billion US Dollars)	
United States	465	
China	284	
Japan	165	
Germany	92	
India	44	

Table 2-5: **Global R&D Spending**

Source: 2014 Global R & D Funding Forecast
http://www.battelle.org/docs/tpp/2014_global_rd_funding_forecast.pdf?sfvrsn=4

Research and development spending is also funded by the federal government and by universities and nonprofit research centers. Excellent business conditions in the 1990s, a strong economy, and enhanced tax revenues fueled a federal budget surplus, thus potentially easing some past pressures on government support of research and development. Furthermore, the budget surpluses eased the cost of money and effectively reduced the costs of investing in research and development.[19]

The United States spends more on research and development than any other country in the world. In the year 2014, spending on research and development was estimated to be $465 billion.[20] However, more recently, a troubling trend emerged: Corporate research and development spending is on the decline. In particular, technology companies have cut back on R&D funding heavily. The National Science Foundation states that private sector funding for research and development has declined dramatically. Among the companies that have drastically cut R&D spending are Hewlett-Packard Co. and Microsoft Corporation.

It is essential for the marketing department to work closely with research and development to ensure that the firm as a whole pursues a market orientation (see Chapter 1). The marketing department should ensure that the new products and services and all innovations are directed at effectively meeting the needs of consumers and that research and development maintains a constant market focus.

2-6   THE POLITICAL ENVIRONMENT

Business must constantly scrutinize the political environment, which includes federal and local government policies as well as labor and political action groups that could have an impact on their operations. Multinational corporations have an even greater burden. They must evaluate political developments in the host country of operations and in the home country where the parent company is headquartered. The next section addresses the different types of political risks that currently confront businesses.

2-6a: Risks Related to Economic Performance

A poor economic performance and forecast are likely to lead to greater levels of risk for companies. Of particular concern are high inflationary rates and high unemployment rates, both of which could lead to higher taxes, regulatory restrictions, an increasingly active labor movement, and even political instability.

During downturns in the economy, federal, state, and local governments often resort to increasing taxes to provide a source of valuable revenue. The government may also reduce expenditures that facilitate industry performance, the government may spend less on improving the transportation infrastructure, it might reduce expenditures for the military, or it may limit lucrative industry contracts on government-subsidized economic development projects.

2-6b: Risks Related to Government Economic Policy

Government elections, especially elections in which a change in the governing party occurs, usually signal a change in policies in general. The new policies may increase or decrease tax burdens or tighten or loosen industry regulations. The Republican victory in 2001 set the stage for a pro-business agenda and corporations quickly brought their wish lists to the new administration.

The subsequent 2006 elections, however, brought the Democratic Party in power in the Senate, and, in 2008, in both houses and the wish list items met with forceful challenge. These themes continued to resonate well into the 2014 elections and beyond.

2-6c: Risks Related to Labor and Action Groups

From labor unions to political action groups, many political forces, in addition to the government, can greatly affect a company's operations. In many countries, labor unions are very powerful and can readily influence national policies. In the United States, labor unions have lost some ground in recent years as a result a history of abuses and a strong economy that ensured solid bonuses for workers. Unions in the United States are organized under the umbrella of the American Federation of Labor-Congress of Industrial Organizations (AFL-CIO), which represents more than 13 million workers.

Action groups can also affect company operations. For example, Exxon recently was the victim of a "Boycott Esso" (Exxon's name outside the United States) campaign aimed at U.S. environmental policies. Groups such as the Public Citizen, associated with Ralph Nader, and other consumer groups are constantly monitoring companies to identify issues that may be of interest to consumers and those taking a stand. With the help of the movie industry, action groups can present a veritable threat to business.

Companies have some control over the actions of labor and action groups. Although they cannot control market demand and derived demand for labor, companies can provide severance packages that are fair and invest in the services of job placement businesses in an effort to seek placement for the employees who have been terminated. In addition, companies should be politically neutral and keep some distance from politics to avoid negative public sentiment. Being too closely associated with an administration or political party could result in a negative attitude toward the company and its products.

2-6d: Risks Related to Terrorism

Terrorist attacks against business interests culminated in the United States with the September 11, 2001, attack on the World Trade Center in New York City. In a choreographed operation, terrorists hijacked four planes that took off within minutes of each other and crashed into each of the World Trade Center's twin towers, as well as the Pentagon. Experts evaluated these attacks as the culmination of a 20-year trend toward assaults aimed to kill many people in technically complex operations.

Corporate terrorism has been on the rise in the past decades, with many U.S. interests being targeted worldwide. As a result, the cost of protecting corporations has increased greatly. Moreover, companies worldwide have reassessed their corporate preparedness programs after the April 2013 Boston Marathon bombings to focus on protecting operations, finances, business strategy, and brand reputation and to maintain good corporate governance.[21]

In addition to training employees in terrorism avoidance, such as briefing personnel on what to expect when in high-risk areas, companies can also purchase insurance against terrorist acts from private insurance companies. Cigna International's International Specialty Products & Services offers insurance products that cover kidnapping, detention (kidnapping without asking for ransom), hijacking, evacuation, business interruption and extra expenses, product recall expenses, and expenses arising from child abduction (e.g., hiring private investigators or posting rewards for information).[22] The private and public sectors have learned to deal more effectively with terrorism and a number of advances have mitigated terrorism risk: security controls, better political understanding, and a more efficient management of terrorism events when they take place.[23]

As a result of these controls, the United Kingdom thwarted a plot to blow up aircraft between Britain and the United States. Moreover, the United States is improving its tracking of imports and exports through its Automated Commercial Environment (ACE) system. ACE is a commercial trade processing system developed by the U.S. Customs and Border Protection to facilitate trade while strengthening border security. It allows customs agents to centralize all information regarding cargo systems through mandatory electronically filed manifests. In the United States, there are 72 ACE ports, and soon the system will be available at all U.S. ports, with capabilities for air, rail, and sea cargo processing.[24]

A company has several resources at its disposal to evaluate country risk. The Department of State, the Department of Commerce, and other governmental and nongovernmental agencies provide data on country political risk that are current and continually updated to reflect new developments in each country around the world (see an example of country risk evaluation in Table 2-6).

Table 2-6:   **Country Risk Scores: Countries That Offer the Lowest Risk**

Rank	Country	Overall score*
1	Norway	89.70
2	Switzerland	87.44
3	Luxembourg	87.21
4	Singapore	86.59
5	Sweden	86.41
6	Finland	84.54
7	Denmark	82.49
8	Canada	82.45
9	Hong Kong, China	81.74
10	Australia	81.53

*Score out of 100

Source: "Euromoney Country Risk:*Euromoney,* July 2013.

Summary

1. Provide an overview of the marketing microenvironment and all of its components. A major function of marketing is to develop a company's customer base. Potential customers must be identified, targeted with appropriate marketing strategies, and persuaded to purchase a company's goods or services. Although this task may appear to be rather simple, it becomes daunting when the company's microenvironment is considered. Strengths and weaknesses in internal company dynamics, current and potential customers and suppliers, and competing firms can influence how successfully the marketing function is performed. It is the responsibility of the marketing department to manage these various components of the microenvironment, addressing their weaknesses and focusing on their strengths in a manner that is congruent with the company's marketing and organizational goals.

2. Provide an overview of the sociodemographic and cultural environment components of the macroenvironment and related trends. The sociodemographic and cultural environment comprises elements such as demographics, subcultures and cultural values, and all other elements in the environment related to consumers' backgrounds, values, attitudes, interests, and behaviors. Sociodemographic trends that will affect marketing in the future include a slower population growth rate, an aging population, and a more diverse population. Because individuals are waiting longer to get married and are having smaller families than in the past, the U.S. population is not expected to grow as fast during the twenty-first century as it did during the twentieth century. Although the growth is slower, the average age of the American population will increase. This is primarily a result of advances in medical knowledge. In addition, the diversity of the U.S. population will increase primarily as a result of higher birth rates among minorities than among the Caucasian population. Continuing immigration is also a factor in this increase in diversity.

3. Address the economic and natural environment components of the macroenvironment and the topic of economic development. The economic environment encompasses all the factors in the environment that affect the use of resources, including the limited natural resources, the production of goods and services, and the allocation of goods and services to individual and organizational consumers. Marketing is an important driver of the economy; in turn, the economy has a profound impact on marketing decisions and on consumers, determining consumer income and spending, borrowing decisions, and savings—which, in turn, affect the economy. There is a large degree of interdependence among the economies of the world, regardless of whether they are those of high-income, middle-income, or low-income countries. Economic development is a function of productivity, economic exchange, technological improvements, and income, and according to the Rostow modernization model, societies must go through different phases to achieve a developed state. These phases are traditional society, transitional society, takeoff, drive to maturity, and high mass consumption.

4. Examine changes in the technological environment component of the macroenvironment. Technology is the primary driver of change in the environment. Companies are under constant pressure to develop new and better products, with new technologies, to gain advantage over competitors, or simply to keep up. The continued growth of research and development spending is largely attributed to industry's realization that structural and operational changes are not the only road to profitability. The United States spends more on research and development than any other country in the world.

5. Address the political environment component of the macroenvironment and discuss indicators of political risk and company approaches to political risk management. Businesses must constantly scrutinize the political environment, which includes federal and local government policies and labor and political action groups that could have an impact on their operations. Companies can experience political risks attributed to economic performance, to government economic policy, to labor and action groups, and to corporate terrorism.

Key Terms

big emerging markets (BEMs)	low-income countries	takeoff
cultural values	lower-middle-income countries	traditional society
demographics distributors	macroenvironment	transitional society
drive to maturity	McMansions	upper-middle-income countries
emerging markets	microenvironment	younger boomers
Generation X	middle-income countries	zoomers
Generation Y	older boomers	
high mass consumption	Rostow model of economic development	
high-income countries	sociodemographic and cultural environment	

Discussion Questions

1. Comment on the following statement: "Strengths and weaknesses in internal company dynamics, current and potential customers, and suppliers and competing firms can influence how successfully the marketing function is performed." How do suppliers affect the company's ability to optimally address consumers' needs?

2. Examine Figure 2-5, Burger King's competitors. Create a similar figure for your favorite brand of jeans. When you finish your figure, explain why you placed the various brands and products in the layers you did.

3. Compare Generation X-ers with boomers. Can marketers target them similarly? Why or why not?

4. Which generation segment do you fit into? Explain your personal purchases and philosophies with what is contained in this chapter. In what ways do you fit the description? In what ways are you different? Be specific.

5. Pick two of the age groups discussed in this chapter. Compare and contrast their purchases of the following product categories and how they would affect the way brands would be marketed to each group.

a. Clothes	c. Investment services
b. Vacation packages	d. House cleaning and lawn services

6. Pick two products from this list. Discuss how a company would market to each of the age groups and ethnic groups mentioned in Section 2-3a:

a. Lawn service

b. Hiking boots

c. Mexican restaurant

d. Condoms

e. Ski resort in Colorado

f. Mayoral political candidate

7. Economic interdependence exists today among countries of different levels of development. Assume that China and India experience a downturn in their economies. How could companies in the United States be affected by changes in the economies of these countries?

8. What are the factors driving up the costs of technology? Why is there a need for constant emphasis on research and development and technological change?

9. Describe indicators of political risk in the world. Examine current events and identify some of the political risks that companies could encounter.

10. How can companies reduce political risk? Be specific, provide examples.

Review Questions
(Answers are on Last Page of the Chapter)

True or False

1. The political and legal environment is not a component of the macroenvironment.

2. To evaluate competitive forces, it is important to take into consideration several layers of competition.

3. Marketing managers do not typically consider the limited company's resources.

4. Generation Y is a segment of consumers who spend heavily on clothing, automobiles, college education, and rental apartments.

5. Cultural norms are defined as beliefs about a specific mode of conduct or desirable end state that guide the selection or evaluation of behavior.

6. Since the United States became such a powerful leader in information technology, the fluctuations in the economy in the rest of the world barely affect its domestic market.

7. Countries in Central and Eastern Europe are considered as emerging markets, which both grow rapidly and have great potential.

8. Middle-class consumers are the least likely to be affected by downturns in the economy.

9. Private industry is accountable for all the research and development spending in the United States.

10. Companies have no control over the activities of labor and political action groups.

Multiple Choice

11. Which of the following categories relate to the microenvironment?
   a.   Strengths and weaknesses of the company
   b.   Consumers and suppliers
   c.   Wholesalers, facilitators of marketing functions, and competitors
   d.   All of the above

12. The elements of sociodemographic and cultural environment are
   a.   federal and local government.
   b.   expenditures for different household items.
   c.   labor and action groups.
   d.   none of the above.

13. Which of the following consumer segments are more likely to have large proportions of disposable income and would tend to purchase luxurious items?

    a.   Empty nesters

    b.   Older boomers

    c.   Seniors

    d.   None of the above

14. The characteristics of the high mass consumption modernization stage are

    a.   leading sectors shifting toward durable goods.

    b.   surge in per capita income.

    c.   increased allocation to social welfare programs.

    d.   all of the above.

15. What stage of economic development in the Rostow model is characterized by the adoption of modern technology in all economic activity?

    a.   Transitional stage

    b.   Traditional stage

    c.   Takeoff stage

    d.   Drive-to-maturity stage

16. Protecting natural resources is an important societal concern. The most appropriate action is

    a.   demarketing the use of environmentally harmful products.

    b.   outsourcing the production of harmful products to other countries.

    c.   providing more power to environmental protection agencies.

    d.   none of the above.

17. Most research and development spending takes place in the

    a.   pharmaceutical industry.

    b.   information technology hardware.

    c.   chemical industry.

    d.   automotive sector.

18. Which of the following is not a political risk that currently controls businesses?

    a.   Risk related to labor and political action groups

    b.   Risk related to competitive action

    c.   Risk related to terrorism

    d.   Risk related to government policies

19. During a period of poor economic performance, the government might reduce the expenditures that facilitate industry performance. What strategies are appropriate at this time?

    a.   Reducing the expenditures on the transportation infrastructure

    b.   Reducing the expenditures for the military

    c.   Limiting contracts on government-subsidized development projects

    d.   All of the above

20. How could companies reduce the risk and/or costs of terrorism?

    a.   By training their employees in terrorism avoidance

    b.   By purchasing additional insurance against terrorism

    c.   By considering the cultural, ethical, religious, and political issues of globalization

    d.   All of the above

Blog

Clow-Lascu: *Marketing: Essentials 5e Blog*

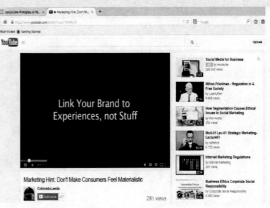

Screenshot of YouTube Video highlighted in
Clow-Lascu *Marketing Essentials 5e* blog.

What Is Happening Today?

Learn More! For videos and articles

that relate to Chapter 2:

blogclowlascu.net/category/chapter02

Includes Discussion Questions

with each Post!

Notes

1. Susan Greco, "How to Benchmark Sales-and-Marketing Budgets," *Inc.* 21, no. 2 (February 1999): 1c.

2. Dana-Nicoleta Lascu, Lalita Manrai, Ajay Manrai, and Ryszard Kleczek, "Interfunctional Dynamics and Firm Performance: A Comparison between Firms in Poland and the United States," *International Business Review* 15, no. 6 (2006): 641–659.

3. Ibid; Ajay K. Kohli and Bernard J. Jaworski, "Market Orientation: The Construct, Research Propositions, and Managerial Implications," *Journal of Marketing* 54 (April 1990): 1–18.

4. Jim Duffy, "Cisco product delays opening doors for rivals," Network World (April 13, 2010), accessed on June 20, 2014 at http://www.networkworld.com/article/2206932/lan-wan/cisco-product-delays-opening-doors-for-rivals.html

5. "Tale of Three Trends," *Monthly Labor Review* 125, no. 4 (April 1, 2002): 64.

6. www.usatoday.com/money/workplace/2005-11-06. Nielsen, "Millennials: Breaking the Myth" (January 27, 2014), accessed on March 14, 2014, at http://www.nielsen.com/us/en/insights/reports/2014/millennials-breaking-the-myths.html.

7. "The Gen Y Budget," *American Demographics* 24, no. 7 (July/August 2002): S4.

8. "The Gen X Budget," *American Demographics* 24, no. 7 (July/August 2002): S5.

9. "The Younger Boomer Budget," *American Demographics* 24, no. 7 (July/August 2002): S6.

10. "The Older Boomer Budget," *American Demographics* 24, no. 7 (July/August 2002): S7.

11. Elliot Gluskin, "Healthy, Adventurous 'Zoomers' Are Potential New Customers," *Bicycle Retailer & Industry News* 15, no. 10 (June 15, 2006): 38.

12. "The Empty Nester Budget," *American Demographics* 24, no. 7 (July/August 2002): S8.

13. "The Senior Budget," *American Demographics* 24, no. 7 (July/August 2002): S10.

14. See Milton J. Rokeach, *The Nature of Human Values* (New York: The Free Press, 1973); Jan-Benedict E. M. Steenkamp, Frenkel ter Hofstede, and Michel Wedel, "A Cross-Cultural Investigation into the Individual and National Cultural Antecedents of Consumer Innovativeness," *Journal of Consumer Research* 63 (April 1999): 55–69.

15. Michael J. Mandel, "In a One-World Economy, a Slump Sinks All Boats," *Business Week Industrial Technology Edition*, no. 3738 (June 25, 2001): 38–39.

16. See Walt W. Rostow, *The Stages of Economic Growth: A Non-Communist Manifesto* (London: Cambridge University Press, 1960); Walt W. Rostow, "The Concept of a National Market and Its Economic Growth Implications," in *Marketing and Economic Development*, ed. P. D. Bennett (Chicago: American Marketing Association, 1965): 11–20; Walt W. Rostow, *The Stages of Economic Growth,* 2nd. ed., (London: Cambridge University Press, 1971).

17. Terry Pristin and Marianne Rohrlich, "Latest Word in Luxury Is Haggling," *New York Times* (October 16, 2002): A2.

18. Tim Studt and Jules J. Duga, "Smaller Increase Forecast for U.S. Research Spending," *Research & Development* 44, no. (January 2002): F3–F8.

19. Ibid.

20. 2014 Global R&D Funding Forecast http://www.battelle.org/docs/tpp/2014_global_rd_funding_forecast.pdf?sfvrsn=4

21. Marsh 2013 Risk Insurance Report, April 2014, available at http://usa.marsh.com/Portals/9/DocumentsSecure/6307%20-% 202014%20Terrorism%20Risk%20Insurance%20Report_MRMR.pdf

22. "Counter-Terrorism Driver Training May Thwart Executive Kidnapping," *Best's Review* 98, no. 2 (June 1997): 95.

23. World Economic Forum, *Global Risks* 2007.

24. www.cbp.gov

Cases

Case 2-1 The House-Proud Consumers

Homeowners spend approximately $130 billion on remodeling projects every year. One in ten homeowners spends more than $5,000 a year on remodeling.

Home renovation has become a national pastime. Whether hiring contractors or as do-it-yourself mavericks, consumers are transforming their living quarters at a breakneck pace and with committed passion. Quality-of-life improvements are high on people's lists since the Great Recession and September 11, 2001. Before these events, if consumers had an extra $15,000 to spend, they were likely to spend it on two weeks in Europe. Today they are putting in a media room or a steam shower. They have come to realize that $15,000 could buy major home improvements that they could have for years, compared with something that may last for just weeks.

Young couples prepare rooms for their first child and then build an addition to accommodate family life with two children. Later, bright playrooms become teenagers' hangouts. Empty nesters reinvent the home as an expression of their tastes, comfort, and status and then sell it to buyers who tear it apart to renovate to their own tastes. These individuals could move to a house in the Sunbelt that better fits their needs, but they might still have to renovate for a perfect fit—and spend $10,000 on a move and six percent in brokerage fees.

But renovation makes perfect sense. House prices have risen faster than the dollar-per-square- foot cost of renovating, which suggests that investing in your home is wise. The cost of buying a new home has escalated an average of 3.7 percent a year since 1994 (and double or triple that number in the country's hottest markets), whereas the cost of remodeling has gone up just 2.8 percent annually. Moreover, properties that are not properly maintained deteriorate. Kitchens and baths should be redone every 15 to 20 years to preserve the value of the house investment. Houses built in the 1960s had 1.5 baths, a small kitchen, and no family room, whereas today's new homes have three baths, great rooms, and master bedrooms you can land a plane in. The price of not keeping your home up to date is that it may eventually sell for significantly less than others of the same size, or it may linger on the market for months.

The house-proud constitute an attractive target market for home improvement stores, magazines, television programs, and contractors. These consumers rummage through expensive, glossy magazines for renovation and decoration inspiration— Kitchen and Bath, Elle Décor, Southern Living, Coastal Living, and This Old House— spending hundreds of dollars on do-it-yourself books and videos, and call on friends and colleagues for contractor referrals. They tour appliance and furniture design showrooms and rummage through tiles in tile specialty shops. In the evening, they are glued to Home and Garden Television (HGTV) programs, such as This Old House, Weekend Warriors, Curb Appeal, and Before and After.

These glossy magazines, books, and programs present a cornucopia of styles and choices—fanciful, practical, cutting-edge, and neotraditional; Italian, British, Danish; stainless and distressed— and direct-to-consumer retailers where good taste in the form of mass-produced distinction and democratized connoisseurship is finally available to all, regardless of income and social class. Like the food revolution, the home design revolution is built on the paradox that what is special should be available for everyone's enjoyment and that good taste can at last shed its residue of invidious social differences.

Questions

1. Which demographic segments described in the text represent the best market for renovation businesses? Explain why.

2. What types of industries and businesses can take advantage of this trend for renovation? How should each industry or business market itself to this group?

3. What is the economic motivation behind renovation? How does consumer income influence this decision? How does the economic cycle influence it?

4. What type of influences has the technological environment had on home renovation over the past 20 years? What technological advances might affect this market in the future?

Sources: Kris Hudson, "Americans Boost Spending on Remodeling: Homeowners Doled Out $130 Billion Last Year for Renovations, The Wall Street Journal, Feb. 3, 2014, accessed at http://online.wsj.com/news/articles/SB10001424052702303743604579355250986245422; A. O. Scott, "Interior Life," *The New York Times Magazine* (December 1, 2002): 19–20; Jean Sherman Chatzky and Lysa Price, "Home Remedies," *Money* 31, no. 5, (May 2002): 108–120; Sheila Muto, "Home and Family: Repairs and Improvements Totaled $233 Billion in 2003," *The Wall Street Journal* (January 13, 2005): D5.

Case 2-2 *smart fortwo*—An Automobile for Drivers Over 50?

DaimlerChrysler AG introduced the smart car—a two-seat, almost nine-foot-long *smart fortwo* automobile—to consumers in the United States in 2008. The automobile, now the sole property of Daimler AG, starts at about $14,000 for the *smart fortwo pure*, and reaching $19,000 for for Cabriolets, and even more for the electric version, is fun to drive—at about 40 miles per gallon of gas—and easy to park.

smart fortwo began in the early 1990s as a joint venture between Mercedes-Benz and Swatch—the company that makes Swatches, watches with colorful designs, whose mission was to enhance the Mercedes portfolio with an "ultraurban" automobile. The automobile has had a distinctive presence in the United States. It had already been on display at the Museum of Modern Art in New York as a work of art. It was developed with safety in mind, with a tridion safety shell—a hard shell aimed at protecting its two occupants. It is also equipped with Electronic Stability Control, and an antilock brake system. It has a high driving position to ensure the greatest visibility, and it is made of energy efficient and recyclable materials. These design elements are going to be of great value, especially in the land of sport utility vehicles (SUVs), where consumers may wonder about the safety of a miniature automobile.

In the United States, the subcompact automobile has been the fastest-growing automobile segment since gasoline prices have increased rapidly. Automobiles such as the Toyota Yaris, Ford Fiesta, Honda Fit, Nissan Versa, and Hyundai Accent have done well. They are about four feet longer than the *smart fortwo*. Its closest competitor, the Mini Cooper is about three feet longer. The problem with the size of the *smart fortwo* and for the other subcompacts is that, in the United States, they share the road with SUVs that are double their size, such as the Chevrolet Tahoe, the top-selling full- sized SUV. So far, only the Nissan Versa has received good ratings on crashes; however, the Insurance Institute for Highway Safety found that the driver death rate in all minicars was higher than for any other vehicle.

The distribution of *smart fortwo* was initially handled by smart USA, headquartered in Bloomfield Hills, Michigan, its exclusive distributor for the United States and Puerto Rico. In the United States, smart USA, started out as a division of Penske Automotive Group, and was solely responsible for distributing the smart.

The *smart fortwo* was designed to appeal to teenagers, urban residents, baby boomers, and retirees. Of these categories, especially appealing are baby boomers and retirees, who have the disposable income necessary for the rapid success of the *smart fortwo*. Moreover, these two segments often live in retirement communities where they often get around in golf carts for their daily activities. The *smart fortwo* would compete successfully with the golf cart in terms of a transportation vehicle, allowing them mobility beyond the community itself. It would also be a status brand, with established European roots as a Mercedes offering, and one that conveys a hip image, with its different striking colors.

Lori Felder, a specialist in zoomer boomers and president of Zoomer Inc., believes that she can increase the *smart fortwo's* inroads into the boomer and retiree market. She is planning to approach Stephen Cannon, president of Mercedes USA, to pitch to him a marketing plan that would help his company market the automobile more effectively to zoomers.

Questions

1. Which demographic segments and subsegments should Lori target if she is planning to appeal to the over-50 consumer? How are these segments different? How are they similar?

2. Provide a psychographic profile of all the different consumers that the *smart fortwo* is targeting.

3. Analyze the *smart fortwo* in terms of its appeal to young families. In which cases would the automobile appeal to families and in which cases would it not appeal to them?

4. How would the economic environment impact the sales for the *smart fortwo*? Explain.

5. In looking at the global market, in what countries should Lori market the *smart fortwo*? Why? Justify your choices.
6. Does ethnicity impact the sales of the *smart fortwo*? Why or why not?

Sources: Karla Sanchez, "Smarter Car: 2013 Smart Fortwo Electric Drive Starts at $25,750 – Photos Galore" (October 4, 2012), *Motor Trend*. Retrieved 2012-10-10. Gina Chon and Stephen Power, ''Can an Itsy-Bitsy Auto Survive in the Land of the SUV? *Wall Street Journal* (January 9, 2007): B1; www.smartusa.com/company.html.

Answers to Review Questions

Answers: 1) False, 2) True, 3) False, 4) True, 5) False, 6) False, 7) True, 8) False, 9) False, 10) False, 11) d, 12) d, 13) a, 14) d, 15) d, 16) a, 17) b, 18) b, 19) d, 20) d.

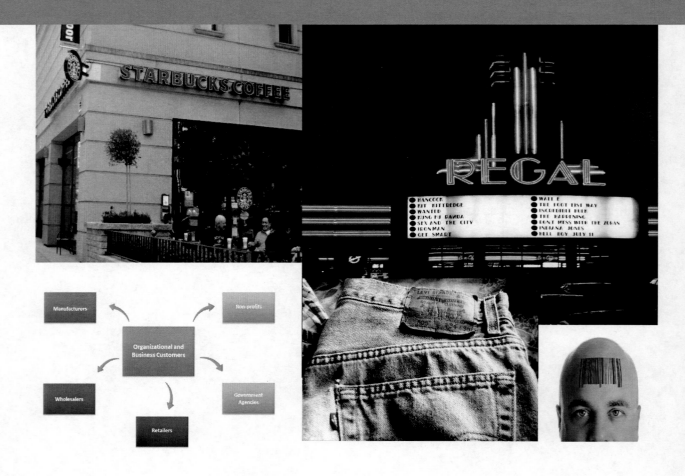

Foundations
of
Marketing

Chapter 3

Marketing Ethics, Regulations, and Social Responsibility

Learning Objectives

Chapter Outline

After studying this chapter, you should be able to:

1 Identify the ethical issues faced by marketers and discuss the pros and cons of each issue.

2 Discuss the legislation and regulatory agencies that affect marketing.

3 Describe the role of the Federal Trade Commission as it relates to marketing and discuss how it investigates complaints.

4 Discuss the role of the Better Business Bureau in regulating marketing activities.

5 Discuss the social responsibility of business firms and provide examples showing how a firm can demonstrate its social responsibility.

3-1 CHAPTER OVERVIEW

A primary goal of marketing is to develop a customer base that will desire and purchase a firm's products. In this process, marketing material is developed that will persuade consumers and businesses to make a purchase. Ethical issues will arise about the material that is developed and about how it is transmitted, and even to whom it is transmitted. For example, teenagers represent a huge market for goods and services, spending more than $75 billion a year on various items.

Advertising to teens requires nontraditional approaches and ads that are often cutting edge. Not all critics approve of these methods of targeting teens. Although they are not children, teenagers are not yet adults. Questions arise as to which goods and services are safe to promote to teens and which are not. In terms of advertising, debate centers on what approaches are appropriate for teens and what are not. Certainly, advertising soft drinks would be appropriate, but questions were raised when 7-Eleven did it with an ad where a Slurpee was used to freeze a teen's tongue in preparation for piercing it. Questions were raised when Scary Movie 3 included Coors Brewing Company's scantily-clad Coors Twins and then Coors heavily promoted the movie. A beer company promoting a movie with a PG-13 rating was seen as advertising to children because one-third of the audience would be below the legal drinking age of 21.

This chapter discusses the ethical issues that arise when marketing material is developed to persuade consumers and businesses to purchase products. Section 3-2 presents both criticism of and a defense for marketing to familiarize the reader with both sides of the issues.

Because companies and organizations do act in unprofessional and even illegal ways, a number of laws have been passed to protect consumers and businesses. Section 3-3 addresses the legal environment of business, described in Chapter 2 as a component of the macroenvironment of the company. It is important to present the legal issues involved in marketing alongside ethics-related concerns and company self-regulation attempts. The section highlights the primary legislation that affects marketing and the agencies that are responsible for regulating marketing activities. Of special importance to marketing is the Federal Trade Commission (FTC). This section closes with a discussion of industry regulatory agencies available through the Council of Better Business Bureaus (CBBB).

Section 3-4 presents the positive side of the ethical issue —social responsibility. Firms are expected to act in a socially responsible manner. Two ways in which they can do this are cause-related marketing and green marketing. Both are discussed.

3-2 ETHICAL ISSUES IN MARKETING

> **Ethics:**
> Philosophical principles that serve as operational guidelines for both individuals and organizations concerning what is right and wrong.
>
> **Morals:**
> Personal beliefs or standards used to guide an individual's actions.

In understanding ethical issues in marketing, it is important to differentiate between ethics and morals. **Ethics** are philosophical principles that serve as operational guidelines for both individuals and organizations concerning what is right and wrong. **Morals** are personal beliefs or standards used to guide an individual's actions. Morals direct people as they make decisions about everything from personal conduct, to sexual behavior, to work activities, to family life, to interaction with other individuals. A person's feelings about companies can be based on his or her moral feelings. For example, numerous citizens believe the United States should not conduct business with countries that have a history of human rights violations or exploit child labor. Some will even boycott brands that operate in these countries.

Ethics help us as individuals and organizations to establish boundaries regarding acceptable and unacceptable conduct. Many leaders in organizations assert that they wish to be ethical in their decisions.

Yet recent events with companies such as Enron and WorldCom have shown the need for a higher level of ethical behavior within corporations. The public is now demanding that companies, their leaders, and their employees act in an ethical manner. How are your ethics? Before proceeding any further with this chapter, take "The Top 10 Test" on marketing ethics found in Table 3-1.

Table 3-1: The Top Ten Test of Right or Wrong

Answer right or wrong to each of the following ethical situations. Be honest. Do not give the answer you think is right, but what you would do in that situation. No one will know your score, but you.

1. **Share the Glory** —You are writing the monthly status report to the board detailing the performance of your division. The talk in the corridor is about the incredible success resulting from an innovative strategic suggestion championed by a competitor in your division. Trouble is, you really dislike the guy. It is a personal thing. You deliberately fail to acknowledge his contribution and take all the glory yourself. Right or wrong?

2. **The Silent Kickback** —You are a consultant. A client, who trusts you implicitly, asks you to recommend a third-party vendor for a planned capital purchase. You provide a vendor recommendation but fail to mention that the vendor is going to commission you on the lead ... the classic 10-percent-off-the-top routine. Incidentally, the vendor in question does good work, and there is no fiddling with the pricing structure because of your referral fee. You choose not to say anything to your client about the arrangement. Right or wrong?

3. **He Is Not in Right Now** —You do not use voice mail. Your assistant, who screens your calls, informs you that Mr. Unhappy, who has been trying to track you down for the past week, is on the line. You have time to take the call. Courtesy alone dictates that you take it, but you choose to blow it off with any one of the common excuses (i.e., he is in a meeting, he is on the phone talking to London). Right or wrong?

4. **Promises Not Kept** — You run a research firm and recently sold a proposed industry study to a group of clients based on the guarantee that you will be conducting interviews with 100 industry influentials. Because of timing and logistical difficulties, you complete only 75 of the interviews. However, you are still going to lose a ton of money on the deal. You priced the study too low to begin with, and it ended up absorbing more time than you had projected. Your clients, those who bought the study, have already prepaid and like the results even though you fell short of the guaranteed interview count. You choose to remain silent and not proportionally rebate your clients for the shortfall. Right or wrong?

5. **The Refund Not Refunded**— You are flying to meet a client in another city. At the last minute, you decide to extend the trip to visit a second client while you are on the road. The deal is that your clients always rebate you in full for travel expenses. You bill both clients for the full return airfare from your city to theirs, despite the fact that you were able to secure a multicity, discounted fare and in the process made money on the deal. Right or wrong?

6. **The Money-Back Guarantee** — Your sales literature clearly states that a dissatisfied customer is entitled to a full refund or credit irrespective of the reason or the cause. You do a job for a client, but because of contributory negligence on both sides and a lack of clear definition and cause of the problem, your client chooses to pay you and let the matter drop. You believe that you went above and beyond the call of duty in addressing the client's needs. But you still do not offer a refund. Right or wrong?

7. **The Plane Crash**— You are the marketing director of a major airline. One of your planes crashes because of airline negligence. You know that you have to expose the airline's insurance representatives to the next-of-kin as soon as possible to negotiate quick settlements. The longer the delay, the greater the risk that an attorney will get to them first and force protracted litigation in a class-action suit, which, in turn, will result in higher settlement costs. It does not feel right to force a confrontation with the next-of-kin at their moment of greatest vulnerability, but you do it anyway. Right or wrong?

8. **The Name Dropper** —You and I meet for the first time. During the meeting, you ask me to provide names of friends and associates, people who might be prospects for your product or service. You subsequently write them a letter, and in the opening paragraph, you mention that the referral came from me. The problem is, you did it without my permission. When I gave you the names, I neglected (and you deliberately failed) to mention the issue. Right or wrong?

9. **The Fake Request for Approval (RFP)** —You are the head of a young, aggressive advertising agency, and you would love to know how your competitors package and present themselves. Therefore, you fake an RFP for an imaginary account that is up for review, send it out, and specify that responses be mailed to a blind postal address. Your competition wastes precious time responding to a fictitious RFP, and you gain valuable insights into your competitors' psychology and marketing technique. Right or wrong?

10. **Fresh from the Faucet**— You are in the bottled water business. Unlike your competitors' products, your water does not come from a natural source. No gurgling springs for you. You take good old-fashioned town water, distill it, treat it, and package it with a fake, natural-sounding name, together with label artwork resplendent with waterfalls and bubbling brooks, a classic case of the reality not matching the perception. But it is great marketing. Right or wrong?

(See next page for results).

Table 3-1: The Top Ten Test of Right or Wrong (continued)

Results:

If you answered "right" to 0–1 of the situations: Congratulations! You make good ethical decisions.

If you answered "right" to 2– 3 of the situations: Congratulations! You tend to make good ethical decisions, but at times you are not sure what is the correct course of action.

If you answered "right" to 4– 10 of the situations: Ethics is an important issue that you will want to study further. It is important not only to recognize ethical situations but also to make good ethical decisions.

Source: From Alf Nucifora, "How Is Your Marketing Conscience?" *Fort Worth Press,* October 20, 2000. Reproduced with permission of the author. Alf Nucifora is a nationally syndicated marketing columnist and consultant. He can be contacted by phone at 404-816-6999 (Atlanta) or by e-mail at alf@nucifora.com. His Web site is **www.nucifora.com.**

Over the years, marketing has come under attack for questionable activities. Some of the major criticisms of marketing are listed in Table 3-2. It is important to examine these criticisms in an introductory course in marketing. Although unfair and unethical behavior has occurred and will undoubtedly occur in the future, it is important to examine both sides of the issue and see how marketing can benefit society as a whole. If conducted in an ethical manner, marketing not only is a powerful force in the success of organizations but also can provide the opportunity for consumers to become more enlightened consumers of goods and services.

Table 3-2: Ethical Issues in Marketing

Marketing causes people to buy more than they can afford.

Marketing overemphasizes materialism.

Marketing increases the prices of goods and services.

Marketing capitalizes on human weaknesses.

Marketing shapes inappropriate cultural values.

Marketing uses deceptive and misleading techniques.

Marketing violates consumer rights to privacy.

3-2a: Marketing Causes People to Buy More Than They Can Afford

Marketing critics have voiced the concern that marketing persuades individuals to purchase goods and services that they do not need and cannot afford. Although it is true that millions of marketing dollars are spent to influence purchase decisions, and sometimes people buy more than they should, the easy acquisition of credit and the overuse of credit cards make it possible to overbuy.

The average credit card debt per household is now at $15,191, which is an increase of 3.7 percent from the previous year. The average number of bank credit cards per household is 19.3. Typically, that includes eight bank cards, eight retail cards, and three debit cards.[1] But should the entire blame lie with credit companies? No, not any more than it should be blamed on marketing. Overspending appears to be an epidemic, cultural change in our society caused by people seeking immediate gratification (see Figure 3-1). Few are willing to save and make a purchase only when they have the cash. This tendency to live beyond one's means, however, has been exacerbated by the opportunity offered by U.S. bankruptcy laws. Although many bankruptcies are caused by a major illness or loss of employment and are unavoidable, others are the result of overspending and inability to control personal gratification. This has resulted in an increase in personal bankruptcy filings in the United States by nearly 350 percent over the past 25 years, to 1.2 per 1,000 individuals currently.[2]

Figure 3-1: Overspending using credit cards is a national and international epidemic: the average credit card debt per U.S. household is now at $15,191!

3-2b: Marketing Overemphasizes Materialism

Closely tied to the notion that people buy goods and services they cannot afford is the criticism that marketing has created a materialistic society. The debates center on one issue: Has the marketing of goods and services created an attitude of materialism, or has marketing merely responded to the materialistic desires of society?

Underlying this argument is the assumption that materialism is wrong. In response, those who defend this aspect of free enterprise suggest that materialism, like many other things, is bad only if carried to an extreme. In comparing developing countries with the United States and other developed countries with high-consumption cultures, it is easy to show how materialism has created a positive impact on society and the standard of living people enjoy.

3-2c Marketing Increases the Prices of Goods and Services

Does marketing increase the prices of goods and services? Yes, it does. There is no doubt prices would be lower if marketing were eliminated. But before marketing is cut out, the following four factors must be considered:

- Marketing creates intangible benefits for a product.
- Marketing provides information that allows consumers to become better informed.
- A company can reduce its marketing efforts only if all the competitors within the industry do the same.
- Marketing is a significant contributor to the nation's gross domestic product (GDP).

Marketing can be used to create intangible benefits for goods and services. Consider the case of Nike shoes, Jaguar, Häagen-Dazs ice cream, Levi jeans, McDonald's restaurants (see Figure 3-2), Tide detergent, American Express credit cards, and Southwest Airlines. Each of these brands conveys a meaning beyond the product category. Nike and Jaguar can command higher prices because of the brand name, which is the result of their marketing effort. McDonald's and Southwest Airlines enjoy a large market share in their respective industries because they have been able to position themselves in a highly competitive market as the low-cost provider. Tide and American Express are highly recognizable brands because of intensive advertising. Consumers purchase these brands and many others because of intangible benefits, such as the trust and quality that stands behind the name. Consumers know that every time they purchase Tide, it will perform.

Figure 3-2: Advertising is an important component in building a strong brand for products like McDonald's.

Through marketing, consumers have the opportunity to become better informed. Marketing can provide consumers with knowledge about specific brands and product categories. Until Rogaine advertisements appeared, consumers had no idea that there were products that could be used to prevent hair loss. Until Rogaine targeted some of its ads to females, consumers thought the product was only for men. Other forms of marketing communications such as point-of-purchase displays, product labels, and salespeople can provide valuable information to consumers to assist them in making wiser purchase decisions. For example, the advertisement for Family Care in Figure 3-3 provides information about its after-hours clinic for individuals who may be sick on the weekends or in the evenings.

Figure 3-3: Advertising provides important information to consumers, such as this ad for Family Care, informing consumers about its after-hours clinic.

Source: Courtesy of Newcomer, Morris & Young.

Firms within highly competitive industries, such as soft drinks, automobiles, and athletic shoes, would like to reduce the size of their marketing budget. But if competitors do not reduce their marketing budget, it will be difficult for a firm to remain competitive with the firms in the industry. Table 3-3 provides a list of the top eight restaurant chains by market share. Notice that the advertising expenditures tend to be correlated with the market share. That does not necessarily mean that spending more in advertising will result in higher market share. Rather, to maintain a high market share, brands must continue to advertise. See Table 3-4 for a list of the top 10 megabrands and how much each spends on advertising alone. It is interesting to note that in the top 10 brands in terms of advertising spending, five are automobile brands, three are telecommunications companies, one is a restaurant, and one is a computer manufacturer.

Table 3-3: Comparison of Market Share to Advertising Expenditures for the Top Restaurant Chains

Rank	Brand	Market Share	Ad Spending (in millions)
1	McDonald's	8.18%	$957
2	Subway	2.78%	$516
3	Starbucks	2.44%	$70
4	Wendy's	1.98%	$280
5	Burger King	1.97%	$256
6	Taco Bell	1.74%	$280
7	Dunkin' Donuts	1.44%	$119
8	Pizza Hut	1.32%	$239
9	KFC	1.07%	$263
10	Chick-fil-A	1.06%	$32

Source: Adapted from www.AdAge.com; Accessed on March 30, 2014

Within the restaurant chain category, if Burger King chose to reduce its advertising expenditure, it is highly likely it would lose market share unless McDonald's, Wendy's, Subway, and Taco Bell also reduced their advertising spending. If all of these brands agreed to reduce their advertising expenditures, then it is likely they would face collusion charges for restraint of free trade. We do not want competitors making agreements among themselves that will in any way hinder the free market system.

Advertising in the United States alone stands at 4.1 percent of the U.S. GDP, and is projected to grow to 5 percent of GDP within the decade.[3] This does not include dollars spent on promotions, personal selling, and other forms of marketing communications. Traditionally, advertising accounts for about 25 percent of all marketing dollars. This means that the total marketing-related expenditures at well over $3 trillion. Eliminating marketing would create a tremendous loss of jobs and create a serious blow to the nation's GDP.

Rank	U.S. Measured-Media Spending	(in millions)
1	AT&T	$1.59
2	Verizon	$1.43
3	General Motors Co.	$958
4	McDonald's Corp.	$957
5	Berkshire Hathaway (GEICO)	$921
6	Toyota Motor Corp.	$879
7	Ford Motor Co.	$857
8	T-Mobile US	$773
9	Macy's	$762
10	Walmart Stores	$690

Table 3-4: Top 10 U.S. Megabrands and U.S. Ad Spending

Source: Adapted from www.AdAge.com; Accessed on March 30, 2014

3-2d: Marketing Capitalizes on Human Weaknesses

A sensitive ethical issue in marketing is the promotion of goods or services of a highly personal nature or during times of human vulnerability. For example, after the terrorist attacks of September 11, 2001, it was thought that some companies used patriotic themes to promote sales rather than to display genuine concern for the situation and victims of the attacks. Funeral homes and other similar services have been accused of taking advantage of grieving loved ones to encourage purchases beyond an individual's means.

In terms of personal services, marketers have been criticized for promoting the idea that happiness depends on physical attractiveness.[4] Appearance is a critical issue. To create an advertisement that feeds on insecurities about looks is considered by some to be unfair. Think about the various ads for weight loss programs. Most display both "before" and "after" pictures, with the person, usually a female, looking forlorn in the before photo, whereas the after shot depicts a much happier person.

In addition to weight loss programs, companies also offer consumers who are unhappy with their appearance services such as abdominoplasty (tummy tuck), electrolysis (hair removal), breast enhancements, and liposuction. All of these services are based on dissatisfaction with one's physical appearance. Critics say these efforts create unrealistic goals regarding personal appearance and cause people to examine self-worth in an unfair, shallow, and sexist manner.

Recently, more men have been attracted by this desire to enhance their physical appearance as well as their desire to improve their sexual performance. Hair coloring products, hair transplants, facelifts, penile enlargement programs, and erectile dysfunction treatment advertisements all feed on a person's insecurities. The issue here is similar to the first one that was raised about materialism: Is marketing driving human behavior or just responding to human desires (i.e., is marketing responding to society's preoccupation with personal appearance, or is marketing taking advantage of a person's insecurities)?

3-2e: Marketing Shapes Inappropriate Cultural Values

In terms of marketing's influence on cultural values, several issues are at stake. For example, marketing has been attacked for promoting products that are not good for public consumption. Alcohol and tobacco, especially, are believed to have a negative impact on people and on society as a whole. This has led some activists to object to the advertising of these products. The first issue here is one of free speech and free enterprise. As long as the firms are not violating the law (e.g., selling to minors), then why should companies not have the same right to market their products as any other organization?

The second issue is more philosophical. Does the promotion of such products shape cultural values, and, if so, then is it ethical to encourage individuals to consume a product (e.g., tobacco) that is known to be harmful to their health and results in millions of dollars of health care costs? If marketing, and especially advertising, indeed shapes cultural values, then it would appear that marketing should be regulated and controlled. The difficulty lies in the decision about who should determine what is appropriate and what is not appropriate. If, however, marketing just reflects the morals and values of our cultural environment, then regulating marketing would not be helpful in shaping cultural values.

To understand this dilemma better, consider the marketing of personal products, such as condoms, feminine hygiene items, male sex enhancement drugs, bras, and underwear. In the 1960s, none of these products were advertised on television. Now all are advertised. Is this change a reflection of changing social and cultural values, or has the promotion of these types of products molded social and cultural values to a point where this is now acceptable?

Many citizens believe that advertisements are becoming more offensive. Sexuality and nudity are the most troubling and controversial issues. For example, Calvin Klein has been highly criticized for the level of nudity and sexual suggestiveness in its advertisements. Calvin Klein has a history of pushing sexuality and nudity to the limit. More recently, it has been cited for the manner in which children are used in its promotions. The objections began years ago when a 15-year-old Brooke Shields was featured in a Calvin Klein ad proclaiming "Nothing comes between me and my Calvins." People not only objected to Calvin Klein using a 15-year-old but also objected to the sexual innuendo of a 15-year-old not wearing underwear. Viewers protested more strongly about a series of Calvin Klein television ads featuring underage girls being asked about their bodies. At the same time, a series of magazine ads featured partially clothed young models posing in sexy and suggestive ways to expose their underwear. Many magazine editors refused to run the print advertisements, and some television stations objected to the television commercials. Because of the complaints, the Federal Bureau of Investigation (FBI) investigated Calvin Klein to see if the magazine models were indeed 18 years old.

Later, in an attempt to sell children's underwear, Calvin Klein decided to prepare a large billboard in Times Square to accompany a series of magazine advertisements. The billboard promoting its line of children's underwear was to show two six-year-old boys arm wrestling and two girls about the same age jumping on a sofa. All were to be clad only in their underwear. Based on public opinion and strong objections from conservative groups, psychologists, and even the mayor of New York that such advertisements bordered on child pornography, Calvin Klein canceled the proposed billboards.[5]

Calvin Klein is not the only company using sexuality to sell its products. Sex is used overtly or subtly in many ads because it helps sell products. But in discussing the use of sexuality in marketing material, it must be kept in mind that what is offensive to one individual or group may not be to another (see Figure 3-4). In a nation that proclaims freedom of speech and expression, this is a very controversial issue. Company leaders must decide if they are going to use marketing material that contains sexuality or nudity. If so, then they must examine how their customers will view the ads. Ultimately, it is the customers who decide if the advertisements are acceptable, and as long as using sexuality in ads increases sales, companies will continue to use it.

An especially controversial area of marketing is that of advertising to children. Advertisers spend more than $12 billion a year on marketing products to children ages four to twelve. More than $2 billion is spent on print advertising, $2.5 billion each for TV and radio advertising, and the remaining $5 billion is used for public relations and marketing of events attended by

Figure 3-4: Sexuality is often a theme in window displays in Europe.

children. To snag these children, advertising agencies and marketing managers are hiring child psychologists. They want to know what kids think and how best to reach them (see Figure 3-5).[6]

Figure 3-5: Kid chic: Children are targeted with drama and style .

Why are children such an attractive market? Sheer numbers, for one thing. Tweens, children between nine and thirteen years old, control an estimated $43 billion in spending power, and marketers that try to reach them will need to have a keen understanding of how these kids interact online. They are known as mobile mavens, as Generation Z, children with digital in their DNA, who don't know a world without the social and mobile Web. Today's little kids and tweens having buying power to the tune of $1.2 trillion per year; this figure also includes the degree to which the children are influencing their parents' purchases – for example, 60 percent of all tweens today have influenced their parents' decision on which car to purchase.[7]

Are children a fair target for marketers? Children have not reached maturity and do not have the reasoning power of adults. It is difficult for children to distinguish between fact and fiction. They are easily influenced and misled. They develop strong feelings toward brands at an early age and by the early teenage years, insist upon designer clothes and brand-name products. Although some would like to ban all advertising to children, others would like no restrictions at all, claiming First Amendment rights. Somewhere between these two extremes is the right answer.

3-2f: Marketing Uses Deceptive and Misleading Techniques

For many consumers, the statement that "salespeople cannot be trusted" applies to more than just car salespeople. From the business-to-business perspective, many buyers feel that every salesperson will say and promise anything to make a sale. Often the relationship becomes almost adversarial, pitting buyers against sellers. Although it is true that some salespeople do use deceptive and misleading statements to sell, most do not. It is not in their best interests to do so. Salespeople rely on word-of-mouth communication from current customers to attract new business as well as repeat business from current customers. Dishonesty will be punished by customers who will make purchases elsewhere, tell others to avoid the business, and file complaints with agencies such as the CBBB. The long-term benefits of being honest far outweigh the short-term benefits of high-pressure and deceptive sales tactics.

For the business-to-business sector, more serious ethical issues include gifts and bribery. To influence sales, purchasing agents and other decision makers within a company are often the recipients of gifts, meals, entertainment, and even free trips. From a personal ethics standpoint, many concerned leaders wonder if personal gifts should be accepted if they are designed to influence a business purchase decision.

Closely tied with the issue of receiving gifts is one that is even more complex and difficult. In many countries, bribery is an accepted practice. To obtain government permits and business contracts, it is a common practice to offer bribes. Without them, permits and business contracts are not granted or are difficult to obtain. In Germany and France, the government actually permits companies to write off bribes as tax deductions. Dealing with these ethical issues is a major concern for business-to-business operations and businesses operating in the international environment.[8]

> **Bait and Switch:**
> A marketing tactic in which a retailer promotes a special deal on a particular product and then, when consumers arrive at the store, the retailer attempts to switch them to a higher-priced item.

In the retail area, a marketing tactic occasionally used is **bait and switch**. When using bait and switch, retailers promote a special deal on a particular product, and then, when the consumer arrives at the store, they attempt to switch the consumer to a higher-priced item. Often, advertised specials are stripped-down versions of a product or the low end of a product line. Once the consumers are in the store, salespeople will attempt to switch them to a better, pricey model. This tactic becomes illegal under two conditions. The first is when the retailer does not stock enough of the sale item, with the intention of not having it in stock when the consumer arrives. The second is when the salespeople use undue pressure to influence the customer to switch. As you can imagine, the second would be harder to prove.

Deceptive or misleading advertising is even more difficult to judge. When does an advertisement become misleading or deceptive? A Botox ad promised that use of the product would reduce all wrinkles, although the Food and Drug Administration (FDA) had approved the product for use only between a person's eyebrows. Furthermore, the ad did not tell viewers that the result is temporary, and that, for lasting results, injections of Botox have to be taken every three to four months.[9] Certainly, regulating authorities have concluded that this particular ad is deceptive and misleading. Section 3-3 includes a more detailed explanation of the standards used in determining whether an advertisement is deceptive or misleading.

Another concern is ads that are legally not deceptive or misleading but are clearly biased. For example, consider the numerous ads for cologne and perfume. Many promote the idea that you will become instantly appealing to members of the opposite sex and that your dream mate will suddenly discover you. Most people would consider these events unlikely to occur, but the message is still there. Use the cologne or perfume and you will become more sexually attractive. How far can an advertiser go with themes like this before it becomes misleading? As you can imagine, that question is difficult to answer because everybody will have a different opinion about where that point is.

3-2g: Marketing Violates Consumer Rights to Privacy

The more marketers understand about you as a consumer, the more efficient they can become in developing marketing material that will influence your purchase behavior. Although age, gender, income, and education are important pieces of information, if marketers can learn about your hobbies, interests, attitudes, and opinions, then it will be easier to design a message that will attract your attention. If marketers know where you shop and what you purchase, then the picture of you becomes even clearer. To learn all of these things about you, the marketer must gather information. That is where the right-to-privacy issue comes into play. Consumers want to protect their personal information, but marketers need it to promote their goods and services.

Where do marketers typically obtain information? Information comes from many different sources. For example, magazines sell their subscription lists. A firm that sells fishing supplies or equipment would like to purchase subscription lists from magazines about fishing so that it can send direct-mail pieces and catalogs to people who like fishing. By targeting people who like fishing, a company like Yamaha can reduce costs, and the material sent to the targeted individuals is more likely to be noticed and the probability of purchasing a boat increases (see Figure 3-6). Other sources of information include warranties that are filled out when purchasing a new product, surveys sent by magazines or other companies, credit card companies, banks, and schools.

Figure 3-6: By targeting individuals who like saltwater fishing, Yamaha is more successful than if this ad were shown to the general public.
Source: Courtesy of Newcomer, Morris & Young

The information-gathering source that has raised the most controversy is the Internet. Through cookies, information can be gathered from a computer about what sites the user has visited, how long he or she was at each site, and any other activity he or she conducted while on the Internet. This information becomes extremely valuable to marketers in understanding habits, interests, and purchases. Tied in with demographic data, this information is a gold mine for marketers.

In discussing this controversy, it must be kept in mind that marketers are interested in groups of people who fit a certain pattern, not individuals. It is not cost effective to market to every person with a different marketing message; however, it is cost effective to market to a group of consumers who have the same interests, habits, and purchase behavior. For example, the goal of the company that sells camping supplies is to obtain a database of people who would be inclined to purchase camping supplies. From this information, the company can better understand this group's thinking, interests, and attitudes, which can be used in preparing marketing communications material. Although it is important to protect the privacy of consumers, it is also important for consumers to understand how marketers are using the information.

3-2h Marketing's Role in Society

Although the criticisms of marketing have an element of truth, it is necessary to realize that marketing is an important ingredient of society and does perform a valuable role. While marketing's primary function is to promote the purchase and consumption of goods and services, consumers have the opportunity to gather information that will allow them to make better decisions.

It is also important to remember that some marketing tactics may be legal but are still perceived by a large segment of society to be unethical or in bad taste. When one is making marketing decisions, it is important to keep in mind that individuals, groups, states, nations, and societies differ in their beliefs about what constitutes both ethical and unethical behavior, and about what should be considered legal or illegal (see Figure 3-7). To help guide marketers in making ethical decisions, the American Marketing Association (AMA) adopted the code of ethics, which is highlighted in Table 3-5.

Figure 3-7: Beliefs about ethical and unethical behavior and what is considered legal and illegal vary from country to country and across cultures within a country. Counterfeit purses are sold in many stalls in this central Swiss marketplace.

Table 3-5: AMA's Code of Ethics

Members of the American Marketing Association (AMA) are committed to ethical professional conduct. They have joined together in subscribing to this Code of Ethics embracing the following topics:

Responsibilities of the Marketer

Marketers must accept responsibility for the consequences of their activities and make every effort to ensure that their decisions, recommendations, and actions function to identify, serve, and satisfy all relevant publics: customers, organizations, and society.

Marketers' professional conduct must be guided by:
1. The basic rule of professional ethics: not knowingly to do harm;
2. The adherence to all applicable laws and regulations;
3. The accurate representation of their education, training, and experience; and
4. The active support, practice, and promotion of this Code of Ethics.

Honesty and Fairness

Marketers shall uphold and advance the integrity, honor, and dignity of the marketing profession by:
1. Being honest in serving customers, clients, employees, suppliers, distributors, and the public;
2. Not knowingly participating in conflict of interest without prior notice to all parties involved; and
3. Establishing equitable fee schedules, including the payment or receipt of usual, customary, and/or legal compensation or marketing exchanges.

Rights and Duties of Parties in the Marketing Exchange Process

Participants in the marketing exchange process should be able to expect that:
1. Products and services offered are safe and fit for their intended uses;
2. Communication about offered products and services is not deceptive;
3. All parties intend to discharge their obligations, financial and otherwise, in good faith; and
4. Appropriate internal methods exist for equitable adjustment and/or redress of grievances concerning purchases.

Table 3-5: AMA's Code of Ethics (continued)

It is understood that the above would include, but is not limited to, the following responsibilities of the marketer:

In the area of product development and management,
  Disclosure of all substantial risks associated with product or service usage;
  Identification of any product component substitution that might materially change the product or impact on the buyer's purchase decision;
  Identification of extra-cost added features.

In the area of promotions,
  Avoidance of false and misleading advertising;
  Rejection of high-pressure manipulation;
  Avoidance of sales promotions that use deception or manipulation.

In the area of distribution,
  Not manipulating the availability of a product for purpose of exploitation;
  Not using coercion in the marketing channel;
  Not exerting undue influence over the reseller's choice to handle the product.

In the area of pricing,
  Not engaging in price fixing;
  Not practicing predatory pricing;
  Disclosing the full price associated with any purchase.

In the area of marketing research,
  Prohibiting selling or fund raising under the guise of conducting research;
  Maintaining research integrity by avoiding misrepresentation and omission of pertinent research data;
  Treating outside clients and suppliers fairly.

Organizational Relationships
Marketers should be aware of how their behavior may influence or impact the behavior of others in organizational relationships. They should not demand, encourage, or apply coercion to obtain unethical behavior in their relationships with others, such as employees, suppliers, or customers:

1. Apply confidentiality and anonymity in professional relationships with regard to privileged information;
2. Meet their obligations and responsibilities in contracts and mutual agreements in a timely manner;
3. Avoid taking the work of others, in whole or in part, and represent this work as their own or directly benefit from it without compensation or consent of the originator or owner;
4. Avoid manipulation to take advantage of situations to maximize personal welfare in a way that unfairly deprives or damages the organization of others.

Any AMA members found to be in violation of any provision of this Code of Ethics may have his or her
Association membership suspended or revoked.

Source: Reprinted by permission of American Marketing Association.

Figure 3-8: A Framework for Ethical (and Unethical) Decision Making

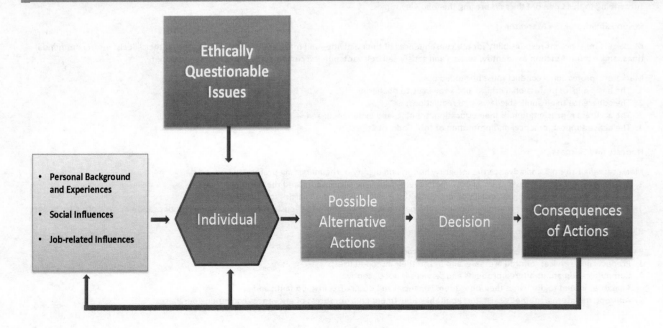

3-2i: Individual Roles in Marketing Ethics

When thinking about individuals and ethical decisions that each person faces, one should consider the two extremes. At one extreme are marketing decisions that are viewed as unethical only by a few individuals because they do not have a serious impact on other people, firms, or society. At the other extreme are marketing decisions that are viewed as unethical by most people and do have a potentially lasting and serious impact on individuals, firms, or society.

Figure 3-8 (previous page) provides a useful framework for examining how someone in marketing would make a decision that can carry some ethical ramifications. For purposes of illustration, suppose you are the marketing director of a video game company that wants to market a new video game to males ages 13 to 18. Although the game has some violence, the sexy attire of the female characters disturbs you. When you are preparing the marketing material for the game, your dilemma is how sexy to make the ads. More important, is using sex appeal even appropriate for this age group?

As illustrated in Figure 3-8, your decision is influenced by your personal background and experiences. If you grew up in a liberal environment where sexuality was discussed openly, you may not see an ethical dilemma at all. But if you grew up in a religious or conservative environment where sexuality was a taboo subject, you may feel sexuality is not an appropriate marketing appeal for young teenagers. If you were the parent of a teenage boy or a teenage girl, your feelings may be different than if you were 25 years old and had no children.

Although society and its views will have an influence on your decision, a more relevant influence will be the forces within your company. If you were just appointed the marketing director and your career will be influenced by the sales of this video game, your decision may be different than if you have been with the company for 20 years and have proved your ability to make good decisions. A major difficulty for employees in these situations is the attitude and beliefs of the company. If the chief executive office (CEO) of this video game company feels it is not ethically wrong to use sex appeal for males between 13 and 18 years of age, then you will have less latitude to make a decision.

In most ethical decisions, there are consequences to the decision. In this situation, your decision will affect the success of this video game. Although there is no guarantee that using sex appeal will increase sales, you suspect that teenage boys would be more inclined to pay attention to such an advertisement. However, if you take a stand and say no, will those in the company, especially your boss, respect your decision, or will you soon be looking for another job? Your decision and the consequences that occur as a result will then become part of your personal experience that will be used in future decisions.

3-3 MARKETING REGULATIONS

Because of the ethical issues discussed in Section 3-2, the federal and state governments of the United States have passed a number of laws to protect consumers from unethical corporate practices. These laws pertain to price fixing, free enterprise, food quality, fair interest rates, product safety, protection of children, deceptive advertising, and a variety of other issues. Table 3-6 (next page) lists the major federal legislation, along with a description of each.

Two overriding principles are behind the legislation mentioned in Table 3-6. First is the objective of ensuring free trade and open competition among firms. Second is the need to protect consumers from unscrupulous actions of business firms. As businesses grew in size during the 1800s, the federal government realized that, if left unchecked, these businesses would create monopolies and eventually dominate the marketplace. With no competitors, the large businesses could dictate prices, distribution, and access to goods and services. Consumers would be forced to pay the price charged or do without, especially if no substitutes existed.

To prevent monopolies and trusts that could restrict trade, the Sherman Antitrust Act was passed in 1890. This was followed in 1914 by the passage of the Clayton Act and in 1936 by the Robinson-Patman Act. These last two acts were designed to prevent price discrimination by sellers. When businesses could no longer form monopolies or large trusts, they controlled buyers by using "tying contracts" and price discrimination. Charging small businesses more for the same merchandise and forcing them to buy an entire line of merchandise allowed the manufacturers to choose who would be allowed to purchase from them. The Clayton Act and Robinson-Patman Act prevented this type of behavior.

Table 3-6: Major Federal Legislation Affecting Marketing Activities	
Legislation	**Description**
1890 Sherman Antitrust Act	Prohibits trusts, monopolies, and activities designed to restrict free trade.
1906 Federal Food and Drug Act	Created the Food and Drug Administration and prohibits the manufacture and sale of falsely labeled foods and drugs.
1914 Clayton Act	Prohibits price discrimination to different buyers, tying contracts that require buyers of one product to also purchase another item, and combining two or more competing firms by pooling ownership of stock.
1914 Federal Trade Commission Act	Created the Federal Trade Commission (FTC) to address antitrust matters and investigate unfair methods of competition.
1936 Robinson-Patman Act	Prohibits charging different prices to different buyers of the same merchandise and requires sellers that offer a service to one buyer to make the same service available to all buyers.
1938 Wheeler-Lea Amendment	Expanded the power of the FTC to investigate and prohibit false and misleading advertising and practices that could injure the public.
1946 Lanham Act	Established protection of trademarks.
1966 Fair Packaging and Labeling Act	Requires that manufacturers provide a label containing contents, who made the product, and how much of each item it contains.
1972 Consumer Product Safety Act	Established the Consumer Product Safety Commission (CPSC), which sets safety standards for products and ensures that manufacturers follow safety standard regulations.
1976 Hart-Scott-Rodino Act	Requires corporations wanting to merge to notify and seek approval of the government before any action is taken.
1990 Children's Television Act	Limits the number and times advertisements can be aired during children's programs.

To protect consumers from unethical, deceptive, and misleading marketing tactics, the Federal Food and Drug Act, the Federal Trade Commission Act, the Wheeler-Lea Amendment, the Fair Packaging and Labeling Act, the Consumer Product Safety Act, and the Children's Television Act were passed. Although the focus of each piece of legislation was slightly different, the overarching principle of each was to ensure that consumers were treated fairly and protected from deceptive and misleading marketing practices.

Passing laws to prevent monopolies and to protect consumers did not ensure that businesses would comply. Using federal authorities, state authorities, and the court system became too burdensome. Therefore, a number of federal agencies were created to ensure that laws were upheld. Table 3-7 (next page) lists the primary agencies involved in regulating marketing activities and has a description of each agency's responsibilities. These various agencies were given the authority to set standards, investigate cases of wrongdoing, and punish those who did not comply. Although all are important, we will discuss only the FDA and the FTC because they are the most relevant to marketing.

Table 3-7: Primary Federal Agencies Involved in Regulating Marketing Activities	
Agency	**Responsibility**
Food and Drug Administration (FDA)	Regulates and oversees the manufacturing, distribution, and labeling of food and drugs.
Federal Communications Commission (FCC)	Regulates the television, radio, telephone, and Internet industries.
U.S. Postal Service (USPS)	Responsible for mail delivery and investigating mail fraud schemes and any other illegal marketing activities using
Bureau of Alcohol, Tobacco, and Firearms (ATF)	Oversees the manufacture, sale, and distribution of tobacco and alcohol.
Federal Trade Commission (FTC)	Primary agency responsible for ensuring free trade among businesses and investigating false, deceptive, or misleading claims in advertising and other types of marketing communications.
Consumer Product Safety Commission (CPSC)	Sets safety standards for products used by consumers in or around their home.

3-3a: The Food and Drug Administration

The FDA has the responsibility of overseeing the sale of all food and drug products. Before a drug can be used by physicians or sold to the public, the FDA must approve it. Strict tests and guidelines are used to ensure that there are no detrimental side effects. Occasionally, the FDA will allow doctors to use a drug under test conditions to measure its impact and side effects before it is released for public use.

For food products, the FDA is responsible for ensuring that food is safely processed and packaged. Because labels were often misleading, the Fair Packaging and Labeling Act (see Figure 3-9) was passed in 1966. This law requires that all food products have a label stating every ingredient in an order that corresponds to its relative content.

Phrases such as "contains 220 calories per serving" have to be explained in terms of what constitutes a serving size. Often, the typical serving size that an individual eats is not the same as that designated by a manufacturer. For example, a low-fat granola cereal that states it has 220 calories and three grams of fat per serving size is required to state on the label that a serving size is only two-thirds of a cup, not the two or three cups a typical person may eat at a meal.[10]

Table 3-8 (next page) contains information about the sugar and caffeine content of selected beverages. You may be surprised at the differences among the various brands.

Figure 3.9: To protect consumers from misleading labels, the Fair Packing and Labeling Act, passed in 1966, set standards for what should be on a label.

3-3 b The Federal Trade Commission

The agency with the most impact on marketing is the Federal Trade Commission (FTC). In addition to ensuring free trade among businesses, the FTC is responsible for investigating claims of false, deceptive, or misleading marketing communications. Deceptive or misleading marketing communications can stem from any type of marketing source, such as advertising, billboards, direct mail, corporate literature, oral and written communications by sales people, or corporate Internet materials. The Wheeler-Lea Amendment, passed in 1938, gave the FTC authority to investigate claims of false advertising and prohibit any marketing practice that might injure the public or be deceptive in any way.

Table 3-8: Sugar and Caffeine Content of Selected Beverages		
Soft Drinks	**Serving Size**	**Caffeine (mg)**
FDA official limit for soft drinks	12 oz.	71 (200 parts per million)
Pepsi MAX	12 oz.	69
Mountain Zevia (Zevia)	12 oz.	55
Mountain Dew, regular or diet	12 oz.	54 (20 oz. = 90)
Diet Coke	12 oz.	47 (20 oz. = 78)
Dr Pepper or Sunkist, regular or diet	12 oz.	41 (20 oz. = 68)
Pepsi	12 oz.	38 (20 oz. = 63)
Coca-Cola, Coke Zero, or Diet Pepsi	12 oz.	35 (20 oz. = 58)
Barq's Root Beer, regular	12 oz.	23 (20 oz. = 38)
Dunkin' Donuts Coffee with Turbo Shot	large, 20 fl. oz.	436
Starbucks Coffee	venti, 20 fl. oz.	415
Starbucks Coffee	grande, 16 fl. oz.	330
Panera Frozen Mocha	16.5 fl. oz.	267

Sources: Adapted from Center for Science in the Public Interest, "Caffeine Content of Food & Drugs," http://www.cspinet.org/newcafchart.htm, accessed on July 17, 2014.

A firm can violate this law even when the company did not expressly intend to deceive or mislead consumers. According to the FTC, an advertisement or marketing communication is deemed to be deceptive or misleading when:

1. A substantial number of people, or the "typical person," is left with a false impression or misrepresentation that relates to the product; or

2. The misrepresentation induces people, or the typical person, to make a purchase.

A violation is deemed to have occurred if one or both conditions are met. Businesses and individuals can sue under the guidelines of the FTC.[11]

When investigating complaints, the FTC does not consider subjective or puffery claims to be a violation. **Puffery** exists when a firm makes an exaggerated claim about its goods or services, without making an overt attempt to deceive or mislead. Terms normally associated with puffery include words such as best, greatest, and finest. For example, in the advertisement in Figure 3-10 the headline reads "The Best Seat in the House." The FTC sees this as puffery and would take no action. When Ol'Man states that its deer treestand is the "most comfortable," the "easiest to use," and the "highest quality," these are all statements of puffery. However, when Ol'Man states it is the "safety leader," then it becomes deceptive and misleading if indeed the Ol'Man treestand is not the safety leader. The company must be able to back up this type of statement. Obviously, there is quite a bit of gray area when a claim about a false or misleading statement is made.

The FTC can receive a complaint from any of the following sources:

- Consumers
- Businesses
- Congress
- The media
- The FTC itself

Puffery:
When a firm makes an exaggerated claim about its goods or services, without making an overt attempt to deceive or mislead.

Figure 3-10: This advertisement by Ol'Man uses puffery in the statements "The Best Seat in the House," "Most Comfortable," "Easiest to Use," and "Highest Quality."
Source: Courtesy of Newcomer, Morris & Young.

Each entity can raise concerns about what appears to be an unfair or deceptive practice by a particular business, group of businesses, or even an industry. In the beginning, FTC investigations are often confidential, but they do not have to be. The initial confidential investigation protects both the FTC and the company being investigated if no violation has occurred. However, if the FTC believes a law has been violated or a marketing practice is viewed as deceptive or misleading, the first step in resolving the issue will be to issue a consent order. If the company agrees to the consent order, it agrees to stop the disputed practice but does not admit any guilt. Most investigations of the FTC end with a signed consent order.

An illustration of this process involved two companies that collected extensive information from high school students that was to be shared with colleges, universities, and other education-related services. These companies — the National Research Center for College and University Admissions (NRCCUA) and American Student List (ASL) —distributed questionnaires in high schools, collecting from students information such as their name, address, gender, grade point average, academic and occupational interests, athletic interests, extracurricular interests, ethnicity, and religious background. Both firms claimed that this data collection request was funded by colleges and universities and that the data would be shared with educational institutions. The FTC found both claims to be false. Although the data were shared with educational institutions, they were also sold to commercial firms for marketing purposes. In addition, commercial entities provided financial support to both companies. Because neither of these facts was shared with the high school students or the schools, the FTC found the marketing approach to be misleading and deceptive.

Both companies signed a consent order agreeing that information collected in the past would not be sold to any commercial firm. They also agreed to properly disclose in future data collection efforts that the companies were also supported by commercial entities and that the data could be sold to commercial firms for marketing purposes. By signing the consent agreement, both firms agreed to stop the potentially "deceptive and misleading practices," while at the same time not admitting they were guilty of breaking any FTC regulations.[12]

If a consent agreement cannot be reached, the FTC may issue what is called an administrative complaint. A formal proceeding similar to a court trial is held before an administrative law judge. Both sides submit evidence and testimony to support their case. At the end of the administrative hearing, the judge makes a ruling. If the judge feels a violation has occurred, a cease-and-desist order is prepared. This order requires the company to immediately stop the disputed practice and refrain from any similar practices in the future. If the company is not satisfied with the decision of the administrative law judge, it can appeal the case to the full FTC commission.

The full commission holds a similar type of hearing in which evidence and testimony can be presented. The full commission can issue a cease-and-desist order if it believes the company is guilty or dismiss the case if it feels the administrative judge and previous rulings were incorrect. Companies not satisfied with the ruling of the full FTC commission can appeal the case to the U.S. Court of Appeals and even up to the U.S. Supreme Court. The danger in appealing to the Court of Appeals is that the court has the power to provide consumer redress (i.e., the power to levy civil penalties).

A complaint does not have to go to the Court of Appeals, however, for civil penalties to be assessed. The FTC also has the power to do so. E-Babylon, Inc. agreed to pay a $40,000 civil penalty as part of its consent agreement. The FTC accused E-Babylon, Inc. of misrepresenting its products as being new, brand-name inkjet cartridges, when in fact they were either remanufactured or generic cartridges (see Figure 3-11). In addition, E-Babylon, Inc. advertised that any dissatisfied customer could receive a "no questions asked" re-

Figure 3-11: The FTC ordered E-Babylon, Inc., to pay a $40,000 civil penalty as part of its consent agreement for misleading and deceptive marketing practices for its inkjet cartridges.

fund, but in reality, customers had an extremely difficult time in obtaining refunds. Furthermore, E-Babylon, Inc. did not comply with the FTC's mail order rule because it did not advise customers who purchased its products that they had the right to cancel their orders and receive a refund if E-Babylon, Inc. could not ship the merchandise on time. Lastly, the company was ordered to pay redress to all consumers who were entitled to refunds either under the FTC's mail order rule or E-Babylon, Inc.'s money-back guarantee. Rather than risk a greater penalty by appealing to the court system, firms like E-Babylon, Inc. will usually agree to consent orders.[13]

In more severe instances of deceptive or misleading advertising, the FTC can order a firm to prepare corrective advertising. These situations are rare and occur only when the FTC believes that discontinuing a false advertisement will not be a sufficient remedy. In ordering corrective advertising, the FTC concludes that consumers believed the false or misleading information, and the goal of having the company issuing corrective ads is to bring consumers back to a neutral state that existed before the misleading ads.

Corrective advertising orders are rare but were used by the FTC following a judgment against Volvo Cars of North America. The company had created an advertisement showing a row of cars being destroyed by a monster truck as it ran over them. Only the Volvo was not smashed. After investigation, the FTC discovered that the Volvo automobile had been altered with steel bars to prevent it from being crushed. The FTC concluded that the ad would cause consumers to believe that Volvo was a safer automobile than it actually was. Consequently, the FTC not only ordered Volvo to discontinue the ad but also to run a new advertisement explaining how the car had been altered in the previous commercial.[14] The FTC seldom orders corrective ads because, in most cases, it is extremely difficult to eliminate the impact of a misleading ad and take consumers back to a neutral point.

The FTC rules cover every aspect of marketing communications. Regardless of the type of communication, unfair or deceptive marketing communications are prohibited. Marketers must be able to substantiate claims through competent and reliable evidence (see Figure 3-12). If endorsers are used, their statements must be truthful and represent their experiences or opinions. If expert endorsements are used, their statements must be based on legitimate tests performed by experts in the field. All claims must reflect the typical experience that a customer would expect to encounter from the use of the product or service, unless the advertisement clearly and prominently states otherwise.[15]

One of the keys to FTC evaluations of advertisements and marketing communications is the idea of substantiation. Firms must be able to substantiate (e.g., prove or back up) any claims made. Failure to do so can result in some form of FTC action. The marketers of Xenadrine EFX, a weight-loss pill,

Figure 3-12: It would be difficult to substantiate claims such as "fabulous" and "best tasting".

paid $20.8 million to settle FTC allegations of false and unsubstantiated advertising claims. Xenadrine EFX made claims that the product was clinically proven to cause rapid and substantial weight loss and clinically proven to be more effective than leading ephedrine-based diet products. The FTC conducted independent studies of Xenadrine EFX and found no substantial weight loss. In fact, in one study, the control group taking a placebo lost more weight than the Xenadrine EFX group. The complaint by the FTC also stated that EFX falsely represented people in the ads as having achieved weight loss entirely through the use of Xenadrine EFX, when the weight loss was actually the result of rigorous diet or exercise. In addition, the endorsers were paid from $1,000 to $20,000 for their testimony, which Xenadrine EFX failed to disclose in their advertisements.[16]

If a firm makes a claim about its product, it must be able to substantiate that claim. If a firm says, "Brand X reduces the symptoms of the common cold," it must be able to prove that Brand X does indeed reduce the symptoms of the common cold. In this case, an independent study would be the best substantiation. If the company performs the study itself, it must be careful to follow good scientific procedures. The

FTC examines company-sponsored research more closely than research by an independent firm.

In addition to investigating individual businesses, the FTC can also investigate an industry and provide what is called a trade regulation ruling. Normally, the FTC will hold a public hearing and accept both oral and written arguments from companies in the industry concerned. They will then make a ruling that would apply to every firm within an industry. As with other rulings made by the FTC, decisions can be challenged in the U.S. Court of Appeals. For instance, the FTC investigated the pricing practices of funeral homes and issued a trade regulation ruling that required funeral homes to provide customers with an itemized list of charges.[17] The FTC will also aggressively pursue industries or practices that it believes are not in the best interest of the public or that violate current laws or acts.

The FTC may also issue industry guidelines. Because celebrities and experts are frequently used in advertisements to endorse a product, the FTC issued guidelines concerning the use of celebrity endorsements and testimonials. Not to be deceptive, the following criteria must be met:

1. Statements must reflect the honest opinion, findings, beliefs, or experience of the celebrity.
2. The accuracy of the celebrity's claims must be substantiated by the advertiser.
3. If the advertisement claims the celebrity uses the product, the celebrity must in fact be a bona fide user of it.
4. The advertiser can use the endorsement only as long as it has good faith belief that the celebrity will continue to hold the views expressed in the advertisement.[18]

3-3c Industry Regulations

Because of the volume of complaints, the federal regulatory agencies would have a difficult time investigating them all if it were not for the industry regulatory system. Although the various industry regulatory agencies have no legal power, they can reduce the load on the FTC and the legal system. Many allegations or complaints about unfair and deceptive marketing practices are handled and settled within the advertising and business industry. Although various industry agencies exist for monitoring marketing activities, the most common is the Council of Better Business Bureaus and its three subsidiary agencies: (1) the National Advertising Division (NAD), (2) the Children's Advertising Review Unit (CARU), and (3) the National Advertising Review Board (NARB).

The Council of Better Business Bureaus, Inc. (CBBB) and local Better Business Bureaus (BBB) are venues available to both consumers and businesses. Unethical business practices or unfair treatment can lead to the filing of complaints against a business with the CBBB. The CBBB will compile a summary of charges leveled against individual firms. Although the charges are not investigated, they are kept on record for potential customers who want to learn about a particular business. When asked by an individual or business, the CBBB will provide a carefully worded report that will raise cautionary flags about a firm that has received a great number of complaints and state the general nature of the complaints.

In 1971, the National Advertising Review Council (NARC) was formed by the Association of National Advertisers, the American Association of Advertising Agencies, the American Advertising Federation, and the CBBB. The purpose of NARC is to foster truth, honesty, and accuracy in advertising through industry self-regulation. NARC also establishes policies and procedures for the NAD, the CARU, and the NARB.[19]

When complaints about advertising are received, the CBBB refers them to either the NAD or the CARU of the CBBB. The agency concerned will collect information and evaluate data concerning the complaint to determine whether the complaint is legitimate. In most cases, the NAD and the CARU are looking for evidence of substantiation. If the firm's advertising claim is substantiated, then the complaint is dismissed. If it is not, the NAD and the CARU will negotiate with the business to modify or discontinue the advertisement. If the advertiser disagrees with the decision, then it can be appealed to the NARB of the

CBBB. From there, the appeal would go to the FTC or other appropriate federal agency.

Recently, CARU recommended that 20th Century Fox Entertainment refrain from advertising films rated PG-13 on children's television programming. The ruling came from an investigation by CARU into the advertising of the movie "X-Men: The Last Stand," which was rated PG-13, on Nickelodeon during children's programming. CARU stated that the advertisers of videos and movies "should take care that only those which are age-appropriate are advertised to children." It further stated that because the movie had been rated PG-13 by the Motion Picture Association of America as a result of intense sequences of violence, some sexual content, and language, it was not appropriate to advertise the movie to children younger than 13. Although the advertiser disagreed with CARU and did not believe the content of the movie was inappropriate for children, they complied with the ruling and discontinued advertising the movie during children's programming.[20]

Complaints are often filed by a competitor because of unfavorable depictions of their brand versus the advertised brand. Such was the case when Procter & Gamble filed a complaint with the NAD concerning Unilever's ad for Degree Ultra's Clear Antiperspirant, which claimed:

"Unless they're using New Degree Ultra Clear, those white marks may just show up later."

"Others go on clear. New Degree Ultra Clear stays that way."

"100% Little Black Dress Approved."

After viewing demonstrations of Unilever's brand (New Degree Ultra Clear) and Procter & Gamble's brand (Secret Platinum Invisible Solid), the NAD stated that both brands left perceptible white residue, although the Procter & Gamble brand did leave substantially more than the Unilever brand. The NAD ruled, however, that leaving "substantially less residue" is significantly different than stating it "leaves no residue." Therefore, the NAD recommended that Unilever discontinue all television, Web site, and print advertising making such claims. Although Unilever disagreed with the NAD decision, they stated that it "fully supports the self-regulation program and will take NAD's opinion into consideration in future advertising."[21]

Not all of the NAD rulings are against the advertiser. The NAD determined that Starbucks had substantiated claims made in its "Fair Trade Certified" coffees. The issue was that Starbucks claimed that 21 percent of the Fair Trade Certified Coffee imported into the United States was purchased by Starbucks, making it the largest purchaser of such coffee. Fair Trade Certified Coffee is coffee bought at a fair price from developing countries, and that encourages environmental sustainability and community development; the claim was used by Starbucks to highlight its concerns for the people in these countries. Upon review of reports issued by Transfair USA, the organization that helps developing countries import coffee to the USA, the claims made by Starbucks was found to be truthful and correct.[22]

In some cases, the advertiser is dissatisfied with the ruling of the NAD and appeals the decision to the NARB. Such was the case with Perdue Farms, Inc. when the NAD ruled against Perdue's claims of "fresh fully cooked" and "no preservatives." The NAD had ruled that the product being sold by Perdue misled the public because it was labeled "fresh fully cooked" when it could stay on the shelf for three to six months before being sold. Furthermore, although Perdue labeled the product as having no preservatives, two well-known antimicrobial agents (sodium lactate and sodium diacetate) had been added. Perdue Farms, however, contended the label had been approved by the FDA's Food Service and Inspection Service, and therefore the NAD should defer the ruling to that agency and allow the terms to be used.[23]

Most cases investigated by the NAD, the CARU, and the NARB are resolved. Occasionally, an advertiser refuses to participate in the self-regulation process or ignores the ruling. For example, the NAD investigated claims made by Spitz Sunflower Seeds that its brand was the "#1 sunflower seed" and contained "all natural ingredients." ConAgra filed the complaint because they believed their brand, David, was the number one brand and they also believed the Spitz Sunflower brand did not use "all natural ingredients." When Spitz Sales, Inc. refused to participate in NAD's investigation and provide substantiation for their claims, the case was referred to the FTC and the FDA for review. As noted previously, the FTC and FDA do have legal authority and can require Spitz Sales, Inc. to participate in the investigation. Spitz Sales also faced the risk of being forced to pay civil penalties. Because of this risk and the additional cost required to defend their case before the FTC or FDA, most companies willingly participate in the advertising industry's self-regulation system.[24]

3-4 SOCIAL RESPONSIBILITY

Consumers today expect companies to act responsibly and to be good citizens. In a recent survey, 83 percent of Americans indicated that it is important for corporations to support the needs of society.[25] This can be done by producing environmentally safe products, by controlling for emissions and wastes that contaminate the environment, or by becoming involved in meeting the social needs of society. In the past, most corporations fulfilled the requirement of meeting the needs of society through philanthropy. Then, in 1984, American Express promised to donate one cent for the Statue of Liberty restoration project for every cardholder transaction. In three months, $1.7 million was donated. Transactions rose by 28 percent, and new card applications rose by 17 percent.[26] It was a whopping success for the Statue of Liberty restoration effort and for American Express. It was also the beginning of a movement from philanthropy to cause-related marketing (see Figure 3-13).

Figure 3-13: This advertisement by Plum Creek shows its commitment to social responsibility. Although Plum Creek provides timber for the lumber industry, it is committed to preserving hunting, fishing, and outdoor recreation habitats.

Source: Sample print advertisement courtesy of The Miles Agency and Alliance One Advertising, Inc.

3-4a: Cause-Related Marketing

Writing a check to a local charity or even a national charity is not cause-related marketing, but rather philanthropy. **Cause-related marketing** is a long-term partnership between a nonprofit organization and a corporation and is integrated into the corporation's marketing plan. Both parties must benefit from the relationship for it to be an effective cause-related marketing effort (see Figure 3-14) .

> **Cause-related Marketing:** A long-term partnership between a nonprofit organization and a corporation that is integrated into the corporation's marketing plan.

The Cone/Roper Corporate Citizenship Survey found, shortly after the events of September 11, 2001, that 81 percent of Americans would switch brands to help support a cause if price and quality were equal, and 92 percent indicated they felt more positive about a corporation that supported a cause.[27]

To be successful with a cause-related program, the firm must demonstrate a genuine support for a cause. If it does not and if customers suspect a firm is using the nonprofit cause to benefit itself, it will backfire. To ensure that

Figure 3-14 Esso, an ExxonMobil company, partnered with Junior Achievement Young Enterprise in a number of European countries to develop the Sci-Tech challenge to encourage high school students to consider mathematics and science oriented careers.

a cause-related program will work, a firm first must align itself with a cause that fits its mission and its products. Avon's support for breast cancer research is a logical fit.

How companies promote the cause is extremely important. If they spend $3 million to advertise their $100,000 donation, as Philip Morris did after the September 11 terrorist attacks, consumers will see it as exploitation. If they mention it in their advertising, on point-of-purchase displays, and in their facility but do not make it a big deal, consumers will accept it. Consumers are looking for a genuine relationship between the nonprofit organization and the company, not a gimmick by the corporation to boost its sales. One method of demonstrating this genuineness is getting employees involved. If employees do not support and believe in the cause, the public will be suspicious of the motives. Employees of corporations with legitimate cause-related programs are 38 percent more likely to say they are proud of their employer than employees who work for a corporation that is not involved with a cause.[28]

3-4b: Green Marketing

> **Green Marketing:** The development and promotion of products that are environmentally safe.

Cause-related marketing is one way a company can demonstrate its social responsibility; green marketing is another. **Green marketing** is the development and promotion of products that are environmentally safe. Although almost all Americans support the concept of green marketing, few really support it with purchases. For example, more than 11,000 different products have the U.S. Environmental Protection Agency's (EPA's) ENERGY STAR label for energy efficiency. More than 40 percent of consumers recognize the label, but only a small percentage demand the label when making a purchase. Despite advances in technology, a study by Roper found that 42 percent of consumers interviewed still believe that "environmentally safe products don't work as well" as regular products (see Figure 3-15). [29]

Global warming has received considerable press lately. Of Americans, 58 percent agree that there has been a global warming and 50 percent believe it is serious. Yet consumers are reluctant to turn off lights and drive more fuel-efficient cars. For example, hybrid cars account for only 1.3 percent of U.S. light-vehicle sales.[30]

The key to successful green marketing is the same as developing a strong brand name for any product. First, the product must be of high quality. Although marketing may be able to entice some people to purchase, a poorly built product will eventually lose. Consumers will not continue to purchase poorly built products to support the environment. Although in the past green marketing products such as laundry detergents were inferior, such is not the case anymore.

Second, the cost of producing green products must be reduced. This has been a challenge because of the lack of acceptance by the public. Companies are reluctant to invest huge dollars in research on green products that may not do well in the marketplace. This will change, however, if companies continue to have success with green products. Phillips Lighting recently introduced the "Marathon" fluorescent light bulb that has a longer life and lower operating costs. It has done well in the marketplace.

The last key to successfully marketing green products is to make these green products attractive to the public. If products like Pepsi and Coke can be made "sexy" through shrewd marketing and advertising techniques, so can products that are environmentally friendly. Companies that recognize this opportunity and jump on it now will build an advantage for the future when the world's petroleum supply and other natural resources do become a factor. At the rate of current consumption, the cost of producing environmentally friendly products, such as synthetic carpet, will someday be cheaper than carpet made with petroleum chemicals.

Figure 3-15 Products often are packaged in green containers to communicate that they are as close as feasible to nature.

Summary

1. Identify the ethical issues faced by marketers and discuss the pros and cons of each issue. A number of ethical issues have been raised concerning marketing. First, marketing causes people to buy more than they can afford. Although some would feel this overspending is the result of marketing, others would claim marketing is just responding to what consumers want. Second, marketing overemphasizes materialism. Again, although some would argue that marketing creates materialism, others would say marketing is merely responding to materialistic desires. Third, marketing increases the prices of goods and services. Although this is true, marketing also provides information so consumers can make intelligent consumption decisions. Fourth is the criticism that marketing capitalizes on human weaknesses. Marketers would argue that they are just responding to personal needs. Fifth, critics would suggest that marketing shapes and encourages inappropriate cultural values. Marketers would contend that marketing responds to current cultural values and would not be effective in promoting desires that do not conform to cultural values. Sixth, marketing uses deceptive and misleading advertising. Although some marketers do use deceptive and misleading advertising, agencies such as the FTC have been created to protect consumers. Last, critics contend that marketing violates consumers' right to privacy. Although marketers do gather personal information, it is used to better market to people's needs.

2. Discuss the legislation and regulatory agencies that affect marketing. A number of laws have been passed to protect consumers and to ensure free trade among businesses. Antitrust legislation includes the Sherman Antitrust Act, Clayton Act, Robinson-Patman Act, and the Hart-Scott-Rodino Act. Legislation to protect consumers includes the Federal Food and Drug Act, the Federal Trade Commission Act, the Wheeler-Lea Amendment, the Fair Packaging and Labeling Act, the Consumer Product Safety Act, and the Children's Television Act. These laws were passed to prevent misleading and deceptive marketing practices and ensure honest labeling of foods, drugs, and safe products for consumer use. From these acts, a number of agencies were established, including the FDA, FCC, ATF, FTC, and CPSC. Each of these agencies is responsible for regulating business and investigating activities of wrongdoing.

3. Describe the role of the Federal Trade Commission as it relates to marketing and discuss how it investigates complaints. The role of the FTC is to investigate activities that restrict free trade and claims of misleading or deceptive marketing communications. Complaints can be filed by consumers, businesses, Congress, the media, or the FTC itself. An advertisement or marketing communication is said to be deceptive or misleading if the typical person is misled. Any claims made by a company must be substantiated in some way. If the FTC finds that a violation has occurred, it can issue a consent order or a cease-and-desist order. It can also levy civil penalties. Appeals from the FTC go to a federal court of appeals.

4. Discuss the role of the CBBB in regulating marketing activities. Complaints about advertising are referred to the CBBB's NAD, the CARU, or the NARB. Complaints not settled by the NAD or CARU are referred to the NARB. Both operate similarly to the FTC but without obligatory power. However, in most cases, decisions by the NAD, CARU, or NARB are followed.

5. Discuss the social responsibility of business firms and provide examples showing how a firm can demonstrate its social responsibility. Businesses are expected to behave in a socially responsible manner and be supportive of societal needs. This social responsibility can be met through cause-related marketing programs or green marketing programs.

Key Terms

bait and switch	ethics	morals
cause-related marketing	green marketing	puffery

Discussion Questions

1. Marketing to teenagers has raised a number of ethical issues, as was discussed in the chapter opener. Do some research on the Internet or with an electronic database to find at least two articles that discuss the ethical issues in marketing to teenagers. Summarize what you find and compare it to your personal thoughts about advertising to teens.

2. Pick one of the ethical issues presented in Section 3-2. Talk to five people you know of various ages, genders, and ethnic backgrounds. Summarize how each felt about the issue you picked.

3. Pick one of the ethical issues presented in Section 3-2. Discuss how you feel about the issue. Find articles from the Internet or an electronic database that either support or refute your view.

4. Look through the list of criticisms identified in Table 3.2. Which one concerns you the most? Why? Which one is of the least concern to you? Why? How does your age, gender, ethnicity, religious background, family, and environment affect your choices? Explain.

5. Pick one of the pieces of legislation listed in Section 3-3. Research its background and the impact it has on business.

6. Access the website of the FTC at http://www.ftc.gov. Review the press releases and past decisions. Find one that interests you to discuss. Write a report summarizing the case.

7. If you came across an advertisement that you thought was misleading and wanted to report it, would you report it to the FTC or the BBB? Why?

8. What are your thoughts about e-mail spam? What approach do you think the FTC should take towards spam? Would you be willing to turn in a friend, relative, or business associate who was violating the law? How much of a reward would it take?

9. What is your opinion of cause-related marketing? What causes do you support? Do you modify your purchase decisions based on causes a company supports? Why or why not?

10. What is your attitude toward green marketing? Name the last product you purchased because of green marketing. How much impact does green marketing have on your purchase behavior?

Review Questions
(Answers are on Last Page of the Chapter)

True or False

1. Ethics help individuals and organizations to establish boundaries regarding acceptable and unacceptable conduct.

2. Morals are personal beliefs or standards used to guide an individual's actions.

3. Marketing has been criticized for creating a materialistic society.

4. Bait and switch tactics used by retailers provide more product options to the consumer.

5. Personal information gathered through the Internet should allow marketers to advertise specific products of interest to each individual.

6. To determine whether a company used deceptive or misleading advertising, the FTC will examine the company's intentions to design a deceptive and misleading ad.

7. The FTC does not have the power to levy civil penalties; only the U.S. Court of Appeals has this power.

8. Decisions by the NAD, CARU, or NARB cannot be appealed to the FTC or to the federal court system.

9. Historically, green marketing has not been successful because green products were considered to be of inferior quality.

10. Cause-related marketing is a strategy used to promote a product line by advertising donations made to nonprofit organizations.

Multiple Choice

11. Easy consumer credit is partially to blame for which of the following criticisms of marketing?
    a. Marketing causes people to buy more than they can afford
    b. Marketing increases the prices of goods and services.
    c. Marketing capitalizes on human weaknesses.
    d. Marketing violates consumers' rights to privacy.

12. Which of the following is an example of the criticism that marketing shapes inappropriate cultural values?
    a. An advertisement for weight-loss programs
    b. An advertisement offering a complete computer system for only $299
    c. An advertisement for Rogaine, a hair-growth product
    d. An advertisement for birth control pills

13. Which of the following statements defines the marketing role in society?
    a. Marketing uses unethical methods to lure customers.
    b. Marketing reduces tension between competing companies.
    c. Marketing has a limited commercial role.
    d. Marketing allows consumers to make better decisions.

14. The agency responsible for regulating the radio industry is the
    a. FDA.
    b. FCC.
    c. FTC.
    d. CPSC.

15. The legislation that prohibits false and misleading advertising is the
    a. Fair Packaging and Labeling Act.
    b. Lanham Act.
    c. Wheeler-Lea Amendment.
    d. Robinson-Patman Act.

16. The legislation that prohibits price discrimination to different buyers is the
    a. Sherman-Antitrust Act.
    b. Clayton Act.
    c. Fair Packaging and Labeling Act.
    d. Lanham Act.

17. When making a claim about a product, the FTC will look for
    a. puffery statements.
    b. substantiation of the claim.
    c. a testimony of an expert witness.
    d. overly complex claims.

18. Decisions by the NAD, CARU, and NARB are
    a. not binding, but most companies abide by their decisions
    b. binding only if ruled by the NARB.
    c. as binding as rulings of the FTC.
    d. none of the above.

19. Advertisers engage in puffery
    a. when the ad contains an obscene message.
    b. when the ad makes reference to a competitor's product.
    c. when the ad includes such words as ''greatest,'' ''finest,'' and ''best.''
    d. when the ad is obviously designed to mislead.

20. If the FTC believes that a company used unfair or deceptive practices, the first step in resolving the problem will be to issue a(n)
    a. consent order.
    b. administrative complaint.
    c. cease and desist order.
    d. judgment for approval by the federal court.

Clow-Lascu: *Marketing Essentials 5e Blog*

Screenshot of YouTube Video highlighted in
Clow-Lascu *Marketing Essentials 5e Blog.*

What Is Happening Today?

Learn More! For videos and articles

that relate to Chapter 3:

blogclowlascu.net/category/

chapter03

Includes Discussion Questions

Notes

1. American Household Credit Card Debt Statistics: 2014, nerdwallet.com, available at www.nerdwallet.com/blog/credit-card-data/average-credit-card-debt-household. Rob Kelley, "Debt: Consumers Juggle Big Burden," *CNN Money*, available at http://money.cnn.com/2005/10/07/pf/debt/debtmeasures, accessed on January 28, 2007.
2. ACA International, "Bankruptcy Filings Declined in 2013," http://www.acainternational.org/creditors-bankruptcy-filings-declined-in-2013-30843.aspx, accessed on July 17, 2014. Thomas A. Garrett, "The Rise in Personal Bankruptcies: The Eighth Federal Reserve District and Beyond," *Federal Reserve Bank of St. Louis Review* (January/February 2007): 15.
3. JCDecaux, "Global Ad Spend Forecast 2013," December 2012, http://www.jcdecaux-oneworld.com/wp-content/uploads/2013_/06/OneWorld_GlobalAdspend_Forecast_032013.pdf, accessed on March 30 2014.
4. D. Kirk Davidson, "Marketing This 'Hope' Sells Our Profession Short," *Marketing News* 32 (July 20, 1998): 6.
5. Andy Newman, "Calvin Klein Cancels Ad with Children Amid Criticism," *New York Times*, (February 18, 1999): 9; Suzanne Fields, "Calvin Klein Ads Again Use Kids and Sex to Sell," *Philadelphia Business Journal* 18 (March 5, 1999): 47; Kirk Davidson, "Calvin Klein Ads: Bad Ethics, Bad Business," *Marketing News* 29 (November 6, 1995): 1–12.
6. Faye Rice, "Superstars of Spending," *Advertising Age*, 72 (February 12, 2001), 9c.
7. Sharon Goldman, "The Social Tween: Marketers Take Aim at Kids Raised on Smartphones and Facebook," Adweek, June 24, 2012, http://www.adweek.com/sa-article/social-tween-141314, accessed on March 12, 2014; Center for Digital Democracy, "The Next Generation of Consumers," Jan. 12, 2012, http://www.democraticmedia.org/kids-spending-and-influencing-power-12-trillion-says-leading-ad-firm, accessed on March 30, 2014.
8. Brian Marchant, "Bribery and Corruption in the Business World," *Credit Control* 18, no. 7 (1997): 27–31.
9. Lisa Stein, "Furrowed Brows," *U.S. News & World Report* 133 (September 23, 2002): 18.
10. "Portion Sizes Growing Out of Control," *USA Today Magazine* 128 (April 2000): 10–11.
11. James A. Calderwood, "False and Deceptive Advertising," *Ceramic Industry* 148 (August 1998): 26.
12. Federal Trade Commission, "High School Student Survey Companies Settle FTC Charges," press release, available at www.ftc.gov/opa/2002/10/student1r.htm, November 6, 2002.
13. Federal Trade Commission, "On-Line Sellers of Inkjet Cartridge Refills Agree to Pay $40,000 Civil Penalty to Settle with the FTC," press release, available at www.ftc.gov/opa/2002/ebabylon.htm, November 6, 2002.
14. R. Serafin and G. Levin, "Ad Industry Suffers Crushing Blow," *Advertising Age* 61 (November 12, 1990): 1,3.
15. Jack Redmond, "Marketers Must Be Familiar with FTC Guidelines," *Inside Tucson Business* 5 (March 18, 1996): 18–19.
16. Federal Trade Commission, "Federal Trade Commission Reaches 'New Year's' Resolutions with Four Major Weight-Control Pill Marketers," available at www.ftc.gov/opa/2007/01weightloss.htm, accessed on January 4, 2007.
17. Federal Trade Commission, "FTC Reviews Funeral Rules," available at www.ftc.gov/opa/1999/9904/fun-rule.rev.htm, November 7, 2002.
18. "False Advertising and Celebrity Endorsements: Where's My Script?" *Sports Marketing Quarterly* 15, no. 2 (2006): 111–113.
19. National Advertising Review Council, available at www.narcpartners.org, accessed on January 27, 2007.
20. Children's Advertising Review Unit, "CARU Reviews Ad for X-Men: The Last Stand," December 20, 2006 press release, available at www.narcpartners.org.
21. National Advertising Division, "Unilever, P&G Participates in NAD Forum," October 4, 2006 press release, available at www.narcpartners.org.

22.   National Advertising Division, ''Starbuck's Participates in NAD Forum,'' November 21, 2006 press release, available at www.narcpartners.org.

23.   National Advertising Division, ''Perdue Farms Appeals NAD Decision to NARB,'' November 2, 2006 press release, available at www.narcpartners.org.

24.   National Advertising Division, ''NAD Refers Spitz Sales to the FTC and FDA,'' January 19, 2007 press release, available at www.narcpartners.org.

25.   Kevin T. Higgins, ''Marketing with a Conscience,'' *Marketing Management* 11 (July/August 2002): 12–16.

26.   Beth Armknecht Miller, ''Social Initiatives Can Boost Loyalty,'' *Marketing News* 36 (October 14, 2002): 14–15.

27.   Ibid.

28.   Higgins, Marketing with a Conscience.

29.   Jacquelyn A. Ottman, ''Green Marketing,'' *In Business* 24 (July/August 2002): 30–31

30.   Jim Johnson, ''Growth in Sales of Hybrids to Continue, Forecasts Say,'' *Waste News* 11 (January 16, 2006), 1c.

Cases

Case 3-1 The New Video Game

Normally, the initial marketing meeting for a new video game was not a big deal. However, this one was different for a number of reasons. Company sales had been flat; combined with increased costs, profits had been down for the past two quarters. With the Christmas season approaching, Brad knew this was an opportune time to push a new product. Sales could be generated quicker than at any other time of the year. The last two new video games had fallen under projected sales. Fingers were pointed at the marketing department, especially at Brad because he was the marketing manager, a position he had held for the past three years. But the CEO stood up for Brad, suggesting that maybe research and development had not done their homework in creating games that would appeal to the company's young male market.

Feeling some heat to produce a winner, Brad slid into his seat beside Amy, the new public relations director. She had made a huge impression on the management team in the four months she had been there. She was attractive, witty, and with a double degree in marketing and public relations from the University of Georgia, well qualified for the position she held. She had already earned the respect of the CEO and other top management personnel with the way she handled a recent negative press situation.

Across the table were the Vice President of Research and Development, Stewart Hanks, and two of the ''techies'' from the video game division. At the head of the table was Alex Olfermayer, the CEO. He had been with the company for 23 years and had served as CEO for the past seven. During his tenure, the company had grown from $3 million in annual sales to more than $9 million.

Brad turned his attention to Mr. Hanks, who explained the newest video game. It was based on the game player rooting out terrorists from around the world before they destroyed major American targets like the Pentagon and the White House. The terrorists were not easily identifiable, and if innocent people were killed, then the probability of the terrorists hitting American targets increased. Time and skill would be needed to beat the terrorists before the ultimate disaster hit, the assassination of the president.

Just listening to the description of the new game got Brad excited. As the video game team went through a simulated version of some of the graphics, Brad looked over at the CEO. He could see that he was also impressed. Brad had a gut feeling this was going to be a big winner.

When the presentation was over, the CEO expressed his enthusiasm for the game. Brad joined in the discussion, telling the group this would be an easy marketing sell. Turning to Amy, he asked her opinion. With a solemn look on her face, she replied, ''Our competitor is already developing a similar game, but they are at least a month ahead of us.''

''When is their game coming out? They've beat us with the last three games, they're not beating us this time!'' Mr. Olfermayer snapped.

''I don't know,'' Amy replied.

''Can you find out?''

''How do you know they are producing a similar game?'' Brad asked before Amy could reply to the CEO's question.

''I know somebody who works over there.''

''You need to get us the scoop on what is going on over there and when they plan to introduce their version. We have to make sure our game is better,'' the CEO replied.

"He's not going to tell me confidential information like that. He just happened to let it slip about this new game. It was just by accident I found out."

Looking at Amy, the CEO narrowed his eyes. "You find out about this game so we can beat them. We are not losing on another game." Turning to Brad, he continued as he stood up to leave the room. "You understand what I am saying, don't you?"

"Yes, sir."

Feeling the tension in the room, the research and development staff quickly slipped out behind the CEO. For a few minutes, neither Amy nor Brad spoke.

Turning to Amy, Brad asked, "Can you get the information?"

"It will cost $10,000."

"That's blackmail."

"How bad do you want it?" Amy replied coolly.

"Not bad enough to pay someone $10,000. It would be my head if an auditor ever found something like that, and I'm not going to Mr. Olfermayer with that type of request."

Standing up, Amy looked down at Brad, a sly grin on her face. "If $10,000 is too risky for you, then I'd settle for the associate marketing director's position."

"I already have someone in that position."

"So, what does that matter?" Amy replied as she walked out of the room.

Never in his 12 years of working in a marketing department, in three different companies, had Brad experienced anything like this. Looking out the window, he noticed his wife and two kids coming toward the building. He had almost forgotten this was his youngest child's birthday. He could not afford to lose his job, at least not right now.

Questions:

1. What options does Brad have for dealing with this situation? What are the ethical implications for each option?

2. If you were in Brad's spot, what would you do? Would your actions be different if quitting was not an option right now because of family concerns and financial obligations?

3. What is your evaluation of Amy and her approach to Brad's dilemma?

4. Although Amy does not report to you, should you have a talk with her boss about her? Should you talk with the CEO about Amy? What are the consequences of each action?

5. If Brad would make the decision to either give Amy the $10,000 or fire his current associate and give her the position, what would be the consequences of the decision?

6.   Discuss the ethical implications of the newly proposed game.

Case 3-2 Tweens

Tweens, children from 9 to 13 years of age, are an important market and a complicated bunch, as parents and marketers know. They are considered too old for toys, feisty, opinionated, honest, sharp, cynical, and responsible for $200 billion in sales a year -- of which $43 billion comes from direct spending of their own disposable income. This is a huge market and one that manufacturers of children's products are eager to tap. The challenge is how, when, and where.

Rena Hawkins, vice president of marketing, examined data recently purchased by her company. The first table was how tweens spend their time. At the top of the list was watching TV, logging on to the Internet, hanging out with friends, listening to music, watching a movie/DVD at home, and playing video games with others or alone. More interesting to Rena was the list of tech products and services kids have. More than two-thirds of tweens have a TV in their room, 40 percent have a video game console, and 15 percent have a DVD player. In homes with Internet access, 57 percent of the tweens have access in their rooms. These media do not sit idle either. On the average, tweens watch 3.1 hours a day of TV and spend 2.9 hours a day with the Internet or video games.

Another area of interest to Rena was the percentage of total purchases made by tweens alone. The findings were not what she expected. Tweens spend most on video games (31 percent), apparel/footwear (20 percent), impulse buys, like snacks (20 percent), consumer electronics (10 percent), music/books (10 percent), and toys/crafts (9 percent). Because her company sold children's clothing, toys, and games, she was glad to see that toys, games, and clothing were on the list but was disappointed that they collectively accounted for only 29 percent of total expenditures.

How Tweens Spend Their Free Time (Weekends)	
Watch TV	83%
Log on Internet	74%
Hang out with friends	68%
Listen to music	67%
Watch movie/DVD at home	64%
Play viceo games with others	60%
Prepare a meal	43%
Read	42%
Go shopping	41%
Exercise	40%

Source: C+R Research Youthbeat Report

The last set of facts she examined was how tweens find out about "cool" stuff. The first item on the list caused Rena to sit upright. She looked again to make sure she read it correctly. At the top of the list was advertising, cited by 76 percent of the tweens. Second was friends and peers at 59 percent. Other influences were relatives (15 percent), the Internet (14 percent), and shopping inside of stores (10 percent).

With this information in hand, Rena was now ready to make some recommendations to the company for the upcoming Christmas holiday season. She had two major proposals. First, she was going to ask for an increase in the advertising budget of 25 percent over last year's budget. She knew that advertising of toys was especially big during the fall, just before Christmas. For instance, she learned Mattel was spending half of their advertising budget on Christmas-related advertising. That would be $230 million. Other research indicated that overall, ad spending for the fourth quarter of the year was 15 percent higher than last year. She believed if her company was to compete effectively, she needed an increase in her ad budget of 25 percent.

Her second proposal was to create a Web site for tweens where they could log on and select the toys they wanted. It would be patterned after Wal-Mart's "wish list" site where two elves nudge kids to select toys by clicking on the word "Yes." If they do, they hear applause. If they select "No," there is silence. Once compiled, the list of toys the child wants is sent to the parents. Rena knew that several consumer groups filed a complaint with Wal-Mart and even with the FTC because they believed the Web site was unethical and created a culture of nagging. Although Rena acknowledged the website would be controversial, she knew a large number of tweens had Internet access in their rooms and she believed the Web site would boost sales of the company's toys and games.

Questions:

1. What is your opinion of Rena's recommendations?
2. From the list of ethical issues discussed in the first part of this chapter, what ethical issues do you see arising from Rena's recommendation of increasing advertising directed to tweens?
3. What is your evaluation of the proposed Web site? Is it ethical? Do you think the FTC would be concerned?
4. What are your thoughts about aggressively marketing clothing, toys, and games to tweens?

Sources: Greg Smith, "Tweens 'R Shoppers: A Look at the Tween Market and Shopping Behavior," Popai, The Global Association for Marketing at Retail, March 12, 2013, http://www.popai.com/store/downloads/POPAIWhitePaper-Tweens-R-Shoppers-2013.pdf, accessed on July 18, 2014. Bruce Horovitz, "6 Strategies Marketers Used to Get Kids to Want Stuff," USA Today (November 22, 2006); 0 b; Marla Weiskott, "Tweens: A Consuming Army," Playthings 03 (September 2005): 42–43.

Answers to Review Questions

Answers: 1) True, 2) True, 3) True, 4) False, 5) True, 6) False, 7) False, 8) False, 9) True, 10) False, 11) a, 12) d, 13) d, 14) b, 15) c, 16) b, 17) b, 18) a, 19) c, 20) a.

Chapter 4

Consumer Behavior

Learning Objectives

After studying
this chapter,
you should be able to:

1. Identify the elements of a consumer behavior model.

2. Describe the different social influences that have an impact on consumer behavior.

3. Describe the different psychological influences that have an impact on consumer behavior.

4. Address the five stages of the consumer decision-making process.

5. Describe variations in consumer decision-making based on whether consumers engage in extensive, limited, or routine problem solving.

4-1 CHAPTER OVERVIEW

Product evaluations and purchase decisions dominate our lives as consumers. We define who we are through consumption. Take, for example, Cheri, a successful artist, who has recently built a 3,000 square foot home with the help of a well-known local architect. Cheri had the living room rug designed to be identical to her painting and paid $8,500 for a local interior design firm to create the rug. She bought an antique grandfather clock for $10,200 and placed it in the center of the living room. The adjoining kitchen combines expensive stainless steel appliances with granite countertops and IKEA cabinets. The dining room is IKEA cheap chic, defined by functionality and simplicity.

Closets prominently display Cheri's designer wardrobe, which is dominated by black and gray Donna Karans and Armanis bought from a local boutique, for about $2,000 per suit. Her casual clothes come primarily from local discounters, T. J. Maxx, Marshalls, and Target. She also purchases many of her everyday clothes from the local Junior League thrift shop, sometimes for as little as $2 per item.

Cheri purchases virtually all her food at Food Lion, a low-priced supermarket, and uses newspaper coupons on almost every item she purchases. For additional savings, she purchases the Food Lion store brand, rather than the national brand whenever she can.

Cheri's decisions require daily planning and decision making to project an image to the outside world, to others who see her on the street, and to her friends who visit her at home. This image also involves cutting costs in areas that are not readily visible to others. Like Cheri, consumers cannot be placed into neat, well-defined categories. Individual motivations, interests, attitudes, and upbringing create complex individuals who may not be easily categorized (see Figure 4-1). The chapter presents a basic model of consumer behavior (Section 4-2), noting the personal and social (interpersonal) influences on behavior. Section 4-3 addresses social influences, such as cultures and subcultures, social class, individual roles and status, family and households, and reference groups, in developing attitudes, interests, opinions, and behavior. Section 4-4 addresses psychological influences, such as motivation, perception, learning, beliefs and attitudes, personality, and lifestyle. The stages of the consumer decision-making process are described in Section 4-5. Finally, Section 4-6 offers insights into variations in decision processes attributed to the extent of problem solving involved in the purchase and the level of consumer involvement.

Figure 4-1: Consumers are complex individuals who are influenced by many factors, such as culture, social class, families, and reference groups.

4-2 A CONSUMER BEHAVIOR MODEL

Marketing managers extensively scrutinize consumer behavior. From national department stores to local convenience stores, from large consumer goods manufacturers to small service providers, businesses strive to acquire timely information about their target consumers. Learning why consumers behave in a particular manner and how their behavior changes over time is essential to the company's bottom line. First, social influences, such as culture and subculture, social class, individual roles and status, family makeup, and reference groups, are instrumental in shaping individual attitudes, interests, opinions, and behavior. In the chapter's opening vignette, Cheri is a single professional woman, upper-middle class, with upper-class tastes, but a middle-class budget. Although she can afford a large home, unique furnishings, and an haute-couture wardrobe, she buys other products at discount stores or thrift stores to save money.

Psychological influences also affect consumer behavior. Individual motivation, perception, learning, personality, and lifestyles, as well as beliefs and attitudes, are likely to influence how consumers behave. Cheri grew up in a materialistic culture and, as a result, buys products that her friends or those that she aspires to have as friends approve of and pays for them using a large amount of her discretionary income. She lives the lifestyle she aspires to, while cutting costs by purchasing less visible products from cheaper sources.

Marketers need to understand what motivates consumers like Cheri in their purchase behavior. What motivates them to purchase certain brands and shop at certain stores? What messages do consumers want to convey about themselves through the products they purchase? Figure 4-2 illustrates the different influences exerted on consumer behavior.

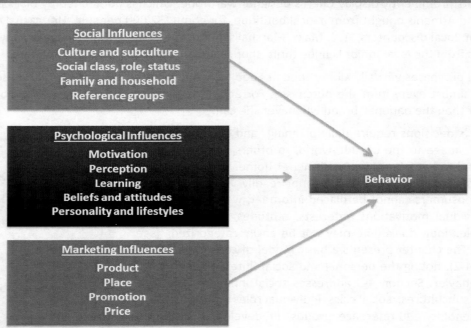

Figure 4-2: **Model of Consumer Behavior**

Sources: Adapted from George Fisk, "Reflection and Retrospection: Searching for Visions in Marketing," *Journal of Marketing* 63, no. 1 (1999): 115–121; William O. Bearden, R. E. Netemeyer, and Jesse E. Teal, "Measurement of Consumer Susceptibility to Interpersonal Influence," *Journal of Consumer Research* 15 (1989): 473–481; Dana N. Lascu, William O. Bearden, and Randall L. Rose, "Norm Extremity and Interpersonal Influences on Consumer Conformity," *Journal of Business Research* 32 (1995): 201–212; J. Paul Peter and James H. Donnelly, Jr., *Marketing Management: Knowledge and Skills, 7th ed.* (Boston: McGraw-Hill Irwin).

4-3 SOCIAL INFLUENCES ON CONSUMER BEHAVIOR

The social influences examined in this chapter are culture, social class, role and status, families and household, and reference groups. Culture is recognized as having an important influence on consumption and consumer behavior in general. Cultural influences are expressed in the consumption of goods and services, in homes, offices, stores, and marketplace sites, with differences noted across various subcultures.[1] Similarly, social class, role, and status influence the types of goods and services consumers purchase. Friends and family are also likely to affect individuals' consumption, the brands that they purchase, the frequency of purchase, the prices they are willing to pay, the stores where they purchase their goods, the service establishments they select, and the media that they are exposed to.

4-3a: Cultural Influences on Consumer Behavior

Culture—a society's personality—is defined as a continually changing totality of learned and shared meanings, rituals, norms, and traditions among the members of an organization or society. **Values** are important elements of culture. Values are enduring beliefs about a specific mode of conduct or desirable end state that guides the selection or evaluation of behavior, and are ordered by importance in relation to one another to form a system of value priorities.[2] Values guide individuals' actions, attitudes, and judgments, which are derived from and continually modified through personal, social, and cultural learning, ultimately affecting their product preferences and their perception of products. Cultures are set apart by their value systems. Western cultures (North American and Western European) place more stress on success, achievement, and competitiveness, whereas Eastern cultures are more likely to be concerned with social welfare. A sample of universally held values is provided in Figure 4-3.[3] According to this classification, values can be related to goals (**terminal values**) or to the processes whereby one can attain those goals (**instrumental values**).

Values are learned from those with whom individuals are in contact: family, friends, teachers, clergy, politicians, and the media. The United States is a melting pot of different cultures that have blended together to create the American culture with its own values and beliefs. Learning a new culture, which most immigrants must do when they live in another country, is known as **acculturation**. Acculturation encompasses interaction with the culture and adaptation to the culture, and it includes the **assimilation** of a new culture, maintenance of the new culture, and resistance to both the new and old cultures. Acculturation does not necessarily mean abandoning all home country traditions; that is, it does not mean complete assimilation of the new culture. For example, recent Asian Indian

> **Values:**
> Important elements of culture defined as enduring beliefs about a specific mode of conduct or desirable end state.
>
> **Terminal Values:**
> Values related to goals.
>
> **Instrumental Values:**
> Values related to processes whereby one can attain certain goals.
>
> **Acculturation:**
> The process of learning a new culture.
>
> **Assimilation:**
> Adapting to and fully integrating into the new culture.

Figure 4-3: Instrumental and Terminal Values

Instrumental Values (the means by which terminal values are achieved)	Terminal Values (goals reached by means of instrumental values)
Ambitious	A comfortable life
Broadminded	An exciting life
Capable	A sense of accomplishment
Cheerful	A world at peace
Clean	A world of beauty
Courageous	Equality
Forgiving	Family Security
Helpful	Freedom
Imaginative	Inner Harmony
Independent	Mature love
Intellectual	National Security
Logical	Pleasure
Loving	Salvation
Obedient	Self-respect
Polite	Social recognition
Responsible	True friendship
Self-controlled	Wisdom

Source: Adapted from Milton J. Rokeach, *"The Nature of Human Values"* (New York: The Free Press, 1973).

immigrants to the United States are less likely to be assimilated in this culture because they maintain their original religious practices, language, food consumption, housing, friendship patterns, and contact with India.[4] Although Indian Americans are not easily assimilated, they are, nevertheless, acculturated in the American culture.

Consumer acculturation refers to contact with a new culture and the resulting change for consumers in terms of their approach to consumption in the new environment.[5] Asian Indian consumers consume fast food, shop at supermarkets, root for their favorite baseball team, and overall, successfully integrate in the American culture without necessarily being assimilated.

> **Subcultures:**
> Groups of individuals with shared value systems based on ethnicity or common background.

Subcultures

Subcultures are components of the broad culture. They are groups of individuals with shared value systems based on ethnicity or some other common background. Subcultures could be based on regional differences. For instance, Southern consumers have different lifestyles than Midwest consumers.

Subcultures are often based on ethnicity or nationality: Italian Americans maintain many of the traditions from their home country and have strong ties to the old country. Or subcultures can be based on religion—an important element of culture. Among the important ethnic and national subcultures in the United States are African Americans, Hispanic Americans, and Asian Americans.

The African American subculture makes up 12 percent of the total U.S. population. African Americans are younger than the rest of the U.S. population, with a large percentage living in cities. They are the most fashion-conscious group of consumers, with 34 percent in a recent poll saying they like to keep up with fashions, compared with only 25 percent for whites. African Americans are more likely to travel a long distance to shop and will go out of their way to find news stores, especially for a bargain. But, they are also more brand loyal and less likely to be innovators and try out new products during the introduction stage of the product lifecycle.[6]

Hispanics account for 16.4 percent of the U.S. population and represent the largest and fastest-growing subculture in the United States. More than half of Hispanic Americans are of Mexican origin, with the rest coming from Central and South America and Puerto Rico. Although Hispanic Americans do not constitute a homogeneous group, they do share a number of traits: the Catholic religion, the Spanish language, and more traditional and conservative values--although that is changing. Hispanic Americans are brand conscious and brand loyal, they adopt primarily well-established brands, and they prefer to shop at national chain retailers rather than at small stores. They are ahead of the digital curve, spending more than eight hours watching online video per month—over 90 minutes longer than the U.S. average--and adopting smart phones at a higher rate than any other demographic group.[7]

The Asian American subculture, which is 4.8 percent of the U.S. population, is the most heterogeneous subculture, consisting of ethnic and national groups with different languages and traditions—Chinese, Asian Indian and Pakistani, Filipino, Japanese, and Korean for instance. They are more affluent and place a high value on education. Asian Americans enjoy shopping, are the most frequent

Figure 4-4: Asian Americans are more affluent and are the most frequent shoppers.

shoppers, and are the most brand conscious. Yet as a group, they also are the least brand loyal, with 25 percent saying they switch brands often, compared with 22 percent of African Americans, 20 percent of Hispanic Americans, and 17 percent of Caucasians (see Figure 4-4).[8]

> **Religion:**
> A way of defining a society's relationship to the supernatural and, as a result, determining dominant values and attitudes.

Religious subcultures are important for marketers because religion defines a society's relationship to the supernatural and, as a result, determines dominant values and attitudes. Religious beliefs are important determinants of consumer behavior because they influence purchase motivation, consumption preferences, purchase patterns, personal customs, and business practices. Attitudes toward authority, family, peers, material possessions, cultural values, and norms, among others, can all be traced to religion.

Religion is linked to cultural behaviors of the different subcultures that have an impact on marketing. The Protestant religion stresses hard work and frugality and is linked to the development of capitalism and economic emancipation. Such attitudes may have created the opportunity for do-it-yourself stores and discounters. Judaism, with its disdain for ignorance and sloth, stresses education. Jewish consumers in the United States are an important target market for educational and professional development. Islam dictates social etiquette between the genders and discourages the consumption of pork products and alcohol. The Hindu religion encourages a family orientation and discourages the consumption of animal products—beef, in particular. Firms targeting these consumers need to be aware of the religious constraints of Muslims and Hindus and offer goods and services that address their special needs. For example, fast-food restaurants find that they can better serve their Asian Indian consumers by offering ample choices of vegetarian food. Vegetarian options may also serve Jewish consumers because they do not compromise consumer kosher requirements. Keeping kosher requires, among other things, the separation of milk products and meat products and of the implements used to serve or process them.

There are, of course, other subcultures that represent important market segments—the different age groups previously described in Chapter 2—Generation X, Generation Y, young boomers, and older boomers all represent different subcultures. Similarly, gay and lesbian consumers represent an important subculture and an important and influential market, with substantial disposable income.

4-3b: Social Class, Role, and Status Influences on Consumer Behavior

> **Social Class:**
> Relatively permanent divisions within society that exist in a status hierarchy, with the members of each division sharing similar values, attitudes, interests, and opinions.

The position of individuals in society can be defined in terms of social class. **Social class** is the relatively permanent divisions within society that exist in a status hierarchy, with the members of each division sharing similar values, attitudes, interests, and opinions. Social class is evaluated as a combination of occupation, education, income, wealth, and personal values, which have a direct impact on consumption. Children are initially socialized in their parents' social class, engaging in activities characteristic of that class.

A brief examination of social classes in the U.S. reveals that there are three main social classes, upper, middle, and lower class, each with subcategories. The upper class is composed of the wealthiest Americans who either inherited money or earned it through business; they spend heavily, sometimes conspicuously, on luxury items and own expensive homes. The middle class is varied, with the upper-middle class earning their money through successful careers founded on professional and graduate degrees. They live graciously, entertaining friends, emulating the upper class in their consumption. Members of the lower-middle social class have skilled jobs founded on technical training. They are price-sensitive, value homes and neighborhoods, and adhere to norms and standards. The lower class consists of employed individuals either working in skilled or semiskilled jobs, living routine lives, have limited social interaction beyond family, and spend impulsively on national brands, or in unskilled jobs. Alternatively, they may be unemployed and on welfare. They have minimal skills and education, and buy impulsively, often on credit and may live in substandard housing.

Figure 4-5: The upper class prefers threadbare rugs, antiques, and so on.

How do the social classes consume differently? The PBS Social Class in America site has a Chintz or Shag game, which offers illustrations of consumption by social class.[9] The upper class, according to the site, prefers threadbare rugs, antiques, and duck decoys as displays; original paintings by recognized artists, and a television set not in the living room. (See Figure 4-5 for an illustration of a home of the old-money class.)

In addition to differences in product preferences and consumption, each social class has other distinctive traits. For example, the upper classes have a broader social circle beyond their immediate community and family, whereas lower classes are more restricted to their home environment and to family life. Upper classes also participate more in activities outside the home, such as theater performances, than lower classes, which engage in physical activities for recreation.

Individuals' positions within a group can also be defined in terms of role and status. **Roles** are based on the activities people are expected to perform according to the individuals around them. In traditional families, women are expected to stay at home and take care of the daily functioning of the household. Women are traditionally assigned to the role of mother and maid. In a more modern rendition of this traditional role, women play the role of soccer moms, carpool drivers, and Parent-Teacher Association (PTA) activists.

> **Roles:**
> The activities people are expected to perform according to individuals around them.
>
> **Status:**
> The esteem which society bestows upon a particular role.

In many developing countries, this traditional role is in fact law. In the most traditional Islamic countries, such as Saudi Arabia, women are not allowed to drive and not permitted to be in public if unaccompanied by a male relative. In these countries, women's business activities are channeled toward interaction in a women-only or family-only environment. Personal services can be performed only by individuals of the same gender. Women can bank only at women's banks, can have their hair done only by other women, and so on. In less-traditional Islamic countries, such as Pakistan, women share responsibility with men in business. It is noteworthy, however, that women play a more limited role politically, where only a few hold notable positions, and when they do, it is often by virtue of their father's position.

In today's Western cultures, women focus on careers, assuming the roles of professionals and managers, and leaving traditional chores to individuals who are considered competent to handle them: maids, day cares, and personal shopping services. Gender roles are not as clearly defined, especially for the upper-middle class. Children and the household become the responsibility of both parents, who take turns in fulfilling the roles that traditionally have been assigned to women. Today's modern society also accepts that the world is not populated only by heterosexual married households. Single parents and gay parent families raise children, adopting the roles that best meet the needs of the children and the family as a whole.

Status is defined as the esteem that society bestows upon a particular role. The role of soccer mom is lower than the role of marketing manager; a woman playing both roles will probably not stress the role of soccer mom in her professional circles for fear of lessening her status of manager. Status defines what products we consume and how we behave. Related to one's background is one's concern with status, or status concern—maintaining it or acquiring it—and with material possessions, or materialism.

Individuals' concern with status is related to the values placed on symbols of status and on the attainment of high status. Often, the products consumed convey messages about the consumer in the same way that language does.[10] Driving a Mercedes or a Porsche advertises that one is a successful professional. The Mercedes station wagon is a typical family automobile for the upper-middle class professional in the United States. In China, Audi is an essential accoutrement of the upper-middle class professional as illustrated in Figure 4-6.

Status—like social class, to which it is related—is easier to transcend in high-income countries than in lower-income countries. In the United States, the Protestant ethic of hard work has led to centuries of individual prosperity

Figure 4-6: This photo is *not* taken at an Audi dealership; these Audi automobiles are in front of an office building located in one of many business districts in downtown Beijing.

and, at the individual level, status advancement. In the United States, it is not perceived as shameful for prominent politicians and businesspeople to refer back to their humble beginnings.

More recently, however, status and social class have become more dynastic than dynamic. The past two decades have seen a substantial increase in inequality in the United States, with real incomes of households in the lowest fifth (the bottom 20 percent) growing by 6.4 percent and the income of the top one percent growing 184 percent. This rise in inequality did not come with a commensurate rise in mobility; in fact, social sclerosis is evident for the middle and lower income population. Clear evidence in this regard is provided in the political arena. In a country where every child aspires to be a president, it appears that the political elite have become a self-perpetuating elite, with prominent politicians in their recent family pedigree coming from the blue-blooded world of private schools and ultra-select Ivy League societies. And, surprisingly, nobody complains that dynastic ties are proliferating, social circles are interlocking, and mechanisms of social exclusion of the vast majority are strengthening.[11]

4-3c: Family and Household Influences on Consumer Behavior

The family exerts probably the most influence on consumers. Consumers continue to purchase the brands they grew up with. Somebody growing up with Ford automobiles will probably continue to purchase them as an adult. If a mother always bought a Butterball turkey for Thanksgiving dinner, her adult daughter will probably continue the Butterball tradition for her family.

Marketers are interested in how decisions are made in the family. Traditionally, food shopping has been the domain of women, whereas automobiles have been the domain of men. Those roles are greatly changing today, with men often taking charge of household purchases in households with dual-career couples. For decades, models of family decision making equated family decisions with husband-wife decisions and excluded or ignored the role of children. More recently, however, the influence of children has received ample attention from marketers, especially when the decision centered on less-expensive products and those products designed for the child's personal use.[12] Yet children's documented buying power and influence on family purchase decisions extend beyond these products. Children are important influencers when it comes to decisions regarding family vacations, the family automobiles, furniture, and the new TV set.[13] Children even determine the brands of products used in daily consumption, such as food and grooming products. In a family household, there may be other decision makers, in addition to the family itself. The residential cleaning service may determine the brands of cleaning products and furniture polish. The family pet may have a preference of one brand of food over another.

Finally, in nonfamily households, roommates bring with them the consumption traditions of their own families and backgrounds. These household members exert an important influence on the types of goods and services consumed by an individual.

4-3d: Reference Groups

> **Reference Groups:** Groups that serve as a point of reference for individuals in the process of shaping their attitude and behavior.
>
> **Associative Reference Groups:** Groups that individuals belong to.
>
> **Dissociative Groups:** Groups that individuals want to dissociate from through their behavior.
>
> **Aspirational Groups:** Groups that individuals aspire to join in the future—for example, by virtue of education, employment, and training.

Reference groups are defined as groups that serve as a point of reference for individuals in the process of shaping their attitudes and behavior. **Associative reference groups** are groups that individuals belong to. As a member of a group, an individual will adopt the group's behaviors, engage in similar activities, and purchase similar brand names as others in the group. For example, members of a sorority are likely to dress similarly, with a preference for the same brand names and retailers. **Dissociative groups** are groups that individuals want to dissociate from through their behavior. Lesbians are rarely dressed in pretty, frilly dresses, and they reject the makeup and accessories that are characteristic of heterosexual women. They tend to dissociate from the more traditional, submissive females through their style, which is simple, assertive, and natural. **Aspirational groups** are groups that individuals aspire to join in the future—for example, by virtue of education, employment, and training. Aspirational groups are important determinants of consumer behavior. Business students aspiring to work on Wall Street will acquire products that fit with their new profile—leather briefcase, designer suit, executive pen set, and other products associated with their coveted professional position.

For Cheri in the chapter-opening vignette, Donna Karan and Armani outfits, expensive antiques, and her house reflect her desire to be accepted by refined locals of taste and means in the town where she recently moved. In cases in which her products are visible and conspicuous, as in the case of clothing or the home itself, Cheri readily spends large amounts of money to signal her preferences to her aspirational group. She purchases products that are privately consumed, such as food, at a discount from off-price retailers. In her public consumption, Cheri distances herself from her associative group, her family on the farm in the Midwest.

4-4 PSYCHOLOGICAL INFLUENCES ON CONSUMER BEHAVIOR

Consumer behavior is likely to be influenced by the following psychological factors: motivation, perception, learning, beliefs, attitudes, personality, and lifestyles. The field of psychology has extensively examined these dimensions and their influence on individual behavior.

4-4a: Motivation

Consumers are motivated by needs and wants. Needs were defined in Chapter 1 as basic human requirements. People are motivated to seek goods and services that satisfy their needs, and marketers attempt to address consumer needs with the different goods and services they offer. A need becomes a want when it is directed to a particular product—wants are shaped by one's culture. We may have a physiological need, such as something to drink, that can become a want—a desire for a particular brand: Coke.

> **Drive (or Motive):** A stimulus that encourages consumers to engage in an action to reduce the need.

When a need is not satisfied, it becomes a **drive** (or motive), which is defined as a stimulus that encourages consumers to engage in an action to reduce the need. **Figure 4-7** illustrates motivation as a process that moves consumers from a latent need (hunger) to the behavior that satisfies that need (going to a restaurant).

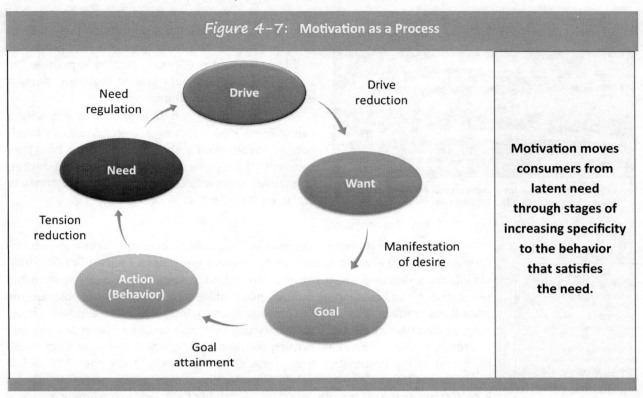

Figure 4-7: Motivation as a Process

Need regulation → Drive → Drive reduction → Want → Manifestation of desire → Goal → Goal attainment → Action (Behavior) → Tension reduction → Need

Motivation moves consumers from latent need through stages of increasing specificity to the behavior that satisfies the need.

Consumers first experience a latent need, such as the need for food. The unsatisfied need becomes a drive or motivation to reduce hunger. The need then translates into a want: a sandwich wrap. The consumer then has a specific goal—searching in his or her memory for various wrap sources—and decides to go to Wawa, a popular gas station convenience store. The behavior that reduces hunger involves eating the Wawa wrap.

One popular theory of motivation, Maslow's theory of needs, explains individuals' motivation to engage in particular behaviors as a function of needs arranged in a hierarchy from the most urgent to the least urgent. Consumers need to satisfy their most urgent needs, such as food and drink, before they can satisfy higher-level needs. As soon as they satisfy their lower needs, their higher needs become more pressing.

Figure 4-8: Maslow's Hierarchy of Needs

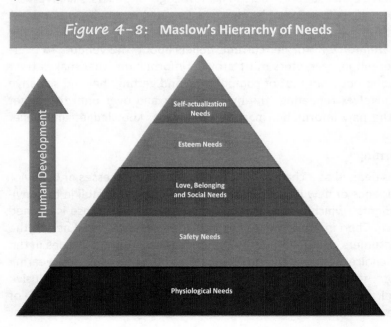

Human Development

Self-actualization Needs
Esteem Needs
Love, Belonging and Social Needs
Safety Needs
Physiological Needs

The Maslow hierarchy of needs is illustrated in **Figure 4-8**. The most basic needs are physiological: the need for food, water, and sleep. At the next level are safety needs, such as the need for shelter and protection from danger or harm. Love, social, or belonging needs are at the following level—the need to be accepted by one's group, family, and friends. Once in a group, individuals crave self-esteem, status and appreciation, respect from others. Finally, individuals need self-actualization, the need to accomplish and realize their own potential. Products can satisfy a number of needs at the same time. Cheri in our example has a strong social need: She needs to

Figure 4-9: Mercedes automobiles often line up at car pools; many consumers believe that they are safer than other brands.

belong to an aspirational group defined as locals of taste and means. To satisfy this need, she purchases visibly consumed products, such as expensive antiques and top designer brands that are popular with this aspirational group.

Consumers can satisfy thirst needs with a can of Pepsi, iced tea, or even water. They can satisfy hunger needs with a steak or a Snickers bar. They can satisfy safety needs with the right brand of tires. "Mercedes automobiles tend to appeal to consumers' need for safety" (see Figure 4-9).

4-4b: Perception

Perception is the manner in which we collect, organize, and interpret information from the world around us to create a meaningful image of reality. Individuals form different images of the same stimulus because of differences in the perceptual processes. One such difference is attributed to **selective exposure**—the stimuli that consumers choose to pay attention to. Individuals are exposed to numerous advertisements every day: They see television and newspaper ads and billboards, and they listen to advertising on radio. Clearly, consumers could not possibly retain all the information from these different sources. They, therefore, selectively choose the messages they will pay attention to. The challenge for advertisers is to create ads that stand out from the multitude of messages consumers see on a daily basis.

Selective distortion involves consumers adapting information to fit their own existing knowledge or beliefs. For example, if a consumer believes that American electronics are inferior to Japanese electronics, then information in an ad that is contrary to this belief will likely be either ignored or distorted to fit into the consumer's current belief structure. After a purchase has been made, consumers often will distort information and evaluate the product to make it conform to their current beliefs and behavior.

Selective retention refers to consumers remembering only information about a good or service that supports personal knowledge or beliefs. An advertisement that does not support a person's current concepts is usually forgotten. A purchasing agent listening to a salesperson may remember only the portions of the conversation that reinforce his or her current beliefs about the vendor. To overcome selective retention, marketers must provide information that makes their good or service stand out from that of competitors, and getting beyond selective retention usually involves repeating the message over and over until the target audience makes the new information part of its current knowledge and belief structure.

4-4c: Learning

Learning is defined as a change in individual thought processes or behavior attributed to experience or new information. It involves **cues** or **stimuli** in the environment, such as products and advertisements, which create an individual response. **Response** is defined as an attempt to satisfy an individual drive. Cheri in our example has a drive to satisfy a social need—the need to be accepted locally by upscale consumers. Her response to this drive is conditioned by cues in the environment that confirm or reject her choices. Cheri may find it rewarding to see celebrities wearing outfits by her preferred designers, to note that these designers are available only in the most exclusive local shops, and, especially, that her aspirational group approves of these designers. The outcome of these desirable cues is a reduction in the drive, known as **reinforcement**—referring to the reinforcement

Perception:
The manner in which people collect, organize, and interpret information from the world around them to create a meaningful image of reality.

Selective Exposure:
The stimuli that consumers choose to pay attention to.

Selective Distortion:
Consumers adapting information to fit their own existing knowledge.

Selective Retention:
Remembering only information about a good or service that supports personal knowledge or beliefs.

Learning:
Change in individual thought processes or behavior attributed to experience or new information.

Cues:
Stimuli in the environment, such as products or advertisements, that create individual responses.

Stimuli:
Cues in the environment, such as products and advertisements, that create individual responses.

Response:
An attempt to satisfy an individual drive.

of the learning process, achieved by strengthening the relationship between the cue and the response. Repeated reinforcement creates a habit. Marketers are keen on making their brands habitual purchases.

4-4d: Attitudes and Beliefs

Attitudes are defined as relatively enduring and consistent feelings (affective responses) about a product. A consumer may like Starbucks, Bose speakers, and Intel processors and dislike fast food, loud music in restaurants, and intrusive salespeople.

Attitudes are difficult to change; therefore, changing attitudes about brands can be quite challenging, depending on how strong the attitudes

Figure 4-10: With time, frozen yogurt has gained a reputation as a health snack.

are. The more firmly held the attitude, the more difficult it is to change. Frozen yogurt (see Figure 4-10) has fought hard to be accepted as a health snack, rather than as a sweet and unhealthy dessert.

Beliefs are associations between a product and attributes of that product. Examples of such beliefs include: "Starbucks sells strong coffee," "Bose speakers are a product of advanced German technology," "Intel processors only exist in quality computers," or "Fast food and smoking cause heart attacks." Marketers attempt to create positive attitudes toward their goods and services and to create beliefs that link their brands to desirable attributes. U.S. multinationals have been successful in creating a positive brand-quality belief in the minds of Japanese consumers as a result of extensive advertising. As a result, Japanese consumers today believe that English-sounding brands are superior brands. Due to this belief, many Japanese brands targeted at the Japanese consumers have English-sounding names (see Figure 4-11).

> **Reinforcement:** Learning achieved by strengthening the relationship between the cue and the response.
>
> **Attitudes:** Relatively enduring and consistent feelings (affective responses) about a good or service.
>
> **Beliefs:** Associations between a good or service and attributes of that good or service.
>
> **Personality:** An individual's unique psychological characteristics leading to specific response tendencies over time.

4-4e: Personality and Lifestyles

Personality is defined as an individual's unique psychological characteristics that lead to specific response tendencies over time. Brands are often positioned to appeal to consumers with a particular personality. High-performance automobiles, such as Porsche and Maseratti, and Rossignol skis attempt to appeal to high-sensation seekers looking for adventure and fun. Variety seekers are a good market to target when introducing a new brand or a new product. Retailers target impulsive consumers by placing impulse items close to the register. Consumers who are more impulsive will buy those products rather than rigidly sticking to the products on the shopping list.

Figure 4-11 Pokari Sweat and Wonda are successful Japanese brands developed based on the Japanese consumer beliefs that brands with English-sounding names have a higher quality.

Lifestyles refer to individuals' style of living as expressed through activities, interests, and opinions. Marketers have made numerous attempts to categorize consumers according to lifestyles—this categorization and measurement is known as psychographics. **Psychographics** incorporate lifestyle and personality dimensions.

SRI Consulting Business Intelligence provides a popular classification of lifestyles: The VALS 2 typology categorizes respondents based on resources and on the extent to which they are action oriented. VALS 2 categorizes consumers as:

Innovators—They are successful, sophisticated, and receptive to new technologies. Their purchases reflect cultivated tastes for upscale products.

Thinkers—They are educated, conservative, practical consumers who value knowledge and responsibility. They look for durability, functionality, and value.

Achievers—They are goal-oriented, conservative consumers committed to career and family. They favor established prestige products that demonstrate success to peers.

Experiencers—They are young, enthusiastic, and impulsive consumers who seek variety and excitement and spend substantially on fashion, entertainment, and socializing.

Believers—They are conservative, conventional consumers who focus on tradition, family, religion, and community. They prefer established brands, favoring American products.

Strivers—They are trendy, fun-loving consumers who are concerned about others' opinions and approval. They demonstrate to peers their ability to buy.

Makers—They are self-sufficient consumers who have the skill and energy to carry out projects, respect authority, and are unimpressed by material possessions.

Survivors—They are concerned with safety and security, focus on meeting needs rather than fulfilling desires, are brand loyal, and purchase discounted products.

Knowledge about consumers' lifestyles is important. Marketers who learn about and adapt to changing consumer attitudes, interests, and opinions will have an advantage in the marketplace.

Innovators:
Psychographic group of individuals who are successful, sophisticated, and receptive to new technologies.

Thinkers:
Psychographic group of individuals who are educated, conservative, and practical consumers who value knowledge and responsibility. They look for durability, functionality, and value.

Achievers:
Psychographic group of individuals who are goal-oriented, conservative, committed to career and family, and favor established, prestige products that demonstrate success to peers.

Experiencers:
Psychographic group of individuals who are young, enthusiastic, and impulsive. They seek variety and excitement, and spend substantially on fashion, entertainment, and socializing.

Believers:
Psychographic group of individuals who are conservative, conventional, and focus on tradition, family, religion, and community. They prefer established brands, favoring American products.

Strivers:
Psychographic group of individuals who are trendy and fun loving. They are concerned about others' opinions and approval, and demonstrate to peers their ability to buy.

Makers:
Psychographic group of individuals who are self-sufficient. They have the skill and energy to carry out projects, respect authority, and are unimpressed by material possessions.

Survivors:
Psychographic group of individuals who are concerned with safety and security. They focus on meeting needs rather than fulfilling desires, are brand loyal, and purchase discounted products.

4-5 THE CONSUMER DECISION-MAKING PROCESS

We have addressed the different influences on consumer behavior—social influences and psychological influences. We are now going to examine the consumer decision-making process, addressing each of the five stages: problem recognition, information search, alternative evaluation, purchase, and post-purchase behavior, as illustrated in Figure 4-12. It should be mentioned, however, that not all consumers go through each stage every time they make a purchase and that certain stages may take more time and effort than others, depending on the type of purchase decision involved— as will be seen later in this section.

Let us, once again, use Cheri from the chapter opening to illustrate different stages of consumer decision making. Cheri is planning to entertain at Thanksgiving and has to engage in a number of purchases. On her most urgent shopping list, she has a new faucet for her guest bathroom, replacing the original

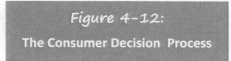

Figure 4-12:
The Consumer Decision Process

Problem Recognition

↓

Information Search

↓

Alternative Evaluation

↓

Purchase

↓

Post-purchase Behavior

faucet, which is a bit too basic for a transitional-style bathroom. She also needs to purchase a turkey and the appropriate trimmings. These purchase decisions will be used to illustrate her decision-making processes, from problem recognition, to purchase, to postpurchase experiences.

4-5a: Problem Recognition

The consumer decision-making process starts when the consumer realizes that he or she has a particular need triggered by the difference between the actual state and a desired state. In the case of the guest bathroom faucet, Cheri has realized that her current faucet is too plain and that it does not convey her sense of style, which is reflected throughout the downstairs entertainment area. Her need for a new faucet is triggered externally: She has seen faucets with Victorian and contemporary designs at the homes of many of her friends, in stores, and in restaurant bathrooms. A contemporary faucet and vanity at a friend's house (see Figure 4-13) may have suggested to her that she really needs to have a faucet that makes a statement in this room as well. She does not exactly know what she wants, but she knows that she wants something other than what she currently has in her guest bathroom.

Her need to have a Thanksgiving dinner party is triggered internally: She has the need to socialize with acquaintances from her new environment. She has a social need to belong to this group of individuals.

4-5b: Information Search

Before making a purchase decision, consumers will search for information. They begin this search by first engaging in an internal information search, which involves thinking back to the different places where they have seen the product displayed or experiences that they themselves had with the good or service. If consumers have previously bought a product (or a particular brand), these consumers could simply engage in a repeat, habitual purchase, buying the same brand at the same store.

As previously mentioned, Cheri is a regular customer at Food Lion. Based on her experience, she knows that the store will carry some brand of fresh turkey, canned cranberries, stuffing, and walnuts for the stuffing. She also has seen pumpkin pie sold at the store. Cheri's mother used to shop at the last minute for products for the Thanksgiving dinner and she always delivered a great meal; her mother was never keen on brand names—any brand of turkey was acceptable, as long as it was fresh. When the time comes, Cheri will spend about half an hour at Food Lion buying all the products she needs for the dinner.

Consumers could also engage in an external information search, taking time to read published information about a product, going through manufacturer or retailer brochures, searching the Inter-

Figure 4-13: Seeing a contemporary faucet at a friend's house, such as this one, could trigger a need for Cheri to purchase a new bathroom faucet for her guest bathroom.

net, or asking friends about various brands. In her search for a new faucet, Cheri would most likely go to specialty stores that specialize in bathroom and kitchen fixtures and appliances and to large home improvement stores to see what brands are available. She would also examine magazines such as *Kitchen and Bath*, looking for specifics about faucets. She is planning to spend quite some time to make sure that she gets the right product at the right price.

It is important for marketers to be aware of the information sources that their target consumers use. For bathroom sinks, for example, the most useful sources are those controlled by the manufacturer and its channel of distribution: Consumers rely on salespeople and manufacturer brochures for information. For turkey purchases, consumers are more likely to rely on

Figure 4-14: Advertising a soothing cream on a lifeguard stand may trigger one to purchase the product after lying all day in the sun.

retail advertising and on word-of-mouth communication for information. Marketers do not control the latter. Advertisements strategically placed in areas where consumers might need a particular product can trigger a need to purchase, for example, a cream that would pamper skin after lying in the sun (see Figure 4-14).

4-5c: Alternative Evaluation

In evaluating product alternatives, consumers compare the different brands and retailers to make sure that the brand they purchase best meets their needs. Often, this step occurs simultaneously with information search. For new product purchases, the alternative evaluation step is very important. Consumers typically use about five evaluation criteria in deciding on the brand that they are going to purchase. Among these criteria are those that a product must meet. For example, the faucet that Cheri is going to purchase must be stylish and unlike most of the other faucets on the market. There are no trade-offs for style and uniqueness. Other important criteria are performance and ease of use. In other respects, Cheri is flexible: Prices for faucets range between $20 and $130, but she is willing to go much higher. She is also flexible with regard to the location of the retailer and is willing to order the product so that it would be conveniently delivered to her home.

In her search, Cheri finds brands such as Moen, FHP, Delta, Grohe, and Hansgrohe. The Moen and FHP brands appear to be rather simple, similar to the faucets that one can find in any public toilet. Grohe, a German manufacturer, seems to have more interesting designs in general, but its sink faucets are unremarkable. Cheri is particularly interested in the Philippe Stark models sold by Hansgrohe, another German manufacturer, under the brand name Axor and the Our Victorian brand sold by Delta.

Cheri finds out that the Axor faucet costs about $670 at the different specialty stores. She tries to find the brand at a lower price on the Internet, without success. All the sites direct buyers to retailers and none offer discounts. One such distributor is Duravit in Germany, which sells the complete Stark line, including toilets, sinks, and accessories. Lowe's, a home improvement store, does not carry the Stark collection. Home Depot, another large home improvement store, can obtain it at a lower price—$458. Cheri finds out that, if she orders the product at Home Depot, the store can put in a rush order so that the faucet can be installed before the Thanksgiving party.

It is possible, however, that the alternative evaluation step may not be part of the decision-making process. For habitual purchases, consumers rely on their memory of a previous purchase and product experience and quickly decide which brand to purchase. Cheri has organized many Thanksgiving dinners before, even when she used to live in a small city apartment while attending the Institute of Fine Arts in New York. Although not a habitual purchase, a turkey is a turkey ... with some caveats. First, her convection oven would choke on anything larger than 20 pounds. Second, she would not consider buying a frozen turkey—her mother fervently believed that they could pose a health danger because they tend not to

Figure 4-15: Appealing attributes to consumers in this coffee shop are its central location and its fair trade coffee.

defrost evenly. And trimmings are trimmings—the store brand is just as good as any other competing national brand. Cheri thought that she could stop at the natural food store to purchase a farm-raised turkey on the way home from her studio in the city but quickly dismissed the idea. It involved complex logistics; moreover, she believed that the turkey would probably not be as plump and juicy as one purchased at Food Lion.

It is important for marketers to understand the consumer evaluation process and focus on the attributes that are used in the decision process. Fair trade coffee and a placement in a chic central mall location (see Figure 4-15) are appealing attributes for consumers.

4-5d: Purchase

There are two important aspects to the purchase process: the purchase intention and the actual purchase. A number of consumer behavior models address the purchase intention and the purchase as two separate steps. Consumers may decide on a particular brand and on the outlet where the product will be purchased. These decisions reflect their purchase intentions. However, between the point where the purchase intention was formed and the actual purchase, there can be many intervening factors that could impede the purchase. The individual may have second thoughts about the brand or the importance of the purchase altogether. In our example, Cheri may decide that it is too expensive to purchase a new faucet and that she would be better off saving the money to purchase a new outfit. Or she may decide to buy the turkey from the natural food store, rather than from Food Lion, to make sure that she will serve the highest quality product—she can also share the information with her guests. If she were to purchase the turkey from Food Lion, then she would be reluctant to share information about the product's source with her guests.

She may go to Home Depot with her best friend to make the faucet purchase. On a closer examination, however, her friend may notice that the Axor faucet does not spray water evenly; Cheri then could decide to purchase the Victorian style Delta faucet, which costs only $179. The job of marketers is to make sure that purchase intentions are translated into purchase behavior. Having a competent salesperson who will handle the order quickly, an appealing store environment with a pleasant atmosphere, and beautiful shiny fixtures could help the consumer to advance from intention to purchase.

4-5e: Postpurchase Processes

The marketing task is not complete at the point where the client purchases the product. As mentioned in Chapter 1, satisfaction and dissatisfaction are important determinants of whether consumers will purchase the brand again. Marketing managers need to persuade consumers that they purchased a quality, reliable brand that addresses the needs consumers identified in the problem recognition stage, and that it is better than the competition. Marketers must also address consumers' feelings of anxiety related to losing the freedom to purchase other brands or products that may or may not compete directly with the one chosen.

Expectations and Satisfaction

As previously explained, consumers anticipate product performance based on their experiences, as well as information received from the media and from other consumers. They have expectations that influence the evaluation of good or service quality and predict how the product will perform on the market. Cheri expects that the Delta faucet she ultimately purchased will be of very high quality. She expects that the faucet will perform well, and more importantly, it will look lovely in her guest bathroom.

If a good or service performs better than expected, then consumers are likely to be satisfied. If satisfied, consumers are likely to purchase the brand in the future. If performance matches expectations, consumers are somewhat satisfied (psychologists refer to this as satisficing). If expectations are greater than performance, then there is a gap between expectation and performance and consumers are likely to be dissatisfied with the brand and may never purchase it again. These consumers are also expected to engage in negative word-of-mouth communication about the brand and switch to a competitor in the future.

If Cheri is satisfied with the Delta brand faucet, she may, in the future, spend thousands of dollars to purchase an entire Victorian style bathroom suite, from the formidable, wall-anchored toilet, to the geometric bathtub marvel, to the modest yet unique shower. If she is dissatisfied, she may return the product to the retailer for a full refund or just bad-mouth the brand to her friends if she does not want to go through the return process.

Cognitive Dissonance and Buyer's Regret

Cognitive Dissonance:
An anxiety feeling of uncertainty about whether or not the consumer made the right purchase decision.

Buyer's Regret:
A feeling of anxiety related to the consumer's loss of freedom to spend money on other products.

Cognitive dissonance is an anxiety feeling of uncertainty about whether or not the consumer made the right purchase decision. This feeling is especially strong if the purchase is important and expensive and if the consumer does not have the option of returning the product if he or she is not satisfied with it. **Buyer's regret** is related to cognitive dissonance, in that it is also a feeling of anxiety; the anxiety is related to the consumer's loss of freedom to spend money on other products. Spending $458 on a faucet will limit the amount that Cheri can spend when her favorite retailer, carrying designer clothing, has its end-of-year sale.

An important task of marketers is to reduce cognitive dissonance and buyer's regret by reassuring consumers that they made the right purchase. Postpurchase installation, service, warranties, advertisements, and direct-mail communications all serve to reduce consumers' cognitive dissonance and dispel any concerns the consumers may have about the purchase. Such communications may compare the brand favorably with competing brands and stress attributes that are important to the consumer. For example, Cheri would be delighted to receive a note from Delta congratulating her on her purchase or a telephone call from Home Depot reassuring her that it stands behind the Delta brand. Table 4-1 (next page) summarizes the consumer decision-making process for Cheri in the purchase of the faucet and the Thanksgiving turkey.

4-6 VARIATIONS IN DECISION MAKING

In the process of making purchase decisions, consumers can engage in extensive problem solving, going carefully through each of the steps of the consumer decision-making process. In this case, consumers will spend substantial amounts of time searching for information about the different brands and outlets where the product may be purchased. **Extensive problem solving** is typical for high-involvement purchases (products that have a high personal relevance). Most consumers purchasing furniture and decor products will engage in extensive problem solving because, for most, it will be a high-involvement purchase decision, as Figure 4-16 (next page) illustrates.

Extensive Problem Solving:
Consumer decision making that involves going carefully through each of the steps of the consumer decision-making process.

High-Involvement Purchases:
Purchases that have a high personal relevance.

Limited Problem Solving:
Consumer decision making that involves less problem solving. This type of decision making is used for products that are not especially visible, nor too expensive.

Cheri considers a faucet a **high-involvement purchase** because the faucet selected is important in projecting her sense of style to her aspirational group. She wanted the faucet to be unique, unlike all the other products on retailers' shelves and in her acquaintances' bathrooms. Cheri went through extensive problem solving when purchasing the Delta faucet, spending large amounts of time and energy to learn about the different faucet brands available on the market.

Consumers can engage in **limited problem solving** for products that

Table 4-1: Cheri's Decision-Making Process for a Faucet and a Turkey		
Stage	**Faucet**	**Turkey**
Problem Recognition	The need for a new faucet was triggered externally because of faucets Cheri had seen with Victorian and contemporary designs at the homes of many of her friends, in stores, and in restaurant bathrooms.	Cheri's need to have a Thanksgiving dinner party was triggered internally because she had the need to socialize with new acquaintances from her new environment.
Information Search	In her quest for a new faucet, Cheri looks externally for information at specialty stores and large home improvement stores to see what brands were available. She also read magazines looking for specifics about faucets.	Cheri conducted an internal search based on her memory of her mother shopping at Food Lion at the last minute for products for the Thanksgiving dinner. Her mother was never keen on brand names--any brand of turkey was acceptable if it was fresh.
Alternative	Cheri located several brands of faucets and spent considerable time evaluating each brand. Price, quality, and appearance were the major criteria she used.	Cheri spent little time evaluating the evaluation various brands of turkey. In fact, she never paid any attention to the brand name. She based her evaluation on the size and the appearance of the turkey.
Purchase	After careful consideration, Cheri purchased the Victorian style faucet made by Delta and sold at Home Depot.	Cheri purchased the turkey from Food Lion because that was the retailer she used for groceries and where she was purchasing her other food items.
Postpurchase	Cheri experienced both cognitive dissonance and buyer's regret. She worried her friends would not like the style she picked out, and if they did not, she did not have the money to buy another new set.	Cheri spent little time evaluating the turkey purchase because it tasted good and her company enjoyed it.

are not especially visible or too expensive. In deciding to purchase the turkey at Food Lion, Cheri wanted to minimize the amount of time and effort dedicated to the purchase. Although buying a turkey was not quite a routine purchase, her once-a-year experience provided enough information to her that she did not need to ask around where she would find a reasonable product. She may have looked at the weekly advertisements from other supermarkets to note whether they offered a greater discount, and she may have examined different brands of fresh turkey at Food Lion. Beyond that, her decision process was relatively simple: She selected the turkey brand, found the right size turkey, and purchased it.

Consumers can also engage in **routine problem solving**. Consumers engage in routine problem solving for habitual purchase decisions involving products that they purchase frequently. Consumers routinely purchase Tropicana juice, Yoplait yogurt, Eggo waffles, Colgate toothpaste, and other similar brands. Consumers do not need to compare these brands with alternative product offerings if these

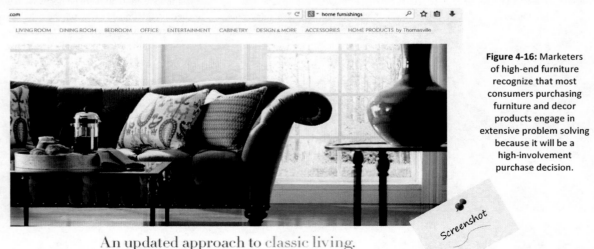

Figure 4-16: Marketers of high-end furniture recognize that most consumers purchasing furniture and decor products engage in extensive problem solving because it will be a high-involvement purchase decision.

brands have provided a satisfactory consumption experience. Routine problem solving is typical for **low-involvement products** (products with limited personal relevance, such as eggs, cheese, and other convenience goods).

Finally, consumers are greatly affected by **situational influences**. When purchasing products for personal private consumption, consumers are more likely to purchase discounted products or to buy store brands. When purchasing products with friends, consumers tend to engage in more limited problem solving in making their purchase decision. And when purchasing a product for gift giving, consumers are likely to engage in extensive problem solving, both with regard to the brand and the retailer, ensuring that the product is impeccably packaged and presented. Marketers need to take note of consumers' situational influences and steer their decision accordingly. Salespeople in boutiques and department stores often take special care to ensure that products targeted for gift giving are attractively wrapped and presented. For a review of the variations in decision making, see Table 4-2 .

Table 4-2: Variations in Decision Making		
Product	**Cheri's action**	**Type of problem solving situation**
Faucet	Cheri spent several days and a lot of time choosing just the right bathroom faucet.	Extensive problem solving.
Turkey	Cheri examined the various turkeys.	Limited problem solving. She was at Food Lion and, after several minutes, picked the one that she thought would be the best.
Candy bar	As Cheri was checking out, she noticed the rack of candy bars and picked out her favorite.	Routine problem solving.
Stereo	Wanting to get the right stereo, Cheri spent several weeks looking in stores and catalogs and online before she made a purchase.	Extensive problem solving.
Soft drink	Thirsty, Cheri went to the soda machine and bought Diet Coke, the same brand she almost always purchases.	Routine problem solving.
McDonald's	Cheri was hungry but did not have much time.	Limited problem solving. She thought about which fast-food restaurants were on her way to work and because McDonald's was on the right side of the street and there did not appear to be a long line of cars at the drive-up window, she chose it.

Summary

1. *Identify the elements of a consumer behavior model. The consumer behavior model addresses the influence of social and psychological factors that affect consumer behavior.* Social influences, such as culture, subcultures, social class, roles, status, families, households, and reference groups, are instrumental in shaping individual attitudes, interests, opinions, and behavior. Psychological influences, such as motivation, perception, learning, personality, and lifestyles, as well as beliefs and attitudes, are likely to influence how consumers behave.

2. *Describe the different social influences that have an impact on consumer behavior.* Among the social influences that affect consumer behavior are culture, social class, role and status influences, family and household influences, and reference group influences. Culture includes the totality of learned and shared meanings, rituals, norms, and traditions among the members of an organization or society. Values are particularly important in that they guide individuals' actions, attitudes, and judgments and thus affect behavior. Values are learned from those with whom individuals are in contact: family, friends, teachers, clergy, politicians, and the media. Learning a new culture is known as acculturation. Subcultures are components of the broad culture; they are groups of individuals with shared value systems based on ethnicity or common background. Among the important ethnic and national subcultures in the United States are the African American subculture, the Hispanic American subculture, and the Asian American subculture. Social class, role, and status influences also have an important impact on consumer behavior. In the United States, the social classes are the upper class, consisting of upper uppers (old money) and lower uppers (new money); the middle class, consisting of upper-middle class (professionals) and lower-middle class (white collar); and the lower class, consisting of upper-lower class (blue collar) and lower-lower class (unskilled and unemployed). Additional social influences are exerted by one's family and household and by reference groups, especially by aspirational reference groups that one would like to belong to.

3. *Describe the different psychological influences that have an impact on consumer behavior.* Consumer behavior is influenced by motivation, perception, learning, attitudes, beliefs, personality, and lifestyles. Consumers are motivated by needs and wants, which create a drive to engage in behavior. In the hierarchy of needs, physiological needs, such as food and water, are the most basic. They are followed by safety needs and social needs—for love and belonging. At the higher levels are the need for self-esteem and status in society, and at the highest level, the need for self-actualization—the need to accomplish and realize one's full potential. Perception is the manner in which we perceive the world around us, the manner in which we notice advertisements and products in a store. Learning, which involves changes in individual thought processes or behavior attributed to experience, influences consumer behavior. Attitudes and beliefs involve developing feelings about products and associations between a good or service and attributes of that good or service. Finally, individuals' enduring traits and responses to stimuli around them (personality) and individuals' style of living as expressed through activities, interests, and opinions (lifestyles) also influence consumer behavior. Marketers have devised modalities to cluster individuals based on personality and lifestyle through psychographic measurement.

4. *Address the five stages of the consumer decision-making process.* The stages of the consumer decision-making process are problem recognition, information search, alternative evaluation, purchase, and postpurchase behavior. Problem recognition develops when there is a difference between the actual state and a desired state. It can be triggered externally, by advertising or store displays or by observing others consuming a product; or it can be triggered internally, through an individual need. Consumers could search for information internally, by searching their own memory about a product experience, or externally, by consulting magazines or salespeople. After evaluating the different brand and retail outlet alternatives, consumers typically develop the intention to purchase a product; barring any intervening events or concerns, the consumer engages in the purchase. After purchase, marketers need to ensure that consumers will be satisfied with their purchase by offering guarantees and prompt postpurchase service and by ensuring that the product functions optimally. They also have to reduce consumers' cognitive dissonance (the anxiety that consumers associate with the concern that they may not have bought the best product) and buyer's regret (the regret for the loss of freedom to purchase other products with the money).

5. *Describe variations in consumer decision making based on whether consumers engage in extensive, limited, or routine problem solving.* Depending on the product purchased, consumers could engage in extensive problem solving, where they will go through each stage of the decision-making process. This is typical for products of high personal relevance—high-involvement products—that may have been expensive or may be closely tied to the consumer's self-image. Limited problem solving takes place in the case of products that are not especially expensive or important (low-involvement products), and only minimal problem solving takes place for routine purchase decisions, many of which are habitual.

Key Terms

acculturation	innovators	selective distortion
achievers	instrumental values learning	selective exposure
aspirational groups	lifestyles	selective retention
assimilation	limited problem solving	situational influences
associative reference groups	low-involvement products	social class
attitudes	products makers	status
beliefs	perception	stimuli
believers	personality	strivers
buyer's regret	psychographics	subcultures
cognitive dissonance	reference groups	survivors
cues	reinforcement	terminal values
dissociative groups drive (or motive)	religion	thinkers
experiencers	response	values
extensive problem solving	roles	
high-involvement purchases	routine problem solving	

Discussion Questions

1. What are the primary subcultures in the United States based on nationality and ethnicity? Can you identify other subcultures based on age and geographic location?

2. Identify the subcultures that you are part of. How have these subcultures affected your consumer purchases? Be specific.

3. Discuss the affect of religion on your personal consumer purchases. What about your sexual orientation? How does that impact your purchase behavior. Provide specific illustrations.

4. Which social class do you belong to? How does this affect your purchase decisions? Describe the role(s) that affect you. What about status? How does status affect your behaviors?

5. Discuss the impact of your family on your consumer purchases? Which member or members of your household have the most impact on your purchase behavior? Why?

6. Identify your reference groups. What groups do you belong to (associative groups)? What types of products do you consume based on these affiliations? What groups do you aspire to belong to? What products do you consume or purchase by virtue of this projected affiliation?

7. Take the VALS 2 typology test, available at www.sric-bi.com/VALS. What psychographic category do you belong to? Are your friends in the same category? How do you explain the differences?

8. Identify a low-involvement product and a high-involvement product that you have recently purchased. Attempt to reconstruct the consumer decision-making process involved for each product.

9. Identify a recent high-involvement purchase you made. Discuss each of the five stages of the decision-making process in terms of the purchase. Especially highlight your mental thought processes and any influences that affected the decision you made.

10. Identify products and brands that fit into each of the following categories: extensive problem solving, limited problem solving, and routine problem solving. Provide explanations for each product and brand you classified.

Review Questions
(Answers are on Last Page of the Chapter)

True or False:

1. The consumer behavior model is based on social influences, such as culture, subculture, social class, individual roles and status, and family.

2. Values are defined as a continually changing totality of learned and shared meanings, rituals, norms, and traditions among the members of society.

3. The lower-upper class accounts for two percent of the U.S. population; the class earned new money through business ventures and are most likely to show off their possessions.

4. Consumers are motivated by needs and wants.

5. Selective retention involves consumers adapting the information to fit their own existing knowledge or beliefs.

6. A consumer's personality is expressed through activities, interests, opinions, and lifestyle.

7. The customer decision-making process consists of five stages: defining the desired social status, seeking information, searching for the best discounts, making the purchase, and postpurchase behavior.

8. The consumer decision process starts with the consumer realizing that a particular need is triggered by the difference between the actual state and the desired state.

9. Alternative evaluation is a necessary step in the decision-making process for all purchases.

10. When purchasing low-price products for personal private consumption, consumers tend to follow the extensive problem-solving pattern.

Multiple Choice

11. Which of the following categories relate to the psychological influences of consumer behavior?
   a. Family and households
   b. Personality and lifestyles
   c. Individual roles and status
   d. Culture and subculture

12. Which of the following categories relates to subculture?
   a. Ethnicity and nationality
   b. Age groups
   c. Religion
   d. All of the above

13. Which of the following statements defines status?
   a. The products people consume and individuals' behavior
   b. Activities people are expected to perform
   c. Emphasis on the individual materialistic perception of success
   d. a and b

14. Which of the following are reference groups?
   a. Aspirational groups
   b. Associative groups
   c. Dissociative groups
   d. All of the above

15. Reinforcement in the context of the learning process refers to
   a. strengthening the relationship between the cue and the response.
   b. change in the contents in an advertisement.
   c. applying more aggressive direct sales techniques.
   d. all of the above.

16. Which of the following characteristics describes the psychographic profile of the VALS group called "survivor"?
   a. Focused on meeting needs rather than fulfilling desires
   b. Sophisticated
   c. Goal oriented
   d. b and c

17. When making a purchase, what information source do consumers typically use?
   a. Internal or external information sources
   b. Internal information sources
   c. External information sources
   d. None of the above

18. Different factors could interfere and prevent the purchase in the _____ phase of the purchase process.
    a. purchase intention
    b. actual purchase
    c. postpurchase
    d. a and b

19. Which of the following statements describes cognitive dissonance?
    a. Dissatisfaction with product performance
    b. Consumers trying out a different brand each time when making a purchase
    c. Anxiety feelings of uncertainty about the right purchase decision
    d. None of the above

20. The purchase of a new suit or dress will normally require
    a. extensive problem solving.
    b. situational problem solving.
    c. limited problem solving.
    d. routine problem solving.

Blog

Clow-Lascu: *Marketing: Essentials 5e Blog*

Screenshot of YouTube Video highlighted in
Clow-Lascu *Marketing: Essentials 5e Blog.*

What Is Happening Today?

Learn More! For videos and articles

that relate to Chapter 4:

blogclowlascu.net/category/chapter04

Includes Discussion Questions

with each Post!

Notes

1. Lisa Penaloza and Mary C. Gilly, "Marketer Acculturation: The Changer and the Changed," *Journal of Marketing* 63, no. 3 (July 1999): 84–104.

2. See Milton J. Rokeach, *The Nature of Human Values:* (New York: The Free Press, 1973); Jan-Benedict E. M. Steenkamp, Frenkel ter Hofstede, and Michel Wedel, "A Cross-Cultural Investigation into the Individual and National Cultural Antecedents of Consumer Innovativeness," *Journal of Consumer Research* 63 (April 1999): 55–69.

3. Rokeach, *The Nature of Human Values.*

4. Raj Mehta and Russell W. Belk, "Artifacts, Identity and Transition," *Journal of Consumer Research* 17 (March 1991): 398–411.

5. Penaloza and Gilly, Marketer Acculturation.

6. 2010 Census Briefs, "Overview of Race and Hispanic Origin," at http://www.census.gov/prod/cen2010/briefs/c2010br-02.pdf, accessed on March 23, 2014; David Sokol, "The United Colors of Retailing," *Shopping Center World* (February 2003): 24–30.

7. Nielsen, The Digital Consumer, February 2014, at http://www.nielsen.com/us/en/insights/reports/2014/the-us-digital-consumer-report.html, accessed on March 23, 2014; 2010 Census Briefs, accessed on March 23, 2014; Linda Lane, "Marketing to Hispanics Is Complex, But Essential," *DSN Retailing Today* 42, no. 8 (April 21, 2003): 8–9.

8. 2010 Census Briefs, accessed on March 23, 2014; Sokol, The United Colors of Retailing.

9. Linda P. Morton, "Segmenting Publics by Social Classes," *Public Relations Quarterly* 44, no. 2 (Summer 1999): 45–46; PBS "People Like Us: Social Class in America," available at www.pbs.org/peoplelikeus, accessed on February 6, 2007.

10. David K. Tse, Russell W. Belk, and Nan Zhou, "Becoming a Consumer Society: A Longitudinal and Cross-Cultural Content Analysis of Print Ads from Hong Kong, the People's Republic of China, and Taiwan," *Journal of Consumer Research* 15 (March 1999): 457–472.

11. "Special Report: Ever Higher Society, Ever Harder to Ascend—Meritocracy in America," *The Economist* 374, no. 8407 (January 1, 2005): 35.

12. Ellen Foxman, P. Tanshuaj, and K. Ekstrom, "Family Members' Perception of Adolescents' Influence on Family Decision Making," *Journal of Consumer Research* 15 (March 1989): 482–491.

13. Marla Weiskott, "Tweens: A Consuming Army," *Playthings* 103 (September 2005): 42–43.

Cases

Case 4-1 Tapping into the Sharing Economy with Airbnb

Marissa Smith just graduated from college with a degree in marketing and is currently renting a condo on the Upper East Side, in a middle-class neighborhood in Manhattan known as Yorkville. Her rent is steep, at $2,400 for a small one-bedroom, and electricity costs her an average of $200 a month. Her income is limited as she just started a new position as a marketing assistant at a small Midtown firm. Moreover, she spends little time in the apartment with long hours at work and her weekends in Long Island with her family. She has always contemplated sharing the space with someone who could benefit from living weekends in the City, but she did not have any idea how to go about it.

One of her colleagues at work suggested that she examine some possibilities for extra income with Airbnb, a company that provides a platform for people to rent their apartments, rooms, homes, and even castles with great ease. Marissa has heard of the company: many of her friends traveled all over Europe with Airbnb and reported great experiences.

Airbnb co-founder, Brian Chesky, believes that the new sharing economy, where people share their home or a room in the home typically for less than the price of a hotel room, and where they give rides to individuals for less than the cost of a taxi cab, is going to be the direction business is likely to take in the twenty-first century. Airbnb, according to Chesky, has "over 3,000 castles, 2,000 treehouses, 900 islands and 400 lighthouses available to book on the site. On a recent night, over 100 people were staying in yurts…"Fifty-six percent of guests staying on Airbnb on a recent weekend were doing so for their first time. Over 17 million total guests have stayed on Airbnb. It took Airbnb nearly four years to get its first million guests. Now one million guests stay on Airbnb every month."

Marissa searched the Airbnb listings and found several one-bedroom apartments listed in Yorkville, for about $150 per night. To that amount, a guest would add the Airbnb service fee and, in some instances, owners charged a cleaning fee averaging about $75. Assuming she would be renting the apartment for four nights a month, she would net about $600.

One concern Marissa has is that her lease is strict with regard to subletting, but the landlord is out of town, and condos in Manhattan are not nearly as strict as co-operative apartment buildings, which closely monitor rentals and subletting. Newspapers are replete with stories of individuals in rent-controlled apartments – which are very difficult to come by – evicted for subletting with Airbnb. Worst case for Marissa: she would have to find another apartment, not a minor pursuit, but still a hassle in a relatively competitive environment.

On the other hand, Marissa trusts Airbnb, which, in fact, acts as a platform of trust, where everyone can see everyone's identity and also rate the host or the guest for everyone else to see. Thus, everyone would develop a reputation visible to everyone. According to Chesky, "in this hyperconnected world, reputation will give you access to all kinds of things now... Your reputation now is like having a giant key that will allow you to open more and more doors," allowing you to define yourself as a trustworthy renter, and, respectively, as a trustworthy host.

The apartment is located centrally in a safe, family-oriented part of town, within easy reach of Central Park, the Metropolitan Museum of Art, and the park-like East River boardwalk. There are several D'Agostino supermarkets nearby, a couple of gourmet stores like Food Emporium, and many corner shops selling anything from pastries to hospital supplies.

Marissa thinks Airbnb might be a good opportunity for her potential guests to enjoy life in the City, and for her to earn some income that will lessen the high rent burden she is presently carrying.

Questions

1. Describe the social factors that are influencing Marissa to contemplate renting her apartment with Airbnb and the social factors that influence travelers to use Airbnb instead of traditional hotels.

2. What psychological factors are influencing Marissa's decision to rent her apartment? Be specific and explain why.

3. How would Marissa's apartment meet the needs of tourists in Manhattan?

4. What other "sharing economy" business ideas can you come up with to appeal to younger consumers?

5. Discuss the steps of the consumer decision-making process as it relates to Marissa deciding to rent her apartment with Airbnb.

Sources: Thomas Friedman, "And Now for a Bit of Good News," *The New York Times,* July 19, 2014, accessed at: http://www.nytimes.com/2014/07/20/opinion/sunday/thomas-l-friedman-and-now-for-a-bit-of-good-news.html?_r=0 on July 19, 2014; www.airbnb.com, accessed July 19, 2014.

Case 4-2 The Hispanic Market

Albertsons LLC is a supermarket chain with 655 locations in Arizona, California, Colorado, Florida, Louisiana, Oklahoma, and Texas. Because Hispanic Americans account for 14 percent of the U.S. population, Albertsons sees it as an attractive market, especially because Hispanic Americans are the fastest- growing ethnic segment in the United States. To reach this market segment, Albertson's hired Anton Estrada to design and direct the company's Hispanic American marketing effort. Management believed that having someone of Hispanic American background to develop the Hispanic American marketing program would be a huge asset and increase their chances of succeeding.

Anton immediately began assessing the various markets where Albertsons operated stores. Although there were 35 million Hispanic Americans in the United States, they were not evenly distributed throughout the states where Albertsons had stores. Anton was able to collect the following percentages of the state's population that was Hispanic American.

- Arizona—18.7 percent
- California—25.8 percent
- Colorado—12.8 percent
- Florida—12.1 percent
- Louisiana—2.3 percent
- Oklahoma—3.1 percent
- Texas—25.5 percent

Based on personal experience and facts he had learned in college, Anton knew that Hispanic Americans tended to be more brand and store loyal than the population as a whole. If a retail store, such as a supermarket, treated Hispanic Americans right, they would be loyal to that store. He also knew that Hispanic Americans are willing to pay more money for a name brand product that they believe is of high quality, durable, and dependable.

In terms of grocery shopping, Hispanic Americans prefer fresh food. Because they cook more from scratch, a greater percentage of their grocery money is spent on fresh fruit, vegetables, meat, poultry, fish, and eggs. Instead of shopping once a week like most Caucasians, Hispanic Americans tend to shop more frequently, as much as four to five times a week. Furthermore, they spend an average of $133 per week on groceries compared with $91 for the non–Hispanic American family.

A study by FMI (Food Marketing Institute) provided specific information about what store attributes were important to Hispanic Americans. The percentage of Hispanic Americans who rated the following store attributes as important or somewhat important is given here.

Store Attribute	Rate
A clean, neat store	98%
Fresh, high-quality fruits & veggies	97%
Fresh, high-quality meats & poultry	96%
Courteous, friendly employees	96%
Low prices	96%
Carry Hispanic	91%
Bilingual employees	88%
Bilingual signage	84%
Store active in Hispanic American	84%
Bilingual packaging	82%

Now let us turn to the challenges faced by Estrada. Not all Hispanic Americans are the same. Although most are from Mexico, many Hispanic Americans are from Central and South America, Cuba, the Caribbean, Honduras, and Puerto Rico. Just as Caucasians are not all the same, neither are all Hispanic Americans the same. Although they share a common Spanish language, they do not all share the same cultural views. Furthermore, the level of acculturation into the American culture varies considerably. Some are fully acculturated, whereas others have accepted and adopted little of the American culture. Some speak English well, others do not. Most, however, live in a world of dual languages. They watch and read both English and Spanish programs and magazines. Overall, 70 percent of Hispanic Americans identify the Spanish language as the most important cultural aspect that they want to retain. However, four out of 10 Hispanic Americans prefer to use English, and 54 percent of Hispanic Americans watch English-speaking television programs. The differences among the generations is evident with children growing up in the United States and Hispanic Americans who have lived in the United States for a number of years showing a higher level of acculturation than Hispanic Americans who have recently moved to the United States.

Questions

1. Should Estrada develop a program that is used in all of the Albertsons stores, or should he concentrate on only certain states? If only certain states, which states would you suggest? Also, within those states, should he concentrate only on certain stores? Explain your reasoning.

2. Because of the different nationality backgrounds of Hispanic Americans, how does Estrada handle development of marketing materials?

3. What specific marketing recommendations should Estrada make to management to reach the Hispanic American market?

4. Based on the information provided in this case, how has culture affected the Hispanic American grocery shopper and how does it affect the marketing approach Albertsons would use to reach them?

Sources: Fictitious case based on "Study Sheds Light on Latino Shopping Preferences," *DSN Retailing Today* (June 27, 2005): 18; Robert Vosburgh, "Target: Marketing to Hispanics Worth Effort," *Supermarket News* 53, no. 32 (August 8, 2005): 38039; Amanda Lintott, "Marketing to Hispanics in the US," *Brand Strategy* no. 186 (October 2004): 48–50.

Answers to Review Questions

Answers: 1) False, 2) False, 3) True, 4) True, 5) False, 6) False, 7) False, 8) True, 9) False, 10) False, 11) b, 12) d, 13) c, 14) d, 15) a, 16) a, 17) a, 18) b, 19) c, 20) a.

Chapter 5

Business-to-Business Behavior

Learning Objectives

After studying
this chapter,
you should be able to:

1. Identify the types of goods and services that businesses purchase.

2. Identify the types of business customers.

3. Explain the concepts of derived and joint demand and why they are important for the business-to-business market.

4. Identify the types of buying situations and when each is used.

5. Describe the concept of the buying center and the different roles employees can play.

6. Discuss the factors that influence business-to-business buyer behavior.

7. List the seven steps in the business-to-business buying process and explain what occurs in each step.

Screenshot

5-1 CHAPTER OVERVIEW

For business travelers, the routine at airports has become time consuming and is often frustrating. Long lines, inconvenient rules, and high fares with commercial airlines have caused business travelers to examine other options including hiring private charter jets, flying one of the new startups that fly only business travelers, or purchasing a jet plane or a share in a corporate jet.

The real interest in owning a jet aircraft was given a boost by the terrorist attacks of September 11, 2001, and the ensuing changes in airport security. Since then, the sale of private planes has increased about 35 percent per year to $8.8 billion. This jump in sales of jet airplanes is a result in part of lighter, faster jets now on the market, such as the Eclipse 500, that sells for $1.5 million. But for many companies, the $1.5 million price tag, plus operating and maintenance costs, is too high. Instead, they have pursued part ownership in a jet aircraft, with the most common portion being a one-sixteenth share. Twenty years ago, only 730 individuals and businesses owned fraction shares of a jet aircraft; today, more than 5,000 are part owners.[1]

Although the marketing of goods and services to businesses has some similarities to the marketing of goods and services to individual consumers, there are also some significant differences as illustrated by the sales of jet aircraft. This chapter addresses those differences. Section 5-2 begins with a discussion of the various types of goods and services purchased by businesses. They range from multimillion-dollar projects, such as new buildings and jet aircraft to low-cost items, such as paper clips and copy paper.

Section 5-3 presents the different types of business customers and the way businesses determine demand for their products. In the consumer market, if a firm wishes to stimulate demand, it can offer a price discount, coupons, or some other promotion to encourage consumers to make a purchase. A supplier of raw materials, such as lumber to a furniture factory, cannot stimulate demand just by offering some type of special deal because the amount of lumber, a furniture factory will buy depends on how much furniture it sells to retail stores, who in turn sell the furniture to consumers.

Section 5-4 examines the business-to-business purchase process. In many situations, more than one person is involved in the purchase decision, with each performing a different role. Some will be instrumental in making the decision, whereas others provide information or work out the details of the purchase. The section concludes with a discussion of the various factors that influence how individuals act within the business-to-business purchasing process and what affects the purchase decision that is made.

The last section of the chapter, Section 5-5, identifies the seven steps of the business purchase process. The buying process begins with the identification of a need, goes through identifying potential vendors, and ends with the selection of a vendor who can meet the company's need.

5-2 TYPES OF BUSINESS GOODS AND SERVICES

In understanding business buyer behavior, it is helpful to identify the types of goods and services that businesses purchase. They include major equipment, buildings and land, accessory equipment, fabricated and component parts, process materials, maintenance and repair parts, operating supplies, raw materials, goods for resale, and business services. Each of these requires a slightly different marketing approach and is purchased by a different kind of customer.

5-2a: Major Equipment, Buildings, and Land

The purchase of buildings, land, and major equipment, such as factory machines, mainframe computers, and robotic equipment, requires considerable time and thought. Top management is almost always included in the decision and often in the selection process because the cost of these items is normally quite high. These types of purchases are often the result of strategic decisions made by executive management, and financing is a consideration because few companies would have the cash to pay for them. In the case of major equipment, leases could be examined as an option because they may be more cost effective than a purchase. From a seller's standpoint, these types of purchases require a long period of time, often several months, and the involvement of the top management of the selling company.

5-2b: Accessory Equipment

Accessory equipment consists of items used by a business but that are not typically directly involved in the production or sale of the firm's products. Accessory equipment would include furniture; office equipment, such as personal computers and copy machines; forklifts; and vehicles such as a company truck. Trailers are examples of accessory equipment used by German beer manufacturers (see Figure 5-1). These items are not purchased on a regular basis and therefore require some extra effort when the purchase is made. Because most are not high-ticket items, top management is not normally involved in the selection but may be involved in the final approval. This would likely depend on the ticket price. For a fax machine, top management probably would not be involved, but for a company truck that may cost $30,000, it may be. At a minimum, a vice president will probably be involved in the truck purchase. As with major equipment, leases are sometimes considered rather than a purchase. For example, rather than purchase copy machines or a fleet of cars, these items can be leased.

Figure 5-1: Examples of accessory equipment are trailers used in the distribution of beer.

5-2c: Fabricated and Component Parts

Fabricated and component parts are identifiable products that are incorporated into another product. In automobiles, component parts include the spark plugs, the battery, the radio, and the tires. These parts are not made by the automobile manufacturer but are purchased from outside vendors and installed on the vehicle. Fabricated parts are a type of component part. However, the difference is that the fabricated parts are not as easily identifiable. For instance, most computer manufacturers use fabricated parts in building their computers. The processor, the CD-ROM drive, and the speakers used in your computer were all purchased from various vendors. Your computer manufacturer just assembled them into a computer for you. Unless you are a computer wizard, the only fabricated part you can probably identify is the Intel Pentium processor. The sink shown in Figure 5-2 is a component part used in the construction of kitchens by building contractors.

Because fabricated and component parts become a part of a finished product, quality and dependability become important issues. If the motherboard on your computer or the radio in your automobile is of inferior quality, then it will reflect on the product being purchased. If you purchased a Mercedes, your

Figure 5-2: FHP is promoting its line of sinks for building contractors to use in the construction of homes and business facilities.

Source: Sample print advertisement courtesy The Miles Agency and Alliance One Advertising, Inc.

expectations of radio quality would likely be different than if you purchased a Mini Cooper. Therefore, Mercedes is likely to purchase a higher-quality radio or stereo system. The key is to match the quality of the component part to the quality of the finished product.

The second important factor is dependability. If the stereo installed in your Mercedes is not dependable, then Mercedes will spend time and money replacing it. Ford found itself in a costly situation with Firestone tires that were installed on new Ford vehicles. The recall of all of the vehicles to replace the Firestone tires not only cost Ford a lot of money, but it also damaged Ford's reputation, even though Ford did not manufacture the tires. The Firestone situation was also a major factor in the ouster of Ford's CEO at the time, Jacques Nasser. Consumers blamed Ford for purchasing defective tires for its new vehicles, and Nasser was blamed for the way he handled the situation.[2]

5-2d: Process Materials

Process materials are used in the manufacture of other products but lose their identity. Process materials include items such as cement, aluminum, steel, plastic, and wire (see Figure 5-3). Because process materials are used in the building of other products, specifications are an important issue. The metal and plastic used in building a clothes dryer must meet certain grade, quality, and durability specifications. The grade of electrical wire required varies depending on whether it is used for the switch on the dryer's console or the cord that is plugged into the home's 220-volt electrical outlet.

As with fabricated and component parts, quality, delivery, and cost are important issues. Because process materials lose their identity, any defects will be directly attributed to the manufacturer. But it is also the case that because they lose their identity, they achieve a commodity status with buyers. The electrical wires used in the General Electric (GE) clothes dryer can be purchased from a number of firms that manufacture electrical wiring. The quality is often the same, so factors such as price, deals, and dependable delivery become more important in the purchase decision. GE would be inclined to go with the lowest cost as long as the firm could provide quality and dependable delivery of the wire. However, if another company offers GE a special deal on wire, GE may be willing to switch vendors. All of this is said with the understanding that dependable delivery is crucial. If the wire is not delivered to the GE factory in a timely manner, it could cause a shutdown of the assembly line and cost GE money. Therefore, buyers often build in penalties or fines if a supplier's failure to deliver their materials causes a shutdown of an assembly process.

Figure 5-3 Cement is a process material used in the construction of buildings and other products.

5-2e Maintenance and Repair Parts

Items such as oil, grease, filters, gears, switches, and motors are maintenance and repair parts. These items are needed to keep a machine running or to repair a machine when it is broken. Maintenance items are normally kept in stock and are replenished on a regular basis. As with process materials, maintenance items are often commodity products with no or little brand-name recognition. Because the brand of grease used on a machine is usually not a factor in the purchase decision, price becomes an important determinant.

Repair parts are not usually kept in stock unless they are items that break down often or may be extremely critical to an operation. For example, a mill that uses a large number of electrical motors will usually keep motor parts on hand so that a motor can be repaired quickly. It may even keep spare motors that can be switched out while the broken one is being repaired.

For accessory equipment that a firm purchases, instead of the buyer taking care of the repairs and keeping repair parts on hand, it may opt for a maintenance contract. Copiers are an excellent example. With the purchase of a Konika Minolta copier, a business may also purchase a three-year maintenance agreement whereby Konika Minolta agrees to maintain the copier and repair anything that is broken. These maintenance contracts are especially important for technical equipment requiring specialized knowledge to repair.

5-2f: Operating Supplies

Operating supplies tend to be low-cost items a company needs for day-to-day operations. Light bulbs, paper, pencils, paper clips, and cleaning chemicals would be examples. These types of products are purchased on a regular basis by the purchasing department's staff or secretarial staff. Price and convenience are usually the most important criteria in purchasing. Little effort or time is devoted to purchasing operating supplies.

5-2g: Raw Materials

Raw materials are supplied by the agriculture, fishing, mining, and timber industries. Raw materials must go through some type of manufacturing process before they can be used in building a product. Timber must be cut into some type of board or chips at a sawmill before it can be used. Minerals must be mined and impurities taken out before the minerals can be used. Corn, wheat, and other agricultural products must be cleaned and processed before they can be used as ingredients in food or feed products.

Raw materials are purchased in bulk based on some type of grading process. The price a farmer will be paid for wheat is determined by the grade and quality of the wheat. When it is sold, it loses its identity because it is often mixed with grain from other sources. The mill that grinds the wheat into flour has no idea what farmer's wheat is used but does know the grade and type of wheat. Because the wheat has no brand identity, brokers, agents, and distributors are often used (see Figure 5-4). General Mills does not want to deal with every farmer to purchase wheat for its needs. Therefore it will deal with a broker or distributor who has purchased wheat from a number of sources and pooled it together.

For a company like General Mills, the two most important factors in purchasing an ingredient like wheat are the price and a dependable supply. Because wheat is graded by

Figure 5-4 Wheat is a raw material that food manufacturers purchase through brokers and distributors.

quality, General Mills will tend to go with the supplier who offers the best price with an acceptable level of quality and delivery.

Because of the commodity nature of raw materials, the Internet has gained in popularity as a mode of purchasing. For example, Allactiontrade.com is a business-to-business auction marketplace for both buyers and sellers. Companies can sell excess inventory and liquidate stock they own and purchase materials and products for themselves. Sellers can post raw materials and other products on the site, inviting potential buyers to bid on it. Buyers can post particular needs, inviting suppliers to offer bids.[3]

5-2h: Goods for Resale

As you will learn in future chapters, wholesalers, distributors, and retailers purchase many goods for the purpose of resale. **Wholesalers and distributors** are companies that purchase goods from a manufacturer for resale to other members of the channel. In most cases, wholesalers and distributors sell to retail outlets. But in recent years, retailers have started buying directly from the manufacturer to reduce costs.

> **Wholesalers and Distributors:** Intermediaries that purchase goods from a manufacturer for resale to other members of the channel.

Manufacturers who are producing goods for end-user consumption must understand the consumer market. To be successful, Reebok must understand what consumers want in shoes, even though it does not sell directly to consumers but through retail shoe stores. In addition, Reebok must understand that shoe retailers are not particularly concerned about selling a specific brand, but in selling shoes. If Reebok's advertising can increase the sales for a retail store, then the store will display and push Reebok products. However, if consumers walking in are demanding Skechers, then shoe stores will feature Skechers. Reebok may have to offer shoe stores larger discounts or other incentives to encourage them to give a higher priority to Reebok shoes. You can quickly see that if Reebok does this, then other shoe manufacturers may have to counter with their own set of incentives and deals.

The same philosophy applies to wholesalers or distributors. Because their goal is to earn a profit, they will push the brand that benefits them the most. Suppose an office supply distributor carries multiple brands of staplers. Unless there is demand for a specific brand by the retail stores, the distributor will push the brand that generates the highest profits and sales for them. As a result, pricing and trade deals become significant components of the selling process of goods for resale.

5-2i: Business Services

Business services consist of professional services and operating services. Professional services would include legal counsel, medical services, certified public accountants (CPAs), auditing services, and consulting services. Operating services would include the telephone service, Internet provider, insurance carrier, lawn care service, janitorial service, and shipping services. Professional services tend to be hired for a particular situation or on retainer when they are needed. Operating services tend to be hired on contract to supply the service on a continual basis for a fixed period of time. For many companies, these types of services are let out for bid on a routine basis, often once a year (see Figure 5-5).

In recent years, there has been a trend to outsource some of a company's operation to outside vendors. Large companies that have a cafeteria

Figure 5-5: This advertisement by OccuMed promotes its occupational medicine program and is directed at businesses.
Source: Courtesy of Newcomer, Morris & Young.

will often contract with an outside vendor, such as Aramark, to operate the food service for them. Other companies have outsourced human resource functions, information technology (IT) functions, and payroll. They believe doing this will allow them to obtain better service at a lower cost than if they did it themselves.

Marketing of a service to another business is a greater challenge than marketing a good because the business cannot see the service before making the purchase. Personal relationships and trust become more important. If the members of an office complex decide that they want to hire a service to take care of their lawns, they must make a decision on proposals submitted and the work they believe the service will provide. Because of the risk of not knowing how well a service will perform, most companies do not switch service providers unless they are unhappy with their current provider. Seldom will coming in with a lower price be enough, unless the price is substantially lower than the company's current vendor. Even then, the company may have doubts whether the new service provider can provide the same service level at such a reduced price.

5-3 CHARACTERISTICS OF BUSINESS-TO-BUSINESS MARKETS

Business-to-business markets differ from consumer markets in a number of ways. Fewer buyers, larger purchase volume, geographic concentrations, and a formal buying process are the major differences. A manufacturer of computer chips has a limited number of computer manufacturers who will buy its computer chips. Boeing has a limited number of businesses that will purchase its commercial jumbo jets. Even a steel mill has a limited number of buyers of its products.

Because there are a limited number of buyers, the purchase volume of each is much higher. Dell, IBM, and other computer manufacturers will purchase computer chips by the thousands and will expect volume discounts and other services as a result of the purchase. If a computer chip manufacturer loses a large account like Dell, the loss can be devastating to the business. Because of the high cost of airplanes, a manufacturer like Boeing will not even start production until it receives an order from a major airline like Southwest Airlines.

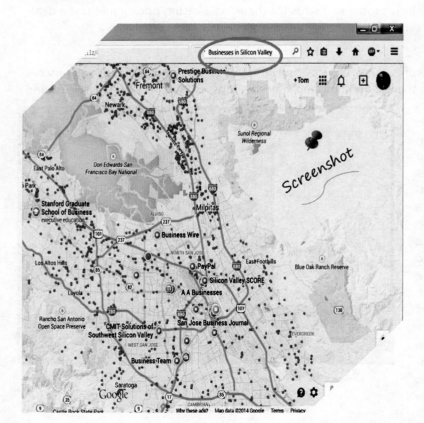

It is common for businesses to cluster in specific geographic areas. Most people know that the computer industry is concentrated in the Silicon Valley in California. That makes it easier for a company selling component parts because it can call on a number of companies within the valley. It is not unusual for these suppliers to build offices and factories around their market. This has occurred around Wal-Mart's office in Bentonville, Arkansas. Because of the size of Wal-Mart and the size of the orders it places, a number of companies, such as Procter & Gamble, General Mills, and 3M, have built offices nearby to service the Wal-Mart account. A similar scenario has occurred with Del Monte and its supplier of corrugated boxes used to ship Del Monte's food items. The supplier of Del Monte boxes has built a facility close to each Del Monte factory.[4]

Figure 5-6: Organization and Business Customers

Manufacturers

Non-profits

Organizational and Business Customers

Wholesalers

Government Agencies

Retailers

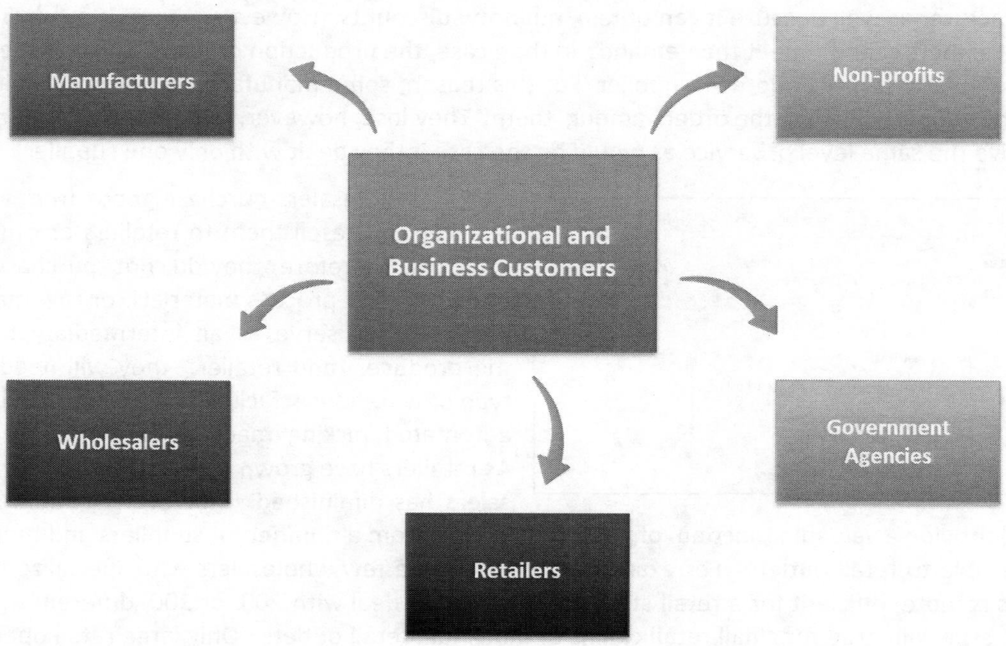

5-3a: Types of Customers

In developing an understanding of business buyer behavior, it is helpful to examine the different types of customers available to a business. They include manufacturers, wholesalers, retailers, government agencies, and nonprofit organizations. These customers are highlighted in Figure 5-6.

Not all of the customer types are viable customers for the goods and services discussed in Section 5-2. Table 5-1 provides a summary of each customer type and the types of goods and services each would likely purchase.

Table 5-1: Types of Customers and Types of Goods and Services They Are Likely to Purchase

Types of Goods or Services	Nonprofit Organizations	Manufacturers	Wholesalers	Retailers	Government Agencies
Major equipment	X	X	X	X	X
Accessory equipment	X	X	X	X	X
Fabricated & component parts	X	—	—	—	—
Process materials	X	—	—	—	X
Maintenance & repair parts	X	X	X	X	X
Operating supplies	X	X	X	X	X
Raw materials	X	—	—	—	X
Goods for resale	—	X	X	—	—
Business Services	X	X	X	X	X

Manufacturers are involved in producing goods for resale. They take raw materials, process materials, and component parts and combine them into a new good to be sold to consumers or other businesses. A manufacturer of jeans will need sewing machines, cutting machines, and other types of equipment to make the jeans. It will also need cloth, buttons, zippers, and thread. To supply these important ingredients, the manufacturer must choose reliable suppliers, and suppliers, in turn, would like to gain exclusive contracts with the manufacturer to increase the size of the order. This arrangement is desirable for the manufacturer as well because it can obtain quantity discounts. However, there is a risk. Suppose the supplier of zippers cannot meet the demand. In that case, the production of jeans stops, or the manufacturer has to quickly contact another supplier. For this reason, some manufacturers prefer dealing with more than one vendor, dividing the orders among them. They lose, however, the quantity discounts and may not receive the same level of service as would be the case if they dealt with only one supplier.

Wholesalers purchase goods from a manufacturer and resell them to retailers or other distributors. Therefore they do not purchase component parts, process materials, or raw materials. Because they serve as an intermediary between the producer and retailer, they will need some type of warehouse facility and offices. Forklifts and automated picking machines are primary needs. As retailers have grown larger, the need for wholesalers has diminished. However, in some industries, they still provide a valuable function of gathering goods from a number of suppliers and then making them available to retail outlets. For example, dealing with a few wholesalers who specialize in hardware supplies is more efficient for a retail store than having to deal with 200 or 300 different manufacturers. This is especially true for small retail chains or individual retail outlets. Only large retail operations, like Home Depot, Lowe's, or True Value, would have sufficient staff and purchase volume to make it feasible to deal with each manufacturer individually.

Because of the rise of large retail chains, many manufacturers are selling their goods directly to the retailer. Doing so reduces the costs of the goods because there is no intermediary who must earn a profit. It also is faster because the goods do not have to be shipped to a wholesaler, sorted, and then regrouped to be sent to a retailer. The reduced costs can be passed on to consumers by offering the merchandise at a lower price, or the retailer and manufacturer can use the reduced costs to increase profit margins. The disadvantage of this direct channel, however, is that, in most cases, the retailer will have considerably more manufacturers to deal with than if it used wholesalers.

Federal, state, and local governments represent huge opportunities for businesses. They purchase major equipment, land, and buildings. They purchase accessory equipment, maintenance supplies, repair parts, operating supplies, and business services. The major difference with government entities is the bidding process that must be used. Almost all governments have regulations that dictate how the bids have to be submitted and the manner in which the vendor is selected. For businesses willing to devote the time to submit bids, government contracts can be very lucrative.

Nonprofit organizations are similar to governments in the process they use to make purchases. Hospitals and schools are the two largest nonprofit institutions. In many locations, these two nonprofit organizations are the largest employers in the area. All need equipment, supplies, and services.

5-3b: Understanding Business-to-Business Demand

Demand for business goods and services is not as easy to determine as for consumer goods and services because of a concept called derived demand. **Derived demand** is the demand for a good or service that is generated from the demand for consumer goods and services. To illustrate, think about the

> **Derived Demand:** Demand for a good or service that is generated from the demand for consumer goods and services.

demand for major appliances, such as refrigerators, stoves, washers, and dryers. The number of appliances that a retail store like Sears will order depends on the demand it sees in the consumer market. If it is planning a big holiday promotion and the economy is doing well, it may see an increase in demand and will therefore place a larger order with the various appliance manufacturers, such as GE, Whirlpool, Maytag, and its own in-store brand, Kenmore.

The manufacturer's orders for metal, plastic, switches, motors, wires, and other parts used in the manufacturing of appliances depend on how many orders it receives from retailers such as Sears, Basic, Best Buy, and other retailers that sell appliances. In turn, the suppliers of motors, electrical switches, metal, and plastic will order raw materials and processing materials based on the number of orders they receive from the appliance manufacturers. Thus a company that makes plastic that is used in the manufacturing of major appliances depends on the demand that is derived all the way down from the consumer. The concept of derived demand is illustrated in Figure 5-7.

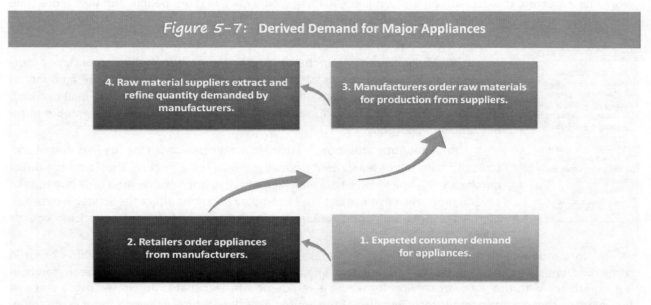

Figure 5-7: Derived Demand for Major Appliances

4. Raw material suppliers extract and refine quantity demanded by manufacturers.

3. Manufacturers order raw materials for production from suppliers.

2. Retailers order appliances from manufacturers.

1. Expected consumer demand for appliances.

All intermediate levels of demand are derived from final consumer demand.

Because of derived demand in the business-to-business sector, it is much more difficult to predict demand and to control production the further distant a business is from the end user. The company that mines iron ore that is used for metal cannot stimulate demand by running an advertisement for metal. Consumers are not going to buy raw metal. The only way the demand can be stimulated is for other companies that use metal in their products to run ads, offer rebates, and create other special promotions for consumers.

Because of the concept of derived demand, businesses face a much more volatile sales situation than consumer markets. Fluctuations and swings in demand are common and can be extreme. This fluctuation and wide swing in sales are due to a concept called the **acceleration principle**, which states that an increase or decrease in consumer demand for a product can create a drastic change in derived business demand. For example, a small increase of 10 to 15 percent in the demand for major appliances can cause as much as a 200 percent increase in the demand for major equipment to boost production of the appliances. Unfortunately, the reverse is also true. A 10 to 15 percent decline in orders for appliances can cause a complete collapse in the demand for the machines and equipment used in the manufacturing of appliances.[5]

Acceleration Principle: An increase or decrease in consumer demand for a product that can create a drastic change in derived business demand.

Joint Demand: Demand for one product that is affected by the level of demand for another product.

Another concept that is important in the business-to-business sector is **joint demand**. Joint demand means that the demand for one product is affected by the level for demand of another product. The demand for operating system software is directly related to the demand for computers. If sales of computers decline, the demand for operating system software will also decline. Although operating systems are sold independently of new computers, the vast majority of the operating systems are sold to computer manufacturers for installation on new computers. There is little a manufacturer of operating systems software can do to stimulate demand independent of computer demand.

5-4 BUSINESS-TO-BUSINESS PURCHASING

In most cases, making purchases for a business is more complex than making personal purchase decisions. However, just like personal purchase decisions, not all business decisions are the same. Deciding on where to locate a plant or whether to build a $13 million building is certainly different than deciding where to purchase copier paper or ink pens. Purchase decisions vary because of the dollar value involved, the people involved in the decision process, and the amount of time spent making a decision. As would be expected, the decision on a $13 million building would involve more people and take more time than the decision about where to purchase copier paper.

5-4a: Types of Buying Situations

> **New Buy Situation:** Purchases made by a business for the first time or purchases for which no one in the organization has had previous experience.
>
> **Modified Rebuy Situation:** Occasional purchases or purchases for which the members of the buying center have limited experience.

Although business purchases tend to be more formal than consumer purchases, they do vary in terms of the number of people involved, the amount of time spent on making the decision, and the individuals who make the final decision. Business buying situations fall into one of three categories: new buy, modified rebuy, and straight rebuy.[6]

In a **new buy situation**, a business makes purchases for the first time. Land, buildings, and major equipment normally fit into this category. They are high-dollar purchases and will involve top management. It is not unusual for a new buy to take several months or even years. These complex decisions affect the strategic direction of the business and often require substantial research before a decision can be made.

In a **modified rebuy situation**, a business makes occasional purchases. Modified rebuys occur in three different situations. The first is a situation in which the person making the purchase has limited buying experience with the good or service. It may be a vehicle or a forklift that is purchased every three to five years or shelving for a retail store. Because of the limited experience, time will need to be taken to develop specifications and to examine the possibilities. The process is not as complex, however, as the new buy primarily because it involves lower dollar purchases with less impact on the strategic direction of the company (see Figure 5-8).

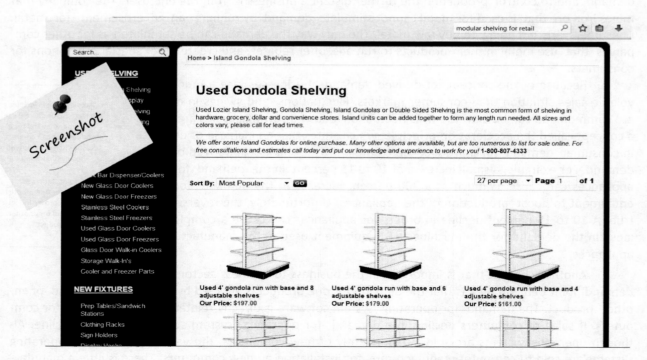

Figure 5-8: Because shelving at a retail store is not purchased on a regular basis and many products, such as t-shirts, are seasonal, it is normally a modified rebuy purchase situation.

A second situation that involves modified rebuys is dissatisfaction with the current vendor. It can be the supplier of aluminum to a factory that manufactures aluminum cans, or it can be the janitorial service for a large office building. The current vendor may not be reliable with delivery, the quality of work may not be up to the firm's specification, or the current vendor may have increased prices. Regardless of the reason for the dissatisfaction, the business decides to solicit bids from other vendors. In many cases, these new bids are compared against the current vendor's contract. Depending on the reason for seeking new bids, the current vendor may or may not be allowed to submit a new bid.

The third situation that causes modified rebuys is the end of a contractual relationship or an offer from a new firm that is substantially better than that of the current vendor. The firm is not dissatisfied with the current vendor but at the expiration of the contract may seek new bids. Government and non-profit institutions are often required by regulation or bylaws to seek new bids at the end of each contractual period. The current vendor is allowed to rebid and often has the best chance of obtaining the contract unless the agency is required to go with the lowest bidder. This is often true for government entities.

Occasionally, a potential supplier will make an offer that is substantially lower than that of the current vendor. When this situation occurs, the firm may decide to open the contract for bid, allowing the current vendor as well as others to bid. Alternatively, the firm may go to the current vendor and see whether it can reduce its prices to meet the new offer that the firm has received. Or the firm may simply switch without giving the current vendor an opportunity to renegotiate. In all three cases, the firm making the purchase will have to study the specifications and spend some time making a decision. Although not as involved as the new buy situations, these modified rebuys do require some effort and time in making the best decision.

The last purchase situation is the straight rebuy, in which a business routinely purchases from a vendor without modifying specifications or without renegotiating new terms. Purchasing office supplies for a large office building is likely to fall into this category. Supplies are purchased from a chosen vendor on a regular basis through a phone call, e-mail, the Internet, fax, or personal sales call. For a selling firm, this is the best situation. The buyer does not consider other firms, and as long as the buyer is pleased with the product and service, purchases continue on a routine basis.

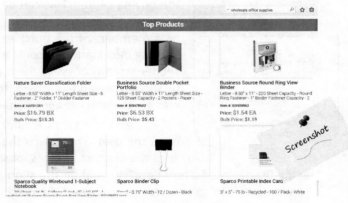

When one examines the types of goods and services firms buy in relation to the buying situation, typical patterns do emerge. For major equipment, buildings, and land, it is virtually always a new buy situation. These high-expenditure, new situations will involve the CEO and other top management personnel. Accessory equipment will vary between the new buy situation and modified rebuys. The type will depend on the price of the accessory equipment and the experience the firm has with it. For some firms, purchasing a new company truck may be a rare occasion and therefore will involve the top management, whereas for other firms, it is a modified rebuy situation that involves only the purchasing department. Major factors in this decision are experience and cost relative to the size of a firm. For a small firm, the truck may be a major purchase and therefore a new buy situation. For a large firm that already owns 50 trucks, purchasing a new truck is not a major purchase, but neither is it a routine purchase that is made on a regular basis.

Fabricated and component parts, process materials, maintenance and repair parts, operating supplies, raw materials, and goods for resale all tend to be straight rebuy situations after a vendor is chosen. Companies develop relationships with a certain vendor or vendors, and they tend to remain in the relationships. It is difficult for a new vendor to receive an order, or to even be considered, unless the company becomes unhappy with its current supplier.

Business services vary widely across the three types of buying situations. For a consulting service that is rarely used, it would probably be a new buy situation. For legal services that are used on occasions when legal situations arise, it may be a modified rebuy situation. For telephone, Internet, and janitorial services, it is likely a straight rebuy situation. Keep in mind, however, that the cost of the service relative to the size of the company, the frequency of purchase, and the experience with the service being purchased determine what type of buying situation it is. For example, a factory with its own janitorial staff would be facing a new buy situation when deciding to use an outside vendor for the first time. But it would be a modified rebuy situation when contacting an outside vendor to come in once a year to clean the carpets, tile floors, and do other special tasks.

5-4b: The Buying Center

Buying Center:
Group of individuals who are involved in the purchase process.

Gatekeeper:
Individual who is responsible for the flow of information to the members of the buying center.

User:
An individual member of the buying center who actually uses the product or is responsible for the product being used.

Influencer:
A member of the buying center who influences the decision but may not necessarily use the product.

Decider:
The member of the buying center who makes the final decision.

Purchaser:
The member of the buying center who makes the actual purchase.

Business-to-business buying decisions often involve more than one individual. The group of individuals involved in the purchase process is called the buying center. This can be as few as one individual in a family-owned business or as many as 20 or more in a large corporation. The rank and roles of the various members of the buying center are determined by factors such as the dollar value of the purchase relative to the size of the company, the impact the purchase has on company operations, and the type of purchase situation. But within the buying group, regardless of size, there are five distinct roles. One individual can play multiple roles, or there can be a number of individuals within each role. The roles can also change over time and from one purchase situation to another. The roles in the buying center are gatekeeper, user, influencer, decider, and purchaser.[7]

The **gatekeeper** is responsible for the flow of information to the members of the buying center. This can be a secretary who screens phone calls and salespeople wanting to see the purchasing agent or other members of the buying center. It can be a member of the purchasing department who is responsible for gathering and filtering information. It could even be the purchasing agent. Not only does the gatekeeper screen access to the members of the buying center, but he or she may also be the one asked to gather information for the group. By having control over information, the gatekeeper will have a large impact on the decision that is made.

An important member of the buying center is the **user**. The user is the individual who actually uses the product or is responsible for the product being used. On a factory floor, it could be the shop supervisor, the line supervisor, or in some cases, even one of the machine operators. The user's task is to provide information about the current product being used as well as the current vendor. For a factory that uses plastic in building its product, the user will know if the grade of plastic currently being used is causing problems on the assembly line. If so, this information can be relayed to other members of the group. If several vendors are being considered, the user will have some insight into the different grades, types, and durability of the plastics being considered from the vendors.

The **influencer** is someone who can influence the decision but may not necessarily use the product. It could be an engineer who knows the specifications that are required of specific process materials or fabricated parts. Through testing and information supplied by various vendors, the engineer could provide information as to which vendor is offering the best quality or the best materials. But the role of influencer can also be played by others in the company. It may be a vice president, someone from the accounting or business department, or a representative from the marketing area. Influencers are individuals who have some stake in the vendor selection and strive to influence the purchase decision.

The person who makes the final decision is the **decider**. This could be the president of the company, a vice president, the controller, the purchasing agent, the secretary, or even the janitor. The decider is the individual or individuals who make the decision on which vendor to use and which products to purchase. This may be a routine process that requires little or no input from others in the buying center if it is a straight rebuy situation. However, in a new buy situation, it may involve input from a large number of people, and the actual decision is made by a group of individuals rather than just a single person.

The **purchaser** is the one who makes the actual purchase. In a large company, this usually is someone in the purchasing department. In a smaller company, it may be a secretary, the owner, the manager, or one of the other employees. Even for a large purchase, the president may make the decision, but it will likely be someone else who actually makes the purchase and works out the details of the purchase arrangement. In straight rebuy situations, the purchasing process may be automatic and just require a phone call, online submission form, or e-mail message (see Figure 5-9).

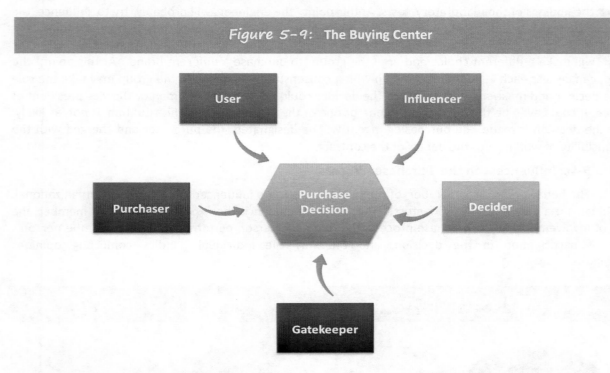

Figure 5-9: The Buying Center

To understand how the buying center operates, suppose John Deere wants to purchase a hydraulic pump for a particular line of its tractors. Let's assume that John Deere is dissatisfied with the current supplier, which makes this a modified rebuy situation (see Figure 5-10). Let us also assume that John Deere put the item out for bids and has received offers from nine different companies. The purchasing agent for John Deere may ask an associate to screen the bid proposals to make sure each is legitimate. In the screening process, the associate purchasing agent is to make sure that the bidder has the capability of supplying the quantity of pumps that are needed each month, is financially solvent, and has experience selling hydraulic pumps to large manufacturers like John Deere. In this capacity, the associate purchasing agent is serving as a gatekeeper because he or she will control the information that is forwarded.

Assume that three companies are screened out, leaving six. The bid information is then sent to John Deere's engineering department. The members of the engineering department look through the specification information and suggest that two firms be eliminated because they are not sure that the du-

Figure 5-10: Purchasing a component part, such as hydraulic pumps, for the manufacturing of John Deere tractors would be a modified rebuy situation involving several members of the buying center.

rability and quality of the firms' hydraulic pumps will meet John Deere's standards. Although the decision to leave them in the pool or not is the purchasing agent's, the engineering department is serving the role of influencer by suggesting that two companies be dropped.

After accepting the information of the engineering department, the purchasing agent reduces the list to four viable vendors. Each is contacted, asked to make an oral presentation to John Deere, and asked to provide three hydraulic pumps for testing by John Deere's engineering lab. At the presentation are two engineers, the plant foreman, the vice president of operations, and the associate purchasing agent. Two weeks after the presentation by the vendors, the buying center meets to make a decision. The engineers report the findings of their laboratory tests. At this point, the engineers will probably try to influence the decision on which brand should be used. The other individuals in the group may agree and a joint decision is made to accept the brand chosen by the engineers. But it is highly likely that someone in the group will make a different choice and urge the group to purchase a different brand. At this point, the group can discuss each vendor and come up with a consensus, or someone in the group may take the role of the decider and make the final decision. The decider could be the plant foreman or the vice president of finance. It could even be the purchasing agent or one of the engineers, but this situation is not as likely. After the decision is made, the purchasing agent will be designated the purchaser and charged with the responsibility of working out the details of the contract.

5-4c: Influences on the Purchase Process

The behaviors of each member of the buying center are influenced by a variety of organizational, individual, social, and temporary factors.[8] These factors influence the expectations of each member, the level of involvement in the purchase process, the role each person performs in the process, the person's level of participation in the decision, and the way the individual handles conflicting opinions (see **Figure 5-11**).

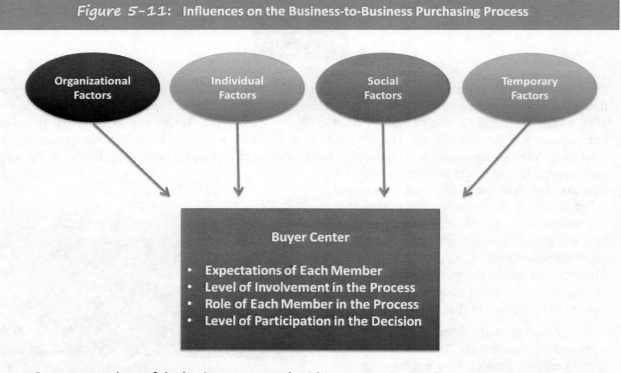

Figure 5-11: Influences on the Business-to-Business Purchasing Process

- Organizational Factors
- Individual Factors
- Social Factors
- Temporary Factors

Buyer Center

- **Expectations of Each Member**
- **Level of Involvement in the Process**
- **Role of Each Member in the Process**
- **Level of Participation in the Decision**

Because members of the buying center work within an organizational structure, a number of organizational factors affect purchase decisions and the roles an individual performs within the buying center. Especially important are the organization's goals and objectives. Decisions must be made within the framework of these goals and objectives. For example, Wal-Mart's goal of being the low-cost leader means that cost will be a major factor in purchase decisions. For FedEx, a major goal is fast delivery of packages. Therefore decisions are made relative to how it may affect the speed of delivery. Although a purchase decision may be more cost effective, if it slows down the sorting process and packages do not reach customers in time, customer service may decline, causing a loss of business.

A company's organizational structure has an impact on the various buying center roles. In an organization with a centralized structure, decisions are made by a few individuals, with others providing input or information. In a decentralized organization, decision making is moved down the organization, allowing more individuals to make decisions and be involved in decisions. Thus, in a decentralized organization, buying centers will tend to be larger, with buying center members participating more actively.

For many purchase situations, companies have a large number of options. Manufacturers who need to purchase nuts and bolts have a large number of possible vendors, more than they have time to examine. To be able to eliminate possible vendors and narrow the list to a few that can be examined closely, most employees adopt some type of heuristic. **Heuristics** are decision rules adopted by individuals to make the decision process more efficient. For example, an individual within a buying center of a small manufacturer may decide that all large vendors should be eliminated. This decision could be based on his or her belief that a large vendor would not devote sufficient resources to a small account to provide good service and that, in an emergency, the vendor would neglect the small manufacturer to take care of larger clients.

> **Heuristics:**
> Decision rules that individuals adopt to make a decision process more efficient.

Because of the large amount of information available from each vendor and independent information that is available, buying center members often adopt a heuristic called satisficing. Satisficing is the process of making a decision that is satisfactory but not necessarily optimal. Often a buying center will make a decision when its members locate a vendor or arrive at a purchase decision that is satisfactory and meets the goals of the organization. It may or may not be the optimal solution. Individuals may feel making the optimal decision would require too much time or require additional resources and that the extra investment is not worth the possible payoff. Often, there is not time to solicit all the information needed before a decision must be made.[9]

Finances and budget constraints constitute organizational factors that affect the purchase decision. If engineers are involved in the buying center, it is not unusual for conflict to arise concerning which component parts or processes should be used. Engineers will push for the part or process that enhances the finished product, whereas the accountants will push for the lowest cost part or process that will get the job done.

Again, the idea of satisficing will surface. If the $15 component part will suffice, then, from an accounting perspective, using it is wiser than using the $19 component part. The engineers will argue, however, that the $19 part will produce a superior product and fewer defects. However, if the $19 part will increase the cost of the product above the competition, the firm may have no choice but to use the $15 part. Financial constraints may restrict the company from using the better part.

Although a number of individual factors influence each member of the buying center, the primary individual factors include personality traits, level of power, stakeholder interest, and personal objectives.[10] Each factor influences how an individual acts within the buying center and how he or she reacts to other members of the buying center.

An individual's personality traits are an important factor in determining how a person behaves and interacts with others. A person who tends to be an extrovert will spend more time interacting with other members of the buying center than someone who is an introvert. However, an introvert is more likely to listen to a salesperson and gather more information than an extrovert. Another personality trait that is important is that of decisiveness. Some individuals are comfortable making decisions and recommendations, whereas others tend to be less decisive: They will wait and follow the recommendations of someone else. Decisiveness is closely tied with a person's level of risk taking and confidence. A person who is willing to take risks will be more likely to switch to a new vendor than someone who is risk averse. Individuals who have a high level of self-confidence will be more likely to share their opinion and persuade other members of the group that they are right, whereas a person who has a low level of self-confidence will tend to follow the recommendation of others. Table 5-2 summarizes these personality traits and ways they can affect the various members of the buying center.

Table 5-2: Personality Traits and Buying Center Functions					
Personality Trait	**Gatekeeper**	**User**	**Influencer**	**Decider**	**Purchaser**
Degree of extroversion	A gatekeeper who is an extorvert is more likely to pass information on to other members of the buying center than an introvert.	A user who is an introvert will not be as likely to speak up about a purchase situation as an extrovert.	An extrovert has more influence on a buying center than an introvert.	A decider who is an extrovert is willing to state his or her decisions and usually not as willing to listen to other viewpoints.	An extrovert purchaser is well-liked by vendors and is likely to be good at negotiations, but he or she may not be as careful about details.
Degree of decisiveness	A gatekeeper with a high degree of deciveness is inclined to make decisions about what information should be passed on to members of the buying center and what should be discarded.	A user who is decisive strives to have more influence on the purchase because he or she is using the product and will be more inclined to make a definitive stand on specific brands or vendors.	Once the influencer has made a decision about the right product or vendor, someone who is high on decisiveness will make a forceful argument to the other members of the buying center, especially the decider.	A decider who is decisive is not as open to other views and is not as likely to be swayed by opinion of the users or the influencers in the buying center.	The purchaser who is high in decisiveness tends to dictate purchasing terms to vendors and is not as likely to compromise and work out details.
Level of risk taking	A gatekeeper who is risk averse tends to screen out all brands and vendors he or she perceives to be risky.	A risk-averse user will tend to stay with current vendors or brands and is reluctant to switch. Only strong evidence or a poorly performing vendor leads to switching vendors.	A risk-averse influencer tends to stay with the current vendors or brand and to persuade other group members to stay with known brands and vendors with good records.	A decider who is risk averse is harder to persuade than someone who is willing to take risks.	A purchasing agent who is risk averse will stay with the current methods of purchasing and current terms.
Level of confidence	A gatekeeper with a high level of confidence will feel more comfortable in screening out information and vendors that she or he feels are not acceptable.	A user with a high level of confidence is more likely to argue for her or his view and insist that the buying center let the user make the decision.	An influencer with a high level of confidence strives to convince other members of the buying center that she or he is right.	A decider with a high level of confidence can be persuaded if given strong evidence but is less likely to change her or his mind once the decision is made.	A purchaser who has a high level of confidence takes the lead in the purchase negotiations.

In addition to personality traits, a person's level of power within an organization has an influence on how he or she behaves within a buying center. The higher ranking a person is in an organization, the more legitimate power he or she will have in each of the buying center roles (see Figure 5-12). Others within the group will have a tendency to follow his or her suggestions, ideas, and decisions. This power tends to be formal and is based on the person's position in the firm. For instance, a vice president's comments are more likely to be accepted by the buying group than the comments of a shop foreman or a supervisor. This formal power, however, can be an impediment to an open discussion about a vendor, even if the person with the formal power strives for it.

All organizations include individuals with informal power. These people have earned the respect of coworkers because of their expertise or ability to make good decisions. Such an individual might be the shop foreman or someone who does not have the formal power but is highly respected by the other members of the buying center. Recommendations and comments made by this type of person will carry considerably more weight than others within the group.

Figure 5-12: Sales Managers typically have the legitimate power to make all the purchase decisions for their respective firm. Courtesy of U.S. Bureau of Labor Statistics

Stakeholder interests and personal objectives are critical factors in how a person functions within the buying center.[11] A person who has a high level of stakeholder interest will be more inclined to be involved and more forceful in influencing the decision. To illustrate, suppose a major portion of a branch manager's evaluation is how well he or she reduces expenses. The more emphasis that is placed on reducing costs by management, the more active the branch manager will be in selecting the low-cost option. If this is coupled with personal objectives, such as his or her desire to become a vice president, then the incentive to be actively involved is even greater.

Although we would like to believe that business purchase decisions are made on a rational basis and in terms of what is best for the firm, that is not always the case. Personal objectives, such as seeking promotions, building a good reputation with the boss, or making a rival look bad, will influence how a person acts within the buying center. Gifts or bribes offered by a salesperson can influence a purchase decision, especially in other countries where this practice is more common.

A salesperson operating in a transition economy must identify all the individuals in the buying group and those outside the buying group who might influence purchase decisions, such as brothers, cousins, and friends of the decision makers, and offer the appropriate bribes to the right individuals. This is common procedure in many developing countries. The World Bank surveyed 3,600 companies in 69 countries and found that 40 percent of the firms paid bribes. U.S. firms, however, have to abide by the U.S. Foreign Corrupt Practices Act, which prohibits bribing, and even prohibits payment to third parties when the company has good reason to assume that part of that payment is used for bribery purposes.

Employees tend to act in ways that enhance their personal career and personal objectives. These actions may not always be visible to other members of the group but are closely connected with the concept of stakeholder interests. The more that individuals have at stake in a purchase decision, the higher will be their involvement and the more forceful they will be in the decision-making process. Even individuals who tend to be introverts will exert a stronger voice in deliberations and decisions if they have a high stake in the outcome of the decision and their job performance will be affected by the purchase decision.

Closely tied with personal characteristics are social factors. Because individuals work within a social environment, social acceptance, norms, and rules of behavior will be factors in how members of the buying center interact with each other. Each person will have his or her own ideas of what is socially acceptable behavior and what is not. Each person will have his or her own ideas about how others ought to act and the roles they should perform within the group. Each business or organization tends to adopt over time a set of social norms. These norms are rules of behavior regarding the proper way to behave within the workplace. For example, most companies believe  employees should treat others with respect and allow each person to express his or her views. With this open environment, better purchase decisions can be made. Although an open environment is ideal, social norms have developed in some companies that do not allow for open communication. Instead, it may be expected that individuals with formal power will not be questioned and that others are expected to demonstrate their loyalty by showing support for these individuals. Social norms are created in companies by management over a period of time. Employees learn what is acceptable and what is not acceptable. These norms affect the buying center because they influence how individuals interact with each other.[12]

The last factor influencing purchase behavior is temporary situations. Because we live and work in a dynamic world, situations faced by businesses change daily. These changes affect purchase decisions. The terrorist attacks of September 11, 2001, changed a number of business decisions. A large number of companies grounded their salespeople and purchased video conferencing equipment to transact business.

E-mail, the Internet and telephones were used more frequently to contact clients and negotiate contracts. Shipments were delayed, rerouted, and modified to ensure employee safety. Other temporary factors, such as declining sales, budget cuts, change in personnel, labor strikes, special interest groups, and vendor delivery problems, can all affect purchase decisions. These temporary situations often force a buying center to make an alternative decision or one that is suboptimal.

To understand this organizational purchase decision process, examine **Figure 5-13.** During the first step, purchasing agents, engineers, users, and other members of the buying center bring their expectations to the process. These expectations are based on their past experiences with the various vendors and their knowledge of the purchase decision that is to be made. Their expectations are also based on the individuals who will be involved in the purchase decision and their past behaviors.

Figure 5-13: The Business-to-Business Purchasing Process

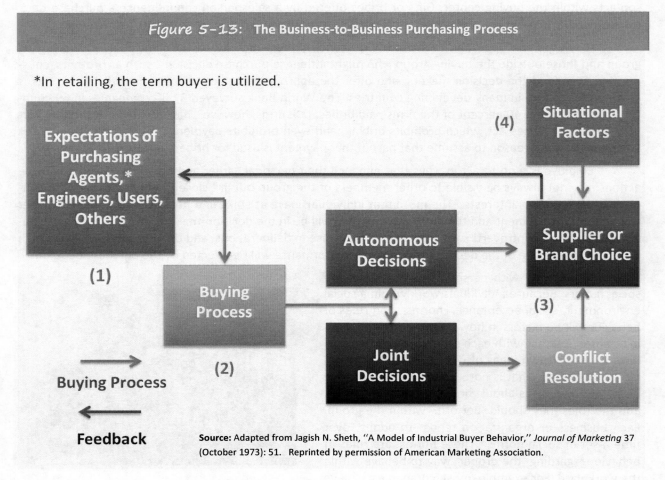

*In retailing, the term buyer is utilized.

Source: Adapted from Jagish N. Sheth, "A Model of Industrial Buyer Behavior," *Journal of Marketing* 37 (October 1973): 51. Reprinted by permission of American Marketing Association.

In the second step, the responsibility for the decision is determined. Some decisions are autonomous, meaning that one person will make the decision, whereas others will involve multiple people and will be joint decisions. Factors determining who will be involved in the decision include the type of purchase decision, buying center makeup, social norms, relative cost of the purchase, and past experiences. Straight rebuy situations will tend to be autonomous, whereas new buys will tend to be joint decisions. Modified rebuys may go either way. If company executives or high-ranking personnel are in the buying center, joint decisions are less likely. Social norms that have been established and past experiences are usually followed unless they did not work in the past or someone specifically states, "We are using a different method for making this decision." Lastly, as would be expected, the higher the cost, the more likely it will be a joint decision.

In the third step, conflict resolution will be required if members of the buying center have different opinions about the decision. Social norms and past experiences will determine the conflict resolution method that will be used. It can vary from an open debate about the various vendors to someone taking charge and making the decision. During the fourth step, situational factors will be considered. These temporary factors will often force the group to make an alternative choice.

After the decision is made, members of the buying center will use the results to develop their expectations of future purchase decisions. If a member of the group was not allowed to express an opinion or was put down by others when trying to speak, it is likely that individual will be less involved in the next decision. If a member of the group took an autocratic approach when it was supposed to be a joint decision, it is likely that fewer people will participate in the next decision, and the decision process may become autonomous. Over time, these experiences often become the social norms for the company, at least in terms of how the buying center operates.

5-5 THE BUSINESS-TO-BUSINESS BUYING PROCESS

The number of steps in the business-to-business process will vary, depending on the type of purchase situation. For a new buy situation, all seven steps listed in Table 5-3 are followed. For a modified rebuy situation, all seven can be followed, or the process can be reduced to five or six steps. For a straight rebuy, only two or three steps are involved.

Table 5-3: Steps in the Business-to-Business Process

Step	New Buy	Modified Rebuy	Straight Rebuy
1. Identification of needs	X	X	X
2. Establishment of specifications	X	?	?
3. Identification of feasible solutions	X	?	—
4. Identification of feasible vendors	X	X	—
5. Evaluation of vendors	X	X	—
6. Selection of vendor(s)	X	X	—
7. Negotiation of purchase terms	X	X	X

To illustrate the steps in the business-to-business buying process, let us consider the case of a local office supply store, Dalton Office Supply, that is contemplating the purchase of a delivery truck. The truck the firm currently has is 12 years old, has almost 200,000 miles, and is too small for the number of deliveries Dalton must now make every day. Because the last purchase was 12 years ago, this purchase situation would be a new buy for the current staff of Dalton.

Before we examine the step-by-step process Dalton will go through, it is beneficial to examine the steps of the buying process and how they relate to the buying center. Table 5-4 indicates which members of the buying center are likely to be involved in each step of the process. The involvement does vary, however, based on the makeup of the company, and the type of purchasing situation. A new buy situation will normally involve more people than a modified rebuy. A large company with a purchasing department will tend to use specialists for each of the buying center roles, whereas a small company will have one individual performing several roles.

Table 5-4: Participation of Buying Center Members in the Buying Process

Step	Gatekeeper	User	Influencer	Decider	Purchaser
1. Identification of needs	X	—	—	—	—
2. Establishment of specifications	X	X	X	X	—
3. Identification of feasible solutions	X	X	X	?	X
4. Identification of feasible vendors	X	X	X	?	X
5. Evaluation of vendors	X	X	?	X	—
6. Selection of vendor(s)	X	X	X	X	—
7. Negotiation of purchase terms	X	—	—	X	—

Figure 5-14: The purchase of a delivery truck is an important decision for any small business owner.

For our Dalton Office Supply illustration, the user would be the truck driver. Because this is a local, two-store operation, the influencers are the two managers of the office supply stores. The decider will be the owner of Dalton, and the buyer is the assistant manager of the larger store because he serves as the purchasing agent for both operations. The gatekeeper, in this illustration, is the assistant manager of the larger store. In this purchase situation, he will serve both as the buyer and the gatekeeper (see Figure 5-14).

5-5a: Identification of Needs

The first step in the business-to-business buying process is the identification of a need. Although advertising and marketing can create desires and needs for consumers, this phenomenon is not as likely to occur in the business environment. In most cases, needs are the direct result of a firm's operation. A bakery needs flour, sugar, and other ingredients to bake its products, and when these ingredients run low, it is time to purchase more. Manufacturers must keep an eye on all of the components and materials used in the production process to make sure they have a sufficient quantity on hand to keep production going. In these types of situations, the purchase process is normally just a straight rebuy. The supplier is notified, and products are shipped to the manufacturer. This is an ideal situation for the supplier because no other vendors or options are even considered. With this type of purchase situation, the company will skip to the last step and negotiate terms of the purchase.

Modified rebuy needs arise from dissatisfaction with the current vendor, a sales pitch by a potential vendor, or the need to purchase a product that is not purchased too frequently. The identification of a need with a new buy situation is the result of a strategic decision or the need to purchase a product that is seldom purchased.

5-5b: Establishment of Specifications

The second step in the purchase process is the development of specifications. In straight rebuy situations, the specifications remain the same or are only slightly modified. In situations in which the specifications need a greater level of modification, a firm will usually enter into the modified rebuy situation, which involves examining other alternatives and vendors.

To ensure that vendor bids can be compared, it is important to establish specifications. When each vendor bids on the same set of specifications, a firm is able to compare bids and make a better decision. Sometimes firms are not sure what the specifications should be. This is especially true for new buy situations. A firm desiring to upgrade its computer system will often seek the help of vendors to establish the specifications. This makes the bidding process more difficult if the same specifications are not used by every firm submitting a bid.

In choosing a truck, Dalton developed two sets of specifications. The first are the specifications for the truck; the second are the purchase criteria. In terms of minimum specifications, the truck must be one ton with a box bed, power lift, and a diesel engine. The criteria that would be used for selecting the truck are listed in Table 5-5. Notice that in addition to the required specifications, Dalton has listed a number of specifications it will use to evaluate each vehicle. Dalton has also identified three additional criteria that will be used in the process. The first is the level of business the truck dealer does with Dalton. This is a common practice in business and is known as **reciprocity**, which means that a business will purchase from businesses that in turn patronize them. Although it will not be the only criterion Dalton uses, it will favor a truck dealer that purchases office supplies from Dalton. Also used in the decision will be any personal experience the members of the buying center have had with the dealers. When this list is completed, the Dalton group is ready to move to the next step—identification of feasible solutions.

> **Reciprocity:**
> The practice of one business making a purchase from another business that, in turn, patronizes the first business.

Table 5-5: Dalton Truck Specifications

Required Truck Specifications
- One-ton box truck
- Power lift
- Diesel engine

Truck Specifications to Be Evaluated
- Fuel mileage
- Consumer report for quality
- Cost of repairs
- Warranty
- Price

Other Purchase Criteria
- Level of business with Dalton
- Brand name (preference for American brand)
- Previous personal experience with dealership

5-5c: Identification of Feasible Solutions

At the third step in the process, a business needs to examine various ways of handling the need. The three most common are to purchase the product from an external business, produce the product itself, or lease it. Companies examining shipping needs have the options of purchasing their own trucks, hiring an independent firm to ship the merchandise for them, or using a commercial service such as United Parcel Service (UPS).

Some decisions are more difficult. For example, suppose Avon has several pieces of equipment used in the production of lipstick that are quite old and labor intensive. For $200,000 to $300,000, Avon can automate the machine and virtually eliminate the human operators. Avon must compare the labor savings of a new machine to the cost of the machine and the level of production that will result. For a high-production item, the labor savings will likely exceed the cost of the new machine. However, for a low-production item, Avon may be better off keeping the old machine, repairing it, and paying out more in labor.

Another option, especially for equipment, land, and buildings, is leasing. This is something Dalton Office Supply could consider. Instead of purchasing a new truck, Dalton could lease a vehicle. The advantages would include always having a newer model that can be used. Because maintenance is the responsibility of the dealer, the company can expense the cost of the lease. Of course, the disadvantage includes not owning the truck. In addition, if the mileage exceeds the lease limits, there is normally a penalty. Dalton must carefully calculate the total cost of owning the vehicle over the life of the truck versus the cost of leasing.

5-5d: Identification of Feasible Vendors

If the decision to use an external source is made, then someone must contact possible vendors and ask them to submit bids. This is one of the tasks of the gatekeeper, and in the process of identifying possible vendors, he or she controls the information flow. If the gatekeeper does not like a particular vendor, that vendor may never be notified. However, some possible vendors may be left out by accident. Just the process of selecting and notifying possible vendors may cause some to be eliminated.

After possible vendors have been located, then someone must screen the list for firms that are not feasible. In this process, firms that may not be able to meet production schedules or that are too small may be eliminated. For example, if the process is the construction of a $20 million facility, small contractors with only a few employees do not have the capability of handling such a large job. Del Monte requires that all the vendors who supply corrugated boxes be located close to the Del Monte facilities because of the high cost of shipping box material a long distance.[13]

For Dalton, initial screening at this stage is to eliminate any trucks that do not have a diesel engine because that was set as a basic requirement. Suppose that in gathering information about the various dealers, the assistant manager finds two dealers who have trucks that meet the specifications but not the criterion of being current customers of Dalton. One has never been a customer; the other used to be a customer but gradually reduced purchases to less than $25 a month. Should these two possible vendors be eliminated? Suppose the dealer that has never been a customer has the lowest-priced truck. Because the assistant manager has been charged with the responsibility of gathering a list of possible trucks, he would have to make a decision. He can leave these two dealers on the list, he can eliminate them, or he can ask someone else in the buying center for advice. It is unlikely that the assistant manager would call a meeting of the entire buying center. Instead, if he wants advice on what he should do, he will go to one of the influencers or the decider. In this case, that would be one or both of the store managers or the owner of Dalton. The person or people he would approach would depend a great deal on the organizational structure and the social norms for Dalton. If it is a company that encourages open communication and the owner is available, the assistant manager may go straight to the owner and ask whether the dealers should be left on the list, because the owner will ultimately make the decision. However, if the company social norms dictate a strong chain of command, then he will go to his boss, the store manager, for counsel.

5-5e: Evaluation of Vendors

Evaluation of vendors normally occurs at three levels. The first level is an initial evaluation screening of candidates. This evaluation screening is different from the screening in the previous step. Vendors who make this list are qualified and meet the minimum specifications. Screening at this level entails evaluating how well a vendor meets the specifications and purchase criteria identified in step two. One or two individuals within the buying center might perform this initial evaluation screening, or the whole group might be involved. The person or persons responsible will largely depend on how many vendors are on the initial list, the type of buying situation, and the relative cost of the purchase. If there are a large number of vendors, normally one or two individuals will be asked to pare down the list. If it is a new buy situation, more individuals will be involved in the initial screening process than if it is a modified rebuy situation. The same is true for the relative cost of the purchase. The greater the cost, the more people are likely to be involved. The purpose of this initial evaluation screening is to reduce the list of feasible vendors down to a smaller manageable list.

Suppose, in our Dalton example, that the assistant manager has a list of nine dealers and 12 possible trucks in the two towns where the company has offices. It is possible that everyone involved in the decision will want to be involved in this initial evaluation screening. However, it is more likely that the assistant manager and another person or two will be asked to narrow the list. The user—in this case, the firm's truck driver—may be asked to work with the assistant manager, or it may be one of the store managers, or both. It is unlikely that Dalton's owner will be involved with this initial screening.

The second level of evaluation is a vendor analysis. This is a formal evaluation of each vendor. **Table 5-6** provides a vendor analysis for a supplier of denim cloth to a manufacturer of jeans. Each denim supplier will be evaluated on each of the seven criteria. This process will allow the jeans manufacturer to narrow down the list of feasible vendors to two or three.

Table 5-6: A Vendor Analysis for Denim Suppliers for a Jeans Manufacturer

	Excellent	Superior	Acceptable	Inferior
1. Speed of delivery	____	____	____	____
2. Handling of emergency and rush orders	____	____	____	____
3. Quality of denim material	____	____	____	____
4. Availability of different colors/styles	____	____	____	____
5. Handling of defective denim	____	____	____	____
6. Percent of denim that is defective	____	____	____	____
7. Purchase terms	____	____	____	____

The last level of the evaluation process is the vendor audit or presentation. At this level, members of the buying center either visit the prospective vendor's site or have the prospective vendor make a presentation to the buying center. Typical questions asked during a vendor audit include:

- What are the vendor's production capabilities?
- What quality control mechanisms and processes does the vendor have in place?
- How closely does the vendor follow the processes?
- What is the defective material rate, and how does the vendor handle defective merchandise?
- What type of equipment is used, how old is the equipment, and how dependable is the equipment?
- What telecommunication and electronic data interchange (EDI) capabilities does the vendor have?
- Can the vendor handle order fluctuations?
- What is the financial stability of the company?
- How many customers does the firm have, and how many are competitors?
- What type of relationship does the vendor have with its suppliers? Will there be an interruption in supplies to the vendor that would affect the vendor's ability to fill orders?
- How stable is the vendor's labor pool? Will a strike or other labor problems cause an interruption in the ability to fill orders?

The primary purpose of the vendor audit is to ensure that the vendor has the capability of meeting the supply demands of the purchaser. If the vendor is supplying denim for a manufacturer of blue jeans, the manufacturer must be sure that the supply of denim will be met, that the quality meets its specifications, and that special orders can be filled quickly. Because the production of blue jeans cannot occur without the denim material, supply capability is crucial (see Figure 5-15).

Figure 5-15: Jeans manufacturers depend on a regular supply of denim.

To ensure a regular supply of raw materials, as well as fabricated and component parts, a large number of buyers are using EDI technology with their vendors. **Electronic data interchange (EDI)** means that data from the manufacturer's production facility are sent directly to suppliers through computers. This allows the suppliers to see how much material is being used, which material is being used, and what level of inventory is left. By receiving data from the actual production process, the vendor knows what type, color, and style of material it needs to produce and when it needs to be sent to the manufacturer.

> **Electronic Data Interchange (EDI):**
> A trust relationship that includes the sharing of data between the buying and selling firm.

This same technology is used at the retail level to ensure that store shelves remain stocked with the correct merchandise. These data can be extremely valuable to manufacturers, not only in what needs to be produced and when it needs to be shipped, but also in what is selling well and what is not. By monitoring actual sales of merchandise, the manufacturer knows which styles and colors are in high demand. This allows the firm to modify its production schedule to produce more of the items that are selling well and fewer of the items that are not selling.

Instead of visiting the vendor's place of business, the vendor may make a presentation to the members of the buying center at their place of business. This is often the case with services, such as an advertising agency, a public relations firm, or a lawn service. For modified rebuy situations, this procedure is likely to be used. The same vendor questions will likely be asked, but the setting is different.

5-5f: Selection of Vendor(s)

Before a final selection is made, the business must decide whether it will go with one vendor or more. For Dalton, because only one truck will be purchased, only one vendor will be selected. But for a supplier of raw materials or component parts, the decision is more complicated. The advantage of choosing one vendor is lower prices through quantity discounts, but the disadvantage is that a greater risk occurs if, for some reason, the one supplier cannot fill all of the orders or is late with the shipment. If the business has an EDI relationship with its vendors, then having more than one supplier creates a higher risk in terms of data exchange. Sharing production schedules and sales data with suppliers assumes a high level of trust between the parties concerned. If more than one vendor is involved with a particular product, maintaining a high level of trust becomes much more difficult. Each vendor is vying for a larger share of the business and can easily see from data it receives how much of the business it has and how much is being given to the competition. For this reason, if more than one vendor is used, EDI relationships are either not established or are established with only the primary vendor. The business may use another vendor for a small amount of the raw material or component parts just to ensure a safe backup to the primary vendor.

5-5g: Negotiation of Purchase Terms

In most purchase situations, the last step, negotiation, is merely a formality because most of the purchase terms have already been worked out during the evaluation and selection process. But for those terms that have not been agreed on, it will be the responsibility of the buyer to negotiate. Payment method, due date, size of order, delivery schedule, and method for handling defective merchandise are a few of the terms that will be agreed on at this stage. After a contract or agreement has been reached, the unsuccessful bidders are informed that the bidding process has been concluded and that a vendor has been chosen.

Although the buying process is over at this point for members of the buying center, evaluation of the purchase process occurs. It may be a formal evaluation, or it may be informal. Users will evaluate the decision based on the criteria used in the selection process. If the new vendor meets everyone's expectations, then, for products used on a regular basis, the company will move to a straight rebuy situation with the vendor. For both the buyer and seller, this relationship is the most desirable, and as long as it remains satisfactory for both parties, it will continue.

For products that are in the modified rebuy situation, the results of the purchase will be remembered by those involved, and the next time the product has to be purchased, the chosen vendor will have a greater chance of being selected. If Dalton purchases a Ford truck and is pleased with the truck's performance, then Dalton will be more likely to purchase a Ford truck the next time. Even in a modified rebuy situation, this will save members of the buying center a considerable amount of time.

For new buy situations, the results of the current purchase are of little value. If it is another 12 years before Dalton purchases another truck, it is likely that the company will spend the same amount of time during the purchase process. Most of the members of the buying center will be new, and the makes, models, and vehicle dealers will have all changed. It is very likely that the dealer the truck was purchased from will have a new owner, so there is no longer any guarantee of the same level of satisfaction. If the dealership is still owned by the same individual, personnel at the dealership have probably changed. That is why, for new buy situations, firms go through all seven steps, and decisions can take anywhere from a few months to a few years.

Summary

1. Identify the types of goods and services that businesses purchase. Businesses can purchase major equipment, buildings and land, accessory equipment, fabricated and component parts, process materials, maintenance and repair parts, operating supplies, raw materials, goods for resale, and business services.

2. Identify the types of business customers. The types of business customers include manufacturers, wholesalers and distributors, retailers, governments, and nonprofit organizations.

3. Explain the concepts of derived and joint demand and why they are important for the business-to-business market. The demand for many business-to-business products is dependent, or derived, on the demand for consumer products. The demand for parts that are used in the manufacturing of a washing machine is derived from the consumer demand for washing machines. With joint demand, the demand for a product is dependent on the supply of other products used in the manufacturing of a product. For example, the demand for electrical switches for washing machines will be affected by the supply of the other parts used in the construction of the washing machines. For business-to-business markets, joint and derived demand determine the demand for a product. Often, there is little a business-to-business firm can do to modify demand for its products.

4. *Identify the types of buying situations and when each is used.* Types of buying situations include new buy, modified rebuy, and straight rebuy. Organizations purchasing a product for the first time or products with which no one has any relevant experience are involved in a new buy situation. In a modified rebuy situation, a product is purchased infrequently and the organization has little experience with the product, or the organization is dissatisfied with its current vendor or receives an attractive offer from another firm it wants to consider. Modified rebuys can also occur at the end of a contract period. Straight rebuy situations occur when orders are placed with the current vendor without considering any other vendors.

5. *Describe the concept of the buying center and the different roles employees can play.* Many buying decisions within a business are joint decisions and involve more than one person. Members of the buying center can play the roles of gatekeeper, user, influencer, decider, and purchaser. The gatekeeper is responsible for filtering information to the other members of the buying center. The user is the individual who actually uses the product or oversees its use. Influencers are individuals who have a significant influence on the decision but do not actually make the decision. The decider is the individual who makes the final decision. The purchaser is the one who negotiates the terms of the contract and actually makes the purchase.

6. *Discuss the factors that influence business-to-business buyer behavior.* The behaviors of each member of the buying center are influenced by a variety of organizational, individual, social, and temporary factors. These factors influence the expectations of each member, the level of involvement in the purchase process, the role each person performs in the process, the person's level of participation in the decision, and the way the individual handles conflicting opinions. The organizational factors include the corporate goals and objectives, the firm's organizational structure, and the finances and budget of the firm. Individual factors that influence each member of the buying center are personality traits, level of power, stakeholder interest, and personal objectives. Each factor influences how an individual acts within the buying center and how he or she reacts to other members of the buying center.

Closely tied with personal characteristics are social factors. Because individuals work within a social environment, social acceptance, norms, and rules of behavior will be factors in how members of the buying center interact with each other. Temporary factors, such as declining sales, budget cuts, changes in personnel, labor strikes, special interest groups, and vendor delivery problems, can all affect purchase decisions. These temporary situations often force a buying center to make an alternative decision or one that is suboptimal.

7. *List the seven steps in the business-to-business buying process and explain what occurs in each step.* The first step in the business-to-business buying process is identification of needs. They can be routine needs, such as those that are part of a manufacturing process, or rare needs, such as a new building. Once the need has been recognized, the next step is the establishment of objectives. For rebuy situations, this is routine and is the same that has been ordered in the past. For modified and new buy situations, time will need to be taken to determine both the product and purchase specifications. During the third step, feasible solutions are evaluated. They often include leasing and outsourcing or using an alternative material. After the decision is made to purchase the product, potential vendors are contacted. Once the list of possible vendors is narrowed down to a smaller, manageable list, evaluation of each vendor occurs. A vendor analysis and vendor audit are often a part of this evaluation. Based on the results of the evaluation, a vendor is selected. The last step is the negotiation of terms with the vendor.

Key Terms

acceleration principle	heuristics	reciprocity
buying center	influencer	straight rebuy situation
decider	joint demand	user
derived demand	modified rebuy situation	wholesalers and distributors
electronic data interchange (EDI)	new buy situation	
gatekeeper	purchaser	

1. Discuss the difference between business buyers and consumers in purchasing airline tickets, automobiles, and cleaning supplies. Be specific.

2. From the list of goods and services purchased by a business, identify at least two examples from each category for each of the following types of businesses:
   a. Bakery
   b. Manufacturer of electric leaf blowers
   c. Pizza restaurant
   d. Tree removal service
   e. Wholesale distributor of hardware supplies

3. Discuss how the concepts of derived demand and joint demand would be relevant to each of the following suppliers:
   a. Supplier of sand to a concrete mixing company
   b. Lumberyard that supplies lumber and other building materials for home construction companies
   c. Supplier of wire that is used in building electrical motors
   d. Food processing factory that makes tomato paste that is sold to other businesses making various types of foods
   e. Company that mines iron ore

4. For each of the following situations, discuss what type of buying situation it is and identify who might serve in each of the buying center roles:
   a. Construction of a new 10,000-square-foot addition to a current 40,000-square-foot factory
   b. Purchase of a new photographic developing machine for a commercial photographic developing service
   c. Purchase of furniture for a new office complex that has just been built
   d. Because of dissatisfaction with the last vendor, the selection of a new company to supply the flour used in baking pizza crusts for the retail food market
   e. The ordering of an extra 5,000 electrical switches used in the manufacturing of electrical space heaters that are sold to retail stores

5. Do some research on the impact on business-to-business markets of the Great Recession of 2008. What types of business-to-business markets were adversely affected? What business-to-business markets benefited from the recession in terms of increased sales?

6. Reread section 5-4c, Influences on the Purchase Process and selling in international markets and the use of gifts and bribes. How do you stand on this issue? Is it ethical for sales people working in another country, where gifts and bribes are used, to use the same methods? What might happen if they do not follow the local customs? What might happen if they do, in terms of U.S. laws?

7. Do some research on Web EDI. Who else uses it—in addition to Wal-Mart? What are the advantages and disadvantages of Web EDI?

8. How important is the Internet in identifying possible vendors? Are companies located through the Internet viable vendors? How can a business determine whether a business is legitimate?

9. Assume you have been given the responsibility of searching the Internet for viable companies for each of the following purchase situations. Use the business-to-business section under business and economy at Yahoo or another search engine. Locate two feasible companies and discuss why each is a viable company.
   a. Fresh fish for a retail grocery store
   b. Circuit boards for a computer manufacturer
   c. Electric motors to be used in electrical leaf blowers
   d. Translation services for a company wanting to do business in Argentina
   e. Shipping company to transport grain to South America

10. Suppose you have been asked to locate feasible vendors for a restaurant seeking to upgrade its dining room furniture. Locate five different vendors on the Internet. Create a table with four columns. The first column should have

the name of the possible vendor and the second column is the vendor's URL address. In the third column identify reasons to select the vendor and in the fourth column identify doubts you have about the vendor or reasons the firm should not be selected. Assume this is a chain of 25 restaurants located in the U.S. Southeast. When you finish with the evaluations, select one vendor and justify why that firm was chosen.

Review Questions

(Answers are on Last Page of the Chapter)

True or False:

1. Top managers normally participate in the purchase of major equipment, buildings, and land.

2. To reduce the cost of a finished product, a manufacturer may use fabricated and component parts of inferior quality.

3. The most efficient channel of selling goods to consumers consists of a manufacturer, a wholesaler, and a retailer.

4. Derived demand is a business-to-business demand generated from the demand for consumer goods or services.

5. It is not unusual for a new buy to take several months or even several years to complete.

6. Purchasing office supplies for a large corporation is normally classified as a straight rebuy.

7. In the business-to-business purchasing process, the gatekeeper is responsible for screening the decisions made by the buying center.

8. The user in the buying center is the individual who actually uses the product or is responsible for the product being used.

9. If a group of engineers provides test data or information on quality and reliability, they can decide which vendor to choose.

10. EDI technology allows data from the manufacturer's production facility to be sent directly to suppliers and vendors.

Multiple Choice:

11. Retailers, wholesalers, and distributors purchase goods for the purpose of resale.
Which of the following statements is correct?
    a. Retailers are not concerned with selling a particular brand.
    b. Wholesalers and distributors will push the brand that benefits them the most.
    c. a and b.
    d. None of the above.

12. The fluctuations and wide swing in sales in business-to-business sales can be explained by the acceleration principle. The principle addresses which of the following?
    a. A small increase in the demand for a good can cause a huge increase in demand for production equipment.
    b. A 10 to 15 percent decline in orders can cause a complete collapse in the demand for the raw materials used in making a product.
    c. a and b.
    d. None of the above.

13. Business-to-business markets differ from customer markets in all of the following aspects except
    a. fewer buyers.
    b. large purchase volume.
    c. geographic concentration.
    d. informal buying process.

14. The number of batteries supplied to a Ford automobile manufacturing plant directly relates to the number of other engine components, such as alternators, supplied to assemble a particular model. This is an example of
    a. derived demand.
    b. joint demand.
    c. straight rebuy.
    d. direct demand.

15. A modified rebuy occurs in which of the following situations?
    a. Limited buying experience with the product
    b. Dissatisfaction with the current vendor
    c. Switching to a new vendor by the end of the contractual relationship
    d. All of the above

16. Heuristics are decision rules adopted by the members of a buying center to
    a. make the decision process more efficient.
    b. select vendors based on location.
    c. avoid errors in vendors' evaluation.
    d. none of the above.

17. Satisficing is a heuristic decision rule that
    a. requires consideration of all known information in the final decision.
    b. satisfies the expectations and strategies of the top managers.
    c. is satisfactory but not necessarily optimal.
    d. satisfies the requirements for easy manufacturing.

Blog

Clow-Lascu: *Marketing: Essentials 5e Blog*

Screenshot of YouTube Video highlighted in
Clow-Lascu *Marketing: Essentials 5e Blog.*

What Is Happening Today?

Learn More! For videos and articles

that relate to Chapter 5:

blogclowlascu.net/category/chapter05

Includes Discussion Questions

with each Post!

Notes

1. Douglas MacMillan, "Tomorrow's Business Traveler," *Business Week Online* (August 11, 2006): 15; "One Jet, 16 Owners, Big Problems," available at, www.msnbc.msn.com/id/16947116, accessed on February 19, 2007; Laura DeMars, "Business Travel Goes Private," available at, www.cfo.article.cfm/5348151/c_8509518, February 19, 2007; Marilyn Adams, "Airlines Upgrade Service for Wealthier Fliers," *USA Today* (March 14, 2006): 05b; Barbara DeLollis, "Longest Flights Get Seat-Bed Upgrades," *USA Today* (September 27, 2006): 04b.
2. David Kiley, "While CEOs Take Beating, Ford's Scores with Spots," *USA Today* (July 29, 2002): 04b.
3. www.allactiontrade.com, accessed on February 14, 2007.
4. Will Mies, "Buyers Say Corrugated Suppliers Bring Value, But Business Reinvestment Warrants Concern," *Pulp & Paper* 76 (July 2002): 38–42.
5. Eugene F. Brigham and James L. Pappas, *Managerial Economics*, 2nd ed.: (Hinsdale, Ill: Dryden Press, 1976).

6. Patrick J. Robinson, Charles W. Faris, and Yoram Wind, "Industrial Buying and Creative Marketing," *Marketing Science Institute Series* (Boston: Allyn & Bacon, 1967).

7. Patricia M. Doney and Gary W. Armstrong, "Effects of Accountability on Symbolic Information Search and Information Analysis by Organizational Buyers," *Journal of the Academy of Marketing Sciences* 24 (Winter 1996): 57–66; Kenneth E. Clow and Donald Baack, Integrated Advertising, *Promotion, & Marketing Communications*, 3rd ed.: (Upper Saddle River, N.J.: Prentice-Hall, 2007), 76–77.

8. Frederick E. Webster, Jr., and Yoram Wind, "A General Model for Understanding Organizational Buyer Behavior," *Marketing Management* 4 (Winter/Spring 1996): 52–57; Clow and Baack, *Integrated Advertising*, 77–79.

9. Herbert Simon, *The New Science of Management Decisions* (Upper Saddle River, N.J.: Prentice-Hall, 1977).

10. Webster and Wind, A General Model; Doney and Armstrong, Effects of Accountability.

11. Phillip L. Dawes and Don Y. Lee, "Information Control and Influence in Emergent Buying Centers," *Journal of Marketing* 62 (July 1998): 55–69.

12. Marvin E. Shaw and Phillip R. Costanzo, *Theories of Social Psychology*, 2nd ed.: (New York: McGraw-Hill, 1982).

13. Ibid.

Cases

Case 5-1: Briggs & Stratton

Briggs & Stratton is the world's number one maker of air-cooled gasoline engines used in lawn mowers, garden tillers, and other lawn equipment. Sales of these small gasoline engines account for about 86 percent of the total sales for Briggs & Stratton, which was $1.9 billion last year.

Briggs & Stratton manufactures all of its 3- to 25-horsepower small engines in the United States. Factories are located in Alabama, Georgia, Kentucky, Missouri, and Wisconsin. It also has joint ventures with companies in Australia, Canada, China, Japan, New Zealand, and Latin America. The headquarters for Briggs & Stratton is located in Wauwatosa, Wisconsin.

A major component part of the gasoline engine is the spark plug. With the contract up for its current supplier, the Briggs & Stratton purchasing department in Wauwatosa, Wisconsin, decided to put the contract up for bid. At the current production level, Briggs & Stratton purchased about two million spark plugs a year. Because of the size of the contract, Senior Vice President Paul Neylon and Vice President and General Manager of the Small Engine Division, Joe Wright, were asked to participate in the initial discussion.

The first decision that had to be made was who would be included in the vendor decision. At the first meeting, the group agreed that both Neylon and Wright should be involved in the decision. Neylon suggested, given the size of the contract, that Senior Vice President and CFO James Brenn should also be involved in the purchase decision— at least at the stage of selecting the vendor. Although the foreign joint ventures in China, India, or Japan would not be directly affected by the decision, Neylon suggested that the Vice President of International Operations, Michael Scheon, and the Vice President of European Operations should also be involved. His rationale for inclusion was that any changes in major suppliers in the United States would have ripple effects in the international operations and the same vendor chosen for the United States would be in the bidding for the international production facilities. Wright disagreed, saying that the Far East facilities are different because of the joint ventures and that the factories there tend to use local vendors, not U.S. firms.

Wright felt strongly that the buying center group should also include the plant managers at each of the five manufacturing facilities, an engineer from each facility, and the vice president of distribution, sales, and service, Curtis Larson. He wanted to know first-hand from each facility if there were any problems with the current vendor and what factors were important in the selection of a vendor. He also felt Larson was important because he could relay information about service problems with the engines and about whether the spark plug was a contributor to any service recalls or warranty repairs.

Leaving the final decision of who should be included in the buying center group to Wright, attention was turned to the possible vendors. Wright suggested they consider Autolite, Robert Bosch Corporation, ACDelco, NGK, Champion, Spitfire, and Kingsborne. Each of these brands had a good reputation, was dependable, and was large enough to handle the Briggs & Stratton account.

"We will need to develop the vendor analysis criteria as well as a vendor audit list for the site visit," suggested Neylon. "But the most critical decision is: Do we go with just one vendor, or do we use two or three? With five plants, we could potentially use up to five vendors. By allowing each plant the freedom to use a different vendor, we don't have such a high risk if there are problems with one vendor in meeting our production schedule. We could easily contact one of the others to fill in any slack."

Wright countered that he felt that strategy was not cost effective. First, he did not like the idea of each manufacturing facility choosing the brand of spark plugs. Second, he felt that by consolidating to one vendor, the company could negotiate a better price. Ordering two million from a single vendor would certainly be cheaper than breaking down the order to 400,000 from several vendors. Third, given the EDI relationship the company has with its current vendor, Wright did not want to share production data with four or five different vendors.

Although Neylon understood, he felt strongly that it was too risky to go with just one vendor. "At least use another vendor at one of the plants to ensure a backup vendor," he suggested.

Wright could see this was going to be a difficult decision and would take a long time to accomplish. It was also a critical decision that had significant ramifications for the entire company. He first would have to decide on how many people he wanted in the buying group and who they would be. He then would have to decide on the vendor analysis criteria and the vendor audit checklist. Lastly, he would have to decide about how many vendors to use.

Questions

1. Who should be in the buying center for this decision? Discuss which roles you think each person should play.

2. Develop a list of criteria you think should included in the vendor analysis.

3. Develop the vendor audit checklist that should be used when the buying center visits the facilities of the spark plug manufacturer.

4. Should Briggs & Stratton use only one vendor or more than one? Justify your recommendation. What are the advantages and disadvantages to your decision?

Source: Fictitious case based on Hoover's Company Profiles of Briggs & Stratton Corporation, January 7, 2005; www.briggsandstratton.com, accessed on June 14, 2014.

Case 5-2: Selling Eco-Furniture

Baltix was founded in 1999 and is a unique manufacturer of office and school furniture. It uses only eco-environmentally friendly materials. For instance, one table has silvery legs made of recycled aluminum cans and a top made from shredded dollar bills. The Federal Reserve banks shred about 45 to 60 tons of money a month. Baltix buys the shredded money and mixes it in a slurry and presses it into countertops and tabletops. Other materials used to make furniture include wheat straw and sunflower-waste materials. The goal is to produce furniture that is made from recycled and environmentally friendly material that can, in turn, be recycled rather than discarded in waste dumps or in other ways pollute the environment.

Baltix sells its healthy environmental furniture to city, state, and local governments; to libraries; to corporations and businesses committed to environmental stewardship; and to architects and designers working on buildings for clients who are committed to protecting the environment. Presently, Baltix is pursuing the college and university environment. With recent sales to the University of Minnesota, CSU East Bay, University of Washington, Luther College, and Sonoma State University, Baltix realizes that colleges and universities can be a significant new market for their products.

Because of the role of higher education in society, Baltix management believes that colleges and universities will be more eco-friendly than businesses in general. In developing marketing materials for the college and university market, Baltix developed the following list of the reasons why these institutions should choose Baltix:

- Furniture is flexible and mobile.
- Furniture is easy to assemble and install.
- No harmful adhesives or formaldehyde is used.
- Products are competitively priced.
- Furniture has higher green content than any other company in the market.
- Furniture has reusable materials at the end of the product's life.
- Custom solutions are available.

From the institutions' viewpoint, desks, tables, and chairs used in classrooms and other areas throughout a university must meet the needs of students, instructors, and the institution. For instance, in lecture halls, chairs must be durable, yet comfortable. In computer labs, furniture must allow for various computer configurations and be of the proper height for comfortable use. In dorms, furniture needs to meet various purposes, such as a lounge or study area. Baltix realized that selling to colleges and universities would require a different selling approach.

Questions

1. If Baltix were to make a sales call at your university or college, whom would they contact? Who would fill each of the five roles of the buying center?

2. Which of the three types of buying situations would this be for most colleges and universities? Explain your answer.

3. Look at Section 5-4c. What are the organizational, social, individual, and temporary factors that might affect an institution's decision?

4. How eco-friendly is your college or university? What would be the best approach for Baltix if they wanted to sell thier furniture to your institution?

Sources: Scott Carlson, "What a Difference a Desk Makes: Universities Buy Eco-Friendly Furniture," *Chronicle of Higher Education* 51, no. 37 (May 20, 2005): 27; Mike Kennedy, "Seat Work," *American School & University* 78, no. 6 (February 2006): 24–26; www.baltix.com, accessed on February 15, 2007.

Answers to Review Questions

Answers: 1) True, 2) False, 3) False, 4) True, 5) True, 6) True, 7) False, 8) True, 9) False, 10) True, 11) c, 12) a, 13) d, 14) b, 15) d, 16) a, 17) c

Chapter 6

Marketing Segmentation

Learning Objectives

After studying this chapter, you should be able to:

1. Identify the rationale for adopting a target marketing strategy.

2. Identify the bases for consumer segmentation and offer company application examples.

3. Identify the requirements necessary for effective market segmentation.

4. Describe the three targeting strategies that companies use.

5. Describe the six positioning strategies that companies can use to position their brands in the minds of target consumers

Chapter Outline

6-1 CHAPTER OVERVIEW

With the exception of very narrow markets, one single company, however large its resources and capacity, cannot possibly serve all customers. Consumers are too numerous, and their needs and wants are too diverse. For example, social media took the global community by storm, with youth falsely declaring to be 13 before turning 10 just to be able to sign up and join Facebook, and with older boomers posting photos of their latest visit to the Golden Gate Bridge or their kale juice recipe. Facebook was founded in 2004, and today, it has over one billion active users.[1] However, today, teenagers in the U.S. view Facebook as their parents' and grandparents' social medium. While most teens continue to use Facebook occasionally, most are migrating to Snapchat, a photo messaging app that allows Apple and Android users to take photos, record videos, add text and drawings, and send them to recipients. Snapchat users control how long recipients can view their messages. They set the time up to ten seconds and send – then the message disappears forever. Moreover, Snapchat, founded in 2011 and deemed the fastest rising startup,[2] lets you know if the recipients have taken a screenshot. According to Snapchat, in May 2014, the application's users were sending about 700 million photos and videos per day, while Snapchat Stories content was being viewed 500 million times per day. The application's main demographic consists of users between 13 and 23 years of age, and 80 percent of Snapchat's users are located inside the U.S.

Consumers have unique needs and different attitudes, interests, and opinions, and these can change with time. Given this diversity, it is important for companies to focus on those segments that they can serve most effectively and to design goods and services with these segments in mind—that is, to engage in target marketing.

Companies use **target marketing** to:

1. Identify segments of consumers who are similar with regard to key traits and who would respond well to a product and related marketing mix (market segmentation).

2. Select the segments that the company can serve most efficiently and develop products tailored to each (market targeting).

3. Offer the products to the market, communicating through the marketing mix the products' traits and benefits that differentiate the products in the consumer's mind (market positioning).

> **Target Marketing:**
>
> The process of focusing on those segments that the company can serve most effectively and designing products, services, and marketing programs with these segments in mind.

Market segmentation, targeting, and positioning constitute the focus of this chapter. Section 6-2 focuses on market segmentation, identifying the requirements for successful segmentation and the bases for segmentation. Section 6-3 addresses the three strategies used in targeting: differentiated, concentrated, and undifferentiated, and Section 6-4 addresses the different approaches to positioning brands in relation to other competing products, based on product traits and benefits that are relevant to the consumer.

6-2 MARKET SEGMENTATION

The marketplace is composed of consumers with unique needs and preferences. Firms find that it is difficult to satisfy all consumers; consequently, they simplify their marketing task by appealing to those consumers whose needs are most effectively met by their own offering. Market **segmentation** involves identifying consumers who are similar with regard to key traits, such as product-related needs and wants, and who would respond well to a similar marketing mix.

> **Segmentation:**
>
> The process of identifying consumers or markets that are similar with regard to key traits, such as product-related needs and wants, and that would respond well to a product and related marketing mix.

It is important to realize that not all market segments are financially feasible to explore because they are either too small or their characteristics are not that different from the population as a whole or other market segments. As will be illustrated in Chapter 7, most companies conduct some type of segmentation study to identify profiles of different types of consumers that the company could target. Marketing managers are especially interested in identifying those segments composed of consumers who are heavy product users. Research sponsored by KitchenAid suggested that the company should focus on "the culinary-involved" consumers, a segment of heavy users of kitchen appliances. The company successfully targeted these consumers, and its sales experienced a double-digit increase.[3] For other products, income may be the primary basis for segmentation. Luxury brands target high-income consumers. Yet other products are targeted at the mass market—the manufacturer mass-produces the product, promotes it, and distributes it widely to the mass market. But even these products need to be appropriately targeted, as Figure 6-1 illustrates. The following section addresses the different bases for identifying market segments that share similar needs and wants.

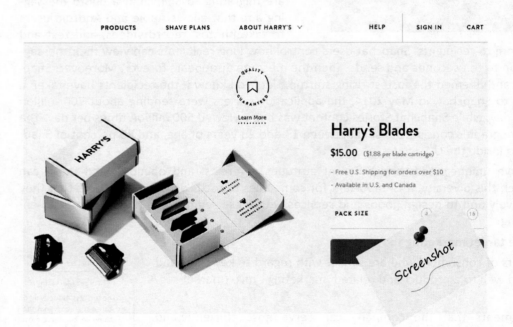

Figure 6-1:
Razor blades are aimed at the mass market, but even they need to be appropriately targeted. This is a screenshot of Harry's website. Harry's is a relative newcomer to the industry and is positioning its brand as a high quality, affordable alternative to premium blades, using sleek, contemporary designs for both its product line and marketing campaigns.

www.harry's.com

6-2a: Levels of Segmentation

As mentioned in the preceding paragraphs, the marketplace consists of consumers with unique needs and preferences. Individual buyers have unique product needs, and a company that has all the resources available at its discretion—including time—can potentially target each prospective buyer individually. However, for most firms, that is a difficult and costly proposition. It is virtually impossible to satisfy every consumer, and thus companies will simplify their marketing task by appealing to those consumers whose needs are most effectively met by their own offering. Some firms may not even segment the market at all, marketing to the masses. Figure 6-2 identifies the three levels of segmentation: mass marketing, segment marketing, and micromarketing.

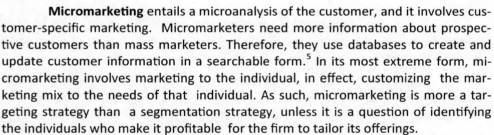

Figure 6-2: Levels of Segmentation

Mass Marketing → Segment Marketing → Micromarketing

Mass marketing is the shotgun approach to segmentation. It involves identifying the product-related preferences of most consumers and then targets the product broadly to everyone. Mass marketing allows firms to subsequently target these consumers while incurring minimal costs. The outcome of this strategy is ultimately low prices for the consumer or high profit margins for the seller. Mass marketing by itself is a rather difficult proposition in industrialized markets, where consumers are highly differentiated in their preferences. In the aggregate, there is a move from mass marketing to micromarketing. But for individual firms, a mix of strategies is necessary. For example, Procter & Gamble uses more precise segmentation approaches that coexist with mass marketing. In developing countries, however, mass marketing plays a key role—a central role in some areas.[4]

Segment marketing involves identifying consumers who are similar with regard to key traits, such as product-related needs and wants, and who would respond well to a similar marketing mix. BMW offers the Mini to young consumers who have just finished college and to singles and couples living in cities, the 300 series to young professionals, and the 500 and 700 series to mid-level professionals and families. Section 6-2 in this chapter focuses primarily on segment marketing.

Micromarketing entails a microanalysis of the customer, and it involves customer-specific marketing. Micromarketers need more information about prospective customers than mass marketers. Therefore, they use databases to create and update customer information in a searchable form.[5] In its most extreme form, micromarketing involves marketing to the individual, in effect, customizing the marketing mix to the needs of that individual. As such, micromarketing is more a targeting strategy than a segmentation strategy, unless it is a question of identifying the individuals who make it profitable for the firm to tailor its offerings.

> **Segment Marketing:** A process that involves identifying consumers who are similar with regard to key traits, such as product-related needs and wants, and who would respond well to a similar marketing mix.
>
> **Micromarketing:** A process that involves a microanalysis of the customer and customer-specific marketing.

6-2b: Bases for Segmentation

The purpose of segmentation is to identify clusters of consumers that respond in a similar fashion to a company's marketing strategies. Identifying individual market segments will enable the company to produce products that meet the precise needs of target consumers with a marketing mix that is appropriately tailored for those segments. The company typically conducts extensive marketing research to identify such segments.

In the process of analyzing consumer demand and identifying clusters of consumers that respond similarly to marketing strategies, firms must identify those bases for segmentation that are most relevant for their goods or services. Figure 6-3 identifies the bases for segmentation that companies could use in the process of analyzing their markets.

Demographic Segmentation

Demographics are statistics that describe the population, such as age, gender, race, ethnicity, income, education, occupation, social class, life cycle stage, and household size. There are many differences among consumers with regard to demographic variables. The following examples demonstrate how these differences have important implications for marketing.

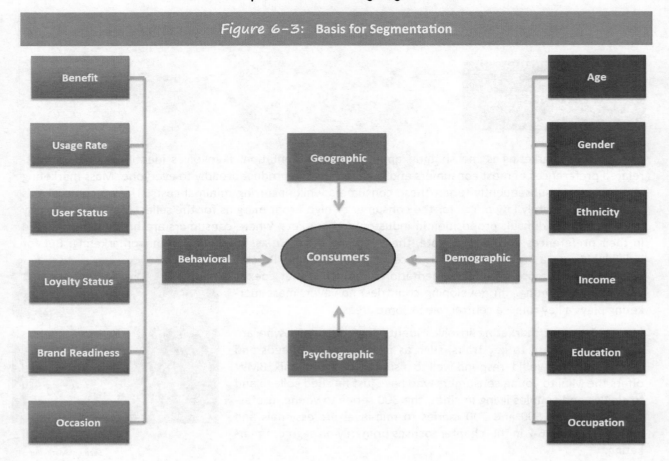

Figure 6-3: Basis for Segmentation

Benefit

Usage Rate

User Status

Loyalty Status

Brand Readiness

Occasion

Behavioral

Geographic

Consumers

Psychographic

Demographic

Age

Gender

Ethnicity

Income

Education

Occupation

Two major **demographic segmentation** variables are age and life cycle stage. As individuals age and enter different life cycle stages, their product preferences also change.

In Chapter 2 an age categorization of sociodemographic groups examined Generations X and Y, baby boomers, empty nesters, and seniors. Each of these categories has been identified as a viable target segment for certain products. For example, Generation Y consumers tend to spend more on entertainment, whereas baby boomers and Generation X consumers' spending has a family focus. The needs and preferences of each segment vary substantially. Generation Y consumers have grown up in a media-saturated, brand-conscious world. The intense marketing efforts aimed at Generation Y have taught them to assume the worst about companies trying to coax them into buying something. Consequently, advertisements meant to look youthful and fun may come off as merely opportunistic, as PepsiCo's "Generation Next" campaign was viewed. This group of consumers responds better to humor, irony, and the "unvarnished" truth, as Sprite (see Figure 6-4) has done with advertisements that parody celebrity endorsers and carry the tagline, "Image is

Figure 6-4: Many products are marketed based on a person's age or life cycle stage. Sprite's website features the "Sprite Style" Gallery, with posts of crowd-sourced photos from Sprite's targeted demographic segment.

www.sprite.com/style/sprite-style-gallery/

nothing. Thirst is everything. Obey your thirst.''[6] These consumers tend to be more blasé and less suscepti-
ble to influence.

Baby boomers, who are in a different life cycle stage, have different interests and concerns. As baby boomers are rapidly entering the 55- to 74-year-old age category, they are creating a surge in the number of affluent households, with incomes over $100,000. Boomers have already demonstrated a penchant
for trying to delay the aging process. As they move into their sixties, they will almost certainly avail themselves of such cosmetic procedures as Botox shots to erase wrinkles, skin treatments at health spas, and
highly personalized health care services . Even periodic house calls by a doctor to check on health status
may not be a stretch for this market.[7]

Products such as clothing, cosmetics, and hair products are among the obvious products that are
tailored based on a person's gender. Companies may elect to target either men or women with their products. Yet often success in one category may compel the company to target the other gender. For instance,
clothing brands such as Liz Claiborne and DKNY, which have traditionally targeted women, find their men's
lines to be increasingly successful. Alternatively, clothing brands such as Armani, which have initially targeted men, have subsequently become established in women's fashions.

Even Nike, a company that has traditionally targeted hardcore sports guys, is now actively courting
women. Nike has even plunged into the yoga market with everything from shoes to balance boards. The

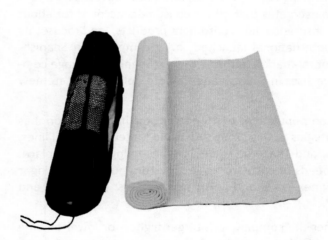

company's unfolding women's initiative is considered its most important strategic undertaking of
the new millennium. Every new resource allocation at Nike now is considered with at least one
eye toward the female consumer. Although
women's products have been generating less
than 20 percent of Nike's overall sales, the company's goal is to double that number in the next
few years. Nike is planning to target women
differently than it targets men. The company decided to innovate products specifically for wom-
en, based on their unique needs. NikeWomen,
formerly Nike Goddess, is successful with women.
It is designed and merchandised with women in
mind, from the assortment to the atmospherics
to the dressing rooms.[8]

Targeting men and women with different products and marketing strategies makes good business sense. Women are receptive to different messages than men and have different interests than men.
One illustration of these differences is in Internet usage, as illustrated in Table 6-1. Notice that each gender
is subdivided into five different market segments. When various market segments are identified, descriptive names are often given to each group. For instance, the male Internet segment that has a high level of
computer usage and likes to use the Internet to research investments and locate software is called
''Bits and Bytes.'' This segment has a special interest in computers, and most of their hobbies are computer
related, so calling this market segment ''Bits and Bytes'' makes sense. However, the female group that uses the Internet for chats and a personal Web page is called ''Social Sally.'' Their lives revolve around making friends, and the Internet is a means of socializing. Understanding the broad differences between men
and women and the differences between the behavioral segments within each gender category helps
marketers target these segments more efficiently. The marketing message designed for the ''Bits and
Bytes'' male segment will look different from the marketing message designed for the ''Social Sally'' segment.

As seen in Chapter 4, subcultures constitute important markets of consumers with shared value
systems that are based on ethnicity or common backgrounds. Marketing managers increasingly focus on
individual ethnicities, directing their marketing efforts to meet their specific needs. JPMorgan Chase fo-

Table 6-1: Male and Female Segments on the Internet		
Segments	**Usage Situations**	**Favorite Materials**
Male		
Bits and Bytes	Computers and hobbies	Investments, discovery, software
Practical Pete	Personal productivity	Investments, company listings
Viking Garner	Competing and winning	Games, chat, software
Sensitive Sam	Help family and friends	Investments, government information
World Citizen	Connecting with world	Discovery, software, investments
Female		
Social Sally	Making friends	Chat and personal Web page
New Age Crusader	Fight for causes	Books and government information
Cautious Mom	Nurture children	Cooking and medical facts
Playful Pretender	Role-play	Chat and games
Master Producer	Job productivity	White pages, government information

Source: Scott M. Smith and David B. Whitlark, "Men and Women Online: What Makes Them Click?" *Marketing Research* 13, no. 2 (Summer 2001): 20–25.

cuses its marketing efforts on multicultural market segments. Its corporate branding campaign targets Hispanic Americans in New York and Texas with Spanish-language TV, radio, and print advertising and is actively targeting Asian American consumers. MetLife estimates that ethnic consumers account for about 30 percent of the company's retail business, including insurance and retirement products, and focuses its marketing efforts on these segments. MasterCard International launched a TV campaign on Spanish-language networks, which adapted its "Priceless" general-market effort with new Spanish-language commercials. And Washington Mutual, which already advertises in Spanish and Chinese, plans to create new campaigns in Vietnamese and French.[9]

Growth, in particular, of the Hispanic American population, to 16 percent of the population, has challenged businesses to rethink their marketing strategies to this group. Hispanic-targeted apparel lines, such as Lucy Pereda at Sears, Daisy Fuentes at Kohl's, and Thalia at Kmart, are becoming commonplace. Similarly, Wal-Mart customizes its assortment to the needs of each store's unique community, breaking it down by country of origin. They sell Maseca flour, Jumex, Valle and Kerns fruit nectars, Las Costna and Goya food brands, and Herdez salsas, among others.[10]

Product price is often a determinant of whether the company will target higher- or lower-income consumer segments. In general, luxury designers target their products at high-income consumers. Bvlgari, Fendi, Hermès, Prada, and Escada brands retail for prices prohibitive for middle- and lower-income consumers. The converse is not necessarily true: Lower-priced products do not necessarily appeal only to lower-income consumers. Wal-Mart consumers come from all economic strata of society, all with the same goal: to get value at everyday-low prices.

Psychographic Segmentation

Demographics are closely linked to **psychographic segmentation**, which includes lifestyles, values, attitudes, interests, and opinions. It is difficult to describe psychographics without demographics. Cultural variables, such as religion, norms, and even language, influence consumer product preferences as well.

> **Psychographic Segmentation:** The use of values, attitudes, interests, and other cultural variables to segment consumers.
>
> **Target Market:** Consumers or markets that are similar in aspects relevant to the company.

One vehicle for segmenting consumers psychographically that was addressed in detail in Chapter 4 is the VALS typology provided by SRI Consulting Business Intelligence. The VALS typology categorizes respondents based on resources and on the extent to which they are action oriented. The VALS psychographic categories and their descriptors are listed in Table 6-2.

Marketing managers must understand the psychographic and demographic makeup of their **target market** to effectively address its needs. The Fresh Market, a specialty food chain present primarily on the East Coast, uses a different appeal to

VALS Category	Characteristics
Innovators	Successful, sophisticated, and receptive to new technologies, their purchases reflect cultivated tastes for upscale products.
Thinkers	Educated, conservative, and practical consumers, they value knowledge and responsibility and look for durability, functionality, and value.
Achievers	Goal-oriented, conservative, and committed to career and family, they favor established, prestige products that demonstrate success to peers.
Experiencers	Young, enthusiastic, and impulsive, they seek variety and excitement and spend substantially on fashion, entertainment, and socializing.
Believers	Conservative, conventional, and focusing on tradition, family, religion, and community, they prefer established brands, favoring American products.
Strivers	Trendy and fun loving, they are concerned about others' opinions and approval.
Makers	Self-sufficient, they have the skill and energy to carry out projects, respect authority, and are unimpressed by material possessions.
Survivors	Concerned with safety and security, they focus on meeting needs rather than fulfilling desires, are brand loyal, and purchase discounted products.

Table 6-2: VALS Psychographic Categories

consumers in the various neighborhoods where they have stores. Their merchandise mix varies to best address the needs of each neighborhood. For example, in their upscale neighborhoods, they carry exclusive French cheeses, such as Chaumes, Morbier, and Roquefort. In their more bohemian neighborhoods, they carry a wider selection of natural foods. And in their ethnic neighborhoods, they attempt to carry products that appeal to their ethnic consumers. Figure 6-5 illustrates products with, initially, a specific subculture appeal which, with time, have become mainstream.

Figure 6-5 Chemeneas, open fire garden heaters originally from Mexico, were first adopted in the South-West, but, today, there are equally popular on the East Coast. Courtesy of Sting-Ray's.

Another example of a psychographic segment is the high-sensation seeker. High-sensation seekers thrive on high stimulation and hedonic consumption. Their behavior translates into a windfall for manufacturers of high-risk products and entertainment—and even for the armies of psychologists, psychiatrists, and geneticists who specialize in sensation seekers. Medical research has found that the traditional attribution of high-sensation seeking to high testosterone levels is, in fact, a myth and that people hooked on thrills have a low cortisol level, which is remedied promptly by high excitement. Marvin Zuckerman, a professor of clinical psychology who has studied high-sensation seekers for four decades and developed well-known psychometric measures for sensation seeking, has identified certain common characteristics of the sensation-seeking market. High-sensation seekers drive fast, are drawn to excitement and to exciting people, and "in every aspect of their lives, they are looking for the latest thing."[11]

Frank Farley, a well-known psychologist, describes high-sensation seekers and individuals with Big-T (thrill-seeking) personalities. Individuals with Big-T personalities are mountain climbers, hot-air-balloon racers, parachuters, race-car drivers, hang-gliders, and creative artists.[12] Examples of Big-T artists are the Young British Artists (YBA) group—a group of conceptual artists, sculptors, and installation artists, most of whom attended Goldsmiths College in London and then took the United States by storm with shock art, placing animals in formaldehyde, for instance. This group is best represented by Damien Hirst. In other examples, Hermann Nitsch stages crucifixions and animal slaughter, incorporating ritual, music and dance.

Behavioral Segmentation

Behavioral segmentation is used to identify clusters of consumers who seek the same product benefits or who use or consume the product in a similar fashion. Behavioral variables include benefits sought, usage status, user rate, loyalty status, buyer-readiness stage, and occasion.

Benefit segmentation is defined as the process of identifying market segments based on important differences between the benefits sought by the target market from purchasing a particular product. Marketers who understand the motivation behind consumer purchases will be able to send the appropriate message to the relevant market segments. Notice in Table 6-1 (page 148) the benefit sought by each segment is different. Bits and Bytes men use the Internet to find out more about the latest computer models and software, to keep up with their hobbies, and to manage their investments. The Viking Garner segment seeks opportunities to chat with others and to play games. Social Sally women seek similar benefits, making friends and chatting, as well as sharing their news with friends and relatives through their Web page. New Age Crusaders use the Internet to fight for their causes and to find related books and government information.

Usage rate segmentation is defined as the process of segmenting markets based on the extent to which consumers are nonusers, occasional users, medium users, or heavy users of a product. Segments of consumers identified as heavy users of a product category would constitute prime target markets for new brands in the category. Taco Bell introduced the Grilled Stuft Burrito backed by an advertising campaign with the tag line "Ooh, fajitas," and Border Bowls, with beans and salad topped with meat and cheese, to its heavy users—between the ages of 18 and 34, who, according to company research, wanted "the beef to be beefier, the beans to be chunkier, the restaurants to be cleaner, and the service to be faster."[13]

Heavy users of one offering should not be overlooked by businesses that may be serving a different type of consumer. In a study on restaurant-related consumption behavior, Scarborough Research found that seven percent of adults are heavy users of quick-serve restaurants and of sit-down restaurants. These consumers are young, with 40 percent between the ages of 18 and 34, with above-average income; they go to McDonald's and also to Chinese and Mexican restaurants.[14]

Benefit Segmentation: The process of identifying market segments based on important differences between the benefits sought by the target market from purchasing a particular product.

Usage Rate Segmentation: The process of segmenting markets based on the extent to which consumers are nonusers, occasional users, medium users, or heavy users of a product.

User Status Segmentation: The process of determining consumer status—as users of competitors' products, ex-users, potential users, first-time users, or regular users.

User status segmentation is defined as the process of determining consumer status—as users of competitors' products, ex-users, potential users, first-time users, or regular users. Although the ideal consumer may be considered to be the regular user, companies should not limit their marketing efforts to just reinforcing the user behavior of this market. Although it is true that introducing a product for the first time to a market of nonusers will create enormous and costly challenges for the company, in that it has to educate consumers about the brand and convince them to buy, it is also true that such markets may present great potential. Yum! Brands Inc. unveiled its breakfast offering at its Taco Bell restaurants, in an attempt to revitalize the brand after the Escherichia coli outbreak. Similarly, Wendy's is testing the breakfast market, and Starbucks is expanding its offerings to hot breakfast items, such as Black Forest ham, egg and cheddar; eggs Florentine with baby spinach and Havarti; peppered bacon, egg, and cheddar; sausage, egg, and cheddar; and whole grain, and Western omelet wrap.

Loyalty segmentation is defined as the process of segmenting the market based on the degree of brand preference, commitment, retention, allegiance, and the extent to which consumers engage in repeat purchases.[15] Loyal consumers are valuable to companies; these are the consumers that the company does not need to persuade to buy its products. Marketing managers strive to create consumer loyalty by offering consistently high-quality goods and services. Marketers also tie the consumer to the brand by offering loyalty programs that direct individual consumer's consumption to the company. Airlines and hotel chains ensure consumer loyalty by offering rewards tied to the extensive use of that airline or hotel chain. Retailers offer various promotions only to consumers who use their loyalty cards frequently; for instance, Home Depot e-mails its loyal and valued customers an offering of 10 percent off all purchases from its online store for a limited time, typically one week.

Buyer-readiness stage segmentation is defined as the process of segmenting the market based on individuals' stage of readiness to buy a product. For laser-assisted in situ keratomileusis (LASIK) surgery aimed at correcting hyperopia, myopia, and astigmatism, the market can be segmented into consumers who are not aware of the service, consumers who are aware of it and may need it in the future, consumers who are aware of it but will never need it, consumers who are interested to find out more about LASIK surgery, consumers who would like to have the surgery but cannot afford it, and consumers who intend to have the surgery. A company such as Virginia Eye Institute, a heavy promoter of this type of surgery, will need to create different promotion campaigns for each viable segment. Examples of such campaigns are awareness campaigns for those who do not know about this type of surgery or about the fact that Virginia Eye Institute offers this surgery, informational campaigns for consumers who might want additional information, and persuasive campaigns for those who are still debating about whether they should have this type of surgery.

> **Loyalty Segmentation:** The process of segmenting the market based on the degree of consumer loyalty to the brand.
>
> **Buyer-Readiness Stage Segmentation:** The process of segmenting the market based on individuals' stage of readiness to buy a product.
>
> **Occasion Segmentation:** The process of segmenting based on the time or the occasion when the product should be purchased or consumed.

Figure 6-6: Candy is packaged for special occasion promotions.

Occasion segmentation is defined as segmentation based on the time or the occasion when the product should be purchased or consumed. Champagne is normally consumed to celebrate a special occasion, on New Year's Eve, or at Sunday brunch. Cosmetics companies increase their advertising, promoting extensively before Mother's Day. Different types of candy are promoted for special occasions. For Halloween, candy is sold in large packages that include small portions. And for Valentine's Day, candy is presented in red, heart-shaped packages (see Figure 6-6). And Table 6-3 (next page) summarizes the various behavioral segmentation strategies.

Geographic Segmentation

Geographic segmentation is defined as segmentation based on geographic location, such as region, state, or city. Small companies typically limit their marketing to segments within the proximity of the firm. Large companies may elect to target various regional segments differently, based on regional preferences. For example, Coke and Pepsi taste different in different parts of the United States and in the world—sweeter in the South of the United States and with a stronger lemon flavor in Europe.

> **Geographic Segmentation:** Market segmentation based on geographic location, such as country or region.

Table 6-3: Behavioral Segmentation Strategies		
Behavioral Segmentation	**Definition**	**Typical Categories**
Benefit segmentation	Market segments based on important differences between the benefits the target market seeks from purchasing a particular product	Varies
Usage rate segmentation	Market segments based on the extent, or quantity, to which consumers use a product	Nonusers; Occasional users; Medium users; Heavy users
User status segmentation	Market segments based on the current usage of a product	User of competing brands; Ex-user; Potential user; First-time users; Regular users
Loyalty status segmentation	Market segment based on the degree of brand preference, commitment, retention, and allegiance to a brand	No loyalty; Low loyalty; Medium loyalty; High loyalty
Buyer-readiness stage segmentation	Market segments based on individuals' stage of readiness to buy a product	Consumers who are not aware; Consumers who are aware of it but will never need it; Consumers who are aware of it and may need it in the future; Consumers who are interested and want to learn more; Consumers who are ready to purchase
Occasion segmentation	Market segments based on the time or the occasion when a product should be purchased or consumed	Varies

Often, firms are organized geographically, with different divisions specializing in particular markets. Stihl, a manufacturer of chain saws, sells its products primarily to individual consumers in the southeastern United States and to professional loggers in the northwestern United States. In another example, the advertising agency that created the advertising campaign for the Snoring Center used geographic segmentation placing the billboards along major highways in Dallas, Texas (see Figure 6-7).

Figure 6-7: In promoting the Snoring Center, geographic segmentation was used with ads on billboards and in magazines in the Dallas, Texas area.

Multiattribute Segmentation

Multiattribute segmentation is defined as a process that uses multiple bases for segmenting consumers. Companies rarely use only demographic variables in their segmentation approaches. Typically, they also add psychographic and behavioral variables to the demographic information to determine the best approach to reach their target market. For example, Reynolds aluminum foil is targeted to women ages 24 and older—women who cook or at least store food.

> **Multiattribute Segmentation:** The process of segmenting the market by using multiple segmentation variables.

Many management consulting firms have come up with systems for segmenting consumers using multiple bases for segmentation: demographics, psychographics, and behavior. Two popular classification systems based on zip code are

PRIZM (a Nielsen product) and Community™ Tapestry™ (offered by ESRI Business Information Solutions). PRIZM was the first lifestyle segmentation system and is still widely used. Based on the principle of "birds of a feather flock together" (i.e., that people of similar demographic and lifestyle characteristics tend to live near each other), PRIZM assigns every neighborhood in the United States to one of 67 clusters. Each cluster describes the predominant demographics and lifestyles of the people living in that neighborhood. Among the classifications used by PRIZM are rural, small town, second cities, suburbs, urban, and upper market, middle market, and lower market in terms of social rank—based on income, household wealth, education, occupation, and home value. A PRIZM segment, Blue

Highways, are lower-middle-class couples and families who live in isolated towns and farmsteads, where boomer men hunt and fish, women enjoy sewing and crafts, and they all go to a country music concert. On the other hand, the segment Suburban Sprawl consists of a collection of middle-aged singles and couples living in the heart of suburbia who are members of the baby boom generation, hold decent jobs, and own older homes and condos, and pursue conservative versions of the American Dream. Both have similar household incomes—the median income is just under $50,000—and they have no children.

Community™ Tapestry™, ESRI's market segmentation system, classifies neighborhoods into 65 market segments based on social, economic, and demographic characteristics. According to the Community Tapestry classification, one of the authors of this text lives in an area composed of primarily three segments: (1) college towns, representing on- and off-campus living, where convenience is the main consideration for food purchases and where residents eat out, order in, and access the Internet; (2) metro renters, who are young, well-educated professionals in large cities, renters in high-rise units, living alone with roommates; and (3) dorms to diplomas, where most dwellers are college students. This segment is 44.5 percent white, 47.9 percent black, and the median income is just over $30,000. To find out how your zip code is classified, refer to ESRI's Web site at www.esribis.com and proceed to Community Tapestry to enter your zip code.

6-2c: Segmenting Business Markets

Business markets can be segmented based on similar variables as used with the consumer market: geographic location, behavioral dimensions such as benefits sought, user status and usage rate, buyer-readiness stage, degree of loyalty, and other adapted dimensions. For example, instead of demographics, segmentation can take place based on firm size and industry sector.

The following are examples of four behavioral segments of business markets:[16]

- The **relationship-seeking segment** consists of relatively sophisticated service users who believe that the user-provider relationship is important. This segment has a "realistic" level of expectations for the service requirements and does not expect to pay a low price—these businesses understand the trade-off between service levels and price.

- The **price-sensitive segment** is looking for low prices but also has low service requirements; it wants the work done at the lowest possible cost.

- The **high-expectation service segment** is the most demanding and needs extensive customer focus, placing considerable demands on service providers while demanding low prices.

- The **customer-focus needs segment** is prepared to pay for higher-than-average service that is tailored to meet their business needs.

6-2d: Requirements for Successful Segmentation

Identifying the bases that the company will use for segmentation is important. Equally important is ensuring that the segments are large enough to warrant investment, that they are relatively stable over time, and that they are going to respond to the company's marketing efforts. For segmentation to be effective, marketing managers need to assess the measurability, substantiality, stability over time, accessibility, and actionability of the market segments.

Measurability is defined as the degree to which individual market segments are easy to identify and measure or the ability to estimate the size of market segments. In highly industrialized countries, such as the United States, it is relatively easy to measure or estimate market segments. Government and marketing data are readily available to help companies in the process of making decisions: Census data are reasonably accurate, TV viewing data can be relatively easily collected with the cooperation of cable companies, and shopping behavior can readily be evaluated by linking universal product code (UPC) data to loyalty cards' use.

> **Measurability:**
> The ability to estimate the size of a market segment.
>
> **Substantiality:**
> The extent to which the market is large enough to warrant investment.
>
> **Stability:**
> The extent to which preferences are stable, rather than changing, in a market segment.

Yet even in our data-rich environment, marketers will find that important segments may not be fully measurable. For example, a company advertising to Hispanic American consumers can only partially estimate its reach in markets where there is a large seasonal and unregistered migrant population. Companies targeting products to gay and lesbian consumers find that only about six percent of the population self-identifies as gay and lesbian. Limiting targeting strategies to the self-identified segment ignores the large closeted gay and lesbian segment.

Substantiality is defined as the degree to which a segment is large enough and profitable enough to warrant investment. After measuring the size of a market segment, a company needs to determine whether the segment is large enough to earn a decent return on its investment. For example, it would not make sense for a retailer to position itself as specializing in selling clove cigarettes because the market for clove cigarettes is limited, even in large cities.

Stability is defined as the degree to which segment consumer preferences are stable over time. This is an important consideration in an environment where products are in different life cycle stages and where preferences are continually changing. For decades until the late 1980s, dealers of artifacts and antiques prominently displayed elephant tusks and rare leopard skins in Fifth Avenue and 57th Street store windows in Manhattan. Chinatown retailers experienced brisk sales of ornately carved elephant tusks.

However, a change in public opinion took place after the U.S. government and various international organizations revealed the cruelty of these trades and stressed the distinct possibility that these animals may become extinct. The movie and book *Gorillas in the Mist*, also popular in the 1980s, further convinced consumers that the trade in rare animals is cruel. The trade in objects made from rare animals fell out of favor with the consuming public, and this once-substantial market segment quickly diminished (see Figure 6-8).

Figure 6-8: Leopard skins that were once prominently displayed have fallen out of favor.

It is important to note that segments do change with time, especially early in the product life cycle or when new technologies appear. As discussed in the chapter opening, the traditional segments of Internet users changed substantially after the technology became more affordable and computers were bought by the mass market.

Accessibility is defined as the ability to communicate with and reach the target market. Some markets cannot be accessed with marketing communications. A large proportion of children cannot easily be reached through marketing communication.

Many children spend their weekdays in day cares that have a policy not to expose children to TV programming. At home, their parents may decide not to allow them to watch TV programs and show them, instead, educational videos. In their everyday lives, these children may never be exposed to children's advertising.

Working mothers are also difficult to target: Most have little time to watch TV and read women's magazines. They spend their free time catching up on home chores and tending to their spouse or children, rather than in front of the TV set or leafing through nonessential magazines. Marketers often can reach them only relatively late during the consumer decision-making process, when they are already at the store and they may have already made their purchase decision.

> **Accessibility:**
> The ability to communicate with and reach the target market.
>
> **Actionability:**
> The extent to which the target market segment is responsive to the marketing strategies used.
>
> **Differential Response:**
> The extent to which market segments respond differently to marketing strategies.

Actionability is defined as the extent to which marketers are capable of designing effective programs that can effectively serve the market segment. An important question that marketing managers must ask is whether they can effectively serve the market segment. Do they have the product that the market needs? Are they pricing it based on the needs of the market? Small and large firms alike find that they cannot predict well the actionability of their target segment when they go abroad. A small boutique Italian wine bar attempting to introduce authentic Italian wines in Germany finds that the market expects it to be primarily a restaurant. The largest retailer worldwide, Wal-Mart, found that it cannot compete effectively for consumers in Germany, where the market is saturated with low-service, low-priced local competition. An insufficient a priori assessment of actionability will often lead to failure.

Figure 6-9: Water is segmented based on its origin, its mineral content, and on whether it is still or sparkling.

Differential response is defined as the extent to which market segments are easy to distinguish from each other and respond differently to company marketing strategies. If consumers are similar or have identical preferences—and this is hardly ever the case—there is no need for target marketing. Even the market for water is segmented into sparkling or still, based on its provenance, based on its mineral content, and so on (see Figure 6-9).

6-3 TARGET MARKETING DECISIONS

Companies that have ample resources can, and often do, address the needs of all segments of consumers. Procter & Gamble and Kraft attempt to target all consumers with the products they sell, filling the supermarket and discount store shelf space with what seemingly are competing brands and saturating the media with their communication, meeting all related needs of target consumers at a nice profit. Other companies with sufficient resources choose to focus on one well-established brand, improving it continually, offering alternatives under the same umbrella brand name. Boeing uses such a strategy. To date, it has only one true direct competitor—Airbus Industrie. Not all companies have the resources of the companies mentioned here. Frequently, small and medium-size businesses are successful by best addressing the needs of one or two segments or a small niche. One common trait of all these companies is that they research their consumers closely and target and position their products accordingly. Companies can use three main strategies to target their markets: differentiated, concentrated, and undifferentiated.

6-3a: Differentiated Marketing Strategy

Companies that use a **differentiated marketing strategy** identify, or even create, market segments that want different benefits from a product and target them with different brands, using separate marketing strategies. Some companies have the necessary resources to offer at least one brand to every conceivable market segment. Procter & Gamble offers a variety of laundry detergents to consumers all over the world: Cheer, Dreft, Era, Febreze, Gain, Ivory Snow, and Tide. To European consumers, the company offers combinations of the following brands: Ace, Alfa, Ariel, Bold 2 in 1, Bonux Biomat, Dash, Daz, Dreft, Fairy, Febreze, Moher, Tide, and Vizir.[17] Each of these laundry detergents appeals to a different market, consumers who want a detergent that has an excellent cleaning ability, consumers who need whitening, consumers who need fabric softening agents in the washing process, consumers who need a product for sensitive fabrics or for babies' sensitive skin, and consumers who may be allergic, to name a few.

Differentiated Marketing: A targeting strategy identifying market segments with different preferences for a particular product category and targeting each segment with different brands and different marketing strategies.

Concentrated Marketing: The process of selecting only one market segment and targeting it with one single brand.

Such strategies, whereby companies offer brands for every market segment, require significant resources on the part of the company. It is much more costly to develop a marketing strategy for each market segment than to address a single segment or to offer only one brand targeted at all consumers.

6-3b: Concentrated Marketing Strategy

Not all companies can afford to offer something for everyone. Not all companies desire to meet the needs of all consumers in the marketplace. In fact, many companies select only one market segment and target it with one single brand, using a **concentrated marketing strategy**. Montblanc, a company manufacturing pens, fountain pens, jewelry and accessories, offers a relatively limited product selection that it markets to a professional class. See Figure 6-10 for a sample of concentrated marketing.

Figure 6-10: The Sagres brand of beer is the only offering of SCC – Sociedade Central de Cervejas e Bebidas, S.A, in Portugal.

Companies that cannot afford to compete in a mature market with an oligopoly may choose to pursue a small segment—a niche. This option may be the only one available for the company's limited resources. Retailers often use a niche strategy. The Body Shop caters to consumers who are environmentally concerned and who want to purchase natural products that have not been tested on animals.

6-3c: Undifferentiated Marketing Strategy

An **undifferentiated marketing strategy** is one in which the product is aimed at the entire market using a single marketing strategy. The company using this strategy chooses to ignore differences among consumers and offers the entire market one single brand. Many bulk products are aimed at all consumers, regardless of demographics, psychographics, and behavioral differences. For branded products, this is difficult to achieve: Even salt brands offer low-sodium and kosher versions.

Undifferentiated Marketing: A targeting strategy aiming the product at the market using a single strategy, regardless of the number of segments.

Using an undifferentiated strategy offers the company economies of scale in manufacturing and promotion and the ability to cut costs. Although this strategy may appear as the most efficient, marketers are aware that segment needs may be better served by tailoring offerings to various segments of the market. In that sense, manufacturers of branded products will benefit from using a differentiated strategy, if they can afford it; if not, they can offer a concentrated strategy, meeting the needs of a target segment more efficiently than they would those of the entire market.

6-4 POSITIONING THE BRAND

Positioning entails placing the brand in the consumer's mind in relation to other competing brands, based on brand traits and benefits that are relevant to the consumer. Such a process involves identifying competitors, determining how the competitors are perceived and evaluated by target consumers, determining the competitors' positions in the consumers' mind, analyzing the customers, selecting the position, and monitoring it.[18]

There are six approaches to the brand positioning strategy: attribute/benefit positioning, price/quality positioning, use or applications positioning, product user positioning, product class positioning, and competitor positioning (see Figure 6-11). [19]

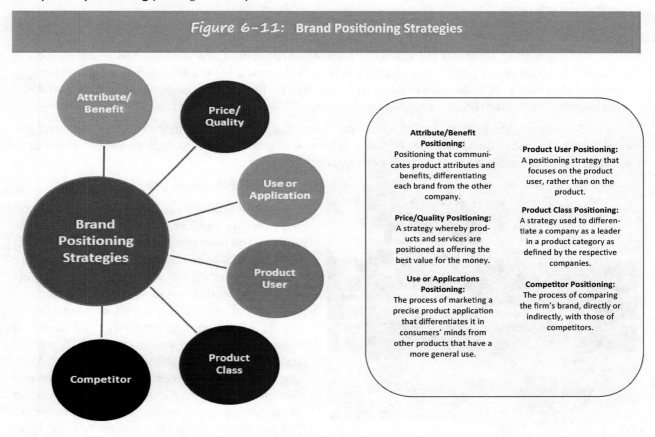

Figure 6-11: Brand Positioning Strategies

Attribute/Benefit Positioning: Positioning that communicates product attributes and benefits, differentiating each brand from the other company.

Price/Quality Positioning: A strategy whereby products and services are positioned as offering the best value for the money.

Use or Applications Positioning: The process of marketing a precise product application that differentiates it in consumers' minds from other products that have a more general use.

Product User Positioning: A positioning strategy that focuses on the product user, rather than on the product.

Product Class Positioning: A strategy used to differentiate a company as a leader in a product category as defined by the respective companies.

Competitor Positioning: The process of comparing the firm's brand, directly or indirectly, with those of competitors.

6-4a: Attribute/Benefit Positioning

Procter & Gamble focuses on product attributes and benefits to position many of its brands within a single product category. An **attribute/benefit positioning** strategy uses product or service attributes and benefits to position it in the consumers' mind relative to competitors' brands. The following are examples of product positioning by Procter & Gamble (www.pg.com):

• Cheer, in powder or liquid, with or without bleach, is positioned as protecting against fading, color transfer, and fabric wear.

• Dreft is positioned as a detergent that removes tough baby stains and protects garment colors.

Part Two: Foundations of Marketing

• Gain, as a liquid and powder detergent, is positioned as having exceptional cleaning and whitening abilities.

• Procter & Gamble's premium product, Tide, in powder or liquid, with or without bleach, is positioned as a laundry detergent with exceptional cleaning, whitening, and stain removal abilities.

Such precise positioning, which is reflected in the company's communication with its respective segments, clearly differentiates each brand from the other company brands and from those of competitors such as Unilever and Colgate-Palmolive.

6-4b: Price/Quality Positioning

The **price/quality positioning** strategy positions goods and services in terms of price and quality. Manufacturers such as Toyota, Daewoo, and Philips, as well as retailers such as Wal-Mart and Sears, emphasize the value aspect of their offerings. Alternatively, goods and services can be positioned at the other end of the price/ quality continuum, as the best product that money can buy. In addition to stressing high quality, such positioning also entails an exclusive distribution or access, an expert sales force and service, and advertising in publications aimed at an upscale market. Mercedes-Benz claims that, in a perfect world, everyone would drive a Mercedes. Kempinski Hotels and Resorts, an upscale German chain, reflect "the finest traditions of European hospitality," is synonymous with distinctive luxury, and "style, nobility, and efficiency."[20]

6-4c: Use or Applications Positioning

How a product is used or the various applications of a product are often used to position products in the **use or applications positioning** strategy. Procter & Gamble's Era is positioned as a high-technology detergent that pretreats and washes fabrics to suspend dirt. This very precise application differentiates it in consumers' minds from other laundry detergents that have a more general use.

Sometimes, the uses or applications differ from one market to another. A bicycle manufacturer would most likely position its offerings in Asia and Europe as efficient transportation, whereas in the United States, it would position them as high-performance recreation.

Figure 6-12: Skeeter Performance Fishing Boats uses a product user positioning strategy with this advertisement directed to bass anglers.
Source: Courtesy of Newcomer, Morris & Young.

6-4d: Product User Positioning

The **product user positioning** strategy focuses on the product user, rather than on the product. The marketing mix for Jeep is targeted at the individual who wants to go places where trucks and cars do not have access. All product descriptions and advertising emphasize this aspect. Jeep itself has the aspect of an all-terrain vehicle. GE Monogram appliances are aimed at those who have a Hatteras yacht, Barcelona chairs, and Noguchi tables. Phoenix Wealth Management is positioned to appeal to the woman who gives her broker investment ideas, who is taking her company public, or who earns more than her CEO husband. The Skeeter boat in Figure 6-12 is positioned as the best boat for bass anglers.

6-4e: Product Class Positioning

Pizza Hut has used the approach saying it is the best dine-in pizza establishment. It wants to be in the dine-in pizza product class, not the delivery business. Products using a **product class positioning** strategy differentiate themselves as leaders in a product category, as they define it. Milk, for most people, is considered a breakfast drink. For others, milk is consumed with cookies by children after school. To increase sales, the milk industry wants to reposition its product to be consumed at any time of the day, for any reason. Thus it does not want consumers to put milk in the breakfast drink category; the milk industry wants milk to be a beverage (see Figure 6-13). The danger, of course, of such a strategy is that now milk must compete with soft drinks, coffee, tea, and other drinks, instead of breakfast drinks like orange juice.

Figure 6-13: To boost sales, the milk industry would like consumers to consider milk a beverage that can be consumed anytime, rather than just at breakfast.

6-4f: Competitor Positioning

When a firm compares its brand with those of competitors, it uses a **competitor positioning** strategy. Some comparisons are direct. Others are subtle. When Airbus asks readers of *The Financial Times* if they would be more comfortable with two or four engines when they are up in the air, it makes an implicit reference to Boeing, which has only two engines.

All positioning, ultimately, is relative to competition, only not always explicitly so. Even symbols hint at competition: Merrill Lynch is bullish on the market (it is portrayed by the bull); all other competitors are probably wimps. *The New York Times'* celebrated slogan coined in 1897, "All the news that's fit to print," ultimately states that, if it is not published there, it is not newsworthy. Similarly, Bata shoes' tag line is 'we know shoes' – all about feet, all about shoes, having delivered high-quality hand-crafted footwear for over 100 years (see Figure 6-14).

Figure 6-14:

Bata Shoes claims that they know shoes and have delivered high-quality hand-crafted footwear for over 100 years – something that few manufacturers can claim. This is a screenshot from their website:

www.betashoes.com

6-4g: Positioning Maps

Positioning is all about perception—it is in the consumer's mind and is the consumer's perception of a brand relative to the competition. Brands can be mapped on a positioning map based on their attributes, allowing them to be compared relative to other brands with which they are competing. According to Trout and Ries, a company should ask the following questions:[21]

1. What place does a product occupy in most consumers' minds?
2. What place does the company want to occupy?
3. What competitors does the company have to defeat to occupy the position it desires?
4. Does the company have the resources to attain this position?
5. Can the company persist until it gets there?
6. Are the company's tactics supporting its positioning objectives?

Let us assume two attributes, price and strength of automobiles, where strength is defined as a tank-like safety quality, which offers the consumers the comfort (justified or not) that they will survive any collision. We are using only two attributes because they are easier to map than multiple attributes. However, marketers use three-dimensional maps routinely to position their brands. The two attributes, price and strength (or safety), will be mapped on the x and y axes, respectively, as shown in Figure 6-15.

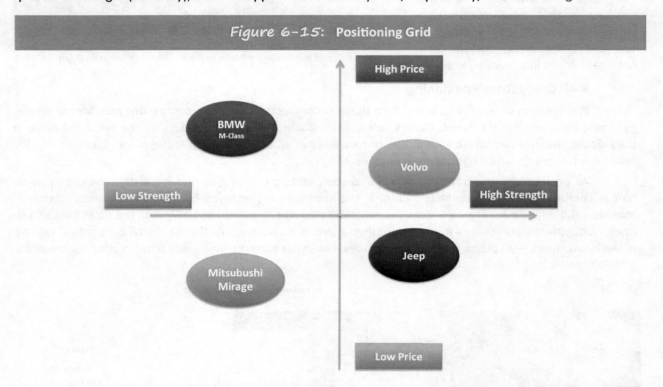

Figure 6-15: Positioning Grid

We have four quadrants. Volvo occupies a position in the high-price/high-strength quadrant. This position was achieved with extensive advertising over decades of Volvo attempting to convince buyers of the strength of its automobile. Jeep lies in the lower-price/high-strength quadrant. It is sturdy but more affordable than the Volvo. The BMW M-Models are very expensive and smaller automobiles, which, with their soft-top, can be easily flattened by a collision with just about any sports utility vehicle. It occupies the low- strength/high-price quadrant. The Dodge Neon is cheap but also not sturdy, therefore, it occupies the low-price/low-strength quadrant.

An automobile manufacturer can use this map in many ways, to determine its position on this positioning map or on another map with different attributes. It can also use the map to determine where, in the consumers' minds, it should position its new models. By mapping all competing brands on the price-strength dimensions, the company can identify gaps that are not addressed by competitors and offer a new model that fits in the respective position. Alternatively, if the company determines that the automobile is in an undesirable quadrant, from the consumer's point of view, it can advertise itself as occupying a different position—as long as that position is plausible. For example, the Dodge Neon probably wants to maintain its position as low price; however, assuming that buyers want a higher-strength position, it can communicate (advertise) its performance in collisions, assuming that the respective record supports a higher-strength position.

Summary

1. Identify the rationale for adopting a target marketing strategy. Target marketing is used to identify segments of consumers who are similar with regard to key traits, who would respond to a particular marketing mix (i.e., to segment the market); to select the segments that the company can serve most efficiently and develop products tailored to each (i.e., to target the market); and to offer the products to the market, communicating through the marketing mix (i.e., positioning) the product traits and benefits that differentiate the product in consumers' minds.

2. Identify the bases for consumer segmentation and offer company application examples. Consumers are segmented based on the following variables: demographics, which are statistics that describe the population, such as age, gender, ethnicity, education, income, and occupation; psychographics, which refer to values, attitudes, interests, and other cultural variables used to segment consumers; geographic location; and behavior. Behavior segmentation is composed of using variables such as usage rate and user status, loyalty status, and the benefits sought from purchasing the product or service. Business segments are based on some of the same criteria, with some adaptation. For example, demographic variables for businesses may consist of company size and industry sector. In addition, other behavioral variables could be used in the case of businesses. Examples are relationship-seeking segments, which consist of relatively sophisticated service users who believe that the user-provider relationship is important but have realistic expectations for the service requirements and do not expect to pay a low price; price-sensitive segments, which consist of businesses that are looking for low prices but also have low service requirements; high-expectation service segments, which are the most demanding, need extensive customer focus, and place considerable demands on service providers while demanding low prices; and customer-focus needs segments, which are prepared to pay for higher-than-average service that is tailored to meet these users' needs.

3. Identify the requirements necessary for effective market segmentation. For segmentation to be effective, segments must be easy to measure, stable over time, accessible via marketing communication and distribution, actionable through marketing strategies, and able to respond differentially from other segments to a company's marketing strategy.

4. Describe the three targeting strategies that companies use. These strategies are differentiated marketing, whereby companies address the needs of different segments by offering them different brands and using different marketing mix strategies; concentrated marketing, whereby companies address a single consumer segment that is large and stable enough to warrant the investment; and undifferentiated marketing, whereby a company can reap the benefits of standardization by using the same strategy to market to all consumers.

5. Describe the six positioning strategies that companies can use to position their brands in the minds of target consumers. Companies can position products by focusing on product attributes or benefits; by positioning the brand as a high-price/high-quality product or as the best value for the money; by positioning the brand based on use or applications; by positioning the brand based on traits of product use or by positioning it as the best product in its class.

Key Terms

accessibility	high-expectation service segment	relationship-seeking segment
actionability	loyalty segmentation	segment marketing
attribute/benefit positioning	mass marketing	segmentation
benefit segmentation	measurability	stability
buyer-readiness stage segmentation	micromarketing	substantiality
competitor positioning	multiattribute segmentation	target market
concentrated marketing	occasion segmentation	target marketing
customer-focus needs segment	price/quality positioning	undifferentiated marketing
demographic segmentation	price-sensitive segment	usage rate segmentation
differential response	product class positioning	use or applications positioning
differentiated marketing	product user positioning	user status segmentation
geographic segmentation	psychographic segmentation	

Discussion Questions

1. Demographics and psychographics are often used in the process of conducting multiattribute segmentation. You have been hired by a new gardening magazine to identify the different market segments that the magazine could target. Conduct your segmentation analysis by identifying various segments of gardeners. Describe them in terms of demographics, psychographics, and behaviors.

2. Look at Table 6-1. Identify the Internet segment that fits you. Discuss your usage situations and favorite materials. How closely does it fit the information provided in the table? Identify the Internet segment of one sibling, your parents, and your closest friend. Discuss their usage situations and favorite materials as well.

3. Identify five products that you believe are segmented on the basis of gender. Identify what your think is the top brand in each product category. Explain why you think it is the top brand. Discuss how the brand is marketed to your gender.

4. Describe the different bases for behavioral segmentation. What are some of the relevant behavioral market segments for individuals who use a fitness center or gym? Describe a segmentation strategy a fitness center could use based on benefit segmentation, usage rate segmentation, user status segmentation and occasion segmentation.

5. Marketing managers use a number of criteria to ensure effective segmentation. Assume that you are working for a manufacturer of children's haircare products. What are the criteria that you would use for effective segmentation?

6. Look at Table 6-2, VALS Psychographic Categories. Which VALS category would you fit into? Why? How accurate are the characteristics listed in terms of your personal characteristics. Identify two close friends or relatives. Identify their VALS category and discuss each of their characteristics.

7. Go to ESRI's Web page at **www.esribis.com** and enter the following zip codes: 23220, 90210, 10022, and 23229. Type in your zip code. What makes of automobiles would sell well in these target markets? Explain. What other product categories should be targeted to these markets?

8. What are the six positioning strategies? What strategies does Mercedes USA use for its U.S. market? Does Mercedes use different strategies for its international markets? (Go to the other English-language Mercedes sites to answer this question.)

9. For each of the positioning strategies discussed in Section 6-4, identify a brand that uses the respective strategy. Explain your choice.

10. Write down the names of the restaurants that are close to your college or where you live. Create a position grid using price and quality as the two dimensions. Place each restaurant on the grid. Discuss why the restaurants are placed where they are. Would the map be different if someone else drew it? Why or why not?

Review Questions

(Answers are on Last Page of the Chapter)

True or False

1. Market segmentation is defined as identifying the segments of consumers who are similar with regard to key characteristics and who would respond well to a product and related marketing mix.

2. The purpose of segmentation is to identify all consumers' needs and develop a specific marketing strategy for each segment.

3. User status segmentation is defined as the process of segmenting the markets based on the extent to which consumers are nonusers, occasional users, medium users, or heavy users of a product.

4. Multivariable segmentation is based on benefits sought and usage status.

5. Measurability for successful segmentation is defined as the degree to which an individual market segment is easy to identify and measure or the ability to evaluate the market segment's size.

6. Stability, as a basis for successful segmentation, is defined as the degree to which the segments are large enough to warrant the investment.

7. Companies that use a differentiated strategy identify or even create market segments that want different benefits from a product and target them with different brands.

8. A company that pursues a small market segment—a niche—is engaging in differentiation.

9. A company that offers a brand that is positioned as an advanced formula detergent that can suspend dirt engages in product user positioning.

Multiple Choice

10. Which of the following categories relate to selecting segments that the company can serve most efficiently and developing a product mix tailored to each segment?
        a. Market segmentation
        b. Market targeting
        c. Market positioning
        d. All of the above

11. Demographic segmentation includes which of the following categories?
        a. Motivation
        b. User status
        c. Income
        d. None of the above

12. Companies that attempt to provide skin treatment products for baby boomers are engaged in which of the following types of segmentation strategies?
        a. Behavior segmentation
        b. Multiattribute segmentation
        c. Segmenting business markets
        d. Demographic segmentation

13. Two popular classification systems based on zip codes are PRIZM and Community™ Tapestry™. They aid in _____ segmentation.
        a. Behavior
        b. Geographic
        c. Multivariable
        d. Occasion

14. In segmenting business markets, the relationship-seeking segments are characterized as
        a. Seeking low prices and accepting low service levels.
        b. Understanding the trade-off between service levels and price.
        c. Demanding low prices but extensive customer service.
        d. Accepting higher prices to address their own specific needs.

15. Which strategy would offer the best value for the money spent on goods and services?
        a. Price/quality positioning
        b. Use or application positioning
        c. Product user positioning
        d. Competitor positioning

Blog

Clow-Lascu *Marketing: Essentials 5e Blog*

Screenshot of YouTube Video highlighted in Clow-Lascu *Marketing: Essentials 5e Blog.*

What Is Happening Today?

Learn More! For videos and articles that relate to Chapter 6:

blogclowlascu.net/category/chapter06

Includes Discussion Questions with each Post!

Notes

1. www.facebook.com
2. Frederic Lardinoid, "Snapchat Wins the Fastest Rising Startup at the 2012 Crunchies," Accessed at http://techcrunch.com/2013/01/31/snapchat-wins-fastest-rising-startup-at-the-2012-crunchies/ on June 14, 2014.
3. Alison Stein Wellner, "Culinary Feat," *American Demographics* 23, no. 3 (March 2001): S16.
4. Jack Neff, "P&G Chief: We Need a New Model—Now," *Advertising Age* 75, no. 46 (November 15, 2004): 1–2.
5. Michael R. Pearce, "Succeeding with Micromarketing," *Ivey Business Quarterly* 62, no. 1 (1997): 69–72.
6. Joyce M. Wolburg and James Pokrywczynski, "A Psychographic Analysis of Generation Y College Students," *Journal of Advertising Research* 41, no. 5 (September/October 2001): 33–52.
7. Peter Francese, "Older and Wealthier," *American Demographics* 24, no. 10 (November 2002): 40–41.
8. Thomas J. Ryan, "Just Do It for Women," *SGB* 39, no. 3 (March 2006): 25–26.
9. Mercedes M. Cardona, "Segment Marketing Grows as Tool for Financial Services Leaders," *Advertising Age* 71, no. 48 (November 20, 2000): S1, S11.
10. Debbie Howell, "Targeting Ethnicity," *Chain Store Age* 82, no. 2 (March 2006): 58–59.
11. Sharon Begley, "Researchers Delve into the Darker Side of Scary-Ride Junkies," *The Wall Street Journal* (May 31, 2002): B1.
12. Christopher Munsey, "Frisky, But More Risky," *Monitor on Psychology* 37, no. 7 (July-August 2006): 40.
13. Bob Sperber, "Taco Bell Builds beyond Border Bowls," *Brandweek* 43, no. 40 (November 4, 2002): 6.
14. Mark Dolliver, " . . . .Which Helps Explain Why There Are So Many Eateries Around the U.S.," *Adweek* 47, no 30 (August 7–14, 2006): 22.
15. Rebekah Bennett and Sharyn Rundle-Thiele, "A Comparison of Attitudinal Loyalty Measurement Approaches," *Journal of Brand Management* 9, no. 3 (January 2002): 193–209.
16. Bill Merrilees, Rohan Bentley, and Ross Cameron, "Business Service Market Segmentation," *Journal of Business and Industrial Marketing* 14, no. 2 (1999): 151–164.
17. www.pg.com, accessed July 21, 2014.
18. Adapted from David A. Aaker and Gary J. Shansby, "Positioning Your Product," *Business Horizons* 25, no. 3 (May/June 1982): 56–62.
19. Ibid.
20. See www.kempinski.com.
21. Jack Trout and Al Ries, *Positioning: The Battle for Your Mind* (New York: McGraw- Hill, 2000).

Cases

Case 6-1 The World—Vegas Style

Before 1990, the word elegance was never used in the same sentence as Las Vegas. The dominant traits of an earlier Las Vegas were excess and tackiness, not elegance. Vegas was about ogling long-legged cocktail waitresses in Daisy-Duke tights, eating thick steaks, drinking scotch, and wearing gaudy fashions.

In an attempt to outgrow its tacky past and create fantasy excursions to faraway places, Las Vegas has created an opulent international oasis in the desert. Evocative of Italy, the $1.8 billion, 3,000-room Bellagio Hotel opened in October 1999; followed by the $950 million, 3,700-room Mandalay Bay, recreating the South Seas; the Venetian, with 6,000 rooms at a cost of $1.3 billion; the $760 million, 2,900-room Paris–Las Vegas; and a 2,600-room Arabian-themed Aladdin. In 2007, the venerable Stardust Hotel and Casino was demolished with great pomp to make way for a new $4 billion, 5,300-room mixed-use complex called Echelon, built by Boyd Gaming Inc. Las Vegas visitors today can choose between a gondola ride through an indoor canal ($12), a trip to the top of the Eiffel Tower ($8), or an expensive dinner at the Wolfgang Puck eateries, which make Vegas one of the best restaurant cities in the United States. Inspired by the Bellagio Hotel's shows O (Cirque du Soleil) and Mystère, the new Paris hotel has put on its own French musical, Notre Dame de Paris.

A unique city in the middle of the desert, Las Vegas draws numerous visitors attracted to gambling opportunities, conferences, entertainment, and the Strip's new hotels (see Figure 6-16). Las Vegas does not share its visitors with any other attraction: They are captivated and captured by gambling, attending shows, and shopping within the environment. It is a marketer's dream that resort mogul Steve Wynn would like to capture yet again, through Winn Las Vegas, inspired by a Picasso painting he owns. This is a $2.8 billion resort, 50 story, 2,716-room hotel with an 18-hole golf course, an art gallery with Mr. Wynn's collection, 19 restaurants, and a Ferrari-Maserati dealership.

Figure 6-16 Las Vegas at night.

So far, the Wynn Las Vegas is the most expensive resort ever built in Las Vegas, topping the $1.8 billion Bellagio, another Wynn property. Built on the site of the old Desert Inn at the north end of the Strip, Wynn Las Vegas is comparable in size to Bellagio, featuring an 111,000-square-foot casino with 2,000 slot machines and 136 table games, and a water-based entertainment complex.

Who is the target market for these grandiose plans? Most likely, the yuppies who are expected to take their morning stroll in Bellagio's botanical garden, splendid with blooms. These are the consumers who marvel at original paintings in the hotel's art museum, who dine in French restaurants, and who buy gowns they will wear proudly to a black-tie fund-raiser in Middle America.

Questions

1. Describe the different visitor market segments that Las Vegas appeals to. Use demographic, psychographic, behavioral, and geographic bases for segmentation in creating your descriptions.

2. What are the target markets of the new international hotels in Las Vegas? Go to the Bellagio Hotel and Casino web site at www.bellagio.com to find out more information about the hotel's target market.

3. What types of targeting strategies are these international hotels using? Be specific explaining your reasoning.

4. What is the positioning strategy that the Winn Las Vegas hotel is using to attract its visitors? Justify your answer.

Sources: Tony Illia, "Vegas Readies Itself for Yet Another Boom," *ENR* 253, no. 21 (November 29, 2004): 17; Richard Corliss, "Spotlight on . . . Las Vegas," *Time* 155, no. 7 (February 21, 2000): 132; Andrew Baby, "Just a Dream?" *Barron's* 82, no. 41 (October 14, 2002): 29; www.1st100.com; Steve Friess, "Stardust Hotel-Casino Is Demolished," *New York Times* (March 13, 2007): 1; Laura Landro, "Weekend Journal; Vegas's Class Wars: As Giant Wynn Hotel Tries to Rise Above the Glitz, We Put It to the Test, *Wall Street Journal* (February 17, 2007) W1.

Case 6-2 Dressing the Consumers Who Give Back: BeGood Clothing

Mark Spera and Dean Ramadan were roommates during their junior and senior years at the University of Richmond. After graduation, both started in traditional corporate jobs, but were quickly disappointed that the companies that hired them were only focused on making money, without examining the social implications of what they were doing, without giving back to society or to the environment. Inspired by a book by Patagonia's founder, Yvon Chouinard, "Let My People Go Surfing," they founded BeGood Clothing in August 2012, and after an enthusiastic customer response, they opened a store in San Francisco. According to Spera, "local customers said they had been waiting for a store like BeGood Clothing to open."

The store's mission is to "open customers' eyes to alternate ways to spend money", and, as such, almost all the brands that they carry have their own giveback programs. These are brands such as "Toms Shoes, which gives a pair of shoes to a child in need for every pair bought, and Patagonia, which gives one percent of total revenue to eco-causes," according to Spera. For each item purchased from BeGood Clothing, the company donates to a local charity and to fundraisers of local charities. Customers also get a 10% discount if they bring used clothes for donating to Goodwill to the store. BeGood Clothing is able to offer very high quality clothing at reasonable prices by selling only through their website or through their San Francisco store.

Consumers respond well to the company's marketing strategy. When accessing the company Web site, you have to register and receive in return an email that states the following: "Working at a huge San Francisco retailer left us craving radical innovation. We couldn't accept being plagued by doing as we've always done. So we set out to change retail by creating clothing that is timeless in profile, outrageously affordable and unprecedented in its organic quality."

Shoppers are giving this retailer high marks: "I started browsing through the jewelry when I finally discovered that everything in the store gives back to either the environment or a humanitarian cause!! If I wasn't already impressed with the clothing selection, I had yet another reason to shop! Honestly, it's very cool that this store provides such fashionable items when I'm assuming that they're limited to very few brands. I will definitely return and bring friends! BeGood redefines the notion of 'shopping for a cause!'"

Questions

1. Discuss the consumer who is likely to purchase clothing at BeGood Clothing. What bases of segmentation can be used for this market? Justify your segmentation bases.

2. What are the desirable benefits that BeGood Clothing provides to consumers? Be specific.

3. How does BeGood Clothing differentiate itself from competitors such as the Gap?

4. Who would be the primary competitors of BeGood. Draw a perceptual map of BeGood Clothing and the competition you identified. Use environmental concern (high, low) and quality (high, low) for your map

5. Identify the brand positioning strategy being used by BeGood. Justify your choice.

Sources: Rebecca Wilson, "Richmond alumni start charitable clothing retailer, The Collegian, February 26, 2013, available at http://thecollegianur.com/2013/02/26/; https://begoodclothes.com, accessed on July 21, 2014; company email, received on July 21, 2014; Yelp.com review, March 7, 2013, accessed at http://www.yelp.com/biz/begood-clothing-san-francisco-2, July 21, 2014.

Answers to Review Questions

Answers: 1) True, 2) False, 3) False, 4) False, 5) True, 6) False, 7) True, 8) False, 9) False, 10) b, 11) c, 12) d, 13) c, 14) b, 15) a

Chapter 7

Marketing Research

Learning Objectives

After studying this chapter, you should be able to:

1. Define marketing research, provide a description of its scope, and offer examples of each type of research conducted in marketing.

2. Describe the steps involved in the marketing research process.

3. Introduce the concept of decision support systems for marketing and describe the sales forecasting process.

7-1 CHAPTER OVERVIEW

Marketing requires a thorough understanding of the product's target market and its ever-shifting preferences. Marketers must continually monitor the market and its preferences through systematic marketing research. With all its success, Google could rest on its laurels and reap high profits from its ever-evolving search engine. However, in its ongoing quest to understand consumers and to meet their needs, the company has developed a revolutionary product: Google Glass, named by Time Magazine as one of the best inventions of 2012. Google Glass is in fact a computer with a head-mounted optical display, a hands-free, quick-to-use alternative to a smartphone.[1] It was released in 2014 at just under $1,500.[2] The company partnered with the Italian eyewear company Luxottica, owners of many eyewear global brands, such as Ray-Ban, to offer different frame designs.[3] There are still concerns with privacy, with 70% of individuals polled showing concern with hackers accessing personal data, including location information,[4] but the product is predicted to become a success once these concerns are addressed.

Successfully marketing innovative products like Google Glass requires a thorough understanding of the product's target market. Numerous marketing plans fail as a result of an incomplete understanding of the market, and, if privacy fears prevail in the end, this could be the end of the phenomenal Google Glass.

Critical to Google in this endeavor is marketing research. This chapter defines marketing research in Section 7-2 and examines its broad scope within marketing across all components of the marketing mix (product, place, price, and promotion) in Section 7-3. Section 7-4 addresses the marketing research process and the different steps involved in defining the research problem, developing a research plan, collecting information, conducting primary research, and interpreting the results. Section 7-5 addresses the decision support systems used in marketing and how they can help marketers forecast sales.

7-2 DEFINING MARKETING RESEARCH

Marketers need to constantly monitor the different forces affecting their operations and the products they sell. Marketing information, which should constitute a basis for all executive action, must be taken into consideration to improve the chances of success in a complex marketing environment. An important caveat is that such information needs to be carefully evaluated and viewed in light of the purpose for which it was collected. Complex environmental factors complicate the task of marketing researchers, who should have not only an expertise in the most advanced techniques of scientific inquiry but also a profound understanding of the markets under investigation.

As readily seen in the Google Glass situation, not all products perform as predicted in the marketplace. Google could not have anticipated that individuals' concern with privacy would constitute a greater deterrent to purchase than the product's initial price of almost $1,500.

> **Marketing Research:**
> The systematic design, collection, recording, analysis, interpretation, and reporting of information pertinent to a particular marketing decision facing a company.

Research does not provide all the answers, but it does provide solid information that marketing managers can use to make intelligent decisions. **Marketing research** involves the systematic design, collection, recording, analysis, interpretation, and reporting of information pertinent to a particular marketing decision facing a company.

7-3 THE SCOPE OF MARKETING RESEARCH

Marketing research addresses both broad and specific issues that are relevant to the company and its operations. It ranges from monitoring developments in the marketing environment—or general **marketing intelligence**—to anticipating a product's performance in the marketplace, to evaluating consumers' specific brand-related or advertisement-related attitudes. Figure 7-1 highlights the scope of marketing research and the components of marketing research that will be examined in this section.[5]

> **Marketing Intelligence:** Results obtained from monitoring developments in the firm's environment.

Figure 7-1: The Scope and Components of Marketing Research

Research of Industry, Market Characteristics, and Market Trends

Buyer Behavior Research

Product Research

Distribution Research

Promotion Research

Pricing Research

7-3a: Research of Industry, Market Characteristics, and Market Trends

Studies of industry trends, market characteristics, and market trends are conducted regularly by marketing research suppliers, such as Nielsen, and shared with subscribers. In one study Nielsen found that consumers are too tired to clean and prepare dinner. Nielsen examined data regarding convenience-oriented product categories and found that, indeed, semiprepared food and products that offer cleaning convenience are among the top industry sellers.[6]

Why would such data and information be valuable? First, understanding industry and market characteristics and trends will tell a firm what products should be produced and how those products should be marketed. For instance, Nielsen's research indicated that firms producing cleaning products should produce products that offer consumers cleaning convenience. The research also indicated that firms should use convenience-oriented advertisements to promote the products. A company like Pillsbury can focus advertisements on how easy it is to make its brand of muffins.

7-3b: Buyer Behavior Research

Buyer behavior research examines consumer brand preferences and brand attitudes. Nielsen found that high-income consumers in search of a deal purchase their products at warehouse clubs and discount stores such as Target. Affluent shop-

> **Buyer Behavior Research:** Research examining consumer brand preferences, brand attitudes, and brand-related behavior.

pers are described by Nielsen as concerned with product freshness: They make 56 percent more trips to the supermarket in search of fresh produce.[7]

The study found that, while those making over $100,000 a year shop at all the mainstream retailers, they are more than twice as likely to frequent a mass merchandiser compared with households earning $20,000 or less.[8] Interestingly, Wal-Mart is clearly a favorite retail outlet for higher-income consumers (see Table 7-1).

Table 7-1: Household Purchases and Retailer Patronage: Percentage of Households Served		
Percentage of U.S. Household Penetration by Household Income		
Retail Channel	**Household Income**	
Traditional Channels	<$20,000	$100,000 +
Grocery	99	100
Drug	82	84
Mass Merchandiser	79	86
Dollar Store	80	46
Supercenter	63	52
Convenience/Gas	47	33
Warehouse Club	31	70

Source: Nielsen, "Affluent consumers want and use broad range of shopping choices," available at www.factfiguresfuture.com, March 2007.

Brand Awareness Research: Research investigating how consumers' knowledge and recognition of a brand name affects their purchasing behavior.

Consumer Segmentation Studies: Research conducted to identify market segment profiles.

In developing strong brands, brand-name recognition and awareness are important. A component of buyer behavior research, called **brand awareness research**, investigates how consumers' knowledge and recognition of a brand name affects their purchasing behavior. Such studies are often conducted by companies to assess the position of their brands in the marketplace relative to the competition. For instance, the International Research Institute on Social Change launched a study of luxury goods in the United States. A total of 3,000 respondents were interviewed in person at home and were asked about their familiarity, at least by name, with a set of 34 luxury brands. They were asked the following question: "Here is a list of luxury brands. Please indicate which ones you know at least by name." The researchers found that, in the United States, global brands of crystal and fine china, such as Daum, Christofle, and Bvlgari, were relatively unknown. Consequently, consumers were less likely to indicate an intention to purchase these brands.[9] Because of this low brand awareness, Daum, Christofle, and Bvlgari realized that if they were going to be successful in the United States, they would first have to launch an advertising campaign to build brand awareness. Only then would consumers consider purchasing the brands.

Other useful studies that belong to this category are **consumer segmentation studies**, which are conducted to identify profiles of different consumers that the company could target. Marketing researchers often attempt to identify those segments composed of consumers who are heavy product users. KitchenAid commissioned a battery of ethnographic studies, which found that consumers were not interested in the appliance for the appliance's sake. They were interested in what the appliance could do for them and how it could help them prepare delicious food and be able to entertain friends and family. To confirm and quantify these results, KitchenAid commissioned a segmentation study that found that the company should

focus on "the culinary-involved," a segment of consumers who were heavy users of kitchen appliances and who believed in using the best products for their homes. These "wannabe chefs" are passionate about cooking, and, most important to KitchenAid, the segment cuts across all demographic groups. It is not confined to upper-income households. As a result of the consumer segmentation study, KitchenAid's advertising agency created an advertising campaign featuring a picture of lemon souffle´ pancakes drizzled in lemon sauce and topped with raspberries. Beneath the picture were images of the large and small appliances that helped to prepare the dish. Six months after the campaign was launched, sales for both the KitchenAid countertop and major appliances were showing double-digit growth.[10] The segmentation study provided the right information about who purchased KitchenAid products and what type of advertising approach would appeal to them.

Faced with stagnating sales, the milk industry conducted research to see how much milk girls drank and how much they should drink. Using this information, the Bozell Agency developed an advertisement campaign to encourage girls to drink milk so their bodies would have the correct amount of calcium. Similarly, research has shown that children who include 100% fruit juice in their diet have higher quality diets (see Figure 7-2), and the juice industry is using this information to increase consumption.

7-3c Product Research

Most product research is directed to new product development. A brief overview will be given in this section, but a more thorough discussion is found in Chapter 8. Typical product research includes:

- Concept development
- Competitive product studies
- Brand-name generation
- Product packaging design
- Product testing
- Test marketing

Figure 7-2: The orange juice industry, which recently has found itself under attack from certain health critics, is fighting back using social media.

Concept development research studies evaluate the viability of a new product and the composition of the other marketing mix elements in light of the product's intended target market. Activities research includes investigating the feasibility of a new product idea through generating a concept statement, determining technical feasibility for the concept, testing the concept with customers, and defining the product and target market. In the U.S. consumer packaged-goods industry, it is estimated that a company spends at least $20 million to introduce a new product and that about 80 percent of the products fail.[11] With such a high cost to develop new products and such a high failure rate, it is essential that companies test the product concept before they ever start investing money into actual product development.

Brand-name generation involves the development and testing of brand names and logos. These studies are used not only by companies manufacturing consumer goods, where their importance is obvious, but also by industrial marketing companies and agricultural goods companies. For example, when American Cyanamid Company created a new herbicide-tolerant crop production system, it used a research firm that started out with 600 possible names and then narrowed the list to 30, which were then tested for linguistic appropriateness. After the company decided on the Clearfield brand, it tested the brand for six different crops (see Figure 7-3). Testing showed the Clearfield name and logo to be meaningful, credible, appropriate, memorable, and likable.[12]

The annals of marketing are replete with examples illustrating the importance of testing a global brand name in all the countries where the product is to be sold. Rolls-Royce planned on marketing its Silver Mist model in German-speaking countries,

> **Concept Development Research:** Concept tests that evaluate the product or service offering and the related marketing mix in light of the different target markets.
>
> **Brand-Name Generation:** The testing of brand names and logos.

Figure 7-3: When American Cyanamid Company created a new herbicide-tolerant crop production system, the company used brand-name studies to narrow the 600 possible names down to the one that was chosen — Clearfield.

Product Testing: Studies that estimate product preference and performance in a given market.

Competitive Product Studies: Studies that help in determining the overall product strategy for the product, the price that the market will bear for the respective product category, and the promotion that is appropriate in light of the competition.

Product Packaging Design: Studies that evaluate consumers' reaction to a package, the extent to which the package adequately communicates information to the consumer, and the distribution implications of the package.

Test Marketing: Evaluating product performance in select markets that are representative of the target market before launching the product.

Channel Performance and Coverage Studies: Studies investigating whether existing channels are appropriate for the marketing task at hand.

only to find out before the launch that "mist" means "dung" in German.[13] Sunbeam Corporation, however, entered the German market without testing the name of its product, Mist-Stick, before introduction.[14] As you would expect, the product did not do well. **Product testing** estimates product performance and preference in a given market, whereas **competitive product studies** are helpful in determining the overall product strategy for the product, the price that the market will bear for the respective product category, and the promotion that is appropriate in light of the competition. **Product packaging design** studies help firms determine consumers' reactions to various package designs, the extent to which the package adequately communicates information to the consumer, and the distribution implications of packaging decisions.

After a product has been developed, many companies will use **test markets** to fine-tune the marketing approach that will be used and to make modifications in the product itself. Test marketing involves testing new product performance in a limited area of a target market to estimate product performance in the overall market. In the late 1990s, Procter & Gamble test-marketed Swiffer, a new disposable mop. Based on sales in the test markets, they decided to launch the Swiffer mop in all of the company's major markets.[15]

More recently, after conducting additional product research using focus groups, Procter & Gamble introduced the Swiffer Sweep+Vac, a small, battery-operated vacuum cleaner with a Swiffer mop attached. They found that people would go on their hands and knees to wipe up the pile of dirt that was left behind after mopping with a dry Swiffer cloth. But the new product was then quickly recalled because it presented a potential fire hazard.[16] Perhaps the company focused too much on what consumers wanted, rather than on product performance.

7-3d Distribution Research

Examples of distribution research are **channel performance and coverage studies**, which investigate whether existing channels are appropriate for the marketing task at hand. Channel performance and coverage studies are usually the first steps that the company undertakes in the process of channel design. The analysis involves identifying the threats, opportunities, strengths, and weaknesses that will influence channel performance and viability. Research should evaluate competitors' share of existing channels, the relative profitability of each channel, the coverage of the market served, and the cost of each channel function. Research should also evaluate likely changes in buying patterns, potential competitive entrants, long-run cost pressures, and new technologies, such as the Internet or multimedia retail kiosks. Research should assess what customers are seeking from the various channels by asking the following questions:

• What service attributes do the target customers value?

• How can we use the differences in preferences to segment customers with similar needs?

• How well do the available channels meet the needs of each market segment?[17]

To evaluate the appropriateness of plant or warehouse locations to the needs of a company, a **plant/warehouse location study** can be used. Such research evaluates variables such as the cost of transportation, real estate, labor costs, the availability of power sources, and tax rates. Also important in the analysis is the proximity to the customer. Although it may seem like a minor detail, plants and warehouses located in the wrong places can add considerable costs to the price of a product and create a situation in which a company cannot compete effectively. A major reason Wal-Mart has been so successful is its understanding of distribution costs and the need to minimize the costs through optimal locations of its distribution systems.

7-3e: Promotion Research

Promotion research evaluates, among other factors, the extent to which the company effectively communicates with the market, the extent to which certain promotional strategies are appropriate for a particular market, and the extent to which the media used are appropriate for the intended message.

Studies of premiums, coupons, and deals determine the appropriateness and effectiveness of these types of promotions for a given target market. For example, Promotions Decisions Inc., a Cincinnati-based research firm, uses the Coupon Prophet Model to compare coupon redeemers and nonredeemers using detailed consumer information gained from frequent shopper data. The company then analyzes prior purchase behavior to identify those segments that responded well to couponing strategies.[18]

Increasingly, coupons are delivered via e-mail and cell-phone text messages. Cellfire, a downloadable application that provides coupons from retailers in the user's area, allows the user to scroll through offers, select, and show the coupon to the cashier. The program automatically deletes used coupons. Studies of couponing have shown redemption rates of 15 to 23 percent, with strong brands being the most successful, compared with 1.2 percent for coupons distributed via free-standing inserts. Cellfire's research has shown strong demand across demographic groups, with a skew toward the younger consumer. Among advantages of Cellfire are that the company can monitor Cellfire offer usage as well as calculate the reaction time for the redemption.[19]

Advertising effectiveness research is frequently conducted to examine the effectiveness and appropriateness of advertisements aimed at individual markets. Advertising effectiveness can be evaluated by measuring viewers' recall of an advertisement, their attitude toward the ad, and the extent to which the ad persuaded the consumer to purchase the sponsor's product. Figure 7-4 exemplifies the outcome of consumer demand. The owner of these drugs, a middle-aged woman who closely follows advertising, asked her doctors, after an accident, for every imaginable pain pill in common advertisements—and had most of them prescribed.

Media research is an important component of promotional research. Identifying the media that best fit with the company's target market and the company's advertising needs ensures that advertising dollars are well spent. It is critical that the product's target market match the viewing audience of the   media being used. Nielsen Media Research is an important research provider in this category. It uses the National People Meter service to provide audience estimates for all national program sources, including broadcast networks, cable networks, Spanish-language networks, and national syndicators. It also provides local Nielsen ratings for television stations, regional cable networks, and Spanish-language stations in each of the 210 television markets it serves.

Other promotion-related research studies may address personal selling activities. Examples

> **Plant/Warehouse Location Study:**
> A study that evaluates the appropriateness of plant or warehouse location to ensure that it is in accordance with the needs of the company.
>
> **Studies of Premiums, Coupons, and Deals:**
> Studies that determine the appropriateness and effectiveness of premiums, coupons, and deals for a given target market.
>
> **Advertising Effectiveness Research:**
> Studies conducted to examine the effectiveness and appropriateness of advertisements aimed at individual markets.
>
> **Media Research:**
> Studies that evaluate media availability and the appropriateness of the medium for a company's message.

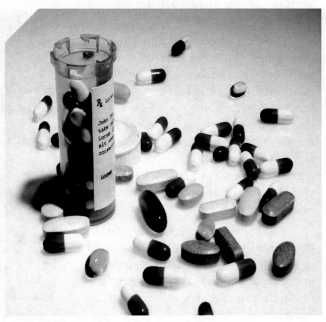

Figure 7-4: Prescription drugs are often readily prescribed.

of such studies are **sales force compensation, quota, and territory studies**, which are crucial in helping to determine the appropriate sales and incentive strategies for certain markets. Sales force studies will also determine the performance of salespeople by territory, which will guide sales managers in placing salespeople in territories and redeploying salespeople to territories that may have greater potential.

7-3f: Pricing Research

There are numerous examples of pricing research. Pricing is a key determinant in research studies attempting to project demand, such as market potential studies, sales potential studies, and sales forecasts. Pricing research is also an important determinant in **cost analyses, profit analyses, price elasticity studies**, and **competitive pricing analyses.**

Today, product quality is important, but the dealmaker is often the price tag. A decade ago, consumers were attracted by store atmosphere, the assortment of brand names, and customer service. To buy a brand name, one had to shop in a department store, and that alone carried cachet—to be a discount shopper meant being lumped with the proletariat. Today, research reveals that the once-mysterious ways of merchandising have been reduced to a single element: price. According to Marshal Cohen, co-president of NPD Fashionworld, a company tracking retail sales, you could be at a dinner party on Fifth Avenue and millionaires will be talking about what deals they were able to get at Wal-Mart.[20] Much of the recent pricing research confirms that shoppers' economic status does not determine where they shop; they just do not want to pay a lot for that muffler, sweater, or digital camera.[21]

On the other hand, pricing research has persuaded companies to introduce downmarket versions of their upmarket brand. For example, Procter & Gamble has introduced a low-rent cousin, Charmin Basic, which is almost as squeezably soft as the original, and Bounty Basic, which is equally basic and not as fancily packaged as the original. Research has determined that consumers are more deal prone these days, as a result of the high gas prices, the proliferation of high-quality store brands, and the Wal-Marts, Costcos and other big-box retailers enabling consumers to pay generic prices by buying brand names in bulk. Pricing research has also shown that attitudes have changed, and even well-off consumers flaunt their bargain-hunting abilities.[22]

Pricing research can help companies find the optimal price that will help meet a company's pricing objectives—even when it comes to canned fruits and vegetables (see Figure 7-5). Understanding pricing is essential for marketers. Consumers' need for a deal and price competition must be aligned with businesses' need to make a profit and with all of their other marketing mix strategies.

Figure 7-6 reviews examples of the various types of research discussed in this section. It also highlights the operational and managerial uses of the research and the strategic use of the information.

Figure 7-5 Pricing research helps determine the optimal price that will meet the company's pricing objective — even for products such as guitars!

Sales Force Compensation, Quota, and Territory Studies: Different studies pertaining to personal selling activities; they are crucial in helping to determine the appropriate sales and incentive strategies for certain markets.

Market Potential Studies: Studies conducted to evaluate the potential of a particular market.

Sales Potential Studies: Studies forecasting optimal sales performance.

Sales Forecasts: Projected sales for a particular territory.

Cost Analyses: Methods used for projecting the cost of research.

Profit Analyses: Studies that estimate product profit in specific markets.

Price Elasticity Studies: Studies examining the extent to which a particular market is price sensitive.

Competitive Pricing Analyses: Pricing studies that determine the price the market will bear for the respective product category based on a survey of competitors' prices.

Figure 7-6: Summary of Marketing Research

Marketing Research	Operational Resources	Managerial Uses	Strategic Uses
Research of Industry, Market Characteristics, and Market Trends	Evaluate industry and market trends.	Modify product attributes and promotion to meet changes in the industry and market.	Ensure that the company is producing the product desired by the consumer.
Buyer Behavior Research	Understand why, how, and when consumers purchase the product.	Modify the promotional approach to ensure that the message matches the needs and interests of the target market.	Ensure that the product is being promoted to correct target market in the correct manner.
Product Research	Review current product features.	Assess new product features.	Use computerized design to devise new products.
Distribution Research	Monitor supply-demand imbalances.	Manage supply-demand imbalances.	Strengthen distribution channels.
Promotion Research	Evaluate effectiveness of promotions such as advertising, and consumer and trade promotions.	Adjust promotional methods and media outlets to ensure that the target market is being reached.	Ensure that the product is being correctly promoted.
Pricing Research	Measure consistency and accuracy.	Adjust prices to reflect elasticity.	Ensure long-run competitiveness.

7-4 THE MARKETING RESEARCH PROCESS

The marketing research process follows the steps outlined in Figure 7-7. The first step in the process is to define the issue or problem faced. The second step is to examine secondary data for relevant information. If the problem cannot be solved with secondary data, then a primary research study needs to be conducted. This is the third step. The fourth step involves analyzing the data, making recommendations, and implementing the findings of the research.

Marketing research can be done with in-house staff or through a marketing research firm. Using an in-house staff reduces the cost of the research, and staff members normally have a better understanding of the problem being researched and how it needs to be done. However, they are likely to lack the marketing research expertise that an outside vendor would have. It is because of this expertise that most companies look to outside vendors, especially for major research projects.

7-4a: Problem Definition

The first step in the marketing research process requires that marketing managers and marketing researchers define the research problem and jointly agree on the research objectives. It is possible that the

Figure 7-7: Summary of Marketing Research

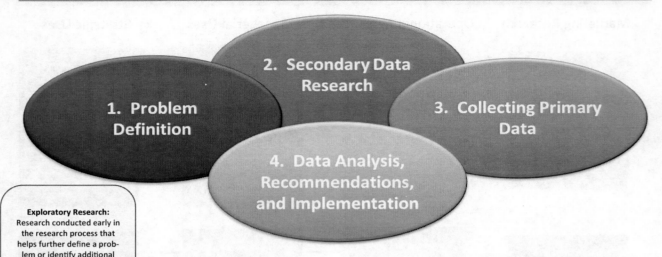

Exploratory Research:
Research conducted early in
the research process that
helps further define a problem or identify additional
problems that need to be
investigated.

Research Approach:
The method used to collect
data.

Descriptive Research:
All research methods observing or describing phenomena.

**Causal (Experimental)
Research:**
Research that examines
cause-and-effect
relationships.

Secondary Data:
Data collected to address a
problem other than the
problem at hand.

Internal Secondary Data:
Data previously collected by a
company to address a
problem not related to the
current research question.

External Secondary Data:
Data collected by an entity
not affiliated with
the company.

marketing manager does not have a clear idea of the research problem that needs to be investigated. For the situation previously described for Google Glass, a key problem that warrants further investigation is why prospective consumers entertain such strong privacy fears for this product. How can the company alleviate this fear?

To help in defining a marketing problem, researchers often conduct **exploratory research**, which is research conducted early in the research process to assist researchers in defining a problem or identifying additional problems that need to be investigated.

In understanding the issue to be examined, researchers will also discuss the **research approach** that will provide the best answer. Marketers have two approaches that can be used: descriptive research and causal (experimental) research. **Descriptive research** involves observing or describing a phenomenon. For example, the study might involve collecting information about consumer privacy fears when wearing Google Glass, and how those privacy concerns differ from similar concerns regarding smartphones. A descriptive study should also assess tangential issues, such as attitudes toward the price for the product. **Causal (experimental) research**, however, examines cause-and-effect relationships. For Google Glass, a casual research study could test consumers' reactions to different advertising messages designed to alleviate privacy intrusion concerns.

7-4b: Secondary Data Research

Researchers first must determine whether any information is available on the topic being researched. Researchers should start by examining secondary data, which are data collected to address a problem other than the problem currently facing the company. **Secondary data** offer the advantage of low cost and ready availability; data collection also takes less time and effort. The data that may be most relevant to the researcher's study, however, will most likely not exist, or if they do, they may be dated or unreliable.

There are two categories of secondary data. **Internal secondary data** are collected by the company to address a different problem or collected by the company to address the same problem, but in a different environment or for a different brand. Prior research reports on the company's other brands, sales figures for different territories, and inventory reports are types of secondary data. For Google Glass, especially useful are internal data sources that Google might have regarding the consumer concern for privacy for its other products.

External secondary data are defined as data collected by an entity not affiliated with the company.

Table 7-2: External Secondary Data

General Interest and Business Publications
American Demographics
Business Horizons
Business Week
Forbes
Fortune
Harvard Business Review
Newsweek
Time
U.S. News & World Report

Trade Publications
Advertising Age
Adweek
Brand Marketing
Brandweek
Catalog Age
Chain Store Age
Discount Store News
Marketing
Marketing Management
Marketing News
Marketing Research
Mediaweek
Sales & Marketing Management
Stores
Target Marketing

Academic Marketing Journals
Journal of Advertising
Journal of Business Research
Journal of Consumer Research
Journal of Consumer Marketing
Journal of Consumer Psychology
Journal of Macromarketing
Journal of Marketing
Journal of Marketing and Public Policy

Journal of Marketing Research
Journal of Retailing
Journal of Services Marketing
Marketing Science
Psychology & Marketing

Marketing Organizations
Academy of Business
Academy of Marketing Science
Advertising Research Foundation
American Academy of Advertising
American Marketing Association
American Psychological Association
Association for Consumer Research
Center for Service Marketing
Chartered Institute of Marketing
Direct Marketing Association
Institute for the Study of Business Markets
Interactive Marketing Institute
Marketing Research Association
Marketing Science Institute
Medical Marketing Association
Sales & Marketing Executives Association
Society for Marketing Advances

Government Sources
Advance Monthly Sales for Retail and Food Services
Annual Retail Trade Survey
Annual Survey of Manufacturers
Census of Wholesale Trade
Current Industrial Reports
Monthly Retail Sales & Inventories
STAT-USA/Internet
Statistical Abstract of the United States
U.S. Census Bureau

Table 7-2 lists a number of reliable sources for data that companies might use in the early stages of their research. Local libraries have readily available general interest and business publications. Most university libraries that have a business school are likely to carry the trade publications and marketing journals listed. Many of the government sources listed in Table 7-2 are readily available online. The marketing organizations listed can also provide access to relevant data at a reasonable fee.

For its research on privacy concerns and effectiveness of privacy appeals, Google might consult a number of marketing articles published in *The Journal of Marketing* over the years.

Valuable secondary data can be provided by marketing research firms, such as Nielsen, which offer extensive information to subscribers on different markets, products, and topics. Table 7-3 lists the top 10 U.S. research firms in terms of sales revenue.

Table 7-3: Top U.S. Market Research Operations

U.S. Rank 2012	U.S. Rank 2011	Organization	Headquarters	Website	U.S. Research Revenue ** ($ in millions)	% Change From 2011 ***	WW Research Revenue** ($ in millions)	Non-U.S. Research Revenue** ($ in millions)	% Non-U.S. Revenue	U.S. Full-Time Employees
1	1	Nielsen Holdings N.V.	New York	Nielsen.com	$2,651.0	4.0%	$5,429.0	$2,778.0	51.2%	10,486
2	2	Kantar*	London & Fairfield, Conn.	Kantar.com	929.4	-4.8	3,338.6	2,409.2	72.2	3,930
3	3	Ipsos	New York	Ipsos-NA.com	590.0	-5.5	2,300.0	1,710.0	74.3	1,996
4	4	Westat Inc.	Rockville, Md.	Westat.com	491.1	-3.1	495.9	4.8	1.0	2,019
5	5	Information Resources Inc. (IRI)	Chicago	IRIworldwide.com	478.7	2.9	763.8	285.1	37.3	1,325
6	6	Arbitron Inc.	Columbia, Md.	Arbitron.com	444.1	6.7	449.9	5.8	1.3	982
7	7	GfK USA	Nuremberg, Germany	GfK.com	330.9	0.5	1,946.9	1,616.0	83.0	1,131
8	8	IMS Health Inc.	Norwalk, Conn.	IMSHealth.com	271.3	-4.0	775.0	503.7	65.0	540
9	9	The NPD Group Inc.	Port Washington, N.Y.	NPD.com	191.8	1.5	272.0	80.2	29.5	875
10	10	ICF International Inc.	Fairfax, Va.	ICFI.com	191.2	7.5	239.7	48.5	20.2	1,152

Source: Jack Honomichl, "The 2013 Honomichl Top 50 Report," accessed at https://www.morpace.com/Honomichl-Top-50-Chart.pdf on June 1, 2014.

An examination of Nielsen will provide an excellent example of the many marketing research services available to a company. These services are listed in Table 7-4. One service, Consumer*Facts, could be useful to Google Glass in an assessment of the demographic profile of its target market. Consumer*Facts offers information on household purchase behavior and demographic profiles on an all-outlet basis. The service provides category and brand details for more than 1,000 product categories (dollar sales, dollar share, number of buying households, percent household penetration, buying rate, and purchase frequency). The most valuable information to Google Glass might be the insights that the research company can provide into demographic trends of the digital consumer.[23]

Quality secondary data will help companies further refine problems and objectives and, if necessary, even redefine them. But even the highest-quality secondary data alone usually do not provide an answer to a specific research problem. Effectively addressing a research problem often requires the collection of primary data. The process of collecting primary data is examined in the next section.

Table 7-4: External Secondary Data
ACNielsen AdEx International
Account Shopper Profiler
Intended User Survey
Cross Outlet Facts
Fresh Foods Consumer Panel
Fresh Foods Syndicated Reports
Consumer*Facts
Channel Facts
Panel*Views
Promotion Planner
Strategic Planner
Super SCANTRACK
SPINS Natural Track
Syndicated Trade Marketing Services
Chain-Level Trading Areas
Store-Level Trading Areas
Consumer Marketplace Report
A.C. Nielsen Convenience Track
A.C. Nielsen Homescan
Homescan Basket*Facts
Homescan New Product*Facts
Market*Track International Panorama
Retail Account Reports
SCANTRACK Services
SCANTRACK Ethnic Services
A.C. Nielsen SCANTRACK In Store Conditions Service
SCANTRACK Key Account Causal

Source: www.nielsen.com

7-4c: Collecting Primary Data

Most marketing research projects involve the collection of **primary data**, which is information collected for a specific purpose: to address the problem at hand. Collecting primary data requires substantial expertise in both instrument design and administration and, as a consequence, it is expensive and time-consuming. Collecting quality primary data requires a concerted effort on the part of marketing managers and researchers to identify the appropriate research approaches, **data collection instruments**, sampling plans, and **contact methods** that are capable of providing primary data of high **reliability** and **validity** that best address the research problem and research objectives.

The Research Methodology

When collecting primary data, researchers can use two different methods: qualitative research or quantitative research. **Qualitative research** typically involves a small number of respondents answering open-ended questions. Results are usually subjective because the researcher must interpret what respondents are saying. Alternatively, qualitative research could also involve observation that is not systematically structured but rather open to a subjective analysis. **Quantitative research**, however, is a more structured approach involving responses that can be summarized or analyzed with numbers. Descriptive and causal research approaches discussed in Section 7-4a would use a quantitative research methodology, whereas exploratory research would typically use the qualitative methodology. It is interesting to note that, in certain countries such as France and Italy, there is a preference for qualitative data as a complement to quantitative data, whereas in others such as Germany, the United States, and Scandinavian countries, quantitative data are deemed as more valuable.

Qualitative research has been particularly useful either as a first step in studying marketing phenomena—when conducting exploratory research—or as one of

Primary Data: Data collected for the purpose of addressing the problem at hand.

Data Collection Instruments: The instruments used to collect data, such as a questionnaire, a paper-and-pencil measure, or an electronic measurement device.

Contact Methods: Methods used for approaching study respondents.

Reliability: The ability of the service firm to perform the service provided in a dependable and accurate manner [service]; the extent to which data are likely to be free from random error and yield consistent results [scale].

Validity: The extent to which data collected are free from bias.

Qualitative Research: Research that involves a small number of respondents answering open-ended questions.

Quantitative Research: A structured type of research that involves either descriptive research approaches, such as survey research, or causal research approaches, such as experiments in which responses can be summarized or analyzed with numbers.

the methods of exploring the problem at hand using multiple methods. Among the more popular qualitative research approaches are focus group interviews, depth interviews, and observation.

Focus group interviews typically involve six to 12 participants recruited to meet some previously decided characteristics—for instance, ethnic background, certain age groups, social class, and use of certain products—and a moderator who guides the discussion based on a certain discussion agenda. Frequently, representatives of the sponsor observe the group's deliberations through a one-way mirror or on closed-circuit television. A video camera or tape recorder may also be used to record the group's deliberations on a certain topic of interest to the sponsor. The participants are typically given a small financial reward or products, such as free product samples or food, for participating in the study.

Another approach that is helpful for collecting qualitative data is the **depth interview**. Depth interviews are one-on-one attempts to discover consumer motivations, feelings, and attitudes toward an issue of concern to the sponsor, using a loose and unstructured question guide. They are typically used if the issue under study is a complex behavioral or decision-making consideration or an emotionally laden issue. Professional interviewers are typically well trained in keeping the respondent focused on the problem addressed and in handling complex interviewing situations. In addition to guiding respondents to address the problem investigated, interviewers can demonstrate the product and its features, and further probe into issues that are relevant to the research.

Depth interviews can take place in person—these are referred to as personal interviews. There are cheaper alternatives to personal interviews: For instance, computer-assisted telephone interviewing (CATI) is a telephone data collection method whereby the interviewer sits in front of a computer terminal, reads the questions on the screen, and promptly enters the answers.

Using interviewers to conduct research is very expensive and more time consuming than other research methods; however, the data they collect are normally more robust because interviewers can further address issues that come up during the interview. Consequently, the method offers insights that quantitative research approaches cannot provide.

Observational research (or observation) is a particularly useful research approach for gathering qualitative data. It is defined as a research approach in which subjects are observed interacting with a product and reacting to other components of the marketing mix and the environment. Numerous approaches are used in observational research. One method, known as **naturalistic inquiry**, is an observational research approach that requires the use of natural rather than contrived settings because behaviors take substantial meaning from their context.[24] The researcher is directly involved in the data collection as a participant in the group whose verbal and nonverbal behaviors are observed. The analysis performed by the researcher is inductive, rather than deductive; that is, unlike in conventional research methods, the researcher

does not rely on previous theory in the process of developing hypotheses, but rather develops theories from the data. **Ethnography**—the study of cultures—is largely based on naturalistic inquiry. Both academic researchers and practitioners have used this approach to better understand consumers and consumer motivations. This technique is frequently used by researchers who attempt to increase the validity of their studies by acquiring an intimate knowledge of a culture's daily life through personal observation.[25]

Quantitative research methods are structured research approaches involving either descriptive research, such as observation, survey research, and content analysis, or causal research approaches,

---

Focus Group Interviews:
A qualitative research approach investigating a research question, using a moderator to guide discussion within a group of subjects recruited to meet certain characteristics.

Depth Interviews:
A qualitative research method involving extensive interviews aimed at discovering consumer motivations, feelings, and attitudes toward an issue of concern to the sponsor, using unstructured interrogation.

Observational Research (or Observation):
A research approach whereby subjects are observed interacting with a product and reacting to other components of the marketing mix and the environment.

Naturalistic Inquiry:
An observational research approach that requires the use of natural rather than contrived settings because behaviors take substantial meaning from their context.

Ethnography:
The study of cultures.

Quantitative Research:
A structured type of research that involves either descriptive research approaches, such as survey research, or causal research approaches, such as experiments in which responses can be summarized or analyzed with numbers.

such as experiments. Observation, previously noted as a type of qualitative research, can also be quantitative when the subjects are systematically observed interacting with a product and reacting to other components of the marketing mix and the environment. An example of a quantitative observational method is the study of garbage (garbology). Garbology studies could examine if consumers' reported diet matches the packages identified in their garbage bins.

Physiological instruments can also be used as an observation method to measure a respondent's involuntary responses to stimuli. An instrument called a pupillometric meter can be used to measure eye movements and the dilation of a person's pupil. Another instrument, the psychogalvanometer, attached to a respondent's fingers, can measure an individual's perspiration level. These instruments are often used in advertising research to measure the physiological reaction to particular ads. Some researchers see these instruments as more accurate than verbal or written responses in which a respondent may give researchers the socially acceptable answer. For instance, in measuring the impact of nudity in an ad, respondents may indicate on a paper-and-pencil test that they do not notice the nudity in an ad any more than an ad with a fully-clothed model, whereas a physiological test may indicate otherwise. Physiological instruments are good for evaluating an individual's level of arousal to ads and other marketing material. They are also good for packaging research—not only to measure physiological reaction but also to track eye movement across the package. Such research helps marketers identify whether people are paying attention to the ad and if they are focusing on the brand name and logo.

Content analysis is a quantitative methodology that entails counting the number of times preselected words, themes, symbols, or pictures appear in a given medium, such as a print advertisement, or any medium with verbal or visual content. One area in which content analysis is used extensively in an attempt to discover emerging themes and patterns is advertising research. Here is an example of a content analysis study that a company could conduct.

Please look at each advertisement and indicate to what extent you believe the ad appears to have the following characteristics *by circling the corresponding number,* as follows using the following 1 to 5 scale:

1 = if the ad **DOES NOT AT ALL HAVE** the respective characteristic;
2 = if the ad **DOES NOT HAVE** the respective characteristic;
3 = if you are **NOT SURE** if the ad has the respective characteristic;
4 = if the ad **HAS** the respective characteristic;
5 = if the ad **DEFINITELY HAS** the respective characteristic.

The ad appears to be:			
Interesting	5 4 3 2 1	Stressing safety	5 4 3 2 1
Funny	5 4 3 2 1	Stressing excitement	5 4 3 2 1
Seductive	5 4 3 2 1	Stressing adventure	5 4 3 2 1
Joyful	5 4 3 2 1		
Scary	5 4 3 2 1	**Now, please fill in the following information:**	
Colorful	5 4 3 2 1	The ad features _____ people.	
Dull	5 4 3 2 1		
Spartan	5 4 3 2 1	The age of the Google Glass owner is approximately _____ years.	
Stressing practicality	5 4 3 2 1		

> **Content Analysis:**
> Method that assesses the content of advertisements in a medium with verbal or visual content.
>
> **Survey Research:**
> Descriptive research that involves the administration of personal, telephone, or mail questionnaires.

Survey research, another example of widely used descriptive research, typically involves the administration of structured questionnaires in a personal interview, by telephone, the Internet, e-mail, or by mail. The use of the questionnaires assumes that respondents are both capable and willing to respond to the questions. A relatively low-cost survey method is mail questionnaires; however, this method has a high nonresponse rate. Many mail surveys are discarded, even if they come from establishments that consumers patronize. The most expensive survey method is the personal interview—a method that provides valuable data. Such an interview would be highly structured, compared with the depth interview discussed in the qualitative research approach section. However, even a structured personal interview allows the interviewer to probe into issues that the respondent may raise or to answer questions, thus providing valuable additional information to the researcher.

Causal (experimental) research looks at cause-and-effect relationships, eliminating or controlling for other extraneous factors that may be responsible for the results and eliminating competing explanations for the observed findings. It requires the use of matched groups of subjects who are subjected to different treatments, to ascertain whether the observed response differences are statistically significant.

Although difficult to do, causal research provides marketers with reliable data. Figure 7-8 summarizes the various research methods that can be used in collecting primary data.

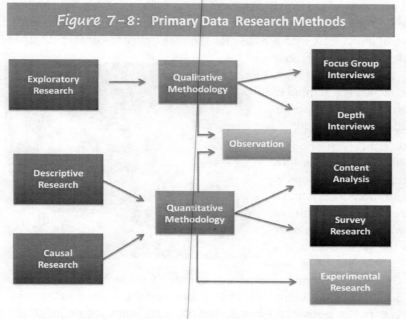

Figure 7–8: Primary Data Research Methods

Data Collection Instruments

Although electronic measurement devices are used to collect data, most data are collected using some type of questionnaire with either paper-and-pencil forms or a computer. In developing a questionnaire, researchers must come up with an appropriate format that will accurately collect the data. The questionnaire could use **open-ended questions**, which allow respondents to use their own words in responding to the questions. Alternatively or in addition, the questionnaire could use forced-choice questions, which include the possible responses of which respondents must select one. Examples of the latter are the **semantic differential scale**, a scale anchored by words with opposite meanings (good . . . bad, important . . . not important), and the Likert scale, anchored by "strongly disagree" and "strongly agree" statements. Clear instructions would help respondents in filling out the questionnaire appropriately.

A semantic differential questionnaire is illustrated in Figure 7-9. Notice that in this case, the respondent is asked to evaluate a particular flat screen television brand along 12 criteria. The respondent is also asked to evaluate the leading competitor and the ideal rating for a flat screen television. Charting all three measures on one graph allows researchers to determine how well their brand compares to the leading competitor and the ideal brand.

> **Open-ended Questions:**
> Questions with free-format responses that the respondent can address as he or she sees appropriate.
>
> **Semantic Differential Scale:**
> Scale that is anchored by words with opposite meanings.

Sampling Plan

The sampling plan calls for the marketing manager and researcher to jointly decide on the **sample**, that is, a segment of the population selected for the study and considered representative of the total population of interest.

Among sampling decisions are the selection of the **sampling unit**—determining who will be included in the survey. Should the researcher interview anybody in the household, including children? Should the researcher interview only the driver? Should the sample include people from all over the United States or just certain regions? Should the sample include individuals from other countries?

Figure 7–9: A Semantic Differential for a Flat Screen T.V.

Please mark the blanks that best indicate your feelings about Brand A, your feelings about Brand B, and your ideal rating for a 27" flat screen television.

Expensive		Inexpensive
Innovative		Conservative
Low quality		High quality
Disreputable		Reputable
Unattractive console		Attractive console
High status		Low status
Well-known		Unknown
Excellent picture		Poor picture
Poor value for money		Good value for money
Like other brands		Unique
Reliable		Unreliable
Unavailable		Readily available

Legend: A = brand of the company
B = leading competitor
I = ideal rating for a brand by respondent

Sample:
A segment of the population selected for the study and considered to be representative of the total population of interest.

Sampling Unit:
The individuals or groups included in the study.

Sample Size:
The number of study participants.

Sampling Procedure:
The procedure used in the selection of sampling units.

Random Probability Sample:
A sample in which each individual selected for the study has a known and equal chance of being included in the study.

Convenience Sample:
Sample composed of individuals who are easy to contact for the researcher.

Judgment Sample:
A sample of individuals thought to be representative of the population.

Sampling Frame:
The list from which sampling units are selected.

Researchers must also decide on the **sample size**—determining how many individuals will be surveyed. Ideally, a larger sample should be chosen to ensure that accurate results are obtained. The **sampling procedure**—determining how the sampling units will be selected—is also important. The most representative sample of a particular population is a **random probability sample**, in which each individual selected for the study has a known and equal chance of being selected. A less representative but easier method of selecting a sample would be to use a **convenience sample**, which is composed of individuals who are easy for the researcher to contact. Another

sampling method that does not pose much effort for the researcher is a **judgment sample**, which is a sample of individuals thought to be representative of the population being studied.

The most critical criterion in selecting a sampling technique is how well the sample represents the population under consideration. The population could be students at a university or all consumers who own a mobile phone. Although the ideal is to use a random probability sample, it is not always practical. Obtaining a random probability sample of students at a university may be possible, but it would not work for mobile phone owners. As long as the sample selected represents the population being studied, a convenience or judgment sample is adequate.

The last decision researchers must make, in terms of sampling, is the **sampling frame**—the list from which sampling units are selected. Examples of sampling frames are mailing lists or telephone books. **Figure 7-10** reviews the sampling decisions that must be made.

Collecting Data

Data can be collected using the various contact methods, such as mail, e-mail, Internet, telephone, and personal interview. **Table 7-5** addresses the advantages and disadvantages of each type of contact method. For decades, the traditional forms of data collection have been mail, telephone, and personal interviews. E-mail and online surveys are very popular today.

The best method for a research study is a function of researcher needs, the size of the sample desired for the study, the amount of data needed, and other considerations. For a very large sample, using a mail and e-mail questionnaire is appropriate. If a large amount of

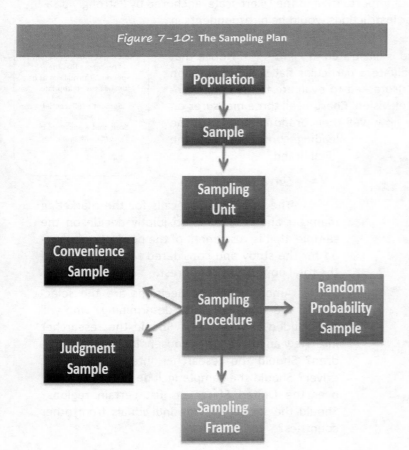

Figure 7-10: **The Sampling Plan**

Population
↓
Sample
↓
Sampling Unit
↓
Convenience Sample ← Sampling Procedure → Random Probability Sample
Judgment Sample ←
↓
Sampling Frame

data needs to be collected, then a mail questionnaire would be the best contact method. Alternatively, if researchers want to further probe into a particular response, personal interviews offer more flexibility. A higher response rate is obtained with a personal or a telephone interview than with other methods.

After the instrument is designed and the sample is selected, the researcher or research team is ready to collect the primary data. This expensive undertaking can be eventful. The data collectors need to be briefed appropriately. Researchers must decide how **nonresponse**—defined as the inability or refusal by a respondent to participate in a study—should be handled. In some instances, it makes sense to go back and identify the traits of the respondents who refused to participate to compare them with those of respondents who participated to be sure the sample who responded is the same as those who did not respond. For mail surveys, the nonresponse rate can be high, at 90 percent or even more. So for valid research, it is essential that individuals who participated in a study represent the population being studied and are not different from individuals who did not participate.

Table 7-5: Advantages and Disadvantages of Different Contact Methods

Method	Advantages	Disadvantages
Mail	Inexpensive No interviewer effects Large amounts of data Reasonable sample control	Slow Low response rates Lack of flexibility
E-mail	Inexpensive No interviewer effects Reasonable amount of data Fast Reasonable sample control	Low response rates Lack of flexibility
Internet	Inexpensive No interviewer effects Reasonable amount of data Fast	Low response rates Not much flexibility Poor sample control
Telephone	Reasonable cost Few interviewer effects Reasonably fast Reasonable response rates Reasonable sample control	Lower amounts of data Higher cost
Personal and Focus Group Interviews	High flexibility High response rate Large amounts of data Reasonably fast High sample control Personal and focus	Expensive Large interviewer effects

Nonresponse: The inability or refusal by a respondent to participate in a study.

7-4d Data Analysis, Recommendations, and Implementation

Data collected should be coded, entered into the analysis program, and analyzed. Researchers will tabulate the results and put them in a form that is meaningful and that will answer the problems introduced in the beginning of the research process. To understand these last three steps in the research process, study Figure 7-11.

Figure 7-11: Data Analysis, Recommendations, and Implementation of Findings for a Study on Coffee.

1. Do you drink coffee?	☐ Yes	01	300
	☐ No	02	200
2. In general, how frequently do you drink coffee? (Check only one answer.)	☐ Two or more times per day	03	142
	☐ Once per day	04	84
	☐ Several times per week	05	42
	☐ Once or twice per week	06	20
	☐ One to three times per month	07	12
	☐ Never	08	200
3. During what time of day do you drink coffee? (Check all answers that apply.)	☐ Morning	09	270
	☐ Lunchtime	10	165
	☐ Afternoon	11	100
	☐ Dinnertime	12	150
	☐ Evening	13	205
	☐ None	14	200

Coding: Questionnaires numbered A001 to A500. Each response is labeled 01 to 14 (e.g., Morning is 09, Evening is 13.) Question 3 is a multiple-response question.

Tabulation: Total responses are shown above right.

Analysis: Sixty percent drink coffee. About 28 percent drink coffee two or more times daily (representing 47 percent of all coffee drinkers); almost 25 percent of coffee drinkers (74 people) consume coffee less than once per day. Ninety percent of coffee drinkers consume coffee in the morning; only one-third consume it in the afternoon.

Recommendations: The coffee industry and individual firms need to increase the advertising geared toward noncoffee drinkers, as well as infrequent coffee drinkers. Emphasis should also be placed on lifting coffee consumption during afternoon hours.

Implementation: New, more aggressive advertising campaigns will be developed, and the annual media budgets devoted to increasing overall coffee consumption will be expanded. One theme will stress coffee's value as an afternoon pick-me-upper.

Notice in the first step of the analysis that 500 questionnaires were collected and that each questionnaire was numbered from A001 to A500. Each response was then coded and tabulated. The results of the tabulations appear on the right portion in the left panel Figure 7-11. Notice that out of the 500 respondents, 300 drink coffee, and 270 drink coffee in the morning. The right panel in Figure 7-11 presents some of the analysis of the data. For instance, because 500 respondents took the survey and 300 said they drink coffee, we can say that 60 percent of the respondents drink coffee. Notice that 142 said they drink coffee two or more times per day. Because we know that 300 drink coffee, we can say that 47 percent of coffee drinkers consume coffee two or more times per day (142 divided by 300). Likewise, we can say that 90 percent of the coffee drinkers consume coffee in the morning. (Supermarkets offer an extensive array of coffee choices to meet consumers' coffee-drinking needs— see Figure 7-12.)

Figure 7-12: Research can help businesses like Starbucks determine the
appropriate coffee flavors for their coffee-drinking shoppers.

Based on this research and the analysis, a possible recommendation could be that the coffee industry and individual firms need to increase the advertising geared toward noncoffee drinkers because 40 percent of the sample does not drink coffee. For those who drink coffee, advertising could focus on drinking coffee in the afternoon, the period with the lowest consumption.

Implementation of the findings might include a more aggressive advertising campaign that is aimed at noncoffee drinkers. This would require an increase in the media budget and could also require an additional study to see what media outlets would be the best for reaching noncoffee drinkers. For the current coffee drinkers, to stimulate additional consumption, the theme that coffee is "an afternoon pick-me-upper" could be used.

7-5 MARKETING DECISION SUPPORT SYSTEMS

Marketing decision support systems (MDSS) are defined as a coordinated collection of data, systems, tools, and techniques, complemented by supporting software and hardware designed for the gathering and interpretation of business and environmental data.[26] Ideally, a marketing decision support system should be:[27]

- Computerized—Having a computerized support system is now possible even for small and medium-sized businesses because of the increase in the capability of personal computers to perform more and more complex tasks.

- Interactive—Managers can use online instructions to generate on-the-spot reports, without assistance from a programmer, who will be involved only in system updating and training.

- Flexible—Managers can access and integrate data from a variety of sources and manipulate the data in a variety of ways (e.g., producing averages and totals, sorting the data).

- Discovery-oriented—Such systems should produce diagnostics that reveal trends and identify problems.

A number of areas lend themselves well to MDSSs. A common use is that of sales forecasting. The more complex the techniques used in forecasting sales, the more their efficiency can be improved in an MDSS environment. Nevertheless, input obtained from using the simpler methods (sales force composite estimates, jury of executive opinion, and the Delphi method) can be used to cross-validate the estimates given by the more sophisticated forecasting techniques (time series and econometric models).

Forecasts from **sales force composite estimates** are based on the personal observations and "hunches" of the sales force. Salespeople are in close contact with the consumer; therefore they are in the best position to find out about consumer desires and overall changing market trends. Forecasts from the **jury of expert opinion** are based on the opinions of different experts about future demand. The experts' opinions are then combined, and an aggregate demand estimation is offered. Another method, the **Delphi method**, entails asking a number of experts to estimate market performance, aggregate the results, and share this information with these experts. This process is repeated several times until a consensus is reached.

Among the more sophisticated forecasting techniques are time series methods, which use data of past performance to predict future market demand. Typically, these methods give more weight to more recent developments. They assume that the future will be similar to the past. Econometric methods, however, take into account different deterministic factors that affect market demand—factors that may or may not depend on past performance trends. **Time series and econometric methods** are dependent on the availability of historical data. For markets where historical data are unavailable, such as developing countries, it is appropriate to estimate demand by analogy, noting responses of markets with similar relevant characteristics, markets with similar levels of economic development, markets with similar cultural characteristics, and so on.

The **analogy method** is an estimation method that relies on developments and findings in markets that are relatively similar. For example, to estimate the anticipated adoption rate of cellular phones in Latvia, it may be appropriate to identify the proportion of new adopters in a more advanced country in the Baltics—Estonia, which is more developed—where cellular phone service is widely available, but which shares a similar history and similar geopolitics with Latvia. This would be a country performance analogy. However, to estimate the adoption rate of Internet service in Sri Lanka, it may be appropriate to evaluate the adoption rate of computers in Sri Lanka. This is would be a product performance analogy.

Important forecasting methods for retailers and other channel members involve **point-of-sale (POS)-based projections**, which are performed with the help of store scanners, such as those used in super markets (Figure 7-13). Research suppliers increasingly use store scanners to assess market share and other relevant market dimensions. Weekly or biweekly store audits reveal the movement of goods within the store and from warehouses.

Marketing Decision Support Systems (MDSS):
A coordinated collection of data, systems, tools, and techniques, complemented by supporting software and hardware designed for the gathering and interpretation of business and environmental data.

Sales Force Composite Estimates:
Research studies in which sales forecasts are based on the personal observations and forecasts of the local sales force.

Jury of Expert Opinion:
An approach to sales forecasting based on the opinions of different experts.

Delphi Method:
A method of forecasting sales that involves asking a number of experts to estimate market performance, aggregating the results, and then sharing this information with the said experts; the process is repeated several times, until a consensus is reached.

Time Series and Econometric Methods:
Methods that use the data of past performance to predict future market demand.

Analogy Method:
A method for estimation that relies on developments and findings in similar markets or where the product is in the same life cycle stage.

Point-of-Sale (POS)-Based Projections:
Market projections based on the use of store scanners in weekly and bi-weekly store audits.

Chapter 7: Marketing Research

Figure 7-13: Researchers use scanners to assess market share, as well as to track current sales of products.

Summary

1. Define marketing research, provide a description of its scope, and offer examples of each type of research conducted in marketing. The chapter offers examples of each type of research conducted in marketing. Marketing research involves gathering information for marketing decisions. It is wide in scope, covering industry research, market traits and trends, buyer behavior, and the marketing mix. Examples of product research are product testing, product package studies, and competitive product analysis. Distribution research covers areas such as channel performance and coverage and plant/warehouse location studies. Promotion research has a wide scope, with studies of premiums, coupons, and deals; advertising effectiveness; media research; and sales force analyses. Pricing research involves studies projecting demand, as well as market potential studies, sales potential studies, cost analyses, and profit analyses, among others.

2. Describe the steps involved in the marketing research process. The first step of the research process involves defining the research problem and setting the research objectives; this is usually done in conjunction with the research team and the marketing managers initiating the research. The development of the research plan involves deciding on the information sources—primary and secondary—and determining the appropriate research approach. The research approach may involve collecting qualitative data, using focus groups or observation methods, or collecting quantitative data, using descriptive (surveys, content analyses) or causal research methods (experimental research). They, in turn, determine the contact methods: mail, e-mail, Internet, telephone, and personal interviews. The sampling plan must be determined: selecting the sampling procedure, sample size, frame, and unit. Finally, the researcher must collect, analyze, and interpret the information.

3. Introduce the concept of decision support systems for marketing and describe the sales forecasting process. Decision support systems represent a coordinated approach to collecting and interpreting business and environmental data. Methods used in sales forecasting are sales force composite estimates, which are based on the personal observations or hunches of the sales force; jury of expert opinion, which involves the aggregate opinions of different experts about future demand; the Delphi method, which entails asking a number of experts to estimate market performance, aggregate the results, share the information with the experts, and repeat the process several times until a consensus is reached; time series and econometric models, which use data of past performance to predict future market demand; the analogy method, which is an estimation method that relies on developments and findings in markets that are relatively similar; and POS-based projections, which perform sales forecasts with the help of store scanners.

Part Two: Foundations of Marketing

Key Terms

advertising effectiveness research	focus group interviews	random probability sample
analogy method	internal secondary data	reliability
brand awareness research	judgment sample	research approach
brand-name generation	jury of expert opinion	sales force compensation, quota, and
buyer behavior research	market potential studies	territory studies
causal (experimental) research	marketing decision support systems (MDSS)	sales force composite estimates
channel performance and coverage studies	marketing intelligence	sales forecasts
competitive pricing analyses	marketing research	sales potential studies
competitive product studies	media research	sample
concept development research	naturalistic inquiry	sample size
consumer segmentation studies	nonresponse	sampling frame
contact methods	observational research (or observation)	sampling procedure
content analysis	open-ended questions	sampling unit
convenience sample	plant/warehouse location study	secondary data
cost analyses	point-of-sale (POS)-based projections	semantic differential scale
data collection instruments	price elasticity studies	studies of premiums, coupons, and deals
Delphi method	primary data	survey research
depth interviews	product packaging design	test marketing
descriptive research	product testing	time series and econometric methods
ethnography	profit analyses	validity
exploratory research	qualitative research	
external secondary data	quantitative research	

Discussion Questions

1. Using the example of Google Glass, describe the types of promotion-related research that could be conducted that would help the company more effectively promote its brand.

2. You have been hired by Procter & Gamble to conduct a study that investigates whether consumers are likely to purchase a new product: Dero Lux. Procter & Gamble envisages the product as a quality detergent to be used only on the highest-quality fabrics—silk, wool, and fine cotton blends. Take this study through all the steps of the research process and elaborate in detail on the investigation.

3. Assume a local business person wants to open a restaurant near your university. For each of the following types of research, identify research that would be beneficial, explain why it would be important, and describe what you would do.

    a.   Buyer behavior research

    b.   Product research

    c.   Promotion research

    d.   Pricing research

4. Assume a local business person wants to open a tanning salon near your university. From the various studies described in the chapter, identify four that you feel would be beneficial. Explain why you think they would be beneficial and describe what you hope to learn from the research.

5. What is the difference between qualitative and quantitative research approaches? Give examples of each.

6. Suppose your university wanted to know when, how , and why students use the computer labs on campus. Discuss how your university could use each of the following types of qualitative studies to gather this information.

    a.   Focus group

    b.   Depth interview

    c.   Observation research

7. Suppose the marketing department at your school wanted to survey students about why they chose marketing as a major. Which approach should they use – qualitative, quantitative, or both. Justify your answer. Then identify which research methods should be used, again, justifying your answer. Lastly, discuss the sample that should be selected, how you would select it, and how you would guarantee it would be representative of marketing majors at your school.

8. Design a content-analysis questionnaire that evaluates the portrayal of women in advertising.

9. One of the sororities at your school wants to study body image and how female students feel about their bodies and how that image affects their lifestyle and performance in college. Discuss an appropriate sampling plan identifying a sampling unit, sample size, sample frame, and sampling method. Justify your choices. If the sorority decided on a survey instrument, what method of collecting data would be the best? Why? What would be the advantages and disadvantages of the method you selected if the goal was to have a sample that represented all female students at your school?

10. Going back to the Dero Lux example in question 2, explore different methods for forecasting sales for the new brand.

Review Questions

(Answers are on Last Page of the Chapter)

True of False

1. Channel performance and coverage studies are examples of distribution research.

2. Focus group interviews typically involve randomly selected groups of people who share their opinion about a product in front of TV cameras.

3. Observation is a type of research approach in which subjects are observed interacting with a product and reacting to other components of the marketing mix and the environment.

4. Exploratory research is conducted early in the research process; it is the research that helps to further define a problem or identify additional problems that should be investigated.

5. Observational analysis is a quantitative method that counts the number of times preselected words, themes, symbols, or pictures appear in a given media with verbal or visual content.

6. The questionnaires that use open-ended questions are based on semantic differential scales or Likert scales.

7. Marketing researchers should eliminate nonresponse cases—defined as the inability or refusal of respondent to participate in a study—because they do not provide conclusive information.

Multiple Choice

8. Marketing research addresses which of the following issues?
    a. Monitoring developments in the market environment
    b. Anticipating product's performance in the marketplace
    c. Evaluating customer-specific brand-related or advertisement-related attitudes
    d. All of the above

9. _____ research examines consumer brand preferences, brand attitudes, and brand-related behavior.
    a. Buyer behavior
    b. Purchase-related
    c. Brand loyalty
    d. Brand management

10. Advertising effectiveness research measures which of the following?
    a. Viewers' recall of an advertisement
    b. Viewers' attitude toward the ad
    c. The extent to which the ad persuaded the consumer to purchase the product
    d. All of the above

11. Which of the following categories relate to pricing research?
    a. Cost analysis and profit analysis
    b. Price elasticity studies
    c. Competitive price analysis
    d. All of the above

12. Naturalistic inquiry is a method used in observational research in which information is gathered using
    a. one-on-one interviews with loose and unstructured questions.
    b. natural rather than contrived settings.
    c. an analysis of verbal and nonverbal behavior.
    d. b and c.

13. Which of the following types of research looks at cause-and-effect relationships and eliminates other extraneous factors that may be responsible for the results?
    a. Observation
    b. Content analysis
    c. Descriptive research
    d. Experimental research

14. Which of the following categories is used to determine who should be included in the marketing survey?
    a. Sampling unit
    b. Sampling procedure
    c. Sampling size
    d. Sampling frame

15. Which of the following methods asks a number of experts to estimate the market performance and then aggregates the results and shares this information with the same experts, repeating the procedure until a consensus is reached?
    a. Jury of executive opinion
    b. Analogy method
    c. Delphi method
    d. Time series model

Blog

Clow-Lascu: *Marketing: Essentials 5e Blog*

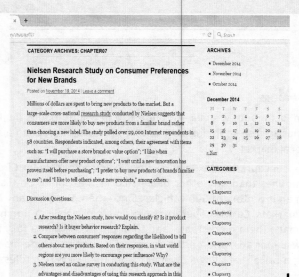

What Is Happening Today?

Learn More! For videos and articles

that relate to Chapter 7:

blogclowlascu.net/category/chapter07

Includes Discussion Questions

with each Post!

Notes

1. Leon Kelion, "Google Glass Eyewear on Sale in the UK," 23 June, 2014, ", accessed at http://www.bbc.com/news/technology-27926352 on June 28, 2014.

2. Coldewey, Devin, "Google Glass to launch this year for under $1,500", NBC News.com Gadgetbox, 23 February 2013, accessed at http://www.nbcnews.com/technology/gadgetbox/ google-glass-launch-year-under-1-500-1C8503747, July 21, 2014.

3. Glass Almanac, "The History of Google Glass," accessed at http://glassalmanac.com/history-google-glass/4/ on June 24, 2014. Danny Hakim, "Detroit's Hottest Seller Is Its Biggest Gas Guzzler," New York Times (November 2, 2002): B , B3.

4. Karissa Bell, "72% of Americans Refuse Google Glass Over Privacy Concerns: Report ", Mashable, April 8, 2014, accessed at http://mashable.com/2014/04/07/google-glass-privacy/ on May 25, 2014.

5. This section is organized based on a framework provided in a table in Thomas C. Kinnear and Ann R. Root, eds., *1988 Survey of Marketing Research: Organization, Functions, Budgeting, and Compensation* (Chicago: American Marketing Association, 1989): 43.

6. See www.acnielsen.com.

7. "The Affluent Can Afford to be Choosy: Nielsen Study," *Progressive Grocer,* (March 1, 2007): 86.

8. ACNielsen, "Affluent Consumers Want and Use Broad Range of Shopping Choices," available from, www.factsfiguresfuture.com, March 2007.

9. Bernard Dubois and Claire Paternault, "Observations—Understanding the World of Luxury Brands: The 'Dream' Formula," *Journal of Advertising Research* 35, no. 4 (July/August 1995): 69–74.

10. Alison Stein Wellner, "Culinary Feat," *American Demographics* 23, no. 3 (March 2001): S16.

11. "Special Report: New Products," *Ad Age International* (April 13, 1998): 17–20.

12. Erika Rasmusson, "Growing a Global Brand," *Sales and Marketing Management* 151, no. 8 (August 1999): 17.

13. Charlotte Clarke, "Language Classes," *Marketing Week* 20, no. 17 (July 24, 1997): 35–39.

14. David Ricks, *Big Business Blunders* (Homewood, Ill.: Dow Jones Irwin, 1983).

15. James I. Steinberg and Alan L. Klein, "Global Branding: Look Before You Leap," *Brandweek* 39, no. 43 (November 16, 1998): 30–32.

16. Deborah Ball, Sarah Ellison, and Janet Adamy, "Just What You Need!: It Takes a Lot of Marketing to Convince Consumers What They're Lacking," *Wall Street Journal* (October 28, 2004): B1; "Procter & Gamble Co.: Vacuum Cleaner Is Recalled for Posing Possible Fire Hazard," *Wall Street Journal* (November 29, 2004): 1.

17. Erin Anderson, George Day, and V. Kasturi Rangan, "Strategic Channel Design," *Sloan Management Review* 38, no. 4 (Summer 1997): 59–69.

18. See www.promotiondecisions.com.

19. Debbie Howell, "Couponing Goes High-Tech," *Chain Store Age*, 82, no. 8 (August 2006): 161.

20. Constance L. Hays, "One-Word Shoppers' Lexicon: Price," *New York Times* (December 26, 2002): C1, C3.

21. Ibid.

22. Claudia Deutsch, "Name Brands Embrace Some Less-Well-Off Kinfolk," *New York Times*, (June 24, 2005): C1.

23. See www.acnielsen.com.

24. See Yvonna S. Lincoln and Egon G. Guba, *Naturalistic Inquiry* (Beverly Hills: Sage Publications, 1985); Laura A. Hudson and Julie L. Ozanne, "Alternative Ways of Seeking Knowledge in Consumer Research," *Journal of Consumer Research* (March 14, 1988): 508–521.

25. Jerome Kirk and Marc L. Miller, *Reliability and Validity in Qualitative Research* (Beverly Hills: Sage Publications, 1986).

26. William R. Dillon, Thomas J. Madden, and Neil Firtle, *Marketing Research in a Marketing Environment,* Burr Ridge, IL: Irwin, 1993.

27. Ibid.

Cases

Case 7-1 Directory Advertising by Automobile Dealers

Dean Dietrich owns a marketing consulting firm in Richmond, Virginia. Autohouse, a new automobile dealership planning to open its stores in the area, is creating a hassle-free shopping environment for used European automobiles, and the company hired Dietrich to research the local market.

The Autohouse concept is replicating the CarMax concept. CarMax, a spin-off of electronics retailer Circuit City and a Fortune 500 company, sells more used automobiles than any other dealership in the United States. It opened its first auto superstore in Richmond in 1993, with an inventory of 500 vehicles. Since then, the company has sold millions of used cars in 80 used car superstores in 38 markets. CarMax operates on a simple principle. It purchases used cars, tests them extensively and repairs them to make them marketable, and then prices them at a fair, no-haggle, price. The prices are listed on the vehicles, in newspaper ads, and on the company's website. Trade-ins are performed as separate transactions, with CarMax offering a price that allows owners to sell their cars regardless of whether they are going to purchase an automobile from CarMax. Moreover, to avoid any propensity to haggle, sales people are paid a per-unit fixed commission. All vehicles are backed with a five-day, 250-mile, money-back guarantee.

Autohouse is using a similar concept in its approach, with a twist: It relies on its competent mechanics hired mostly from Volkswagen and Mercedes dealerships. These mechanics have had extensive training in European automobile repair and certification. Many of them have had experience in providing "certified preowned" certification of foreign automobiles. The automobiles Autohouse will have a 10,000-mile, one-month warranty, which will allow the buyer to bring the car to Autohouse repairs, should there be any problems with the vehicle. Autohouse will accept any European make sold in the United States and in good condition as a trade-in—and, similar to CarMax, trade-ins are also performed as a separate transaction.

Dean's job is to figure out how to advertise this new offering. Autohouse management suggested that, in addition to newspaper and television advertising, Autohouse should advertise in the local telephone directory, under the listing of each European make. Dean is not fully convinced that this should be a primary venue that Autohouse should select for its marketing communications. He decided to design a questionnaire to find out the extent to which local new-car dealerships use directory advertising and how and why they advertise in their selected directories. The following is the questionnaire used.

Richmond-Area Car Dealership Directory Advertising Questionnaire

1. What factors does your dealership consider before advertising in a directory? List all.

2. What size and color advertisement does your dealership use in your dealership's directory advertising? (Please highlight.)

> *Two Page*
>
> *Full Page*
>
> *Half-Page*
>
> *Quarter Page*
>
> *Smaller*
>
> *Color*
>
> *Black & White*
>
> *Other (Please explain.)*

3. List the top three reasons your dealership would choose to advertise in a particular directory:

> 1.
>
> 2.
>
> 3.

4. List the desired traits for a directory that your dealership would advertise in.

5. What directories does your dealership advertise in? List the directory, the year, and the reason.

6. How satisfied has your dealership been with directory advertising in the past? (Please highlight.)

> *Completely Satisfied*
>
> *Very Satisfied*
>
> *Satisfied*
>
> *Somewhat Satisfied*
>
> *Unsatisfied*

Dean approached 10 dealerships to collect this data and four of the dealerships agreed to respond. Their answers follow.

1. What factors does your dealership consider before advertising in a directory?

Dealer 1 Where are the books circulated?

What have we done in the past?

Has our past advertising in the directory led to any sales?

What's the price and size of the ad?

Are directories still the customer's choice for finding out information?

How strong of a presence does my competition have in the directory?

Dealer 2 The number of people that will see it, the potential return on investment and the cost.

Dealer 3 We don't advertise in directories.

Dealer 4 What's the price?

2. What size and color advertisement does your dealership use in your dealership's directory advertising? (Please highlight.)

Dealer 1 Other (simple listing under brand authorized sales and service)

Dealer 2 Color

Dealer 3 None

Dealer 4 Simple telephone listing

3. List the top three reasons your dealership would choose to advertise in a particular directory.

Dealer 1 1. Value price on the ad that I would feel would easily generate a monetary return

2. Get my name on the list for customers who use the directory to call for quotes

3. Promote another aspect of my business, for example, collision repair

Dealer 2 1. Demographics

2. Proximity to dealership

3. Branding

Dealer 3 Choose not to because it's ineffective

Dealer 4 1. Price

2. Effectiveness

3. Name recognition

4. List the desired traits for a directory that your dealership would advertise in.

Dealer 1 1. Serve the market that I feel would choose my dealership based on location

2. Provide a respectable price for the services they provide in today's Internet age

3. Follow up on a yearly basis in ample time to make an educated decision

4. Provide a listing online with a link to our Web site

Dealer 2 1. In our market, to our demographic customer, and good potential return on investment.

Dealer 3 1. n/a

Dealer 4 1. Inexpensive yet reaches a lot of households

5. What directories does your dealership advertise in, for how long, and why?

Dealer 1 Verizon Yellow Pages

Dealer 2 Goochland Chamber of Commerce

Dealer 3 Jewish Community Center

Dealer 4 Verizon Yellow Pages

6. How satisfied has your dealership been with directory advertising in the past?

Dealer 1 Somewhat Satisfied

Dealer 2 Very Satisfied

Dealer 3 Unsatisfied

Dealer 4 Somewhat Satisfied

Questions

1. Evaluate the questionnaire that Dean used.

2. Evaluate the sampling procedure of the study.

3. Look over the results. What do you think Dean should recommend to Autohouse management with regard to directory advertising?

Sources: CarMax.com; Bradley Johnson, "No-Haggle Pricing Climbs Higher, Finds Fans Among Affluent, Educated," *Advertising Age,* (August 1, 2005): 23; Dana-Nicoleta Lascu, Dealership Survey.

Case 7-2 Starting a Modeling Agency

Karen Johnson is contemplating starting a modeling agency in Flagstaff, Arizona. She has previously worked for two top New York modeling agencies and believes that she has sufficient experience, both as a model and as a modeling agency employee, to create a successful agency of her own. Because Flagstaff is somewhat off the beaten path of these agencies, her scouting capabilities in this remote location and her connections in the fashion world may prove to be valuable for her new enterprise.

Although Karen has a feel for what fashion magazines and the fashion industry want in a model, she would like to create a better match between her models and the industry by creating for her models portfolios of photographs that present the prevailing "look"—what is considered the in-look. To better define the in-look, she has hired KD Research to perform a content analysis on the most recent advertisements that appeared in last month's issues of Vogue, Elle, and Cosmo.

KD Research recruited judges to fill out the following questionnaire. Each ad in the three magazines was evaluated separately by three judges.

KD Research Questionnaire

Please look at each ad and indicate to what extent you believe that THE WOMAN IN THE AD appears to have the following characteristics by circling the corresponding number, as follows:

The woman in the ad appears to be					
Soft	5	4	3	2	1
Cool	5	4	3	2	1
Seductive	5	4	3	2	1
Scornful	5	4	3	2	1
Kitten-like	5	4	3	2	1
Optimistic	5	4	3	2	1
Maternal	5	4	3	2	1
Loving	5	4	3	2	1
Practical	5	4	3	2	1
Proud	5	4	3	2	1
Comical	5	4	3	2	1
Calm	5	4	3	2	1
Superior	5	4	3	2	1
Elegant	5	4	3	2	1

(a total of 30 adjectives)

The woman in the ad appears to be					
Caucasian	5	4	3	2	1
African American	5	4	3	2	1
Hispanic	5	4	3	2	1
Asian	5	4	3	2	1

The woman is looking at					
People	5	4	3	2	1
An object	5	4	3	2	1
Nothing	5	4	3	2	1
The reader	5	4	3	2	1

The woman's age is approximately ____ years.

1 = if the ad/woman DOES NOT AT ALL HAVE the respective characteristic
2 = if the ad/woman DOES NOT QUITE APPEAR TO HAVE the respective characteristic
3 = if the ad/woman APPEARS TO HAVE the respective characteristic
4 = if the ad/woman HAS the respective characteristic
5 = if the ad/woman DEFINITELY HAS the respective characteristic

The researchers then attempted to identify the characteristics that were the most prevalent in the ads. They calculated the averages for all the advertisements; the table on the next page shows the results.

Questions:

1. Advise Karen on the prevailing "look" that she should create for her models.
2. Evaluate the research process that KD Research used.
3. In determining what individuals Karen should target for her modeling agency, she again wants to hire KD Research. Outline a research approach for KD Research. Be sure to include all of the components discussed in Section 7-4c, especially the sampling plan.

Emotion / Expression	Mean	Standard Deviation
Soft	3.264	1.035
Poised	3.256	1.004
Confident	3.058	1.072
Youthful	3.019	1.124
Calm	3.001	0.898
Warm	2.977	1.042
Cool	2.975	1.037
Elegant	2.968	0.93
Daydreaming	2.947	1.099
Good girl	2.946	1.016
Seductive	2.901	0.959
Pensive	2.857	1.013
Proud	2.854	0.947
Sexy	2.826	0.988
Sophisticated	2.821	0.961
Sexual	2.791	0.976
Loving	2.786	0.976
Self-loving	2.781	0.921
Snobbish	2.756	1.115
Natural	2.743	0.983
Smiling	2.731	1.135
Humble	2.686	1.031
Happy	2.679	1.007
Sassy	2.678	0.958
Mannequin	2.672	0.991
Demure	2.67	1.064
Anxious	2.641	0.954
Tease	2.623	0.937
Stiff	2.603	0.977
Superior	2.529	0.874
Socialite	2.521	0.982
Coy	2.496	0.884
Reluctant	2.456	0.951
Emotionless	2.438	1.175
Nostalgic	2.432	0.837
Caucasian	3.704	1.373
Hispanic	1.745	1.096
African American	1.314	0.818
Asian	1.29	0.67
Nothing	2.706	1.679
Reader	2.495	1.813
People	1.867	1.279
Object	1.832	1.153

Prevalent

Characteristic

Averages

Answers to Review Questions

Answers: 1) True, 2) False, 3) True, 4) True, 5) False, 6) False, 7) False, 8) d, 9) a, 10) d, 11) d, 12) d, 13) d, 14) a, 15) c

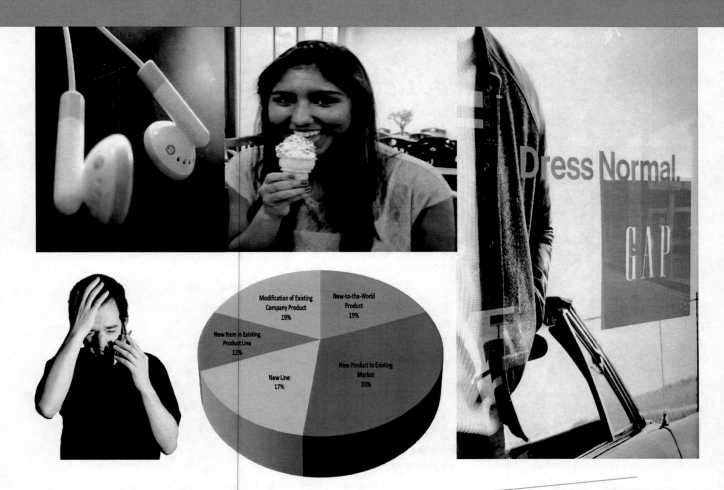

Marketing Mix

Strategies

Chapter 8

Product Strategies

8-1 CHAPTER OVERVIEW

Mick Jagger, Keith Richards, Charlie Watts, Ron Wood, and Brian Jones belong to a brand that is as much in demand today as it was 40 years ago: the Rolling Stones. The veteran rock band has managed to fill and rock the house at New York's Madison Square Garden, the Los Angeles Forum, and Toronto's Air Canada Centre, surviving more than four decades in a fickle, trend-driven, cutthroat, turbulent, insanely competitive music industry. Today, the Rolling Stones, ''the greatest rock 'n roll band in the whole world ever,'' according to former President Bill Clinton and millions of others, are the most successful rock band in history, having generated more than $1.5 billion in revenues—and that is only since 1989.

The Stones are, in fact, a brand, and their brand management skills are the reason for their remarkable success. From the beginning, the Rolling Stones positioned themselves strategically. They were not the Beatles or the Beach Boys—they were different, a little rougher, more in your face. And it paid for them to be a differentiated brand that stayed true to their original formula.

The Stones also seek business partnerships that are harmonious with their own, both in stature and shared relevance with their target audience—among their partners are Sheryl Crow, Anheuser-Busch, Microsoft, Sprint, and E*Trade.[1] Jagger readily understood the power of branding from the beginning of his career because he commissioned a graphic design student at the Royal College of Art in London to create the Stones' tongue logo, a design that was easy to reproduce and that could withstand the test of time. This is one of the strongest and most recognizable logos in the global market.[2]

The Stones' survival is attributed to a clear differentiation of their brand from that of the competitors, and consistency—staying true to their winning core product formula—over time. Most other similar music brands have not encountered the same resonant appeal over time. Twisted Sister, Front 242, Cyndi Lauper, Styx, and Sisters of Mercy have held a fraction of the music audience's attention for a fraction of the Stones' time. Like most products, they have advanced through the product life cycle (PLC) rapidly, from introduction to decline in just a few years. This chapter will address product-related issues—from new product development decisions, to challenges presented by new product launch decisions, to issues involving managing the product mix and the product portfolio in line with the company strategy and the demands of different consumers.

Section 8-2 provides a product definition and addresses the different product dimensions and classifications. Section 8-3 addresses product decisions regarding branding, logos, trademark protection, and brand strategy. Section 8-4 addresses the packaging and labeling decisions of the firm, and Section 8-5 examines product mix management decisions and issues related to product length, width, and depth. Section 8-6 addresses the new product development process and new product-related decisions. Section 8-7 addresses product diffusion and the different types of adopters, and Section 8-8 addresses the PLC stages—introduction, growth, maturity, and decline. Section 8-9 addresses issues related to the management of the product portfolio.

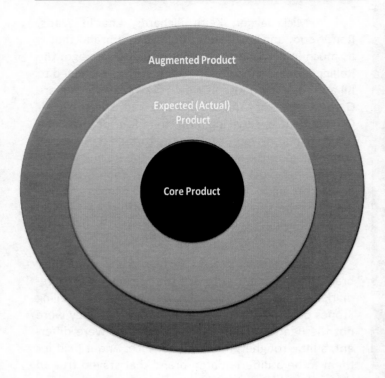

Figure 8-1: The Core, Expected and Augmented Product

Augmented Product

Expected (Actual) Product

Core Product

8-2 PRODUCT DEFINITION AND CLASSIFICATION

A Rolling Stones performance, merchandise sold at the concert, hair highlights at the Frederic Fekkai hair salon, a burger at Burger King, and landscaping by the local landscaping service are all examples of products. A **product** is defined as any offering that can satisfy consumer needs and wants. As mentioned in Chapter 1, products include goods, which refers to tangible products, and services, which refers to intangible activities or benefits that individuals acquire but that do not result in ownership, and ideas and experiences that consumers perceive as valuable because they fulfill their needs and wants.

8-2a: Core, Expected, and Augmented Products

Products can be conceptualized at three levels, as illustrated in **Figure 8-1**.[3] The **core product** is the fundamental benefit, or problem solution, that consumers seek. An individual who purchases aspirin is actually buying relief from headaches. Another individual buying an automobile is purchasing transportation. Another individual purchasing a massage is buying relief from muscle ache. Relief and transportation are the fundamental benefits that the respective consumers are seeking.

The **expected (or actual) product** is the basic physical product, including styling, features, brand name, and packaging, which delivers those benefits. An individual purchasing a massage at her health club also expects to have a gentle masseuse with magic fingers, calming music, clean sheets, and clean covers. The consumer purchasing the automobile expects it to have comfortable seats, a reasonable radio with a CD player, power steering, power windows, and, in North America, air-conditioning and automatic transmission.

The **augmented product** is a product enhanced by the addition of extra or unsolicited services or benefits to the consumer to prompt purchase—such as warranty, repair services, maintenance, and other services that enhance the product's use (see **Figure 8-2**). Most of the competition today takes place in the augmented product arena. A children's dentist provides a Mermaid toothbrush and fun-colored gel, sends a birthday card with a smiling cartoon character, and has toys ready for the tots in the waiting room. Some automobile dealers offer breakfast and a free car wash every Saturday. When all competitors offer extra or unsolicited services or benefits, that augmented product becomes the expected product. Turndown hotel service, where the bed is arranged for sleeping and a chocolate mint is placed on the pillow, becomes the expected product. Liquid washing detergents are expected to have a measuring cap indicating amounts required for different size loads.

8-2b: Product Durability

Durable goods are defined as tangible products that have a prolonged use. Automobiles, appliances, and furniture are types of durable goods that last over many years of use. Most definitions suggest that durable goods are goods that have

Product:
Any offering that can satisfy consumer needs and wants.

Core Product:
The fundamental benefit, or problem solution, that consumers seek. expected (or actual)

Expected (or Actual) Product:
The basic physical product, including styling, features, brand name, and packaging, that delivers the benefits that consumers seek.

Augmented Product:
A product enhanced by the addition of extra or unsolicited services or benefits, such as a warranty, repair services, maintenance, and other services that enhance product use to prompt a purchase.

a life of more than two years. **Nondurable goods** are defined as tangible products that are consumed relatively quickly, purchased on a regular basis, and last less than two years. Examples of nondurables are food, clothing, shoes, gasoline, and natural gas. Services are defined as intangible activities or benefits that individuals acquire but that do not result in ownership. Examples of services are medical care, legal counseling, accounting, and marketing services. Services are further examined in Chapter 9.

8-2c: Product Classification

Marketing managers have classified consumer products into four basic categories,[4] based on the level of risk attributed to the purchase and the amount of effort involved in purchasing the product.

Figure 8-2 In this advertisement by Community Trust Bank, augmented services such as no monthly service fee, no per check charges, no charge for first order of checks, and overdraft advantage are being promoted to differentiate the bank from its competitors. **Source:** Sample print advertisement courtesy of Miles Agency and Alliance One Advertising, Inc.

Convenience goods are relatively inexpensive and frequently purchased products. Relative to the other three categories, convenience goods are considered to have the lowest level of perceived risk and purchase effort. Examples of convenience goods are bread, milk, beer, and snacks. Among examples of convenience goods are **impulse goods**, which are goods bought without any earlier planning, such as candy, gum, and magazines. Retailers place these goods conveniently within reach of the checkout aisle. However, for those consumers who cannot resist candy, supermarkets are now offering candyfree checkout aisles (see Figure 8-3). Other examples of convenience goods are **staples**, which are products that are bought routinely, such as milk, cheese, bread, and soap; and **emergency goods**, which are purchased to address urgent needs, such as candles, lanterns, and bottled water when a hurricane is announced, and salt and snow shovels when snow is in the forecast.

Preference goods are defined as convenience goods that become differentiated through branding and achieve some degree of brand loyalty. Preference goods are higher risk and higher in terms of purchase effort compared with convenience services. To indicate that a preference exists, the term *favorite* can be attached to the product category. For example, if one's favorite cola is Pepsi, one will most likely shop only in larger stores that are more likely to sell the brand than in smaller stores that could have an exclusive arrangement with Coke.

Shopping goods are defined as goods that consumers perceive as higher-risk goods, which they are willing to spend a greater amount of purchase effort in searching for and evaluating. Among examples of shopping goods are home appliances, clothing, and furniture. Shopping goods can be classified further based on their degree of homogeneity.

Figure 8-3: Supermarkets in Europe rarely offer candy in the check-out aisle.

Durable Goods:
Tangible products that have a prolonged use.

Nondurable Goods:
Tangible products that are consumed relatively quickly and purchased on a regular basis; they last less than two years.

Convenience Goods:
Relatively inexpensive and frequently purchased products.

Impulse Goods:
Goods bought without any earlier planning, such as candy, gum, and magazines.

Staples:
Goods that are bought routinely, such as milk, cheese, bread, and soap.

Emergency Goods:
Goods purchased to address urgent needs.

Preference Goods:
Convenience goods that become differentiated through branding and achieve some degree of brand loyalty.

Shopping Goods:
Goods that consumers perceive as higher risk but for which they are willing to spend a greater amount of purchase effort to find and evaluate.

Homogeneous shopping goods are goods that vary little in terms of physical characteristics or functions but differ in terms of style and price sufficiently to warrant a search. Example of homogeneous shopping goods are tires and stereo equipment. For homogeneous shopping goods, price is an important variable: After consumers decide on the desired characteristics of the good, the next step is to look for the lowest price. **Heterogeneous shopping goods** are products that vary significantly in terms of functions, physical characteristics, and quality, and they require a physical evaluation by the buyer. These goods—clothing and furniture, for example—vary greatly in their characteristics. Retailers need to carry a wide assortment of these goods to appeal to enough individuals, and they need to have highly trained sales people to assist customers. For these products, price is not as important as other product characteristics.

Specialty goods are goods that reach the ultimate in differentiation and brand loyalty, where only the chosen brand is acceptable to the consumer. These goods are conceptualized as high risk and are distinguished from shopping goods primarily in terms of higher purchasing effort. Consumers are willing to wait, search high and low, and not settle for anything less. Examples of specialty goods are gourmet foods, such as aged Gouda cheese and Mousse Royale pâté; designer clothes, such as Dana Buchman knits and Hugo Boss suits (see **Figure 8-4**); and other goods, such as Dunhill cigarettes and Rissy Lyn frames (available from Henri Bendel in New York).

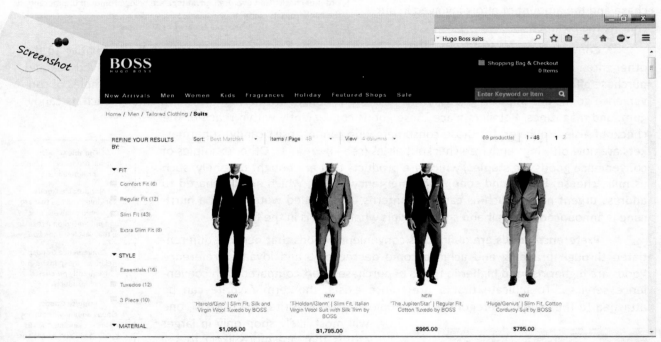

Figure 8-4: Hugo Boss is a brand of high-end, luxurious tuxedos and velvet sport coats with first-class finishing touches and impeccable tailoring. They are one-of-a-kind, handmade creations. http://www.hugoboss.com/us

Homogeneous Shopping Goods:
Goods that vary little in terms of physical characteristics or functions.

Heterogeneous Shopping Goods:
Goods that vary significantly in terms of functions, physical characteristics, and quality, and that require a physical evaluation by the buyer.

Specialty Goods:
Goods that reach the ultimate in differentiation and brand loyalty in that only the chosen brand is acceptable to the consumer.

The following is a summary of the classification categories of products:

1. Convenience goods are relatively inexpensive and frequently purchased products (examples: bread, milk, beer, and snacks).

- Impulse goods are goods bought without any earlier planning (examples: candy, gum, and magazines).

- Staples are products that are bought routinely (examples: milk, cheese, bread, and soap).

- Emergency goods are purchased to address urgent needs (examples: medicine, bandages, candles, lanterns, and bottled water when a hurricane is announced).

2. Preference goods are goods that become differentiated through branding and achieve some degree of brand loyalty (examples: Coke, Pepsi, Nike shoes, and Levi jeans.)

3. Shopping goods are goods that consumers perceive as higher-risk goods, which they are willing to spend a greater amount for which they are willing to spend a greater amount of effort during the search and evaluation process (examples: home appliances, clothing, and furniture).

4. Specialty goods are goods that reach the ultimate in differentiation and brand loyalty, where only the chosen brand is acceptable to the consumer (examples: BMW car and Rolex watch).

8-3 BRANDING

One of the most important roles played by marketing involves branding the product. Branding adds value to products because it makes products appear more distinctive and valuable.

A **brand** is defined as a name, design, symbol, or a combination thereof that identifies the product or the seller and is used to differentiate the product from competitors' offerings. A brand also serves as a guarantee to consumers that the product will be identical each time consumers purchase it, with the same features, design, and performance.

> **Brand:**
> A name, design, symbol, or a combination thereof that identifies the product or the seller and that is used to differentiate the product from competitors' offerings.
>
> **Brand Equity (or Brand Franchise):**
> Brands with high consumer awareness and loyalty.

All products benefit from branding—from turkeys (Butterball) to eggs (Eggland's Best), to oranges (Jaffa and Sunkist), to couscous (Near East), to beer (Michelob and Corona), and to cereal (Total and Cheerios). Brands that have high consumer awareness and loyalty are said to have high brand equity (or brand franchise). **Brand equity (or franchise)** is defined as a set of brand assets and liabilities linked to a brand and its name and symbol, adding or subtracting from the value provided by a product or service to a firm or to that firm's customers. Brand loyalty is an essential asset of brand equity. The epitome of brand equity is the Harley-Davidson aficionado who wears the Harley symbol as a tattoo.[5]

Marketers have attempted to evaluate brand equity and establish the actual value of the brand. A widely accepted brand value ranking is compiled by Interbrand with the help of data from Citibank and currently is considered the most valuable indicator of the financial health of the global elite. The ranking is determined by a collation of brand strength (based on factors such as leadership and market stability), financial and analyst reports, revenue, and profit figures.[6]

Table 8-1 ranks the top 20 brands in terms of brand equity worldwide. Coke, for example, has lost substantial brand value. It appears to be vulnerable because it has a single product offering, and the brand reached its peak in Europe and Latin America.[7] In particular, it has not recovered from recent employee lawsuits over diversity issues, fizzling bottler relations, plunging demand for syrup that forced a production stoppage, and a disastrous product recall in Belgium.[8] However, Coca-Cola has introduced a number of new competitive brands, including Coke Zero, which has achieved a 1.3 percent market share in the United States and shows no signs of slowing down.[9] At the top in terms of brand value are Apple and Google, innovative companies that provide customers with consistency and strong brand equity.

Table 8-1: The Leading Brands of the World		
Rank	**Brand**	**Brand Value ($m)**
1	Apple	98,316
2	Google	93,291
3	Coca-Cola	79,213
4	IBM	78,808
5	Microsoft	59,546
6	GE	46,947
7	McDonald's	41,992
8	Samsung	39,610
9	Intel	37,257
10	Toyota	35,346
11	Mercedes-Benz	31,904
12	BMW	31,839
13	Cisco	29,053
14	Disney	28,147
15	HP	25,843
16	Gillette	25,105
17	Louis Vuitton	24,893
18	Oracle	24,088
19	Amazon	23,620
20	Honda	18,490

Source: Adapted from Interbrand's Best Global Brands 2013,
http://www.interbrand.com/en/best-global-brands/2013/Best-Global-Brands-2013-Brand-View.aspx

The important branding decisions involve deciding on the brand name, mark, logo, character, the brand sponsor, and the brand strategy. These elements help create the **brand image**, defined as the consumer perception of the particular brand. Consumers associate certain brand characteristics with a particular brand. Marketers, through advertising, can help in forming that brand image through appropriate positioning strategies.

Brand name decisions include the selection and protection of the brand name. Brand sponsor decisions involve determining whether the brand should be sold as a manufacturer brand, also known as a national brand; a dealer brand, also known as a private label brand; or a generic brand. The brand can be licensed or co-branded. Brand strategy decisions center on creating brand extensions or line extensions or using or creating family brands, new brands, or multibrands.

8-3a: Brand Identity

Brand Image:
The consumer perception of the particular brand.

Brand Name:
The part of a brand that can be spoken; it may include words, letters, or numbers.

Brand Mark:
The part of a brand that can be seen but not spoken.

Brand Logo:
A distinctive mark, sign, symbol, or graphic version of a company's name that is used to identify and promote the company's product.

Brand Character (or Trade Character):
A character that personifies the brand.

Selecting the instruments that identify the brand—that is, the **brand name**, the brand mark, the brand logo, and the brand character—constitutes very important decisions. A brand name is defined as the part of a brand that can be spoken. It may include words, letters, or numbers. Toyota, McDonald's, Coach, and Delta Airlines (see Figure 8-5) are all brand names. Successful brand names have the following characteristics:

• They are easy to pronounce, memorable, and distinctive. Celebrex, Cingular, and Gateway are memorable names that are easy to pronounce. Distinctive fun names with memorable alliterations are Jolly Green Giant and Colgate Total.

• They suggest product traits or benefits—for example, Hefty bags suggest product strength. Other brand names that are indicative of product traits and benefits are Skin So Soft, Pampers, Huggies, Lean Cuisine, Healthy Choice, Taster's Choice, GoPro, and Head & Shoulders.

• They should also be easy to translate into other languages. A number of international market research firms help companies test brand names in international markets. In global marketing, the wrong brand name can make or break a product.

In addition to the brand name, there are other means for product identification. For example, a **brand mark** is part of the brand that can be seen but not spoken. For McDonald's, the brand mark is the

Figure 8-5: When Northwest Airlines and Delta merged, the Delta brand was selected to represent their combined business.

golden arches. A **brand logo** is a distinctive mark, sign, symbol, or graphic version of a company's name used to identify and promote its product. The Pepsi logo is the half-white, half-blue circle with a white curved dividing line. The Rolling Stones' logo consists of the well-known red lips and tongue. A **brand character (or trade character)** is a character that personifies the brand, such as Tony the Tiger for Kellogg's Frosted Flakes and Ronald McDonald for McDonald's. These elements together help build the brand's identity and are valuable and well-protected trademarks. The Rolling Stones' brand character is depicted by its logo in motion. A **trademark** consists of words, symbols, marks, devices, and signs that are used in trade to indicate the source of the goods and to distinguish them from competitors. A trademark is legally registered with the U.S. Patent and Trademark Office for use by a single company.

A **servicemark** is the same as a trademark, but it identifies and distinguishes the source of a service, rather than a good. The terms trademark and mark are used to refer to both trademarks and servicemarks. Rights for a federally registered trademark can last indefinitely, as long as the owner continues to use it and continues to apply for renewal. A **patent** is the grant of a property right to the inventor. New patents are valid for 20 years from the date on which the patent was filed, and under special circumstances, they can be extended beyond the 20 years. Patents and trademarks are issued by the U.S. Patent and Trademark Office, and they are effective only in the United States and its territories and possessions. It is the responsibility of the firm to protect its trademarks and patents.[10] It should be noted that the 20-year period is not typically the period that the invention is available on the market. For example, in the case of pharmaceuticals, drugs are registered long before they are available on the market. Internationally, firms must apply with the national or local governments for protection.

> **Trademark:**
> Words, symbols, marks, and signs that are legally registered for a single company's use.
>
> **Servicemark:**
> Words, symbols, marks, and signs that are legally registered for a single company's use that identify and distinguish the source of a service.
>
> **Patent:**
> The grant of a property right to the inventor.

The next section addresses some of the challenges firms encounter when protecting their valuable brands and related trademarks and patents.

8-3b: Protecting the Brand

Brand names are valuable assets to a company, as established in Section 8-3, which addressed brand equity. Companies pay millions to protect their brand names from dilution by registering them anywhere they are present and defending them in court. Companies are proactive, rather than reactive, primarily because counterfeit merchandise harms the brand's reputation, its value, and company profits.

In many parts of the world, brands are readily counterfeited. To illustrate, Yiwu, a city five hours from Shanghai, China, is one of the largest wholesale centers of China, where 200,000 distributors purchase up to 2,000 tons of goods daily. It also is China's counterfeit capital, where counterfeit products bearing established brand names—such as Procter & Gamble's Safeguard soap and Rejoice shampoo, Gillette razor blades, and other brands belonging to companies such as Philip Morris, Anheuser-Busch, Prada, Robert Bosch, Kimberly-Clark, and Nike—are sold at a fraction of their genuine counterparts' cost.[11] Counterfeiters in China range from manufacturers of shampoo and soap in back rooms to large state-owned enterprises or joint-venture partners making their profits selling knockoffs of soft drinks and beer, to factories producing car batteries, motorcycles, and even mobile CD factories with optical disc machines. These products are distributed all over the world, including the United States.[12]

It is estimated that companies lose approximately $125 million yearly in licensing revenues alone to counterfeiters, most of this occurring in luxury goods industries, such as watches and accessories.[13] It is also estimated that six percent of the global market is composed of counterfeits.[14]

Examples of counterfeiting are design counterfeiting and brand-name counterfeiting. Design counterfeiting includes copying designs or scents. This practice is quite common and risk free. Many companies replicate the polo-style shirt with a design that approximates the polo rider. The design of women's Peugeot watches is close to that of the Rolex Oyster Perpetual. Unknown perfume manufacturers suggest that their brand is similar in scent to a particular brand of perfume, which they name in their product packaging and advertising. At the next level is brand-name counterfeit purses with names such as Prada, Fendi, and Louis Vuitton are sold practically on the steps of the actual retailer on Fifth Avenue in New York City, as are fake Rolex watches. Counterfeit products even make it to flea markets all over the United States. Companies work diligently to develop a strong brand identity, so they do not want to see counterfeiters use their brand name.

Several factors contribute to the counterfeiters' success. First, consumers are willing to purchase counterfeit goods. Studies have shown, for example, that a large proportion of consumers are likely to select a counterfeit apparel item over a genuine good when there is a price advantage, primarily because function risks are low for apparel, whereas prestige gains are high.[15] In this sense, products that are visible or consumed publicly are more likely to be in demand than products that are less visible or consumed privately. Second, the spread of advanced production technology (affordable, quality, color-copying machines), as well as production lines supplied by pirates, makes it possible for counterfeiters to make perfect replicas of the original products. Frequently, neither the manufacturer nor the consumers can tell fakes from the real product.[16] Third, supply chains are not adequately controlled. Traders use Internet chat rooms and unauthorized dealership networks to sell the products and mix counterfeit products with legitimate products sold on the secondary gray market.[17] Finally, governments in many developing countries are reluctant to crack down on counterfeiters, especially when state-owned enterprises are involved in the operations. In the case of China, for instance, local governments hesitate to crack down on product pirates because they create thousands of jobs and keep the local economy going.[18] Even though China has made a considerable effort to combat the rampant counterfeiting in many areas of the country, closing down the prominent Xiangyang market for counterfeit items in Shanghai,[19] it, nevertheless, has not done enough.

Companies have used a number of strategies to combat counterfeiting. Lobbying the U.S. government, as well as the governments allowing counterfeiting, is a first step. Alternatively, companies could engage in a concerted action to combat counterfeiting by changing a product's appearance to differentiate authentic products from fakes. Budweiser embedded special images in its beer bottles that appear only when the product is chilled, rendering them difficult to copy. Microsoft included holograms on its software boxes and inside user manuals, but pirates quickly learned the trick.[20] But the most successful attacks have been launched with the cooperation of governments of developing countries. In China, for example, a raid was launched by seven battery makers, including Gillette, Energizer, and Panasonic, with the help of 200 government agents, on 21 factories in a southwestern city. As a result of the raid, a total of 150 pieces of manufacturing equipment and three million counterfeit batteries were confiscated.[21]

8-3c: Brand Sponsor Decisions

Brand sponsor decisions involve determining whether the brand should be sold as a manufacturer brand, also known as a national brand; a dealer brand, also known as a private label brand; a retailer brand; wholesaler brand; distributor brand; or as a generic brand. Brand sponsor decisions also involve determining whether the brand can be licensed or co-branded.

Branding today is more complex than ever. In the past, **manufacturers' brands (or national brands)**, defined as brands owned by a manufacturer, dominated retail shelves. Today, **private label brands,** defined as reseller (wholesaler or retailer) brands, abound on the retail shelves. Alongside the national megabrands, such as Procter & Gamble and Rubbermaid, there is now an increasingly large mix of store brands. According to the Private Label Manufacturers Association, store brands currently account for one out of five items sold at supermarkets, drug chains, and mass merchandisers in the United States. [22]

The Private Label Manufacturers Association reports that four out of ten adults now consider themselves "frequent" purchasers of store brand products. The association also reported that consumers on average fill their grocery shopping carts with 32 percent store brand items.[23]

Private label brands are much more profitable for retailers, compared with manufacturers' brands. Of these, the most profitable for retailers are, of course, store brands. For consumers, private label brands represent a guarantee of quality at a lower price. Consequently, they increase store loyalty and patronage. Among successful private label brands are Kmart's Jaclyn Smith, Martha Stewart, and Kathy Ireland,

Manufacturers' Brands (or National Brands): Brands owned by a manufacturer.

Private Label Brands: Reseller (wholesaler or retailer) brands.

which appeal to working- and middle-class mothers; Target's Honors brand; Kohl's Sonoma brand; Nordstrom's Classiques; and Macy's Cellar brand. In recent years, groceries and canned goods represented the product category where consumers were most willing to try store brands. Table 8-2 provides some insights into how consumers perceive private labels in terms of risk.

Table 8–2: Level of Risk Associated with Buying a Private Label Brand (1=Extremely Low Risk and 7=Extremely High Risk)	
Product Category	**Mean Value**
Baby food	6.34
Sunscreen	5.75
Facial care products	5.75
Dairy products	5.67
Milk	5.54
Diapers for children	5.33
Frozen food	5.00
Beverages	4.90
Chocolate	4.54
Pet food	3.80
Liquid soap	3.35
Toilet paper	3.09
Paper towels	2.53

Retailers are aggressively promoting their own brands, placing them typically side-by-side with the national brands, offering consumers the choice of the purchase of the retailer's brand at a lower price. Often, even the packaging is quite similar to that of the manufacturers' brands. This is an example of the **battle of the brands**, defined as a conflict between manufacturers and resellers to promote their own brands. In this battle, manufacturers' advantage lies in the consumers' preference for the manufacturer's brand. But to build this preference requires extensive expenditures on advertising. For example, on the Eastern Shore of Virginia, Sting-Ray's store brand is seen at the same level as, if not better than, national brands for peanuts. Sting-Ray's markets their brand as fresh and local, which gives them a strong competitive advantage over national brands (see Figure 8-6).

Retailers, however, have substantial bargaining power in this battle. They control the shelf space and manage it much like real estate, promoting their own brands by placing them, as mentioned, side-by-side with competing national brands to stress the price difference and offer consumers the option to purchase the product at a lower price. They have central displays with their own brands, creating convenience for consumers looking for that particular

FRESH LOCAL

Figure 8-6: Fresh local peanuts marketed under the local retailer Sting-Ray's brand are perceived as superior to national-brand peanuts: they are perceived as both local and fresh.
Courtesy of Sting-Ray's.

Battle of the Brands:
The conflict between manufacturers and resellers to promote their own brands.

Generics:
Products that emphasize the product, rather than the brand of the manufacturer or reseller.

Licensing:
A process that involves a licensor, who shares the brand name, technology, and know-how with a licensee in return for royalties.

product category (see Figure 8-7, illustrating a prominent Sting Ray's brand display). **Generics**, products that emphasize the product rather than the brand of the manufacturer or reseller, represent the third brand category. They are rarely, if at all, advertised. There is minimal expense associated with their manufacturing, packaging, and distribution, and their shelf location is confined to the bottom shelves in low-traffic areas. This strategy allows them to be significantly cheaper than branded product alternatives. Generics are popular in the drug industry, where the cost of certain brand-name products is often prohibitive for individuals living on low fixed incomes.

Licensing involves the owner of the brand name allowing a manufacturer or a reseller to sell the product under the owner's brand name in return for a licensing fee. Bayerische Motoren Werke AG (BMW) created quite a buzz when it bought the Rolls-Royce name, without the product, for $60 million. BMW then agreed to license the rights to

Figure 8-7: Sting-Ray's Peanut Brittle is a favorite purchase for both locals and tourists visiting the Eastern Shore of Virginia.
Courtesy of Sting-Ray's.

Chapter 8: Product Strategies

Volkswagen. This followed Volkswagen's agreement to purchase Rolls-Royce and Bentley cars for more than $700 million from Vickers PLC, a deal in which VW outbid BMW. The licensing agreement enabled Volkswagen to manufacture and distribute Rolls-Royce automobiles only until 2002, when BMW took control of Rolls-Royce production.[24] The first Rolls-Royce was built in 1904,[25] and it took the company many years to develop this reputable brand that stands for excellence in the automotive industry. Licensing the Rolls-Royce name offered the licensee an instant brand name of the highest resonance.

Numerous brands are licensed in the clothing industry. Oleg Cassini, Pierre Cardin, and Bill Blass have almost lost their cachet as high-quality exclusive brands as a result of extensive licensing. Barney, Teletubbies, Bob the Builder, and other popular children's programs have successfully licensed their popular brand names to create equally popular toys. Keds, a shoe manufacturer, has acquired the licenses for Tommy Hilfiger and Levi's shoes. Joseph Aboud, a high-couture clothing brand, was licensed to mid-price bed linen products. Eskimo Pie ice cream has become a successful international brand through licensing.

It should be mentioned that it is not only manufacturers' brands that are licensed. Private label brands are also sold under license. For example, Kmart's Martha Stewart line was licensed to Sears in Canada.[26]

A fourth brand strategy is **co-branding**, which involves using the brands of two different companies on one single product. For example, American Express co-brands with Delta Airlines to offer the Delta Skymiles Credit Card; Kellogg currently co-brands with Disney in the United Kingdom, using Mickey Mouse and Winnie the Pooh on its products. Breyer's Ice Cream Parlor brands are co-brand offerings (see Figure 8-8), with Almond Joy, Klondike, Reese's, Oreo, and Hershey's. And Esso (Exxon) co-brands with Disney in Europe.

Another example is the co-branding partnership between JPMorgan Chase and USA Hockey. JPMorgan Chase issues two different cards every year bearing the USA Hockey name, and every time a purchase is made using the card, a small amount of the purchase is donated to USA Hockey.[27]

Co-branding can be a profitable strategy for firms. In one example, Jack Daniel's co-branded a line of grilling sauces with H. J. Heinz. Because Jack Daniel's stands for Southern heritage, original high-quality craftsmanship, and flavor, and because grilling and bar-

Figure 8-8: Breyer's Ice Cream Parlor uses a co-brand strategy with a number of well-known candy brands.

becue also have long-standing roots in the South, it was believed that this relationship would create the synergy needed for success. The Jack Daniel's grilling sauce line has captured 12 percent of the premium barbecue sauce segment since the product's introduction.[28]

8-3d: Brand Strategy

Co-Branding:
Using the brands of two different companies on one single product.

Line Extension:
The process of extending the existing brand name by introducing new product offerings in an existing product category.

In deciding on brand strategy, a company has a number of options. **Line extension** involves extending the existing brand name by introducing new product offerings in an existing product category. Examples of line extensions are new flavors. For instance, Celestial Seasonings introduced a raspberry-flavored Green Tea, in addition to its already existing Green Tea. Pepsi introduced lime flavors for Diet Pepsi and regular Pepsi. St. Francis Hospital created a new Kids Surgery Suite designed "especially for kids" (see Figure 8-9). New product forms are also popular line extensions. Most detergents introduced liquid versions that they sell in addition to the traditional powder versions. Added ingredients, such as Palmolive dish detergent with antibacterial soap, or removed ingredients, such as low-fat versions of products, are also examples of line extensions. Size can also be varied: Dove ice cream now offers bite-size versions of its popular ice cream.

Companies must be careful when attempting line extensions. In the process, they could sabotage their core brand. Any extension called ultra, plus, or extra may be problematic. The introduction of Alka-Seltzer Plus, for example, was very successful—at the expense of the Alka-Seltzer brand.[29]

In another example, Hershey Chocolate introduced several limited edition line extensions, yielding a gain of eight percent to quarterly sales. However, Hershey allowed this limited edition to drag on for too long, and consequently, they have had to cut a significant amount of the portfolio. Relying on short-term line extensions as a long-term growth plan has been a problematic strategy.[30]

Figure 8-9: This advertisement for the St. Francis Kids Surgery Suite promotes a line extension service designed especially for children.

Source: Courtesy of Newcomer, Morris & Young.

Another strategy involves introducing **brand extensions**—that is, using an existing brand name to introduce products in a new product category. The assumption, for brand extensions, is that the brand is quite successful and enjoys substantial consumer franchise. In fact, if a brand is well known and enjoys substantial consumer franchise, it is only natural for firms to attempt to leverage that into new products. Many strong brands, such as Disney and Taco Bell, have transformed themselves into megabrands through brand extensions.[31] Kodak disposable cameras, Crest toothbrushes and Porsche apparel and sunglasses are all examples of brand extensions.

It is important to note that the wrong extension could create damaging associations that may be expensive to change. Moreover, the decision usually involves an important strategic growth thrust, thus causing the company to lose substantial time and resources and to miss important opportunities.[32]

A third strategy is **family branding (or blanket branding)**, whereby one brand name is used for more than one product. Stihl sells chain saws for individual use and industrial use under the same brand name. Volvo sells automobiles and trucks under the Volvo umbrella name. And the Rolling Stones sell tickets, T-shirts, and other paraphernalia under their well-known brand name.

> **Brand Extensions:**
> The use of an existing brand name to introduce products in a new product category.
>
> **Family Branding (or Blanket Branding):**
> Branding strategy whereby one brand name is used for more than one product.
>
> **Multibranding:**
> Using different brand names for products that the firm sells in the same product category.
>
> **New Brands:**
> New brands in new product categories for the firm.

The reverse of this strategy is **multibranding**, which involves using different brand names for products that the firm sells in the same product category. For example, Procter & Gamble sells an array of products in the laundry detergent category, positioned to address every imaginable laundry need: Tide, Bold, Cheer, Dreft, and Era, among many others.

Yet another strategy involves creating **new brands** in new product categories for the firm. This strategy is often pursued through acquisitions. For example, when Kraft bought Jacobs Suchard, it expanded into the chocolate product category—a category consistent with its cookies and crackers. In the process, it acquired the Toblerone brand, as well as other famous European chocolate brands, Milka and Suchard, engaging in a large number of foreign acquisitions to penetrate even more new markets and new product categories.[33]

8-4 PACKAGING AND LABELING

An important feature of the product is the package. **Packaging** is defined as all the activities involved in designing the product container. Packaging is a very important product feature whose cost ranges from less than 10 percent for a simple plastic wrap to more than 50 percent for a fancy golden mirror that is part of a purse-size compact powder or an elaborate lipstick package. The package contains and protects the product during shipping, handling, and storage.

> **Packaging:**
> All the activities involved in designing the product container.

The primary package may be a single container or wrapper—this is the immediate package. Bread, for example, is wrapped in one single plastic container. Almond Joy and Snickers bars are wrapped in a single wrapper. The primary package may also be enclosed in a secondary package. For example, Toblerone bars are wrapped in an aluminum wrapper and then in the distinctive triangle-shaped yellow box. Chewing gum is wrapped in a primary package for individual pieces of gum and a secondary package that holds five or 10 pieces of gum. An important consideration in designing the package is its storage. For example, products in round packages cannot be efficiently stored on the store shelves and result in substantial wasted space for the retailer, which manufacturers must take into consideration when designing the package. Ocean Spray recently heavily promoted its new square package that now fits in home refrigerator doors, saving valuable space.

The shipping package is usually a larger corrugated box that contains a number of products and protects them during shipping and storage. For Almond Joy, a shipping package contains 40 Almond Joy bars.

The package contains the product label, which performs the following functions:

- Identifies the product or brand—it carries the brand name, logo, and brand mark.
- Describes the product in terms of ingredients or components, weight, or volume. For food products, the label contains nutritional facts, such as calories, fat, cholesterol, sodium, carbohydrates, sugars, and protein based on serving size, and number of servings per package.
- Informs consumers when the product expires and classifies the product based on quality or size.
- Identifies the manufacturer or the distributor and has the UPC for easy inventory processing and scanning.
- Promotes the product. The label advertises the product to the consumer every time the consumer handles it. It is the last brand communication that reminds the consumer to purchase the product when it runs out.

- Directs the consumer on product use, offering recipes for food products or instructions on assembly and safety.

The information that cannot be communicated in the label because of space restrictions can be included in an insert within the package. Inserts include information on assembly and safety in different languages, or for drugs, they could include information on ingredients and side effects.

Packaging is a very important marketing function that must be appropriately coordinated with the company's marketing mix. Consumers expect that, if they pay $200 for a one-ounce bottle of perfume, the package will be unique and plush, not just functional. And they react positively to innovative packaging ideas: The Hershey's Kiss is one unique package that consumers are fond of.

Consumers also expect a package to resist reasonable stress in handling, while maintaining an attractive appearance. However, they also expect that packaging should not be excessive. In response to this expectation, more and more consumer product manufacturers are attempting to cut down on waste and pollution by offering a product in a single primary package, rather than multiple packages. For example, Uncle Ben's rice is no longer packaged separately, in a secondary package, next to the seasoning package. It is placed directly in the box. Similarly, the Manischewitz matzo meal, used as bread and seasoning for frying or for making matzo balls, is now simply offered in a cardboard container, rather than in one-use size secondary packages. And with regard to packaging convenience, Nabisco's Chewy Chips Ahoy cookies have a resealable package to ensure freshness and ease of use for the consumer, and, so far, feedback has been positive.[34]

8-5 THE PRODUCT MIX

The product offering of a firm is usually diversified into various products to ensure a more stable income over time. The **product mix** is defined as the complete assortment of the products that a company offers to its target consumers and has a number of important dimensions. One dimension of the product mix is the **product line**, which consists of the related brands in the same product category. Companies use different line strategies to achieve market share and profitability goals. For example, companies engage in line extensions to target consumers who otherwise cannot afford a particular product. In the fashion realm, for example, numerous top-line designers attempt to increase their profits by targeting the masses with bridge offerings (secondary, more affordable lines): Escada with Laurel, Anne Klein with Anne Klein II, Donna Karan with DKNY, Armani with Emporio Armani, and so on.

Other important product dimensions are the **product length**, which is the total number of brands in the product mix or all of the brands sold by the company; the **product width**, which is the total number of product lines the company offers; and the **product depth**, which is the number of different offerings for a product category. To illustrate these product dimensions, we will use the example of Unilever, one of the largest consumer product companies in the world. Although Unilever is organized primarily into two divisions—the foods division and the personal care division—the company has a number of product lines that are addressed as separate

strategic business units. Let us assume that Table 8-3 comprises all the Unilever brands. The total product length, then, is 22. Counting the different product lines (culinary products, frozen foods, ice cream, margarine, tea, detergents, deodorants, shampoos, personal care, oral care, and fragrances), the total product width is 11. To explain product depth, Lipton tea comes in at least three variants: Lipton Yellow Label, Lipton Ice Tea, and Lipton Brisk. The depth of the tea category (the Lipton brand), therefore, is three. Product depth for the tea line is thus calculated by adding all the variants under the Lipton brand.

Another important dimension of the product mix is **product consistency**, the extent to which the different product lines are related and use the same distribution channels and have the same final consumers. The Unilever brands are consistent within each of the company divisions: the foods division and the personal care division.

Product Mix:
The complete assortment of the products that a company offers to its target consumers.

Product Line:
The related brands the company offers in the same product category.

Product Length:
The total number of brands in the product mix—all the brands the company sells.

Product Width:
The total number of product lines the company offers.

Product Depth:
The number of different offerings for a product category.

Product Consistency:
The extent to which the different product lines are related, use the same distribution channels, and have the same final consumers.

Table 8-3: Unilever Products Aimed at the U.S. Market

Product Area	Brand Names
Culinary products	Ragu Spaghetti Sauces Hellmann's Mayonnaise Knorr Soups
Frozen foods	Gordon's Tenders
Ice cream	Breyers Ben & Jerry's
Margarine	I Can't Believe It's Not Butter
Tea	Lipton
Detergents	Snuggle
Deodorants	Sure Dove
Shampoos	Sunsilk Thermasilk Organics
Personal care	Dove Vaseline Intensive Care Pond's
Oral care	Mentadent Close-Up
Fragrances	Valentino Cerruti Calvin Klein

8-6 *NEW PRODUCT DEVELOPMENT*

To maintain their competitive advantage and to ensure survival and growth, companies must develop and introduce new goods and services that meet the needs of their markets. New product development is a costly and risky process that involves the firm at all levels. The following are examples of risks and difficulties companies face when developing new products:

- Competitors could appropriate the good or service idea and deliver the final good or service to the market more swiftly, economically, and with stronger company backing (brand reputation, financial support) than the initial good or service developer.

- Target consumers might not respond as anticipated to the offering because it does not meet their needs, because they cannot afford it, or because they prefer to adopt a product later in the PLC stage, when the product is proven and more affordable.

- The government might impose restrictions on product-testing procedures.

Figure 8-10 illustrates the product development process. At each step, the process can be either terminated or restarted for each individual product idea. Consequently, a product will go through each stage, or at least through some of the stages, to reach the product launching stage. Throughout the product development process, maintaining a strong market orientation is important. A thorough understanding of consumers' needs and wants, of the competitive situation, and the nature of the market are critical to product success.[35]

Figure 8-10: Steps in the New Product Development Process.

Generating New Product Ideas

Screening New Product Ideas

Developing and Evaluating New Product Concepts

Performing a Product Business Analysis

Designing and Developing the Product

Test Marketing

Launching the Product

8-6a: Generating New Product Ideas

The first step in the new product development process is generating new product ideas—that is, systematically searching for ideas for new products. Depending on the products provided or company philosophies, ideas will be sought using different strategies. Most firms are driven by the marketing concept, and their product development decisions are based on identifying the needs, wants, and desires of consumers. For technology-driven firms, the focus is more likely to be on the product itself, and thus the research and development division may be responsible for developing product ideas. Even in this second instance, however, products are developed with the needs of the consumer in mind.

Companies use multiple sources for ideas. The most obvious sources for ideas are consumers. As salespeople interact with consumers, the company's customer service employees can be queried about customers' reactions to products and about product preferences and needs. Marketing research firms can collect data on consumer preferences as well. They can conduct qualitative research with consumers to explore and identify their needs, gripes, complaints, and hassles.[36]

Internal idea sources, within the company, are also useful. Company idea schemes, even though they tend to focus on cost reduction through process streamlining, waste reduction, and productivity improvement, can also be a good source for ideas. Internal brainstorms can generate innovative ideas. Brainstorming sessions represent a venue for conducting internal qualitative research and may also be used in the process of generating product ideas.[37]

Suppliers and channel members could provide important input. For example, in the cosmetics and toiletries industry, many innovations are driven by raw materials, the properties they bestow on formulations, and the beneficial claims that are associated with their inclusion in formulations.[38] Competition represents an obvious source for ideas. Products that are in the test market phase or that are just being launched are always vulnerable to having their ideas copied. Other sources of ideas are consultants, nonprofit research laboratories, universities, and research firms.

8-6b: Screening New Product Ideas

In the process of screening new product ideas, the goal is to ensure that the product fits well with the target consumers' needs, as well as with the overall mission of the organization.[39] At this stage, a checklist is usually developed to screen out product ideas that do not meet these criteria.

In the screening process, the following should be taken into consideration: [40]

- The product to be developed should be superior, delivering unique benefits to users, rather than a "me-too" undifferentiated product. Such superiority is derived from design, features, attributes, specifications, to product positioning.

- The target market should be a large, attractive, growth market, where the product is perceived as important, where demand for it has been stable over time, and where customers are profitable and price insensitive.

- There should be a fit between the new product requirements and the resources, skills, and experiences of the firm with regard to management capabilities, technical support, research and development, manufacturing skills, sales and distribution skills, and the firm's channel of distribution.

8-6c: Developing and Evaluating New Product Concepts

The next stage, developing and evaluating concepts, entails developing product concepts and determining how consumers will view and use the product. This information can be determined by having the target consumers test the idea to gauge its usefulness.[41] Typically, the process involves developing a detailed description of the product and asking prospective consumers to evaluate it and to indicate their willingness to purchase the hypothetical product. Most often, this is done using a focus group of representative target consumers.

One method that is frequently used at this stage is conjoint analysis. In this method, respondents receive descriptions of different hypothetical products with varying levels of the same attributes, which they are then asked to rank. Analysts can determine the ideal combination of attributes, ascertain the importance of each attribute, and, assuming the data were collected from a sufficiently large sample of the target population, estimate market share.

The creation of new products may range from the substitution of a cheaper material in an existing product to a better way of marketing, distributing, or supporting a product or service.[42] **Degree of product newness** refers to the extent to which a good or service is new to the market. The creation of new products can be accomplished using different strategies. The marketing literature uses various classifications for different categories of innovation. At a basic level, new goods and services can be classified in one of the five categories highlighted in **Figure 8-11**.[43]

Figure 8-11: Types of New Products

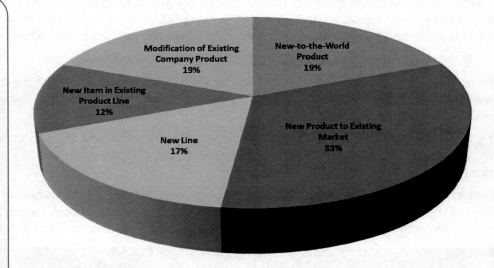

Degree of Product Newness:
The extent to which a product or service is new to the market.

Radical Innovations (or Discontinuous Innovations):
Innovations that create new industries or new standards of management, manufacturing, and servicing, and that represent fundamental changes for consumers, entailing departures from established consumption.

Dynamically Continuous Innovations:
Innovations that do not significantly alter consumer behavior but represent a change in the consumption pattern.

Continuous Innovations:
Innovations that have no disruption on consumption patterns and involve only product alterations, such as new flavors or a new product that is an improvement over the old offering.

Another popular classification organizes innovation into the *radical, dynamically continuous*, and *continuous* categories. **Radical innovations (or discontinuous innovations)** create new industries or new standards of management, manufacturing, and servicing, and they represent fundamental changes for consumers, entailing departures from established consumption.[44] Examples of relatively recent radical innovations are the Internet and endoscopy. **Dynamically continuous innovations** do not significantly alter consumer behavior, but they represent a change in the consumption pattern. Cellular phones are an example of such an innovation. **Continuous innovations** have no disruption on consumption patterns and involve only product alterations, such as new flavors or a new product that is an improvement over the old offering. They usually are congruous, in the sense that they can be used alongside the existing systems. For example, a new Microsoft Windows version will work with computers that are only a few years old or older computers with enhanced capacity. Its newest operating system, Windows Vista, however, is much different from past operating systems, and although it will work with older computers, it requires a much greater amount of memory to operate. This forces consumers to contemplate their purchase decision not because of compatibility considerations, but because of additional products that may need to be purchased for the software to operate more effectively.[45] Most of the innovations taking place today are continuous.

8-6d: Performing a Product Business Analysis

Performing a product business analysis should include calculating projected project costs, return on investment, cash flow, and determining the fixed and variable costs for the long term.[46] However enthusiastic the target consumers' response, if these figures do not fit the company budget, the project will be high risk. For many product categories, product price is a critical characteristic. At this stage, it is important to identify the price level at which revenue or profit best fit the manufacturer's goals.[47]

8-6e: Designing and Developing the Product

At the next stage, designing and developing the product, product prototypes are developed. It is important that product prototypes precisely match the concept description developed in the concept development and evaluation stage. If the company strays from the initial description, it is crucial that the revised product description be tested first.[48] The product now acquires a name, a brand identity, and the marketing mix is developed.

The cross-functional team developing the product—research and development, engineering, operations, marketing, and finance—must come together for this process.[49] This team must be focused on the project in such a way that a large percentage of team members' time is devoted to this particular project, rather than to other projects. It also is important that the team acts as a unit, focusing on the project itself, rather than on departmental interests.[50]

Product Design:
The aesthetic traits, style, and function of the product.

Simulated Test Marketing:
Test marketing that simulates purchase environments in that target consumers are observed in the product related decision-making process.

For multinational companies, it is advisable that coordination takes place across subsidiaries or in conjunction with international partners. Companies such as Boeing and Motorola coordinate research and development activities globally by establishing worldwide information systems to coordinate product and design development. For example, in developing the Boeing 777, the company used real-time computer-aided technology to design components jointly with Japanese partners.[51] Boeing's development of the 787 Dreamliner has also involved extensive cooperation with Japanese partners, such as Fuji Heavy Industries, who developed the wings of the plane.[52]

Companies also tend to encourage communication among research and development facilities in different countries. Procter & Gamble and Unilever, for example, require extensive communication and information sharing among units.[53]

Another important consideration is **product design**, defined as the aesthetic traits, style, and function of the product. Research points to the importance of design and aesthetics in developing products. The iPhone is particularly popular and has substantial brand franchise and cachet, especially because of its sleek, minimalist design. As with the iPod, which was transformed into a veritable fashion statement, with iPod tattoos, so one could change the look of the MP3 as often as one changes clothes, [54] Apple's iPhone, has a design unlike anything seen before, with the capability to change the layout on the screen to landscape or portrait, and is based on touch controls. [55]

8-6f: Test Marketing

Test marketing a product can provide a good indication of how the product will be received when it is in the marketplace, but this stage can also be expensive, time consuming, and open to competitive sabotage.[56] The following are test-marketing options firms can use to evaluate the reaction of the market to their product. Because eight out of ten products fail, **simulated test marketing** is often used to reduce the risks a company would incur in terms of marketing, sales, and capital expenses; in terms of cannibalization of the original brand through line extension; and in terms of competitive reaction to the new product.[57] Among the simulated test marketing research systems used today are LITMUS, which is used especially for new packaged goods, consumer durables, and services; ASSESSOR, which is used for packaged goods; BASES, which is used primarily for food and health and beauty products; and ESP, which is used primarily for packaged goods.[58]

To illustrate, the LITMUS simulated test-marketing study[59] recruits about 600 representative consumers who participate in a research study in a central facility in a number of markets. After responding to questions about their product-related attitudes and purchase behavior, the consumers in the sample view advertising of the new brand and of competitive brands that are embedded in a television program. The respondents then comment on the television program and the advertising and then proceed to a simulated store stocking test brands and competitive brands where they can buy the products at a substantial discount. The proportion of individuals purchasing the test brand is then used to estimate product trialability.

> **Controlled Test Marketing:**
> Offering a new product to a group of stores and evaluating the market reaction to it.

Usually conducted by a research firm in industrialized countries, **controlled test marketing** involves offering a new product to a group of stores and evaluating the market reaction to it (consumer reaction as well as competitive reaction). In the process, different aspects of the marketing mix are varied—price, in-store promotion, placement in the store, and so on. A more informal controlled test marketing involves simply asking a number of stores to carry the product for a fee. Depending on the outcome, the manufacturing firm may decide to produce the product on a larger scale, or not.

A number of important decisions are involved in the full-blown actual test marketing, in which the product and related marketing mix are tested in a large test market area. Companies at this stage must decide on the cities that are most appropriate for testing the product, based on the availability of retailers and other necessary distribution and logistics service providers, and on the availability of the infrastructure needed to conduct the test market, such as the necessary media, research firms, direct-mail providers, and so on. For companies selling financial products and for companies that cannot afford large-scale testing in the marketplace, test marketing may be limited to direct mail. For example, MasterCard continually tests new products by using direct mail. This strategy also appeals to service providers from developing countries.

Visa is also test marketing the text-messaging function of cell phones. It involves sending a select group of consumers a text message with a coupon inside, which consumers can redeem at the point-of-purchase. This strategy has also been adopted by a number of other companies.[60]

Although test marketing can provide valuable information for the manufacturer, anticipating product performance in the short run, its usefulness is often questioned given the high expense it necessitates. In a rapidly changing competitive environment, being first in the market constitutes an important competitive advantage addressed earlier, the first-mover advantage. As such, the company is the first to attract consumers and to commit channel members for its new product. A company is also vulnerable to competitive reaction during the test-marketing stage. On one hand, competition could appropriate the product idea and be the first to offer the product to the market. On the other hand, competition could sabotage the new brand, cutting prices for all competitive offerings.

Test marketing, nevertheless, can be a reliable predictor of market share, costs, and profitability and a tool to assess and compare between alternative product strategies. Yet, surprisingly, this tool is frequently overlooked in marketing.[61] Among errors to avoid in test marketing are incorrect forecasts, unrealistic market conditions, and choice of the wrong test market.[62]

8-6g: Launching the Product

Launching the product, also known as **commercialization**, involves introducing the new product to the market. Strategies for launching the product have an impact on later product performance. Products launched using a successful strategy have a higher rate of success and score high ratings on profitability, technical success, and positive impact on the company.[63] Quality of launch is characterized by the following, in order of impact: high service quality, on-time shipment and adequate product availability, quality sales force and enough sales effort and support, quality of promotion, and sufficient promotional effort.[64]

Commercialization: Stage in the new product development process when the product is introduced to the market.

An important decision is the timing of the new product launch. Companies often attempt to gain the first-mover advantage by being the first to launch the new product. Alternatively, they could engage in later entry. The advantage of later entry is that a firm's competitors would have to incur the costs of informing the market about the new product and its features. Also, the company could market the product as a "me-too" product, reducing advertising costs significantly.

Figure 8-12 illustrates the new product development process used by Coors Brewing Company. The company stresses the role of research and development, as well as the involvement of the other functional areas of the company, in most steps of the process. As the figure indicates, part of the process involves evaluating the overall product portfolio balance.

As many companies have found out over time, planning and timing are crucial elements of new product development. Poor planning and timing can lead to product failure.

Figure 8-12: The New Product Development Process.

Idea Generation

Idea Documentation and Evaluation within Each Research and Development Area

Multifunctional Review, Reprioritize Projects, and Recommend Cut Lines

Project Portfolio Multidimensional Data Analysis

Senior Review: Team Assesses Portfolio Balance

Building Project Milestones into Researchers' Annual Accountabilities

Learning Sessions on Planning to Identify Next Cycle Improvements

Source: Hugo Patino, "Applying Total Quality to R&D at Coors Brewing Company," *Research Technology Management* 40, no. 5 (September/October 1997): 32–36. Reprinted by permission of Industrial Research Institute.

8-7 NEW PRODUCT DIFFUSION

Product diffusion refers to the manner in which consumers accept new products and the speed of new product adoption by various consumer groups. A number of factors influence the speed of product adoption.[65] First, the new product must offer a commercialization *relative advantage* compared with the other offerings available on the market and must be *compatible with the needs of consumers*. In addition, the good or service use must be observable (or communicable to others) and have a high trialability (e.g., consumers can try the product on a limited basis, by renting it).

Target consumers can be segmented based on the manner in which they adopt new products throughout the respective products' life cycle. The segments and their characteristics, also shown in **Figure 8-13,** are as follows:

Innovators—These few risk takers (2.5 percent of the total market) can afford to pay the higher purchase price charged by companies during the introduction stage of a new product. They are willing to accept risk, and they like to be known as the first to try out product concepts among their peers.

Early adopters—The next consumers to purchase the product tend to be opinion leaders in their communities who take risks, but with greater discernment than innovators. They constitute about 13.5 percent of the total population.

Early majority—These consumers, who account for 34 percent of the total market, are more risk averse than individuals in the first categories but enjoy the status of being among the first in their peer group to buy what will be a popular product.

Late majority—These consumers, who account for 34 percent of the total market, are individuals of limited means who are likely to adopt products only if the products are widely popular and the risk associated with buying them is minimal. The products themselves are much more affordable at this stage.

Laggards—These consumers, who account for 16 percent of the total market, are the last to adopt new products and often do so reluctantly. In general, laggards are risk averse and very conservative in their spending.

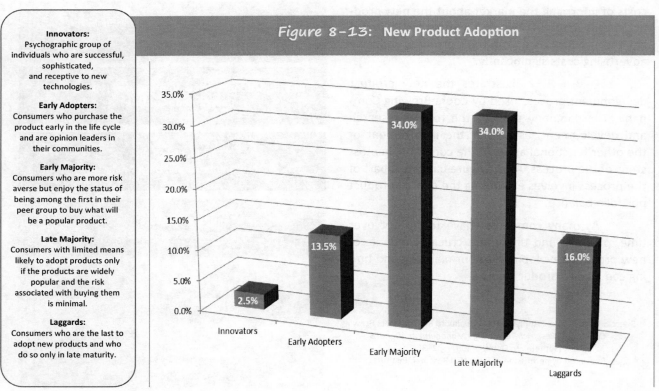

Innovators:
Psychographic group of individuals who are successful, sophisticated, and receptive to new technologies.

Early Adopters:
Consumers who purchase the product early in the life cycle and are opinion leaders in their communities.

Early Majority:
Consumers who are more risk averse but enjoy the status of being among the first in their peer group to buy what will be a popular product.

Late Majority:
Consumers with limited means likely to adopt products only if the products are widely popular and the risk associated with buying them is minimal.

Laggards:
Consumers who are the last to adopt new products and who do so only in late maturity.

Figure 8-13:   New Product Adoption

- Innovators: 2.5%
- Early Adopters: 13.5%
- Early Majority: 34.0%
- Late Majority: 34.0%
- Laggards: 16.0%

8-8 THE PRODUCT LIFE CYCLE (PLC)

After new products are launched, marketing managers need to ensure that their products perform well on the market for a very long time—long enough to generate sufficient profits that can be used to finance other items in the product portfolio. Products pass through distinct stages in their evolution, during which sales and profits rise and fall. In this evolutionary process, products require different marketing strategies at each stage. The **product life cycle (PLC)** is defined as the performance of the product in terms of sales and profit over time. The PLC can apply to a product category or to a particular brand. The traditional PLC is illustrated in Figure 8-14.

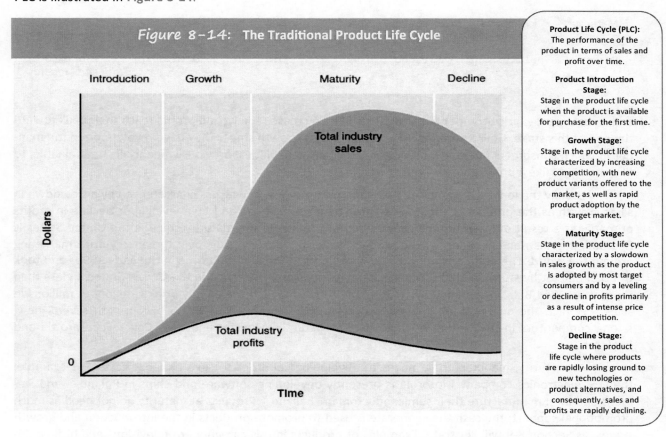

Figure 8–14: The Traditional Product Life Cycle

Product Life Cycle (PLC): The performance of the product in terms of sales and profit over time.

Product Introduction Stage: Stage in the product life cycle when the product is available for purchase for the first time.

Growth Stage: Stage in the product life cycle characterized by increasing competition, with new product variants offered to the market, as well as rapid product adoption by the target market.

Maturity Stage: Stage in the product life cycle characterized by a slowdown in sales growth as the product is adopted by most target consumers and by a leveling or decline in profits primarily as a result of intense price competition.

Decline Stage: Stage in the product life cycle where products are rapidly losing ground to new technologies or product alternatives, and consequently, sales and profits are rapidly declining.

The characteristics of each stage are further explained in Table 8-4, in terms of industry sales, profits, price, promotion, competition, and target market.

The **product introduction stage** is the PLC stage when the product is available for purchase for the first time. During this stage, products are developed in industrialized countries and supported by a firm's substantial research and development budgets and by highly skilled product research teams. To quickly recover the high costs of product development and launching, a firm markets products in industrialized countries to consumers who can afford the high prices that need to be charged. The firm at this stage still has control of the market. It is the only manufacturer or one of the few manufacturers of the product.

In the introduction stage, firms—or the one firm first introducing the product—have negative or very low profits. They are attempting to recover the high product development costs. Sales are low, but increasing. And the company (companies) spends heavily on promotion to encourage product innovators to adopt the product and on developing a viable distribution channel for the product, if such a channel is not yet established.

The **growth stage** is the PLC stage characterized by increasing competition, with new product variants offered to the market, as well as rapid product adoption by the target market. Toward the end of this stage, the focus is on developing economies of scale in the manufacturing process. A standard is reached

Table 8-4: Product Life Cycle (PLC) Strategies

PLC Stage	Industry Sales	Industry Profit	Product Price	Promotion	Competition	Target Market
Introduction	Low	Low	High	High	Low	Innovators
Growth	Increasing	Increasing	Decreasing	High	Increasing	Early adopters and early majority
Maturity	High and stable	Decreasing	Lower	Decreasing	High	Early and late majority
Decline	Decreasing	Decreasing	Low	Low	Decreasing	Late majority and laggards

and, subsequently, price competition is intense. Sales increase rapidly, and profits reach their peak toward the end of this stage. GoPro cameras are currently in the growth stage. They have revolutionized the manner in which consumers interact with images, providing capabilities, previously financially unattainable, to film the world like a pro.

Usually the longest stage in the PLC is the **maturity stage**, which is characterized by a slowdown in sales growth as the product is adopted by most target consumers and by a leveling or decline in profits primarily as a result of intense price competition. A product in the maturity stage in the United States is Red Bull, the Austrian energy drink. The product has systematically taken over the energy drink marketing around the world. The drink was adopted by consumers in the rest of Europe in the early 1990s and took the U.S. market by storm in 1997. Today, it is in nearly every retail shop in the United States. In less than three years, Red Bull single-handedly created and then propelled the energy drink category to millions in sales.[66] In fact, the energy drink industry now accounts for more than $27.5 billion, with several new, strong competitors in the market, such as Hansen Natural's Monster and Coca Cola's Full Throttle and Rockstar.[67]

At maturity, manufacturing moves to developing countries to save on labor costs. For example, the U.S. electronics company Motorola is presently developing software and chips in Poland,[68] and Siemens and Intel manufacture their semiconductors in Thailand.[69] Products at maturity do not need as much promotional support; the cash they generate is used to promote products in the introduction and growth stages, as Section 8-9 will illustrate. Examples of products in this category are television sets, hi-fi equipment, and video cameras, among others. In general, the electronics industry is in the maturity stage, and many firms have begun outsourcing jobs to reduce costs. Electronics companies save on average between 10 and 39 percent yearly by outsourcing.[70]

Products in the **decline stage** are rapidly losing ground to new technologies or product alternatives. Sales and profits are rapidly declining at this stage, and the firm is likely to cut back on production, distribution, and promotional support. Alternatively, management may decide that it is not worthwhile to maintain the product on the market because the costs of even minimal product maintenance are high. Firms still have to pay the costs of manufacturing and distributing the product. Among these costs are those of maintaining the sales staff, of managing the distribution channel, of maintaining shelf space (slotting fees and other expenses), and so on. Dropping the product has many costs associated with it. In addition to the overall losses that it incurs in the divestiture of equipment and physical manufacturing facilities, the company may have dissatisfied employees and unhappy formerly loyal consumers.

Products vary in the length of time needed for them to go through the life cycle. Although most products go through the traditional life cycle, fashion, fads, and styles, for instance, have a much shorter cycle (see Figure 8-15). For example, a style is defined as a general form of popular expression that could last for a longer period of time—even decades—or that could be cyclical in nature. The traditional home is an example of a **style**. It has traditional elements, such as molding, traditional mantle pieces, and modern bathrooms and kitchens. Louis XV is a furniture style characterized by slightly curved legs for chairs and tables. Current Louis XV designs are rendered in dark wood; the original style was popular gilded, white, or a combination thereof. The black-tie dress style for men has been a constant for more than a century, with small variations.

A **fashion** is defined as a current style. In the 1960s, polyester leisure suits and Nehru jackets became popular, followed by bell-bottom pants. In the 1980s, the more dressy yuppie look became popular. In Germany, hip-hop fashion is taking the country by storm. A **fad** is a fashion that quickly becomes very popular and just as quickly disappears. An example of a fad is tooth jewelry. Another example is Tickle Me Elmo, which had a short duration—just one pre-Christmas sales season.

> **Style:**
> A general form of popular expression that could last for a longer period of time or that could be cyclical in nature.
>
> **Fashion:**
> A current style.
>
> **Fad:**
> A fashion that quickly becomes very popular and just as quickly disappears.

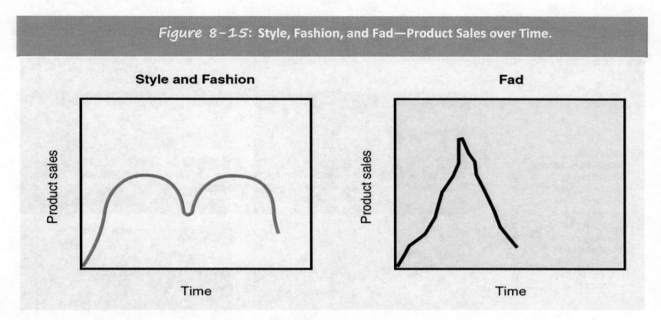

Figure 8–15: Style, Fashion, and Fad—Product Sales over Time.

8-9 MANAGING THE PRODUCT PORTFOLIO

The **product portfolio** is defined as the totality of products managed by the company as separate businesses. Product portfolio decisions are an important aspect of strategic planning, as will be seen in Appendix A. Companies periodically review their different businesses and make decisions on whether to acquire new ones or divest those that might be unprofitable, or that do not represent a good fit with the company. For example, PepsiCo decided to focus more on the Pepsi and Frito Lay brands and divest the restaurant business by spinning off its fast-food restaurants, Taco Bell, KFC, and Pizza Hut. And in the process of expanding their product portfolio, PepsiCo entered the health food industry by acquiring Stacy's Pita Chip Company and Duyvis in the Netherlands—primarily a nuts company. In its future expansion, PepsiCo is strongly betting that the health food and convenience industry is an up-and-coming market and will be profitable for a long time to come.[71]

As we have seen in previous examples, Kraft bought Jacobs Suchard and thus acquired the popular chocolate brands Toblerone, Suchard, and Milka, as well as the very popular European coffee brand Jacobs. Unilever decided to enter the gourmet ice cream business by acquiring Ben & Jerry's. These are all portfolio decisions that involve substantial resource allocations. Companies must constantly reevaluate their portfolios to make sure that they are appropriately allocating their resources to ensure firm success. Two models exist to evaluate portfolios: the growth-share matrix and the product-market matrix.

The **growth-share matrix** was developed by the Boston Consulting Group in the 1970s and remains one of the most popular bases for evaluating company product portfolios. The assumption of the matrix is that a company should have a portfolio of products with different growth rates and different market shares to be successful—high-growth products require cash inputs to grow, whereas low-growth products should generate excess cash, and both types of products are needed simultaneously.[72]

Products are evaluated on two dimensions: relative market share and industry growth rate. Evaluating each dimension in terms of high and low generates a 2 X 2 matrix, illustrated in Figure 8-16. A high relative market share would indicate that a particular brand has a high percentage of the market compared with competitors. A high industry growth rate would indicate an industry that is growing at a rate higher than 10 percent per year.

Figure 8-16: The Boston Consulting Group Matrix

Relative market share in an SBU's market share in comparison to the leading competitors in the industry. Industry growth rate is the annual growth of all similar business in the market (such as sugarless gum).

A balanced product portfolio consists of **stars, cash cows,** and **question marks (or problem children).** Companies should drop **dogs.** All products either become cash cows or dogs eventually.

Most firms do rely on some type of matrix for portfolio planning. A drawback of relying on a particular model is that it keeps the firm focused on the matrix dimensions—in the case of the growth-share matrix, industry growth rate and market share. Other important market dimensions could be neglected in the analyses. Moreover, abandoning a product because it has become a dog may be premature. The dog could quickly become a star if the target market becomes a niche market.

Another approach to evaluating products is the **product-market matrix,**[73] which helps companies identify future products that should be considered for its portfolio. Figure 8-17 identifies four strategies depending on market saturation and contingent on the firm's ability and desire to introduce new products. The following is a brief summary of each strategy with corresponding examples:

- **Market penetration** is defined as selling more products to present customers without changing the product. Approaches include increasing the usage rate of current customers and attracting competitors' customers. Improving product visibility through promotion and through securing better shelf space are two strategies that could be used to this end. Often, companies attempt to penetrate the market further by selling bundles of goods, that might or might not be complementary. Research has demonstrated that consumers who buy products in larger packages are likely to consume more. This strategy, thus, might increase consumption.

- **Market development** is defined as increasing product sales by developing new markets for the company's existing product or by creating new product uses. Many companies increase their sales substantially by going international.

- **Product development** is defined as developing new products to appeal to the company's existing market. Apple could easily increase sales if they were to sell products other than those in their current portfolio. Apple devotees are rapid adopters of new company offerings.

- **Diversification** is defined as developing or acquiring new products for new markets. For example, Heinz Ketchup has developed a variety of new products to increase their revenues, including a fit-in-the door ketchup bottle and various new colors, such as purple and blue, to appeal to their younger audience.[74]

Figure 8-17: The Product-Market Opportunity Matrix

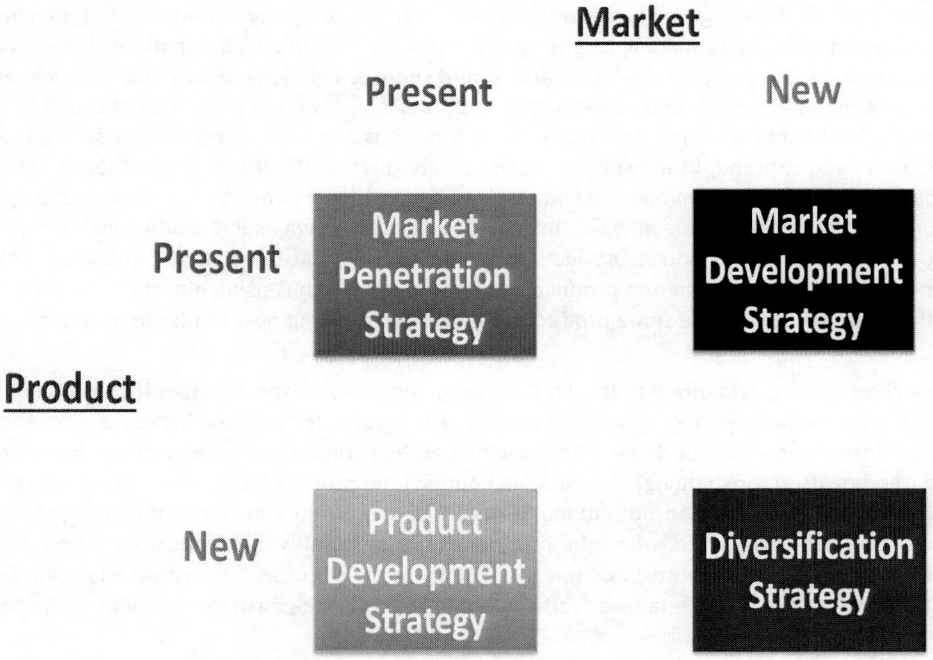

Product-market Matrix: A matrix used to identify future products and opportunities for companies.

Market Penetration: The process of increasing the usage rate of current customers and attracting competitors' customers to sell more products to present customers without changing the product.

Market Development: The process of developing new markets for the company's existing product or creating new product uses.

Product Development: The process of developing new products to appeal to the company's existing market.

Diversification: Opportunity for expansion involving developing or acquiring new products for new markets.

Source: Adapted from H. Igo Ansoff, "Strategies for Diversification," *Harvard Business Review* 35 (September-October 1957): 113–124.

Summary

1. Define and classify products into relevant categories. A product, an offering developed to satisfy consumer needs, can be conceptualized at three levels. The core product is the fundamental benefit, or problem solution, sought by consumers. The expected or actual product is the basic physical product, including styling, features, brand name, and packaging, which delivers those benefits. The augmented product is a product enhanced by the addition of extra or unsolicited services or benefits to the consumer to prompt purchase, such as warranty, repair services, maintenance, and other services that enhance product use. In terms of durability, products are classified as durables (tangible products that have a prolonged use, such as automobiles and appliances), nondurables (tangible products that are consumed relatively quickly and purchased on a regular basis), and services (intangible benefits or activities that individuals acquire but that do not result in ownership). Consumer products are classified into convenience goods, preference goods, shopping goods, and specialty goods. Convenience goods are inexpensive and purchased frequently and include impulse goods that are bought without earlier planning: staples, which are bought routinely; and emergency goods, which are bought to address urgent needs. Preference goods are convenience goods that become differentiated through branding and achieve some degree of brand loyalty. Shopping goods are perceived as higher-risk goods that consumers are willing to spend a greater amount of purchase effort in searching for and evaluating. Specialty goods are highly differentiated and enjoy high brand loyalty, such that they are the only brand acceptable to the consumer.

2. Address issues related to branding, such as the brand name, mark, logo, and character; brand sponsor; and brand strategy decisions. A brand is a name, design, symbol, or a combination thereof that identifies the product or the seller and is used to differentiate the product from competitors' offerings. Brand marks are part of the brand that can be seen but not spoken, and a brand logo is a distinctive mark, sign, symbol, or graphic version of a company's name and is used to identify and promote its product. A brand character or trade character is a character that personifies the brand, such as Tony the Tiger for Kellogg's Frosted Flakes and Ronald McDonald for McDonald's. These together help build the brand's identity and are valuable and well-protected trademarks. A trademark consists of words, symbols, marks, and signs that are legally registered for use by a single company. Counterfeiting, ranging from direct copying to design counterfeiting, is flourishing as a result of improved technology, inadequate channel control, lax enforcement locally and worldwide, and consumer demand. Brand sponsor decisions involve determining whether the brand should be sold as a manufacturer brand (a national brand), a dealer brand (a private label brand, a retailer brand, a wholesaler brand, or a distributor brand, depending on whether it is a retailer or wholesaler selling the product under its own name), or a generic brand. Brand sponsor decisions also involve determining whether the brand can be licensed or co-branded. Brand strategies involve extending the existing brand name by introducing new product offerings in an existing product category, such as new flavors, colors, or sizes (known as line extensions); brand extensions, using an existing brand name to introduce products in a new product category; family (blanket) branding, whereby one brand name is used for more than one product; multibranding, which is using different brand names for different products that the company sells in the same product category; and creating new brands in new product categories for the firm.

3. Address product packaging and labeling issues. Packaging addresses all the activities involved in designing the product container. The primary package may be a single container or wrapper; this is the immediate package. The secondary package may enclose the primary package. The shipping package contains a number of products and typically consists of a corrugated box used for shipping. The package contains the product label, which identifies the product or brand. It carries the brand name, logo, and brand mark; describes the product in terms of ingredients or components, weight, or volume; informs consumers when the product expires; classifies the product based on quality or size; identifies the manufacturer or the distributor; and has the UPC for easy inventory processing and scanning. The package also promotes the product because the label advertises the product to the consumer every time the consumer handles it.

4. Analyze the different dimensions of the product mix. The product mix is the complete assortment of products that a company offers to its target consumers. The product line consists of the related brands in the same product category. Other important product dimensions are the product length (the total number of brands in the product mix), the product width (the total number of product lines the company offers), and the product depth (the number of different offerings for a product category).

5. Describe the new product development process and the different degrees of product newness. The new product development process starts with idea generation, inside and outside the company. The next step involves idea screening using predetermined criteria, followed by concept development and evaluation. Product business analysis determines the extent to which the product is likely to be viable. In the next stage—product design and development—product prototypes are developed and evaluated by target consumers. Test marketing involves great expense on the part of the company; it also leaves the company vulnerable to competitive idea theft. The final stage—launching—requires significant commitment to the product and to the target market. There are different types of new products: products that are new to an existing market or new to an existing company; new lines (i.e., new products or product lines to a company but for a company already operating in that market); new items in an existing product line for the company; modifications to an existing company product; and innovations.

6. Examine the new product diffusion process and the different categories of product adopters. The new product diffusion process involves the following stages: innovators, early adopters, early majority, late majority, and laggards. Product diffusion begins when innovators try the product during the introduction stage of the PLC. If the product is successful, then early adopters will start using it. These are opinion leaders who others will follow. The early majority is ready to try the new product after it is established and prices have come down. The late majority purchases the product only during the mature stage of the PLC when competition is high, prices are lower, and product differentiation has occurred. The laggards resist the new product and buy only when older alternatives are not available.

7. Address the different stages of the product life cycle. The first stage of the PLC is the introduction stage, when the product is first introduced to the market. The product most likely has no or only minimal competition, and it is targeted to innovators who are willing to try new products and spend substantial amounts for the product. The firm has negative profits in the sense that it is attempting to recover product development costs. In the growth stage, sales and profits are increasing rapidly, and more and more competitors are offering the product. In the maturity stage, there is a slowdown in sales growth as the product is adopted by most target consumers and as profits level off or decline primarily as a result of intense price competition. Products are rapidly losing ground to new technologies or product alternatives in the decline stage. Sales and profits are rapidly declining, and the firm is likely to cut back on production, distribution, and promotional support.

8. Examine the challenges involved in managing the product portfolio. The product portfolio consists of the totality of products managed by the company as separate businesses. A popular matrix used for portfolio assessment is the Boston Consulting Group growth-share matrix. Its assumption is that a company should have a portfolio of products with different growth rates and different market shares to be successful. The matrix consists of cash cows, which are products with a high market share and slow growth that generate large amounts of cash, in excess of the reinvestment required to maintain market share; dogs, which have a low market share and slow growth; question marks or problem children, which are low market share and high-growth products that require more cash investment than they generate; and stars, which are high-share, high-growth products that create profits but may require additional investment. A product-market opportunity matrix is used to identify future products that companies should consider for their portfolio. Companies have the option to pursue one of four strategies: market penetration, which involves selling more products to present customers without changing the product by increasing usage rate of current customers and attracting competitors' customers; market development, which involves developing new markets for the company's existing product or by creating new product uses; product development, which involves developing new products to appeal to the company's existing market; and diversification, which involves developing or acquiring new products for new markets.

Key Terms

augmented product	decline stage	homogeneous shopping goods
battle of the brands	degree of product newness	impulse goods
brand	diversification	innovators
brand character (or trade character)	dogs	laggards
brand equity (or brand franchise)	durable goods	late majority
brand extensions	dynamically continuous innovations	licensing
brand image	early adopters	line extension
brand logo	early majority	manufacturers' brands (or national
brand mark	emergency goods	brands)
brand name	expected (or actual) product	market development
cash cows	fad	market penetration
co-branding	family branding (or blanket branding)	maturity stage
commercialization	fashion	multibranding
continuous innovations	generics	new brands
controlled test marketing	growth-share matrix	nondurable goods
convenience goods	growth stage	packaging
core product	heterogeneous shopping goods	patent

preference goods	product life cycle (PLC)	servicemark
private label brands	product line	shopping goods
product	product-market matrix	simulated test marketing
product consistency	product mix	specialty goods
product depth	product portfolio	staples
product design	product width	stars
product development	question marks (or problem children)	style
product introduction stage	radical innovations (or discontinuous	trademark
product length	innovations)	

Discussion Questions

1. Identify 10 brand characters and 10 brand logos. What makes these characters and logos memorable?

2. Try to think of brand names for medicine that you do not normally take. What traits of these brand names made them memorable?

3. Go to Unilever's home page at www.unilever.com and access the brands sold to consumers in the United States. Comment on the product depth, width, and length, as well as on product consistency.

4. How could Unilever take advantage of opportunities in each of the four quadrants of the product market matrix? Give examples in each category.

5. What are the activities involved at each stage of the new product development process? Where are most new products developed?

6. Many products are advertised in the United States as ''new and improved.'' What does this description mean in terms of new product classifications?

7. Recall the last time you remember a product launch that was accompanied by aggressive advertising. What brand was advertised? What traits of the introductory communication campaign do you recall?

8. Describe the PLC and the activities involved at each stage. Offer examples of products at each of the four stages.

9. Differentiate between a fad and a fashion. Can a fashion be really a fad? When can marketing managers find out whether this is the case? Can marketing managers influence fashion and fads? Explain.

Review Questions

(Answers are on Last Page of the Chapter)

True or False

1. The expected, actual product is enhanced by the addition of extra and unsolicited services or benefits to the consumer, which help promote the purchase.

2. As a subgroup of convenience goods, impulse goods are those products bought routinely, such as groceries.

3. Manufacturing brands are also sold as private labels.

4. Licensing involves the owner of the brand name allowing a manufacturer or reseller to sell the product under the owner's brand name in return for a licensing fee.

5. Packaging has a minimal influence on the product's purchase price.

6. Companies' success depends on internal research and brainstorming sessions to generate new product ideas.

7. Products launched with a well-determined strategy have a higher rate of success and score high in profitability technical success, and have a positive effect on the company's performance.

8. Innovators and early adopters constitute the majority of consumers throughout the life cycle of a product.

9. The maturity stage of the PLC is characterized by increasing competition, with new product variations offered to the market, and rapid market adoption.

Multiple Choice

10. Which of the following categories is indicative of high consumer awareness and loyalty?
    a. Brand equity
    b. Brand franchise
    c. Brand identity
    d. a and b

11. Which of the following categories characterize brand names? Brand names
    a. are easy to pronounce and memorize.
    b. suggest product benefits.
    c. are easy to translate into other languages.
    d. all of the above.

12. The battle of the brands is defined as
    a. a conflict between manufacturers and retailers to promote their own brands.
    b. a similarity in packaging of manufacturers' and retailers' brand products.
    c. the selling of the retailer brand at a lower price than the national brand.
    d. all of the above.

13. Which of the following categories is related to the product mix?
    a. Product length
    b. Product width
    c. Product depth
    d. All of the above

14. The product introduction stage is characterized by
    a. negative or low profits.
    b. low but increasing sales.
    c. promotions to encourage product innovators.
    d. all of the above.

15. Which of the following groups in the growth-share matrix is characterized by low market share and high-growth products that require more cash investment than they generate?
    a. Cash cows
    b. Dogs
    c. Question marks (or problem children)
    d. Stars

Blog

Clow-Lascu: *Marketing Essentials 5e Blog*

Tomorrow is Yours to Claim

KelloggsUS

236 vie

Screenshot

What Is Happening Today?

Learn More! For videos and articles

that relate to Chapter 8:

blogclowlascu.net/category/chapter08

Includes Discussion Questions

with each Post!

Part Three: Marketing Mix Strategies

Notes

1. www.rollingstones.com, accessed June 12, 2014; Ian Mirlin, ''The World's Greatest Rock 'n' Roll Brand,'' *Marketing Magazine* 107, no. 43 (October 18, 2002): 16.

2. ''Mouthing Off,'' *Financial Times* (December 5, 2005) 18.

3. Peter S. Menell, "Brand New World: Distinguishing Oneself in the Global Flow – 2014: Brand Totalitarianism," UC Davis Law Review, February , 2014, 787; Theodore Levitt, ''Marketing Success through Differentiation—Of Anything,'' *Harvard Business Review* (January–February, 1980): 83–91.

4. Casey Donoho, ''Classifying Services from a Consumer Perspective,'' *The Journal of Services Marketing* 10, no. 6 (1996): 33–44.

5. Robert W. Pimentel and Kristy E. Reynolds, ''A Model for Consumer Devotion: Affective Commitment with Proactive Sustaining Behaviors,'' *Academy of Marketing Science Review* 1(2004): 1; David A. Aaker, *Managing Brand Equity* (New York: Maxwell Macmillan International, 1991).

6. Jane Bainbridge, ''Global Forces,'' *Marketing* (July 20, 2000): 24–25.

7. Ibid.

8. Kate MacArthur, ''Coke Crisis: Equity Erodes as Brand Troubles Mount,'' *Advertising Age* 71, no. 18 (April 24, 2000): 3, 98.

9. Kate MacArthur, ''Coke Bets on Zero to Save Cola Category,'' *Advertising Age*, (March 17, 2007): 77.

10. www.upsto.gov, accessed on June 14, 2014.

11. Dexter Roberts, Frederik Balfour, Paul Magnuson, Pete Engardio, and Jennifer Lee, ''China's Pirates: It's Not Just Little Guys—State-Owned Factories Add to the Plague of Fakes,'' *Business Week* no. 3684 (June 5, 2000): 26, 44.

12. Ibid.

13. John Zarocostas, ''EU Survey Cites China as Primary Source of Counterfeits,'' *WWD: Women's Wear Daily* 192, no. 79 (2006): 12.

14. Bill Roberts, ''Knocking Off the Counterfeiters,'' *Electronic Business* 32, no. 6 (2006): 10–12.

15. Brandon A. Sullivan and Steven M. Chermak, "Product Counterfeiting and the Media: Examining News Sources Used in the Construction of Product Counterfeiting as a Social Problem," International Journal of Comparative and Applied Criminal Justice, Vol. 30, 4, 15 November 2013, 295-316; Peter H. Bloch, Ronald F. Bush, and Leland Campbell, ''Consumer 'Accomplices' in Product Counterfeiting,'' *Journal of Consumer Marketing* 10, no. 4 (1993): 27–36.

16. Ibid.

17. Ibid.

18. Ibid.

19. Theresa Howard, "Coke Finally Scores Another Winner," USA Today, October 28, 2007, accessed at http://usatoday30.usatoday.com/money/advertising/adtrack/2007-10-28-coke-zero_n.htmon, June 14, 2014; Frederik Balfour, ''China's Fight Against Fakes,'' *Business Week Online* (2006): 10.

20. Roberts et al, China's Pirates, 2000, 26, 44.

21. Ibid.

22. Mike Duff, ''Top Brands 2002: Private Label—Drop-Off Begs Question, How Much Is Too Much?'' *DSN Retailing Today* 41, no. 20 (October 28, 2002): 37, 43.

23. ''Private Label Gaining Popularity in U.S.'' *Retail Merchandiser* 46, no. 12 (2006): 8.

24. Michelle Wirth Fellman, ''Just the Name, Thanks: Why Beemer Bought Rolls,'' *Marketing News* 32, no. 19 (September 14, 1998): 6.

25. www.rolls-royce.com, accessed on June 14, 2014.

26. Duff, Top Brands 2002, 37, 43.

27. Will Wade, ''JPM Chase, USA Hockey Extend Pact,'' *American Banker* 171, no. 31 (2006), 7:.

28. Lisa Marchese, ''Brand Schizophrenia: Today's Epidemic,'' *Brandweek* 43, no. 38 (October 21, 2002): 28.

29. Jon Berry, ''Brand Equity: How Much Is Your Brand Worth?'' *Brandweek* 34, no. 26 (June 28, 1993): 21–24.

30. Stephanie Thompson, ''Hershey Reaches Limits of Limited-Edition Candy,'' *Advertising Age* 77, no. 18 (2006): 12.

31. Berry, ''Brand Equity,'' 21–24.

32. David Aaker and Kevin Lane Keller, ''Consumer Evaluations of Brand Extensions,'' *Journal of Marketing* 54, no. 1 (1990): 27–41.

33. Julie Jargon, ''Kraft Sets Path for Overseas Expansion,'' *The Wall Street Journal* available at www.online.wsj.com, March 22, 2007, B4.

34. ''Chewy Chips Ahoy Launches Unique, Resealable Packaging,'' *Packaging Digest* 42, no. 9 (2005): 6.

35. Robert G. Cooper, ''New Products: What Distinguishes the Winners?'' *Research Technology Management* 33 (November/December 1990): 27–31.

36. Scott M. Davis, ''Bringing Innovation to Life,'' *Journal of Consumer Marketing* 14, no. 5 (1997): 338–361.

37. Gordon A. Wyner, ''Product Testing: Benefits and Risks,'' *Marketing Research* 9, no. 1 (Spring 1997): 46–48.

38. Patrick Love, ''Driving Productivity in Product Innovation,'' *Management Services*, 45, no. 1 (January 2001): 8–13.

39. Lisa Susanne Willsey, ''Taking These 7 Steps Will Help You Launch a New Product,'' *Marketing News* 33, no. 7 (March 29, 1999): 17.

40. See Cooper, ''New Products,'' 27–31.

41. Willsey, ''Taking These 7 Steps,'' 17.

42. Nicholas Valery, ''Survey: Innovation in Industry: Industry Gets Religion,'' *The Economist*, 350, no. 8107 (February 20, 1999): S5–S6.

43. Robert G. Cooper, ''Debunking the Myths of New Product Development,'' *Research Technology Management* 37, no. 4 (July/August 1994): 40–50.

44. See Michael-Jorg Oesterle, ''Time-Span until Internationalization: Foreign Market Entry as a Built-in-Mechanism of Innovations,'' *Management Review* 37, no. 2 (1997): 125–149.

45. ''Five Things You Need To Know About Windows Vista.'' *Office Pro 67*, no. 2 (2007): 6.

46. Willsey, ''Taking These 7 Steps,'' 17.

47. Wyner, ''Product Testing,'' 46–48.

48. Robert S. Doscher, ''How to Create New Products,'' *Target Marketing* 17, no. 1 (1994): 40–41.

49. Willsey, ''Taking These 7 Steps,'' 17.

50. Robert G. Cooper, ''How to Launch a New Product Successfully,'' *CMA*, 69, no. 8 (1995): 20–23.

51. Shaoming Zou and Aysegul Ozsomer, ''Global Product R&D and the Firm's Strategic Position,'' *Journal of Marketing* 7, no. 1 (1999): 57–76.

52. ''Assembly Starts on Dreamliner, The 'Future of Aviation','' *Professional Engineering*, 19, no. 13 (2006): 8.

53. Zou and Ozsomer, ''Global Product R&D,'' 57–76.

54. Lianne George, ''Style—An iPod Interface-Lift,'' *Macleans* 117, no. 47 (November 22, 2004): 56.

55. "IPHONE," *Black Enterprise*, 37, no. 9 (2007): 56.
56. Willsey, "Taking These 7 Steps," 17.
57. Kevin J. Clancy and Robert S. Shulman, "It's Better to Fly a New Product Simulator than Crash the Real Thing," *Planning Review* 20, no. 4 (July/August 1992): 8–16.
58. Ibid.
59. The LITMUS test is the creation of Kevin J. Clancy, who describes the procedure used in Clancy and Shulman, It's Better to Fly, 10–16.
60. "Visa Goes Mobile," *Chain Store Age* 83, no. 1 (2007): 114.
61. Tamer S. Cavusgil and Ugur Yavas, "Test Marketing: An Exposition," *Marketing Intelligence and Planning* 5, no. 3 (1987): 16–20.
62. Ibid.
63. See Cooper, "Debunking the Myths," 40–50.
64. Ibid.
65. See Everett M. Rogers, *Diffusion of Innovations*, 3rd ed., (New York: Free Press, 1983).
66. Kenneth Hein, "Bull's Market," *Brandweek* 42, no. 22 (May 28, 2001): 21, 23.
67. Roberto Ferdman, "The American energy drink craze in two highly caffeinated charts," Quarts, March 26, 2014, accessed at http://qz.com/192038/the-american-energy-drink-craze-in-two-highly-caffeinated-charts/ on June 14, 2014; Matthew Boyle, and Dana Vazquez Castillo, "Monster on the Loose." (Cover story), *Fortune* 154, no. 13 (2006): 116–122.
68. Milton Keynes, "Motorola Chooses Poland for New Site," *Corporate Location*, European Edition (May/June 1998): 7.
69. Faith Hung, "Consortium Looks to Build Thailand Fab—Siemens, Intel and Macronix Want to Jumpstart Country's Semi Industry," *Electronic Buyers' News* no. 1214 (June 5, 2000): 4.
70. James Carbone, "Outsourcing by the Numbers," *Purchasing* 135, no. 8 (2006): 31.
71. MarketWatch, "Company Spotlight: PepsiCo." *Food* 5, no.1 (2006): 29–35.
72. See www.bcg.com.
73. H. Igor Ansoff, "Strategies for Diversification," *Harvard Business Review* 35 (September–October 1957): 113–124.
74. Aaron Pressman, "Who's Really Shaking Up Heinz," *Business Week* (2007): 64.

Cases

Case 8-1: GoPro Cameras – Is This the Future of Photography?

In July 2014, investors coughed up $437 million for the camera maker at the company's initial public offering, with GoPro valued at almost $3 billion at the time. That is quite impressive for a company that makes its profit by making just one camera and gadgets for the camera, to mount it everywhere, on people, babies, eagles, you name it. With sales surging at 87% in 2013, and profits at six percent so early in its life cycle, this product has promise! GoPro makes the world's most versatile cameras that produce high-definition video photography – the cameras are small, lightweight, waterproof, wearable and gear-mountable.

Switching from a GoPro is a low-cost proposition for consumers who like to purchase the newest gadget to record their newest adventures. Switching to a new, more established brand, like Sony, is not exactly a stretch. GoPro could either create more and more innovative cameras to keep customers interested, or hold content captive. Apparently, GoPro is doing both, spending 12 percent of revenue on R&D, creating, among others, a gooseneck and a bracket that works with night-vision goggles, and packaging its videos into its media platform. The company already has content deals with Virgin America and Xbox Live. Last year, people loaded to YouTube 2.8 years' worth of video with GoPro in the title. However, individuals making videos with a GoPro will not hand them over for free.

Questions

1. Is the GoPro camera a fad, fashion, or style? Explain.
2. What life cycle stage would you attribute to the GoPro? Justify your answer.
3. Comment on the degree of product newness for the GoPro camera.

Sources: Adapted from Kyle Stock, "GoPro Goes Big, but Customers Are Still Free to Jump," Bloomberg Businessweek, June 26, 2014, accessed at http://www.businessweek.com/articles/2014-06-26/gopro-goes-big-but-customers-still-free-to-jump on July 14, 2014; http://www.fool.com/investing/general/2014/06/16/gopro-will-be-an-ipo-to-watch-in-2014.aspx, accessed on July 24, 2014; http://gopro.com accessed on July 24, 2014.

Case 8-2 Partnering with TerraPass

Gene Wyatt lives and drives in Scottsdale, Arizona, where he owns an environmentally friendly used golf cart dealership. The dealership property is painted green, in line with the positioning of the store and its merchandise. The Phoenix area, already heavily polluted, benefits as more and more Arizona retirement communities encourage golf cart and scooter transportation. As a result, Gene's dealership is very popular.

Gene has been reading about the impact of automobiles on the environment. In the nineteenth century, climate science was developed, along with the discovery that carbon dioxide traps heat in the atmosphere. It took until the 1980s to develop climate models and computers that could quantify the "greenhouse effect." Gene feels that there is much to be done to fight environmental pollution. Modeled after Ford's "Greener Miles" program, Gene is considering teaming up with TerraPass. TerraPass, invented in 2004 by Wharton business school students working toward their master's degree, is a for-profit firm that has automobile owners investing in clean technologies at a level that will compensate for the amount of carbon dioxide that their own automobile produces. For example, owners of small automobiles who drive 12,000 miles per year will have to pay TerraPass $49.95 per year. This amount is then invested into clean technology: solar energy, wind farms, methane capture facilities, and so on. Those investing in TerraPass receive a certificate, money-back guarantee and window decals and bumper stickers that proclaim membership in this avant-garde program.

Golf cart and scooter owners will likely not have to spend much for an annual TerraPass. Although, at present, TerraPass offers offsets only for automobiles and airplane flights booked through Expedia or Travelocity, and not scooters or golf carts, it is a good bet that the company will charge the minimum amount of $49.95 for owning and driving these vehicles. Gene believes that this is not a large amount of money that would create hardships for his vehicles' buyers and that environmentally concerned buyers would normally welcome the opportunity to take action to protect the environment.

Gene still has some lingering uncertainty about the status of TerraPass. On one hand, it could be an invention that will change our consumption of fossil fuels. On the other hand, what if this is a fad? Carbon-offset markets are still works-in-progress and demand for their offerings depends on dogooders, such as Google billionaire Sergey Brin, who travels around the world in a Boeing 767 and buys offsets to make up for it. The system is not capable of handling large orders of vehicles. If Ford decided to pay for the Green Miles program mentioned at the beginning of this case, the company would clearly be overwhelmed. In the case of Gene's dealership, this may be less of a problem, but it could still affect timely transactions. As Gene ponders the opportunity to partner with TerraPass, he comes across a 2007 article stating that the Supreme Court ruled that the federal government had the power under the Clean Air Act to regulate carbon dioxide emissions from automobiles, setting an important precedent for treating carbon dioxide as a threat to human welfare and allowing for regulations that may potentially tighten fuel-economy standards. These developments should bode well for Gene's business.

Questions
1. Is TerraPass a fad, fashion, or style? Explain.
2. Describe the new-product diffusion process for TerraPass, and comment on the different categories of product adopters.
3. In which stage of the PLC does TerraPass belong?

Sources: Jerry Adler, "Moment of Truth: Is the Push to Save the Planet a Fad or a Turning Point?'s *Newsweek*, (April 16, 2007) 45; www.terrapass.com/howworks.html; "Ford Promotes Driving Greener Miles," *Business Credit* 108, no. 6 (June 2006): 48; Lauren Tara Lacapra, "Take My Emissions, Please," *The Wall Street Journal*, (March 1, 2007): D1; Alan Murray, "Corporate Focus: How an Open Market Might Save the Planet," *The Wall Street Journal*, (March 28, 2007): A11

Answers to Review Questions

Answers: 1) False, 2) True, 3) False, 4) True, 5) False, 6) False, 7) True, 8) False, 9) False, 10) False, 11) d, 12) d, 13) a, 14) d, 15) d, 16) a, 17) b, 18) b, 19) d, 20) d.

Chapter 9

Services Marketing

Learning Objectives

After studying
this chapter,
you should be able to:

1 Discuss the impact of the services sector on the gross domestic product and what has led to the growth of the service sector.

2 Identify the four unique characteristics of services and how each affects the marketing of services.

3 Explain the components of the purchasing process for services.

4 Identify the factors that affect the purchase decision during the prepurchase phase of the purchase process.

5 Discuss the relevant elements of the service encounter and why they are important.

6 Describe the postpurchase evaluation of services and its impact on future purchase behavior.

7 Discuss how service quality is measured.

8 Describe an effective service recovery process.

9 Explain the importance of the customer value package and list the steps required to develop a customer value package.

9-1 CHAPTER OVERVIEW

Digital cameras and smart phones have replaced traditional cameras, as consumers readily embraced easy picture taking and sharing of pictures (see **Figure 9-1**). With the traditional camera technology, individuals dropped off their film at the local drugstore to be processed. With digital photography becoming mainstream, drugstores were forced to adapt the services they offer, and many left the photo-processing business altogether. Consumers today make their own prints rather than rely on a commercial photo-processing service. Most save, store, and keep their images in digital format, which has led to online photo printing services to become the new standard. Newer sites like Snapfish and Shutterfly and traditional providers like Walgreens and CVS offer online photo services such as storage, sorting, editing, sharing, and printing of photos, providing software that allows people to edit and touch up their images, or the service will do it for them.

Figure 9-1: Digital cameras make sharing pictures with family and friends easier and have also created a new online photography service industry.

With new technology inventions like digital cameras and camera phones often come changes in services supporting that technology. Making prints from film is in the decline stage of the product life cycle (PLC), but this decline has spurred a whole new industry, now in its growth stage: digital online photography services.[1]

Services are an integral part of the U.S. economy. They furnish the majority of jobs and contribute the major portion of the nation's gross national product (GNP). Some marketers would consider that marketing of goods and services is the same, whereas others will contend that it takes a different marketing approach. Although it is true that the principles are the same, the unique characteristics of services discussed in Section 9-3 do make it apparent that the application of those principles may vary. Services face some unique challenges that often require a different approach.

The purchase process for services is described in Section 9-4. Understanding how services are purchased, consumed, and evaluated is critical to understanding how services are marketed. Section 9-5 presents the concept of service quality, how it is measured, and what happens when a service failure occurs. The last section, Section 9-6, discusses the services customer value package. Understanding service quality and the customer value package will make it easier for a service business to attract customers and to retain them.

9-2 THE SERVICE SECTOR

When you think of services, it is helpful to think of a continuum with pure services at one extreme and pure goods at the other extreme. A pure service does not have any type of good attached to it. Examples would include personal fitness training, legal services, medical services, and driver education instruction. A pure good is something that is sold without any type of service component attached, such as a computer, exercise equipment, socks, or gasoline at a self-serve convenience store. Most products fall somewhere between a pure service and a pure good. A restaurant is a service because you are paying the business to prepare the food (a good) for you. Computers are a good, but if you have difficulty with your computer, you can call a toll-free number for assistance, contact the company using e-mail, or call a local computer repair company. Figure 9-2 illustrates this goods and services continuum.

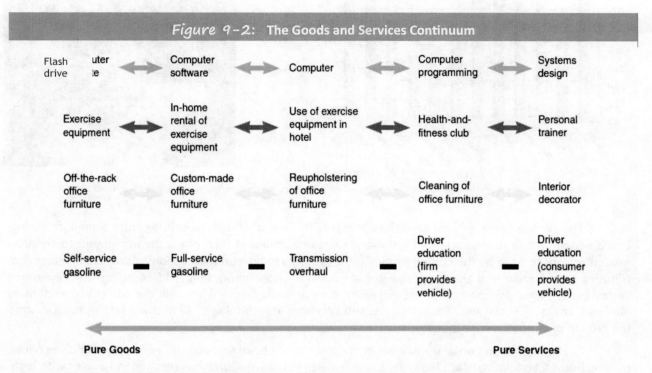

Figure 9-2: The Goods and Services Continuum

Please note: The above continuum should be viewed from left to right. Within each row, there is a consistent pattern from pure good to pure service. In comparisons of different rows, there is somewhat less consistency, due to the diversity of the examples shown.

Services are a vital component of the U.S. economy and that of most industrialized nations. The service sector in the United States accounts for 79.4 percent ($13.34 trillion) of the country's gross domestic product (GDP) and 79.7 percent of the total U.S. employment.[2] Figure 9-3 highlights the size of the service sector in a few selected countries throughout various regions of the world. The GDP is the sum of all goods and services produced within the boundaries of a country. In the United States the GDP would include the production by U.S.-owned and foreign-owned firms. Goods and services produced by U.S.-owned firms outside the country are not calculated in the GDP of the United States.

Between 2010 and 2020, the service sector in the United States is expected to have the most job growth, with the number of wage and salary workers increasing from 112.7 million to 130.7 million, an annual growth rate of 1.5 percent, a growth rate faster than the 0.4 percent experienced during the 2000–2010 period.[3] The fastest growth will be in the Internet, cable, and telecommunications industry; computer software industry; professional and business services; medical services; and employment services.[4] To learn more about the top ten job growth occupations, see Table 9-1.

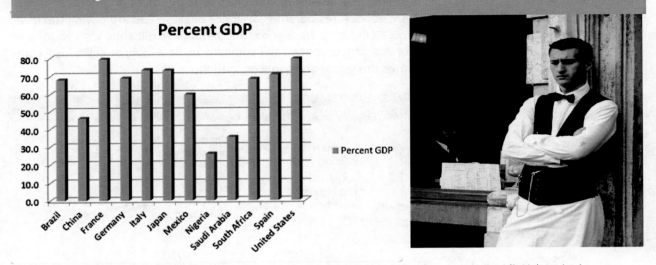

Figure 9-3: The Service Sector as a Percentage of the GDP in Selected Countries.

Source: Adapted from the CIA Fact Book, https://www.cia.gov/library/publications/the-world-factbook/fields/2012.html, accessed on June 12, 2014.

The service sector's rapid growth is primarily the result of nations shifting from a manufacturing-based economy to a service-oriented economy. A major stimulus in this shift is the movement to an information society spurred by the computer and advancements in telecommunications. Additional factors contributing to the growth of the service sector are an aging population, longer life expectancies, increased leisure time, higher per-capita income, increased time pressure, more women in the workforce, sedentary lifestyles, changing social and cultural values, and advances in technology.[5] All of these factors have spurred the growth of various service industries.

The aging population and increase in life expectancy have spurred the need for medical services, nursing homes, and limited-care facilities. More females in the workforce has resulted in families with higher incomes, which translates into a larger discretionary income to spend on luxury-type goods and services, such as entertainment, dining out, vacations, and recreation. With both work and family responsibilities, individuals are stressed for time; consequently, services that save time, such as housecleaning and lawn care, are in higher demand.

Table 9-1: The 10 Occupations with the Largest Employment Growth, 2008-18 (in thousands)

Rank	Occupation	2012	2020	Number	Percent
1	Personal care aides	1,190	1,771	580	48.8
2	Registered nurses	2,711	3,238	526	19.4
3	Retail salespersons	4,447	4,881	434	9.8
4	Home health aides	875	1,299	424	48.5
5	Combined food preparation and serving workers, including fast food	2,969	3,391	421	14.2
6	Nursing assistants	1,479	1,792	312	21.1
7	Secretaries and administrative assistants, except legal, medical, and executive	2,324	2,632	307	13.2
8	Customer service representatives	2,362	2,661	298	12.6
9	Janitors and cleaners, except maids and housekeeping cleaners	2,324	2,604	280	12.1
10	Construction laborers	1,071	1,331	259	24.3

Source: http://www.bls.gov/emp/ep_table_104.htm, accessed July 12, 2014.

Advances in technology have led to a rise in the demand for maintenance and computer-related services. Even automobiles have become more computerized, requiring skilled mechanics. The so-called shade tree mechanic who repairs his own car has become virtually obsolete. Because of cultural and social changes, society no longer places a stigma on individuals who hire someone else to take care of personal chores. Mothers are no longer seen as shirking their duty if they do not stay home with their children, cook the meals, and clean the house. Society no longer feels a man is neglecting his responsibilities when he hires someone to repair his car, mow his lawn, or repair his home.

The service sector is a critical component of our economy, and the successful marketing of services requires an understanding of how services are different from goods. Although the principles of marketing are the same, the application of those principles will be different for a service operation.

9-3 CHARACTERISTICS OF SERVICES

Services possess four inherent characteristics not found in goods: Intangibility, perishability, inseparability, and variability (see **Figure 9-4**).[6] **Intangibility** refers to the lack of tangible assets that can be seen, touched, smelled, heard, or tasted before a purchase, and **perishability** refers to the inability of a service to be inventoried or stored. **Inseparability** is the simultaneous production and consumption of a service, and **variability** is the unwanted or random levels of service quality customers receive when they patronize a service. These characteristics create unique marketing challenges for services not only in terms of attracting new customers but also in retaining current customers.

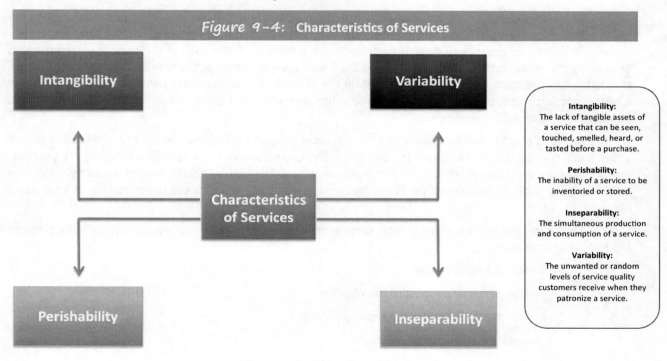

Figure 9–4: **Characteristics of Services**

Intangibility:
The lack of tangible assets of a service that can be seen, touched, smelled, heard, or tasted before a purchase.

Perishability:
The inability of a service to be inventoried or stored.

Inseparability:
The simultaneous production and consumption of a service.

Variability:
The unwanted or random levels of service quality customers receive when they patronize a service.

9-3a: Intangibility

Services vary in the degree to which they are intangible. Services such as a music concert, legal counsel, medical treatments, and a college education are highly intangible. The service cannot be seen, touched, smelled, heard, or tasted before the purchase. However, for each of these services, tangible items are used to perform the service. For example, for a musical concert, there are chairs, a stage, musical instruments, and loudspeakers. For legal services, clients see an office, desks, and law books. For a medical treatment, there are medical instruments and equipment. For a college education, there are the physical structures such as buildings and classrooms. But for all of these services, the actual outcome of the service cannot be seen until the service is performed or the event has taken place (see **Figure 9-5**).

Figure 9-5: Services vary in the degree to which they are intangible. Services such as a music concert, legal counsel, medical treatments, and a college education are highly intangible. For example, for a rock concert, there are chairs, a stage, musical instruments, and loudspeakers.

Some services offer a tangible good with their service, but the service itself is still intangible because consumers are purchasing the service, not the good. For instance, restaurants offer food and a dentist uses crowns and other materials to perform his or her work. In the case of the restaurant, consumers are paying the restaurant to prepare the food for them. An evaluation of the service is based on how well the restaurant prepares the food and serves it. In the second case, patients are paying the dentist to repair a tooth, not just to supply the tooth crown and other materials. The quality of both services will be based on how well the service is performed.

Because of intangibility, consumers have greater difficulty in judging the quality of a service before a purchase. A good can be examined in advance, offering consumers some idea of what they are purchasing. Services are much more difficult to examine in advance. The haircut you receive at a beauty salon cannot be known until the beautician performs the work. This intangibility makes the purchase of a service a higher risk.

To reduce the risk consumers face, service firms strive to reduce the level of intangibility through the following strategies:

- Stress tangible cues.
- Use personal sources of information.
- Stimulate word-of-mouth communication.
- Create a strong corporate image.
- Encourage employees to communicate with customers.

To reduce intangibility, attorneys can feature tangible assets such as their building, their office, or other personnel in an advertisement. A college can feature its facilities, students, athletes, and professors. Using testimonials of students for a college and clients for an attorney can reduce the level of risk and intangibility. Personal sources of information and word-of-mouth communications are excellent ways of making a service appear more tangible. Employees can talk about the service. A beautician, through communicating with the customer, can reduce the intangibility of getting a haircut. An attorney, during an initial visit, can discuss the process he or she will use in handling the case. Because a service is intangible, communication becomes an important element in marketing the service. Although word-of-mouth communication from one customer to another is the best, anything a service can do to communicate with consumers about the service will help reduce the level of intangibility.

9-3b: Perishability

The second characteristic of services is perishability. If a sweater does not sell today, a retailer can keep it and sell it at a later time. If the sale occurs much later, the retailer will sell it at a discount but, most likely, will still make a profit on it. This feature allows firms to mass-produce goods and store them in warehouses and in retail stores until consumers are ready to make a purchase. For services, this is not possible. A Delta Airlines flight that sells only 120 of the 160 seats will lose the revenue of the 40 empty seats once the plane takes off. This revenue is lost forever. It cannot be sold at a later time.

Concerts and sporting events are live events. Fans have no choice as to when or where they can watch the events unless there are multiple performances. If they want to see a particular band, they must go where the performance is being held at the time it is occurring. Again, empty seats are lost revenue because they cannot be inventoried and sold later. To maximize revenue, sports teams, bands, and airlines want to fill every seat.

Perishability can also cause the reverse situation. Demand can be greater than supply. In this situation, Delta Airlines does not have enough seats for everyone. Passengers are unhappy because they cannot book a particular flight. A Dallas Cowboys' game is sold out, and fans are unhappy because they cannot see a particular game. A Beyoncé concert is sold out; fans wanting to see her performance either have to go to another location, hoping they will get a ticket, or forgo the opportunity of seeing her perform live. In every case, potential revenue is lost because of the fixed-seating capacities of each venue.

To reduce the negative impact of perishability, services can develop strategies to deal with fluctuating demand through simultaneously making adjustments in demand, supply, and capacity. The goal is to achieve parity among the three. At the optimum, demand will equal supply, which in turn will equal capacity.

Perishability for Beyoncé concerts can be managed in a number of ways. First, demand can be reduced through increasing ticket prices. As prices are increased, the number of people willing to pay the higher prices declines. Second, demand at various locations can be managed through a Web site that indicates sold-out concerts and locations where tickets are still available. This will shift some of the demand to locations where empty seats are still available. Beyoncé can manage the supply side of perishability by increasing the number of live concerts, thus allowing more people the opportunity to see her perform. The capacity component can be managed by finding larger facilities. Using all three components simultaneously, Beyoncé can maximize her revenue from the live concerts while providing fans the opportunity to see her perform. Her goal would be to fill every location to capacity with no empty seats and no fans turned away because the concert was sold out.

For a restaurant, the same principles apply. Demand can be managed through advertising, special promotions, and pricing. Having a higher dinner price will reduce demand during the evening dinner hours, whereas having a lower lunch price will stimulate demand at lunchtime. Advertising specials for breakfast meals will encourage people to eat breakfast at the restaurant. Supply can be managed by hiring part-time employees during meal times. Unlike the Beyoncé concerts, a restaurant does not have the ability to expand its physical capacity. The number of customers it can have at any one time is controlled by the seating capacity of the facility (see **Figure 9-6**).

Figure 9-6: A convenient location and a reputation for fresh, local seafood has brought many customers back to this popular restaurant.

Part Three: Marketing Mix Strategies

Managing perishability is critical to the success of a service. When demand is less than supply, revenue is lost and the firm has excess capacity. A facility or equipment that is not used to capacity increases the total average unit costs to operate. For example, a movie theater that has a capacity of 175 will have a higher total average cost per customer to operate when the theater averages only 90 people per night, compared with 160 per night. Fixed costs remain the same, but the theater has fewer customers to spread the costs over.

When demand exceeds capacity, potential revenue is lost. Because the facility is filled or equipment is being used to its full capacity, businesses often do not worry about the customers that are turned away. But if customers cannot get tickets to a basketball game or make an appointment with an attorney, they will seek other alternatives. The basketball fan may switch to another sport and never come back to watching basketball games, and the person seeking legal counsel may choose another attorney. In the long run, these lost customers can be detrimental to a firm that may need them during a later time, when demand is less than supply.

9-3c: Inseparability

Goods can be produced in one location, warehoused in another, and then sold at a later time in a retail store; services cannot. For example, getting a cavity filled in a tooth involves a patient going to a dentist and being present while the service is being performed. Because the service must be performed and consumed at the same time, the quality of the service is highly dependent on the ability of the service provider and the quality of interaction between the service provider and the customer.

Figure 9-7: This kiosk for Allied Irish Banks features an ATM that does more than distribute cash. AIB customers can a variety of banking transactions using AIB's BANKLINK service.

To reduce the importance of the customer-employee interaction, service firms look for methods of automating their service through the use of machines, computers, or other technology. The more that a service can be automated, the less it will be reliant on human performance, and the greater will be its availability to consumers. Banks now use automated teller machines (ATMs) to conduct business with customers. ATMs provide efficiency for the bank and convenience for the customer. To further reduce the interaction with bank personnel, most banks now offer online banking services (see **Figure 9-7**). With both the ATM and online banking, employees are not needed to perform the transaction at the time it is desired by customers. This not only increases the availability of banking services to customers to 24 hours a day, 7 days a week, but also reduces the level of human interaction between bank personnel and customers. It also reduces the cost involved for a bank to handle transactions. Banks have estimated the average cost per transaction using a human teller to be $2.50. The cost of a check transaction is $1.07, a telephone transaction is $0.55, an ATM transaction is $0.27, and an online transaction is $0.01.[7]

Realizing the benefit of online services, Citibank was the first financial institution to offer consumers consolidated personal account service—known as My Citi. Customers could log onto one account and conduct all of their banking transactions, pay credit card bills or obtain loans, obtain insurance and investment information, and use an online payment service. Through Travelers Insurance, online quotes and information on life, auto, and homeowners insurance can be gathered. Through Citigroup's subsidiary, customers can now obtain free wireless access and portfolio tracking services, and through C2it, a Citibank system, customers can send payments to anyone via the Internet.[8] By offering all of these services on one consolidated online account, Citibank effectively reduced the inseparability nature of its services.

Service providers such as hair salons have a more difficult situation because they have a high degree of inseparability. Customers are involved in the production of the service, other customers are usually present, and centralized mass production of the service is not possible. Because of the importance of the customer-service provider interaction, it is essential for service businesses like hair salons and restaurants to reduce any negative consequences that might be due to the inseparability. These negative consequences can be reduced if companies emphasize the selection and training of employees. Training should include how to perform the service, as well as how to interact with customers. This training will increase the probability of a positive interaction between the customer and the service provider. In addition, the service operation must provide the proper type and level of motivation.

Hair salons also should have a process for managing customers because more than one customer usually will be in the facility at any one time. This process may include a receptionist greeting customers as they enter and notifying the particular beautician that the customer has arrived. The process may include providing a comfortable waiting area with appropriate reading material. While some customers are having their hair cut, others may be getting a shampoo or having their hair styled. To ensure that each customer is satisfied with the service, the hair salon must manage every step in the customer service process.

Because of inseparability, the number of customers that a hair salon can serve is limited by the time required for each haircut and the size of the facility. If a hair salon has six beauticians and six chairs, then only six customers can be served at one time unless other customers are under the hair dryer or waiting for a perm to set. A hair salon can reduce the negative impact of this inseparability and serve more customers by opening multiple sites. Because customers have to be present for the service, this strategy offers customers multiple sites to receive the service. The multiple-site strategy will also reduce the number of customers present at any one time in a facility. This should allow employees more time with each customer, increasing the quality of service and interaction with the customer.

9-3d: Variability

The last unique characteristic of services is variability. Variability is primarily caused by the human element (although machines may malfunction), thus causing a variation in the service. Each employee will perform a service in a slightly different way with various levels of quality, and even the same employee will provide different levels of service from one time to another. For example, in getting a haircut, the outcome will differ if you use a different beautician each time you go to a salon. The outcome also will vary from one time to another even if the same person is cutting your hair.

Although machines are much more reliable, differences in service can occur. If the computerized testing equipment at an auto repair facility does not operate properly, it may not detect a problem with an engine or it may misdiagnose the problem. However, when these problems do occur, the problems often are not with the computerized equipment but with the person operating the equipment.

Part Three: Marketing Mix Strategies

Although most variability is caused by the service provider, it also can be caused by a variance in the inputs. Computer consultants staffing hotlines face the challenge of dealing with the various levels of knowledge and expertise customers bring to the service process. The same would be true for a consulting service handling situations for various clients.

Industrialization: The use of machines and standardized operating procedures to increase the productivity and efficiency of a business.

Because of this variability characteristic of services, standardization and quality control are the primary methods used to ensure a consistent level of quality across different service providers and across different service experiences with the same provider. A restaurant such as McDonald's will industrialize operations. In this context, **industrialization** refers to the use of machines and standardized operating procedures to increase the productivity and efficiency of a business. Hamburgers, French fries, and other foods are prepared in advance and put in warming bins. By producing these items in advance, more customers can be served during peak demand times. Employees are also trained to follow a specific procedure in preparing each food item. Through standardization and industrialization, customers can expect the same quality of food and service at all of the McDonald's locations.

Keep in mind that variability refers to unwanted or random variations in service quality. Thus a restaurant like Outback Steakhouse will use industrialization and standardization procedures to improve productivity, but customers do not all want their food exactly the same. The cooking of steaks must be customized to meet the customer's desire, or a dish that has shrimp on it may be cooked without the shrimp upon a customer's request. Thus customers at Outback want variability. They want food prepared differently. What they do not want is unwanted or random variability. Therefore, to reduce this unwanted or random variability, it is the responsibility of the wait-staff to ask how food items are to be prepared. This will ensure that the particular requests of each customer are met and the unwanted variability in the service does not occur (see **Figure 9-8**).

Figure 9-8: This photo was used in a blog for a popular, higher-end steakhouse chain. The blog features an article written by the head chef explaining how they approach cooking their steaks to meet the variable demands of their customers.

Enterprise Holdings, comprising Enterprise Rent-A-Car, Alamo Rent A Car and National Car Rental, is the world's largest rental car company, with a revenue of $16.4 billion, and with 8,100 rental car locations in 50 countries and territories and more than 1.4 million cars and trucks in its fleet. The company was recently recognized as a J.D. PowerCustomer Champion, one of just 50 annually. But not so long ago, Enterprise Rent-A-Car experienced a fall in the quality of service. Letters and phone calls from customers indicated that their expectations were not being met. The Enterprise Service Quality Index, which had been developed to measure service quality at each of the branches, indicated that only about 65 percent of its customers were "completely satisfied." But more alarming was the wide range of scores: More than 28 points separated the branches with the highest service quality score from the branches with the lowest. This wide degree of variability troubled Enterprise management as much as did the average score of 65 percent. To ensure that customers received the same level of service at all of its locations, Enterprise took several steps. First, service quality was emphasized at training sessions, in the firm's correspondence with managers, and in its reports. Second, the score for each branch location was published monthly so that everyone in the organization would know how they scored and how their score compared with other branches. Third, the Enterprise Service Quality Index became a prominent factor in promotions. Branch managers whose facilities were not at or above the average score for comparable branches were not considered for promotion. Furthermore, if a branch did not achieve or exceed the company's average index score, the entire team was ineligible for promotion. With management emphasis and support on improving quality and reducing variability, the average index has moved to the high 70 percent range, with a spread of only 11 percent between the highest and lowest.[9]

To be successful, service businesses must understand the characteristics of intangibility, perishability, inseparability, and variability. For examples of all four unique characteristics of services, see Table 9-2.

9-4 THE PURCHASE PROCESS FOR SERVICES

Because of the unique characteristics of services, it is beneficial to examine the services purchase process. When you understand the process consumers use in choosing and evaluating a service, developing an effective marketing approach will be easier. The purchase process for services can be divided into three phases: the prepurchase phase, the service encounter, and the postpurchase phase. During the prepurchase phase, consumers evaluate alternatives, make a purchase decision, and finalize a brand choice. At some point after the decision is made, the consumer will move into the second stage, the service encounter, which is the actual interaction point between the customer and the service provider. Sometimes, the service encounter immediately follows the decision, whereas at other times, it may occur later. For example, when you are on vacation, deciding to patronize a particular restaurant and stopping to eat at the restaurant are virtually simultaneous. At other times, the decision to patronize a particular restaurant may be made hours or even days in advance. During the service encounter, the service is performed or provided to the customer. Because of the inseparability of services, what transpires at the time of consumption has a significant impact on the way customers evaluate the quality of the service and their future purchase decisions. The last phase of the services purchase process is the postpurchase evaluation, which begins upon completion of the service. During this phase, consumers make evaluations concerning the quality of service, their level of satisfaction or dissatisfaction, and future purchase intentions.

9-4a Prepurchase Phase

During the prepurchase phase, consumers evaluate alternatives and make purchase decisions. A number of factors affect the evaluation and decision. These factors can be grouped into internal factors, external factors, firm-produced factors, and perceived risk. Table 9-3 lists each of these factors.

Internal Factors

For most purchase situations, internal factors are the most critical. Internal factors consist of individual needs and wants of the consumer, past experience, expectations of the service alternatives, and level of purchase involvement. To understand these elements, assume that you are looking for a vacation spot

Table 9-2: Understanding the Unique Characteristics of Services

Intangibility

Definition: Lack of tangible assets that can be seen, touched, or smelled before the purchase.

Business-to-business example: A professional janitorial service cannot be seen, touched, or smelled before the service. A firm hiring a professional janitorial service will have to rely on what the janitorial service tells it about the services to be performed.

Consumer example: The food at a restaurant cannot be seen, touched, or smelled before the service. The waiter or waitress can describe the food, and the restaurant may have a picture of the food on the menu or a written description of the particular dish, but consumers cannot actually see what will be served to them.

Strategies to reduce negative impact: Intangibility can be reduced by stressing tangible cues when marketing the service, using personal sources of information, stimulating word-of-mouth communications, creating a strong corporate and brand image, and encouraging employees to communicate with the customers during the service.

Perishability

Definition: Inability of a service to be inventoried or stored.

Business-to-business example: The janitorial service cannot be inventoried or stored. Every day or week, depending on the contract, the service will have to be performed again. The same set of tasks will be performed each time the building is serviced.

Consumer example: The food is prepared when the customer places the order. Some food may be cooked in advance, but the actual order is prepared only after it is ordered. It cannot be inventoried or stored for a later time.

Strategies to reduce negative impact: The service firm has to develop strategies to deal with demand, supply, and capacity. The goal is for demand and supply to match, which should be close to the capacity of the firm. For example, when demand is high, the restaurant will need to expand supply by hiring additional wait-staff and cooks.

Inseparability

Definition: Simultaneous production and consumption of a service.

Business-to-business example: The janitorial service cannot be separated from the individuals doing the service, and it must be performed at the customer's place of business.

Consumer example: The restaurant prepares the food for a customer when it is ordered. The customer consumes the food at the restaurant, and the customer's perception of quality will be partly due to the customer's interaction with the restaurant employees.

Strategies to reduce negative impact: It is important for the service firm to hire competent employees and then train them to perform the service. The service firm needs a process for managing customers so customers will have positive feelings about the interaction between employees and themselves. Inseparability can also be managed by having additional restaurant locations and by offering carryout and home delivery services.

Variability

Definition: Unwanted or random levels of service quality that customers receive when they patronize a firm.

Business-to-business example: The quality of the service will depend on who does the work and how well they are trained.

Consumer example: The quality of service will depend on how well the cook prepares the food. Even the same cook may not prepare the food exactly the same way each time.

Strategies to reduce negative impact: Standardization and quality-control measures can reduce the variability of services. Standardization means that customers will tend to receive the same quality of service, regardless of who performs the service and when. In addition, if machines can be incorporated into the service, machines tend to be more consistent, in terms of quality production, than humans.

for spring break. The most important internal element in the decision will be your particular needs and wants. What do you want to do during spring break? What types of activities do you want to participate in? If you want to go swimming, then you will likely choose the beach or a lake. If you want to go scuba diving, you may choose a resort that teaches scuba diving or has excellent scuba facilities. If you are interested in nightclubs, you will choose a larger town, but if you want peace and quiet, you will choose an isolated, out-of-the way location. If you want to snow ski, you will look for a place in the mountains. If you want to explore another country, then you may choose Europe or a location in South America (see **Figure 9-9**).

Your past experience will factor into this decision. If your past experience with a particular location was positive, then you will be more inclined to go back to the same place. If your past experience was negative, then it is highly probable that you will choose a different place for your spring break. The expectations of the various spring break locations will factor into your evaluation and decision. These expectations are

Table 9-3: Factors Affecting the Prepurchase Phase			
Internal Factors	**Firm-Produced Factors**	**External Factors**	**Perceived Risk**
1. Individual needs and wants	1. Promotions	1. Competitive options available	1. Performance risk
2. Past experience	2. Price	2. The social context of the purchase	2. Financial risk
3. Expectations of service alternatives	3. Distribution	3. Word-of-mouth communications	3. Time-loss risk
4. Level of purchase involvement			4. Opportunity risk
			5. Psychological risk
			6. Social risk
			7. Physical risk

based on past experience, word-of-mouth communications from others, and promotional materials produced by the various resorts and spring break locations. The higher the expectations you develop for a specific location, the greater the likelihood you will choose that location.[10] Of course, the reverse would also be true: The lower the expectations you have for a location, the less likely it will be chosen.

Figure 9-9: When you choose a spring break location, the most important internal element in the decision will be what you want to do during the week: swim, ski, paddle, or hang out with friends.

The last internal factor affecting your purchase decision in the prepurchase phase is the level of your involvement. **Involvement** refers to the level of mental and physical effort exerted by a consumer in selecting a good or service.[11] In high-involvement purchase decisions, consumers spend considerable time searching for information, both internally and externally (see **Figure 9-10**). They are also inclined to spend more time in deliberating and weighing the various alternatives. In contrast, in low-involvement purchase decisions, consumers spend minimal time searching for information and in deliberation. In many cases, it becomes a habitual purchase that is performed with little thought. For example, selecting a car wash would be considered a low-level involvement situation and would involve little thought or deliberation. In most cases, consumers patronize the car wash facility closest to them or one they have patronized in the past. Unless you are going back to the same location for spring break, it is likely that selecting a spring break location will be a high-involvement decision that will require searching for information and then carefully evaluating the alternatives.

> **Involvement:**
> The level of mental and physical effort a consumer exerts in selecting a good or service.

External Factors

The external factors that influence the purchase decision during the prepurchase phase are the competitive options available, the social context of the purchase, and word-of-mouth communications. Going back to our example of a place for spring break, your decision will be influenced by the competitive options available to you. Some options will come from your own memory, others from individuals around you, and others through your external search for information on the Internet or other sources, such as an advertisement. If scuba diving is on your agenda for things to do, your options will be more limited because not all resorts and spring break locations are ideal for scuba diving.

For spring break, the social context of the purchase is usually very important. In fact, it may have a greater influence than even your own personal desires. If you want to spend spring break with college friends, a significant other, or family members, where you go will depend on where they want to go. Your choice will be more of a group decision than your individual decision unless you can convince everyone within your group to choose the location you desire.

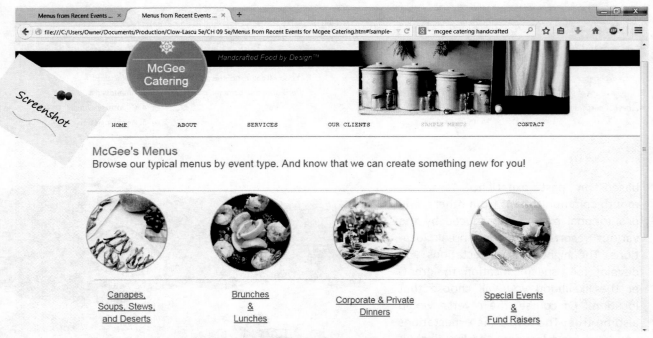

Figure 9-10: Selecting a caterer *and* a menu for a special event is a high-involvement decision that requires considerable time and effort in making the right choice.

Word-of-mouth communications are likely to have a significant impact on the purchase decision.[12] In the process of selecting a service, it is not unusual for consumers to ask other people for their recommendations or evaluations of specific vendors. Consumers feel that word-of-mouth communications from other people are more reliable than any company-sponsored communication, such as an advertisement. In choosing a spring break location, you will undoubtedly seek information from individuals who went on spring break last year. You will want to find out where they went, what they did, and how they liked it. You will especially want this information for locations that you are considering. While internal information may help you narrow the list of possible locations down to a smaller subset, external information can help you develop more concrete views of each location and influence your actual choice.

Figure 9-11: Client listings and testimonials found at a service firm's Web site bear credible testimony for service providers.

Firm-Produced Factors

The firm-produced factors affecting the purchase decision include promotions, pricing, and distribution. From a consumer's viewpoint, firm-produced factors are the least reliable because consumers realize that the goal of the firm is to encourage and persuade consumers to make a purchase. From the service firm's perspective, firm-produced factors are its primary method of reaching consumers with information and persuading them to purchase its service.

Firms have several forms of promotion that can be used, such as advertising, sales promotions, and personal selling. Testimonials are especially useful for services (see **Figure 9-11**).

Service organizations can provide consumers with information that can be used as they make decisions about what service to purchase and which vendor to patronize. For spring break locations, advertising on college campuses and in newspapers in the area is an effective way to communicate with the target market. Television, magazine, and radio ads can be used during the winter months to encourage students to start thinking about spring break and to book their location early. Often, special deals encourage college students to act.

Pricing is an important element of the prepurchase evaluation process. Consumers often compare the prices charged by competing firms. For services, more so than for goods, prices are seen as an indicator of quality. An attorney who charges $100 per hour is normally perceived as more competent than an attorney who charges $75 an hour. A carpet-cleaning service that charges $29.99 per room will be seen as superior to one that charges $19.99 per room. This does not, however, mean that consumers will choose the higher-priced firm. They may choose the lower price for one of several reasons. They may not have the money to pay a higher price. They may feel the higher-priced service is overpriced. They may rationalize that, although the service quality will not be as good, it is still a good value for the price being charged.

For services, **service distribution** is defined as the availability and accessibility of a service to consumers. It would include the firm's physical location, its hours of operation, and its access availability. A bank may operate several branches and place ATMs at various locations. Although actual bank hours are limited, customers have 24-hour-a-day access to their accounts through ATMs and online banking.

Perceived Risk

The last factor in the prepurchase phase is perceived purchase risk. Because of the unique characteristics of services, the purchase decision for services is perceived to be a higher risk than for goods.[13] Before a purchase, consumers will seek a means to reduce the risk involved in the decision, primarily through obtaining additional information. Consumers use the internal factors, external factors, and firm-produced factors just discussed to reduce this purchase risk.

Risk has two components: uncertainty and consequences.[14] **Uncertainty** is the probability that a particular outcome or consequence will occur. **Consequence** is the degree of importance or danger of the outcome itself. For example, there is risk in heart surgery. The uncertainty is the unknown probability of the surgery not being successful, and the consequence, if the surgery does not go well, is death or serious side effects. Because the procedure is now well developed and the probability of something going wrong during the surgery is low, most patients no longer view heart surgery as a high-risk medical procedure, even though the seriousness of the consequences is high.

> **Service Distribution:** The availability and accessibility of a service to consumers.
>
> **Uncertainty:** The probability that a particular outcome or consequence will occur.
>
> **Consequence:** The degree of importance or danger of the outcome itself.

In the purchasing of services, there are seven types of risk. They are performance risk, financial risk, time-loss risk, opportunity risk, psychological risk, social risk, and physical risk (see Table 9-4).

Table 9-4: Perceived Purchase Risk

Risk	Definition
Performance	The chance that the service will not perform or provide the benefit expected
Financial	The amount of monetary loss incurred if the service fails
Time-loss	The amount of time lost as a result of a service failure
Opportunity	The risk of losing other choices when one choice is selected
Psychological	The chance that the service will not fit the individual's self-concept
Social	The chance that the service will not meet the approval of others
Physical	The chance that the service will actually cause physical harm

Performance Risk:
The chance that the service will not perform or provide the benefit for which it was purchased.

Financial Risk:
The amount of monetary loss the consumer incurs if the service fails.

Time-loss Risk:
The amount of time the consumer lost as a result of the failure of the service.

Opportunity Risk:
The risk involved when consumers must choose one service over another.

Psychological Risk:
The chance that the purchase of the service will not fit the individual's self-concept.

Social Risk:
The probability that a service will not meet with approval from others who are significant to the consumer making the purchase.

Physical Risk:
The probability that a service will actually cause physical harm to the customer.

Performance risk is the chance that the service will not perform or provide the benefit for which it was purchased. For example, in the selection of a spring break location, there is the risk that the services the resort promises to provide are not available or are performed poorly. For an automobile repair service, performance risk would be the garage not fixing the problem properly.

Financial risk is the amount of monetary loss incurred by the consumer if the service fails. Money invested in personal tutoring that does not help a student is money poorly spent, or money lost. Money spent on a haircut that is not satisfactory is lost. In addition to the financial loss, there is the possibility of time loss. **Time-loss risk** refers to the amount of time lost by the consumer as a result of the failure of the service. If a consumer has to return to a garage to have his or her car repaired again because the problem was not taken care of the first time, then the consumer has lost the time required to drop off the vehicle and pick it up. In addition, the consumer could not use the vehicle during the time it is in the shop the second time it is being repaired.

Opportunity risk refers to the risk involved when consumers must choose one service over another. After a spring break selection is made, the opportunity to go to other locations is lost. You will never know if the other locations would have been better or worse. **Psychological risk** is the chance that the purchase of the service will not fit the individual's self-concept, and **social risk** is the probability that a service will not meet with approval from others who are significant to the consumer making the purchase. Choosing a resort that friends do not like is a high risk for the person who values friendships. Choosing a resort that does not meet with your self-concept is equally risky. The last type of risk that consumers of services face is **physical risk**. Physical risk is the probability that a service will actually cause physical harm to the customer. Medical procedures, such as plastic surgery, have physical risk.

During the prepurchase phase, consumers evaluate the type and extent of risk involved in the purchase decision. They will often compare service firms to see how much risk would be involved with each option. It is normally the uncertainty component being examined because the consequence component is usually the same. The first step most consumers take in reducing prepurchase risk is to examine their own personal experiences. The tendency is to patronize service firms they have used in the past because they know what type of service will be received. People tend to use the same hair stylist or barber because they know what to expect. Only if they are unhappy with the last haircut will they be inclined to switch.

To further reduce risk, consumers will often seek the opinion of others, such as friends, relatives, business associates, or experts in the field. When looking for a dentist, consumers usually ask other people for recommendations. When looking for spring break locations, the opinions of others will be valuable. The higher the perceived risk, the more likely that the opinion of someone else will be sought. Consumers will sometimes seek service-produced sources of information during the deliberation stage or information-collecting stage. Before deciding on a spring break location, you may collect information on several resorts. Common sources of information include advertising, promotions, and the Internet.

Service firms must be aware of the risk consumers perceive during the prepurchase phase and take appropriate steps to reduce it. It is important to understand the difference between the uncertainty component and the consequence component. To reduce the uncertainty component, services must reduce the perceived probability of a service failure. It is important to recognize that the perceived risk may not be the same as the actual risk. Although the actual risk of a parachute not opening for a skydiver is extremely low, most consumers perceive the risk to be relatively high. Airlines face a similar problem in that it is statistically safer to fly than it is to drive one's own automobile, yet most people perceive flying to be riskier. In both cases, the perception is greater than reality, but consumer decisions are based on the perception, not reality. Therefore, firms must deal with reducing the perceived risk consumers have, regardless of what the actual risk may be (see Figure 9-12).

Communication is a key in reducing the uncertainty component of risk. Through advertising, brochures, and certification, the perceived probability that something will go wrong can be reduced. Having a strong brand name is extremely beneficial. Most travelers feel more comfortable eating at a brand-name restaurant, such as Applebee's, than at a restaurant with an unfamiliar name. The brand-name restaurant is perceived to be more likely to have consistent quality at all of its restaurants. The traveler has no idea what to expect at an unknown local restaurant.

Figure 9-12: Service firms must be aware of the risk consumers perceive during the prepurchase phase and take appropriate steps to reduce it. Many consumers prefer eating at a brand-name restaurant to dining at a restaurant with an unfamiliar name.

Reducing the consequence component of risk is achieved by having quality control standards and procedures. Applebee's can reduce the consequence of food poisoning, or just a meal that tastes bad, by ensuring that all of its cooks and employees follow established quality control standards and specific operating procedures.

9-4b: Service Encounter

The second stage of the service purchase process is the service encounter, which is the actual interaction point between the customer and the service provider.[15] In most cases, the service provider is a person, but it can also be a machine, as in the case of a bank's ATM. In most cases, the customer and service provider interaction are in person— as would be the case with a dental procedure; however, it can occur over the telephone—as would be the case with a call center employee helping a customer with a computer problem. In all of these cases, the quality of the service encounter depends on the service environment and the service personnel or the service machine providing the service.

The service environment consists of the tangible elements of the facility, the facility's atmosphere, and other customers who are present at the time of the service. Tangible elements include, for example, the furniture, signs, brochures, and the equipment and tools being used to perform the service.

The atmospheric elements include such things as the office decor, the cleanliness of the facility, and intangible elements like noise, sound, and odors. (Atmospherics are further addressed in the discussion of the retail environment in Chapter 10.) All of these elements affect how customers react to service situations. If a restaurant is cold, consumers are likely to have a lower evaluation of the service. If a dental office is dirty, it will affect patients' evaluation of the dental care they are to receive. If a bakery has the smell of freshly baked cookies, it will positively influence the consumer's evaluation of the pastry just purchased. In all of these cases, the evaluation of the service is affected by intangible elements that are not part of the service itself. The actual service may be performed well, but customers can go away unhappy or extremely pleased because of an intangible element.

If other customers are present during the service encounter, they can affect the quality of the environment. This is especially true for entertainment services such as sports, theme parks, movie theaters, and concerts. A rowdy or drunken fan can destroy the fun of others watching a game. A customer talking at a movie theater can aggravate other viewers to the point they may not even stay for the whole movie.

In service encounters in which service personnel and customers have direct interaction, the conduct of the service personnel becomes a critical factor. If service personnel are polite and show genuine interest in the customer, their behavior will increase the level of customer satisfaction. If service personnel are indifferent or rude, their behavior can create customer dissatisfaction. The food at a restaurant can be excellent, but if the service is poor, it will reflect negatively on the entire experience. For many services, the conduct of the service personnel is as important or more important than the service itself.

> **Blueprinting:**
> The process of diagramming a service operation.

To ensure a positive service environment, many firms use a concept called **blueprinting**, which is the process of diagramming a service operation.[16] Through blueprinting, every step in the purchase process, from the first contact the customer has with a firm to the completion of the service, is diagrammed. Through this blue-printing process, the firm can see how customers and the firm interact. They can see which steps are not being performed efficiently and where improvements need to be made. The blueprint shows at what times during the service are the service environment, other customers, and service personnel involved. By carefully blueprinting every step in the purchase process, a firm can manage the entire experience to increase the probability the customer has a positive experience. Figure 9-13 illustrates a blueprint for an X-ray process.

Each block in the blueprinting diagram is a "moment of truth" when the customer or patient interacts with the service. The total experience is the sum of each of the contact experiences or moments of truth. If one link in the experience is bad, it will result in the negative evaluation of the whole experience. Customers will not remember the ten steps that went right—only the one step where it went wrong. Del Powell, southeast regional director for the former St. Paul Companies (now part of Traveler's Insurance), summed the importance of the service encounter very succinctly when he stated, "People will forget what you say, they'll forget your slogans, they'll forget your advertising, and they'll forget your promises. But what they'll always remember is what it feels like to do business with you."[17]

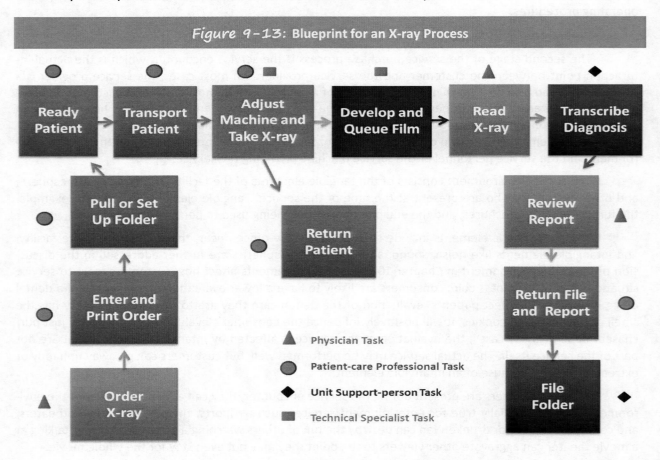

Figure 9-13: Blueprint for an X-ray Process

This service blueprint depicts the 13 steps involved in a typical hospital's X-ray process. The steps can be completed in less than one hour, and they require multiple employees. Without such a blueprint, the X-ray process would probably be less systematic, more time-consuming, and less efficient. Source: Stephen H. Baum, "Making Your Service Blueprint Pay Off!" *Journal of Services Marketing* 4 (1990): 49. Copyright Emerald Group Publishing

9-4c: Postpurchase Phase

The third stage of the purchase process is the postpurchase phase. During this stage, customers will evaluate the quality of service and their level of satisfaction or dissatisfaction. For satisfied customers, future actions include repeat purchases, customer loyalty, and positive word-of-mouth communications. For dissatisfied customers, future actions include switching vendors and negative word-of-mouth communications.[18]

In evaluating service quality, consumers evaluate two components: the technical quality and the functional quality.[19] **Technical service quality** is the outcome of the service, and **functional service quality** is the process whereby the service was performed. For a restaurant, the technical service quality is the food and drinks that are served, whereas the functional service quality is the interaction with the people providing the service (see Figure 9-14). For both components, a consumer will compare the perceived level of service quality that was received to the level of service expected. If expectations are met or exceeded, then consumers are satisfied; if expectations are not met, then consumers are dissatisfied.

In cases in which expectations are not met, the level of customer dissatisfaction will be determined by how and where customers attribute the cause of the service failure or poor service. The process of deciding the cause of the poor service is called **attribution theory**.[20] Customers look at two factors in determining attribution: First, was the cause of the service controllable, and second, could the firm have prevented the service problem? If either factor is confirmed, then the customer will attribute the service problem to the firm and blame it for what occurred.

Figure 9-14: This restaurant relies on a well-informed and courteous wait-staff (functional service quality), and fresh, local seafood (technical service quality).

> **Technical Service Quality:** The outcome of the service.
>
> **Functional Service Quality:** The process whereby the service was performed.
>
> **Attribution Theory:** The process of deciding the cause of a service failure or poor service.

To illustrate, suppose you order some clothes over the Internet, and the package arrives two days late. If the delay is caused by bad weather, you are less likely to be dissatisfied because the Internet company does not have any control over weather conditions. However, if the package is delayed because the company failed to send it out in a timely manner, then it is likely that you will be dissatisfied because the company is at fault and the delay could have been prevented.

Customers who are dissatisfied with a service are likely to choose another firm the next time they purchase that particular service. Few customers actually voice a complaint to the manager or service personnel. The customer may be unhappy with the haircut or the food that was served at a restaurant but will usually not say anything to anyone at the service. In fact, research has shown that only one out of every 25 dissatisfied customers will voice some type of complaint.[21] The remaining 24 say nothing but demonstrate their dissatisfaction by either switching to a different firm, by telling others about the poor quality service, or by doing both. The negative word-of-mouth can be devastating to a business because, on the average, an unhappy customer will tell ten to eleven other people about the bad experience.[22]

For customers who are satisfied, typical future behaviors include repeat purchases, firm loyalty, and positive word-of-mouth communications. Satisfied customers tend to patronize the same firm and, over time, become loyal to that firm. If a person likes the way a service mows the lawn or cleans the house, that person will continue to use the service. He or she may even engage in positive word-of-mouth communications, although usually it does not involve as many people as negative word-of-mouth communications. On average, a satisfied customer will tell only three others of his or her experience, instead of the ten to eleven for customers who are dissatisfied.[23]

9-5 SERVICE QUALITY

A critical component of future purchase behavior is the evaluation of the service a consumer receives. If customers are satisfied with the quality of service, they likely will patronize the firm again. If they are not satisfied, they likely will not patronize the firm in the future. Because future purchase behavior is largely determined by this service experience, it is beneficial to examine how a service business can measure service quality.

9-5a: Measuring Service Quality

In making an evaluation of service quality, customers will compare the service they received to what they expected. This method of measuring service quality is called the **gap theory** because you are measuring the gap between expectations and customer evaluations of the service. Past research has indicated that consumers make this evaluation along the five dimensions of tangibles, reliability, responsiveness, empathy, and assurance.[24]

Tangibles refer to the service provider's physical facilities, equipment, and the appearance of employees. **Reliability** is the ability of the service firm to perform the service promised dependably and accurately. **Responsiveness** is the willingness of the firm's staff to help customers and to provide them with prompt service. **Empathy** refers to the caring, individualized attention the service firm provides each customer. **Assurance** refers to the knowledge and courtesy of the employees and their ability to inspire customers to trust and have confidence in the service provider.

To illustrate these dimensions, suppose you have contacted a company to clean the carpets in your home. The tangibles are the appearance of the equipment being used and the personnel doing the work. If the equipment is old and worn, you may be inclined to believe that the quality of service the company provides is not as good as it would be for a company that has new, clean equipment. If the service is scheduled for 2:00 P.M. and the company shows up an hour late, the response will negatively impact your evaluation of the service quality. If, however, you called a company because of a water pipe break and service technicians are able to get out to your house in the afternoon or the first thing the next day, this quick response would have a positive impact on your evaluation. Employees who are knowledgeable and courteous will enhance your evaluation of the firm's service, whereas employees who do not know how to get particular stains out of your carpet or are rude will have a negative impact. In fact, a rude service technician can create a negative evaluation of the service even though the actual outcome of the service may be satisfactory. Empathy would be the caring, individualized attention the service provides. It may be moving some furniture for you at no additional cost, or it may be spending extra time on a particular spot in your carpet. How you evaluate the quality of service of the carpet-cleaning firm will be a summation of all five dimensions. The firm may do well on four of the five, but doing poorly on one dimension can create a negative overall evaluation of the service (see **Figure 9-15**).

> **Gap Theory:**
> Method of measuring service quality that involves measuring the gap between expectations and customers evaluation of the service.
>
> **Tangibles:**
> The service provider's physical facilities, equipment, and appearance of its employees.
>
> **Reliability**
> The ability of the service firm to perform the service provided in a dependable and accurate (service); the extent to which the data are likely to be free from random error and yield consistent results (scale).
>
> **Responsiveness:**
> The willingness of the firm's staff to help customers and to provide prompt service.
>
> **Empathy:**
> The caring, individualized attention the service firm provides to each customer.

Figure 9-15: Performing well on all five dimensions of service quality is critical for a service like an office or school cleaning business.

In measuring service quality using the gap theory, a service firm has two options. First, it can ask consumers about their expectations before the service and then ask the same series of questions after the service. Subtracting the two scores will give a gap score for each dimension, as well as for the overall service. An alternative method of using the gap theory methodology is to ask customers to evaluate the service along the five dimensions as it relates to what they expected. For example, a question about empathy would read, "The service technician demonstrated he cared about me as a customer." This latter method requires surveying customers only once and will yield similar results.

Instead of using a gap analysis to measure service quality, a company can use internal measures. For airlines, internal measures are such items as the percentage of on-time flights, number of baggage claims, and number of customer complaints. This information has to be filed with the Department of Transportation on a monthly basis, so it is readily available. By tracking these measures over time, an airline can see whether its level of service is increasing or decreasing. It can also compare its data to that of other airlines to see how it stands. These comparative data are especially helpful because they will indicate areas for improvement. If an airline ranks first in the number of baggage claims per 1,000 passengers, then it needs to look at ways of improving its baggage-handling process. If it does not address the problem, passengers are likely to start flying on other airlines.

The advantage of using internal measures of service quality is that weaknesses as well as strengths can be identified. Weaknesses need to be improved to remain competitive, and strengths can be marketed as a reason to patronize the firm. The airline that ranks first in percentage of on-time flights can advertise this as proof of its dependable and reliable service.

9-5b: Service Failure and Recovery

Service failures are defined as instances in which a service is either not performed at all or is poorly performed. Customers are not only dissatisfied, but they may be extremely angry. When service problems occur, customers are less likely to purchase from the firm again in the future and in many cases will tell others about the bad experience. For both reasons, services must develop methods for dealing with service failures.

> **Service Failures:**
> Instances in which a service is either not performed at all or is poorly performed.
>
> **Service Recovery:**
> The process of attempting to regain a customer's confidence after a service failure.

Service firms must realize that a service failure does not automatically result in firm-switching behavior and negative word-of-mouth communications. Customers can be recovered. The manner in which service failures are handled will have a greater impact on future purchase behavior than the original bad experience. Firms often have a second chance to make things right. However, if a firm fails the second time around, the backlash is even stronger because the firm, in essence, has failed twice. This process of attempting to regain a customer's confidence after a service failure is called service recovery.

A successful **service recovery** program can overcome most service failures and diminish the negative impact of the original poor or failed service.[25] The more quickly a service problem is handled, the more likely the customer can be recovered and will purchase from the firm again. If the service problem can be corrected at the time of the service encounter, the negative impact of the experience is almost always diminished. The longer it takes to correct the problem, the less likely it can be resolved satisfactorily and the less likely the customer will be to purchase again. For this reason, most hotels have developed a service recovery program that allows frontline employees to correct problems immediately. At Wyndham Hotels & Resorts, front desk employees can give up to one free night without management approval. This is rarely done, however. In most cases removing a dry cleaning, movie, or restaurant charge from the bill or offering a free meal or spa service is sufficient. At the Ritz-Carlton all employees can settle a dispute up to $2,000 per day.[26] Employees should be trained to defuse the customer's anger as quickly and tactfully as possible. Normally, all this requires is attentive listening, and acknowledging the customer has a right to feel annoyed. Listening will allow customers to vent their anger and explain why they are unhappy. Admitting the firm made a mistake, if indeed this happened, will offset any attribution directed to the firm. It is harder to be mad at someone who admits he or she made a mistake. By agreeing that the customer had a right to be upset and dissatisfied, employees demonstrate empathy and understanding. With this groundwork, the recovery process is ready to move into the resolution stage.

Many companies begin the resolution stage by asking the customer what the firm can do to correct the problem. For example, counter agents at the Dollar and Thrifty car rental companies are trained to immediately ask customers what they think would be a fair settlement.[27] Firms that use this strategy are astounded at the reasonableness of customers and the solutions recommended. Customers seldom recommend drastic solutions. Often, they may suggest a partial refund or a coupon for a discount on another purchase. They may just want the service firm to correct the problem. Few customers will suggest solutions that are unreasonable.

Successful service recovery programs empower employees to correct the wrong. It trusts employees to make the right decision. Baptist Health Care allows each employee to spend up to $250 for service recovery. The money can be used for anything that the employee feels will correct the situation, from giving out a gift certificate, to replacing lost items, to crediting the patient's bill.[28]

After the customer has made a suggestion, the service employee is then ready to negotiate a viable solution to the problem. The goal of the resolution is twofold. First, the firm wants to eradicate the negative experience and change the dissatisfaction into some type of satisfaction. Second, the firm wants that customer to return and purchase again. With these goals in mind, the employee should negotiate a solution that satisfies the customer and is feasible for the firm.

If the problem cannot be corrected at the time it is discovered, then customers need to be informed. The customer needs to be kept up to date on the progress that is made. If the same employee can deal with the customer through the whole service recovery process, it will increase the chances of a positive outcome. In the business-to-business area, keeping customers informed through one contact person is very important. Too often, either the problem is passed around or it is assumed that the customer knows what is happening.

9-6 *CUSTOMER VALUE PACKAGE*

Dissatisfaction and poor service quality are not the only reasons customers switch firms. Customers can be satisfied with a service firm but switch because a competitor offers a better deal or is more convenient. Research has estimated that 65 to 85 percent of customers who switch firms were not dissatisfied with their last vendor.[29] See Figure 9-16 for a breakdown from one study on why customers leave. Because future purchase behavior is determined by more than customer satisfaction, service firms must look at ways to develop stronger relationships with their customers. The key to stronger relationships is in the concept of the **customer value package**, which is the perceived combination of factors that in the consumer's mind creates a superior value for him or her. The components of the customer value package are price, technical service quality, functional service quality, and company image.[30]

Customer Value Package: The perceived combination of factors that in the consumer's mind creates a superior value for him or her.

Figure 9-16: Why Customers Switch Service Firms

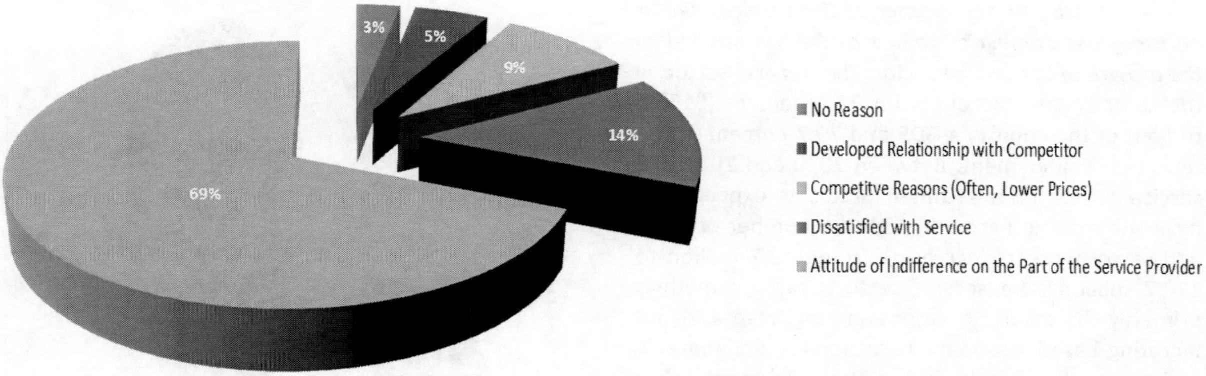

- No Reason
- Developed Relationship with Competitor
- Competitve Reasons (Often, Lower Prices)
- Dissatisfied with Service
- Attitude of Indifference on the Part of the Service Provider

Source: Marc R. Okrant, "How to Convert '3's and '4's into '5's," *Marketing News* 36 (October 14, 2002): 14–15.

Customers will patronize the firm that offers the best value. That value may be a lower price, superior technical quality, superior functional quality, or perceived company image. Customers weigh all four components of the value package and choose the service with the best combination. One consumer may choose a company that has adequate technical and service quality but a lower price, whereas other consumers may choose a different company they perceive to offer high service quality, although the cost is higher.

To develop and manage a customer value package, services will need to:[31]

1. Determine the relative weights customers place on each element of the value package.

2. Determine the value package that will be offered.

3. Develop business objectives and a mission statement that will incorporate the value package.

4. Communicate the values to all company personnel.

5. Develop plans to implement the value package.

6. Monitor the environment for changes in customer value weights.

After a service has determined the relative weights customers place on each element of the service value package, the service must decide what value package they will offer. In addition to meeting the value package desired by customers, firms must examine their own resources and the competitive advantage they can develop. If a service has developed a high level of technical service quality, they will want to look for ways this advantage can be leveraged to produce value for the customer. Hilton, Four Seasons, and other high-end hotels are successful because they provide a customer value package that customers want. Although price is still a component of the value package, it is not as prominent as technical and functional service quality. Firms must carefully look at their target market and develop a value package that meets what their potential customers want (see **Figure 9-17**).

After the value package is developed, the service needs to incorporate the values into the company's business objectives and mission statement. If the company adopts a functional service quality value, the mission statement should address the importance of customer-employee interaction. If the value package stresses price, the mission statement should promote the company's desire to be the low-priced leader. Putting the customer value package in the mission statement and business objectives conveys the message to both employees and customers that providing value to the customer is the driving force behind the company.

Summary

1. Discuss the impact of the services sector on the gross domestic product and what has led to the growth of the service sector. The service sector in the United States accounts for 79.4 percent ($13.34 trillion) of the country's GDP and 79.7 percent of the total U.S. employment. Between 2010 and 2020, the service sector in the United States is expected to have the most job growth, with the number of wage and salary workers increasing from 112.7 million to 130.7 million. The service sector's rapid growth is primarily the result of nations shifting from a manufacturing-based economy to a service economy. A major stimulus in this shift is the movement to an information society spurred by the computer and advancements in telecommunications. Additional factors contributing to the growth of the service sector are an aging population, longer life expectancies, increased leisure time, higher per-capita income, increased time pressure, more female workforce participation, sedentary lifestyles, changing social and cultural values, and advances in technology.

2. Identify the four unique characteristics of services and how each affects the marketing of services. Services possess four inherent characteristics not found in goods: intangibility, perishability, inseparability, and variability. Intangibility refers to the lack of tangible assets that can be seen, touched, smelled,

Figure 9-17: Service businesses must carefully look at their target market and develop a value package that meets what their potential customers want .

heard, or tasted before a purchase, which renders a service relatively difficult for a consumer to evaluate before a purchase. Perishability refers to the inability of a service to be inventoried or stored. This means that one of the goals of marketing is to manage demand so it equals supply and capacity. Inseparability refers to the simultaneous production and consumption of a service, which requires marketing the service at the time and location of the service provider. Variability refers to the unwanted or random levels of service quality that customers receive when they patronize a service. Because of this variability, promises made in advertising and other marketing materials are not always kept; this reflects negatively on the service operation.

3. Explain the components of the purchasing process for services. The purchase process consists of three phases: the prepurchase phase, the service encounter, and the postpuchase phase. During the prepurchase phase, consumers evaluate alternatives, make a purchase decision, and choose a particular brand. At some point after the decision is made, the consumer will move into the second stage, the service encounter, which is the actual interaction point between the customer and the service provider. The last phase of the services purchase process is the postpurchase evaluation, which begins upon completion of the service. During this phase, consumers make evaluations concerning the quality of service, their level of satisfaction or dissatisfaction, and future purchase intentions.

4. Identify the factors that affect the purchase decision during the prepurchase phase of the purchase process. During the prepurchase phase, the factors that affect the purchase decision are internal factors, external factors, firm-produced factors, and perceived risk. Internal factors consist of individual needs and wants of the consumer, past experience, expectations of the service alternatives, and the overall level of purchase involvement. The external factors that influence the purchase decision during the prepurchase phase are the competitive options available to consumers, the social context of the purchase, and word-of-mouth communications. The firm-produced factors affecting the purchase decision include promotions, pricing, and distribution. The types of perceived risk that can affect the purchase decision are performance risk, financial risk, time-loss risk, opportunity risk, psychological risk, social risk, and physical risk.

5. Discuss the relevant elements of the service encounter and why they are important. The service encounter is the actual interaction point between the customer and the service provider. The quality of the service encounter depends on the service environment and the service personnel or service machine providing the service. The service environment consists of the tangible elements of the facility, the facility's atmosphere, and other customers who are present at the time of the service. All of these components of the service encounter affect a customer's evaluation of the service being delivered, as well as the interaction between the customer and service personnel.

6. Describe the postpurchase evaluation of services and its impact on future purchase behavior. During the postpurchase phase, customers evaluate the quality of service and their level of satisfaction or dissatisfaction. For satisfied customers, future actions include repeat purchases, customer loyalty, and positive word-of-mouth communications. For dissatisfied customers, future actions include switching vendors and negative word-of-mouth communications.

7. Discuss how service quality is measured. In the process of evaluating service quality, customers will compare the service they received to what they expected along the five dimensions of tangibles, reliability, responsiveness, assurance, and empathy. Using this method of measuring service quality, companies can ask consumers about their expectations before the service and subsequently ask the same series of questions after the service. Subtracting the two scores will give them a gap score for each dimension, as well as for the overall service. An alternative method is to ask customers to evaluate the service along the five dimensions as it relates to what they expected. Instead of using a gap analysis to measure service quality, a company can use internal measures, such as the number of lost baggage claims or percentage of on-time deliveries.

8. Describe an effective service recovery process. A successful service recovery program is designed to overcome service failures and diminish the negative impact of the original poor or failed service. The more quickly a service problem is handled, the more likely the customer can be recovered and will purchase from the firm again. Employees should be trained to defuse the customer's anger as quickly and tactfully as possible. Normally, all this requires is attentive listening, admitting that the firm made a mistake, and acknowledging that the customer has a right to feel annoyed. Once this is accomplished, it is time for the resolution stage. Many companies begin the resolution stage by asking the customer what the firm can do to correct the problem. Once the customer has made a suggestion, the service employee is then ready to negotiate a viable solution to the problem.

9. Explain the importance of the customer value package and list the steps required to develop a customer value package. Customers will patronize the service that offers the best value package of price, technical service quality, functional service quality, and firm image. To develop and manage a customer value package, services will need to (a) determine the relative weights customers place on each element of the value package, (b) determine the value package that will be offered, (c) develop business objectives and a mission statement that will incorporate the value package, (d) communicate the values to all company personnel, (e) develop plans to implement the value package, and (f) monitor the environment for changes in customer value weights.

Key Terms

assurance	inseparability	service distribution
attribution theory	intangibility	service encounter
blueprinting	involvement	service failures
consequence	opportunity risk	service recovery
customer value package	performance risk	social risk
empathy	perishability	tangibles
financial risk	physical risk	technical service quality
functional service quality	psychological risk	time-loss risk
gap theory	reliability	uncertainty
industrialization	responsiveness	variability

1. Do you own a camera used in extreme action video photography, such as a GoPro? What percentage of your friends own such a camera? Survey at least five individuals who have such cameras. What do they do with the videos they take? What types of service businesses do you foresee developing as a result of extreme action video photography cameras?

2. The majority of new jobs in the future will be in the service sector. Using the Internet and an electronic database, locate articles that discuss future employment and the service sector. Will the service jobs in the future be primarily minimum-wage jobs at service businesses like restaurants, or will they be high-dollar jobs that require a college degree?

3. Select one item from the list of factors contributing to the growth of the service sector discussed in Section 9-2. Using the Internet and an electronic database, locate articles that discuss the factor selected. What types of service industries have benefited in the past, and what types of service industries will benefit in the future? What do you see in the future for the contributory factor you chose in terms of its impact on the service sector?

4. Compare your eating-out habits with those of your parents and grandparents. What changes do you see among the three generations in terms of dining out, purchasing takeout, and eating at home? How has food that is purchased for home consumption changed?

5. For each of the following services, discuss the degree of intangibility, perishability, inseparability, and variability inherent in each service. Pick one service and discuss strategies for reducing the negative impact of each unique service characteristic.

        a. automobile repair service
        b. dentist
        c. photographer's studio
        d. Chinese restaurant
        e. lawn service

6. Pick one of the following services. Discuss each factor of the prepurchase phase and how it would affect your purchase decision.

        a. automobile repair service
        b. dentist
        c. photographer's studio
        d. Chinese restaurant
        e. lawn service

7. Suppose you decided to spend a week on a vacation at a resort in Miami Beach, Florida. Discuss each of the perceived risks involved in making the decision. What would be the uncertainty and consequence factors involved in the decision?

8. On your next dining-out experience, describe your service encounter experience. Discuss each element of the service encounter phase presented in Section 9-4b in terms of your experience. How did each element affect your evaluation of the service?

9. Identify a recent personal service failure situation in which the service was poor or not performed at all. Did you complain to anyone at the service? Why or why not? Have you told any of your friends, relatives, or others about the experience? How many have you told? Did the service make any attempt to make things right with you (i.e., use a service recovery process)? If so, describe the outcome. If not, what could the service have done to correct the situation?

10. Suppose you decide to purchase a year's membership at a fitness gym. What type of value package would you want? Describe how important each element of the customer value package would be to you. Locate three fitness centers or gyms in your area and evaluate them using your customer value package. Which facility would you choose? Why?

True or False

1. Because medical treatment of elderly patients requires special equipment and facilities, such a treatment cannot be characterized as a service.

2. Perishability is directly related to the demand for a particular service. Demand can be managed through advertising, special promotions, and pricing.

3. Variability is a unique characteristic found in most services.

4. Involvement refers to the level of mental and physical effort exerted by a consumer in selecting a good or service.

5. The service encounter is the actual interaction point between the customer and the service provider and consists only of tangible elements.

6. Using the gap theory to evaluate service quality involves measuring the gap between customer expectations and customer evaluation of the service.

7. An alternative to the gap analysis as a measure of service quality is using internal measures performed by the company.

8. After a service failure takes place, dissatisfied customers will be reluctant to make another purchase from the same company despite a successful service recovery program.

Multiple Choice

9. What is the most critical group of factors that affect the prepurchase phase?

      a. internal factors
      b. external factors
      c. firm-produced factors
      d. risk

10. The probability that a particular outcome will occur refers to which component of risk?

      a. uncertainty
      b. consequences
      c. opportunity
      d. performance

11. To ensure a positive service environment, many companies use the concept of blueprinting, which reveals:

      a. every step in the purchase process.
      b. steps where the service is not performed in an efficient manner.
      c. how customers and service personnel interact in the environment.
      d. all of the above.

12. In the postpurchase phase the customer evaluates the following components:

      a. technical service quality
      b. functional service quality
      c. financial benefits
      d. a and b

13. Negative word-of-mouth can be problematic: An unhappy customer is likely to share information regarding his or her bad experience with _____ people.

      a. 1 to 2

      b. 3 to 9

      c. 10 to 11

      d. 20 or more

14. The service staff's willingness to help customers and to provide prompt service is an example of

      a. validity.

      b. reliability.

      c. responsiveness.

      d. responsibility.

15. A customer value package is composed of

      a. price.

      b. company image.

      c. technical service quality and functional service quality.

      d. all of the above.

Blog

Clow-Lascu: *Marketing: Essentials 5e Blog*

What Is Happening Today?

Learn More! For videos and articles that relate to Chapter 9:

blogclowlascu.net/category/chapter09

Includes Discussion Questions with each Post!

Notes

1. Digital Photo Printing Top Ten Reviews, at http://digital-photo-printing-review.toptenreviews.com, accessed on July 16, 2014; Leslie Walker, "Digital-Photo Printing is a Developing Industry," available at *Washingtonpost. com*, June 2, 2005.

2. CIA World Factbook, available at www.cia.gov/publications/factbook, accessed on July 18, 2014.

3. Richard Henderson, "Industry employment and output projections to 2020," Monthly Labor Review, January 2012, 65-83.

4. Gene Koertz, "America's Jobs Are Changing," Business Week (January 24, 2000): 32; Jay M. Berman, "Industry Output and Employment Projections to 2012," *Monthly Labor Review* 127 (February 2004): 63.

5. Kenneth E. Clow and David L. Kurtz, *Services Marketing: Operation, Management, and Strategy*, 2nd ed., (Cincinnati, Oh: Atomic Dog, 2004), 6–7.

6. Valarie A. Zeithaml, A. Parasuraman, and Leonard L. Berry, "Problems and Strategies in Services Marketing," *Journal of Marketing* 49 (1985): 33–46.

7. "The Internet's Place in the Banking Industry," *Chicago Fed Letter, Federal Reserve Bank of Chicago*, no. 163 (March 2001); Joanna Stavins, "ATM Fees: Does Bank Size Matter?" *New England Economic Review* (January/February 2000): 13–25.

8. Eileen Colkin, "Citibank," *Information Week* no. 852 (August 27, 2001): 30–31.

9. Lisa Brown, "Enterprise Holdings' revenue grows to $16.4 billion" St. Louis Post Dispatch, November 6, 2013, accessed at http://www.stltoday.com/business/local/enterprise-holdings-revenue-grows-to-billion/article_3688f927-96e9-5b8b-a922-67d2dd896d80.html on July 21, 2014. Frederick Reichheld and Paul Rogers, "Motivating Through Metrics," *Harvard Business Review*, 83, no. 9 (September 2005), 20–24; Andy Taylor, "Driving Customer Satisfaction," *Harvard Business Review* 80 (July 2002): 24–25.

10. David L. Kurtz and Kenneth E. Clow, "Managing Consumer Expectations of Services," *Journal of Marketing Management* 2 (Fall/Winter 1992–1993): 19–25.

11. Judith Lynne Zaichkowsky, "Measuring the Involvement Construct," *Journal of Consumer Research* 12 (December 1985): 341–352.

12. Keith B. Murray, "A Test of Services Marketing Theory: Consumer Information Acquisition Activities," *Journal of Marketing* 55 (January 1991): 10–25.

13. Ibid.

14. R. A. Bauer, "Consumer Behavior as Risk Taking," in *Dynamic Marketing for a Changing World*, ed. R. Hancock (Chicago: American Marketing Association, 1960): 389–398.

15. Mary Jo Bitner, "Evaluating Service Encounters: The Effects of Physical Surroundings and Employee Responses," *Journal of Marketing* 54 (1990): 69–82.

16. G. Lynn Shostack, "Understanding Services through Blueprinting," in *Services Marketing and Management,* eds. T. Schwartz, D. Bowen, and S. Brown (Greenwich, Conn.: JAI Press, 1992): 75–90.

17. Caroline McDonald, "The Moments of Truth," *National Underwriter/Property & Casualty Risk & Benefits* 105 (July 9, 2001): 25.

18. Diane Halstead, Cornelia Droge, and M. Bixby Cooper, "Product Warranties and Postpurchase Service," *Journal of Services Marketing* 7, no. 1 (1993): 33–40; Mary Jo Bitner, "Evaluating Service Encounters: The Effects of Physical Surroundings and Employee Responses," *Journal of Marketing* 54 (1990): 69–82; William O. Bearden and Jesse E. Teel, "Selected Determinants of Consumer Satisfaction and Complaint Reports," *Journal of Marketing Research* 20 (February 1983): 21–28.

19. Christian Gronroos, *Service Management and Marketing* (Lexington, Mass.: Lexington Books, 1990): 37–39.

20. Valerie S. Folkes, Susan Koletsky, and John Graham, "A Field Study of Causal Inferences and Consumer Reaction: The View from the Airport," *Journal of Consumer Research* 13 (March 1985): 534–539.

21. David Lipton, "Now Hear This . . . Customer Complaints Are Not Bad if Viewed as Business-Building Occasions," *Nation's Restaurant News* 34 (August 29, 2000): 30–31.

22. John Disney, "Customer Satisfaction and Loyalty: The Critical Elements of Service Quality," *Total Quality Management* 10 (July 1999): S491–S497.

23. Barry Farber and Joyce Wycoff, "Customer Service: Evolution and Revolution," *Sales & Marketing Management* (May 1991): 44–48; 50–51.

24. A. Parasuraman, Valarie A. Zeithaml, and Leonard L. Berry, "SERVQUAL: A Multiple-Item Scale for Measuring Consumer Perceptions of Service Quality," *Journal of Retailing* 64 (Spring 1988): 12–40.

25. Tor Wallin Andreassen, "From Disgust to Delight: Do Customers Hold a Grudge?" *Journal of Service Research* 4 (August 2001): 39–50; Clow and Kurtz, Services Marketing, 329–331

26. Gary Stoller, "Companies Give Front-Line Employees More Power," *USA Today*, (June 27, 2005): 1a.

27. Ibid.

28. Martin Wright and Kelly Nemeth, "Making it Right," *Sales & Service Excellence*, 6, no. 6 (June 2006): 9.

29. Joan O. Fredericks and James M. Salter, "Beyond Customer Satisfaction," *Management Review* (May 1995): 29–32.

30. Mokhtar Abdullah, Aamjad D. AlNasser, and Nooreha Husain, "Evaluating Functional Relationship Between Image, Customer Satisfaction and Customer Loyalty Using General Maximum Entropy," *Total Quality Management* 11 (July 2000): S826–S830.

31. Fredericks and Salter, "Beyond Customer Satisfaction," 29–32.

Part Three: Marketing Mix Strategies

Case 9-1 First American Bank

Looking down his attendance list, Thomas Lauden, the Vice President of Marketing for First American Bank, checked off the names. Present were branch managers Brenda Neely and Charles Jones, Vice President of Retail Operations Kristen Hammersmith, Vice President of Consumer Loans Mingshing Liu, and marketing staff members Theresa Hanks and Ollie Jenkins. Lauden called this meeting to discuss the bank's marketing program. Because of declining profits and the emergence of two new banks in First American Bank's area, First American Bank's number of customers had actually declined for the first time in 30 years. Lauden began the meeting by presenting the financial statement for the past year for the 12 facilities in the First American Bank system. All but two had profits decline, and all but four had fewer customers.

Lauden continued by presenting data from the American Bankers Association, showing what customers value in a bank. Trust was at the top of the list, with 83 percent of the respondents indicating it was very important. Reasonable fees were second, competitive interest rates were third, convenience was fourth, financial strength fifth, and reputation sixth, followed by personal attention, up-to-date technology, investment expertise, and a wide range of products and services (see Figure A).

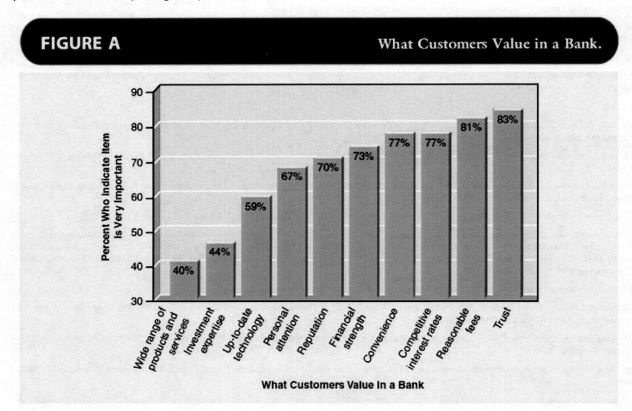

FIGURE A   What Customers Value in a Bank.

Jones was the first to speak. "We have no control over interest rates or fees really. Our fees are similar to those of other banks. So we can toss those out."

"I don't think we should toss them out if they are important," countered Hanks. "If they are important to customers, then we should discuss our fees in the marketing material."

"But what value is it if our fees are the same as those of every other bank? There is no value in promoting something that does not provide a competitive advantage for us or at least makes us stand out from the competition," Jones argued.

"I'm not so sure about that. Maybe our fees are the same and maybe our interest rates are the same, but how do people know that if we don't promote it?" Hammersmith interjected.

"So from this list, it would appear to me we ought to promote the idea of trust, that we have reasonable

FIGURE B

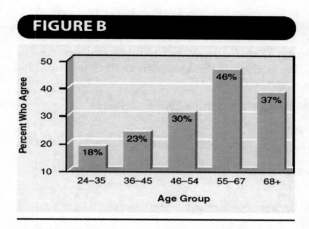

Banks' Commitment to Meeting Customers' Financial Needs by Age Category.
Source: "Customer Views about Banks," *ABA Banking Journal* 93 (September 2001): 6–7.

FIGURE C Perceptions about Banks.

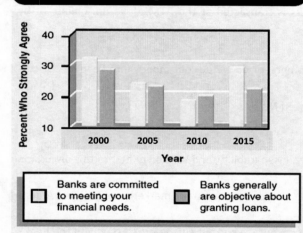

Banks are committed to meeting your financial needs.

Banks generally are objective about granting loans.

fees, competitive interest rates, convenience, and financial strength," Neely spoke up.

"But how do you promote trust? What can you say in an advertisement that conveys that message?" Jones asked.

Smiling, Lauden looked at Hanks and Jenkins as he replied, "That's what I pay my staff to figure out." Putting another slide on the overhead (see Figure B), Lauden continued. "I think this slide is even more startling. When people were asked if their bank was committed to meeting their financial needs, look at the results. The younger the respondent, the less likely they were to agree. That means it's the younger generation that does not believe we are committed to meeting their financial needs."

"And they are our future customers," mused Hammersmith.

"The percentage of 24- to 35-year-olds is half of the percentage of retired people," Ollie pointed out. "In fact, the real problem appears to be the 24- to 45-year-old age group."

"Before we go any further," Lauden suggested, "let me show you the remaining slide, which look at the overall percentages over time, since 2000 (see Figure C). First is the statement that 'banks are committed to meeting your financial needs.' Notice that 31 percent strongly agreed in 2000, which dropped to a low of 17 percent in 2005 and is now up to 28 percent. For the statement that 'banks generally are objective about granting loans,' the percentage for strongly agree was 27 percent in 2000, which dropped to 19 percent in 2005, and is now at 21 percent."

"I thought we were doing a better job of granting loans to all of the different demographic groups," Liu spoke. "But this information indicates that is not the perception."

"Do you think we need to include more minorities in our marketing material?"

"That may be a good idea. Have we examined all of our marketing material to see how minorities, women, retirees, and even college students are represented?" Mingshing asked.

"We have, but not formally," Ollie replied.

"I don't think that is a real issue with us. What I do sense is that we are not attracting the under-30 individual, especially males. We seem to do better with females in that age category," Hammersmith pointed out.

"Do you think it's because they have higher expectations or maybe they are just harder to please? What do you think is the issue?" Mingshing asked.

Lauden responded, "I think they have options, especially Internet options that the older consumer does not have. I also believe they are not as interested in developing a personal relationship with their bank as are older consumers. Look who's in the lobby. Almost everyone out there is over 50. Look who's at the ATM, the drive-up window, and banking with us online. It's almost the opposite."

"I think Tom has a valid point," Jones spoke up. "If our goal is to reach the younger consumer, then we must promote the technology, the online access, the ATMs. That's what they want to see."

"And my experience from the loan area," Mingshing shared, "is that they are concerned about interest rates and reasonable fees. But before we go further on this, let me give you some information I found in my research. We are talking about gaining new customers, but shouldn't we be just as concerned about retaining our current customers? I read that it costs about six or seven times more money to get a new customer than to retain a current customer. I also read that the longer a customer stays with a company, the more profitable they become. They buy more and require less of our time. Here, let me show you some more interesting facts."

Moving to the overhead, Mingshing put up a slide with the following information:

- There is little correlation between satisfaction and retention.

- From 65 to 85 percent of defectors were satisfied with their previous service.

- For those dissatisfied, the primary reasons for leaving were failure to deliver a service as promised and being treated in an unprofessional manner.

- For those satisfied, the primary reasons for leaving were because of perceived better prices or a better value package from a competitor.

Mingshing continued, "As we develop our marketing plan, we need to think about our current customers and encourage them to stay with us. It makes no sense to spend our marketing budget trying to gain new customers if we are losing them as fast as we gain new ones. If the information I read is correct, we have to gain at least six new customers to just break even on the cost of losing one current customer."

"In the study you read, what was the key to retaining customers?"

"Contact with the bank," Mingshing answered.

"But how do you do that if 70 percent of our business is transacted at the ATM, drive-up, online, or by phone?" objected Hammersmith.

"That's the challenge," Mingshing countered.

"So, do we develop a marketing plan to seek new customers, or do we put our money into keeping our current customers?" Jenkins asked.

"Can we do both? Why does it have to be either or?" asked Neely.

Questions:

1. How do the service characteristics of intangibility, perishability, inseparability, and variability fit into this discussion of marketing a bank?

2. Using all of the information presented in this case, what theme would you suggest for marketing of the First American Bank to the under-30 consumer? Why?

3. Can you target new customers and use the same set of ads to encourage current customers to stay with the bank? Why or why not?

4. What should the bank do about the customers they are losing?

5. If trust is an important value to bank customers, how can that message be conveyed to customers who bank primarily using the ATM, driveup, or online facilities?

Sources: Thomas J. Healy, "Why You Should Retain Your Customers," *America's Community Banker* 8 (September 1999): 22–25; "What Customers Value Most," *ABA Banking Journal 93* (September 2001): 17; "Customer Views about Banks," *ABA Banking Journal* 93 (September 2001): 6–7.

Case 9-2 Lori's

Lori Metcalf had always wanted her own restaurant. She had started working at 16 as a waitress and worked her way up until she was managing the local Chili's Bar and Grill. During that time she had worked at six different casual dining restaurants and seen both the good and the bad. With a goal of owning her own restaurant sometime, Lori had skimped and saved money by living in a small apartment and driving an old car. Through her savings, an inheritance she had received, and a personal loan from her sister, she was able to make the down payment on a small chain of six restaurants located in western Tennessee.

Motivation for Choosing a Restaurant and Average Amount Spent per Meal	
• Favorite staff	$21.88
• Ambience	$17.03
• Healthy food	$14.64
• Relaxation	$14.32
• Socialization	$13.38
• Great-tasting food	$12.78
• Fast service	$10.88
• Food variety	$ 9.28
• Good price/value	$ 8.07

Before purchasing the casual dining restaurants, Lori surveyed the current customers as well as individuals who had patronized one of the restaurants in the past. It did not take long for her to see why the restaurant was losing money and why it was for sale. The food was considered average to above average, but that was where the good news ended. Service, cleanliness, and availability of food items varied greatly from day to day. Patrons never knew what to expect.

Lori planned to change the name of the restaurant to "Lori's" feeling that the feminine first name would convey a feeling of personalization and friendliness rather than use her last name of Metcalf. Lori then spent two weeks interviewing restaurant managers and owners she knew. Each had a different idea of what she needed to do to be successful. It was almost more confusing than helpful. The one bottom line, however, that did come through was that customers must enjoy their dining experience and both the good food and service must consistently be there.

In her research, Lori found a study by Restaurant Demand Today that listed the primary goal or motivation of why people ate at a particular restaurant and then how much they spent per meal. The results were enlightening because the individuals who chose a restaurant because they had a favorite staff person who worked there spent the most per meal, $21.88. Great-tasting food was sixth on the list at $12.78 and fast service was seventh. See the accompanying table for the entire list.

Before taking over her restaurant chain, Lori attended a seminar in Atlanta on restaurant management. She attended several sessions that dealt with restaurant trends and what customers want from a restaurant. From these sessions, she made the following notes:

• Successful restaurants must be all-purpose, all-accessible, and all-affordable.

• Patrons want comfort and value.

• Patrons want freedom of choice in menu items.

• Customers like restaurants that know them and treat them with respect and care.

• For families with children, it is the children who often drive the choice of a restaurant.

• The number one reason customers choose a dine-in restaurant is that they "like it there."

• Older Americans are opting away from fast foods and choosing quick service dine-in facilities instead.

• Patrons want a variety of food that includes healthier menu items.

• In the future, more restaurants will explore new marketing tactics, such as cookbooks, local TV shows, and packaging their own foods for sale in grocery stores.

• In the future, more restaurants will use e-mail and social media communications tactics with customers.

• From designer dishware to designer staff uniforms, more restaurants are attempting to create a unique image and design.

• More restaurants are offering pick-up and takeout services.

In two weeks, Lori takes over the management of her small chain of restaurants. She knows marketing is a key to her success, but before she can create her marketing plan, she must make other decisions concerning the operation of the restaurants. For instance, Lori knows changes must be made in the decor of the restaurants and staff must be trained to provide quality service. She has to prioritize. Time and money will not allow her to make all the changes at once.

Questions

1. Based on the table in this case and the other information provided, prioritize the top three tasks Lori should tackle when she takes over this chain of restaurants.

2. What image or feeling do you think the name "Lori's" conveys to customers? How does this fit into the type of service, food, and decor of her restaurants?

3. Discuss each of the characteristics of services (intangibility, perishability, inseparability, and variability) as it relates to Lori's restaurant.

4. How would you motivate the staff at Lori's to provide quality, consistent service? Keep in mind Lori's financial capabilities are extremely limited because she just purchased the restaurants.

5. Would you require the staff to wear a uniform, would you insist on similar attire but no uniform, or to save money at this point in time, would you not worry about wait-staff 's appearance as long as it was neat and clean? Based on your previous responses, how important is the wait-staff 's attire and appearance?

6. From your responses given thus far, briefly outline a marketing plan that Lori can use with a limited marketing budget.

Sources: Paul Frumkin, "Consumer Trends: What Do They Want," *Nation's Restaurant News*, 39, no. 21 (May 23, 2005), 58–68; Michael Sanson and John Mariani, "Full Service Takes a Bigger Bite," *Restaurant Hospitality*, 87, no. 2 (February 2003), 29–34; "Consumer Beat: Dining Motivation and Spending," *Restaurant & Institutions*, 115, no. 1 (January 1, 2005), 24–34.

Answers to Review Questions

Answers: 1) False, 2) True, 3) True, 4) True, 5) False, 6) True, 7) True, 8) False, 9) a, 10) a, 11) d, 12) d, 13) d, 14) c, 15) d

Chapter 10

Channel and Retailing Strategies

Chapter Outline

Learning Objectives

After studying this chapter, you should be able to:

1. Define distribution and identify the different channel functions and dimensions.

2. Identify issues related to channel management, such as channel organization, administration, and relationships.

3. Examine the different logistics functions.

4. Provide an overview and description of the general merchandise retailing category and offer examples and illustrations.

5. Provide an overview and description of the food retailing category and offer examples and illustrations.

6. Provide an overview and description of the non-store retailing category and offer examples and illustrations.

7. Address issues related to merchandise and service mix, location, atmospherics, and future trends in retailing.

Figure 10-1 Gourmet shops often have attractive bakery displays, such as this one ion the East Coast.

10-1 CHAPTER OVERVIEW

Kathleen King rented a bakery in downtown Southampton, New York, in 1979 for $350 a month and spent the winter perfecting her recipes and readying them for mass production. She then opened her doors when the summer crowd descended upon Southampton, and her all-natural (and high-cholesterol) cookies, pies, cakes, and other baked goods were an instant hit.

In 2010, she decided to focus her expansion efforts on wholesaling instead. Today, around 75 percent of King's $1.5-million-a-year revenues come from wholesaling her goods to over 100 gourmet shops on Long Island, in New York City, and in other states. Gourmet shops are popular, and most have an enticing bakery section (see **Figure 10-1**). She also sells through popular upscale grocery chains all over the East Coast. Kathleen's Bake Shop is now named Tate's Bake Shop, in honor of her father. However, the products distributed still carry Kathleen's name. Her primary distributor is Bay View Distributing.[1]

Kathleen's Bake Shop took on the role of manufacturer or producer, selling baked goods through a wholesaler, Bay View Distributing, to gourmet retailers, and directly to Fresh Market gourmet grocery stores on the East Coast.

This chapter addresses issues related to distribution channels and retail outlets. Section 10-2 addresses the need for distribution channels and the different channel functions. Section 10-3 looks at the different channel dimensions, such as direct and indirect channels, channel length and width, and the intensity of distribution. Section 10-4 addresses channel management and Section 10-5 examines the different logistics functions, such as transportation, warehousing, inventory control, and order processing. Section 10-6 discusses the different categories of full-service and limited-service wholesalers and examines the different types of agents and brokers. Section 10-7 examines retailing and its different formats, general merchandise retailing, food retailing, and non-store retailing, and section 10-8 focuses on retailing decisions related to the merchandise and service mix, atmospherics, and location. Finally, Section 10-9 reviews trends in retailing, such as the shortening of retailer life-cycles, technology-based developments, the broadening of the competitive base, and international expansion.

10-2 DISTRIBUTION AND THE CHANNEL FUNCTIONS

Marketing managers understand that the planning of product distribution is among the most important tasks they need to undertake to ensure market success. **Distribution planning** is defined as the planning of the physical movement of products from the producer to individual or organizational consumers and the transfer of ownership and risk. It involves transportation, warehousing, and all the exchanges taking place at each channel level. Distribution planning involves establishing the **channels of distribution**, defined as the totality of organizations and individuals involved in the distribution process who take title to or assist in the transferring of title in the distribution process from the producer to the individual or organizational consumer. The organizations or individuals involved in the distribution process are known as **intermediaries (or middlemen or channel members)**. The decision also involves identifying and managing other intermediaries involved in distribution (e.g., other entities that facilitate the distribution process, such as transportation firms, freight forwarders, and customs brokers for international distribution).

The goal of intermediaries is to offer support for the activities involved in delivering products for the enhanced benefit of the customer. In that sense, intermediaries are active participants in the **value chain (or supply chain)**, the chain of activities performed in the process of developing, producing, marketing, delivering, and servicing a product for the benefit of the customer. Intermediaries are components of the **value delivery chain**, which is composed of all the participants involved in the value chain. Today, many firms partner not just with the channel members or intermediaries, but also with their suppliers to provide optimal efficiencies that enhance profits, as well as customer benefits.

Using intermediaries entails relinquishing control over the marketing mix to a channel member. It also means paying for the channel member's services. Why do manufacturers use distributors to sell their products? Why do they not handle distribution themselves? The answer is that distributors cut down on the cost of distribution, while conveniently providing the desired assortment to consumers at a lower price. The following are the advantages of using intermediaries:

> **Distribution Planning:**
> The planning of the physical movement of products from the producer to individual or organizational consumers and the transfer of ownership and risk; it involves transportation, warehousing, and all the exchanges taking place at each channel level.
>
> **Channels of Distribution:**
> The totality of organizations and individuals involved in the distribution process who take title to or assist in the transferring of title in the distribution process from the producer to the individual or organizational consumer.
>
> **Intermediaries (or Middlemen or Channel Members):**
> The organizations or individuals involved in the distribution process.
>
> **Value Chain (or Supply Chain):**
> The chain of activities performed in the process of developing, producing, marketing, delivering, and servicing a product for the benefit of the customer.
>
> **Value Delivery Chain:**
> The participants involved in the value chain.

- Intermediaries deliver convenience to consumers. Intermediaries help distribute the product to a location that is convenient to the consumer.

- Intermediaries carry and store the product. Intermediaries distribute the product down the channel of distribution, and they store it in warehouses.

- Intermediaries assume risk in the delivery process. Intermediaries typically carry not just the title to the product, but also the risk for the product while it is in their possession, or even beyond.

- Intermediaries lower the cost of the product delivery process by reducing the number of transactions needed to deliver the product to the final consumer. Figure 10-2 illustrates how using a wholesaler can reduce the number of transactions, cutting down on the cost of transportation and handling. In the first scenario, there is no wholesaler; it would take 25 transactions to create an assortment of goods from each of the five manufacturers for each of the five retailers. Introducing a middleman in the second scenario reduces the number of transactions to ten. That, in fact, means fewer shipments are loaded, unloaded, and insured; fewer trucks are used in the transportation of the goods; and less paperwork is filled out by the firms.

- Intermediaries provide an assortment for retailers and, ultimately, for consumers. That is, the wholesaler takes the product from different manufacturers of narrow assortments and delivers it to retailers that can, as a result, provide a wider assortment to consumers.

- Intermediaries buy products in bulk from manufacturers, at a discount. By purchasing larger quantities on behalf of multiple retailers, the wholesaler can negotiate a discount for buying the product in bulk from each individual manufacturer. Then the wholesaler breaks bulk to sell smaller quantities to retailers.

- Intermediaries conduct research for the manufacturer and the channel. Intermediaries are close to retailers and have access to information about changing consumer needs and behavior. They offer important input into the product design, performance, pricing, and promotion. Intermediaries also identify prospective buyers.

- Intermediaries provide credit to other channel members or to consumers, which facilitates transactions.

- Intermediaries often provide service contracts, handling many of the services consumers purchase along with the final product and warranties.

- Intermediaries often pay for part of the promotional expenditures of the manufacturer or retailer. Promotional support includes advertising support and especially sales support.

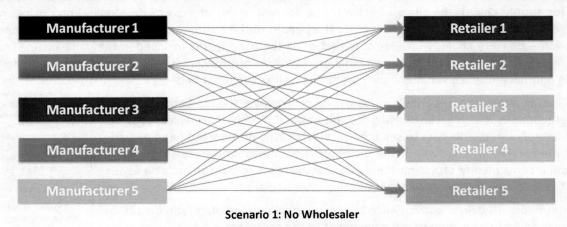

Figure 10-2: The Role of the Wholesaler in Reducing the Number of Transactions

Scenario 1: No Wholesaler

Assume that each retailer needs an assortment of goods from each manufacturer.
The total number of transactions conducted without a wholesaler is 25.

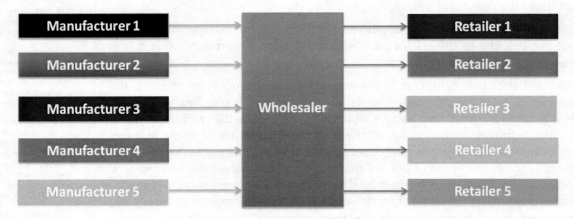

Scenario 2: One Wholesaler

Assume that each retailer needs an assortment of goods from each manufacturer.
The total number of transactions conducted with a wholesaler is 10.

10-3 CHANNEL DIMENSIONS

A **direct channel of distribution** has no intermediaries; the manufacturer sells directly to the final consumer. In the chapter opening, Kathleen selling her baked goods at her Tate's Bake Shop in Southampton, New York, is an example of a direct channel of distribution. In the direct channel, Kathleen has close customer contact and full control over all aspects related to marketing her products.

An **indirect channel of distribution** involves one or more intermediaries between the manufacturer and the consumer. When Kathleen sells her chocolate chip cookies to the Amish Market in New York City, she uses an indirect channel of distribution, with Bay View Distributing acting as wholesaler. She sells the product directly to Fresh Market, a retailer, and thus she uses an indirect channel of distribution since the retailer is between Kathleen and consumers who purchase her bakery goods. These channels are illustrated in Figure 10-3.

An indirect channel does not allow Kathleen close contact with consumers, and she has no control of the marketing. But the indirect channel allows her to increase her presence in the different markets and to increase her sales. It also reduces her marketing expenses and the risk involved in selling in the different locations where she has a presence.

Figure 10-3: Two of Kathleen's Distribution Channels

Kathleen's Distribution Channels

Manufacturer

Indirect Channel   **Direct Channel**

Wholesaler

Bay View Distributing

Retailer

Amish Market, Manhattan   **Fresh Market, North Carolina**

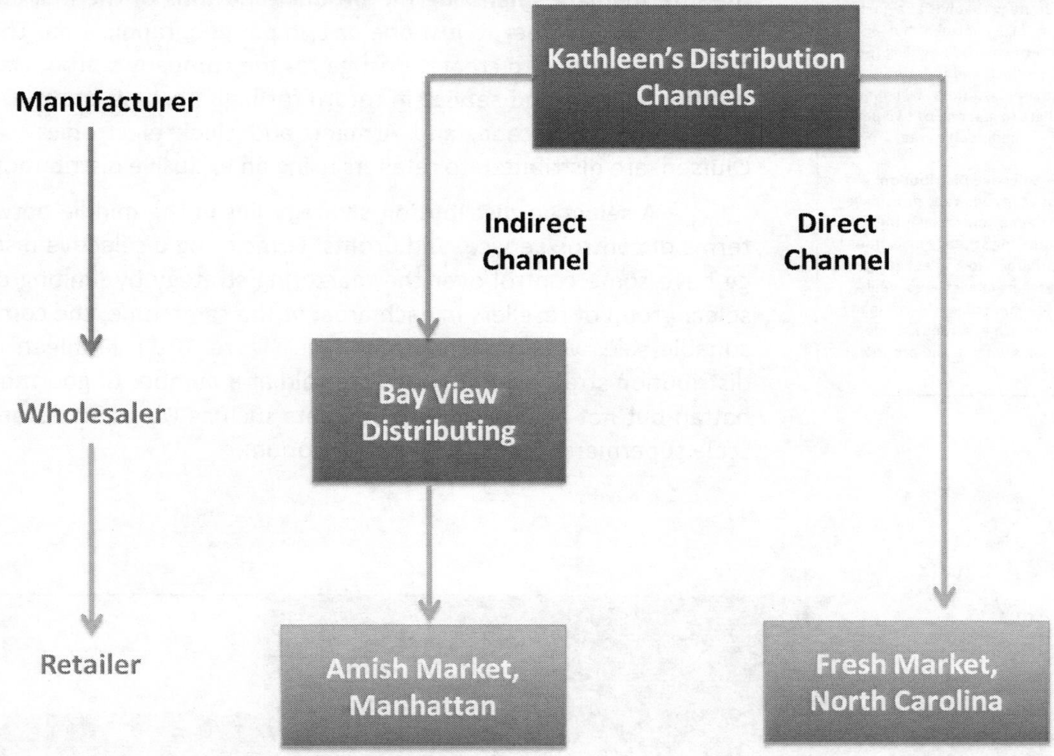

Arrow indicates physical flow of goods and the flow of ownership.

Figure 10-4: Coke wants its brand available to all target consumers when and where they want it, and, as such, deploys an intensive distribution strategy.

Kathleen's two indirect channels in the previous example are relatively short, with one or two intermediaries, respectively. **Channel length** is defined as the number of levels of distributors in a distribution channel. It is not unusual for channels to have multiple levels of wholesalers getting the product closer and closer to the final consumer. In Japan, for instance, multiple levels of distribution are the norm for consumer goods. **Channel width** is defined as the number of independent intermediaries involved at a particular stage of distribution. Kathleen uses a narrow channel, selling through only one wholesaler, Bay View Distributing. This is not unusual for a local bakery. Wide channels involve selling through many distributors.

In addition to channel length, companies need to decide on the number of intermediaries to use at each level of distribution. An **intensive distribution strategy** has as its purpose full market coverage, making the product available to all target consumers when and where they want it. This type of distribution aims at achieving high total sales but is able to recover only low per-unit profits as a result of channel expenses. Staples, such as milk, colas, beer, toothpaste, and snacks, are distributed using an intensive distribution strategy (see **Figure 10-4**).

> **Direct Channel of Distribution:**
> A channel that has no intermediaries; the manufacturer sells directly to the final consumer.
>
> **Indirect Channel of Distribution:**
> A channel that involves one or more intermediaries between the manufacturer and the consumer.
>
> **Channel Length:**
> The number of levels of distributors in a distribution channel.
>
> **Channel Width:**
> The number of independent intermediaries involved at a particular stage of distribution.
>
> **Intensive Distribution:**
> A strategy that has as its purpose full market coverage, making the product available to all target consumers when and where consumers want it.

Exclusive Distribution:
A strategy that has as a goal a high control of the intermediaries handling the product, and thus of the marketing strategy, by limiting them to just one or two per geographic area.

Selective Distribution:
A strategy whereby firms have some control over the marketing strategy by limiting distribution to a select group of resellers in each area, while, at the same time, the company can achieve a reasonable sales volume and profits.

An **exclusive distribution strategy** aims to have a goal a high control of the intermediaries handling the product and thus of the marketing strategy by limiting their number to just one or two per geographic area. This type of distribution is intended to create prestige for the company's products and strong distributor support and service in return for high per-unit profit. Designer clothes, such as Prada, Escada, and Armani, and sleek electronics, such as Bang & Olufsen, are distributed to retailers using an exclusive distribution strategy.

A **selective distribution strategy** lies in the middle between the two in terms of control, service, and profits. Firms using a selective distribution strategy have some control over the marketing strategy by limiting distribution to a select group of resellers in each area; at the same time, the company has a reasonable sales volume and profits (see **Figure 10-5**). Kathleen uses a selective distribution strategy. Her goods are sold at a number of gourmet shops in Manhattan but not at regular supermarkets such as D'Agostino's or even more upscale supermarkets such as Food Emporium.

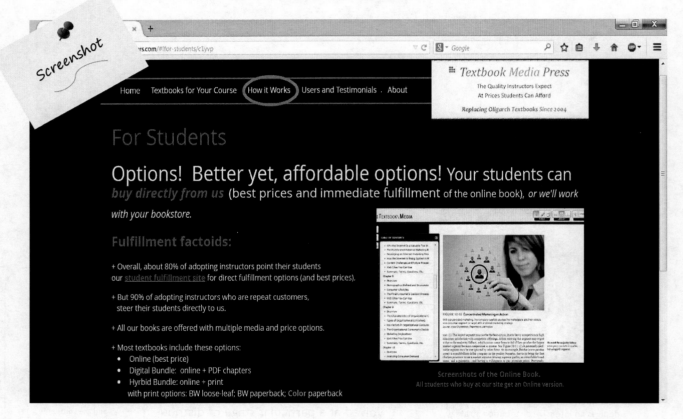

Figure 10-5: The publisher of this textbook, Textbook Media Press, uses a selective distribution strategy. This is a screenshot of its instructor Web site, informing instructors that students can buy the textbook direct at the publisher's fulfillment Web site, or at the campus bookstore. The publisher also uses select online resellers like Chegg.

10-4 CHANNEL MANAGEMENT

Numerous aspects of channel management need to be considered. First, the structure of the channel of distribution is important. Here, decisions must be made with regard to channel organization and administration, as well as channel strategies, such as vertical or horizontal integration. Second, channel relationships must be examined. The use of power in the channel and conflict management constitutes important channel dynamics that can lead to the success or failure of the channel.

10-4a: Channel Organization and Administration

A channel of distribution consists of one or more independent intermediaries, in which each is a separate entity whose goal, in a vacuum, would be resource or profit maximization. Taking the separate goals of each channel member into account, the outcome, within this narrow perspective, would be high margins at each level of distribution, minimal service, and, ultimately, prices that customers are unwilling to pay and service levels that customers would be dissatisfied with. The entire value chain needs to consider the different interests with a marketing perspective in mind: addressing the needs of the consumer. In this sense, a mechanism must exist that assigns marketing responsibilities and addresses channel-wide strategic objectives.

Channels of distribution adopting a **contractual channel arrangement** spell out in a contract all the tasks that must be performed by each channel member with regard to production, delivery strategy, terms of sale, territorial rights, promotional support, the price policies of each intermediary, and contract length.

Channels adopting an **administered channel arrangement** have a dominant member of the distribution channel in terms of size, expertise, or influence who coordinates the tasks of each channel member. The dominant member of the channel, known as the **channel captain**, can be at any level of the distribution channel. A manufacturer with a strong brand pull, such as Coca-Cola or Colgate-Palmolive, could be the channel administrator. Many powerful wholesalers, such as SUPERVALU, that deal with smaller manufacturers or retailers can act as channel captains. Hybrid structures, such as Costco, a warehouse club that sells both to final consumers and resellers, also can administer the distribution channel.

A **dual channel of distribution** is employed by firms that use two different channels. For example, Kathleen uses a dual channel of distribution, selling (1) through a wholesaler to gourmet shops and (2) selling directly to the Fresh Market retail chain. In another illustration, the Donna Karan collection is distributed exclusively, whereas her bridge brand, DKNY, is distributed selectively. It is thus likely that two different channels are used to distribute the two brands: an exclusive distribution channel for the Donna Karan collection and a selective distribution channel for the DKNY brand.

A firm can also use a **multichannel distribution system**, also known as a **hybrid marketing channel**. Before the Internet, multichannel marketing was popular primarily in business-to-business environments. Today, the Internet has completely transformed direct marketing and companies' relationships with customers. By pairing e-mail and the Internet with offline media, marketers can develop compelling campaigns that offer customers important advantages.[2] With multiple channels, customers have an expanding menu of purchase and communication options.

Channel members can strengthen their position in the channel through **vertical integration**, by acquiring or merging with an intermediary in the channel—a sup-

Contractual Channel Arrangement: A contract between intermediaries that defines all the tasks that each channel member must perform with regard to production, delivery strategy and terms of sale, territorial rights, promotional support, the price policies of each intermediary, and contract length.

Administered Channel Arrangement: An arrangement between intermediaries such that a dominant member of the distribution channel in terms of size, expertise, or influence coordinates the tasks of each member in the channel.

Channel Captain: The dominant member of a channel of distribution.

Dual Channel of Distribution: The use of two or more channels of distribution to appeal to different markets.

Multichannel Distribution System (Hybrid Marketing Channel): The use of multiple (more than two) channels of distribution, thus offering customers multiple purchase and communication options.

plier or a buyer. Such integration offers the channel member more control in the channel. Zara, a popular clothing retailer, makes more than half of its clothes in-house, rather than relying on a network of disparate and often slow moving suppliers. Its competitor, H&M, however, buys clothes from more than 900 firms.

Starting with basic fabric dyeing, almost all of Zara's clothes take shape in a design-and-manufacturing center in Spain, with the sewing done by seamstresses from 400 local cooperatives. This setup allows designers to closely follow which items are in demand. They talk daily to store managers to discover which items are selling, and on the basis of this real-time data, they place their orders and ship the inventory directly to the stores twice a week. This procedure eliminates the need for warehouses and for keeping large inventories.[3]

Another strategy that increases intermediary strength in the market is **horizontal integration**, which involves an acquisition or merger at the same level in the distribution channel. Examples of horizontal integration are a manufacturer buying another manufacturer, a wholesaler acquiring another wholesaler at the same level in the distribution chain, or a retailer purchasing another retailer. This strategy, however, may trigger antitrust investigations and create long-term problems for the firms involved.

One of the most important developments in distribution for the past two decades has been the emergence of **vertical marketing systems (VMS)**, which consist of manufacturers, wholesalers, and retailers in the same channel acting as a unified whole. VMS typically involve partial ownership. An example is the wholesaler SUPERVALU purchasing Rainbow Foods grocery stores, and then co-owning these stores, now CUB FOODS, along with other wholesalers. Vertical marketing systems benefit from greater coordination achieved through common ownership.

Horizontal marketing systems (HMS) consist of intermediaries at the same level of the distribution channel pooling resources and achieving economies of scale, thereby playing on their individual strengths. In the manufacturing sector, Porsche is working with Harley-Davidson, the U.S. motorcycle icon, to help it develop low-noise, low-emissions motorcycles. Most recently, Porsche is helping Harley-Davidson develop its water-cooled Revolution engine.[4] At the wholesale level, Mitsui and Mitsubishi, large integrated trading companies, are using their bottling and distribution systems to bottle and distribute all Coca-Cola products in Japan. **Trading companies** are complex marketing systems specializing in providing intermediary services, risk reduction through extensive information channels, and financial assistance. Trading companies have been very successful in Japan and South Korea. Japanese trading companies have operations all around the world, ranging from finance to distribution, technology, mining, oil and gas exploration, and information. They act as intermediaries for half of Japan's exports and two-thirds of its imports. Currently, they are changing from pure traders to more financially sophisticated investment holding companies.[5] The biggest and the best of the traders are members of **keiretsus**, which are families of firms with interlocking stakes in one another. Here, the trading companies' role is to act as the eyes and ears of the whole group, spotting business trends, market gaps, and investment opportunities.[6] The top trading companies in Japan are Itochu Corp., Sumitomo, Marubeni, Mitsui, and Mitsubishi.[7]

Vertical Integration:
The acquisition or merger with an intermediary in the channel that is either a supplier or a buyer.

Horizontal Integration:
An acquisition or merger with an intermediary at the same level in the distribution channel.

Vertical Marketing Systems (VMS):
Intermediary marketing systems that consist of manufacturers, wholesalers, and retailers in the same channel who have partial VMS ownership acting as a unified whole.

Horizontal Marketing Systems (HMS):
Intermediaries at the same level of the distribution channel pooling resources and achieving partial ownership of the system, achieving economies of scale, and playing on their individual strengths.

Trading Companies:
Complex marketing systems that specialize in providing intermediary service and reducing risk through extensive information channels and financial assistance.

Keiretsus:
Japanese families of firms with interlocking stakes in one another.

10-4b: Channel Relationships: Conflict and Power

Intermediaries sometimes disagree on channel goals, on their roles in the channel of distribution, and on the channel rewards. One area of potential is the manufacturer's use of a **pull strategy**, whereby the manufacturer first focuses on consumer demand through extensive promotion, expecting that consumers will request the brand through the channel. The alternative, a **push strategy**, focuses on intermediaries, providing the necessary incentives for them to cooperate in marketing the product to the final consumer. Manufacturers typically use both strategies because using only a pull strategy would create conflict in the distribution channels.

Channel conflict can also be reduced through the appropriate use of power. **Reward power** refers to power over the channel members based on anticipation of special privileges, such as financial rewards for engaging in a particular desirable behavior. Reward power in the form of slotting fees offered by the manufacturer to the retailer will be exerted only as long as the slotting fees are paid. When the manufacturer ceases to pay slotting fees, the products will be removed from the retailer's shelf, unless other types of power exist concurrently. Coercive power refers to power over channel members based on the ability of one or more intermediaries to remove privileges for noncompliance. An example of **coercive power** involves the threat of elimination from the channel of distribution for noncompliance with a particular channel policy. Reward power and coercive power are less persuasive than the other forms of power because when the reward or coercion factors are removed, channel members' behavior reverts to one that is focused on individual goals.

Expert power refers to power over the other channel members based on experience and knowledge that a channel member possesses. **Referent power** refers to power over the other channel members based on the close match in terms of values and objectives shared by members of the channel.

Legitimate power refers to power over the other channel members by virtue of an intermediary's status or position in the channel. A channel captain has legitimate power over the other channel members by virtue of its position and role in the channel. Table 10-1 reviews the various forms of channel power.

10-5 LOGISTICS: OVERVIEW AND FUNCTIONS

Logistics (or physical distribution) is defined as all the activities involved in the physical flow and storage of materials, semi-finished goods, and finished goods to customers in a manner that is efficient and cost effective. The logistics function can be handled by any entity in the distribution channel—the producer, intermediaries, or the customer. An important trait of distribution is that it should meet customers' needs in terms of convenient and timely access to the product at a fair cost.[8]

Pull Strategy:
A strategy whereby the manufacturer first focuses on consumer demand through extensive promotion, expecting that consumers will request the brand through the channel.

Push Strategy:
A strategy that focuses on intermediaries, providing the necessary incentives for them to cooperate in selling the product to the final consumer.

Reward Power:
Power over the channel members based on an anticipation of special privileges, such as a financial reward for conducting a particular behavior.

Coercive Power:
Power over channel members based on the ability of one or more intermediaries to remove privileges for noncompliance.

Expert Power:
Power over the other channel members based on experience and knowledge that a channel member possesses.

Referent Power:
Power over the other channel members based on the close match in terms of values and objectives that members of the channel share.

Legitimate Power:
Power over the other channel members by virtue of an intermediary's status or position in the firm.

Table 10-1: Channel Power	
Type	**Definition**
Reward power	Power over the channel members based on the anticipation of special privileges
Coercive power	Power over channel members based on the ability of one or more intermediaries to remove privileges for noncompliance
Expert power	Power over the other channel members based on experience and knowledge that a channel member possesses
Referent power	Power over the other channel members based on the close match in terms of values and objectives that members of the channel share
Legitimate power	Power over the other channel members by virtue of an intermediary's status or position in the channel

Logistics costs account for as much as 10 to 35 percent of a company's gross revenues, and more than 10 percent of the gross domestic product (GDP) in the United States, making logistics the single highest operating cost.[9] Logistics costs now total more than $1.33 trillion, whereas transportation costs are $835.9 billion.[10] When the U.S. Department of Commerce reported that 60 percent of all Fortune 500 companies' logistics costs are spent on transporting products, it became clear that money saved in this area is likely to lead to more affordable products for consumers.[11] These costs vary greatly by industry sector and by company size and location, as well as other factors. For example, retailers that need to offer wide assortments will spend more on logistics as transportation and storage costs increase. A critical decision in this regard is whether the manufacturer seeks to have an intensive, selective, or exclusive distribution. Logistics involve the following primary functions: transportation, warehousing, inventory control, and order processing, which will be addressed in the following sections.

> **Logistics (or Physical Distribution):**
> All the activities involved in the physical flow and storage of materials, semi-finished goods, and finished goods to customers in a manner that is efficient and cost effective.

10-5a: Transportation

Transportation is an important factor that marketers must consider. The choice of transportation determines whether products arrive at their destination on time and in good condition. The cost of transportation is also an important consideration because transportation costs can increase the product price. Table 10-2 shows the breakdown of the primary modes of freight transportation: truck, railway, airways, waterways, and pipeline. Notice that in terms of volume, the highest percentage of products is moved by rail. See Figure 10-6 for an illustration of volume distribution of the different transportation modes.

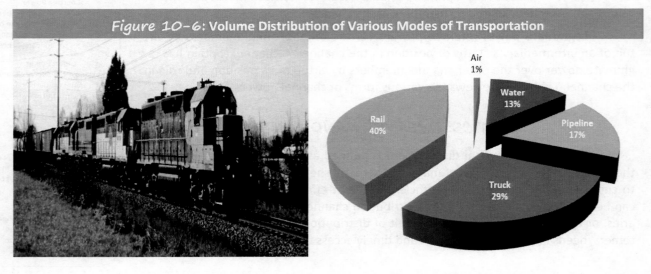

Figure 10-6: Volume Distribution of Various Modes of Transportation

Air 1%
Water 13%
Pipeline 17%
Rail 40%
Truck 29%

Table 10-2: Characteristics of Different Modes of Transportation

Transportation Mode	Flexibility in Terms of Area Coverage	Cost	Speed	Product Examples	Volume of Domestic Traffic*
Truck	High	Higher	Higher	Perishables, clothing, cement, furniture, appliances, electronics, and automobiles	1,051
Rail	Higher	Medium	Lower	Coal, stone, cement, oil, grain, lumber, and automobiles	1,558
Air	Highest	High	High	Jewelry, perishables, electronics, semiconductors, wine, and spirits	15
Water	Low	High	Low	Coal, stone, cement, oil, grain, and automobiles	494
Pipeline	Low	Lower	Low	Oil and gas, chemicals, coal as a semi-liquid	616

*Volume of domestic yearly traffic within the continental United States; freight traffic in billion ton-miles, whereby a ton-mile is the movement of 1 ton (2,000 pounds) of freight for the distance of 1 mile.

Source: *Statistical Abstract of the United States 2004--2005,* U.S. Census Bureau.

Trucks transport smaller shipments over shorter distances than the other freight carriers. Most local transportation is handled by truck, and thus trucks handle a substantial proportion (almost one-third) of all traffic in the continental United States annually. Trucks offer high flexibility, taking products from the factory directly to the destination. Their rates are competitive with the other modes of intracontinental transportation in

Figure 10-7: Trucks are popular for making deliveries within the perimeter of a large metropolitan area.

the United States, and they offer fast service on shorter routes compared with the other modes of transportation. Often, trucks are used in conjunction with other forms of transportation that cannot take the product to the customer's doorstep, in what is referred to as intermodal transportation. Trucks have capabilities, such as refrigeration and processing, which allow them to carry a wide array of products, from perishables to clothing, furniture, appliances, electronics, cement, and automobiles (see Figure 10-7).

Railways remain the primary mode for freight transportation in the United States intracontinentally, accounting for 40 percent of all domestic traffic. They transport over long distances high-weight, high-volume products that have a low per-pound value, such as coal, stone, cement, oil, grain, and lumber, but also more expensive products, such as large equipment and automobiles. (Figure 10-8 illustrates a typical mode of transporting automobiles in Europe, where many road restrictions and high gasoline prices limit the use of the huge auto-transport trucks seen on U.S. highways). Railways are a low-cost mode of relatively low-speed freight transportation. They do not offer the flexibility that trucks do, however, because their mobility is restricted to areas designated for freight handling. Railway freight transportation has been growing consistently over the past decade, but the rate of growth has slowed significantly in the past few years. Nevertheless, railway freight transportation is approximately 1.8 billion tons, bringing in a gross revenue of $72 billion.[12]

Figure 10-8: Railways are a low-cost mode of transportation for shipping high-weight, high-volume products.

Air freight accounts for less than one percent of all intracontinental transportation in the United States. Air carriers offer high-speed, high-cost shipping that is ideal for perishable products, such as cut flowers; for low-volume, lower-weight, high-value products, such as jewelry and electronics; or for documents that necessitate prompt delivery. Companies such as Federal Express base their entire business on air transport, banking on their capability to take products to destinations overnight. Internationally, air freight now makes up a significant portion of total freight transportation, at 16 billion freight ton kilometers, compared to 12 freight ton kilometers in 2009.[13]

Tankers, barges, and other freighters in the inland and coastal waterways account for only 7.5 percent of the total domestic traffic volume. It should be mentioned, however, that water transportation is essential for international trade and accounts for a substantial proportion of international traffic. Waterways are used for transporting high-weight, high-volume products that have a low per-pound value, such as coal, stone, cement, oil, grain, lumber, and petrol, over long distances. In the United States, the use of inland and coastal waterways is currently at 888 million tons.[14]

Pipelines are a low-cost mode of transporting liquid or semiliquid products from the source to the target market in a continuous manner, in which there are no interruptions (unless interruptions are voluntary), and intermediate storage is not necessary. Examples of pipelines are Basin, Bonito, and Capline for offshore and onshore crude oil; Harbor System and Wolverine Line for refined products; and the large, remote, and technically difficult pipeline, the Trans Alaska Pipeline,[15] a feat of engineering running from

> **Intermodal Transportation:** Transportation using two or more different transportation modes—a combination of truck, rail, air, and waterways.

northern to southern Alaska across rough terrain and performing well in extreme weather conditions, transporting more than 1.4 million barrels of crude oil daily. Pipelines are typically owned by the producer or by joint ventures, and they are expensive to maintain.[16]

Firms often resort to **intermodal transportation**, using two or more different transportation modes—a combination of truck, rail, air, and waterways. Intermodal transportation has been greatly facilitated by containerization. Goods can be placed into containers at the factory, taken by truck to a train loading facility, transported to a port, and loaded aboard a ship; after crossing the ocean, the containers are loaded on a truck and transported to their final destination. All of these maneuvers can be accomplished using the initial containers, thus providing greater protection for the products, which do not have to be shifted individually from one vessel to another—and at lower cost because loading the individual products from/into vehicles is more expensive than using containers (see **Figure 10-9**).

10-5b: Logistics Facilitators

Moving goods from the place of origin, normally a manufacturer, to the place of sale, normally the

Figure 10-9: Shipping containers significantly decrease the cost of transportation. Rotterdam in the Netherlands is one of the largest ports in the world, and is a major container traffic hub. This container ship is embarking on a transatlantic voyage.

retailer, requires some type of facilitation. The two most common logistics facilitators are freight forwarders and the hub-and-spoke distribution center.

Freight forwarders are specialized firms that collect shipments from different businesses, consolidate them for part of the distance, and deliver them to a destination, in what is typically a door-to-door service. Many freight forwarders are adapting to fit the needs of their corporate consumers. Many pursue different value-added techniques, such as developing distinctive competencies in terms of geography, type of business, or specific commodities. For example, Kuehne & Nagel is well respected for its ability to expertly handle museum art and valuable exhibition material. The company has also developed expertise with respect to arranging trade fairs and art exhibits, as well as aid and relief for developing countries. Another freight forwarder, DHL, handles shipping for several industry sectors, including health care, fashion, electronics, and live animals, shipping a 15 five-foot-long jellyfish to Australia.[17] Freight forwarding is becoming increasingly important as a result of the rapid globalization of business. DHL, for example, invested $35 million to improve their activities in Hong Kong.[18]

Hub-and-spoke distribution centers are designed to speed up warehousing and delivery by channeling operations to one center (hub) that is particularly well equipped to handle the distribution of products to their destination. The idea of a hub location is to consolidate traffic from different origins and send it directly or via another hub to different destinations (nodes that are not destined as hubs are referred to as spokes), thus achieving economies of scale on hub-to-hub links. Such designs have been popular with airlines as well (e.g., Delta, United). A clear advantage of using them in the distribution network of a supply chain versus a direct airline flight from source to destination is that products, unlike passengers, are insensitive to how many hub stops they need to make. This makes it easier to achieve the goal of making the distribution channel more flexible and responsive to customer needs.[19] Hub-and-spoke network designs have been used by FedEx for a long time and are also used by UPS, Norfolk Southern, and Yellow Freight in some form or another.[20]

One company that takes advantage of this efficient hub-and-spoke distribution model is Carvel. Carvel is offering nationwide delivery for its ice cream cakes. It first promoted its overnight delivery in advertisements in the *New York Times* and the *Wall Street Journal*, listing an 800 number for FedEx delivery anywhere in the continental United States. In terms of logistics, the cakes are made at a Carvel store in Naples, Florida, packed in Styrofoam coolers with dry ice, and shipped within 48 hours via FedEx. The cakes have a "no-melt" guarantee and stay intact in their packaging for about three days. The primary mail-order focus of this strategy is corporate gifts. In the recent past, a New York City promotion agency sent 100 cakes as holiday gifts to its clients, and customer reaction was very positive.[21]

> **Freight Forwarders:** Specialized firms that collect shipments from different businesses, consolidate them for part of the distance, and deliver them to a destination, in what is typically a door-to-door service.
>
> **Hub-and-Spoke Distribution Centers:** Distribution centers designed to speed up warehousing and delivery, by channeling operations to one center (hub) that is particularly well equipped to handle the distribution of products to their destination.

10-5c: Warehousing

Warehousing is defined as the marketing function whereby goods are stored, identified, and sorted in the process of transfer to an intermediary in the distribution channel or to the final consumer. **Inventory** is the amount of goods being stored. Warehousing is necessary when the speed of production does not match demand or consumption. A wholesaler normally gets a break on price for bulk purchases but may have to store products before there are enough retail orders or reorders. The concern, in this regard, is that the cost of storage is significantly lower than the price break the wholesaler received from purchasing the product in bulk, allowing for a profit. Or the wholesaler may have to stock extra products to have them available for immediate delivery to ensure customer satisfaction. If the product is not immediately delivered, the customer may order products from a different wholesaler in the future.

Figure 10-10: Public warehouses facilitate storage for firms that cannot afford to own a private warehouse.

In other examples, many agricultural products, such as corn and wheat, are harvested at the end of the summer or in early fall. Making these products available at once will create excessive supply and depress prices. At the same time, customers are likely to demand these products throughout the year, and if the entire production is sold after harvest, these customers will seek the products from other suppliers.

Companies can use different types of storage facilities. **Private warehouses** are owned or leased and are operated by firms storing their own products. They are used by intermediaries at all levels of distribution: manufacturers, wholesalers, and retailers. These intermediaries typically need to have storage on a regular basis. Public warehouses are independent facilities that provide storage rental and related services (see **Figure 10-10**). **Public warehouses** are used by firms that cannot afford to have their own facilities or that do not have a need for storage on a regular basis. International companies doing business in the United States periodically tend to use public warehouses rather than private warehouses. This is especially true in cases in which they have to store their products in customs-privileged facilities, such as foreign trade zones.

Distribution centers are computerized warehouses designed to move goods. They receive goods from different producers, take orders from buyers, and distribute them promptly. One of the largest distribution centers for electronic components and computer equipment is the Phoenix, Arizona-based Avnet Inc. It has the capability of serving customers ranging from IBM to mom-and-pop shops in the embattled technology market, who demand to have zero-inventory. To keep a handle on inventory, to increase shipping capacity, and to reduce errors, the $2.14 billion company has rolled out Optum Inc.'s MOVE warehouse management system at its 400,000-square-foot Chandler, Arizona, logistics center. This distribution center handles distribution for more than 40,000 customers who do not want any inventory: They expect Avnet to control that.[22]

In addition to the storage function, many warehouses engage in product assembly and packaging. This applies in particular to warehouses located in free trade zones. A **foreign trade zone** (FTZ) is a tax-free area in the United States that is not considered part of the United States in terms of import regulations and restrictions. Products can be shipped to an FTZ, stored and assembled there, and then shipped to the United States or another country. Such products are not assessed duties and cannot be subjected to tariffs or quotas unless they enter the United States. An FTZ is

Warehousing:
The marketing function whereby goods are stored, identified, and sorted in the process of transfer to an intermediary in the distribution channel or to the final consumer.

Inventory:
The amount of goods being stored.

Private Warehouses:
Warehouses that are owned or leased and operated by firms storing their own products.

Public Warehouses:
Independent facilities that provide storage rental and related services.

Distribution Centers:
Computerized warehouses designed to move goods; they receive goods from different producers, take orders from buyers, and distribute them promptly.

Foreign Trade Zone (FTZ):
Tax-free area in the United States that is not considered part of the United States in terms of import regulations and restrictions. Also called a free trade zone.

considered an international area; merchandise in the FTZ, both foreign and domestic, is outside the juris-diction of U.S. Customs.[23] FTZs are usually located in or near a port of entry and operated as a public utility by a public entity, such as the Port of Portland, the Indianapolis Airport Authority, or the Crowfield Corporate Center in Charleston, South Carolina.[24] FTZs are used to show the product to customers and pay duties only when the goods are sold;[25] to break bulk or store products and postpone the payment of duties until the product is shipped to the customer; and to assemble products (goods that are unassembled are cheaper to transport, and duties are assessed at lower rates for them than for assembled goods). Foreign trade zones exist throughout the United States.

10-5d: Stock Turnover

A central aspect of inventory management is **stock turnover**, defined as the number of times per year that the inventory on hand is sold. The stock turnover annual rate is calculated as follows:

$$\frac{\text{Number of Units Sold}}{\text{Average Inventory}} \quad \text{OR}$$

$$\frac{\text{Net Sales}}{\text{Average Inventory (\$ sales)}} \quad \text{OR}$$

$$\frac{\text{Cost of Good Sold}}{\text{Average Inventory (\$ cost)}}$$

A high stock turnover rate is a goal that allows companies to perform optimally in terms of inventory costs, but at the same time, companies do need to be careful that they do not run out of stock. Companies typically establish a **reorder point**, an inventory level at which new orders are placed.

10-6 WHOLESALING

Wholesaling encompasses all the activities involved in buying and handling the goods intended for sale to resellers or other organizational users. Wholesalers sell goods and services to manufacturers, to other wholesalers, to retailers, to the government, and to nongovernmental organizations. As mentioned in Section 10-2, wholesalers provide the advantages of distributing the product down the channel of distribution to a location that is convenient to consumers, warehousing it in the distribution process. California Almonds, for example, are distributed all over the country by the wholesaler (see **Figure 10-11**). Wholesalers take risks of product obsolescence or theft, or even beyond. They reduce the number of transactions needed to deliver a wide product assortment to retailers and ultimately, to consumers. They buy products in bulk from manufacturers at a discount and then break the bulk to distribute smaller quantities to retailers. Last, they conduct research for other channel members, provide service and credit to consumers and other channel members, and pay for promotional expenditures.

10-6a: Merchant Wholesalers

Merchant wholesalers are independent intermediaries who take title to and possession of products they distribute to resellers or organizational consumers. Merchant wholesalers constitute more than half of all wholesalers. There are two types of merchant wholesalers: full-service wholesalers and limited-service wholesalers.

Full-service wholesalers provide a wide range of distribution tasks, such as product delivery, warehousing, sales force assistance, credit, research, planning, and installation and repair assistance, among others. Full-service wholesalers sell primarily to retailers, either to general merchandise retailers or to specialty stores.

Stock Turnover:
The number of times a year that the inventory on hand is sold.

Reorder Point:
An inventory level at which new orders are placed.

Wholesaling:
All the activities involved in buying and handling the goods intended for sale to resellers or other organizational users.

Merchant Wholesalers:
Independent intermediaries who take title to and possession of products distributed to resellers or organizational consumers.

Full-Service Wholesalers:
Independent intermediaries who provide a wide range of distribution tasks, such as product delivery, warehousing, sales force assistance, credit, research, planning, and installation and repair assistance, among others.

Figure 10-11: Wholesalers provide important functions in the process of distributing products such as almonds from trees in California to grocery stores throughout the United States.

Rack jobbers are wholesalers who manage the store shelves carrying their products, assemble the point-of-purchase displays, and determine product prices. They take title to the products they sell on consignment but are allowed to take unsold items back to the manufacturer or wholesaler selling the product.

Limited-service wholesalers offer fewer services than full-service wholesalers. They may not provide distribution tasks, such as sales force assistance, credit, research, planning, or installation and repair assistance, but they do normally provide delivery and storage. They sell perishables, such as seafood, construction materials, tobacco, dairy products, office supplies, and small business equipment.

10-6b: Agents and Brokers

Agents represent buyers or sellers; they do not take possession of or title to the merchandise, and they work based on commission or fees. **Brokers** bring buyers and sellers together; they too do not take possession of or title to the merchandise, and they work based on commission or fees.

A **manufacturers' agent (or manufacturers' representative)** usually works as the company's sales representative, representing manufacturers in a particular market, and is paid on a commission basis. Manufacturers' agents can represent one or more noncompeting manufacturers. They are typically hired by small- and medium-sized businesses that cannot afford their own field force but then need the sales function covered. In that sense, they have a specified territory coverage and need to adhere to specific order-processing procedures.

A **selling agent** has an exclusive arrangement with the company, representing all of its operations in a particular market and acting as the sales or marketing department of the firm. Selling agents do not take title to the goods and are usually paid a percentage of sales. Given their broad responsibilities, their commission is higher than that of manufacturers' representatives. They are common for the clothing and furniture industries.

Purchasing agents have a long-term relationship with a buyer. They select, receive, and ship goods to buyers and are paid on a commission basis. Purchasing agents know their markets well and are familiar with the needs of their customers. Examples of purchasing agents are smaller agents in Italy who purchase designer clothes that are not very popular in the United States but are regarded as solid in Europe. Purchasing agents scour the garment districts in Milan and Rome and bring the newest designs to U.S. buyers in the New York or West Coast garment districts or to another location in Europe.

A **commission merchant** takes possession of goods on consignment from the local markets and then sells them at a central market location. Commission merchants are prevalent for agricultural products, taking products from farmers and selling them to a central market, or for furniture, taking products from furniture manufacturing plants to a large central market that deals in furniture. Many such furniture markets are located in North Carolina.

Rack Jobbers:
Wholesalers that manage the store shelves carrying their products.

Limited-Service Wholesalers:
Wholesalers who offer fewer services than full-service wholesalers, such as delivery and storage.

Agents:
Intermediaries who represent buyers or sellers; they do not take possession of or title to the merchandise, and they work based on commission or fees.

Brokers:
Intermediaries who bring buyers and sellers together; they do not take possession of or title to the merchandise, and they work based on commission or fees.

Selling Agent:
Agent that holds an exclusive arrangement with the company, represents all its operations in a particular market, and acts as the sales or marketing department of the firm.

Manufacturers' Agent (or Manufacturers' Representative):
Representative who works as the company's sales representative, representing noncompeting manufacturers in a particular market, and is paid on a commission basis.

Purchasing Agents:
Agents with a long-term relationship with buyers who select, receive, and ship goods to buyers and are paid on a commission basis.

Commission Merchant:
Agent who takes possession of goods on consignment from the local markets and then sells them at a central market location.

10-7 RETAILING AND RETAIL FORMATS

Most consumers think of grocery stores and department stores as retailers because they are stores that sell products to consumers for final consumption. Yet retailing has a much broader spectrum that includes vending machines, catalog stores, manufacturers' outlet shops, wholesale warehouses selling to consumers, Amway salespeople, and Internet sites selling products. Retailing is defined as all the activities involved in the final stage of distribution—selling goods and services to final consumers for their consumption. Retailers perform the following distribution functions (also illustrated in Figure 10-12):

• Creating convenience for consumers. Retailers offer assortments of goods and services from different manufacturers. Consumers do not have to go to each manufacturer's outlet or wholesaler distributing the manufacturer's product; instead, they shop at a conveniently located single retail outlet.

• Informing consumers. Salespeople in the store, advertisements, and point-of-purchase displays all serve to inform consumers about the products they sell.

• Serving the other channel members (manufacturers and wholesalers). Retailers place individual products, rather than bundles, on the shelves (i.e., they break bulk), mark product prices, store the products, and take ownership of the products, while assuming all related risks (e.g., theft, loss).

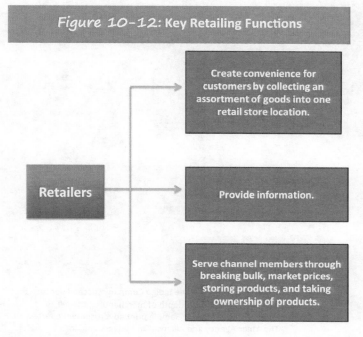

Figure 10-12: Key Retailing Functions

The three main retail formats are general merchandise retailing, food retailing, and non-store retailing. The top U.S. retailers in terms of revenues belong primarily to the first two categories—the top 10 retailers are listed in Table 10-3. However, many of the general merchandise retailers and food retailers also sell through their Web sites, which places them in the non-store category as well.

Table 10-3: Top 10 U.S. Retailers (Ranked by Revenues)		
Rank	Company	Revenues (million U.S.$)
1	Wal-Mart Stores, Inc.	466,114
2	Costco Wholesale Corp.	97,062
3	Kroger Co.	96,751
4	The Home Depot	74,757
5	Target Corp.	73,301
6	Walgreens	71,633
7	CVS Caremark Corp.	63,654
8	Amazon.com	61,093
9	Lowe's Cos. Inc.	50,208
10	Safeway Inc.	44,207

10-7a: General Merchandise Retailing

General merchandise retailers are composed of specialty stores, department stores, general merchandise discount stores, off-price retailers, and catalog showrooms. Approximately 55 percent of all retail sales are made in this category.

Specialty Stores

Specialty stores offer a narrow product line and wide assortment. In this category are clothing stores, which are usually further specialized into women's, men's, or children's clothing stores, such as Gap, Victoria's Secret, and Acorn; bookstores, such as the local retailer of alternative books or the large Barnes & Noble's chain; toy stores, such as Toys "R" Us; office supply stores, such as Office Max and Staples; home improvement stores, such as Lowe's and Home Depot; and consumer electronics stores.

Figure 10-13: Specialty stores like the Indigo Company succeed because they offer consumers a greater depth of merchandise, as well as hard-to-find unique items. **Source:** Sample print advertisement courtesy of The Miles Agency and Alliance One Advertising, Inc.

The largest of these stores (i.e., Barnes & Noble, Toys "R" Us, Office Max, Staples, Lowe's, and Home Depot) offer a huge selection of products in the category in which they are specializing. These are known as category specialists (category killers) and carry a narrow variety of merchandise but offer a wide assortment. Traditionally located in suburbia, category specialists are now migrating to urban areas. For example, Home Depot has a large, luxurious store in Midtown Manhattan, and one can often see people in the neighborhood carrying large merchandise on foot in bags with the Home Depot logo.

Specialty stores—chains in particular—are expanding at the expense of all forms of non-food retailing Specialty store chains are taking market share away from traditional department stores in the United States because they can offer a greater depth of merchandise within a product category. Shoppers looking for a new camera, stereo, kitchen utensils, or clothing will find more brands and selections in a specialty store than they would in a department store. Stores like the Indigo Company, featured in Figure 10-13, succeed because they offer a better selection of merchandise or hard-to-find unique items than other types of stores.

Department Stores

Department stores offer a broad variety of goods and wide assortments. Among the products they carry are the latest fashions for men, women, and children; household appliances and electronics; kitchenware; china; home furnishings; and toys and games. Department stores most often serve as anchor stores (or generator stores), situated at the end (anchor) positions in a mall to generate consumer traffic to the shopping mall. Outside the United States, department stores typically also have large supermarket sections, and some may even carry fresh produce.

It is typical for department stores to have numerous leased departments— sections that are leased to another retailer (see Figure 10-14). Cosmetics counters at most department stores are leased departments, where the cosmetics companies pay rent to be able to sell their products using their own sales staff. The Estée Lauder counter at Nordstrom's department store is such an example: Its staff is hired, trained, and paid by Estée Lauder. Leased departments create traffic for the department store, bringing in clients to purchase products that are complementary to the store's offerings.

Figure 10-14: This is a leased cosmetic department within a department store.

Department stores have suffered substantial losses in the past decades, mostly attributed to the rise in discount stores, off-price retailers, and category killers. The rental fee in malls tends to be higher than stand-alone facilities, and because of the large size of department stores, rent is a high-expense item for them. Discount stores, off-price retailers, and category killers can purchase large volumes of merchandise and sell it at a lower price than department stores, which puts a squeeze on the profit margins for department stores.

In good times, department stores do okay; in bad times, shoppers buy their merchandise at discount stores and category specialists. So, with each recession, more of the customer base of the department stores is eroded. The future of department stores is certainly a huge question mark.

General Merchandise Discount Stores

General merchandise discount stores sell high volumes of merchandise, offer limited service, and charge lower prices. Discount stores are divided into two categories: **all-purpose discount stores**, which offer a wide variety of merchandise and limited depth, and category specialists (category killers), which carry a narrow variety of merchandise and offer a wide assortment. The all-purpose category is dominated by stores such as Wal-Mart, Kmart, and Target. Category specialists, also known as category killers or stores with category dominance, are large specialty stores that carry a narrow variety of merchandise and a wide assortment. Types of category specialists are office supply stores, such as Staples and Office Depot (see Figure 10-15); home improvement centers, such as Home Depot and Lowe's; bookstores, such as Half Price Books; children's stores, such as Toys "R" Us; and furniture stores, such as IKEA, which dominate the modern, basic furniture market.

Figure 10-15: Discounters like Half Price Books, have forced booksellers to change their retail practices. Some, like Borders Books, waited too long to adapt.

Off-Price Retailers

Off-price retailers sell brand-name and designer merchandise below regular retail prices. The products they sell may include overruns, irregular products, and products from previous seasons. Off-price retailers include the following:

- Factory outlet stores, for designers such as Ralph Lauren, Liz Claiborne, and Jones New York, and for porcelain manufacturers, such as Dansk and Royal Doulton

- Department store outlets, such as Off Fifth for Saks Fifth Avenue, Last Call for Neiman Marcus, or Nordstrom Rack for Nordstrom's (They carry products that did not sell at discounted prices in the respective department stores.)

- Close-out retailers, with broad, inconsistent assortments, such as T.J. Maxx and Marshalls

- Single-price retailers, such as the Dollar Store

Catalog Showrooms

Catalog showrooms offer high-turnover, brand-name goods at discount prices. A typical format for a catalog showroom is one in which customers order from a catalog in the showroom where the product is displayed and then pick up the prod-

General Merchandise Discount Stores: Retailers that sell high volumes of merchandise, offer limited service, and charge lower prices.

All-Purpose Discount Stores: General merchandise discount stores that offer a wide variety of merchandise and limited depth.

Off-Price Retailers: Retailers that sell brand-name and designer merchandise below regular retail.

Catalog Showrooms: Showrooms displaying the products of catalog retailers, offering high-turnover, brand-name goods at discount prices.

Figure 10-16: Superstores have the space to offer an extensive selection--and quantity--of goods. The superstore in this photo is literally overflowing with product!

uct at a designated location. The goods sold in this retail format are not always brand-name goods. Typically, customers receive a catalog, which is also available online and in the showroom; based on the offerings displayed in the catalog and in the showroom, they order the product they would like to purchase in the store and pick it up from a designated location, often in an unassembled state.

IKEA is an example of a catalog showroom that has changed with the times, offering easy access to products that can easily be carried by consumers but maintaining the traditional order process for heavier or special-order products.

10-7b: Food Retailers

Food retailers consist of conventional supermarkets, supercenters, warehouse clubs, and convenience stores.

Conventional Supermarkets

Conventional supermarkets are self-service retailers with annual sales higher than $2 million and less than 20,000 square feet of store space. Conventional supermarkets, such as Kroger, Food Lion, and Fry's, account for almost half of all supermarket sales and offer a one-stop grocery shopping opportunity to consumers. At the Martin's Super Market, consumers can purchase regular groceries, as well as fresh specialty products, such as sushi and panini sandwiches. Consumers who prefer to dine in can drop their children off for an hour at the on-site day care, which is available in a number of the stores, and go to the Martin's Café for a relatively quiet hot lunch. Subsequently, the entire family can shop for groceries and have the products carried to the family van by a courteous store employee.

Superstores

Superstores are stores with more than 20,000 square feet of space and at least $17 million in sales. The superstore category includes **combination stores** (carrying food and drug products, as well as nonfood items that account for at least 25 percent of sales). A number of all-purpose general discount stores - Wal-Mart, for example - have been transformed into superstores to facilitate one-stop shopping for consumers. In their new, enhanced formats, these stores carry an extensive food selection in addition to broad non-food product lines. These stores are known as **supercenters** or **hypermarkets**, and they combine supermarket, discount, and warehouse retailing principles (see Figure 10-16).

Warehouse Clubs, or Wholesale Clubs

Warehouse clubs (or wholesale clubs) require members to pay an annual fee and operate in low-overhead, enormous warehouse-type facilities. They offer limited lines of brand-name and dealer-brand groceries, apparel, appliances, and other goods at a substantial discount (see Figure 10-17). They sell to final consumers who are affiliated with different institutions, as well as to businesses (when sell-

Food Retailers: Retailers selling primarily food products.

Conventional Supermarkets: Self-service food retailers with annual sales of more than $2 million and with an area of less than 20,000 square feet.

Superstores: Large retailers, such as combination stores or hypermarkets, that sell food, drugs, and other products.

Combination Stores: Medium-sized retail stores that combine food and drug retailing.

Supercenters: Stores that carry an extensive food selection and drug products, as well as nonfood items (which account for at least 25 percent of sales), combining supermarket, discount, and warehouse retailing principles.

Hypermarkets: Very large retail stores in Europe that combine supermarket, discount, and warehouse retailing principles—similar to superstores in the U.S.

Warehouse Clubs (or Wholesale Clubs): Stores that require members to pay an annual fee and that operate in low-overhead, warehouse-type facilities, offering limited lines of brand-name and dealer-brand groceries, apparel, appliances, and other goods at a substantial discount.

ing to businesses, they are wholesalers, rather than retailers). The top U.S. warehouse clubs are Sam's Club (part of Wal-Mart), Costco, and B.J.'s. As seen earlier in this chapter, Costco ranks second in terms of net sales, and a typical Costco warehouse is jammed with consumers loading their shopping carts at any time of day.

Figure 10-17: Wholesale clubs have an enormous amount of retail space. This wholesale club has endless aisles of small kitchen appliances and kitchenware.

Convenience Stores

Convenience stores are small retailers located in residential areas convenient to consumers. They are open long hours (often 24 hours a day, 7 days a week); carry limited lines of high-turnover necessities, such as milk, coffee, soft drinks, beer, bread, medicine, and gasoline; and offer the possibility of a one-stop shopping experience. Formats of convenience stores vary from small, independent retailers to chains such as 7-Eleven and Wawa. Convenience stores are able to compete with supermarkets by selling other products, such as gasoline, propane gas tanks, and other products. Wawa, for example, operates a successful convenience store selling healthy fast food, such as wraps and fresh sandwiches.

10-7c: Non-store Retailing

Non-store retailing is extremely small compared with the other two categories but offers the potential of being the fastest growing. Internet retailing, or e-commerce, is the newest participant in this category and has the greatest potential for growth. Other components of non-store retailing include vending machines, television home shopping, catalog retailers, and direct marketers.

Internet Retailing

Internet retailing (or interactive home shopping or electronic retailing) is an important retail format. The Internet retailing category includes both traditional retailers and the new dot-com companies (bricks and clicks, respectively). Traditional retailers are attempting additional market penetration through the Internet, making it convenient for loyal customers to purchase their products, and market diversification, expanding their market to consumers who otherwise would not normally shop in their particular retail establishment (see Figure 10-18). Internet retailing provides opportunities for retail firms to define their market beyond their geographic target regions.

Vending Machines

With the advent of smart phones and smart (chip) cards, **vending machines** have become more popular than ever (and, increasingly, more vending machines worldwide accept credit cards). Technology is now facilitating a more interactive consumer relationship, in which videos illustrate product use and provide more information. Vending machines are conveniently located close to consumers, allow for 24-hour access, and eliminate the need for salespeople. In the United States, they primarily sell beverages and food items. In Japan, they are very popular and sell just about anything one can think of, including beer, sausage, rice, life insurance, eggs, cameras, pantyhose, and condoms. In Munich, Germany, vending machines for fresh flowers are located in the center of town.

> **Convenience Stores:** Small retailers that are located in residential areas, are open long hours, and carry limited lines of high-turnover necessities.
>
> **Internet Retailing (or Interactive Home Shopping or Electronic Retailing):** Selling through the Internet using Web sites to increase market penetration and market diversification.
>
> **Vending Machines:** An interactive mode of retailing convenience goods.

Figure 10-18: This Minnesota-based retailer sells a lot of Irish-themed products both online and at its stores scattered throughout the Twin Cities. In the past ten years, online sales have grown from 5% to 35% of overall revenues.

Television Home Shopping

The **television home shopping** category includes cable channels selling to consumers in their homes, infomercials, and direct response advertising shown on broadcast and cable television. The primary television shopping networks in the United States are the QVC and the Home Shopping Network (HSN). All sell products to consumers in a format that approximates that of a talk show with a primary focus on the product and on making the sale. Infomercials also have a talk-show format, often featuring celebrities or other appropriate spokespeople who, during half-hour-long television programs, attempt to sell a product.

Catalog Retailing and Direct-Mail Retailing

Television Home Shopping:
Retailing through cable channels selling to consumers in their homes, through infomercials, and by direct-response advertising shown on broadcast and cable television.

Direct-mail Retailing:
Retailing using catalogs and other direct mail, instead of brick-and-mortar stores.

Catalog Retailers:
Retailers selling products through mail catalogs.

Direct-mail retailing refers to retailing using catalogs and other direct mail, instead of brick-and-mortar stores. Department stores and supermarkets often send direct mail to their valued customers to inform them about sales. Consumers can go to the store or order the advertised products by telephone or online.

Catalog retailers—retailers selling products through mail catalogs—are very popular in high-income countries, and many products are sold through catalogs. Gardeners ordering from one catalog retailer will find themselves on the list of many other catalog retailers, such as Heirloom Roses, Wayside Gardens, and Edible Landscaping. Most gardening catalog retailers offer a colorful Web site as an alternative to the equally colorful catalog.

Like Internet retailing, catalogs and direct mail are especially popular with consumers because of the ease of shopping.

Direct Selling

In the **direct selling** retail format, a salesperson, typically an independent distributor, contacts a consumer at a convenient location (e.g., his or her home or workplace), demonstrates a product's use and benefits, takes orders, and delivers the merchandise. Retailers involved in direct selling are Avon Products, Nu Skin, and Mary Kay Cosmetics. Cutco knives, Electrolux vacuum cleaners, and encyclopedias are also sold through this venue. **Network marketing (or multilevel marketing)** is a variation on direct selling that involves signing up sales representatives to go into business for themselves with minimal start-up capital. Their task is to sell more "distributorships"— that is, to identify more sales representatives from their own personal network, to buy the product, and to persuade others to buy the product. Among the most successful network marketing firms are Amway, Herbalife International, and Equinox International.

> **Direct Selling:**
> Selling that involves a salesperson, typically an independent distributor, contacting a consumer at a convenient location (e.g., his or her home or workplace), demonstrating the product's use and benefits, taking orders, and delivering the merchandise.
>
> **Network Marketing (or Multilevel Marketing):**
> An alternative distribution structure, using acquaintance networks for the purpose of distribution.

10-8 RETAILING DECISIONS

Retailers need to make a number of important decisions to most effectively appeal to their target market. They need to determine the merchandise assortment, the types of services that need to be offered, the store characteristics likely to appeal to their target consumers, and the store location that is most appropriate for their customers.

10-8a: The Merchandise Mix and the Service Mix

Retailers need to determine the optimal **merchandise mix**—that is, the product assortment and brands that will be carried by the store. Related to the merchandise mix is the **service mix**—the different types of services that will be offered to the retail customers. Decisions such as product assortment and service are important aspects of marketing that necessitate extensive evaluation on the part of retailers.

> **Merchandise Mix:**
> The product assortment and brands that the store carries.
>
> **Service Mix:**
> The different types of services offered to retail customers.

For example, Martin's Super Markets carries the typical supermarket fare that most of its competitors carry. In addition, it features gourmet products, such as specialty cheeses; dinner packages with complete entree, dessert, and bread, waiting to be picked up and served on the dinner table; and hot gourmet food in its café. It has one section dedicated to natural foods and another to international foods. In terms of customer service, Martin 's staff actually takes customers to the location of the merchandise on the shelf and, if their groceries do not fit neatly in a small grocery bag, carries them to customers' automobiles.

Today, many retailers attempt to increase their merchandise mix to become a one-stop shopping experience for consumers. In the process, they add products that are not related to the existing merchandise mix, which is known as **scrambled merchandising**. Scrambled merchandising expands a firm's competitive base: A wine shop could add gourmet products and fresh bread from a local baker and produce from local farmers, thus competing with other gourmet stores, bakeries, and supermarkets. An antique dealer could carry designer pillows and sheets, thus competing with department stores. A home-improvement warehouse could carry furniture, thus competing with furniture stores. From the consumer's point of view, one-stop shopping is clearly an advantage. Inside Indigo, featured in Figure 10-19, carries small furniture items and home decor specialties, along with its clothing and jewelry lines.

> **Scrambled Merchandising:** Scrambled merchandising involves retailers adding complementary product categories not included in the existing merchandise mix and more services to create one-stop shopping convenience for target consumers.

Figure 10-19: Inside Indigo uses a scrambled merchandising strategy to boost its product line beyond apparel and apparel accessories.
Source: Sample print advertisement courtesy of The Miles Agency and Alliance One Advertising, Inc.

Assuming that the retailer's traditional consumers do purchase the additional products added to the merchandise mix through scrambled merchandising, there is still the possibility that the same consumers may eventually become confused as to the precise business of the retailer. There is also the danger that the retailer will start into a never-ending spiral of retailing. To illustrate, suppose a supermarket adds a line of health and beauty aids to increase its profit margins. Drugstores, because they are losing customers now, will add a product to their merchandise line, such as greeting cards, stamps, magazines, and office supplies. Because of this, stationery stores are being threatened, so to remain competitive, they add gift items, toys, novelties, perfume, and inexpensive jewelry. Consumers no longer need to go to a stationery or gift store for gift specialties, so to maintain their customers, stationery and gift stores add candy, party supplies, a deli, and perhaps a small café. What do the supermarkets do now that some of their business is leaving? They need to add new scrambled merchandise. Figure 10-20 illustrates this self-perpetuating nature of scrambled merchandising.

Figure 10-20: The Self-Perpetuating Nature of Scrambled Merchandising

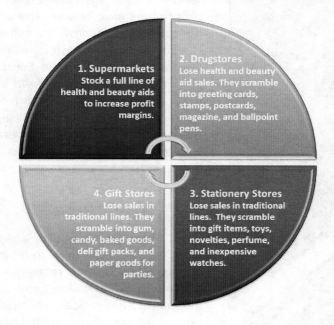

1. Supermarkets Stock a full line of health and beauty aids to increase profit margins.

2. Drugstores Lose health and beauty aid sales. They scramble into greeting cards, stamps, postcards, magazine, and ballpoint pens.

4. Gift Stores Lose sales in traditional lines. They scramble into gum, candy, baked goods, deli gift packs, and paper goods for parties.

3. Stationery Stores Lose sales in traditional lines. They scramble into gift items, toys, novelties, perfume, and inexpensive watches.

10-8b: Atmospherics

Atmospherics refer to the physical attributes of the store or non-store retailer. For a brick-and-mortar store, atmospherics include lighting and music tempo, the fixtures and other displays, colors, and store layout—in other words, all the store characteristics that create the overall mood and image for the store. For example, the Bloomingdale's department store is divided into what appears to be smaller boutiques. Individual designers or groups of designers have their own chambers, which are vividly lit. Perfumes are omnipresent, as are individuals ready to spray any of the passers-by with the newest olfactory attraction. Barnes & Noble bookstore, a large category specialist specializing in book retailing, creates reading nooks and cafés with comfortable armchairs for quiet reading.

10-8c: Location

A critical decision for retailer success is location. It is important for a retailer to be located close to its customer base. Retail location determines in a large part the customer mix and the competition. In the past, most stores used to be located in **central business districts**, in the middle of busy downtowns, and often close to movie theaters and banks. In many urban areas, central business districts continue to thrive as the commercial and cultural heart of the city.

Secondary business districts are shopping areas that form at the intersection between two important streets, consisting primarily of convenience and specialty stores. **Neighborhood business districts** meet the needs of the neighborhood and tend to be located on a main street of a neighborhood; typically, they have a supermarket, a drugstore, and several smaller retailers.

Shopping centers consist of a group of stores that are planned, developed, and managed as one entity. **Regional shopping centers** consist of at least 100 stores that sell shopping goods to a geographically dispersed market; they tend to have three or four anchor stores or generator stores and several other retailers in between. Customers are drawn from the entire area to its stores.

Atmospherics:
The general atmosphere of the store created by its physical attributes, including lighting and music tempo, the fixtures and other displays, colors, and store layout.

Central Business Districts:
Business districts located in the commercial and cultural heart of the city, in the middle of busy downtowns, and close to movie theaters and banks.

Secondary Business District:
Shopping areas, consisting primarily of convenience and specialty stores, that form at the intersection between two important streets.

Neighborhood Business Districts:
Business districts that meet the needs of the neighborhood and that tend to be located on a main street of the neighborhood; typically, they have a supermarket, a drug store, and several smaller retailers.

Community shopping centers have fewer than 40 retailers, with a department store, a supermarket, and several smaller specialty retailers. **Neighborhood shopping centers** have between five and 15 retailers and serve the neighborhood, providing convenience in the form of a supermarket, discount store, a laundry service, and other smaller specialty stores. In Europe, neighborhood shopping centers are likely to have a small pedestrian zone that cannot be accessed with automobiles; these neighborhoods are created for a walking, rather than a driving, shopper. Specialized markets contain stores specializing in a particular product category. An example is the diamond district in New York.

10-9 TRENDS IN RETAILING

Retailers operate in a rapidly changing environment. New retailers need to be innovative and proactive to survive; established retailers can easily fail if they do not keep up with retailing trends and practices. Moreover, the Internet has radically changed retailing practices. For existing retailers, it has created new possibilities for reaching old and new consumers, but it has also created new competition.

10-9a: Shortening Retailer Life Cycles: The Wheel of Retailing

New forms of retailing are quickly emerging and rapidly reaching maturity. Whereas the department store took a century to reach maturity, new formats, such as warehouse clubs and Internet retailing, have reached or are quickly reaching maturity in less than a decade.

The **wheel of retailing** partially illustrates the evolution of retailing. It describes how stores that start out as innovative low-margin, low-cost, and low-price operations seek to broaden their customer base by adding services, upgrading facilities, and thus increasing costs and prices. In the process, they lose their initial customers, who move on to new low-priced retailers, and become conventional retailers. Ultimately, these conventional retailers fall off the wheel because they are replaced with more innovative retailers climbing up on the wheel. The wheel of retailing is illustrated in Figure 10-21.

The wheel of retailing could explain the disappearance of many department stores, like Gimbels and Ames, that lost their middle-class customer base as they attempted to climb higher on the wheel. Another retailer, Bonwit Teller, an upscale clothing specialty store, survived for decades until it decided to climb beyond the stratosphere of established high-end retailers, such as Bergdorf Goodman's and Henri Bendel; initially, all three were competing for the same consumers with robust bank accounts.

10-9b: Technology-Based Developments

Technology is facilitating the retailing function, eliminating the need for salespeople, and increasing the accuracy of transactions. Pumping gas today is

Shopping Centers:
Groups of stores that are planned, developed, and managed as one entity.

Regional Shopping Centers:
Shopping centers that consist of at least 100 stores that sell shopping goods to a geographically dispersed market.

Community Shopping Centers:
Shopping centers with fewer than 40 retailers, containing a department store, a supermarket, and several smaller specialty retailers.

Neighborhood Shopping Centers:
Shopping centers that have between five and 15 retailers and that serve the neighborhood, providing convenience in the form of a supermarket, discount store, laundry service, and other smaller specialty stores.

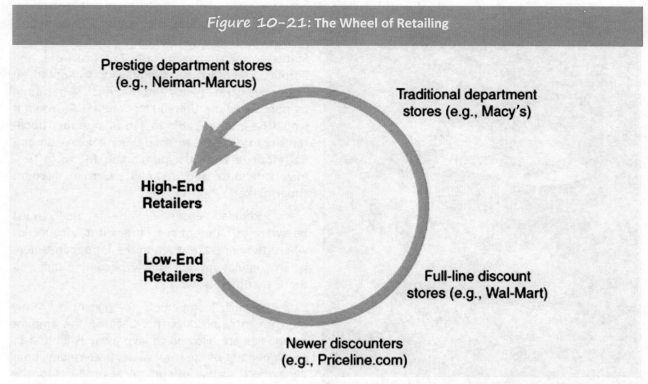

Figure 10-21: The Wheel of Retailing

largely a self-service transaction, as is banking. Optical scanners have greatly facilitated the checkout process, ensuring accurate calculation and facilitating inventory control. At many stores today, consumers can scan their own groceries and pay for them with credit cards, thus lowering the cost of human resources for the retailer.

The Internet enables traditional retailers to further penetrate their current market, offering convenience to loyal customers who purchase their products. It also allows them to diversify and expand their market to consumers who otherwise would not normally use the respective retail establishment, even to consumers in international markets interested in the retailer's offering.

In other developments, retailers are attempting to use technology to create brand experiences. Shoppertainment is the logical blend of retailing and leisure that increases the guests' length of stay and, very important, the total spending on the retailer's premises. World retail brands and consumer product companies in the new millennium are aiming to create entertaining in-store environments that delight customers and increase the likelihood of repeat visits and spending.

10-9c: The Broadening Competitive Base

Retailers are facing increasing competition from competitors who are not in the same retail category. Part of this trend is attributed to scrambled merchandising, whereby retailers add unrelated goods in order to provide one-stop shopping convenience to consumers and increase their own profits. For example, in the past, gourmet coffee was available only at gourmet shops and coffee houses. Today, you can purchase gourmet coffee at gourmet shops, at gourmet coffee houses, at many supermarket chains, at wholesale clubs, at drugstores, and over the Internet. Consumers can purchase books at bookstores, at discounters such as Wal-Mart, at Internet sites such as Amazon.com, at supermarkets, and at drugstores.

10-9d: International Expansion of Retailers

Retailers are rapidly expanding internationally to gain competitive advantage and to increase sales, profits, and overall firm performance. As they expand beyond their home-country borders, retailers also can take advantage of cost savings and learn from experiences in a way that could further enhance home-country operations. For example, Tesco, the British retailer, is using its stores in Central and Eastern Europe as a testing ground for ideas that are intended for application in the home market. The Tesco Extra in New-

castle, United Kingdom, is based on a Tesco hypermarket in Hungary. Retailers from the United States are expanding in Latin America, Asia, and Europe. Wal-Mart, for example, has adopted an aggressive strategy for international penetration by purchasing the United Kingdom ASDA Group. It would be inconceivable to see a large metropolitan city in a European emerging market without a Carrefour, a French hypermarket, Metro, a German warehouse club, and Aldi, a German discount supermarket.

Retailers expanding internationally must be aware of different regulations in the countries where they operate. Even in the European Union, where regulations are slowly becoming uniform, there are differences.

French companies, for example, rarely offer an extra product free because the amount companies are allowed to give away is limited to seven percent of the total value. In Germany, bundling offers, such as offering three products for the price of two, are illegal, and cash discounts to the consumer are limited to three percent. Although these rules are no longer as strict, they have nevertheless created business practices that are entrenched and are unlikely to change quickly.

Furthermore, retailers expanding internationally must be aware of different retail practices from one market to another. Consumers in the United States prefer to shop less frequently and purchase products in bulk, whereas, in Europe, consumers go to the supermarket, the butcher, or the baker daily, or every other day, buying in smaller quantities. Supermarkets in the United States play quiet contemporary music, whereas supermarkets in Asia tend to be bright and loud, with salespeople creating excitement by announcing sales. In many emerging markets, buying at farmers' markets means buying at bargain prices, whereas in most high-income countries, consumers pay a premium price at outdoor markets for what is sold as organic food.

Summary

1. Define distribution and identify the different channel functions and dimensions. Distribution planning is the planning of the physical movement of products from the producer to individual or organizational consumers and the transfer of ownership and risk. It involves transportation, warehousing, and all the exchanges taking place at each channel level. It involves establishing the channels of distribution— the totality of organizations and individuals involved in the distribution process who take title or assist in the transferring of title in the distribution process from the producer to the individual or organizational consumer. It also involves identifying and managing other intermediaries involved in distribution (i.e., other entities that facilitate the distribution process, such as transportation firms, freight forwarders, and customs brokers for international distribution). The goal of intermediaries is to offer support for the activities involved in delivering products for the enhanced benefit of the customer. In that sense, intermediaries are active participants in the value chain (or supply chain), the chain of activities performed in the process of developing, producing, marketing, delivering, and servicing a product for the benefit of the customer. Channels of distribution perform the functions of distributing the product down the channel of distribution to a location that is convenient to consumers, warehousing it in the distribution process. They take risks for product obsolescence or theft, or even beyond. They reduce the number of transactions needed to deliver a wide product assortment to retailers, and, ultimately, to consumers. In addition, they buy products in bulk from manufacturers at a discount and then break the bulk to distribute smaller quantities to retailers. They also conduct research for other channel members, provide service and credit to consumers and other channel members, and pay for promotional expenditures.

Among channel dimensions are channel length (defined as the number of levels of distributors in a distribution channel) and channel width (the number of independent intermediaries involved at a particular stage of distribution). An intensive distribution strategy has as its purpose full market coverage, whereas exclusive distribution has as a goal a high control of the intermediaries handling the product, and thus the marketing strategy, by limiting their number to just one or two per geographic area. Selective distribution opts for some control over the marketing strategy by limiting distribution to a select group of resellers in each area; at the same time, the company has a reasonable sales volume and profits.

2. Identify issues related to channel management, such as channel organization, administration, and relationships. Intermediaries can opt for a contractual channel arrangement, which spells out in a contract all the tasks that must be performed by each channel member with regard to production, delivery strategy and terms of sale, territorial rights, promotional support, the price policies of each intermediary, and contract length. Intermediaries can also have an administered channel arrangement, which has a dominant member of the channel in terms of size, expertise, or influence that coordinates the tasks of each channel member—the channel captain. Firms can also use a dual channel of distribution, or multichannel distribution, appealing to different markets; this strategy is also known as multimarketing. Channel members can strengthen their position in the channel through vertical integration (by acquiring or merging with an intermediary in the channel—a supplier or a buyer). Alternatively, they can increase intermediary strength in the market through horizontal integration, which would involve an acquisition or merger at the same level in the distribution channel.

3. Examine the different logistics functions. Logistics involve the following primary functions: transportation, warehousing, and inventory control, as well as customer service, and plant, warehouse, and reseller location planning. In terms of transportation, firms must decide whether to ship products by truck, water, rail, air, or pipeline, or a combination of these methods— known as intermodal transportation. These decisions depend on the type of product involved, on the urgency of delivery, and on how much the firm can afford to pay for the shipment. Companies must also decide on warehousing, which involves deciding where goods are stored, identified, and sorted in the process of transfer to an intermediary in the distribution channel or to the final consumer. There are different types of storage facilities that companies can use. Private warehouses are owned or leased and operated by firms storing their own products. They are used by intermediaries at all levels of distribution: manufacturers, wholesalers, and retailers. These intermediaries typically need to have storage on a regular basis. Public warehouses are independent facilities that provide storage rental and related services. Public warehouses are used by firms that cannot afford to have their own facilities or that do not have a need for storage on a regular basis. Firms must also determine how to optimally manage their inventories. Inventory control involves ensuring that there is a continual flow of goods to customers that matches the quantity of goods with demand. Reducing inventory costs is essential because high inventories may result in products becoming stale, or large stocks of last year's models may hurt sales of new models.

4. Provide an overview and description of the general merchandise retailing category and offer examples and illustrations. In the general merchandise retailing category are a number of retailers. Specialty stores, offering narrow assortments and deep product lines, are rapidly increasing their presence internationally. Department stores (general retailers that offer a broad variety of goods and deep assortments) are experiencing somewhat of a decline, whereas general merchandise discount stores are rapidly expanding, with great success. Wal-Mart, Kmart, and Target, in particular, have made great strides in attracting consumers. Category specialists, specializing in one product category, are also very successful. Catalog showrooms, selling high-turnover, brand-name goods at discount prices, are going out of business, but of all catalog showrooms, the IKEA "model" has been the most enduring.

5. Provide an overview and description of the food retailing category and offer examples and illustrations. Food retailers include conventional supermarkets, which are dominated by national and regional chains. Superstores are large combination stores (food and drug); in the rest of the world, they are known as hypermarkets. Warehouse clubs are becoming very popular worldwide, and many U.S. retailers in this category are doing very well. Convenience stores abound, with many chains developing in conjunction with gas stations.

6. Provide an overview and description of the non-store retailing category and offer examples and illustrations. Non-store retailing is one of the areas with the highest growth and unlimited opportunities. Internet retailing has vastly expanded opportunities for small and medium-sized retailers all over the world. Vending machines are increasing in sophistication and have different formats and capabilities in each market where they are available; the products they can carry also differ. Television home shopping is attracting more audiences, and today also offers opportunities to brick-and-mortar retailers to expand. Catalog retailers are still strong, expanding rapidly on the Internet. Direct selling and network marketing continue to gain ground, especially in developing countries.

7. Address issues related to merchandise and service mix, location, atmospherics, and future trends in retailing. Retailers need to make a number of important decisions in order to most effectively appeal to their target market. They need to determine the merchandise assortment that they should carry, the type of service that they should offer, the store characteristics likely to appeal to their target consumers, and the store location that is most appropriate for their customers. Among the trends in retailing are the shortening of the retailer life cycle, with new forms of retailing quickly emerging and rapidly reaching maturity; technological changes that facilitate inventory control and the overall retail transaction, as well as access, facilitated by the Internet; broadening of the competitive spectrum, with many stores expanding beyond their traditional product mix; and rapid internationalization to take advantage of new opportunities and increase the retailers' bottom line.

Key Terms

administered channel arrangement	conventional supermarkets	hybrid marketing channel
agents	department stores	hypermarkets
anchor stores	direct channel of distribution	indirect channel of distribution
atmospherics	direct-mail retailing	intensive distribution strategy
brokers	direct selling	intermediaries
catalog retailers	distribution centers	intermodal transportation
catalog showrooms	distribution planning	Internet retailing
category specialists	dual channel of distribution	inventory
central business districts	exclusive distribution channel	keiretsus
channel captain	expert power	legitimate power
channel length	food retailers	limited-service wholesalers
channel width	foreign trade zones	logistics (physical distribution)
channels of distribution	freight forwarders	logistics facilators
coercive power	full-service wholesalers	manufacturers' agent
commission merchant	general merchandise discount stores	merchandise mix
community shopping centers	horizontal integration	merchant wholesalers
contractual channel arrangement	horizontal marketing system (HMS)	middlemen (or channel members)
convenience stores	hub-and-spoke distribution centers	multichannel distribution system

neighborhood business districts

neighborhood shopping centers

network marketing

off-price retailers

physical distribution

private warehouses

public warehouses

pull strategy

purchasing agent

push strategy

rack jobbers

referent power

regional shopping centers

retailing

reward power

scrambled merchandising

secondary business districts

selective distribution channel

selling agent

service mix

shopping centers

specialty stores

supercenters

superstores

supply chain

television home shopping

trading companies

value chain

value delivery chain

vending machines

vertical marketing system (VMS)

warehouse clubs

warehousing

wheel of retailing

Discussion Questions

1. The chapter-opening vignette introduces Kathleen King as the owner of Tate's Bake Shop. Describe and categorize all the distribution activities she is involved in.

2. Assume that you are working for a large competitor of Kathleen's (described in the opening vignette), one that would like to dominate this particular niche market—the gourmet bakery market. Devise a distribution plan for your company that would effectively compete with Kathleen in her target market.

3. The competing company you created in question 2 needs to distribute its bakery goods all over the country. Assume that all the cookies are prepared at a large bakery on the outskirts of Greenwich, Connecticut. Your job is to determine the logistics involved in shipping the cookies to San Francisco, California; Oahu, Hawaii; and Boise, Idaho. What mode of transportation could you use for each destination? Which mode do you plan to use and why?

4. Refer to your and your family's shopping habits. How often do you shop at department stores? What products do you typically purchase there and why do you shop there as opposed to other types of stores? Do the department stores in your hometown appear to be doing well? Explain.

5. Make a list of the various types of general merchandise retail categories discussed in the text. For each category, discuss your personal shopping behavior. Identify a store or stores that you regularly patronize. Which category of general merchandisers to you patronize the most? Why?

6. Do you shop at convenience stores often? Why or why not? What types of products do you typically purchase at convenience stores?

7. How often do you shop online? What types of products do you typically purchase online? Would you say your online shopping has increased over the last few years or decreased? Why?

8. Pick your favorite retail store. Discuss the store's merchandise mix, service mix, atmospherics, and location. How important are each of these to you? Explain.

9. How important is atmospherics in your choice of a retail store? Explain. Pick one retail store you patronize because of the atmospherics. Explain why. Pick another store where you will not go because you dislike the atmospherics. Discuss why.

10. Think of your personal shopping behavior. Rank the following in terms of importance to you in the selection of a retail store: merchandise mix, service mix, atmospherics, location, and brands sold within the store. Explain the rationale for your ranking.

11. Think of your personal shopping experiences. Identify the five retail stores where you shop the most. Explain what you like about each store and why you patronize it. Is there anything you dislike about the five stores? Explain why and how it affects your shopping decisions.

12. Look through the non-store retail formats identified in Section 10-7c. Discuss each type of non-store retailing in terms of your personal experience. What types of products have you or do you purchase from each? How often do you use each? What factors affect your purchase decision with each type?

True or False

1. A direct channel of distribution might have one or two intermediaries.

2. Channel length is defined as the number of independent intermediaries involved at a particular stage of distribution.

3. The channel captain is the dominant channel member in the administered channel arrangement.

4. Trading companies are complex marketing systems specializing in providing intermediary services, risk reduction, and financial assistance.

5. Because logistics can be handled by any entity in the distribution channel, operational expenses for logistics are rather low.

6. As a result of the unpredictable demand for most goods, retailers cannot use JIT inventory systems.

7. Category specialists offer great product depth and narrow product breadth.

8. The wheel of retailing illustrates how stores that start out as innovative low-margin, low-cost operations seek to broaden their customer base by adding services and increasing prices. In the process they lose their initial customer base and become conventional type retailers; soon they fall off the wheel as more innovative retailer chains replace them.

9. A reason for retailers to expand internationally is to increase sales and profits by taking advantage of new consumer markets.

Multiple Choice

10. Which of the following is a component of distribution planning?

a. Planning of the physical movement of products
b. Transfer of ownership and risk
c. Transportation, warehousing, and all exchanges at each channel level
d. All of the above

11. Which distribution strategy aims at full market coverage, making products available to all consumers at the right place and the right time?

a. Intensive distribution
b. Exclusive distribution
c. Selective distribution
d. Contractual distribution

12. Multimarketing or selling through warehouse and retailer chains is an example of

a. Vertical integration.
b. Dual channel of distribution.
c. Horizontal integration.
d. Vertical marketing system.

13. Which type of power is based on a close match in terms of values and objectives shared by other channel members?

a. Coercive power

b. Expert power

c. Referent power

d. Legitimate power

14. Which stores most often serve as anchors in the mall, generating traffic for the stores situated in between?

a. All-purpose discount stores

b. Category specialists

c. Department stores

d. Off-price stores

15. Which of the following categories create atmospherics in a retail store?

a. Lighting and music tempo

b. Interior fixtures and displays

c. Store layout and color selection

d. All of the above

Blog

Clow-Lascu: *Marketing Essentials 5e Blog*

Screenshot

What Is Happening Today?

Learn More! For videos and articles

that relate to Chapter 10:

blogclowlascu.net/category/chapter10

Includes Discussion Questions

with each Post!

Notes

1. Gail Buchalter, "Out of the Nest–Now," *Forbes* 149, no. 11 (May 25, 1992): 64; and www.tatesbakeshop.com.
2. Hallie Mummert, "Lessons in Multichannel Marketing," *Target Marketing* 27, no. 12 (December 2004): 39–41.
3. "Business: Floating on Air," *The Economist* 359, no. 8222 (May 19, 2001): 56–57.
4. Tim Burt, "Porsche Fires Revolution at Harley," *Financial Times* (July 14–15, 2001): 8.
5. "Japanese Trading Companies: The Giants That Refused to Die," *The Economist*, 319, no. 7709 (1991): 72–73.
6. Ibid.
7. Ibid.
8. Adapted from Prabir K. Bagchi and Helge Virum, "Logistical Alliances: Trends and Prospects in Integrated Europe," *Journal of Business Logistics*, 19, no. 1 (1998): 191–213.
9. Sue Abdinnour-Helm, "Network Design in Supply Chain Management," *International Journal of Agile Management Systems*, 1, no. 2 (1999): 99–106.
10. Dan Gilmore, "State of the Logistics Union 2013 ," *Supply Chain Digest*, June 20, 2013, accessed at http://www.scdigest.com/assets/FIRSTTHOUGHTS/13-06-20.php?cid=7172 on July 27, 2014.
11. Abdinnour-Helm, "Network Design," 99–106.
12. Association of American Railroads, accessed at https://www.aar.org/StatisticsAndPublications/Documents/AAR-Stats.pdf on July 26, 2014.
13. IATA, "Air Freight Market Analysis," accessed at http://www.iata.org/whatwedo/Documents/economics/Freight-Analysis-Dec-2013.pdf on July 27, 2014.
14. American Association of State Highway and Transportation Officials, "Waterborne Freight Transportation," June 2013, accessed at http://www.camsys.com/pubs/WFT-1_sm.pdf on July 27, 2014.
15. Randy R. Irvin, "Pipeline Owners Must Reassess Utility of Undivided-Interest Ownership," *Oil & Gas Journal*, 99, no. 30 (July 23, 2001): 60–65.
16. Ibid.
17. www.dhl.com.
18. "DHL Will Spend $35 Million to Boost Hong Kong Operations." Logistics Today 48, no. 2 (2007): 14.
19. Sue Abdinnour-Helm, "Network Design in Supply Chain Management," *International Journal of Agile Management Systems*, 1, no. 2 (1999): 99–106.
20. Ibid.
21. Melissa Dowling, "Carvel Puts Its Ice Cream in the Mail," *Catalog Age* 10, no. 3 (March 1993): 12.
22. Brian Albright, "Better Distribution, Fewer Errors," *Frontline Solutions* 3, no. 13 (December 2002): 13–14.
23. George F. Hanks and Lucinda Van Alst, "Foreign Trade Zones," *Management Accounting*, 80, no. 7 (January 1999): 20–23.
24. Ibid.
25. Ibid.

Cases

Case 10-1 Shipping European Hot Water Radiators

Jane Whitman has spent her junior year in college in a study-abroad program in Germany. It was a frigid winter, and the large apartment she shared with five roommates was toasty for the whole month of February, when the thermometer never climbed above freezing. The apartment was equipped with hot-water heaters that stood flat against the wall and looked like contemporary art, and at the same time, they did not intrude into the space. Jane's parents live in an old Baltimore neighborhood of Victorian-era homes, where they heat their home with heavy, ornate cast-iron radiators, which will soon need to be replaced. In Jane's experience, the cast-iron radiators are not in any way superior to these more modern counterparts, which heat much faster. Jane decided to go to Baumax, a big-box home-improvement warehouse in Berlin, and to her surprise, she found various brands of modern radiators selling for about $25. In comparison, cast-iron radiators cost hundreds, even thousands of dollars, and they are available only in poor condition at architectural salvage firms that charge a lot for discarded goods that must be refinished.

Jane hoped to find similar hot water radiators for her parents' home through distributors in the United States for a comparable price. She searched the web and found that, indeed, there were radiant hydronic heaters selling in the United States. One of the most popular brands is Runtal Radiators, the world leader in this product category. They offer sleek and decorative European Style panel radiators in different formats: baseboard, wall panels, column radiators, and vertical panels. They claim to have invented the Europanel radiator in Switzerland more than 50 years ago. She quickly found a distributor for Runtal, but the prices they charged were around $700 for the radiator alone, without the hardware. She could ship the German private-label brand (Baumax) radiators to Baltimore and the price for delivery duty paid would still be below half of what the Runtal distributors charged.

Her parents had talked to neighbors about Jane's new venture: purchasing modern replacement radiators from Germany. Many indicated that they too were interested in this product. Soon, Jane's order swelled to 122 radiators. Jane quickly came to the realization that this might just be the small business that she would like to be involved in during her senior year in college and, possibly, beyond. She quickly embarked on a study of shipping options and attempted to understand the industry.

Her first challenge was to decide whether she should ship by air or by ocean freight. In the long term, air freight is a possibility. Overall, the world air freighter fleet is forecast to reach 3,563 in the year 2025, and prices are going down. However, new ocean container ships are faster and cheaper to operate, and the price is much lower than air freight. Jane approached one of her roommates, a marketing major, with this information, and asked her for help with ideas on how to transport 122 radiators— and, possibly, many more if this became a successful business.

Questions:

1. You are Jane's roommate. Discuss the advantages and disadvantages of the different modes of transportation—indicate what transportation venues are not appropriate for this shipment.

2. Advise Jane on the appropriate venue for transporting the radiators—air or ocean freight.

3. Create an intermodal transportation plan for the radiators, shipping them from the store's (Baumax) warehouse in the Eastern Berlin suburbs to the North Baltimore neighborhood where Jane's parents live and where the other customers are located.

4. Assume that Jane will be in this cross-border shopping business for the long term—she also found that hardware for doors and bathrooms is much cheaper in Germany than in the United States. Advise her whether, in the long term, she should use air or ocean freight based on the developments described previously.

5. If Jane wants to have the radiators sold through a retail outlet in the United States, which type of outlet would be the best? Justify your choice.

6. Would it be feasible for Jane to sell the radiators directly to consumers through the Internet? Explain why or why not?

7. If Jane decided to sell directly to consumers via the Internet, discuss the issues she would face in shipping the radiators. Would she use a freight forwarder? Why or why not?

Sources: www.runtalnorthamerica.com, accessed on July 27, 2014.

Case 10-2 The Complex World of SUPERVALU

SUPERVALU is one of the largest companies in the U.S. grocery distribution channel, a wholesaler and retailer of note. It has 35,000 employees, and annual sales in excess of $17 billion. The company was named in 2007 as a Fortune Most Admired Company and a Forbes Platinum 400 Company.

In 2003, SUPERVALU's retail store network, including licensed locations, totaled 1,391 stores in 40 states. Since then, the company grew considerably over the years. Recently, however, it was forced to cut over 1,500 jobs in order to compete for cost-conscious customers in a recovering economy. Yet, after selling five of its grocery store chains, SUPERVALU nevertheless continues to have a considerable presence in the market, with 1900 retail locations. The company's retail network includes the retail chains CUB FOODS, FARM FRESH, HORNBACHERS, SHOP 'N SAVE, and SHOPPERS, its very profitable national discounter SAVE-A-LOT, and several in-store pharmacies. The retail banners that SUPERVALU operates are household names in the markets where they compete, many of them holding the number one or two market share positions.

SUPERVALU also provides distribution and related logistics support services to more than 3,420 grocery stores. According to industry assessments, SUPERVALU has also demonstrated a top-down commitment to the creation of a truly superior, consumer-driven private label program.

In 2014, SUPERVALU engaged in what is called "wholesale play," a complex transaction where the company bought 18 of Rainbow Foods stores 27 stores for $65 million. The remaining 9 Rainbow Foods stores are expected to close as Rainbow's parent company, Roundy's, is expected to exit the market. Ten of the stores reopened as CUB FOODS. Interestingly, SUPERVALU's wholesale customers, including Jerry's Foods and Lunds, will share ownership with SUPERVALUE in several of the supermarkets.

Questions :

1. What type of distributor is SUPERVALU?

2. Describe vertical integration at SUPERVALU.

3. Describe horizontal integration at SUPERVALU.

4. Go to SUPERVALLUE'S Web site at http://www.supervalu.com. Identify the various retail outlets and identify the

type of retail format it is.

5. Go to SUPERVALLUE'S Web site at http://www.supervalu.com. Identify the various retail outlets and discuss for each type of outlet the retail store's merchandise mix, service mix, atmospherics, and location.

6. Where would you place SUPERVALUE on the wheel of retailing? Why?

Sources: Anne Gasparro, "Supervalu Profit Falls 49% - Sales Fall as Supermarket Operator Competes for Cost-Conscious Consumers," The Wall Street Journal, July 24, 2014, accessed at http://online.wsj.com/articles/supervalu-profit-falls-49-1406206452 on July 27, 2014; Mike Hughelett, "Supervalu CEO Calls Rainbow Deal a "Wholesale Play," Star Tribune, July 17, 2014, accessed at http://www.startribune.com/business/267353481.html on July 27, 2014. www.supervalu.com, accessed on July 27, 2014.

Answers to Review Questions

Answers: 1) False, 2) False, 3) True, 4) True, 5) False, 6) False, 7) True, 8) True, 9) True, 10) d, 11) a, 12) b, 13) c, 14) c, 15) d

Chapter 11

Pricing Strategies

Learning Objectives

After studying this chapter, you should be able to:

1. Define pricing and examine the external and internal influences on pricing decisions.

2. Examine the different price objectives: sales-based, profit-maximization, product-quality leadership, and status quo.

3. Address the pricing strategies: cost-based, demand-based, competition-based, and combination pricing.

4. Address strategic marketing applications in relation to pricing, such as price variability, price psychology, price discounting, and pricing in relation to the marketing mix.

5. Address strategies that companies use to change prices.

Figure 11-1: Today's deal-prone consumers are looking for storewide sales, clearance sales, price reductions, and any other type of pricing incentive that will result in a good bargain.

11-1 CHAPTER OVERVIEW

According to Marshal Cohen, co-president of NPD Fashionworld, shoppers' economic status no longer determines where they shop.[1] Price has become one of the most important considerations for consumers, who are now more educated than ever. Consumers were once attracted by the atmosphere, assortment, and customer service available at department stores and specialty stores. They also knew that department stores and specialty stores were the only places where they could purchase brand-name merchandise. Today, the mysterious ways of merchandising have been reduced to one dimension: price. Consumers are reluctant to pay full retail price for merchandise. In fact, consumers of all economic strata of society shop at discounters that stack the brand-name merchandise high and offer minimal service. Price-cutting strategies (such as the clearance sale illustrated in Figure 11-1) have proved successful with today's deal-prone consumer.[2]

Pricing is a central marketing strategy element because of its effect on product positioning, market segmentation, demand management, and market share dynamics.[3] Setting prices is a complex undertaking. Numerous internal and external variables, such as the nature of the product, the location of production plants, the type of distribution system used, and the economic climate, must be evaluated before determining the final price of products and services.[4]

This chapter addresses challenges that firms face when setting prices. It also addresses the impact of the competitive, political and legal, and economic and financial environments on pricing decisions. Section 11-2 offers a definition of pricing and addresses external and internal influences on pricing. Section 11-3 addresses the different price objectives: sales-based, profit-maximization, product-quality leadership, and status quo objectives, as well as other objectives involving pricing. Section 11-4 examines the cost-based, demand-based, competition-based, and combination pricing strategies. Section 11-5 addresses strategic marketing applications in relation to pricing, such as price variability, pricing psychology, price discounting, and pricing in relation to the marketing mix, whereas Section 11-6 examines issues related to changing the price.

11-2 INFLUENCES ON PRICING DECISIONS

Price is defined as the amount of money necessary to purchase a good or service. Everything and everyone has a price. A marketing manager's price is his or her salary, which accounts, in part, for the individual's ability, work experience, education, and training. Chief executive officers (CEOs) of large multinationals have a much higher price than supervisors in an industrial supply firm. A hamburger has a price, which captures various costs incurred in obtaining and processing the ingredients, in paying for labor costs, for franchise royalties, facility rent, and advertising. Pets have a price, from a $100 spaying fee for an adorable half-breed street puppy from the local SPCA to $14,000 for a superb Hyacynth Macaw parrot.

As the chapter-opening suggests, in today's economy, price plays an essential part. Many products are standardized in the mature marketplace of the United States, and competition stands ready to chip away at company profits by offering the same product at a lower price. A business can use its pricing strategy wisely to reach its objectives and maximize its revenue. In fact, price is the only element of the company's marketing mix that produces revenue; product, place, and promotion, the other elements of the marketing mix, represent costs to the firm. This section addresses the different external and internal influences on price decisions.

11-2a: External Influences on Price

The primary external influences on price are consumers, economic intermediaries, logistics, competition, and the government.

Consumer Influences on Price

Consumers play an important role in determining the final price of products. According to the **law of demand**, consumers purchase more products at a lower price than at a higher price. For each price the company might charge, there will be a different level of demand. This relationship is illustrated in the **demand curve**, which portrays the number of units bought for a particular price in a given time period. Figure 11-2a shows the demand curve for most products: As price increases, the quantity demanded decreases. Marketing managers can influence the price-quantity demanded relationship to a certain extent. For example, they could increase promotion for the product. This would lead to an increase in the quantity demanded, as illustrated in Figure 11-2b, causing a shift in the entire demand curve.

Figure 11–2: Demand Curves

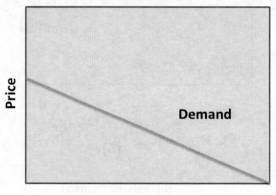

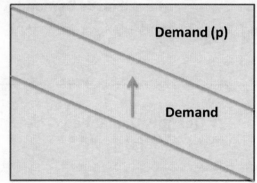

Quantity Demanded
(a) As the price increases, quantity demanded decreases.

Quantity Demanded
(b) Promotion leads to a shift in the demand curve.

(a) Demand curve for most products.

(b) Demand curve shifts as a result of promotion.

However, consumers may or may not be sensitive to price changes. For example, introducing a high excise tax on cigarettes has not led to a change in cigarette demand, regardless of the tax imposed.[5] Cigarette users view cigarettes as necessities and are thus are not likely to give up smoking as a result of price increases. Demand for cigarettes is inelastic; it does not respond to price changes. **Price elasticity** is defined as buyer sensitivity to a change in price. The formula for calculating price elasticity is:

> **Law of Demand:**
> Economic law whereby consumers are believed to purchase more products at a lower price than at a higher price.
>
> **Demand Curve:**
> Curve that portrays the number of units bought for a particular price in a given time period.
>
> **Price Elasticity:**
> Buyer sensitivity to a change in price.

$$\text{Price Elasticity of Demand} = \frac{\text{Percent Change in Quantity Demanded}}{\text{Percent Change in Price}}$$

or

$$\text{Price Elasticity of Demand} = \frac{\dfrac{\text{Quantity 1}-\text{Quantity 2}}{\text{Quantity 1}}}{\dfrac{\text{Price 1}-\text{Price 2}}{\text{Price 1}}}$$

The formula calculates the percentage change in demand for each percentage change in price. Demand is elastic if a small change in price results in a large change in demand (see Figure 11-3a). For cigarettes, demand is inelastic; that is, for a small change in price, there is only minimal, if any, change in the quantity demanded (see Figure 11-3b).

Figure 11-3: Demand Elasticity

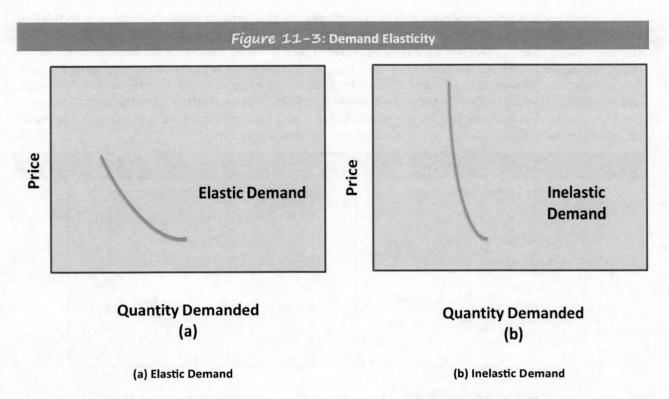

(a) Elastic Demand

(b) Inelastic Demand

If consumers believe that products are relatively similar and there are many product substitutes, they are less likely to purchase at high prices. Thus, for these consumers, demand is elastic. Marketers who understand elasticity price their products and run their promotions accordingly. Delta Airlines, for example, offers lower fares for consumers to fly across country in October or February because the airline understands that, for these consumers, demand is elastic. They are more likely to travel if airfares are discounted. Business travelers, however, must travel on short notice and their travel cannot be postponed until prices are lower (see Figure 11-4). For these consumers, who cannot purchase tickets in advance, airlines maintain high prices during these months, despite the seasonal slowdown in the business.

In addition to a consumer's financial situation, other consumer-behavior-based determinants explain price-related behavior. For example, deal-prone consumers are more likely to respond to deals than consumers who are not deal-prone. Similarly, consumers loyal to a brand will purchase that brand even if prices increase—up to a point. Consumers loyal to a retailer will pay higher prices for the privilege of shopping there because they prefer special treatment.

For example, Martin's Super Markets offer extra services to consumers. Employees carry the products to the shopper's automobile and load them in the trunk. Consumers who ask about the location of a product are taken to the aisle that has the product, and the employee will pick up the product off the shelf for them. Despite the fact that Martin's charges slightly higher prices, the stores are busy at all hours. Martin's consumers are willing to pay higher prices for the extra service and atmosphere.

A company's pricing decisions are also influenced by customer profitability, spending potential and retention. As addressed in Chapter 1, companies are increasingly focusing on customers' lifetime value—that is, the estimated profitability of the customer over the course of his or her entire relationship with the company. Customer lifetime value in essence determines each customer's profit and loss (P&L).[6]

Figure 11-4: Airlines face an elastic demand curve. Many offer lower fares for consumers to fly across country in October or February when traffic (and demand) is low.

- **Customer profit**—Many companies are starting to calculate profit for each of their customers. Customer profit is calculated as revenue minus costs for that particular customer, and it is a measure of past performance. In general, it is believed that a profitable customer needs to be retained, and much of a firm's efforts are concentrated on customer retention, based on the assumption that acquiring new customers takes much more effort and cost than retaining old customers. Under this assumption, a particularly valuable customer is one who has had a profitable relationship with the company.

- **Customer profit potential**—Customer profit potential is an estimate of the individual's contribution to a company's bottom line. This figure is obtained by comparing estimated potential, using external data predictors such as demographics, psychographics, and summarized credit data by geographic location, to actual profit. When estimating customer profit, the company should also find out who is currently not profitable but looks like they should be.

> **Customer Profit:**
> Profit measure calculated as revenue minus costs for that particular customer.
>
> **Customer Profit Potential:**
> An estimate of the individual's contribution to a company's bottom line.
>
> **Retention:**
> The ability of the firm to maintain a particular customer over time.

Figure 11-5: An attractive, airy atmosphere with minimalist displays are attractive to an upscale clientele.

- **Retention**—Customer retention adds value to a company because these customers tend to buy more products and purchase more often (see Figure 11-5). A two-point improvement in retention, for instance, from 82 percent to 84 percent, adds six percent to current value.[7]

Economic Influences on Costs and Price

Economic factors, such as inflation, recession, and interest rates, affect pricing decisions because they affect the cost of producing a product. An inflationary environment places strong pressures on companies to lower prices; often, pricing competitively may mean that companies are not producing a profit. During inflationary periods, firms often find that they must decide between maintaining a competitive presence in a market and weathering the downside of the economic cycle or abandoning the market, which is a high-cost, high-risk proposition.

The cost of materials, supplies, and labor are some of the costs that are not within a firm's control. For example, several factors affect the cost of gasoline at any time. Price increases can be caused by rising crude oil costs (the raw material that accounts for 40 percent of the retail price for gas). Political turmoil in one or more oil-producing countries can reduce the supply available. The Iraq war led to unprecedented increases in the price of oil and a leap in the price of energy worldwide. The price is also affected by the risk premium accompanying the political or economic uncertainty in the Middle East. Environmental regulations, such as the tough Clean Air Act requirements for reformulated gasoline and the proliferation of distinct fuel blends, can create price increases. Similarly, summer is the time of both the highest motor fuel demand and of

Figure 11-6: Gasoline prices in Europe are very high as a result of high taxes and oil prices; by comparison, gasoline prices in the United States, although high, are a bargain.

the imposition in metropolitan areas of costly environmental regulations designed to fight smog. In Europe, consumers are paying higher prices for gasoline as a result of high taxes (see **Figure 11-6**). On the other side, gas prices could be lowered by opening additional U.S. sites to oil exploration and drilling.[8]

Intermediaries' Influences on Price

As seen in Chapter 10, intermediaries attempt to have some level of control over their own markups, while, at the same time, taking into consideration the price that consumers are willing to pay. Intermediaries are becoming more and more efficient at inventory management, using just-in-time delivery methods, quick-response inventory systems, and electronic data interchange, which allow them to lower their inventory carrying costs and facilitate the flow of products. The use of computerized distribution centers and efficient logistic practices also cut intermediary costs.

Competitive Influences on Price

Pricing strategies must take into consideration both the competitive environment and the firm's position relative to competition. Firms can control prices only if their product is in the early stages of the product life cycle and they are one of the market leaders. During the maturity stage of the product life cycle, the competitive field is broad, characterized by products that are relatively similar. In this type of market, individual firms have little control over price. Therefore the goal of firms at this stage is to keep product prices low, for example, by moving production to a low-labor-cost country. In the maturity stage, companies can still maintain some control over price if their products are well differentiated and have a high degree of brand franchise. Finally, in certain markets, such as utilities, the government regulates prices to ensure access to the services for all consumers. Utilities can also be owned and operated by the government. In planned economies, such as those of China and North Korea, the government sets most prices. In Venezuela, the government took over the country's last privately run oil fields, despite complaints from international companies such as Exxon Mobil and Chevron, which are allowed to stay on only as minority partners. Thus, under the new ownership, the government of Venezuela makes all the pricing decisions for the oil exported.

An economics perspective describes four different types of markets based on competition. **Pure competition** characterizes a market that consists of many buyers and sellers, where no buyer or seller can control price or the market. In this environment, marketing plays a minimal role. Because sellers can sell as much as they want and buyers can buy as much as they need, perfect market information is available to both buyers and sellers, and the product sells for about the same price in the marketplace. Although pure competition is difficult to accomplish in the marketplace, commodities come the closest to pure competition.

Monopolistic competition is a market that consists of many buyers and sellers and products that vary greatly in the same product category. Products are differentiated based on price, style, flavor, and other characteristics important for the final consumer. Coffee is this category, with many brands, such as Maxwell House, Folgers, Eight O'Clock, Taster's Choice, Starbucks, store brands, regional distributor brands, and even ethnic brands, such as Vassilaros and Venizelos, appealing to Greek consumers. These brands are clearly differentiated, and price changes for one brand may not lead to a change in pricing strategy for another. See Figure 11-7.

Figure 11-7: Coffee brands are clearly differentiated, and changes in price for one brand does not necessarily lead to a change in the price of another.

Oligopolistic competition consists of a few sellers who dominate the market. Change in the strategy of one seller will directly affect the other sellers in the marketplace. The automobile industry and the airline industry are characterized by oligopolistic competition. In terms of pricing, the airlines follow similar pricing strategies. Similar prices are seen for the same type of consumer: leisure traveler, business traveler, or off-peak traveler. If one airline lowers prices to attract travelers in the low season, then, typically, all the airlines follow suit.

Pure monopoly characterizes a market that consists of only one seller. This seller could be the government, for planned economies, or a government-owned utility company, in the case of market economies. An example of a government-owned monopoly in the United States is the U.S. Postal Service. Other examples of monopolies are private regulated monopolies, such as local power companies, and unregulated monopolies, as in the case of pharmaceutical companies' drugs that are under patent protection. Regulated monopolies are often required to maintain lower prices to ensure access to the good or service to all consumers. Unregulated monopolies can charge any price the market will bear, but often they do not do so because they need brand-loyal consumers or because of concern that the government may interfere.

> **Pure Competition:**
> Market that consists of many buyers and sellers, where no buyer or seller can control price or the market.
>
> **Monopolistic Competition:**
> Market that consists of many buyers and sellers and products that vary greatly in the same product category.
>
> **Oligopolistic Competition:**
> Market that consists of few sellers who dominate the market.
>
> **Pure Monopoly:**
> Market that consists of only one seller.

The Government's Influence on Price

The government plays an important role in pricing. The government has enacted legislation to protect competitors, channel members, and consumers from unfair strategies. Among examples of areas where the government becomes involved in the pricing strategies of the firm are the following:

- **Price discrimination**—Legislation such as the Robinson-Patman Act prohibits charging different prices to different buyers of the same merchandise and requires sellers that offer a service to one

Chapter 11: Pricing Strategies

buyer to make the same service available to all buyers.

Price Discrimination:
The practice of charging different prices to different buyers of the same merchandise.

Resale Price Maintenance:
Manufacturers requiring retailers to charge a particular price for a product.

Price Fixing:
Agreement among channel members at the same level in the channel of distribution to charge the same price to all customers.

Deceptive Pricing:
Strategy used by sellers who state prices or price savings that may mislead consumers or that are not available to consumers.

Predatory Pricing:
Pricing strategies used to eliminate small competitors and to deceive consumers.

Bait and Switch:
A marketing tactic in which a retailer promotes a special deal on a product and then, when consumers arrive at the store, the retailer tries to switch them to a higher-priced item.

Price Confusion:
Strategies to confuse consumers so that they do not quite understand the price that they ultimately have to pay.

Dumping:
Selling products below cost to get rid of excess inventory or to undermine competition.

Unit Pricing:
Pricing that allows consumers to compare among prices for different brands and for different package sizes of the different brands.

• **Resale price maintenance**—Manufacturers are prohibited from requiring retailers to charge a particular price for a product. They are allowed, neverthe-less, to print a suggested retail price on the product package or attached label.

• **Price fixing**—Legislation such as the Federal Trade Commission Act and the Sherman Antitrust Act addresses all types of unfair competition, including price fixing—an agreement between channel members at the same level in the channel of distribution to charge the same price to all customers. Companies are frequently scrutinized for their price-fixing practices: Christie's and Sothe-by's, the most prominent auctioneers of art and antiques, have recently paid large fines and their reputations have suffered greatly after they were found to engage in price fixing.

• **Deceptive pricing**—Stating prices or price savings, that may mislead consum-ers or that are not available to consumers, is known as deceptive pricing. Un-fair pricing tactics can include **predatory pricing, bait-and-switch tactics**, and **price confusion strategies**. Predatory pricing is charging prices below cost to eliminate small competitors. One way to do this is through **dumping**, which is selling products below cost to get rid of excess inventory or to undermine competition. Bait-and-switch strategies advertise items at a low price. Howev-er, when customers arrive, they are told that the store is out of stock, and the retailer attempts to sell them a higher-priced item. The last type of unfair pric-ing is price confusion, which firms use to confuse consumers, so that they would not quite understand the price that they ultimately have to pay. Exam-ples are a wireless company charging for calls that go unanswered for more than 30 seconds; theaters charging a theater restoration fee or a facilities fee; hotels charging a connectivity fee for access to the phone and the Internet, and another fee for safes, whether or not the phone, the Internet, or the room safe are used.[9]

Many states also require retailers to engage in **unit pricing**—that is, pricing that allows consumers to compare between prices for different brands and for different package sizes of the different brands. Table 11-1 addresses different ex-amples of federal government legislation that affects pricing.

The government may also affect pricing through protectionist strategies that protect national industries from international competitors. This, in turn, leads governments of those competitors to retaliate, with a negative effect on price for all. Government protectionism adds to the final price paid by consumers. For in-stance, the costs of protectionism for the European consumer are as high as seven percent of the gross domestic product of the European Union (EU)—some $600 billion. To illustrate, the EU's banana-import restrictions cost European consumers up to $2 billion a year, or about 55 cents per kilogram of bananas. Because the United States has retaliated with punitive tariffs on European imports, the cost of the EU's banana regime is even higher. In other examples, European beef farmers receive large subsidies, while tariffs of up to 125 percent are imposed on beef im-ports. The costs incurred by European beef consumers for subsidies, tariffs, and other restrictions amount to $14.6 billion a year in the form of higher prices and taxes, or around $1.60 per kilogram of beef. Despite the Uruguay round of trade liberalization and the strides made by the World Trade Organization, protectionist actions continue to increase the costs of goods, and hence the price for the final consumer. The cost of protectionism is high in the United States as well, especially in service industries such as shipping and banking.

Part Three: Marketing Mix Strategies

Table 11-1: Major Legislation Affecting Pricing	
Legislation	**Description**
1890 Sherman Antitrust Act	Prohibits trusts, monopolies, and activities designed to restrict free trade. Bans predatory pricing (i.e., charging prices below cost to eliminate small competitors).
1914 Clayton Act	Prohibits price discrimination to different buyers, tying contracts that require buyers of one product to also purchase another item, and combining two or more competing firms by pooling ownership or stock. Bans predatory pricing.
1914 Federal Trade Commission Act	Created the Federal Trade Commission (FTC) to address antitrust matters and investigate unfair methods of competition. Addresses price fixing and price advertising.
1936 Robinson-Patman Act	Prohibits charging different prices to different buyers of the same merchandise and requires sellers that offer a service to one buyer to make the same service available to all buyers.
1938 Wheeler-Lea Amendment	Expanded the power of the FTC to investigate and prohibit practices that could injure the public, and false and misleading advertising. Addresses price advertising. Bans bait-and-switch advertising.
1966 Fair Packaging and Labeling Act	Requires that manufacturers provide a label containing the contents, what company made the product, and how much of each item it contains. Allows for fair price comparisons.

11-2b: Internal Influences on Price

Internal factors, such as the firm size, the organizational structure, and the industry focus, determine who in the company makes pricing decisions. In smaller organizations, it is usually the owner or the top managers who decide on pricing. In larger organizations, pricing is decided by the brand manager or negotiated in a business-to-business setting. In a market-oriented company, pricing is determined based on information shared with the marketing department by the other functional areas, such as finance, engineering, research and development, or sales. In fact, these departments may be allowed to have direct input in pricing decisions.

Costs are also important determinants of price. In pricing products, companies need to take into consideration all product costs and determine a fair rate of return on investment. A company has **fixed costs**, which are costs that do not vary with the amount of output, such as building rental, maintenance, and the costs of the permanent staff. It also has **variable costs**, which vary with the amount of output, such as raw materials, packaging, and shipping costs. Together, variable costs and fixed costs make up total costs at a particular level of production. Production costs typically fall as a function of experience: As companies acquire more experience, they realize economies of scale. This leads to lower prices and increased sales volume, ultimately leading to greater profits for the company.

> **Fixed Costs:**
> Costs that do not vary with the amount of output.
>
> **Variable Costs:**
> Costs, such as raw materials, packaging, and shipping costs, that vary with the amount of output.

11-3 SETTING PRICING OBJECTIVES

Firms set their pricing objectives in line with the company goals. Thus different firms in the same industry may have different pricing objectives predicated on firm size, in-house capabilities, and focus on profit, sales, or government action. Sales-based objectives focus on increasing sales volume, profit-based objectives focus on the total return on investment, and status quo objectives focus on maintaining a good relationship with customers, channel members, and regulatory bodies. Companies may elect to have more than one goal.

A firm that focuses on sales-based pricing objectives attempts to increase its sales volume and its market share relative to competitors. The premise of this strategy is that sales growth will lead to dominance in the marketplace achieved at low per-unit cost. Companies often introduce new products with sales-based objectives in mind. To achieve high sales, a company may resort to **penetration pricing**, whereby firms price the product below the price of competitors to quickly penetrate the market at competitors' expense and acquire a large market share, and then gradually raise the price. Compaq was able to quickly capture the European market by using this strategy. In the Netherlands, Compaq offered deals unmatched by any brand-name competitor and coupled this pricing strategy with excellent warranties and support. This strategy can be used when consumers are sensitive to price, as well as when the company has achieved economies of scale in manufacturing and distribution, and can afford to sell the product at lower prices. The price must be low enough to keep out competition.

> **Penetration Pricing:**
> Pricing strategy whereby firms initially price the product below the price of competitors to quickly penetrate the market at competitors' expense and acquire a large market share, and then gradually raise the price.
>
> **Skimming:**
> Pricing strategy whereby the product is priced higher than that of competitors.

A firm that focuses on profit-maximization pricing objectives attempts to recover the costs of product development quickly, while simultaneously providing value to consumers. Companies estimate the demand and costs at different prices and will select the price that will produce the maximum profit or return on investment. Companies often introduce new products with profit-maximization objectives in mind using **skimming** strategy, whereby the product is priced above that of competitors. The focus of the company is on immediate profit, rather than on long-run performance. This strategy is most effectively used early in the product life cycle when competition is minimal (once there is substantial competition, there is a high likelihood that competitors will undercut the price) or when there is a high degree of brand loyalty. In general, consumers responding to skimming strategies are more concerned with quality, uniqueness, and status, rather than price. In turn, the product's image and quality must warrant the product's high price.

Product-quality leadership objectives do not necessarily mean that the company is reaping the highest potential profits. In this case, the company is not estimating the demand and costs at different prices and selecting the price that yields the maximum profit, or return, on investment; rather, the company is charging a high price to cover the costs of producing a high-quality product and the costs of related research and development.

Firms may set status quo–based objectives when they are facing too much competition, when they want to refrain from disrupting the channel with changes, or when they do not want to be scrutinized by the government. Such objectives are used to minimize the impact of competitors, government, or channel members and to avoid sales decline. This strategy does not mean that the firm does not change prices—it must match competitors' price reductions or price increases. It should be noted that status quo–based objectives can be adopted only in the short-term, to weather a particular condition or challenge. In the long term, companies must be proactive, rather than reactive, to be able to optimally meet the needs of their target consumers.

Companies may pursue other objectives with their pricing strategies. A non-profit restored local theater and architectural gem may charge just enough to be able to maintain the building and the antique Wurlitzer organ that emerges from the platform on Saturday nights for performances with the help of restoration experts. Different establishments may choose not to charge senior citizens for services or charge them a reduced rate to ensure their participation in certain events. Other companies may decide that one particular brand they offer will be a low-cost leader. It should be noted, however, that low-cost leadership can be a problematic strategy if the product is not backed by adequate performance.

A firm must coordinate its pricing strategy with its product image positioning, with product design and performance characteristics, and with its promotion and distribution strategy to optimally address target market needs. Prices need to mesh with the entire product line and and compare favorably with the competition. Coordinating pricing strategies with the overall marketing strategy is complex. Price is a flexible element of the marketing mix that can be changed quickly to respond to new market developments, unlike the product, the distribution, and the promotional strategies, which cannot be changed as quickly. It is important to note that the pricing strategy also poses the greatest challenge to the firm. Even companies that de-emphasize price in their positioning, opting for a quality positioning, need to be mindful of how they use price to communicate. A price that is not high enough may cause consumers to question the product quality. Pricing the product too high may cause consumers to switch to competitors because they feel it is overpriced. In fact, pricing even slightly higher than direct competitors can lead to a substantial loss in market share, while pricing too low may cut severely into profits, because consumers may question product quality.

11-4 PRICING STRATEGIES

Pricing strategies can be cost-based, demand-based, competition-based, or, when these approaches are integrated, the strategy may involve combination pricing.

11-4a: Cost-Based Pricing

In **cost-based pricing**, the firm sets the price by calculating merchandise, service, and overhead costs and then adding an amount needed to cover the profit goal. Cost-based pricing is relatively easy to calculate because there is no need to take into consideration the estimated price elasticity of demand or the reaction of competitors to price changes. Moreover, costs are easier to estimate than demand elasticity, competitive reactions, and market conditions. The firm's goal is to obtain reasonable profits, using a specified **price floor**, that is, the lowest price a company can charge and attain its profit goals. The cost-based pricing techniques are cost-plus, markup, traditional break-even analysis, and target profit pricing.

Cost-Plus Pricing

Cost-plus pricing is relatively simple: It involves adding a target profit to total costs. Let us assume that a "boutique" nursery selling unique plants tailored to business customers' needs in the eastern United States incurs the following costs and wants to earn a $20,000 profit margin:

Variable Cost	$100 per plant
Fixed Costs	$30,000
Number of Plants Produced	4,000
Desired Profits	$20,000

$$\text{Price} = \frac{\text{Fixed Costs} + \text{Variable Costs} + \text{Profit}}{\text{Number of Units Produced}}$$

$$\text{Price} = \frac{30,000 + (4,000 \times 100) + 20,000}{4,000} = \$112.50 \text{ per plant}$$

This method evaluates profits as a function of costs, and the price is not linked to demand. There is no accounting for excess capacity, and there is no attempt to lower costs because profits remain the same regardless of costs. This strategy is appropriate for custom-made products, such as furniture and equipment. Typically, the nursery gets orders for a number of plants from customers, calculates the price using the cost-plus method, and sends invoices to the businesses placing the order after calculating the total costs.

Cost-Based Pricing:
Pricing strategy whereby the firm sets the price by calculating merchandise, service, and overhead costs and then adds an amount needed to cover the profit goal.

Price Floor:
The lowest price a company can charge to attain its profit goal.

Markup Pricing

Markup pricing is a variant of cost-plus pricing, with a markup used to cover selling costs and profits. Using the example of the nursery (see **Figure 11-8**), markup pricing uses the following formulas:

First, the unit cost is calculated; next, the markup price is calculated, as in the following:

$$\text{Unit Cost} = \text{Variable Cost per Unit} + \frac{\text{Fixed Costs} + \text{Desired Profits}}{\text{Units Produced}} = \$100 + \frac{\$30{,}000 + \$20{,}000}{4{,}000} = \$112.50$$

Assuming that the nursery would like to have a 10 percent markup (0.10) on plants that cost $107.50, then the price would be calculated as follows:

$$\text{Markup Price} = \frac{\text{Unit Cost}}{1 - \text{Markup Percentage}} = \frac{\$107.50}{1 - .10} = \$119.44$$

This yields a profit of $11.94 per plant ($119.44 − 107.50).

This method has the shortcoming of not linking to demand. If the company does not meet its sales target, then its unit costs will be much higher, but this method assumes costs remain the same. The markup method makes sense only if the company meets its sales target. And yet, the method is widely used. Translators, accountants, contractors, and many other service providers use this strategy to determine price. It is a method commonly used for pricing at the different levels of the channel of distribution as well. It is a popular method for a number of reasons. First, costs are easier to calculate than demand. Second, this method is based on costs, which are more stable than demand. Third, expenses, trade discounts, and markdowns are expressed as a function of sales or unit prices—and so are markups. Fourth, competitive price data are readily available, whereas cost data are not. Markup pricing thus facilitates comparison with competition. Last, when all competitors use this method, prices tend to be similar. Thus price competition is minimized.

Figure 11-8: Nurseries and flower shops are especially profitable in early spring, when consumers are eager to get back to gardening.

Break-Even Analysis

Break-even analysis identifies the number of units the company needs to sell or the total number of dollars it needs to make on sales to break even with regard to costs, given a particular price. If the sales exceed the break-even quantity, the company earns a profit; if sales come short, the company has a loss. The break-even point can be calculated in terms of the number of units sold or in terms of sales dollars. Let us assume that an art book publisher is planning on publishing a catalog for a new contemporary art exhibition that will travel to numerous museum venues (see **Figure 11-9**). The publisher incurs the following costs and has the following desired profit goals:

Figure 11-9: Art books, especially exhibition catalogs, are often produced in small numbers at a loss. The city or state where the sponsoring museum is located may cover these costs.

Variable Cost $15 per book
Fixed Costs $130,000
Price of Each Book $70
Desired Profits $40,000

$$\text{Break-Even Point (number of units)} = \frac{\text{Fixed Costs}}{\text{Unit Price} - \text{Variable Costs per Unit}}$$

$$\text{Break-Even Point (number of units)} = \frac{\$130,000}{\$70 - \$15} = 2,364 \text{ books (units)}$$

$$\text{Break-Even Point (sales dollars)} = \frac{\text{Fixed Costs}}{1 - \dfrac{\text{Variable Costs per Unit}}{\text{Price}}}$$

$$\text{Break-Even Point (sales dollars)} = \frac{\$130,000}{1 - \dfrac{\$15}{\$70}} = \$165,456$$

The break-even point can also be calculated by taking into account the amount of profit targeted by the firm:

$$\text{Break-Even Point (number of units)} = \frac{\text{Fixed Costs} + \text{Desired Profit}}{\text{Unit Price} - \text{Variable Costs per Unit}}$$

$$\text{Break-Even Point (number of units)} = \frac{\$130,000 + \$40,000}{\$70 - \$15} = 3,091 \text{ books (units)}$$

$$\text{Break-Even Point (sale dollars)} = \frac{\text{Fixed Costs} + \text{Desired Profit}}{1 - \dfrac{\text{Variable Costs per Unit}}{\text{Price}}}$$

$$\text{Break-Even Point (sale dollars)} = \frac{\$130,000 + \$40,000}{1 - \dfrac{\$15}{\$70}} = \$216,365$$

Part Three: Marketing Mix Strategies

Break-even analysis is used by many types of businesses, including intermediaries at different levels of the channel of distribution. The company can create a break-even chart, which shows the total cost and total revenue expected at different sales volume levels.

Break-even analysis has many of the shortcomings of cost-based pricing: It does not take into consideration demand, and it assumes that customers will purchase at the given price, that no purchase discounts will need to be offered over time, and that costs can be fully assessed a priori.

Target Profit Pricing

Target profit pricing is used by capital-intensive firms, such as automobile manufacturers and public utilities, which must make a reasonable return on investment that is typically approved by the different regulatory commissions. The formula used to calculate target profit pricing takes into consideration a standard volume of production that the firm is expected to achieve. For most firms, that target is more than 90 percent of plant capacity. Assume that a motorcycle company has invested $120,000,000 for a new manufacturing plant with a 30 percent target return on investment (ROI). In its first year, its production was 70,000 units. Its average total costs for each motorcycle are $8,500 per motorcycle at a production level of 70,000 units.

Investment Cost	$120,000,000
Target ROI	30 percent
Standard Volume (number of units per year)	70,000
Average Cost per Unit	$8,500

To calculate the selling price for the motorcycle, the firm uses the following formula:

$$\text{Price} = \frac{\text{Investment Cost} \times (\text{Target ROI Percentage} + 1)}{\text{Standard Volume (units per year)}} + \text{Average Costs per Unit (at standard volume)}$$

$$\text{Price} = \frac{\$120,000,000 \times 1.30}{70,000} + \$8,500 = \$10,728.57 \text{ (selling price)}$$

Target profit pricing is likely to understate the selling price for firms with low capital investments. It also assumes a standard volume that may not be achievable by the firm or, if achieved, does not account for the possibility that there may not be enough demand for the units.

11-4b: Demand-Based Pricing

Demand-Based Pricing:
Pricing strategy that takes into consideration customers' perceptions of value, rather than the seller's cost, as the fundamental component of the pricing decision.

Price Ceiling:
The maximum amount that consumers are willing to pay for a product.

Demand-based pricing takes into consideration customers' perceptions of value, rather than the seller's cost, as the fundamental component of the pricing decision. As such, price is considered as part of the marketing mix before assessing the costs involved. Whereas cost-based pricing is product driven, demand-based pricing is consumer driven. For demand-based pricing, firms identify a **price ceiling**, which is the maximum amount that consumers are willing to pay for a product. The ceiling is contingent on the elasticity of demand, which itself is contingent on the availability of product substitutes and urgency of need. Demand estimates are much less precise than cost estimates because they are based on research of consumers' willingness to pay for the product at different price levels and on consumers' perceptions of product value. In highly competitive situations, firms need to lower prices, which, in turn, requires companies to keep costs low. When there is minimal competition, firms can afford to increase prices and obtain high profits from sales.

One type of demand-based pricing is **modified break-even analysis**, which combines break-even analysis with an evaluation of demand at various price levels. This approach assumes that, as the price increases, demand will decrease in an elastic demand environment, where there are many product substitutes and competition is intense. It should be noted, however, that demand estimates are not always going to be on the mark, so this approach, although taking into consideration likely demand, is not as precise as the cost-based, traditional break-even approach. Another approach is price discrimination, in which one higher-priced product is offered to inelastic segments, and lower prices are offered to elastic segments. Discrimination can be based on consumers' ability to pay, the product features, time or season, or place. These issues are further addressed in Section 11-5e on pricing segmentation.

> **Modified Break-Even Analysis:**
> Analysis that combines breakeven analysis with an evaluation of demand at various price levels, assuming that, as the price increases, demand will decrease in an elastic demand environment, where many product substitutes are available and competition is intense.

Key to demand-based pricing is the fact that today's consumers demand value—high-quality products at a fair price. Most consumers also want deals. They are no longer willing to pay high prices, and they refuse to pay the full retail price in general. Offering deals is expected. Fast food restaurants offering 99 cent items are popular with consumers.

The Wal-Mart everyday low price (EDLP) strategy is a clear winner and is adopted by companies that understand that consumers do not want to wait for a sale—they want deals on everything they buy, all the time (see **Figure 11-10**). Consumers have made it clear that they are willing to forgo service if that means being able to purchase quality products at lower prices—hence, the popularity of warehouse clubs.

Figure 11-10 This advertisement for Zeagler Music promotes the idea that the company's cymbals are priced using everyday low pricing.

Source: Sample print advertisement courtesy of The Miles Agency and Alliance One Advertising, Inc.

In its pure form, EDLP means the same low price every time a consumer shops in the store. This also means no price promotions; manufacturers, as a result, must rethink how they are going to attract consumers and maintain brand equity. EDLP also means everyday low cost (EDLC), which means retailers and suppliers have to work on identifying cost-saving initiatives. Nielsen cautions that the absence of promotions removes some of the excitement from the shopping experience, especially for "promotion junkies," that is, individuals who thrive on finding a bargain. Moreover, promotions are essential for impulse goods, such as snacks and soft drinks, to stimulate consumption. For these goods, it is possible that sales are not at their highest in an EDLP environment.

11-4c: Competition-Based Pricing

Many firms choose to use competitors' prices, instead of demand or product costs, to determine the prices of their products. This method is useful when firms compare themselves to companies with similar products that have similar demand patterns and costs. Competition-based pricing may mean that the firm prices its products at the

Price Leadership:
The tendency of one firm or a few firms to be the first to announce price changes, with the rest of the firms following.

Bid Pricing:
Pricing that involves competitive bidding for a contract, whereby a firm will price based on how it believes competitors will price, rather than based on demand or costs.

level of competition, above the prices of competition, or below the prices of competition. Pricing at the level of competition does not lead to competitive retaliation because it does not affect competitors. Pricing below competition, however, is likely to elicit some level of competitive response.

In an oligopoly, typically one firm, or a few firms, tend to be the first to announce price changes, and the rest of the firms follow. This is known as **price leadership**. These firms tend to be the market leaders with well-accepted leadership positions in the industry.

Another form of competition-based pricing is **bid pricing**, which involves competitive bidding for a contract, whereby a firm will price based on how it believes competitors will price, rather than based on demand or costs. The firm that bids lowest typically wins the contract. Most project development for U.S. development bodies, such as the U.S. Agency for International Development, and for international bodies, such as the World Bank and the United Nations Development Program, are contracted using competitive bidding. The federal, state, and local governments, as well as numerous other organizations, require competitive bidding, which gives each bidding company one single chance to make an offer.

11-4d Combination Pricing

Combination pricing is often used in practice. Firms might use cost-based pricing to establish the lowest acceptable price—the price floor—and then use demand and competition-based approaches when pricing their products for intermediaries or for the final consumer. For example, a manufacturing firm might determine the maximum price that consumers are willing to pay for its products—the price ceiling—and then work backward to the product cost to determine the target profit it should achieve.

11-5 STRATEGIC MARKETING APPLICATIONS

This section addresses price variability, pricing psychology, price discounting, and pricing in relation to the overall marketing strategy and the other elements of the marketing mix.

11-5a: Price Variability and Marketing Strategy

Consumers prefer and expect prices to be relatively stable for the most part. **Customary pricing,** whereby a firm sets prices and attempts to maintain them over time, is a strategy used to address this expectation (see **Figure 11-11**). One of the primary reasons for increasing prices is inflation. In this case, manufacturers are forced to pass price increases on to the final consumer. Another reason is excessive demand. In this situation, increasing prices to lower demand may work against the firm at some point, because consumers may move on to competitors who charge lower prices or to product substitutes. And, when the cost of ingredients increases, manufacturers prefer to alter product size or the product ingredients, rather than alter the price. Candy in the checkout aisle has relatively constant prices over time.

Certain products, however, are priced to change. Prices at gas stations change almost daily, in direct response to changes in crude oil costs or to changes in driving behavior— in the summer,

Figure 11-11: Beer prices have remained relatively constant over time.

the cost of gas goes up. Gas stations practice **variable pricing**, changing their prices in response to changes in cost or demand.

Flexible pricing is a strategy that allows a firm to set prices based on negotiation with the customer or based on customer buying power. For example, say a consumer haggles for everything from the price of a cake in a pastry shop that is about to close at the end of the day, to the price of a designer bracelet that stayed too long in a clothing store window, to the price of antiques in an exposed store on the eve of a hurricane. When purchasing a large quantity of goods or when purchasing expensive merchandise, that consumer is likely to garner substantial savings from negotiations.

No-haggle pricing is a strategy that is aimed at consumers who are averse to negotiation, but who want, nevertheless, to have some sort of low-price guarantee. In the automobile industry, where prices are traditionally set based on negotiations, Saturn was the first to advertise itself as haggle-free. Customers responded well to the no-haggle pricing approach because they did not have to focus an inordinate amount of time on price, rebates, coupons, and discounts, and as a result they were very loyal to their local dealer. In the automobile resale business, CarMax pioneered the concept of haggle-free secondhand automobile retailing, with great success. The primary appeal of no-haggle pricing is perceived fairness. A retailer might not have the lowest price every day, but if all consumers are paying the same fair price, then no one feels cheated. In general, about one-fourth of consumers love to deal, another one-fourth detest it, and half would rather not haggle but believe they must to get the best deal. And research shows that men are more willing to haggle than women. Research also shows that no-haggle pricing appeals to younger, better-educated consumers with above-average incomes.

11-5b: Pricing Psychology and Marketing Strategy

Psychological pricing refers to setting prices to create a particular psychological effect. One of the dimensions involved in psychological pricing is the **reference price**, the price that consumers carry in their mind for a particular product or brand. Reference prices can be created or influenced by previous purchase experiences, by advertising, or by the manufacturer's suggested retail price or list prices.

Price is often used as a signal for quality: Consumers tend to believe that higher prices are associated with better quality, especially in cases in which quality is difficult to evaluate (e.g., for unknown brand names). **Prestige pricing** is a strategy based on the premise that consumers will feel that products below a particular price will have inferior quality and will not convey a desired status and image. To support prestige pricing, retailers tend to use a psychological tool known as **even pricing** (setting selling prices at even numbers) to contrast with **odd pricing**, which sets prices at below even dollar values to give the impression that the product is not expensive. Upscale retailers, such as Saks Fifth Avenue and Neiman Marcus, use even pricing for most of their products. They use odd pricing only for those products they place on sale. Odd pricing is used to give the impression that consumers are getting a great value: A dishwashing machine that costs $995 is expensive, but it will not be perceived as expensive as one that is $1,000. Odd pricing typically has decimal prices that end in .99, .97, or .95—as in $999.99, $19.97, or $27.95 (see **Figure 11-12**). The odd pricing and even pricing strategies are not used in many markets. In Europe, even pricing is preferred because it facilitates calculations (see **Figure 11-13**), but, even there, these strategies, pioneered in the United States, are quickly becoming the norm.

11-5c: Price Discounting and Marketing Strategy

Price discounting involves reducing the price for purchasing larger quantities, for responding to a promotion, for paying cash, or responding earlier than a particular set time. There are a number of examples of discounts. One is the *quantity discount*. Both consumers and intermediaries typically get a price break when

Customary Pricing: Pricing strategy whereby a firm sets prices and attempts to maintain them over time.

Variable Pricing: Strategy of changing prices in response to changes in cost or demand.

Flexible Pricing: Pricing strategy that allows a firm to set prices based on negotiation with the customer, or based on customer buying power.

No-Haggle Pricing: Pricing strategy that is aimed at consumers who are averse to negotiation, but who want, nevertheless, to have some sort of low-price guarantee.

Psychological Pricing: Setting prices to create a particular psychological effect.

Reference Price: The price that consumers carry in their mind for a particular product or brand.

Prestige Pricing: Strategy based on the premise that consumers will feel that products below a particular price will have inferior quality and will not convey a desired status and image.

Even Pricing: Setting selling prices at even numbers.

Odd Pricing: Setting prices at below even dollar values.

Figure 11-12: Menu items are priced using odd pricing, with most prices ending in 99 cents.
Courtesy of Sting-Ray's.

Figure 11-13: Even pricing is preferred in Europe.

Price Discounting:
Strategy that involves reducing the price for purchasing larger quantities, responding to a promotion, paying cash, or responding earlier than a particular set time.

Multiple-Unit Pricing:
Pricing whereby consumers get a discount to purchase a larger quantity with the purpose, ultimately, to increase sales volume.

Promotional Pricing:
Strategy that reduces prices temporarily to increase sales in the short run.

Loss-Leader Pricing:
Pricing whereby the firm advertises a product at a price that is significantly less than its usual price to create traffic in the stores for consumers to purchase higher-margin products.

they purchase larger quantities of a particular product. Purchasing a mega-pack of Huggies diapers results in a per-unit price that is almost half of that paid for a small package. Purchasing a package of eight Bounty paper towel rolls is significantly cheaper than purchasing eight separate rolls of identical size. These are examples of **multiple-unit pricing**, whereby consumers get a discount to purchase a larger quantity with the purpose, ultimately, to increase sales volume. The goal of the firm is for consumers to respond to the price incentive by purchasing the product and then to increase consumption—use more paper towels for more household chores or change the baby more often.

Intermediaries can benefit from *trade discounts* for selling or storing the product, *seasonal discounts* for purchasing the product in the off-season, or *cash discounts*, such as a two percent reduction in price for paying within two weeks. Consumers can also benefit from seasonal discounts, such as by going to a resort in the off-season. Or they can qualify for a *trade-in allowance* for turning in their old product when they purchase a new one, such as a trade-in allowance an old automobile for a new one.

Another form of price discounting is **promotional pricing**, which reduces prices temporarily to increase sales in the short run (see **Figure 11-14**). Special event sales, cash rebates, low- or zero-interest financing, and free maintenance are all examples of promotional pricing strategies. One strategy that retailers use and that manufacturers find problematic if it involves their brand is **loss-leader pricing**, whereby the firm advertises a product at a price that is significantly less than its usual price. The goal is to create traffic in the stores for consumers to purchase higher-margin products. Eggs for 99 cents before Easter and turkeys for 59 cents a pound before Thanksgiving are typical loss leaders. The problem with loss-leader pricing, and with promotional pricing in general, is that it can hurt the brand in the long term. Consumers will expect to find the brand at the reduced price and will refuse to purchase it at its regular price. Also, if the product is available for a very low price, consumers may come to question its quality relative to the competitors' product.

11-5d: The Product and Pricing

With regard to the product component of the marketing mix, pricing can be used for numerous purposes. **Product line pricing** involves creating price differences between the different items in the product line, such that specific price points are used to differentiate between the items in the line. For instance, instead of selling products for one price, using one version of a product, the firm may select to identify different market segments and price products differently for the respective segments. Segmented pricing, in this case, adjusts prices to allow for differences in the products. Designers offer collection lines (Ralph Lauren, Anne Klein) at higher prices and the bridge lines (Polo, Anne Klein II) at lower prices. The differences between the prices of the different lines are easily observable—thus the price points are distinct. Ralph Lauren shirts retail for more than $98, whereas Polo shirts can be bought for less than $55. Anne Klein jackets cost at least $400, whereas Anne Klein II jackets retail for less than $400. As these examples illustrate, product line pricing is popular in the clothing industry, where designs are greatly differentiated (see **Figure 11-15**).

Figure 11-14: This store's promotional pricing strategy of "70 Percent Off List Price" is drawing many customers to their front counter.

With multiple product lines, companies can appeal to different market segments, increasing their profit opportunities. Problematic with product line pricing is the likelihood that markdowns taken on the higher-priced merchandise will blur the distinction between the different lines.

Figure 11-15 : Product line pricing Is common in the clothing industry, where designs like these are greatly differentiated.

Other product-related dimensions of pricing include **accessory pricing**, which addresses pricing of accessories and other optional products sold with the main product. Accessories for a bed set are neck pillows, decorative pillows, valances, and other products that have the same design and that would look lovely when used with the main product. **Captive-product pricing** involves pricing of products that must be used with the main product. Companies such as HP offer ink cartridges that must be used with its printers. Consumers tend to spend more on ink cartridges than they do for the printer itself. **By-product pricing** involves pricing of by-products that are of low value to get rid of them. Wood chips produced after shredding the wood of a felled tree can be treated with insecticide and used as mulch.

Bundling refers to the pricing of bundled products sold together. A company can sell a product, warranty, delivery, and installation together in one bundle. Bundling is used in the fast food industry with value meals and in the transportation indus-

> **Product Line Pricing:**
> Pricing that involves creating price differences between the different items in the product line, such that specific price points are used to differentiate among the items in the line.
>
> **Accessory Pricing:**
> Pricing of accessories and other optional products sold with the main product.
>
> **Captive-Product Pricing:**
> Pricing of products that must be used with the main product.
>
> **By-Product Pricing:**
> Pricing of by-products that are of low value to get rid of them.
>
> **Bundling:**
> Pricing of bundled products sold together.

try with vacation packages. The Queen Mary 2 transatlantic cruise includes return air, transportation to London from Southampton, and a week's stay in London, all for an amount that could be used to purchase a nice little car.

11-5e: The Place and Pricing

Distribution can increase product delivery costs and hence the cost of a product. **Geographic pricing** is defined as pricing that accounts for the geographic location of customers. Some IKEA merchandise is cheaper in Europe than in the United States; Levi's jeans are more expensive in Europe than in the United States. Similac, the baby formula manufactured by Abbott Laboratories, sells in Holland for a fraction of its cost in the United States. Geographic

> **Geographic Pricing:** Pricing that accounts for the geographic location of the customers.

pricing takes into consideration the cost of distribution, as well as other factors, such as taxes, competitors who benefit from government subsidies, and consumer demand.

In addition to geographic pricing, place, time, and seasons can be used in pricing segmentation. Seating behind home plate is more expensive than seating in the nosebleed section of the outfield in baseball stadiums. Daytime performances at the theater are cheaper than evening performances. Summer rates tend to be higher than off-season winter rates for beach resorts.

11-6 CHANGING THE PRICE

Companies often find that they have to make pricing changes to remain competitive. In inflationary times, they must pass along costs to consumers. When competition is intense and competitors are slashing prices, the company must go along with the price cuts to avoid losing customers. Cutting prices, however, is not always the solution: In addition to diminishing profit margins, such strategies might bring about price wars with competitors trying to hold on to their market share, crippling the entire industry.

Companies can use a number of methods to pass on increases in costs to the consumers. First, the company can communicate openly the reason for the price increase. Gas companies rely on the media to communicate this information. Because the media are perceived as unbiased, this type of communication is very valuable. The gas companies themselves do not need to justify the price increase to the consumer. Retailers can also communicate price increases to consumers. In times of shortage as a result of drought or other natural phenomena, retailers will communicate the reason behind the high prices of produce. Another method for increasing prices is to do so without the consumer immediately noticing: by eliminating price promotions, by adding more expensive items to the product line and eliminating cheaper ones, and by changing ingredients and lowering the quantity, without altering the package.

One important concern of the firm is the reaction of competitors to price changes. Usually, if more than one competitor follows suit in lowering the price, all the others will follow suit. If more than one competitor follows suit in raising the price, it is uncertain whether the others will do so, leaving the firm that initiated the price increase at a disadvantage, unless the firm repositions itself as a higher-quality prestige brand.

Summary

1. Define pricing and examine the external and internal influences on pricing decisions. Price is the amount of money necessary to purchase a good or service. Among external influences on price are consumers, who, according to the law of demand, purchase more products at a lower price than at a higher price. Economic factors, such as inflation, recession, and interest rates, also affect pricing decisions because they affect the cost of producing a product. An inflationary environment places strong pressures on companies to lower prices. Firms then find that they must decide between maintaining a competitive presence in a market and weathering the downside of the economic cycle or abandoning the market, which is a high-cost, high-risk proposition. The costs of materials, supplies, and labor are among the many costs that are not within a firm's control. Intermediaries also affect product prices, as does competition. In a competitive environment where there is pure competition, the effect is not as great as in an oligopolistic environment. Yet another external influence on the firm is exerted by the government, which takes action against unfair pricing practices, such as price discrimination, resale price maintenance, price fixing, and various deceptive pricing practices. Deceptive practices include predatory pricing, which involves charging prices below cost to eliminate competitors (dumping to get rid of excess inventory is an example of predatory pricing); bait-and-switch tactics, which involve advertising items at a low price, telling customers they are out of stock, and then trying to sell them a higher-priced item; and price confusion, which is a strategy used to confuse consumers with regard to the actual price. Among internal factors influencing pricing are firm size and costs, such as fixed and variable costs, which are important determinants of price.

2. Examine the different price objectives: sales-based, profit-maximization, product-quality leadership, and status quo. Sales-based pricing objectives focus on increasing the sales volume. One way a company can increase sales is through penetration pricing, selling the product for a low price in order to gain market share. Profit-based objectives focus on the total return on investment. With this strategy, a company introducing a new product can use a skimming strategy, pricing the product high to recoup investments quickly in the early stages of the life cycle. Product-quality leadership pricing objectives establish prices based on the performance and image of the product. Status quo objectives focus on maintaining a good relationship with customers, channel members, and regulatory bodies. This strategy cannot be maintained for long, but it is useful, especially if the company is under scrutiny from the government or competition. Companies may elect to have more than one objective.

3. Address the pricing strategies: cost-based, demand-based, competition-based, and combination pricing. For cost-based pricing, a firm sets the price by calculating merchandise, service, and overhead costs and then adding an amount needed to cover the profit goal. Cost-based pricing is easy to calculate because it does not take into consideration the price elasticity of demand or the reaction of competitors to price changes. The cost-based pricing techniques are cost-plus, markup, target, price-floor, and traditional break-even analysis. Demand-based pricing takes consumers' perceptions into account and their potential response to the product at different price levels. With demand-based pricing, firms identify a price ceiling, which is the maximum amount that consumers are willing to pay for a product. This amount is contingent on the elasticity of demand, which itself is contingent on the availability of product substitutes and urgency of need. Demand estimates are less precise than cost estimates because they are based on consumers' willingness to pay for the product at different prices and on consumers' perceptions of value. In competitive situations, firms need to lower prices and thus need to keep costs low. When there is minimal competition, firms can increase prices and obtain high profits. Many firms use competitors' prices, instead of demand or product costs, to determine the prices of their products. This approach is useful when firms compare themselves to similar companies with similar products that have similar demand patterns and similar costs. Pricing at the level of competition does not lead to competitive retaliation because it does not affect competitors. Pricing below competition, however, is likely to elicit some level of competitive response. Companies can also use combination pricing or a combination of these strategies.

4. Address strategic marketing applications in relation to pricing, such as price variability, price psychology, price discounting, and pricing in relation to the marketing mix. With regard to price variability, companies can use customary pricing, keeping the same price over time. They can also use variable pricing, changing their prices in response to changes in cost or demand, and flexible pricing, which allows a firm to set prices based on negotiation with the customer, or based on customer buying power. Psychological pricing refers to setting prices to create a particular psychological effect. Price is often used as a signal for quality; as such, prestige pricing is a strategy based on the premise that consumers will feel that products below a particular price will have inferior quality and will not convey a desired status and image. To support prestige pricing, retailers use even pricing, setting selling prices at even numbers, to contrast with odd pricing, which sets prices at below even-dollar values to give the impression that the product is not expensive. Price discounting involves reducing the price for purchasing larger quantities, for responding to a promotion, for paying cash, or responding earlier than a particular set time. The goal in price discounting is for consumers to respond to the price incentive by purchasing the product, and then to increase consumption in the long term. Intermediaries can benefit from trade discounts, seasonal discounts for purchasing the product in the off-season, or cash discounts for paying within a specified period. Consumers can also benefit from seasonal discounts, or they can qualify for a trade-in allowance for turning in their old product when they purchase a new one. Promotional pricing reduces prices temporarily to increase sales in the short run; loss-leader pricing, whereby the firm advertises a product at a price that is significantly less than its usual price to create traffic in the stores for consumers to purchase higher-margin products, may pose problems to the brand in the long term.

With regard to the marketing mix, product dimensions of pricing are accessory pricing, which addresses pricing of accessories and other optional products sold with the main product; captive-product pricing, which involves pricing of products that must be used with the main product; by-product pricing, which involves pricing of by-products that are of low value to get rid of them; and bundling, which refers to pricing of bundled products sold together. Place dimensions are geographic pricing, defined as pricing that accounts for the geographic location of customers, and place, time, and season pricing segmentation.

5. Address strategies that companies use to change prices. Companies often find that they have to make pricing changes to remain competitive. In inflationary times, firms must pass along costs to consumers. When competition is intense and competitors are slashing prices, the company must go along with the price cuts to avoid losing customers. Companies can use a number of methods to pass increases in costs on to the consumers. First, the company can communicate openly the reason for the price increase. Retailers and manufacturers can also communicate price increases to consumers. In times of shortage as a result of drought or other natural phenomena, retailers will communicate the reason behind the high prices of produce. Another method for increasing prices is to do so without the consumer immediately noticing: by eliminating price promotions; by adding more expensive items to the product line and eliminating cheaper ones; and by changing ingredients and lowering the quantity, without altering the package.

Key Terms

accessory pricing	geographic pricing	price elasticity
bid pricing	law of demand	price fixing
bait and switch	loss-leader pricing	price floor
bundling	modified break-even analysis	price leadership
by-product pricing	monopolistic competition	product line pricing
captive-product pricing	multiple-unit pricing	promotional pricing
cost-based pricing	no-haggle pricing	psychological pricing
customary pricing	odd pricing	pure competition
customer profit	oligopolistic competition	pure monopoly
customer profit potential	penetration pricing	reference price
deceptive pricing	predatory pricing	resale price maintenance
demand-based pricing	prestige pricing	retention
demand curve	price	skimming
dumping	price ceiling	unit pricing
even pricing	price confusion	variable costs
fixed costs	price discounting	variable pricing
flexible pricing	price discrimination	

Discussion Questions

1. Demand for certain products is price inelastic. Identify three goods or services that you would purchase at practically any price. Would most consumers consider your choices to be inelastic? Why or why not?

2. Demand for most products is price elastic. Identify three products that you would purchase in a greater quantity or more frequently if the price were lower. Would most consumers purchase more of those same products. Why or why not?

3. On a continuum where pure monopoly is at one end and pure competition is at the other, where would you place automobiles? Airlines? Telephone companies? Clothing manufacturers? Beer manufacturers? Explain.

4. When Wawa gas stations were first introduced to the market, they had the cheapest gasoline of all competitors. Wawa also had the highest quality sandwich wraps for sale, better than those of most restaurants, at about the same price. What pricing strategy did Wawa use to introduce its gasoline business? What strategy did it use to introduce its wraps? Justify your answers.

5. Recall a recent shopping experiences. What product accessories have you bought? How were they priced relative to the main product? What captive products have you bought? Have you ever bought by-products?

6. Access the website of Ray-Ban sunglasses at www.ray-ban.com. Which pricing objective do you believe Ray-Ban is using? Why? What types of psychological pricing strategy would you advise the company to use for its products?

7. A retired person has decided to make bird houses for some extra income. Use the following information to calculate the selling price using the cost-plus pricing method.

> Variable costs per bird house: $14.00
>
> Fixed costs: $170.00
>
> Number of bird houses being built: 40
>
> Desired profit: $500.00

8. A retired person has decided to make bird houses for some extra income. Use the following information to calculate the selling price using the markup pricing method.

> Variable costs per bird house: $14.00
>
> Fixed costs: $170.00
>
> Number of bird houses being build: 80
>
> Desired profit: $1.000.00

9. A retail store pays $6.65 for a bag of horse feed. The store wants to mark it up 30%. Using the markup pricing method, calculate the selling price.

10. A manufacturer of television is planning to spend $300,000 on an advertising campaign. The television costs $120.00 to build and sells for $160.00. How many television sets must the manufacturer sell to breakeven on the advertising campaign?

11. Refer to the information in Question 10. Suppose the manufacturer wants to earn $200,000 in profit with the advertising campaign. How many televisions must the manufacturer sell to breakeven on the advertising campaign including the $200,000 desired profit margin?

12. The cost of building a theme park is $8 million. The company wants to earn a 20% return on investment. The company estimates 400,000 people will visit the theme park during the year and that variable costs per visit will be $25.00. Using the target pricing method calculate the price the theme park will need to charge for each visitor.

13. Access each of the following websites. For each site discuss the level of price elasticity you believe is present for that product, the factors that most influence prices, type of competitive market (pure competition, etc.), price objective being used, and any price discounts that you observe. For each be sure to justify or explain your rationale.

> a. Taco Bell (www.tacobell.com)
>
> b. Guess (www.Guess.com)
>
> c. John Deere (www.deere.com)

Review Questions

(Answers are on Last Page of the Chapter)

True or False

1. According to the law of supply and demand, consumers purchase fewer products at a lower price than at a higher price.

2. The demand curve portrays the number of units bought for a particular price in a given time period.

3. Monopolistic competition characterizes a market that consists of many buyers and sellers, where no buyer or seller can control price or the market.

4. Legislation such as the Robinson-Patman Act prohibits charging different prices to different buyers of the same merchandise and requires sellers that offer a service to one buyer to make the same service available to all buyers.

5. Predatory pricing and dumping are examples of price fixing.

6. In pricing their products, companies need to take into consideration all product costs to obtain a fair rate of return on investment.

7. Skimming involves firms initially pricing the product below the price of competitors to quickly penetrate the market at competitors' expense and acquire a large market share, and then gradually raise the price.

8. In cost-based pricing, the firm sets the price by calculating merchandise, service, and overhead costs and then adds an amount needed to cover the profit goal.

9. Cost-plus pricing is a variant of cost-based pricing, with a markup used to cover selling costs and profits.

Multiple Choice

10. A market that consists of few sellers who dominate the market is a(n)

     a. pure monopoly.

     b. monopolistic competition.

     c. oligopoly.

     d. monopoly.

11. A market that consists of many buyers and sellers and products that vary greatly in the same product category is a(n)

     a. pure monopoly.

     b. monopolistic competition.

     c. oligopoly.

     d. monopoly.

12. Manufacturers are prohibited from requiring retailers to charge a particular price for a product; they are thus prohibited from

     a. price discrimination.

     b. price fixing.

     c. resale price maintenance.

     d. engaging in odd pricing.

13. The price that consumers carry in their mind for a particular product or brand is known as

     a. referent pricing.

     b. reference pricing.

     c. referral pricing.

     d. none of the above.

14. Which of the following is an example of prestige pricing?

     a. Odd pricing

     b. Even pricing

     c. Cost-plus pricing

     d. All of the above

15. A strategy whereby the firm advertises a product at a price that is significantly less than its usual price to create traffic in the stores for consumers to purchase higher-margin products is known as

    a. loss-leader pricing.

    b. reference pricing.

    c. odd pricing.

Blog

Clow-Lascu: *Marketing Essentials 5e Blog*

What Is Happening Today?

Learn More! For videos and articles that relate to Chapter 11:

blogclowlascu.net/category/chapter11

Includes Discussion Questions with each Post!

Notes

1. http://www.nytimes.com/2002/12/26/business/one-word-shoppers-lexicon-price.html
2. Virginia Citrano, ''The Right Price,'' CFO 8, no. 5 (May 1992): 71–72.
3. Macki Sissoko, ''Cigarette Consumption in Different U.S. States, 1955–1998: An Empirical Analysis of the Potential Use of Excise Taxation to Reduce Smoking,'' Journal of Consumer Policy 25, no. 1 (March 2002): 89–107.
4. Ravi Dhar and Rashi Glazer, ''Hedging Customers,'' Harvard Business Review 81, no. 5 (May 2003): 86–92.
5. Ben Lieberman, ''Why Chicagoans Are Paying More for Gas at the Pump,'' Chicago Sun-Times (February 17, 2003): 53.
6. ''Finance and Economics: Europe's Burden,'' The Economist 351, no. 8120 (May 22, 1999): 84.
7. ''Finance and Economics: Europe's Burden,'' The Economist 351, no. 8120 (May 22, 1999): 84.
8. http://asiapacific.acnielsen.com/pubs/index.shtml, accessed on May 4, 2007.
9. Kim Korth and Erich Merkle, ''The Resurrection of Saturn,'' Automobile Design & Production 119, no. 3 (March 2007): 16–17.

Cases

Case 11-1 Competitive Pricing Strategies: The Airlines Industry

Jeremy Jones is the travel consultant for a large East Coast corporation. His firm was hired to handle travel arrangements for all the corporation's employees, and his primary task was to ensure the lowest cost for the company. Jones had several options. One possibility was to contract with a low-cost airline and receive a minimal volume discount; the airlines did not have sufficiently high margins to allow for a substantial discount to any large client. Another possibility involved working with a major airline serving the East Coast. In this regard, U.S. Airways appears to be a good candidate because, in many respects, its pricing strategy is similar to that of East Coast discounters. However, U.S. Airways was in the same predicament with the discounters. It could not afford to offer a large discount on East

Coast travel; yet, the company could offer substantially reduced deals for transatlantic travel. With any of the airlines, an agreement would mean that the airline would work on the itinerary, identifying the lowest fare for the respective route, and bill Jones' firm. Jones solicited a bid from each airline, and U.S. Airways offered a five percent reduction on transatlantic and continental U.S. routes, with the exception of East Coast travel.

Yet another possibility was to use one of the popular search engines to find the lowest price. This would be the most labor-intensive activity because his consultancy would be responsible for identifying the best fare for the corporate client, rather than the airline. It would also be a negative because the travelers would not be able to earn miles on their travel. But this option is clearly the lowest-cost alternative for his client.

Jeremy reviewed the airlines' pricing strategies for the East Coast. Ticket prices range from $305 to $514 for advance purchases. Last minute ticket prices were typically above $1,000. There appeared to be very little variance among the airlines that served the East Coast, such as JetBlue Airways, Southwest Airlines, and U.S. Airways. Carriers have been slow to increase prices to avoid a sensitive issue for the airlines. American Airlines was unsuccessfully accused by the U.S. Justice Department of predatory pricing after it matched prices of new discounters, flooded markets with additional flights, and raised prices after the discounters folded or retreated. The case was eventually dismissed, but the issue fuels airlines' restraint.

U.S. Airways was clearly a possibility for Jones. On the other hand, using popular search engines could identify better deals than a special deal with U.S. Airways; on the other hand, it would be much more work for Jeremy Jones. Looking at one such search engine, www.airfarewatchdog.com, Jones noted that discount airlines indeed offered the best deal in the continental United States, where his corporate client traveled the most. For example, when he searched the Web site, he found that Southwest Airlines offered for that particular month a system-wide sale for travel on Tuesdays and Wednesdays, with fares ranging from $99 to $119 one way, with no round-trip purchase required.

Jones had the information provided by the airlines, and his finding from search engines such as www.airfarewatchdog.com, www.orbitz.com, and kayak.com. He had a week to prepare a proposal for his corporate client.

Questions

1. Describe the nature of competition in the airlines industry. Describe the nature of information about available services and corresponding pricing strategies in this industry.

2. What are the pricing strategies used by the low-budget airlines? Are their strategies sustainable?

3. Describe the U.S. Airways pricing strategies. How do they position the airlines relative to their direct competitors, American Airlines, and United Airlines?

4. Advise Jeremy on the proposal that he has to present to his corporate client.

Source: Ann Keeton, ''Earnings Digest: US Airways, JetBlue Return to Profitability,'' *Wall Street Journal* (January 31, 2007): C10; Scott McCartney, ''The Middle Seat: Rivals Show Restraint After Independence Fails,'' *Wall Street Journal* (January 17, 2006): D4; www.airfarewatchdog.com, accessed on August 9, 2014.

Case 11-2 The Business Side of Exhibition Catalogs

Karen James, a talented curator and art businesswoman with noteworthy art exhibitions on her resume, is in the process of planning a traveling exhibition of German expressionist painters throughout the United States. She has received commitments, pending adequate insurance, for a number of paintings. To date, Karen has received financial support commitments from two nonprofit foundations—the Goethe Institute and the Institut für Auslandsbeziehungen— to underwrite the cost of transportation of the art pieces from different museums and private lenders to the museums where the art will be exhibited. She is still working with museums to ensure their commitment. She has been able to secure only a handful of venues for the exhibit: a mid-sized museum in central Virginia (with a reasonable contemporary art collection, but with only a small gallery of expressionist paintings), and a small museum in New York City specializing in German expressionist art. She has also been able to persuade one other museum in the Midwest to host the exhibition. Furthermore, Karen needs to cover two additional costs. One is the cost of the exhibition catalog, which she will author. She will have 4,000 copies printed and delivered at a cost of $30 each. Her total cost for the catalog will be $120,000. Another is the cost of insurance. This latter cost is likely to present the most problems. According to Lisa Dennison, a deputy director of the Solomon R. Guggenheim Museum in New York and its chief curator, ''the rising value of art, coupled with the escalating cost of insurance premiums are making these . . . shows prohibitive. . . .This, along with falling attendance, has been one of the most serious repercussions of September 11.'' The art lost in and around the World Trade Center, about $10 million worth of pieces by Calder, Miro, and Lichtenstein, may constitute just a fraction of what could be lost in another massive attack. Collectors also fear for their art, and some insist that museums obtain extra insurance before they agree to lend their art. More recently, artists and collectors have demanded additional earthquake insurance, which museums and galleries rarely carry because it is prohibitively expensive.

Karen's total insurance bill will be a high $18,000 ($13,000 for the New York museum and $5,000 for the other two museums). Her personal additional expenses are $27,000. She has negotiated to receive $62,000 from the three museums, regardless of exhibit attendance. Now she must decide the price that she should charge the museums for the catalogs.

Questions

1. If Karen's fixed expenses are $120,000 for the catalog, $18,000 for insurance, and $27,000 for personal expenses, how much must she charge the museums for the catalog to break even?

2. If Karen wanted to make a total of $100,000—which includes the $62,000 that she was able to negotiate with the museum—how much would she have to charge the museum for the catalogs?

3. What are some of the shortcomings of the method you used to calculate the prices of the catalogs in questions 1 and 2?

4. From Section 11-4, discuss each of the major methods of pricing as it would relate to Karen's pricing of the catalog. Which method should she use? Why?

Sources: Daniel Grant, "Artists: Is Your Work Insured in Your Gallery?," Huffington Post (May 22, 2012), accessed at http://www.huffingtonpost.com/daniel-grant/artists-is-your-work-insu_b_1535342.html; Carol Vogel, "Fear of Terror a Complication for Art Exhibits," *New York Times* (February 25, 2003): A1, A20.

Answers to Review Questions

Marketing

Communications

Chapter 12

Integrated Marketing Communications

Learning Objectives

After studying this chapter, you should be able to:

1. Discuss the concept of integrated marketing communications.

2. Identify the various marketing communication elements.

3. Identify the elements of communication and the importance of AIDA.

4. Discuss the various factors that affect the relative mix of communication elements in an integrated marketing communications plan.

5. Identify the various types of advertising.

6. Describe the appeals that can be used in designing an advertisement.

7. Differentiate between the three types of message strategies.

8. Discuss the advantages and disadvantages of the primary media.

12-1 CHAPTER OVERVIEW

In most purchases, whether a cup of coffee or a high-priced car, emotions are critical part of the decision. Brand loyalty is built on emotions, not facts! Consumers like ads that make them laugh, make them smile, make them feel good. Thus, the popularity of the AT&T "It's Not Complicated" campaign with kids. The Super Bowl ads with horses, puppies, and other animals touch a heart string. Advertising and marketing communications are an integral part of creating those emotions that lead to positive brand feelings.

The fourth component of the four Ps of marketing is **promotion**. Promotion refers to all forms of external communications directed toward consumers and businesses with an ultimate goal of developing customers. In recent years, marketers have been pushing to integrate all forms of promotion, or communication, to ensure that the company speaks with one voice. Section 12-2 presents the concept of integrated marketing communications (IMC), as well as the principal channels of an IMC program (Section 12-3). Marketing communications are based on an understanding of the communication process, which is discussed in Section 12-4.

For an effective IMC plan, a firm must decide which elements of communication it needs to use to communicate effectively with customers. The relative mix of promotional elements will vary depending on the objectives that the firm would like to achieve and the budget that has been allocated for marketing. Section 12-5 discusses the communication mix and the elements that influence how the marketing package is developed.

Advertising is an important component of integrated marketing communications (IMC) and is presented in Section 12.6 and Section 12-7. The last section of the chapter (Section 12-8) discusses the media selection process and the advantages and disadvantages of the primary media.

12-2 INTEGRATED MARKETING COMMUNICATIONS

Although some marketing experts would argue that the integrated marketing communications (IMC) approach is a recent phenomenon, others would argue that it has been around for a long time. The latter view is supported by marketing articles, which for years have promoted the idea of coordinating all of the marketing functions and activities. However, although the concept may have been discussed in marketing articles, few companies practiced IMC until the beginning of the 21st century. Integrated marketing communications has now become the key term and key guiding principle in developing marketing communications. What is **integrated marketing communications (IMC)**? It is the coordination and integration of all marketing communication tools, avenues, and sources within a company into a seamless program designed to maximize the communication impact on consumers, businesses, and other constituencies of an organization.

When Wieden+Kennedy took over the Old Spice account, the agency developed an integrated television, print, and online campaign with the theme "Experience is everything." It was a cheeky look at modern masculinity designed to stimulate sales of specific products such as deodorants, body washes, and fragrances. In all three media, the goal was to recreate the Old Spice brand as an authentic brand and one that would also be trendy to use.[1]

For decades Maxwell House coffee was ranked as the top-selling coffee in America. In recent years, sales have slumped and Maxwell House fell to second place behind J.M. Smucker's Folgers brand. It was time for a brand makeover. Kraft, parent company for Maxwell House, budgeted $25 million for the campaign and hired seven advertising agencies to carry out the work. The lead agency, Wieden+Kennedy, introduced the makeover with the new tagline "Say good morning to a good day." The campaign featured broadcast ads, a digital media component, a strong presence in social media, a new logo, packaging and flavors. By integrating all of these messages and using multiple media, Wieden+Kennedy increased the chances that the consumer would be exposed to one of the new advertisements. Integrating all of these forms of communication resulted in a greater impact than using a different message in each medium or broadcasting messages at different times. This process of marketing of a product through two or more channels is known as **multichannel marketing.**

Customers, both individuals and businesses, are better informed, more price conscious, and more demanding of quality, service, convenience, and speed than in the past. Reaching these potential customers requires a consistent marketing message at every customer contact point. IMC is a holistic approach that involves everyone in the company articulating the same message. For this integration to work, it must occur at three levels. First, there must be open communication vertically within the company, from the employees who interact with customers and perform the day-by-day work to the chief executive officer (CEO). Second, there must be horizontal communication, across functional areas and departments. Third, there must be communication to customers and stakeholders who have an interest in the company (see **Figure 12-1**).

12-3 *COMMUNICATION CHANNELS*

An organization has many potential venues of communication. Traditionally, the promotional mix included advertising, sales promotion, trade promotion, personal selling, and public relations. With an integrated approach, other components of communication have also become important, such as digital marketing, direct response marketing, and social media. Viable venues for communication are traditional media (radio, television, newspapers, and magazines), as well as the Internet, billboards, transit signs, store signage, and company stationery.

Practically every organization uses some type of **advertising** to promote its products. Advertising is any form of paid communication directed to an organization's customers or other stakeholders. Outlets for advertising include the traditional media, such as radio, television, magazines, newspapers, and billboards (see **Figure 12-2**), as well as the Internet and social media. Advertising has a major advantage: It is able to reach a large number of people with a single message. Although cost may be high (as much as $4 million for a 30-second Super Bowl TV spot), the relative cost per person reached is very low. Although a direct-mail piece to

> **Promotion:**
> All forms of external communications directed toward consumers and businesses with an ultimate goal of developing customers.
>
> **Integrated Marketing Communications (IMC):**
> The coordination and integration of all marketing communication tools, avenues, and sources within a company into a seamless program designed to maximize the communication impact on consumers, businesses, and other constituencies of an organization.
>
> **Multichannel Marketing:**
> The marketing of a product through two or more channels.

Figure 12-1: Coyote Wild's message that it is the source for "fine home interior furnishings, accents and gifts" must be communicated to employees and stakeholders, as well as customers.

Source: Sample print advertisement courtesy of The Miles Agency and Alliance One Advertising, Inc.

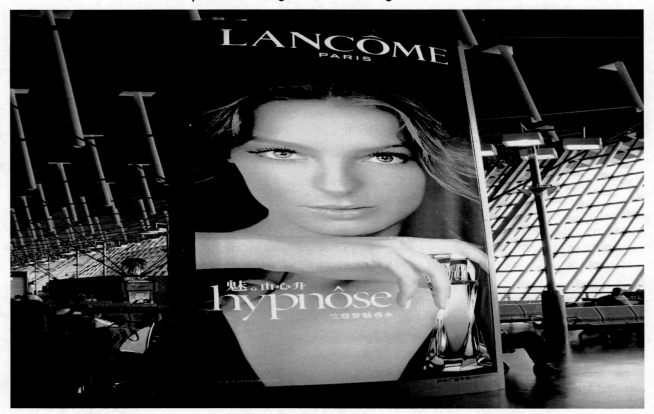

Figure 12-2: Advertising at major airports in high-traffic areas is a cost-effective method to reach target consumers.

consumers may cost as much as $2 per person, a television advertisement that costs $250,000 but reaches 2.5 million people costs only ten cents per person.

Whereas advertising is aimed primarily at customers, **public relations** is aimed at the general public and stakeholders of an organization. Public relations (PR) addresses issues faced by an organization and represents the organization to the public, media, and various stakeholders. The PR department normally handles any event that occurs that has a direct or indirect impact on the public or stakeholders. If an accident occurs at a factory, the PR department will deal with the media and provide information to the public. If a new product is introduced, it is the responsibility of the PR department to send out a news release. If the quarterly earnings are above or below the projection, it is the PR department that deals with Wall Street and other investors.

Publicity is usually an outcome of public relations that is produced by the news media and is not paid for or sponsored by the business involved. A newspaper article about Enron, Coca-Cola, Gap, or any other organization would be publicity. The company has no control over what is being said. It is the responsibility of the PR department to monitor the media and the environment that surrounds a firm—especially the macro-environment—for events that may affect the organization. Businesses should monitor articles that are written about the firm. Rather than react to events, it is better if a business is prepared for them and can act proactively. If a strike in South America is going to interrupt the supply of coffee to Starbucks, the PR department can alert Starbucks's management so another source of coffee beans can be contacted or an alternative plan can be developed. If an article is going to appear in the *Wall Street Journal* about the labor practices of a company, then the firm can be better prepared to counter possible misconceptions.

To stimulate sales, companies will often use either sales promotions or trade promotions or both. **Sales promotions** (often called consumer promotions)

Advertising:
Any form of paid communication directed to an organization's customers or other stakeholders.

Public Relations (PR):
A communication venue that addresses issues an organization faces and represents the organization to the public, media, and various stakeholders.

Publicity:
A form of public relations produced by the news media but not paid for or sponsored by the business concern.

are incentives used to encourage end users to purchase a product. **Trade promotions** are incentives directed toward channel members to encourage them to purchase, stock, or push a product through the channel. Both are short-term tactics used by firms to stimulate sales, demand, or inquiries. Sales promotions include offers such as coupons, premiums, sweepstakes, and contests. Most sales or consumer promotions offer some type of price incentive or additional gift or merchandise to encourage consumers to make a purchase. Coupons offering $1.00 off a bottle of shampoo or 50 cents off a box of cereal are found in almost every Sunday newspaper across the United States. According to Watts NCH Promotional Services, marketers distributed 323 billion coupons during a recent year, with approximately 3.1 billion, 1.07 percent, being redeemed. Of all coupons distributed, food products account for 43 percent and nonfood products account for 57 percent. The three largest categories of coupons are for food and personal care products, pet foods and treats, and household cleaning supplies. The average face value of these coupons is now $1.16 (see **Figure 12-3**).[2]

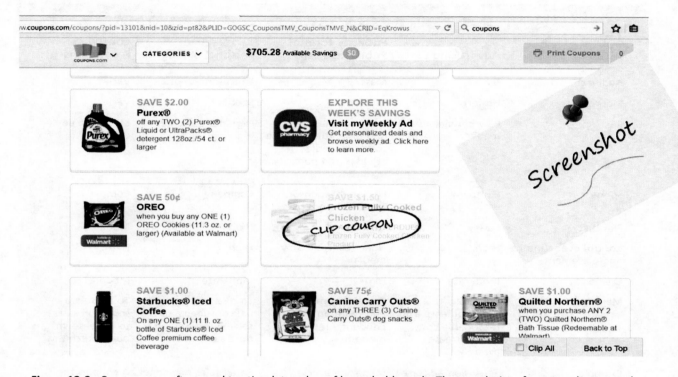

Figure 12-3: Coupons are often used to stimulate sales of household goods. The popularity of coupons has moved from printed media to the Web, including dedicated sites to coupon circulation like **www.coupons.com**.

Trade promotions involve channel members. Similar to consumer promotions, trade promotions are designed to encourage immediate activity. It may be a discount or price-off offer if a retailer will purchase a certain number of cases of cereal by the end of the month. It can be an offer for a free case of motor oil if the retailer will purchase 2,000 cases within the following 30 days. It may be a commitment to pay 75 percent of the cost of a retailer's advertisement in a newspaper if the manufacturer's product is prominently featured. Because of intense competition among manufacturers for retail shelf space, trade promotions have become extremely important in the marketing of products. Manufacturers spend about 14 percent of their total sales on trade promotions. For food manufacturers, this percentage is higher (16 percent). The amount spent on trade promotions has increased dramatically, from $8 billion in 1980 to more than $85 billion today.[3]

Personal selling is an important component of marketing, especially for companies that sell to other businesses, the government, or institutions. It is also important for consumer products, such as real es-

> **Sales Promotions:**
> Incentives to encourage end users or consumers to purchase a product.
>
> **Trade Promotions:**
> Incentives directed toward channel members to encourage them to purchase, stock, or push a product through the channel.

tate, insurance, and high-ticket items like automobiles and furniture. **Personal selling** is a direct communication approach between the buyer and seller with the express purpose of selling a product. In most cases, personal selling takes place between two individuals, but it can also take place between teams of individuals. With large corporate purchases, it is not unusual for the selling organization to use a team approach in selling its products. Even with consumer sales, teams may be used, but it is usually with the buyer, in the form of a couple or family. Home and automobile purchases are normally joint decisions, and vacations may involve the entire family.

Table 12-1 contrasts advertising, the publicity component of PR, personal selling, and sales promotion on factors such as audience, message, cost, sponsor, flexibility, control over the content and placement of the message, credibility, and major goal. An example is also given of each type of promotion as it would relate to a Sony CD player.

Table 12-1: Characteristics of Major Forms of Marketing Communication

Factor	Advertising	Publicity form of Public Relations*	Personal Selling	Consumer Promotions
Audience	Mass	Mass	Small (one-to-one)	Varies
Message	Uniform	Uniform	Specific	Varies
Cost	Low per viewer or reader	None for media space and time; can be some costs for media releases and publicity materials	High per customer	Moderate per customer
Sponsor	Company	No formal sponsor (media are not paid)	Company	Company
Flexibility	Low	Low	High	Moderate
Control over content and placement	High	None (controlled by media)	High	High
Credibility	Moderate	High	Moderate	Moderate
Major goal	To appeal to a mass audience at a reasonable cost, and to create awareness	To reach a mass audience with an independently reported message	To deal with individual consumers, to resolve questions, to close sales	To stimulate short-run sales, to increase impulse purchases
Example	Television ad for a Sony CD player for use in cars	Magazine article describing the unique features of a Sony CD player for use in cars	Retail sales personnel explaining how a Sony CD player for cars works	A coupon for $15 off a Sony CD player

* When PR embodies advertising (an image-related message), personal selling or sales promotion, it takes on the characteristics of those promotional types. However, the goal would be more image-related than sales related.

Personal Selling: A direct communication approach between the buyer and seller with the express purpose of selling a product.

Database Marketing: The collection, analysis, and use of large volumes of customer data to develop marketing programs and customer profiles.

Direct Response Marketing: The promotion of a product directly from the manufacturer or seller to the buyer without any intermediaries involved in the transaction.

Computer technology has facilitated the development of customer databases, which can be used for database marketing programs and direct marketing programs. **Database marketing** refers to the collection, analysis, and use of large volumes of customer data to develop marketing programs and customer profiles. **Direct response marketing** is the promotion of a product directly from the manufacturer or producer to the buyer without any intermediaries involved in the transaction. Because of the development of computerized customer databases, most direct marketing today uses the information stored in company or commercial databases. Both approaches have gained prominence with the increased use of computer technology.

The rise of computer technology has also given birth to **Internet or digital marketing**, which is the promotion of products through the Internet. According to the U.S. Census Bureau, approximately 75% of Americans have access to the Internet at home or have a smartphone with Internet access. As shown in Figure 12.4, overall Internet usage decreases with age, with 87.5% of Americans under 25 having Internet at home, have a Smartphone, or have both. That number falls to 58.4% for individuals 55 and older. The largest decrease is in the use of Smartphones going from 67% for individuals 34 and under to 23.3% for individuals 55 and older. Because of the impact the Internet currently has on marketing and the tremendous impact it could have in the future, all of Chapter 13 is devoted to this topic (see **Figure 12-4**).

> **Internet or Digital Marketing:** The promotion of products through the Internet.

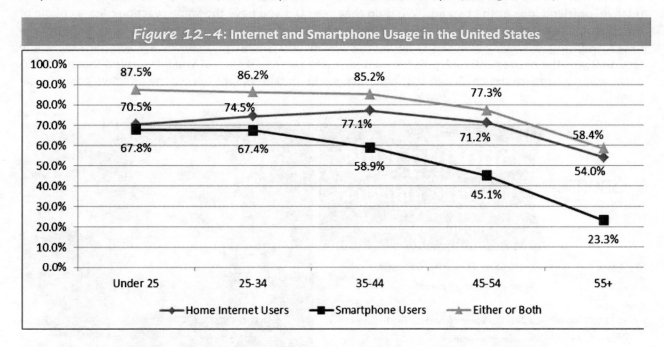

Figure 12-4: Internet and Smartphone Usage in the United States

Source: Adapted from "Computer and Internet Use in the United States", United States Census Bureau, www.census.gov, accessed August 8, 2014.

In recent years, social media has become an important element of marketing communication plans. Social media allows brands to communicate with customers in real time. This instant communication creates the potential to generate buzz and excitement for a brand. More sophisticated interactions with customers can be readily achieved through blogs, websites and social media advertising. At the same time, negative word of mouth and other developments that can quickly damage a brand can be addressed in a tactful manner that reduces any potential harm. Social media is no longer an option for marketing communications. Brands and businesses must develop social media marketing plans or be left behind by competitors.

Part Four: Marketing Communications

12-4 *THE COMMUNICATION PROCESS*

The key to successful marketing is communication. Someone must send a message, and someone must hear and understand the message. The challenge is developing a message that will get the attention of consumers or businesses and that will then move the recipient to respond in the desired manner. With all of us being bombarded by hundreds of marketing messages each day, getting noticed is difficult. Then, if a message is noticed, will the message be interpreted correctly, in the manner the advertiser or business intended? Examine the advertisement in Figure 12-5. What message do you think the advertiser wants to convey? Examine the advertisement in Figure 12-6. What message is it conveying? Have a fellow classmate, relative, or friend look at the two ads. What do they see? Did you have the same reaction? Ask a couple of other people to examine the ads. Was their reaction consistent with yours and those of your friends or relatives? If so, the advertising agencies created effective advertisements that convey a single message—if, in fact, that was the message the advertisers wanted you to receive. If each of you interpreted the ads differently, you now realize the challenge that advertisers and marketers face in creating effective communication.

Figure 12-5: What does this Snoring Center advertisement convey?

Source: Pink Jacket Creative.

Figure 12-6: What message does this advertisement for The Toggery convey?

Source: Sample print advertisement provided courtesy of The Miles Agency and Alliance One Advertising, Inc.

12-4a: Model of Communications

Marketing communications function similarly to other types of communication between two parties. Someone sends a message; someone else receives it. With marketing, however, the message does not always have to be sent through a person. It can be sent using television, radio, magazines, or social media. The channel of communication contains a series of six sequential stages, as illustrated in Figure 12-7.

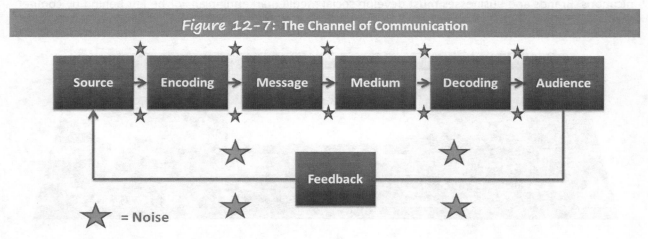

Figure 12-7: **The Channel of Communication**

Source → Encoding → Message → Medium → Decoding → Audience

Feedback

★ = Noise

The message begins with a **source**, which is the organization that originates a marketing communication (see **Figure 12-8.**) The source can be the company itself, or it can be the advertising agency that represents the company. For the "Got Milk?" series of advertisements, the source is the Bozell Agency, hired by the milk industry to develop the advertising campaign. The goal of the campaign was to encourage consumers to drink more milk. With the rise in popularity of soft drinks and other types of drinks, the consumption of milk had declined. To reverse this trend, the milk industry hired the Bozell Agency to create a series of ads to stimulate interest in drinking more milk.

The second step in the communication process is **encoding**, which is the process of transposing the objective or goal of a marketing communication concept into an actual marketing communication piece such as an advertisement, brochure, or sign. With the "Got Milk?" campaign, the creative staff working on the milk industry account wanted to convey the message that drinking milk is fashionable and cool. Therefore they chose a series of celebrities that are well liked by consumers and not only showed them with a glass of milk, but also with a white milk mustache. In addition, copy was added to explain the importance of drinking milk and the fact that milk is a good source of calcium for bones.

When the encoding process is complete, a message has been created. The **message** is the completed marketing communication piece. It may be a 30-second advertisement for television, a point-of-purchase display for a retail store, an interactive website, or post on a social media site. If the message is done well, it will embody the objectives and goals of the creatives who developed it. The "Got Milk" advertisement was just one of a series of messages created for the milk industry by the Bozell Agency.

Figure 12-8: The source for this advertisement for Lucky Strike cigarettes is the British American Tobacco group.

Once the message has been created, it must be sent to the consumer. The **medium** is the venue used by the source to send a marketing communication message to its intended audience. The medium may be television, radio, a magazine, the Internet, an envelope, or a sign on the side of a city bus. The choice of medium is important because, if the intended audience does not receive or see the marketing message, they cannot react to it. For the Bozell Agency, magazines were chosen as the primary medium for its series of print "Got Milk?" advertisements.

As a consumer picks up a magazine and notices the milk advertisement, **decoding**, the process of interpreting the meaning conveyed in a marketing message, begins. One consumer may look at the advertisement, notice the attractive female, and think that milk will promote good looks. That is not the message that was intended. Another person may notice the advertisement and think that drinking milk is cool. If that was the message intended in the original encoding process, then effective communication has taken place. If the consumer thinks that not only is milk cool to drink but that it is an excellent source of calcium, then the agency has effectively communicated the message that was intended.

The **audience** is defined as the individuals who observe a marketing communication and decode the message. It is the individuals who see the ads during a television show, in a magazine, or on a billboard. It is the shopper who sees a point-of-purchase display in a grocery store. It is the person at home who receives a direct-mail piece offer. For effective communication to take place, the audience who re-

> **Source:**
> The organization that originates a marketing communication message.
>
> **Encoding:**
> The process of transposing the objective or goal of a marketing communication concept into an actual marketing communication piece, such as an advertisement, brochure, or sign.
>
> **Message:**
> The completed marketing communication piece.
>
> **Medium:**
> The venue the source uses to send a marketing communication message to its intended audience.
>
> **Decoding:**
> The process of interpreting the meaning conveyed in a marketing message.
>
> **Audience:**
> The individuals who observe a marketing communication and decode the message.

ceives the marketing communication needs to match the audience for which it was designed. If the ad shown in Figure 12-8 had been intended for females 15 to 30 years old, but 80 percent of those who saw the advertisement were males older than 50, the advertisement did not reach its intended target: The message the agency wanted to send to the 15- to 30-year-old female was never received.

The last step in effective communication is **feedback**, which is the response of the audience to the message. For the "Got Milk?" advertisement, the feedback may be the increased consumption of milk or a more positive attitude toward drinking milk. If the sale of milk increases after the launch of the milk ads, then the agency knows that the message was heard and that consumers responded positively. To see if the message was interpreted correctly, the agency will need to interview viewers of the ad to see what they thought about the ad and what message they thought the ad conveyed. For advertising and many types of marketing communications, feedback is informal and indirect, making it difficult for marketers to know how effective the communication was, or even if the intended audience received the message. For personal selling, however, the salesperson can watch the buyer and listen to his or her reaction. Feedback is immediate, allowing the salesperson to modify the message to ensure that the decoding is taking place as intended.

> **Feedback:**
> The response of the audience to the message.
>
> **Noise:**
> Anything that interferes with the audience receiving the message.

The last factor in the channel of communication is **noise**, which is anything that interferes with the audience receiving the message. It can occur anywhere along the channel of communication. It may be someone talking during the airing of a radio advertisement. It may be someone getting something to eat during a television commercial. It may be that the models in the "Got Milk?" ad distract a viewer, and he or she does not even notice the written message in the ad. It may be a shopper thinking about a work situation and not listening to what a salesperson is saying. Noise prevents the audience from seeing a marketing communication message or from correctly comprehending the intended message.

One form of noise that affects the effectiveness of ads is clutter. In many magazines, there are more pages devoted to advertisements than to the magazine's content. In television, approximately 12 to 14 minutes of each hour are spent with advertisements or public service announcements. A study by the Cabletelevision Advertising Bureau indicated that there is an enormous difference in the viewer's ability to recall ads between the first ad in a series and the fourth, fifth, or last ad in the series. In addition, if too many ads are shown then viewers will either switch channels or quit watching.[4] To avoid this high level of ad clutter, advertisers are pursuing various online advertising strategies and utilizing social media. Even these outlets are becoming cluttered with ads.

12-4b: AIDA Concept

The ultimate goal of marketing communication is for the audience to respond in some manner. It may be to make a purchase, to enter a contest, to call a toll-free number, or to shop at a retail store. One method of reaching these goals is to design marketing communication using the AIDA concept. **AIDA** is an acronym that stands for attention, interest, desire, and action.

Before consumers or a business can be influenced to make a purchase, the marketer must get their attention. If it is a salesperson making a sales call, then a smile, a handshake, and a friendly greeting can gain the buyer's attention. If it is a television commercial, the viewer's attention might be gained by having the volume louder; having a sexy, attractive person appear on the screen; playing a familiar tune; or using a tranquil scene. For an online ad, attention may be garnered through a unique, psychedelic array of colors; a large, bold headline; an eye-catching scene; or a well-known celebrity. To get viewers' attention, the advertisement in Figure 12-9 for Ouachita Independent Bank, designed by the Newcomer, Morris & Young agency, used a Dachshund in full color to contrast with the black and blue ink used in the rest of the ad.

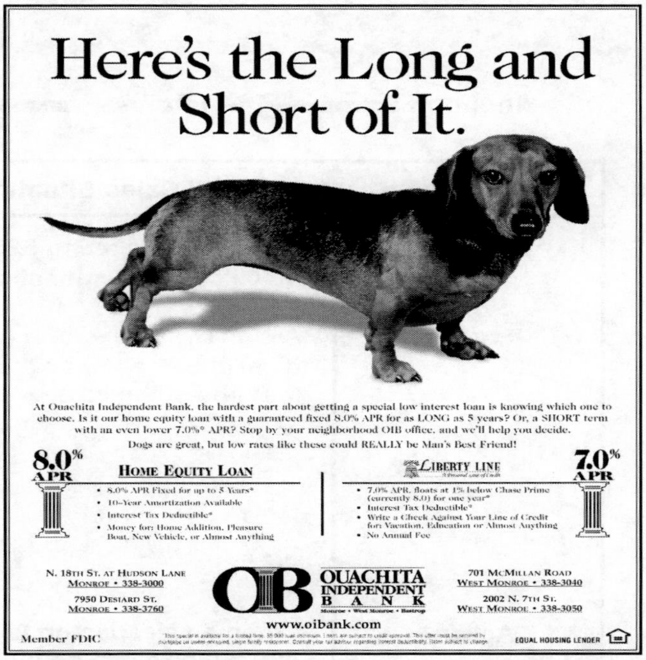

Once the marketer has the person's attention, the next step is to develop interest. The attractive model, the Dachshund, or a familiar tune may catch your attention, but if you do not stop and read the advertisement, the message will not be received. Taglines and written or verbal copy must then express the concept or idea that the advertiser wishes to express to develop your interest in the product. The advertisement for Ouachita Independent Bank used the headline "Here's the Long and Short of It" to tie in with the picture of the Dachshund and the content copy of the ad. The agency that designed the ad is hoping the headline, with the picture, will garner your attention long enough that you will be interested in reading the rest of the ad. A salesperson has an advantage over media advertising because once the salesperson has your attention, he or she can adjust the sales presentation to build interest in the product and answer any questions you may have.

Figure 12-9: Which component of AIDA does this ad primarily convey?
Source: Courtesy of Newcomer, Morris & Young.

AIDA: An acronym that stands for attention, interest, desire, and action.

Once a person's interest has been gained, the third step is to build desire. A purchasing agent for a large company may have four or five vendors from whom she can purchase raw materials. The salesperson has to convince the purchasing agent why his company should be selected. In contrast, it is more difficult for an advertiser to present a message that will lead the viewer from just being interested in the product to wanting to purchase it. A representative at Ouachita Independent Bank talking about the benefits highlighted on the ad would have an easier time developing desire than if someone just read the advertisement itself.

The last step in this process is action. This is the actual decision to make the purchase. For the purchasing agent, it may be signing a contract with a supplier. For the person seeing the Ouachita Independent Bank ad, it may be going to the bank and securing a home equity loan.

The amount of time a person will spend in each step will vary widely. For high-involvement decisions, such as purchasing furniture, clothes, or a vehicle, it may take a marketer a long time to develop desire. For candy bars, simply using a point-of-purchase display near the checkout stand may be enough to urge someone to make a purchase. The time from attention to action may be only a few seconds. If it takes longer, the person is likely to decide that the candy bar has too many calories and that he or she can get by without it. Figure 12-10 summarizes the use of AIDA for an exercise bicycle in a retail sales situation and with a television advertisement.

Figure 12-10: Using the AIDA Concept to Sell an Exercise Bike

Attention ➡ Interest ➡ Desire ➡ Action

AIDA Concept	Retail Sales Situation	Television Advertisement
Attention	A store sign offering $25 off catches your attention.	A well-built young man appears on the screen wearing only shorts.
Interest	A sign by the exercise bike highlights the low cost and features of the bike.	You have been wanting an exercise bike, and this is a model you have not seen before, so you want to see what it looks like and what features it has.
Desire	You sit on the bicycle, and it feels more comfortable than any others you have tried.	After seeing the TV ad, you check the Internet to see where the closest retail store is located and what the Web site says about the bike.
Action	When a salesperson tells you that the bike can be purchased now and, if for any reason, you don't like the bike, you can return it within 30 days for a full refund, you decide to purchase it.	Having thought about the exercise bike, you see another advertisement. You decide this is the right bike and make a decision to purchase it, using the toll-free number listed on the TV screen.

12-5 *THE COMMUNICATION MIX*

In developing an integrated marketing plan, the marketing manager must decide on the relative mix of communication tools. How much will be spent on advertising? How much will be spent on trade promotions and sales promotions? How much will be spent to support personal selling? Will social media be used, or will the company use database marketing? How will the Internet be used? The answer to these questions depends on a number of factors that will be discussed in this section. But first, it is interesting to examine how current marketing budgets are used (see Figure 12-11). Because of the pervasive nature of advertising, students tend to believe that most of a company's marketing budget is spent on advertising. This is not true. In fact, only about 25 percent of all marketing dollars is spent on advertising. The remaining 75 percent is spent on trade promotions and consumer promotions, with trade promotions using up 50 percent of the budget and consumer promotions the other 25 percent.

12-5a: Business versus Consumer Marketing

The communication mix for business-to-business marketing tends to be different than for consumer marketing. Business-to-business marketing relies more on personal selling, trade promotions, digital marketing, and telemarketing, whereas consumer marketing relies more on advertising, social media, and consumer promotion. Because businesses are more concentrated and make larger volume purchases, using a salesperson makes sense. One salesperson may account for annual sales in the millions of dollars. Also,

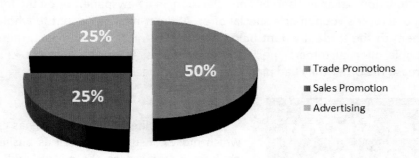

Figure 12-11: How Marketing Dollars Are Used.

because of the high volume of a single purchase, it is important to use the best means of communication: personal selling. For consumers, however, it would not be financially feasible to use a salesperson, except for large ticket items. Advertising and social media can reach more people with a message at a much lower cost per person.

12-5b: Communication Objectives

A major factor in how marketing dollars are allocated and the mix of communication tools is what the firm wishes to accomplish. An IMC plan is often oriented toward a single objective. It is possible, however, for a program to accomplish more than one objective at a time, but this may be confusing to potential customers. Communication objectives can be classified into these six major categories:

- Increase demand
- Differentiate a product
- Provide information
- Build brand equity
- Reduce purchase risk
- Stimulate trial

Each objective requires a different approach, and each requires a different mix of communication elements. Although any of the communication elements, such as advertising, can be used to accomplish any of the objectives, other forms of communication, such as consumer (or sales) promotions or personal selling, may work better for a specific objective. The optimal results occur when the communication tools are used together, integrating them into one common theme. For example, to reduce purchase risk, a firm may use advertising coupled with a $2-off coupon and a special point-of-purchase display. The combined effect of using all three elements together is greater than if only one were used.

Increase Demand

To increase demand, firms usually turn to trade and sales promotions. Offering wholesalers and retailers trade promotions, such as price discounts, quantity discounts, and bonus packs, encourages them to purchase more of a product because they can increase their margins. For example, if a manufacturer of picture frames offers retail stores a 10 percent discount on purchases made by October 1, many of the stores will boost their orders. They can then either pass the savings on to the customer through cheaper prices, or they can charge the customer the same amount, increasing their profit by 10 percent. In most cases, retailers use the latter strategy. Retail prices stay the same. To make the increase in demand more dramatic, manufacturers may offer a manufacturer's coupon to consumers at the same time they are offering the channel discount. Giving a discount to both consumers and channel members drastically reduces the profit margin for manufacturers, but it will create a short-term burst in sales.

Advertising is the least effective promotional element to directly increase demand but can serve a valuable support function. An advertisement on television, in a newspaper, or on the Internet can alert consumers to a manufacturer's coupon or a special offer. A direct-mail piece sent to wholesalers and distributors can alert them to the trade discount being offered. For more of an impact, the manufacturer could have its salespeople offer customers special trade discounts. In these situations, channel members will often either increase the order they had planned or make a special purchase.

Differentiate a Product

The proliferation of brands has created a situation in which most consumers as well as businesses have multiple choices. In many cases, there is little difference between the various brands. If this is perceived to be so by the buyer, then price becomes the determining factor. To avoid situations in which buyers make purchase decisions entirely on price, companies strive to differentiate their product from the competitors' product. Benefits and features not available from competitors are stressed. If there are few or no actual differences, companies will often strive to create a psychological difference. The best communication tool used to differentiate a product is personal selling. A salesperson has the opportunity to explain a product's features and benefits. The message can be tailored to each buyer, and questions can be answered. For business-to-business markets and high-end consumer products that use salespeople, this method is very effective once the salesperson has the ear of a prospective buyer. But in situations in which personal selling is not possible, a product can be differentiated effectively through advertising. Through an ad, a firm has the opportunity to highlight a product's features and benefits and to show how a particular brand differs from competing brands. The Haik Humble Laser Center advertisement in Figure 12-12 highlights a free seminar individuals can attend that will explain the new S3 VISX technology used in laser vision correction.

Trade promotions and consumer promotions are not effective in differentiating a product, unless the differentiation is based on price. If a brand is positioned as the low-cost option, then using trade promotions and consumer promotions can be valuable. But if the differentiation is to be based on a benefit or feature, then using numerous trade and sales promotions can actually make it more difficult to differentiate a product. If Pringles chips are promoted as not being greasy, but the company uses coupons extensively, consumers are likely to see Pringles as a cheap brand of potato chips rather than a brand that has been differentiated in another way.

Figure 12-12 This advertisement by Haik Humble Laser Center strives to differentiate the center's brand name by stressing new laser vision correction technologies that are available to patients and by using an endorsement from pro-football quarterback Doug Pederson.

Source: Sartor Associates, Inc. for Haik Humble Eye Center.

Provide Information

Salespeople and advertising are effective at providing potential customers with information. Salespeople are able to modify the information to meet the needs of individual customers. A retail salesperson can provide a shopper with information on major appliances and features of each brand. A field salesperson can inform clients about a special upcoming sale or a new product recently introduced. Advertising is also an excellent means of providing information. Retailers use advertising on a regular basis to inform customers of their location, their operating hours, and the brands they carry. Advertising can be used to promote special events like a Labor Day sale; the introduction of a new brand, such as Vanilla Coke; or the grand opening of a new business (see Figure 12-13). Trade and consumer promotions are not good venues for providing information because each offers some type of incentive to encourage action on the part of the consumer or business.

Build Brand Equity

For long-term survival, brands must develop a certain level of brand equity that allows them to stand apart from competitors. As mentioned in Chapter 8, brand equity (or franchise) is defined as a set of brand assets and liabilities linked to a brand and its name and symbol, adding or subtracting from the value provided by a good or service to a firm or to that firm's customers.

Brand equity is built on two foundations: quality and awareness. The quality must match or exceed the relative price being charged. The quality of food served at McDonald's does not match that of food served at Outback Steakhouse or Ruby Tuesday's, but it meets the standard relative to the price. If McDonald's did not produce quality fast-food items, it could not stay in business. Part of McDonald's brand equity, however, is not only its food but also its service, convenience, and standardization.

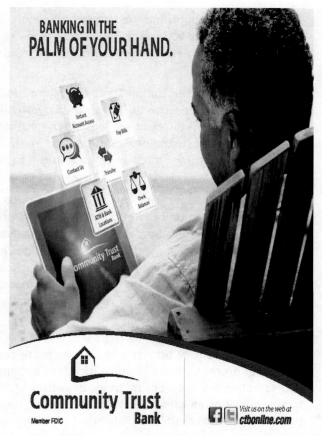

Figure 12-13: The objective of this advertisement is to provide information about the new mobile services offered by a community bank.
Source: Courtesy of Community Trust Bank , Monroe, LA.

The other factor in building brand equity is awareness. Although awareness does not equate to brand equity, you cannot have a high level of brand equity without awareness. McDonald's, Campbell's Soup, Wal-Mart, Nike, and Toyota, are all well known and have a high level of awareness. Kmart, Enron, and WorldCom are also well known, but because of quality or environmental issues, they lack a high level of brand equity.

About the only way to develop a high level of brand awareness is through advertising. Television, radio, digital and print advertising are major avenues for making people aware of a particular brand. For many brand ads, little information is given. The focus is not on differentiating the product, but on building an awareness of the brand name and reminding consumers of the brand. The goal is to build a strong brand name. If awareness and a brand name are backed by quality products, then brand equity will develop. Brand equity is important from a company perspective because it equates to loyal customers.

Reduce Purchase Risk

Reducing purchase risk is important for new products, new brands, and for gaining new customers of current brands. Personal selling is the best communication tool to accomplish this objective, offering the salesperson the opportunity to answer objections and explain features that will reduce the buyer's perceived risk. If safety is a factor, the salesperson can explain the safety features. If performance is a factor, the salesperson can explain the performance features and how the product will provide the benefits the customer wants.

Other communication tools that can reduce purchase risk are consumer and trade promotions. Both are effective because they offer the buyer an incentive, normally a price reduction, to make the purchase. A 25-percent discount reduces purchase risk. With sampling, purchase risk can be reduced even further: If a potential customer can use a gym free for a week, then the risk of making a purchase is greatly reduced. The customer has a good idea of the benefits of membership and can more readily tell if it is a lifestyle fit.

Although advertising can be used to reduce purchase risk, it is not too effective. Viewers know that the ad is going to promote a product and its features, so it will have little effect on their perceived risk of making a purchase. In rare cases, however, an advertisement may point out a feature or statistic that will be effective in reducing purchase risk. The airlines have tried to reduce the perceived risk of flying for passengers who are afraid by pointing out that it is statistically safer to fly than to drive. The advertisements have virtually no impact on perceived risk because of the consequence of an accident: People who fear flying may think that they would be one of those statistics.

Stimulate Trial

To build new brands and to rejuvenate stagnant brands, companies will want to stimulate trial. Consumer promotions are the best means of accomplishing this objective. Coupons, sweepstakes, contests, and sampling are excellent methods of getting someone to try a product (see **Figure 12-14**). Food manufacturers will often offer free samples of their food at grocery stores so people can try it. If they like it, there are coupons readily available that allow the consumers to purchase the product at a reduced price.

Figure 12-14; The craft beer industry relies heavily on free sample to encourage consumers to try new varieties of beer.

Trade promotions are relatively ineffective in stimulating trial. Wholesalers and retailers are reluctant to try new products unless they know consumers will buy them. The trade incentive would have to be substantial, reducing the wholesaler's and retailer's risk, before they would stock an item that no one may buy. For established companies like Procter & Gamble, General Foods, and Kellogg's, retailers are more likely to take the risk because they know that these companies thoroughly test a product in advance, and their history indicates that they have solid brands. But even in these cases, the retailer will want the manufacturer to tie the trade promotion into some type of consumer promotion or advertising.

Advertising and personal selling have moderate success in stimulating trial. Advertising could create interest in the product, but stimulating trial would be slow. If advertising is tied with consumer promotions, then its effectiveness will increase dramatically. The same is true for personal selling. A salesperson has some impact on stimulating trial, but it really takes a trade or consumer promotion offer for the buyer to go ahead and make a purchase. Philips Belgium found a unique method for stimulating trial of its new Philishave Cool Skin Shaver, which proved to be very successful. Philips Belgium created traveling shaving stations complete with barber chair, sink, and Cool Skin hostesses. The portable shaving stations were set up in malls, movie theaters, department stores, and other high-traffic areas. People who bought the shaver onsite received a free shaving kit stocked with Nivea skin products and a Philishave Cool Skin towel. The promotion generated 4,600 trials, with 25 percent of those who tried the shaver purchasing it.[5] Table 12-2 summarizes the relative strength of each communication element for each of the communication objectives.

Table 12-2: Communication Objectives and Communication Elements				
Communication Objective	**Advertising**	**Trade Promotions**	**Consumer Promotions**	**Personal Selling**
Increase demand	Slow, takes time	Excellent for encouraging distributors and retailers to purchase more; impact is immediate and short term	Excellent for encouraging end users to request the product; impact is immediate and short term	Good for items that are sold almost entirely by field salespeople, but poor for retail sales, because the salesperson is dependent on someone coming into the store
Differentiate a product	Excellent	Poor, because differentiation is almost always based on price, not product features	Moderate for encouraging end users to request the brand, but may create price-related differentiation rather than differentiation based on product features	Excellent, because the salesperson has the ability for two-way communication and can often demonstrate how the product is different from that of a competitor
Provide information	Excellent	Poor, because it depends on the type of trade promotion, and the trade offer normally overshadows the information	Poor, because it depends on the type of consumer promotion, and the promotional offer normally overshadows the information	Excellent, because there is two-way communication and the buyer can ask questions
Build brand equity	Excellent	Poor, because most trade promotions focus on some type of price incentive	Poor, because most consumer promotions focus on some type of price incentive	Moderate, because salespeople's primary goal is to sell a product, not to build its equity
Reduce purchase risk	Poor, because advertising can reduce risk only through talking about the features and benefits of the product	Good, because wholesalers and retailers can receive price incentives to make a purchase	Good, because consumer promotions can reduce the financial risk; excellent if the firm can use sampling or trial purchase incentives	Excellent, because the salesperson has an opportunity to answer questions and demonstrate the product
Stimulate trial	Moderate to good success if tied with a sales promotion	Poor, because of so many new products being introduced	Excellent, through offering consumers some type of incentive	Moderate success because of ability to answer questions and demonstrate the product

12-5c: Push/Pull Marketing Strategies

Push/pull marketing strategies relate to how manufacturers market their products. With a push marketing strategy, the manufacturer attempts to push the product through the channels with the belief that if the product is available in retail outlets, consumers will purchase it. With a pull marketing strategy, the manufacturer builds product demand at the consumer level with the belief that consumers will go to retailers and demand that the product be stocked. Manufacturers seldom use either one or the other; instead, they use a combination. Thinking of push/pull marketing strategies along a continuum provides a better understanding of how they work together and what types of communication elements are best suited for each. Manufacturers who place the greatest emphasis on a push strategy will primarily use trade promotions and personal selling. Trade promotions provide incentives to channel members to stock an item and to push it through the channel. Personal sales calls on retailers and wholesalers will then enhance this process. For a pull strategy, the emphasis will be on advertising and consumer promotions. Advertising builds awareness and brand identity, and consumer promotions offer consumers incentives to try the product. Table 12-3 summarizes these relationships.

In the past, pharmaceutical companies relied exclusively on a push strategy. Samples of new drugs were given to physicians and advertisements were taken out in medical journals. The goal was to get physicians to prescribe the drug for their patients. Recently, however, drug companies have turned to a pull strategy. Viagra, produced by Pfizer, relied heavily on this strategy. Using television and print ads with celebrities, Pfizer encouraged patients to talk to their doctor about Viagra. After taking note of Viagra's success, Pharmacia sunk $130.4 million into promoting its arthritis drug, Celebrex. Drug companies are still providing samples to physicians but have moved a large amount of their marketing money into consumer advertising with the goal of building demand with patients, who will then request the drug from their physician.[6]

Table 12-3: The Communication Elements and Push/Pull Marketing Strategies		
Push Strategy	**Communication Element**	**Pull Strategy**
Low	Advertising	High
High	Trade promotions	Low
Low	Consumer promotions	High
High	Personal selling	Low

12-5d: Product Life Cycle

The stage of the product life cycle (PLC) has a strong impact on marketing communications and the elements used. During the introductory stage, the goals of businesses introducing a new product are to promote industry demand and brand awareness, and to stimulate trial. Advertising works best for promoting industry demand and building awareness. For a business-to-business product, personal selling will also work well. Consumer promotions are important to stimulate trial purchases. Normally, trade promotions will not work because channel members are uncertain about the projected consumer demand.

When the product moves to the growth stage, marketing dollars continue to be spent on advertising, but the objective is to develop brand preference and to differentiate the product from the competition, rather than build industry demand, unless the company has substantial market share. When Nintendo owned 80 percent of the video game market, expanding the industry demand was a logical objective because Nintendo would get 80 percent of the new business. Because of increasing demand, dollars are shifted from consumer promotions to trade promotions. With growing consumer demand, companies will spend more on encouraging channel members to push their brand rather than the competition's brand. Because consumers want the product, there is little need for consumer promotion offers.

When the product hits maturity, competition becomes intense. About the only way a company can increase market share is to take it away from the competition. In this environment, expenditures in all four areas are high. Advertising is needed to differentiate the product. Trade promotions are needed to encourage channel members to place a greater emphasis on a particular brand. Consumer promotions are needed to encourage consumers to choose a particular brand over the competition. Personal selling is needed to highlight the advantages of one brand over another.

The reverse situation occurs when the product moves into the decline stage. It does not make sense to advertise, use trade or consumer promotions, or personal selling. Firms reduce their marketing expenditures with the idea of pulling out of the market and discontinuing the product. Table 12-4 summarizes the marketing communication elements as they relate to the PLC.

Table 12-4: Marketing Communication and Product Life Cycle				
The Stage of the Product Life Cycle				
Marketing Communication Element	**Introductory Stage**	**Growth Stage**	**Maturity Stage**	**Decline Stage**
Advertising	Moderate, to develop awareness of a new product and build industry demand	High, to develop brand name and brand awareness	High, to differentiate the product from the competition	Low, because demand is declining and a new product or technology has taken its place
Trade Promotions	Low, because consumers are not familiar with the new product, and for retailers, it would be a high risk	Moderate, since consumers are demanding the product, and manufacturers do not need a high level of trade promotion to push their product	High, to encourage channel members to stock and push the firm's product	Low, because with declining demand, there is no need to encourage channel members to stock the product
Consumer Promotions	High, to encourage trial usage of the product	Low, since consumers are demanding the product, and few sales incentives are needed for purchasing	High, to encourage consumers to choose a particular brand over the competition	Low, because sales promotion incentives will not encourage consumption
Personal Selling	High for business-to-business salespeople because they can explain the new product, but low for consumer products since the salesperson would have to wait for the customer to come to them	Moderate, since salespeople serve primarily as order takers with consumers and businesses demanding the product	High, to encourage customers to purchase a particular brand	Low, because few people or businesses want the product

12-6 ADVERTISING

Advertising is all around us. We see it on TV, view it on the Internet, hear it on the radio, read it in magazines, and see it in social media. It is on billboards, the sides of buses, and even in public bathrooms. No matter where we go, advertising is there. It is an important part of marketing communications. Ad spending in the United States is now over $190 billion per year with an annual growth rate ranging from two to four percent.

In 1969, Condon Bush used his mother's recipe to develop the first can of Bush's Best Baked Beans. Through hard work and perseverance, that first can of baked beans produced a small family business. Primarily using a push strategy, the Bush family was able to grow their business into the number three spot in the baked beans category, behind ConAgra's Van Camp's and Campbell's baked beans. But the family finally made the decision in 1993 to use advertising to promote their product, with the objective of growing even more. Because they did not believe in advertising, convincing them to give advertising a try was a big challenge.

Jay Bush, grandson of the company's founder, was selected to be the company's spokesperson. The first ad featured Jay explaining to consumers that the baked beans tasted so good because they were prepared according to an old family recipe, a secret recipe known only to Duke, the family dog. The ad ends with Duke conveying the idea that, with him knowing the secret, the recipe may not be a secret much

Figure 12-15: Because of a savvy advertising program, Bush's beans are now the market leader in the baked beans category.

longer. The ad was so successful that in just one year, Bush's market share in the baked beans category nearly tripled. It now has a 50 percent share of the $470-million-a-year baked bean market, compared with only 24 percent for Van Camp's and 7.5 per-cent for Campbell's. A major reason for Bush's success is that it spends about $14 million a year on advertising, compared with less than $1 million for Van Camp's and Campbell's combined.[7] Now the Bush family is a strong believer in the benefits of advertising and even sponsored Game Show Network's "Dog Days of Summer," which consisted of a half-day block of a double-dog-dare game show called Dog Eat Dog. It consisted of a fun-in-the-sun pool party/barbecue, dog antics, and sunbathers performing belly flops and cannonballs for "bean-counter judges" (see **Figure 12-15**).[8]

Table 12-5: Top Ten Advertisers		
Rank	**Company**	**Advertising Expenditures**
1	Procter & Gamble	$3.17 billion
2	General Motors	$1.79 billion
3	AT & T	$1.79 billlion
4	Comcast	$1.65 billion
5	L'Oreal	$1.55 billion
6	Toyota	$1.27 billion
7	Berkshire Hathaway	$1.25 billion
8	Verizon	$1.22 billion
9	Pfizer	$1.14 billion
10	Time Warner	$1.13 billion

Source: Adapted from "Kantar Media Reports U.S. Advertising Expenditures Increased 0.9 Percent in 2013," http://kantarmedia.us/sites/default/files/kantar-media-q4-2013-us-ad-spend.pdf, March 25, 2014

Just like Bush's Baked Beans, companies spend millions, even billions of dollars on advertising. The largest advertiser in the United States is Proctor & Gamble, spending $3.2 billion annually. The closest advertisers to P & G are General Motors and AT&T, both at $1.8 billion. Table 12-5 shows the top ten U.S. advertisers. Table 12-6 provides advertising dollars spent in the top categories. Top on the list is retail stores with $16 billion. A close second is the automotive industry at $15.2 billion.

Advertising can be classified into two broad categories: product advertising and institutional advertising. Both categories can be used to accomplish the communication objectives discussed. It is important for marketers to remember that advertising is just one component of the communication mix, and it must fit into the overall IMC objectives and not drive the marketing campaign. Too many marketers fall into the trap of thinking that advertising can solve all of their problems and thus put it into a lead role. For some IMC campaigns, advertising should be in a lead role, but for others, it needs to provide a supporting role.

12-6a: Product Advertising

Most advertising falls into the product advertising category. **Product advertising** is any advertisement that is designed to promote a firm's brand. It can be targeted to end users or channel members. Product advertising can be further subdivided into the following categories:

- Brand
- Informative
- Persuasive
- Pioneer
- Comparative

Rank	Category	Advertising Expenditures
1	Retail	$16.02 billion
2	Automotive	$15.21 billion
3	Telecom	$9.36 billlion
4	Local services	$9.13 billion
5	Financial services	$7.60 billion
6	Personal care products	$7.03 billion
7	Food & Candy	$6.63 billion
8	Restaurants	$6.45 billion
9	Direct Response	$5.63 billion

Table 12-6: Top Ten Advertising Categories

Source: Adapted from "Kantar Media Reports U.S. Advertising Expenditures Increased 0.9 Percent in 2013," http://kantarmedia.us/sites/default/files/kantar-media-q4-2013-us-ad-spend.pdf,

> **Product Advertising:** Advertising designed to promote a firm's brand.
>
> **Brand Advertising:** An advertisement designed to promote a particular brand with little or no information in the advertisement.
>
> **Informative Advertising:** An advertisement designed to provide the audience with some type of information.

In examining the different types of product advertising, you must keep in mind that a good advertisement may have components from more than one category. These categories exist only for the purpose of discussion and to assist you in understanding how advertisements are created.

Brand advertising is designed to promote a particular brand and typically provides little or no information in the advertisement. Figure 12-16 is an advertisement for Aeneas Williams Dealerships. The ad does not provide any information about the product other than placing the various automobile brand names down the left side of the advertisement. The primary goals of brand advertising are to develop a strong brand name and to build brand awareness. To develop brand equity, a firm must first build a high level of brand awareness. Brand advertising can accomplish this goal.

Informative advertising is designed to provide the audience with some type of information. It may be a retail store informing the public of its address, phone number, or operating hours. Figure 12-17 for Zeagler Music is such an

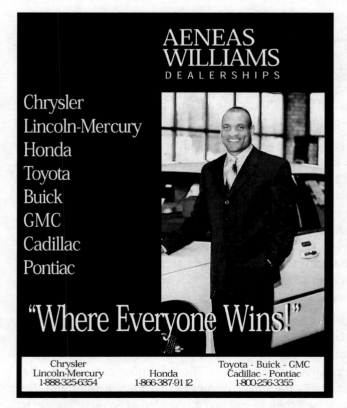

Figure 12-16: This advertisement by Aeneas Williams Dealership is an example of brand advertising.

Figure 12-17: This advertisement for Zeagler Music is an example of informative advertising.

Source: Sample print advertisement courtesy of The Miles Agency and Alliance One Advertising, Inc.

Figure 12-18: This advertisement for Skeeter Performance Fishing Boats is an example of persuasive advertising.

Source: Courtesy of Newcomer, Morris & Young.

advertisement. It provides the phone numbers of the store and informs consumers that Zeagler Music has electric Fender guitars starting at $199. Product manufacturers will sometimes produce informative ads that tell consumers which retail stores carry their brands.

The most common form of product advertising is **persuasive advertising**, which is designed to influence viewers' thinking in some way. The advertisement for Skeeter boats in Figure 12-18 is designed to persuade anglers that owning a Skeeter boat is one of life's breathtaking experiences. The ad creatives wanted to add validity to their statement, so they used the Bass Masters Classic Official Sponsor logo, indicating that Skeeter is an official sponsor of the Bass Masters Classic. Additional detail is then provided in the ad copy to back up the tagline used in the advertisement.

The least-used type of product advertising is pioneer. With **pioneer advertising**, the goal is to build primary demand for a product. It is normally used only in the introductory stage of the product life cycle (PLC). Because the product is new, consumers have to be convinced to buy it. After the product moves into the growth stage of the PLC, advertisers have to switch to another type of advertising, unless they are the industry leader. Even in those cases, they have to be careful because pioneer advertising builds demand for the product category, which means the ad will also help the competition as well. Pfizer used pioneer advertising when it introduced Viagra. The first ads were designed to build demand for the product—the Viagra name was not even mentioned. Men with impotency problems were just encouraged to see their physician and told that there was a drug available that would help.

The last type of product advertising is **comparative advertising**, which compares the featured brand with another brand, either named or implied. Advertisers have to be careful with comparative ads to ensure that they do not violate the FTC rule regarding substantiation of claims. The ads must compare similar products, and any claims made in the advertisement must be substantiated. Because companies do not like to see their brand being ridiculed in an ad or shown to be inferior, most companies examine comparative ads very closely to ensure that they are not violating the law. Comparative ads can be successful, however, espe-

Persuasive Advertising: An advertisement designed to persuade viewers' thinking in some way.

Pioneer Advertising: An advertisement designed to build primary demand for a product.

Comparative Advertising: An advertisement that compares the featured brand with another brand, either named or implied.

cially for new brands. When a new brand is compared to a well-known brand, the new brand will gain recognition and brand equity. Seeing the two brands together in the same ad encourages consumers to see the two brands as equals.

12-6b: Institutional Advertising

Institutional advertising is designed to build the corporate reputation or develop goodwill for the corporation. Seldom is a brand name mentioned in the advertisement and often the corporate name is a minor component of the ad. The advertisement in **Figure 12-19** for Glenwood Regional Medical Center highlights the heart care that is available to patients in the communities surrounding Glenwood.

Institutional ads can also be public service announcements and cause-related promotions. For example, an ad by Glenwood Regional Medical Center provided information about what people can do to prevent encephalitis. Both cause-related advertising and public service ads enhance a brand's goodwill with the public if the ads convey genuine concern. As was presented in Chapter 3, it is important for companies to demonstrate that they care about society and the environment. Consumers also believe that firms should be involved in supporting good causes. Thus, most companies will designate part of their advertising budget to institutional advertising.

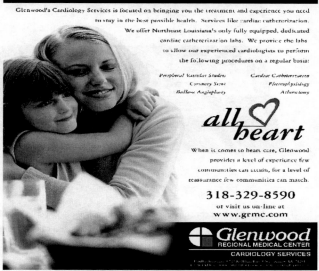

You have a lot to live for. That is why we have expanded our heart program.

318-329-8590
or visit us on-line at
www.grmc.com

Glenwood
REGIONAL MEDICAL CENTER
CARDIOLOGY SERVICES

Figure 12-19: This advertisement for Glenwood Regional Medical Center is an example of institutional advertising.
Source: Sample print advertisement courtesy of
The Miles Agency and Alliance One Advertising, Inc.

> **Institutional Advertising:** Advertising designed to build the corporate reputation or develop goodwill for the corporation.
>
> **Creatives:** Individuals who actually design the advertisements.

12-7 CREATIVE DESIGN

The creative design process begins with information obtained from the a client about the objectives of the advertisement or the ad campaign, the target audience, and any message themes that should be included. The advertising objective would be related to the communications objectives previously discussed. For example, if the communication objective were to build brand equity, then the advertising objective might be to increase brand awareness by 25 percent over the four months of the advertising campaign. If the brand already has a high awareness, then the objective may be to increase brand preference for the product by 10 percent over the life of the advertising campaign. Notice that with advertising objectives, the objective needs to be specific, measurable, and have a specific time frame.

In addition to the advertising objective, the **creative** needs to know who the target audience will be in terms of demographics, psychographics, and lifestyle. Demographic information, such as age, gender, ethnicity, income, education, and geographic region, is essential. A brand awareness advertisement aimed at teenage females is going to be designed differently than one aimed at females older than 60. Psychographics will provide information about the target audience's activities, interests, and opinions. This information is as important as the demographics. If the creative knows about the target audience's lifestyle, such as they like outdoor activities such as hiking, boating, and fishing, this information will help in designing an effective ad. The more the creative knows about how the audience thinks and behaves, the easier it is to design an effective ad.

In advertising campaigns, message themes are often carried over from one ad to another and even from one campaign to another. Allstate Insurance uses the message theme "You're in good hands" in every

Figure 12-20: Most consumers, especially homeowners, would readily associate Allstate Insurance with its message theme, "You're in good hands," and would probably readily consider the company when contemplating a change in insurance providers.

campaign and with almost every advertisement (see Figure 12-20). Capital One has the tagline "What's in Your Wallet?" and Home Depot's ad emphasizes "More savings. More doing." The message theme is a method of ensuring that ads and campaigns are connected and that consumers hear a consistent message.

Once the creative has the background information from the client, she is ready to start working on the ad or the ad campaign. The next set of decisions involves the appeal and the message strategy. Although these decisions will be discussed independently, the creative normally makes the decision about each simultaneously because they are interrelated.

12-7a: Advertising Appeals

The **advertising appeal** is the design a creative will use to attract attention to and interest in an advertisement. The six primary types of appeal are:

> **Advertising Appeal:**
> The design a creative will use to attract attention to and interest in an advertisement.

- Emotion
- Fear
- Humor
- Sex
- Music
- Rational

The appeal chosen will depend on the objective of the ad, the target audience, and how the creative wants to convey the message to the intended audience. Almost every product can be advertised using any of the six appeals, and an advertisement can use two or three appeals together. For instance, in creating advertisements for the milk industry, Goodby, Silverstein & Partners used a deprivation approach with a humor appeal. Bozell, however, used a variety of appeals in its print ads. Some ads used an attractive, sexy model. Others used a rational approach in talking about the importance of milk in providing calcium. Some used an emotional approach, as in the "Got Milk?" ads.

Emotional appeals are an excellent method of building brand preference and brand loyalty. The goal is to build a bond between the brand and the consumer, just as you would between two people. Most of the Effie Award winners, which are presented by the New York chapter of the American Advertising Association, use some type of emotional appeal. The most common emotional appeals focus on the consumer's life and feelings.[9] Because of the capacity to use both sight and sound, TV and videos posted on the Internet are the best media for emotional appeals. Facial expressions, body language, and voice inflections can all be used to demonstrate feelings.

Fear appeals are used for many products such as insurance, fire alarms, deodorant, and mouthwash. With insurance, the fear focuses on what happens if an accident occurs and the person is not insured. With deodorant, the fear focuses on social rejection. Fear appeals work because they increase viewers' attention, interest, and persuasion. Many viewers will remember an ad with a fear appeal better than one with a rational, upbeat argument.[10] But advertisers have to be careful to use the right level of appeal. If the fear level is too low, viewers will not pay attention to the ad; on the other hand, if it is too high, then they will tune the ad out or switch channels. The most effective fear ads are somewhere in between.[11] See Figure 12-21 for an illustration of this concept.

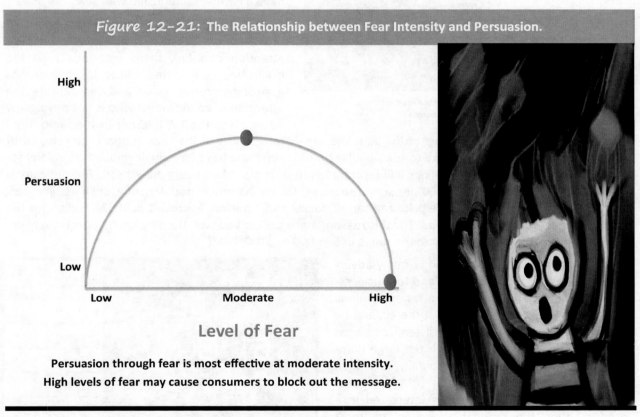

Figure 12-21: The Relationship between Fear Intensity and Persuasion.

Level of Fear

Persuasion through fear is most effective at moderate intensity.
High levels of fear may cause consumers to block out the message.

Humor is used in about 30 percent of all advertisements because it has proved to be one of the best approaches at garnering viewers' attention and keeping their interest.[12] It has intrusion value, which means it has the ability to break through clutter and gain a person's attention. People like to laugh, and they enjoy watching ads that are humorous. Humor provides a way to escape from reality through a comedic view of life. The danger of using humor is that it can overpower the product and the intended message. To be effective, the humor has to grab the viewer's attention and hold it throughout the ad. But if the humor is too strong, then the viewer will remember the ad but not the brand being advertised or the message being conveyed. It is important to tie the humor to the brand and the message.

Many advertisers use sex appeals for a wide variety of products. Research has shown that sex and nudity in an advertisement increase viewer attention, regardless of the gender of the audience or the gen-

Figure 12-22: Fashion designers use sex appeal extensively, even on store mannequins .

der of the models in the ad. The danger, however, is that brand recall for ads with sex appeal is usually lower. Thus, although sex appeal gains attention, it appears that, if it is not done tactfully, the sex appeal may interfere with the person remembering the brand being advertised or the message being conveyed.[13] Sex appeals work best for products that are in some way related to sex. For instance, Guess advertisements use sex appeal effectively because the clothes being advertised are designed to enhance a person's personal, sexual appearance (see **Figure 12-22**). Using sex appeal to sell tools, office furniture, or life insurance will not be as effective because these products do not have a natural relationship with sex.

Music is an important component of broadcast ads because it helps to gain people's attention and link them emotionally to the brand being advertised. Music, like humor, has a strong intrusion value and can capture the attention of an individual who is not paying any attention to the TV, Internet or the radio. With a music appeal, the primary thrust of the ad is the song. The visuals and the copy support the song. With this type of appeal, advertisers like to use popular tunes that people have already developed an affinity for with the hope that the same feelings will be transferred to the product being advertised. The difficulty is the cost, which averages $250,000 per song. However, for an extremely popular song, such as Jimi Hendrix's ''Are You Experienced,'' the price tag can skyrocket to $7 million. Microsoft paid $12 million for the Rolling Stones' song ''Start Me Up.'' For this reason, many advertisers will use new artists or relatively unknown bands, which typically cost in the range of $35,000 to $100,000.[14]

Rational appeals are used in many advertisements, especially in print ads and for business-to-business ads. The premise of a rational appeal is that consumers will stop, look at the ad, and be interested in reading the copy or listening to what is being said. Unfortunately, with the large number of ads everyone is exposed to daily, it is much harder to get a person's attention using a rational appeal. However, if a person is interested in a product, then the rational appeal is the most effective means of conveying information and promoting the brand's benefits. It is also an effective means of advertising high-involvement products about which consumers may want to obtain additional information. If a consumer will stop and pay attention to an ad using a rational appeal, the chances are good that the information will be understood and become a part of the person's memory. **Figure 12-23** illustrates a business-to-business advertisement using a rational appeal.

Figure 12-23: The business-to-business advertisement by OccuMed Network uses a rational appeal.

Source: Courtesy of Newcomer, Morris & Young.

12-7b: Message Strategies

The message strategy is the primary tactic an advertisement will use to deliver a message. The message strategy is what is being said, whereas the appeal is how it is being said. For example, a person may say "look at that" and by the inflection of the person's voice relay fear, shock, love, emotion, or just a matter-of-fact, rational statement with no emotion. Message strategies fall into three categories: cognitive, affective, and conative.

Cognitive message strategies are the presentation of rational arguments or pieces of information to consumers. The message focuses on key product attributes or important customer benefits. Shoes with DMX technology may be described as comfortable. A fishing boat may be featured as being designed for bass fishing with oversized storage, live wells for fish, built-in coolers, and ergonomically designed cockpits with backlit controls. With a cognitive message strategy, creatives assume the audience will read or listen to the ad, pay attention to the message, and cognitively process the information. The goal is to develop cognitive knowledge and beliefs about the brand by presenting information about the product's attributes and benefits the consumer can receive from the brand.

As would be expected, the cognitive message strategy works well with a rational appeal. However, often advertisers will use an emotional, fear, or sexual appeal to get the person's attention, and then use a cognitive message to explain the product's benefit. With this contrasting approach, the visual element or the headline is normally used to grab attention; then the body of the ad is used to explain the product.

Figure 12-24: Marketers would probably use an emotional appeal at first to promote a package tour to Venice. However, the trip is expensive and getting there is no easy feat; ultimately, a cognitive appeal will have to elaborate on the tour benefits.

Affective message strategies are designed to invoke feelings and emotions within the audience. They are based on the belief that if consumers react emotionally to an advertisement, their response will affect their attitude toward the ad, which will then be projected toward the brand. An advertisement that elicits a feeling of warmth and love within the viewer will usually create a liking for the ad, which will enhance positive feelings toward the product (Figure 12-24). Affective emotions can

Cognitive Message Strategies: The presentation of rational arguments or pieces of information to consumers.

Affective Message Strategies: Messages designed to invoke feelings and emotions within the audience.

Figure 12-25: The Mediating Effect of Emotions on Communication Cues and Attitude toward the Brand

Ad Content

↓

Emotional Response

↓

Attitude toward the Ad

↓

Attitude toward the Brand

Emotional response evoked by advertising may, in turn, affect a consumer's attitude toward the advertised brand.

work in the reverse as well. An advertisement that creates anger or disgust will create a negative feeling toward the ad and, in turn, a negative feeling toward the brand. Affective message strategies are used in conjunction with emotional, fear, humor, sex, and music appeals. Seldom will an affective message strategy be coupled with a rational appeal. Figure 12-25 illustrates how an affective message strategy builds a favorable attitude toward the brand.

Conative message strategies are designed to elicit some type of audience behavior, such as a purchase or inquiry. They are normally tied with a promotion that is offering a coupon, a price-off, or some other special deal. An advertisement for Cheerios with a 50-cent coupon and an opportunity to enter a special sweepstakes would be a conative message strategy because the goal of the ad is to have consumers purchase a box of Cheerios and to enter the contest. The advertisement in Figure 12-26 by the Breast Center of Glenwood Regional Medical Center uses a conative message strategy. The ad encourages women to ask their doctor about a Mammotome or to call the Glenwood HealthSource for more information. An emotional and fear appeal is used to send the message by combining a photo of a young, attractive female with the fact that about one out of eight women will be diagnosed with breast cancer.

Conative Message Strategies: Messages designed to elicit some type of audience behavior, such as a purchase or inquiry.

Figure 12-26: This advertisement by the Breast Center of Glenwood Regional Medical Center uses a conative message strategy.

Source: Sample print advertisement courtesy of The Miles Agency and Alliance One Advertising, Inc.

12-8 MEDIA SELECTION

Media selection is a critical component of advertising. If the correct medium is not selected, the target market will not hear the message. Understanding the target audience in terms of media behavior is important. Just as research is conducted to understand consumer behavior in terms of purchasing products, research must be conducted to understand media behavior. How much advertising should be allocated to each medium, such as radio, TV, newspapers, the Internet and so forth? More important, if the members of a particular target market watch TV, which shows do they tend to watch?

Figure 12-27 presents the breakdown by media of the $190 billion spent on advertising media buys in the United States. Notice that the largest category is for television, 39.4%. But a close second and the fastest growing area is for digital advertising, 30.9 percent. Almost half of the digital advertising is for mobile ads. Print media, newspapers and magazines, are still an important media as is radio. The smallest category is out-of-home advertising.

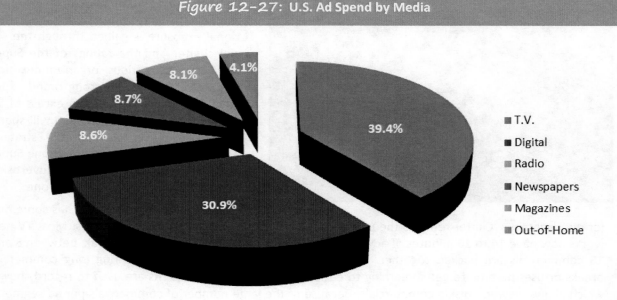

Figure 12-27: U.S. Ad Spend by Media

- T.V.
- Digital
- Radio
- Newspapers
- Magazines
- Out-of-Home

Source: US Total Media Ad Spend Inches Up, Pushed by Digital," *eMarketer*, http://www.emarketer.com/Articles?Print,aspx?R=1010154.)

12-8a: Broadcast Media

Broadcast media consist of television and radio. TV provides excellent opportunities for creating effective advertisements because both visual images and sounds can be incorporated simultaneously. TV also has the advantage of having high **reach**, defined as the number of people, households, or businesses in a target audience exposed to a media message at least once during a given time period. Just one TV advertisement can reach millions of consumers. For example, an advertisement on American Idol reached 18.4 million households, and an advertisement on CSI reached 11.1 million households. Each week, Nielsen Media Research publishes the Nielsen ratings for TV shows.

> **Reach:**
> The number of people, households, or businesses in a target audience exposed to a media message at least once during a given time period.

Nielsen ratings are an important factor in how much it costs to advertise on a TV show. The higher the Nielsen rating, the more it will cost. For example, the average cost of a 30 second ad on network TV during prime time is $126,000. But an ad on CSI will cost around $500,000 because of its high audience viewing and high average Nielsen rating. While the overall cost is high, the relative cost per viewer is low. To be able to compare across media and even across TV shows, advertisers use **cost per thousand (CPM)**,

> **Cost per thousand (CPM):** The cost of reaching 1,000 members of a media vehicle's audience.

which is the cost of reaching 1,000 members of a media vehicle's audience. So for the CSI illustration, if the Nielsen rating indicated an average of 16 million households watched the TV show, then the CPM would be $31.25 ($500,000/16,000,000 * 1,000).

The high reach of television combined with the relative low cost per thousand helps to explain why the Super Bowl has become the showcase of new advertising each year and brands willing to pay over $4 million for just 30 seconds of exposure. Viewership is now over 100 million, which means the CPM is below $40.00. A large percentage of Super Bowl viewers tune in to see the new ads. While they

may watch the football game, their primary interest is the new ads. Social media explodes during and after each game with comments about the various ads and, by the next morning, the best and worst ads of the Super Bowl are announced. For advertisers, in addition to people watching the advertisement during the game, additional exposure is gained through the social chatter and the ratings of the Super Bowl ads by various organizations and Web sites. To ensure strong brand exposure, brands are spending in excess of $1 million to produce the ads and will spend nearly a year in planning the strategy around the ad. Thus, as soon as one Super Bowl ends, brands and their advertising agencies begin work on the next one.

However, television has some major disadvantages. Clutter remains the primary problem , especially on network programs. Most TV networks now have 14 to 16 minutes of advertising per hour. Within each commercial break, between 8 and 15 commercials are packed together. Many viewers simply switch channels during long commercial breaks or use the time to get something to eat or go to the bathroom. DVRs are used to record shows, which allows viewers to skip commercials. Because of the large number of commercials per ad segment, messages at the beginning or near the end of the break have the best recall. Those in the middle often have virtually no impact.[15]

TV commercials have short life spans. Most ads, 91.4 percent, last only 15 or 30 seconds. A recent experiment in TV advertising is the five-second spot, which was designed to counter TiVo. The five-second ad is placed just before the beginning of a TV show. The idea is that when the viewer stops at the beginning of a show after skipping the commercials, the digital video recorder (DVR) will back up a few seconds.[16]

In addition to the high cost of media time, producing a TV ad is expensive, averaging $358,000 for a 30-second spot. But it is not unusual for an agency to spend up to $1 million on producing an outstanding ad, especially for the Super Bowl. Because of the high frequency of TV advertisements, wear-out occurs fast (i.e., the ad quickly loses its ability to hold the viewer's interest). Consequently, agencies have to constantly produce new ads. Often, a series of advertisements will be produced so they can be rotated. Another tactic advertisers use is to create a 30- or 60-second spot and then make 15-second ads from the larger one. All of these tactics create variety and are designed to prevent wear-out from occurring so quickly.

Although radio may not have the glamour appeal of TV, it does offer the advantage of intimacy. Listeners can develop an affinity with the DJs and other radio personalities. This closeness grows over time, especially if the listener has a conversation with the DJ during a contest or when requesting a song.

The bond that develops means the DJ will have a higher level of credibility, and goods or services that are endorsed by the DJ will be more readily accepted.

In addition to providing intimacy, radio is also mobile. People can take radios with them wherever they go. They can listen while at the beach, at home, at work, or on the road in between. No other medium has the power to stay with an audience quite like radio. For business-to-business advertisers, radio provides an opportunity to reach businesses during working hours when businesspeople are likely to be listening to the radio. Even more important is the transit time to and from work when a businessperson is more likely to pay attention to an ad, especially if he or she is stuck in traffic snarl.

Radio stations tend to have definable target markets based on their formats, such as talk radio, country music, rock, pop, oldies, and so forth. This means that a company that wants to advertise on country music stations can find stations all across the country.

Another major advantage of radio is the flexibility and the short lead time for producing commercials. An ad can be recorded and placed on the air within a few days and sometimes within hours. Ads can also be changed quickly. This is especially helpful in the retail sector, where a store may want to change the items featured as being on sale.

Radio has some disadvantages, in addition to the lack of a visual element. Like TV, the short exposure time of most radio advertisements makes it difficult to comprehend what has been said. This is especially true for radio, because people are often involved in other activities, such as working on a computer or driving a vehicle. In many cases, the radio is simply background noise used to drown out other distractions.

For national advertisers, producing a national radio advertisement is challenging because there are few large radio conglomerates and national networks available. To place a national advertisement requires contacting a large number of stations and companies that may own a handful of radio stations. As a result, 67 percent of all radio advertising is for local businesses, with 24 percent being national ads and nine percent being network.

For a summary of the advantages and disadvantages of TV and radio advertising, see Table 12-7.

Table 12-7: Advantages | Disadvantages of Broadcast Advertising	
Advantages	**Disadvantages**
Television	
1. High reach	1. High level of clutter
2. High frequency potential	2. Low recall
3. Low cost per contact	3. Short ad duration
4. High intrusion value	4. High cost per ad
5. Creative design opportunities	
6. Segmentation through cable channels	
Radio	
1. High recall potential	1. Short ad duration
2. Segmented target markets	2. Low attention
3. Flexibility and short lead time in ad production	3. No national audience
4. Intimacy with DJs	4. Difficulty in buying national time
5. Mobility of radios	5. Target duplication in large metropolitan areas
6. Excellent for local businesses	
7. Low cost per contact	

12-8b: Print Media

The primary print media are newspapers and magazines. As previously shown in Figure 12-27, newspapers account for 8.7 percent of total US ad expenditures and magazines are 8.3 percent of total expenditures. While newspaper and magazine readership continues to decline, both are still important venues for advertisers.

Retailers rely heavily on newspapers because they offer geographic selectivity (i.e., access to the local target market area). Sales, retail hours, and store locations are easy to promote in a newspaper ad. Newspapers have relatively short lead times, which allow retailers the flexibility to change ads frequently and keep ads current. They can quickly modify an ad to reflect recent events or to combat a competitor's actions. The ad for The Toggery and Her Toggery in Figure 12-28 informs consumers about an upcoming trunk show.

Newspapers tend to have a high level of credibility because people rely on newspapers for factual information in stories. This carries over to a greater level of credibility for newspaper advertisements. Because readers take time to read a newspaper, they tend to pay more attention to advertisements. This increased audience interest allows advertisers to provide more copy detail in their ads.

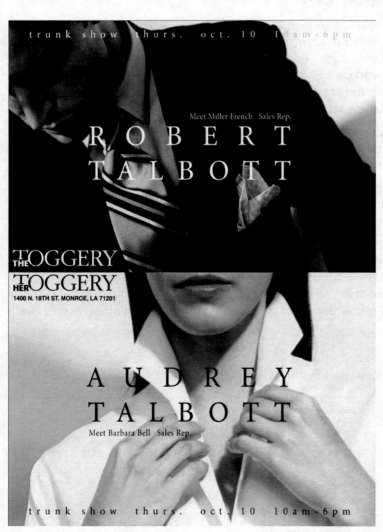

Figure 12-28: This newspaper ad for The Toggery and Her Toggery promotes an upcoming trunk show featuring clothing by Robert and Audrey Talbott.

Source: Sample print advertisement courtesy of The Miles Agency and Alliance One Advertising, Inc.

Newspapers do have some limitations. Except for geographic selectivity, it is difficult to target an advertisement to a specific market segment. Newspapers have a short life span. Once read, most newspapers are discarded. If readers do not see an ad when they first read the paper, it probably will go unnoticed because it is unlikely they will pick up the paper a second time. Compared with other print media, newspaper ads have poor production quality. There are few color ads, because they are expensive, and photos and copy tend to be more difficult to read. Creatives do not have as much freedom to create wild, lavish advertisements because newspapers tend to be more conservative. Newspaper editors are very concerned about offending readers with risqué ads. Just as with radio, it is difficult to purchase national ad space, and because of their local nature, newspapers are a better medium for local businesses than for national firms.

Magazines have become a preferred advertising medium for many products. Research conducted by Marketing Evolution and commissioned by Magazine Publishers of America examined 19 marketers, including Ford, Johnson & Johnson, Target, and Motorola. The study investigated the effectiveness of magazine advertising by examining ad awareness, ad familiarity, purchase intent, and brand imagery for magazines, TV, and online. Magazines led in three of the four categories. Magazines scored highest in brand familiarity (85 percent), purchase intentions (72 percent), and brand imagery (73 percent). TV scored highest in ad awareness.[17] Of course, TV executives debate the validity of both studies. In any case, magazines do provide an excellent medium for advertising.

A major advantage of magazines is the ability to precisely target audience segments. Specialized magazines aimed at specific target markets are more common than general readership magazines. Advertising in these specialized magazines allows advertisers to reach a greater percentage of their audience. Individuals reading Modern Bride will pay more attention to ads about weddings than someone reading People, so advertising wedding products in Modern Bride is likely to be more effective.

Most magazines offer high-quality color reproduction capabilities that allow creatives more freedom in designing advertisements. Color, headlines, and unusual images can be used to attract attention. Magazines such as Glamour, Elle, and Cosmopolitan will use scratch and sniff ads to entice women to smell a particular brand of perfume or cologne.

Magazines have a long advertising life beyond the immediate issue. They are often read and reread by subscribers, which means ads are often seen more than once. Magazine ads last beyond the current issue with people reading the magazine in a doctor's office or the waiting room of a Jiffy Lube. Weeks and even months later, individuals may see an advertisement. In the business-to-business sector, trade journals are often passed around to several individuals or members of the buying center and sometimes kept on file for later reference. As long as the magazine lasts, the advertisement is still there to be viewed. This opportunity for repeat viewings is attractive to advertisers.

Magazines are facing some tough times, however, because of the Internet and TV. A recent study by Media Research Inc. showed an overall decline of readership by 122 titles, or 59.5 percent, of the magazines measured. Six of the eight major magazine categories have seen overall declines. Women's lifestyle, service titles, and business and personal finance publications have all declined. [18] As with other media, clutter is becoming a greater problem for magazines. For example, a recent 318-page issue of Glamour contained 195 pages of advertising and only 123 pages of content. It is easy for ads to be lost in those situations.

Magazines require long lead times, often six months. That makes it difficult to modify ads and to keep ads current. Because of the long life of a magazine ad, people may still see it several months after it appears in the magazine. That means a creative has to think ahead six to 12 months when designing an ad to decide what type of appeal might work.

For a summary of advantages and disadvantages of print media, see Table 12.8.

Table 12–8: **Advantages and Disadvantages of Print Advertising**

Advantages	Disadvantages
Newspapers	
1. Excellent for local businesses	1. Poor buying procedures
2. High flexibility	2. Short life span
3. High credibility	3. Poor quality reproduction
4. Strong audience interest	4. Limited ad design creativity possible
Magazines	
1. High target audience segmentation	1. Declining readership
2. High reader interest	2. High level of clutter
3. High color quality	3. Long lead time to design ad
4. Long life	4. Little flexibility
5. Multiple frequency	5. High cost

Summary

1. Discuss the concept of integrated marketing communications. IMC is the coordination and integration of all marketing communication tools, avenues, and sources within a company into a seamless program designed to maximize the communication impact on consumers, businesses, and other constituencies of an organization. IMC is a holistic approach that involves everyone in the company articulating the same message. There must be open communication vertically within the company, horizontally across functional areas and departments, and outward to customers and stakeholders who have an interest in the company. IMC involves communicating to four primary groups: customers, channel members, employees, and stakeholders.

2. Identify the various marketing communication elements. The marketing communication elements include the traditional promotional mix of advertising, sales or consumer promotions, trade promotions, personal selling, and PR. But with the integrated approach, other components of communication have also become important, such as Internet, database, and direct marketing. Possible communication outlets include traditional venues such as radio, television, newspapers, and magazines, but also the Internet, billboards, transit signs, store signage, and company stationery.

3. Identify the elements of communication and the importance of AIDA. The six steps in communication are the source, encoding, message, medium, decoding, and audience. For communication to occur, the source, which for IMC is normally a business or an ad agency, encodes what it wants to communicate into a message, which is transmitted to an audience via some channel such as a television or point-of-purchase display. The audience, or potential customer, sees the message and decodes the message. If the decoded message matches the encoded message, accurate communication has occurred. Feedback from the audience to the sender alerts the sender to the success of the message and what, if anything, needs to be modified for future messages. Noise is anything that interferes with the delivery of the message from the source to the audience. AIDA is an acronym for attention, interest, desire, and action. It is the process of developing customers, taking them through the stages of getting their attention, building interest in the product, building desire for the product over competitors, and encouraging them to act, ultimately, to purchase.

4. Discuss the various factors that affect the relative mix of communication elements in an integrated marketing communications plan. The factors that affect the relative mix of an IMC campaign include business versus consumer market, communication objective, push/pull strategy, PLC, and communication budget. Business markets tend to rely more on personal selling, whereas consumer markets rely more on advertising. The communication objectives include increasing demand, differentiating a product, providing information, building brand equity, reducing purchase risk, and stimulating trial. The IMC mix will vary depending on which objective is primary. For push strategies, firms will rely more on trade promotions and personal selling, whereas for pull strategies, advertising and consumer promotions are used. The relative IMC mix will vary with each stage of the PLC, with the maturity stage requiring the highest level of all components of the IMC mix. The overall communication budget determines how much is available to divide among the various elements.

5. Identify the various types of advertising. Advertising can be divided into two primary types: product and institutional. Product advertising is any advertisement designed to promote a firm's brand. It can be targeted to end users or channel members. Product advertising can be further subdivided into brand, informative, persuasive, pioneer, and comparative advertising. Institutional advertising is designed to build the corporate reputation or develop goodwill for the corporation; it involves cause-related marketing and public service announcements.

6. Describe the appeals that can be used in designing an advertisement. The advertising appeal is the design a creative will use to attract attention to and interest in an advertisement. The six primary types of appeal are emotional, fear, humor, sex, music, and rational. The appeal chosen will depend on the objective of the ad, the message theme to be used, the target audience, and how the creative wants to convey the message to the intended audience. Almost every product can be advertised using any of the six appeals, and an advertisement will often use two or three appeals.

7. Differentiate between the three types of message strategies. The message strategy is the primary tactic an advertisement will use to deliver a message. The three types of message strategies are cognitive, affective, and conative. Cognitive message strategies are the presentation of rational arguments or pieces of information to consumers that are cognitively processed. The message focuses on key product attributes or important customer benefits with the goal of developing specific beliefs or knowledge about the brand. Affective message strategies are designed to invoke feelings and emotions within the audience. They are based on the idea that if consumers react emotionally to an advertisement, their response will affect their attitude toward the ad, which will then be projected toward the brand. Conative message strategies are designed to elicit some type of audience behavior, such as a purchase or inquiry.

   8. Discuss the advantages and disadvantages of the primary media. TV has the advantages of offering high reach, high frequency potential, low cost per contact, high intrusion value, creative design opportunities, and segmentation through cable channels. The disadvantages of TV are a high level of clutter, low recall, short ad duration, and high cost per ad. For radio, the advantages are high recall potential, segmented target markets, flexibility and short lead time in ad production, intimacy with DJs, mobility of radios, and low cost per contact. The disadvantages are a short ad duration, low attention, no national audience, difficulty in buying national time, and target duplication in large metropolitan areas. In the print media, newspapers offer the advantages of high flexibility, high credibility, and strong audience interest. Disadvantages are poor buying procedures, a short life span, poor quality reproduction, and limited ad design creativity. For magazines, the major advantages include high target audience segmentation, high reader interest, high color quality, long life, and multiple frequency. Disadvantages are a declining readership, high level of clutter, long lead time, little flexibility, and high cost.

Key Terms

advertising	direct response marketing	personal selling
advertising appeal	encoding	persuasive advertising
affective message strategies	feedback	pioneer advertising
AIDA	informative advertising	product advertising
audience	institutional advertising	promotion
brand advertising	integrated marketing com-	public relations (PR)
cognitive message strategies	munications (IMC)	publicity
comparative advertising	Internet marketing	sales promotions
conative message strategies	Intrusion value	source
cost per thousand (CPM)	medium	trade promotions
database marketing	message	
decoding	noise	

Discussion Questions

1. Pick a well-known restaurant, such as Pizza Hut, McDonald's, Outback Steakhouse, or Olive Garden. Discuss how the restaurant integrates all of its marketing messages. What common theme is used? What types of IMC elements are used? Access the firm's Web site. Is the Web site consistent with the television, radio, and other media advertising?

2. Think about purchasing a new car. Identify all of the venues, such as television, radio, magazines, and so on, that you would use to gather information about the various models and list them. In a second list, include any sources of information an automobile dealer may use to communicate with you but that you would not pay any attention to. What are the most effective means of communicating with you? Where would the automobile dealer be wasting money?

3. List the primary media in a table (television, radio, newspapers, and magazines). Add digital (online) to your list. When you think of viewing or listening to the various media, what percentage of your time is spent with each? The total should add to 100 percent. Create a pie chart showing your media consumption. Write a paragraph discussing each of the media in terms of your personal media consumption.

4. Examine the AIDA model. Go to YouTube and locate advertisements that illustrate each of the steps in AIDA. Explain why you think the ad chosen is a good example of the particular AIDA concept, such as getting attention, building interest, building desire, or promoting action. Provide a link to the four YouTube ads you selected in your document.

5. Think about the last major purchase you made. Go through the AIDA concept in terms of what the brand did to get your attention, build interest, build desire, and promote action.

6. Go to YouTube and locate three advertisements you like. Explain why you like the ad. For each ad, identify the type of advertising, such as informative product advertising, comparative product advertising, institutional advertising, etc. Justify your choice. For each ad, identify the appeal used and the message strategy used. Justify these classifications.

7. Review the five types of product advertising. For each type, identify an advertisement that you believe is a good example. Explain why you think it is a good example.

8. Review the six types of advertising appeals. Go to YouTube. For each appeal, locate an advertisement that is a good example. Explain why you think it is a good example. Provide a link to the video in your explanation.

9. Review the three types of advertising message strategies. Go to YouTube. For each message strategy, locate an advertisement that is a good example. Explain why you think it is a good example. Provide a link to the video in your explanation.

10. On the average, how much time do you spend viewing or listening to broadcast media, TV and radio? Discuss your viewing habits of broadcast media in terms of time spent with each, shows or programs you like, and impact of advertising on your purchase behavior.

11. On the average, how much time do you spend with print media, magazines and newspapers? Discuss your reading habits of print media in terms of time spent with each, magazines or newspapers you read, and impact of advertising on your purchase behavior.

12. Create three columns on a piece of paper with the headings (1) Recognize, (2) New, and (3) Not sure. As you watch each advertisement during a 30-minute television show, put a hash mark in the correct column based on whether it was an ad you recognize as having seen before, a new ad, or an ad you are not sure you have seen before. What was the total number of ads aired during the show? Write down the top five ads you recall seeing. What did you like or dislike about each? Do you remember where they were in the sequence of the ad block? Does it make a difference where they are located in the sequence? Why or why not?

Review Questions

(Answers are on Last Page of the Chapter)

True or False

1. The process of encoding begins with the interpretation of the meaning conveyed in the marketing message.

2. The abundance of different communication channels and prolific advertising facilitate the communication process and allow customers to select the right message.

3. Marketing managers allocate at least 75 percent of the marketing budget for advertising because advertising has the most direct impact on sales.

4. AIDA is a concept used by advertisers in designing ads and stands for attention, interest, decision, and advertising.

5. Informational product advertising is the most common form of product advertising.

6. If pioneer advertising worked successfully at the product introduction stage of the PLC, the same ad will most likely be effective in the growth stage.

7. Institutional advertising is designed to build corporate reputation or develop goodwill for the corporation.

8. With most products in the maturity stage of the PLC, advertising is instrumental in the process of developing brand awareness, brand equity, and brand preference.

9. The advertisement message strategy defines the manner in which the advertisement will be presented.

Multiple Choice

10. What is the best description of integrated marketing communications?

    a. Seamless programs designed to maximize the communication effect

    b. Coordination and integration of all marketing communications tools

    c. Coordination and integration of all marketing resources

    d. All of the above

11. Which of the following descriptions refers to multichannel marketing?

    a. Multiple channels for customers to purchase a product

    b. Multiple avenues of communication to gather information

    c. Integration of both distribution and communication channels

    d. None of the above

12. After seeing an advertisement on TV, a consumer checks the Internet to find the closest retail store or searches for more information on the Web as to where the product can be purchased. According to the AIDA concept, these actions belong to which step?

      a. Attention

      b. Interest

      c. Desire

      d. Action

13. Which of the following categories are often used as objectives in the integrated marketing communications plan?

      a. Increasing demand and product differentiation

      b. Providing information and building brand equity

      c. Reducing purchase risk and stimulating trials

      d. All of the above

14. The primary goal of brand advertising is to

      a. build brand awareness.

      b. develop a brand name.

      c. provide detailed information about product features.

      d. a and b.

15. Comparative advertising is most successful in

      a. building primary demand for a product.

      b. introducing new brands.

      c. developing goodwill for the corporation.

      d. providing more information.

16. What should be a key consideration in creating an advertisement that will get attention and produce results?

      a. Advertisement objectives

      b. Demographic information

      c. Psychographics information

      d. All of the above

17. Which message strategy presents a rational argument or pieces of information to consumers?

      a. Cognitive message strategy

      b. Affective message strategy

      c. Conative message strategy

      d. All of the above.

18. Why have magazines become a preferred advertising medium for many consumer products?

      a. Ability to precisely target audience segments

      b. High-quality color reproduction capability

      c. Long advertising life beyond the immediate issue

      d. All of the above

Blog

Clow-Lascu: *Marketing Essentials 5e Blog*

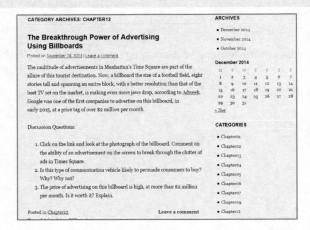

What Is Happening Today?

Learn More! For videos and articles

that relate to Chapter 12:

blogclowlascu.net/category/chapter12

Includes Discussion Questions

with each Post!

Notes

1. Stuart Elliott, "Old Spice Tries a Dash of Humor to Draw Young Men," *New York Times*, available at www.nytimes.com/2007/01/08/business/media/08adcol.html, accessed on January 8, 2007.

2. Carol Angrisani, "Coupon Competition," *Supermarket News* 54, no. 10 (March 6, 2006): 23–25; Noreen O'Leary, "Dealing with Coupons," *Adweek* 46, no. 8 (February 21, 2005): 29.

3. Al Urbanski, "Trade Promo Lowdown," *Progressive Grocer*, vol. 82 (March 1, 2003): 45–46.

4. Katy Bachman, "Cable Clutter On the Rise," *MediaWeek* 13, no. 33 (September 15, 2003), 5–6.

5. Stephanie Thompson, "Grab a Coffee and Shave on the Go," *Brandweek* 40, no. 17 (April 26, 1999): 53.

6. Christine Bittar, "High Anxiety: Patents Expire, Success Wanes," *Brandweek* 43, no. 24 (June 17, 2002): S64.

7. Stephanie Thompson, "Ads Boost Bean Business," *Advertising Age* 72, no. 9 (February 26, 2001): 2.

8. Becky Ebenkamp and Todd Wasserman, "Kids WB's Great Adventure; TNT and Fox's Evil Alien Plot," *Brandweek* 45 (July 26, 2004): 8.

9. Scott Rockwood, "For Better Ad Success, Try Getting Emotional," *Marketing News* 30, no. 22 (October 21, 1996): 4.

10. Jerry Olson and Thomas J. Reynolds, "Understanding Consumers' Cognitive Structures: Implications for Advertising Strategy," in *Advertising Consumer Psychology*, eds. L. Percy and A. Woodside (Lexington, Mass.: Lexington Books, 1983): 77–90.

11. Michael S. Latour and Robin L. Snipes, "Don't Be Afraid to Use Fear Appeals: An Experimental Study," *Journal of Advertising* 36, no. 2 (March/April 1996): 59–68.

12. Harlan E. Spotts and Marc G. Weinberger, "Assessing the Use and Impact of Humor on Advertising Effectiveness," *Journal of Advertising* 26, no. 3 (Fall 1997): 17–32.

13. Jessica Severn and George E. Belch, "The Effects of Sexual and Non-Sexual Advertising Appeals and Information Level on Cognitive Processing and Communication Effectiveness," *Journal of Advertising* 19, no. 1 (1990): 14–22.

14. Wes Orshoski, "Paydays Go By," *Billboard* 118, No. 45 (November 11, 2006), 8; Michael Miller, "Even Out of Context, the Beat Goes On (and On)," *Pittsburgh Business Times* 18, no. 18 (November 27, 1998): 12.

15. Katy Bachman, "Cable Clutter on the Rise," *MediaWeek* 13, no. 33 (September 15, 2003): 5–6.

16. Laura Petrecca, "Five-Second Ads Try to Counter TiVo," *USA Today* available at www.usatoday.com/money/advertising/2006-07-05-5-seconds-ads-usat_x.htm, accessed on July 10, 2006.

17. Steve Miller, "Stop the Presses: Print Still Effective Ad Buy," *Brandweek* 47, no. 39 (October 23, 2006): 8.

18. Katy Bachman, Aimee Deeken, and Jim Cooper, "Media Wire," *MediaWeek* 13, no. 21 (May 26, 2003): 4–5.

Case 12-1 Mudd Jeans: Reaching the Female Teen and Tween

Sales of women's jeans total $7.8 billion. Jeans retailing for less than $40 make up 76.3 percent of this market. Jeans priced at $100 or above make up only 1.5 percent of the market but generate $113.1 million in sales. Jeans no longer are just weekend or home wear; for many they are a fashion statement and appropriate for the office and a night out. For teens and tweens, jeans are an essential component of a girl's wardrobe.

The Mudd jean brand was founded in 1995 by Dick Gilbert and then sold in May 2004 to Hong Kong–based apparel manufacturer Tack Fat Group. The new owner's goal was to make Mudd into a $1 billion business by pushing into Asian markets. The venture failed. In April 2006, the Mudd brand was sold to Iconix Brand Group. Niel Cole, Chairman and CEO of Iconix, stated, "We have a lot of great opportunities with Mudd. We want to grow the different product categories. [Mudd has] an 84 percent brand awareness among young women." After acquiring the Mudd brand, Iconix used marketing research to identify the "Mudd Girl." This girl is between the ages of 11 and 17. She has the following mind-set:

- She is sassy and daring.
- She is part free spirit and part fashionista.
- She is into finding herself, knowing her true voice.
- She is a girl like every other, yet unlike any other.
- She is self-empowered.
- She wants to make a statement and a difference.
- She is independent.
- She wants to accomplish something in her life.
- At the end of the day, she wants to be true to herself.
- She is real.

Iconix established <u>Mymuddworld.com</u> to provide information to teens and tweens and also to be an inspirational Web site for Mudd girls around the country. The site features images from recent ad campaigns, news about fashion, and information about Mudd products. The Web site also provides a social network for girls to share stories, learn about worthwhile social causes, and make new friends.

To connect with their young female market, Mudd launched the "Delicious Curves" for juniors. To pitch this new line, Mudd hired R&B singer Ashanti. It was Mudd's first attempt at using a celebrity spokesperson. Assume you have been selected by the Iconix Group as the advertising agency to promote the Mudd brand to girls 11 to 17.

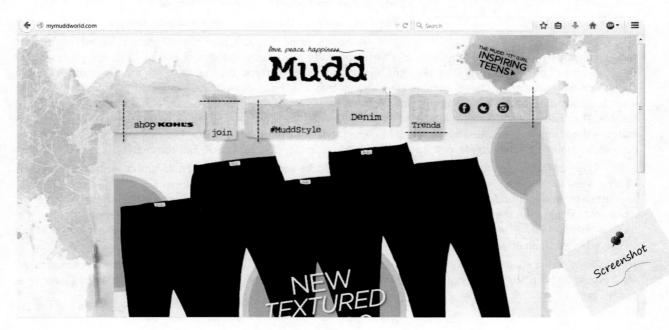

Rules of Advertising to Teenagers

Rule	Percent of Survey Respondents Who Agreed (%)
Be honest.	65
Use humor; make me laugh.	52
Be clear.	45
Show the product.	43
Tell me something important about the product.	37
Do not use sex to sell.	31
Show situations that are realistic.	25
Have a great slogan or jingle.	24
Do not talk down to me.	22
Do not try too hard to be cool.	21
Use great music.	21
Show people/scenes I can relate to.	20
Show people my age.	19
Do not tell me what to do.	19
Show me things I have never seen before.	14
Do not butcher a song I like.	14
Show celebrities who use the product.	8
Show cute animals or babies.	6
Be sarcastic.	5
Show situations that are fantasy.	4

Access the Iconix Brand Web site at www.iconixbrand.com and locate the Mudd brand. Then examine the Mymuddworld.com Web site. Lastly, study the information listed in the accompanying table entitled "Rules of Advertising to Teenagers." This information was the result of a survey conducted by American Demographics. It highlights the most important rules for advertising to the teenage market.

Questions

1. What is your evaluation of the Web sites listed in the case (Iconix Brand, Mudd brand, and Mymuddworld)?

2. Based on the information in this case and the information on the Web sites, what type of advertising campaign would you recommend for Mudd?

3. How would you interpret the information provided by American Demographics concerning rules advertisers should follow for teenagers? How would it affect the design of an advertising campaign?

4. What type of appeal would you use for the Mudd Girl? Why?

5. Discuss the media strategy that you think would be appropriate for the teen market. Where would you advertise?

6. Based on the information in this case, design a print advertisement for Mudd.

Sources: Ross Tucker, "Premium Pops," *Women's Wear Daily* (July 2006): 42; Scott Malone, "Mudd Grows Up," WWD: Women's Wear Daily 188 (August 26, 2004): 10; Iconix Brand Web site, available at www.iconixbrand.html, accessed March 28, 2007.

Case 12-2 Reaching Women

The video gaming business was built on male customers shooting at enemies and destroying foreign invaders. If women played, no one admitted it. That has changed, and changed quite dramatically. Recent research has revealed the following:

- Forty percent of the total gaming audience is female.
- Sixty-four percent of online gamers are female.
- Sixty-one percent of the mobile phone market is female.

Although some females play the violence-oriented games and sports games played by males, females prefer simulation and puzzle-solving types of games. They like games where they can control the characters. They like light humor and fun characters. They want to see more personalization in games and dialogue among the characters. Even though they may be involved in helping destroy an enemy, they also want to heal the fallen friends along the way. Women prefer the kinds of conflicts that you do not have to fight to resolve. The challenge of solving a mystery or a puzzle within the video game is appealing. A popular game with females is the Nancy Drew series, which has sold more than four million copies. The game incorporates a puzzle into each series along with a greater level of socialization, character development, plot, and community.

One of the fastest-growing female segments is middle-aged women. Women 35 and older now average 9.5 hours a week with online gaming, spending twice as much time as men their same age. In the 25 to 34 age group, 65 percent of females play video games, compared with 35 percent of men. But these women play games for a different reason. Men enjoy the me-versus-the computer competition aspect of games. Females turn to games for relief, distraction, and socializing. In addition, females tend to play in shorter time segments and, therefore, like games that can be played in less than 30 minutes.

One of the challenging aspects of marketing games to females is that they do not see themselves as gamers. Most would be horrified if you even suggested they were "gamers." If asked, most would say, "No, I don't have time to play games."

In the past, the video game companies were predominantly operated by males. Game programmers were male. Today, more and more females are entering the video gaming businesses and even are involved in designing video games. Females are developing marketing plans and advertising campaigns to reach female customers. The video gaming business today is very different from the video gaming 25 years ago.

Questions

1. What type of marketing approach would be best for reaching females, considering most do not see themselves as gamers?

2. How would the market approach vary for college and teenage girls versus women in their thirties and forties?

3. In advertising to females 25 to 40, what media would you recommend? Within those media, which specific magazines or television shows would you use?

4. Based on your responses to questions 2 and 3, design a print advertisement that you think would appeal to females for a Nancy Drew video game. What would be your primary message theme?

Sources: Tina Benitez, "The Games Girls Play," *Plaything* 105, no. 1 (January 2007): 19; Beth Snyder Bulik, "Video Games Unveil Feminine Side," *Advertising Age* 77, no. 44 (October 30, 2006): S10; Mike Shields, "The Games Women Play," *Brandweek* 47, no. 19 (May 8, 2006): 36–38; Derek Chezzi, "These Toys Aren't For Boys," *MacLean's* 117, no. 23 (June 7, 2004): 23

Answers to Review Questions

Answers: 1) F, 2) F, 3) F, 4) F, 5) F, 6) F, 7) T, 8) T, 9) F, 10) d, 11) a, 12) b, 13) d, 14) d, 15) b, 16) d, 17) a, 18) d.

.

Chapter 13

Digital Marketing

Learning Objectives

After studying
this chapter,
you should be able to:

1. Discuss current global Internet usage.

2. Identify the benefits of digital marketing.

3. Discuss the importance of e-commerce.

4. Identify and explain the various digital marketing strategies.

5. Explain how firms can use mobile marketing.

6. Examine strategies that can be used in social media marketing.

Chapter Outline

13-1 CHAPTER OVERVIEW

Although marketing has been around for several decades, digital marketing is a recent phenomenon. Consumers and businesses can purchase almost anything over the Internet. They can research brands and companies on the Internet. Because of increased usage of the Internet by both consumers and businesses, having a Web presence has become important, and understanding how to maximize the marketing thrust of a Web site is even more important. In Section 13-2, the makeup of Internet users is presented. Section 13-3 discusses the benefits of digital marketing and functions that are possible with digital marketing. Firms can do more than sell merchandise over the Internet. They can use it for a host of functions that can benefit consumers, other businesses, and even the firm's own employees. Section 13-4 is a presentation of e-commerce and how it affects buyer behaviors today. Section 13-5 discusses various digital marketing strategies that firms can use. Because of the rapid rise of smartphones, mobile marketing (Section 13-6) has become increasingly important. In preparing digital content and advertising, firms have to think about the various platforms consumers utilize. The last section of the chapter addresses ways that businesses can utilize social media to engage with consumers.

13-2 INTERNET USERS

Not since the invention of the automobile or computer has any single invention so radically transformed life and changed the way of doing business as has the development of the Internet. Approximately 2.8 billion people around the globe are using the Internet, with over 300 million of those in North America. The average amount of time each person spends on the Internet is 31.5 hours a month, visiting an average of 59 different sites, going online an average of 30 times per month. Table 13-1 provides penetration statistics for the major regions of the world. North America has the highest penetration rate, at 84.9 percent, followed by Australia and Europe, both around 68 percent. Globally, 39 percent of the world's population use the Internet in some manner.[1]

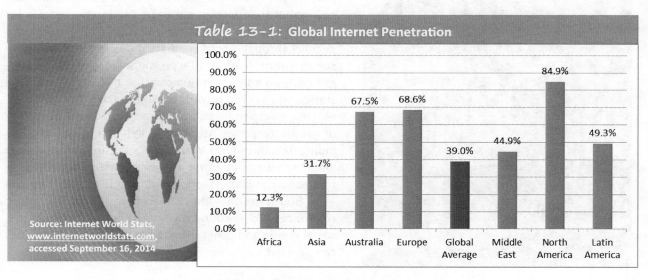

Table 13–1: Global Internet Penetration

Source: Internet World Stats, www.internetworldstats.com, accessed September 16, 2014

Part Four: Marketing Communications

Access to the Internet is no longer restricted through a computer that is hard-wired to the Internet. Multiple platforms exist, including mobile phones and tablets. In the United States, 53 percent of the population now own a smartphone, 31 percent own a tablet, and over 75 percent have a laptop computer. Table 13.2 shows the top five activities for each of the major platforms. Using search engines to locate products and information is near the top of the list for all of the platforms, as well as emailing. But mobile phones and tablets are used more for playing games, texting, viewing photos, and watching videos than a laptop or PC.[2]

Table 13-2: Internet Usage By Platform

Laptop or PC	Mobile Phone	Tablet
Email (92%)	Search engine (91%)	Search engine (88%)
Search engine (92%)	Texting (90%)	Email (84%)
News (76%)	Email (85%)	Playing games (72%)
Shopping (71%)	Social media (70%)	Viewing photos (55%)
Social media (65%)	Playing games (69%)	Watching videos (52%)

Source: How People Use the Internet, http://blog.dashburst.com/infographic/internet-usage-statstics, accessed September 15, 2014.

13-3 DIGITAL MARKETING

The Internet has transformed the way most businesses now operate. At the beginning, many businesses jumped onto the Internet and built Web sites because it was the thing to do. They were not sure how their site would be used or who would use their site. But as Internet usage has continued to increase dramatically, companies have come to realize that the Internet can provide substantial benefits to both customers and the selling firm. Using this information, companies began developing the field of Internet marketing or digital marketing.

The Internet provides numerous benefits for companies, which are highlighted in Figure 13-1. The most obvious use of the Internet is for sales. Although online shopping accounts for only about eight percent of retail sales, it is growing at a much faster pace than retail sales for bricks-and-mortar stores. In the United States, online sales were growing between 30 and 40 percent per year in the early part of the twenty-first century but have recently slowed to about 20 percent per year.[3] The growth rate for offline retailers is only about four percent per year. The Internet allows for a dynamic, interactive communication environment, especially through social media venues. Advertising, consumer promotions, trade promotions, and other integrated marketing communications (IMC) efforts are all static and directed toward consumers or other businesses. Only salespeople and the Internet have the capability of being interactive. Attractive graphics and menus guide individuals through a Web site to the information they want. Yet it can be done at the visitor's own pace. Visitors can skim some sections and read others. They can even bookmark the site or places in the site for future references. To encourage engagement with the brand, social media and other interactive marketing techniques can be used.

Figure 13-1: Company Benefits of Using the Internet in Marketing

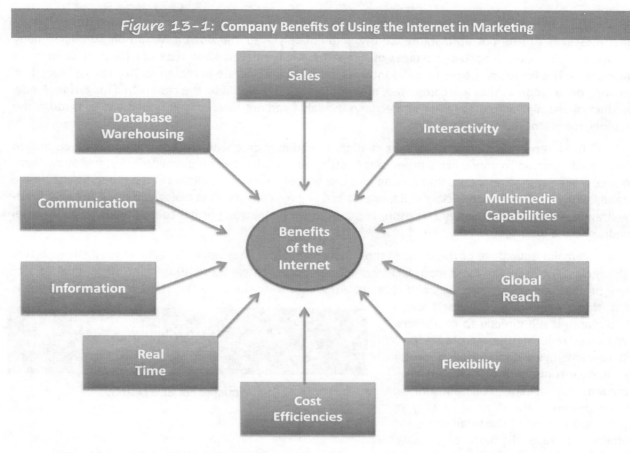

The Internet provides a multimedia environment (see Figure 13-2). Sound, pictures, and videos can provide information or entertainment. A live cam shot can be used for sites such as a college or resort to show a visitor what the actual campus or facility looks like. At a resort Web site, a multimedia presentation could show the different facets of the resort, such as the nightclub, the restaurants, the pool, the beach, and any other amenities that would be appealing. A big benefit of the Internet is that consumers (or businesses) can examine what they want to see, at the pace they want to see it, and as often as they want.

Figure 13-2: The muiltimedia environment of the Internet provides ample opportunities for consumers to view event venues online to assist with ticket purchases. Above is a screenshot from the computer of a baseball fan checking out the view from Section 110 at his favorite ballpark.

Part Four: Marketing Communications

The Internet provides flexibility. Content can be changed quickly, often within minutes or hours. New messages can be put up instantaneously. Immediately after the Boston Marathon bombing, many company Web sites had posted messages of sympathy. Many offered some type of assistance or help for the victims. The flexibility means that the Internet can virtually operate in real time. Ads can be placed on the Internet as soon as they are completed, not months later, as would be the case with a magazine. A new product can be highlighted as soon as it becomes available and not have to wait until it passes through the channel and is stocked on store shelves.

The Internet provides an excellent medium to communicate with customers and prospects and to provide information to various constituencies. Customers can be provided passwords that will allow them to access Web site components that no one else can see. Blogs and newsletters can be used to encourage brand involvement. Through social media, brands can engage consumers in dialog and build stronger loyalty. Brands such as Apple, Harley Davidson, and Jeep have built strong brand communities through social media and the Internet.

A major advantage of the Internet that many companies have not fully realized yet deals with cost efficiencies. For example, most manufacturers spend approximately 20 to 30 percent of the final cost of their products on sales, marketing, and distribution. What makes the potential of the Internet so exciting is that these companies can establish a Web site and sell directly to customers, potentially reducing these costs to 10 to 20 percent. Even for bricks-and-mortar retailers, e-commerce provides an environment for gaining cost efficiencies. When products are shipped directly to customers instead of the retail store, the retailer can save the cost of packing, shipping, and transporting products to retail sites, where they have to be unpacked and stocked on shelves. Also, in most cases, handling and shipping costs can be charged to customers purchasing the product over the Internet.[4]

The last benefit of the Internet is also the most controversial. Because of Internet technology, information about individuals or businesses that visit the site can be gathered, with or without their knowledge. If used ethically, this information can help a firm do a better job of targeting its products to meet the needs of each person who accesses the Web site. This information can be added to the firm's database to build a more robust profile of its customers. For example, an individual who accesses the baseball equipment component of a sporting goods e-commerce site can be provided with a coupon or premium to encourage purchase. If the individual accesses the same site on several occasions, the company can safely assume that the customer has a high level of interest in baseball.

13-4 *E-COMMERCE*

A major use of the Internet is **e-commerce**, which is the selling of goods and services over the Internet. Retailing can be performed in three ways, illustrated in Figure 13-3. The first method is made up of the bricks-and-mortar stores that do not have any presence on the Internet, in terms of e-commerce. These tend to be small stores with regional markets and products that do not lend themselves well to the Internet. In developed countries, bricks-and-mortar firms are a minority and are becoming an even smaller percentage of the total firms every year. However, in developing countries, this form of commerce is still the standard mode of operation.

Figure 13-3: The Three Methods of Retailing

Bricks-and-Mortar Firms:
These organizations operate only with traditional physical facilities and do not yet have a web presence. Given the popularity of the Internet, such companies now tend to be few.

Bricks-and-Clicks Firms:
These organizations recognize the benefits of combining traditional physical facilities with a web presence. Virtually every major firm fits into this category.

Clicks-Only Firms:
These organizations operate only on the web and do not have traditional physical facilities. This has been a popular format for startup firms over the last decade.

In the 1990s, there was a huge burst of dot-com companies, or **clicks-only firms**, which are organizations that sell only over the Internet. Although these firms may have an office somewhere, they do not have a bricks-and-mortar store that a customer can go to. Most shipments are made directly to the customer from the manufacturer or distributor. In many cases, these firms do not even own an inventory but drop ship directly from producer to the customer.

Realizing the impact of the Internet and understanding that it is here to stay, bricks-and-mortar firms began adopting e-commerce Web sites. These firms, which operate both a bricks-and-mortar facility, as well as an Internet e-commerce site, are known as **bricks-and-clicks.** These firms realize that e-commerce can provide customers with a different channel for making purchases and that it can be a valuable tool for providing information about the firms' products (see **Figure 13-4**).

> **e-Commerce:**
> The selling of goods and services over the Internet.
>
> **Clicks-only Firms:**
> Organizations that sell only over the Internet.
>
> **Bricks-and-Clicks:**
> Firms that operate both a bricks-and-mortar facility and an Internet e-commerce site.

Brand-name retailers now realize that the Internet is not a threat to their retail operation but rather can be used to build brand loyalty and increase sales. JCPenney found that shoppers who purchased merchandise from all three channels (retail stores, catalog, and the Internet) spent, on average, more than $800 per year. Individuals who used only one channel spent, on average, $200 per year.[5]

The growth of global Internet retail commerce is impressive. In the United States alone online sales have reached $355 billion, which is about 10 percent of all retail sales. The two major retail categories of products sold are (1) computers and electronics and (2) apparel and accessories. See **Figure 13-5** for a more in-depth breakdown of U.S. Internet retail sales by product categories.

Figure 13-4: Galleries Lafayette, an upscale French Department Store located in Paris, operates as a brick-and-click retailer. Here it is promoting its Web site on a tarp used during remodeling of its physical facility.

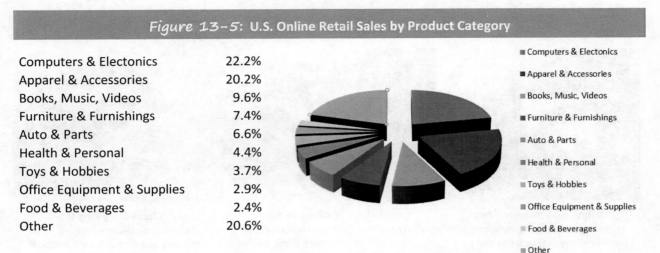

Figure 13-5: U.S. Online Retail Sales by Product Category

Category	Percentage
Computers & Electonics	22.2%
Apparel & Accessories	20.2%
Books, Music, Videos	9.6%
Furniture & Furnishings	7.4%
Auto & Parts	6.6%
Health & Personal	4.4%
Toys & Hobbies	3.7%
Office Equipment & Supplies	2.9%
Food & Beverages	2.4%
Other	20.6%

Legend:
- Computers & Electonics
- Apparel & Accessories
- Books, Music, Videos
- Furniture & Furnishings
- Auto & Parts
- Health & Personal
- Toys & Hobbies
- Office Equipment & Supplies
- Food & Beverages
- Other

Source: Apparel Drives US Retail Ecommerce Sales, www.emarketer.com/newsroom, index.php/apparel-drives-us-retail-ecommerce-sales, April 5, 2012.

An e-commerce site has three primary components: a catalog, a shopping cart, and a payment system. Bricks-and-clicks operations must have a fourth component: a location finder. The catalog can be just a few items displayed on the main screen, or it can be a complex presentation of thousands of products embedded within multiple links and pages. The type of catalog used is determined by how many products the firm sells and the objective of the Web site.

Each site must have some type of shopping cart to assist consumers as they select products. The shopping cart can range from just clicking a circle for an item when only a few products are offered to a more complicated shopping cart that keeps records of multiple purchases and previous purchases. Each site must establish some way for customers to make payments for the items they purchase. For consumers, this is often a credit card system or one of the Internet services such as PayPal. For business-to-business operations, payments are normally made through a voucher system. In other situations, a bill is generated or a computerized billing system is used so that the invoice goes directly to the buyer. In more trusting relationships, the invoice is added to the customer's records without a physical bill ever being mailed.

For bricks-and-clicks operations, buyers need some way of finding the nearest location if the merchandise is not being shipped directly to them. A consumer may examine clothes on the Internet but want to go to the retail outlet, where he or she can try on the clothes and then make the purchase. Businesses that offer merchandise in brick-and-mortar locations normally have some type of store locator software that will tell the consumer or business the closest location by simply typing in the ZIP code.

Although online purchases are growing at a rapid rate, many consumers are still not sure about making online purchases for two reasons: security issues and purchase behavior habits. Many consumers are afraid to use credit cards because of the fear that their credit card number will be stolen. Others are concerned about fraud and dishonest e-commerce Web sites that will take their money and never ship the merchandise or ship poor-quality merchandise. In terms of purchasing habits, consumers feel more comfortable purchasing products from retail outlets because that is the way they have always shopped.

A brief view of history will provide an insight into these two concerns. When mail-order firms first encouraged ordering merchandise by telephone, consumers were fearful about giving out a credit card number to a stranger they could not see. Now, nearly everyone is willing to provide the information while placing orders on the phone. Also, not too long ago credit card holders expressed anxiety about various store employees stealing those numbers. Originally, customers were instructed to "take the carbon" from a credit card purchase to make sure it was torn into shreds to prevent an employee from using the credit card number later. The same pattern is likely to follow with Internet shopping. As consumers become accustomed to using the Web, fears about giving out credit card information will be no greater than they are now for telephone orders or credit card store sales (see **Figure 13-6**).

The second issue is more difficult because it has strong ramifications regarding the future success of e-commerce. Consumers currently feel comfortable buying merchandise at retail stores and through catalogs. It will take time to change these habits, especially the preference for retail shopping. At the retail store, consumers can view and touch the merchandise. They can inspect it for defects and compare brands. Clothes can be tried on to make sure they fit. In addition, customers can see how clothing items look while being worn. As with any new technology, changing habits will require time and the right kinds of incentives.

Before we examine ways to encourage consumers and businesses to shop online, it is helpful to review why anyone would shop online in the first place. **Figure 13-7** provides a more complete list, but the most common reasons given are:

- 24-hour operations
- Convenience
- Time saving
- Lower prices
- No salespeople
- Speed

To encourage consumers and businesses to start making Internet purchases, a firm must provide some type of incentive. This is especially true for the long run. The incentives that can be used are financial incentives, convenience incentives, and value-added incentives.

Persuading an individual or business to change and make that first purchase online normally involves some type of financial incentive, which can be a reduced price, an introductory price, or some type of promotion, such as a coupon. Once the individual or company makes the switch, continuing the financial incentive may not be necessary because of the convenience or added-value features of e-commerce over traditional shopping methods.

Figure 13-6: In the past, consumers were fearful of providing credit card information over the telephone. Today, most people feel secure in doing it. Over time, the fear of providing credit card information over the Internet will also diminish.

Figure 13-7: Why Consumers Purchase Online

Another major incentive that e-commerce can offer buyers is convenience. Instead of making a trip to a bricks-and-mortar location, a consumer or a business can place the order while remaining at home or at his or her place of business. More important, the order can be placed at any time, day or night. Seeking information about various products can be faster and easier on the Internet than using *Consumer Reports*, talking to salespeople, or calling the manufacturer or a retailer. For businesses, ordering merchandise, supplies, and materials over the Internet can save purchasing agents considerable time. In addition to ordering, businesses can check on the status of their orders, shipment information, and even billing data. In most cases, doing so online is considerably quicker than making a telephone call. In this fast-paced world, convenience is a highly attractive incentive for many consumers and businesses (see **Figure 13-8**).

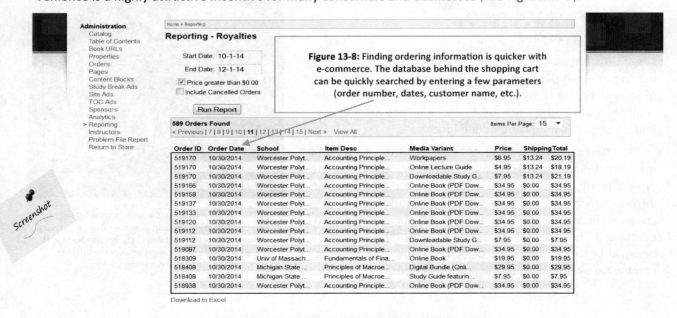

Figure 13-8: Finding ordering information is quicker with e-commerce. The database behind the shopping cart can be quickly searched by entering a few parameters (order number, dates, customer name, etc.).

Although financial incentives can encourage customers to switch to the Internet for their purchasing, it will take some type of value-added incentive (or convenience incentive) to make a more permanent change in purchasing habits. The added value may be personalization, where the firm becomes acquainted with the customer and his or her purchasing behaviors. Through specialized software, past purchase behavior can be tracked, allowing the firm to automatically offer a customer special deals on merchandise he or she is most likely to purchase. For instance, a consumer going through the travel section of an online bookstore may see a banner advertising a special deal on a new travel book. In addition to instant banners, consumers and businesses may also receive e-mails offering new information and other special deals that are available. Again, these deals are based on past purchase behaviors contained within a database. These tools can make it much easier for e-commerce programs to create added value for customers.

13-5 DIGITAL MARKETING STRATEGIES

As society has shifted from desktop computers to laptops, tablets and smartphones, marketers need to adapt to these multi-screen formats. Advances in technology create new digital marketing opportunities along with the need to develop campaigns that can be viewed from any type of screen. Figure 13.9 identifies the primary digital marketing strategies that can be used.

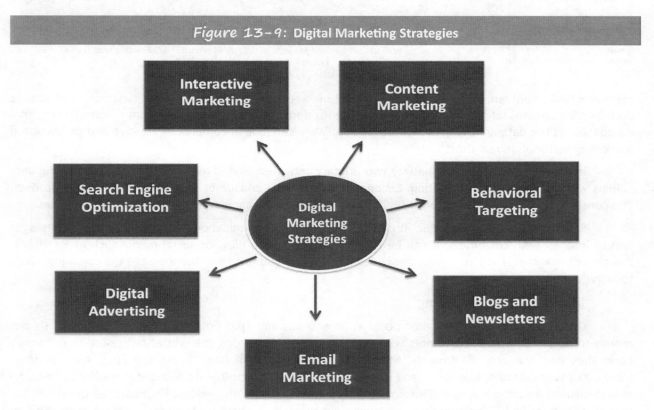

Figure 13-9: Digital Marketing Strategies

13-5a Interactive Marketing

The drive to engage consumers with a brand has led to an increase in **interactive marketing**, which is the development of marketing programs that create interplay between consumers and businesses. The programs feature two-way communication and customer involvement (see Figure 13-10).

The Internet offers the ideal medium for interactive marketing due to the ability to accurately track browser activities and translate the information into in-

> **Interactive Marketing:** The process of individualizing and personalizing everything—from the Web site content to the products being promoted.

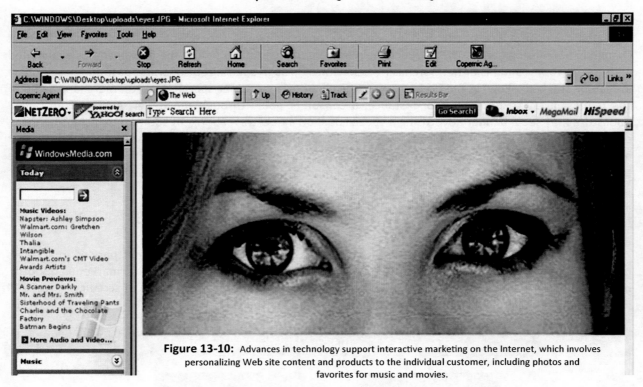

Figure 13-10: Advances in technology support interactive marketing on the Internet, which involves personalizing Web site content and products to the individual customer, including photos and favorites for music and movies.

stant reactions. Software can provide personalized marketing messages. It analyzes customer interactions such as click-stream data traffic and combines it with demographic information from external or internal databases. As the data are being processed, the software can launch complex interactive and personalized marketing materials in real time.

Interactive marketing emphasizes two primary activities. First, it assists marketers in targeting individuals with personalized information. Second, it engages the consumer with the company and product. The consumer becomes an active participant in the marketing exchange rather than a passive recipient.

Several options are available in choosing the best communication channels to present messages and to interact with customers. It can be through a Web site, a blog, or social media such as Facebook, Twitter or Instagram. The best choice depends on the target audience and the message the company wants to convey.

13-5b Content Marketing

Orders for in-ground fiberglass pools at River Pools and Spas declined from an average of six per month to barely two. Four customers who had made deposits during the winter requested their money back; they had changed their minds. Marcus Sheridan, owner of River Pools and Spas, was spending $250,000 a year on radio, television, and pay-per-click online advertising. He reduced the advertising budget and focused on providing useful information through blog posts and videos. He answered questions potential customers had.[6] This approach, called content marketing, saved his business. **Content marketing,** or branded content, consists of providing useful information and product-use solutions to potential customers.

Content Marketing:
Also known as branded content, content that is authentic and useful for businesses and/or consumers.

Content marketing is not self-promotion or advertising to generate sales. It focuses on developing content that is authentic and of interest to consumers or businesses. Marcus Sheridan shared truthful information, good and bad, about fiberglass pools. Customers appreciated his honesty and responded through interactive dialogue and purchases. A company such as Plum Creek Timber can use content marketing to provide information about forestry and ways to protect our environment (see Figure 13-11).

Figure 13-11: In this PR advertisement by Plum Creek Timber Company, Plum Creek emphasizes its concern for the environment. It also lists its Web site so that readers can gather additional information.

Source: Sample print advertisement courtesy of The Miles Agency and Alliance One Advertising, Inc.

To succeed, the information provided in content marketing must be relevant and answer problems faced by customers or in some way improve their lives. The goal is to produce information or solutions that visitors to the site want to share with their friends and relatives. Integrating content with the search and social strategies creates synergy. Using key search words in the content and providing content consumers consider to be valuable enhances the chance that a visitor seeking a solution to a problem will share the Web site with friends through social media.

The content should be updated regularly. Most experts believe two to three times per week is important. Marketers should avoid the temptation to drift into self-promotion and sales talk over time. Staying true to the mission of the branded content, providing information and solutions, is vital.

An alternative to branded content is **sponsored content**, whereby a brand sponsors the content of a blogger or related Web site. A YouTube video about how to get perfect curls had references to the Remington curling iron brand embedded in the video. Spectrum Brands, which owns Remington, pays bloggers to create stories, articles and videos for the Web. An article and video entitled "Get the Right Swimsuit for Your Body" had references to Remington embedded in the content. The goal was for the article and video to be shared through social media venues, such as Twitter and YouTube.

13-5c Behavioral Targeting

Rather than place ads on random Web sites, companies can target individuals most likely to purchase their products. **Behavioral targeting** utilizes Web data to identify these individuals. Behavioral targeting can occur in three different ways. It can be based on:

- Pages a person visits on the Internet
- Keyword searches or content read
- Past visitors to a site

The most common form of behavioral targeting involves tracking a person's movements on the Internet. A cookie is placed on the individual's computer that records data points as she goes from site to site. It records the types of sites visited, the information read, the searches that have been conducted, and products that were purchased. Based on this information, ads will be placed on Web sites that match this browsing history. If an individual has visited a number of Web sites about cooking, the individual will see an advertisement for food and cooking-related products. A coupon or other form of incentive can be placed on the ad to encourage the person to click on it.

The second form of behavioral targeting examines an individual's search behavior. It identifies keywords that are typed into search engines and the content that is read based on the keyword searches. If an individual has used a search engine to locate articles and information about new trucks, then he may see an advertisement by Ford or another truck brand. These ads will typically appear on the search engine being used (see Figure 13-12).

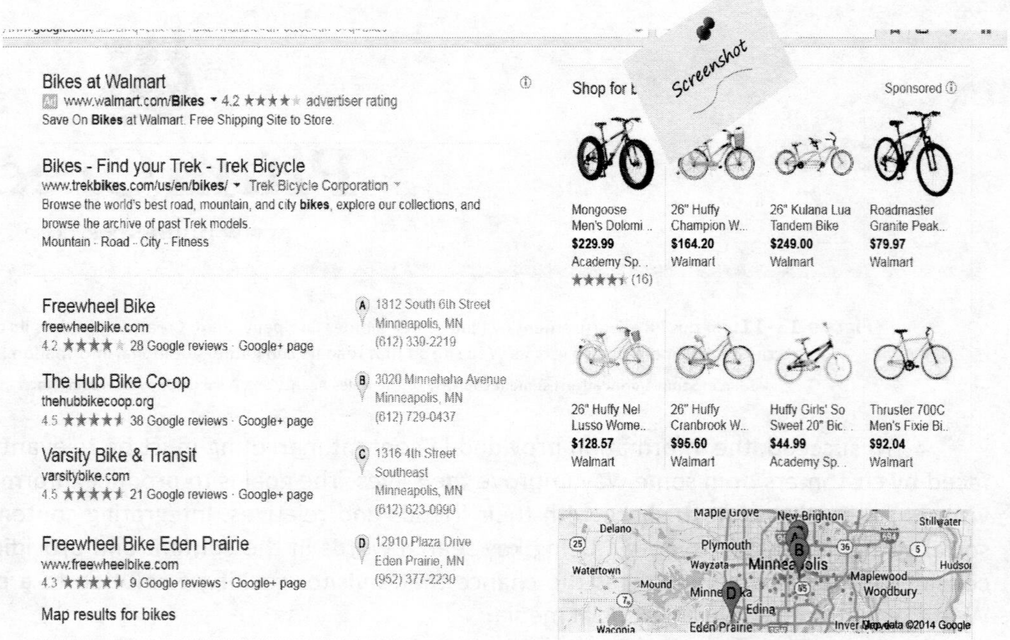

Figure 13-12: Behavioral targeting can be used by bike retailers and manufacturers. Individuals searching online for bikes, or bike paths, or things to do this weekend, can be directed to an ads/links like these that appear in this search.

Sponsored Content: A brand sponsors the content of a blogger or related Web site.

Behavioral Targeting: The utilization of Web data to target individuals.

The final form of behavioral targeting is based on past visitors. Barnes and Noble uses this form of behavioral targeting to suggest books and movies that may interest a person shopping on the company's Web site. This form of behavioral marketing typically is triggered when an individual places a book or movie in a shopping basket or wish list. An ad will be generated that says "Others who purchased this book have also purchased these books." Several suggestions are made based on combinations of purchases of other customers.

Behavioral targeting takes place in micro-seconds without a person even realizing it occurs. Algorithms can be written to trigger these ads as the page loads. Even the brand being advertised may rotate or change based on the bidding process brands use for display advertising. In the above example with keyword behavioral targeting, instead of a Ford ad it may be for a Chevrolet or a Toyota, depending on the result of the bidding process that takes place.

13-5d Blogs and Newsletters

Blogs are online musings that cover a wide range of topics. Some are interactive and permit visitors to post comments; others do not. Setting up company-sponsored blogs can emulate word-of-mouth communication and engage customers with a brand. Fashion retailers entice customers to visit the company's blog to enjoy postings on new styles, upcoming designers, and fashion faux pas. In the past, customers may have relied on magazines for fashion information. Now, company blogs allow them to obtain information faster, and, more important, interactively. This helps brands engage with customers and establishes a two-way communication channel.

> **Blogs:**
> Online musings that cover a wide range of topics.

In developing a blog, analysts stress the importance of identifying a specific reason for the blog before launching it. It may be to make the company more open to its customers, to humanize the company so customers feel the firm cares, or to show a fun-and-happy side of the brand. When Coca-Cola acquired 40 percent of Honest Tea, many customers became unhappy about the move and voiced opinions on the blog. Seth Goldman, CEO of Honest Tea, took time to answer each one. While some customers still did not like the idea, "The blog at least helps people see how we think about it," Goldman said.[7]

Companies have to decide how they will handle negative comments. Most companies have a mechanism for approving comments before they are posted. This policy is to ensure nothing racist or offensive is posted. It should not be to eliminate negative thoughts. Allowing negative comments to be posted shows a company is open, human, and willing to accept feedback, both good and bad. It is important to respond to these negative comments in an honest, straight-forward, and polite manner. Customers will respond to brands that are transparent.

Rather than a blog, some companies prefer to offer consumers (or businesses) a newsletter. The Thrillist (thrillist.com) and UrbanDaddy (urbandaddy.com) Web sites designed newsletters for their customers. Newsletters are sent via e-mail to approximately 1.1 million subscribers. Most subscribers are college graduates with median incomes of $88,000. The UrbanDaddy newsletter emphasizes an exclusive and luxurious approach, advising men on where to shop and how to fit in. The Thrillist newsletter features a fun and relaxed tone. Both organize free, heavily-sponsored events for subscribers of the newsletters. The newsletter becomes a means of engaging the subscribers with the Web sites.[8]

Both blogs and newsletters should follow the same principles outlined as those pertaining to content marketing. Information should be useful and provide solutions to problems customers face. It should be authentic and offer something individuals want to share. It should be integrated with the brand's Web content, search strategy, and social media outreach (see **Figure 13-13**).

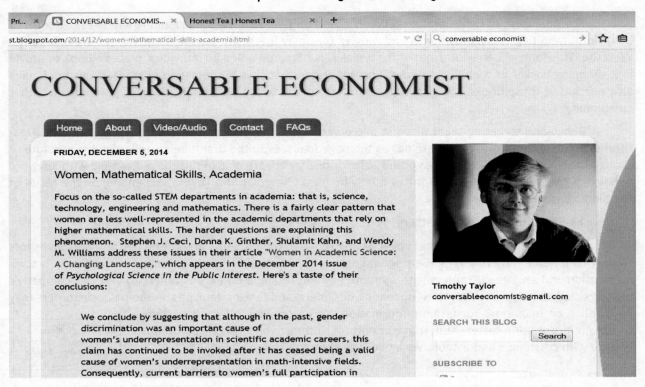

Figure 13-13: Blogs and newsletters that offer highly targeted and specific information are the most effective. The authors of this textbook write a blog designed to update examples provided in this textbook, with the students as the primary target audience (see end of chapter for more info). In a similar fashion, the author of Textbook Media's economics textbook writes a blog, but his overarching goal is to promote the academic journal that he edits, so his target audience is economics professors.

13-5e E-mail Marketing

E-mail can be an important part of a company's digital marketing strategy. To be successful, companies need to integrate the e-mail marketing program with other marketing programs. It cannot simply be a program where mass emails are sent to individuals on a list. Most people resent spam, and response rates are extremely low, in addition to damaging the brand's reputation.

Response rates increase when an e-mail message resembles the information on the company's Web site and coincides with its IMC program. Web analytics can be used to develop email campaigns that offer the greatest chance of response. E-mails can be based on the browsing history of an individual on a particular Web site. Analytics can identify those who made past purchases or put items on a "wish" list but never purchased.

E-mail campaigns can be directed at consumers who abandon shopping carts without making purchases. About 40 percent of online shoppers abandon the shopping cart just prior to the checkout. Only about 30 percent of these shoppers return to complete the transaction. Web analytics can identify the individuals who abandon a shopping basket. Sending an e-mail to these individuals offering free shipping, a discount if they complete the order, or a simple reminder that they have items in their shopping basket can lead to greater sales. Converting these individuals to customers is much easier and more lucrative than sending mass e-mails. Targeted e-mails experience a conversion rate 5 to 10 times higher than mass e-mails sent to a firm's customers. In addition, revenues from these follow-up e-mails are three to nine times higher than other approaches.[9]

In Figure 3-14, Holly Betts, an e-mail expert with Marketing Zen, offers a number of suggestions for developing successful e-mail campaigns. It starts with individuals opting-in to the e-mail program. She emphasizes being upfront and honest with subscribers. Companies should tell recipients what they can expect, when they can expect it, and then deliver on those promises. As with branded content, e-mails should offer subscribers something useful that meets their needs or interests.

Figure 13-14: Developing Successful E-mail Campaigns

- Be upfront, honest with subscribers
- Build list for quality, not quantity
- Give subscribers what they want
- Be familiar with your audience
- Keep e-mails neat and clean
- Be eye-catching
- Integrate social media
- Test, test and test

Source: Interview with Holly Betts, *Marketing Zen* February 14, 2014

Marketing professionals should be sure all e-mails come from the same source so that subscribers instantly recognize the source and know it is an e-mail they gave permission to receive. E-mails should be short, neat, and eye-catching. The message can include links to all of the brand's social media outlets so recipients can increase their engagement with the brand if they desire. Companies should test every e-mail campaign and keep records of what worked and what did not. These records make it possible to build a file of best practices based on results.

13-5f Digital Advertising

Digital, or online, advertising presents a highly effective method for reaching today's consumers, especially the younger, affluent, and Internet-savvy market. Budgets for digital advertising have steadily increased and are now over $500 billion annually. Digital advertising is the fastest growing medium, with annual growth rates exceeding 20 percent. Part of the growth has been fueled by multiscreen advertising, which involves media buys across the various platforms such as the Web, mobile, and tablets.[10]

The first form of Internet advertising involved the use of a display, or banner, ad. In 1994, AT&T ran one carrying the message "Have you ever clicked your right mouse here? You will." This very basic form of advertising generated billions of dollars in advertising revenues. Today, banner ads account for 22.6 percent of digital ads.[11]

Currently, banner ads can be embedded in videos, widget applications, or targeted display ads to increase the chances viewers will see and click the icon. The newest online technology, which has been taken from paid search auction systems, allows advertisers to display a banner ad only to individuals the company chooses. The system is built on a vast warehouse of user Internet data and automated auction advertising exchanges. Advertisers develop messages for specific audiences and set the price they are willing to pay to reach that audience with the banner ad.

When a consumer, such as a 40-year-old male, accesses a particular Web site with the paid search auction technology, in a micro-second the software searches the auction exchange for advertisers matching the profile of the individual who logged onto the page. Once an advertiser has been located, a banner ad instantly flashes on the computer screen. It may be an advertisement for fishing equipment, a pickup truck, or male clothing. If a female with an interest in clothes logs on, an advertisement for current fashions may appear. The automated exchange system grants precise targeting of ads to specific consumers.[12]

Mini-applications embedded in a banner ad, called **widgets**, permit consumer access to some form of dynamic content provided by an external source other than the company where the ad resides. Widgets provide individuals personalized access to Web information or functionality from any device connected to the Internet. Boxcar Creative developed a widget application for ConocoPhillips using RICH expandable banners to create interactive polls, fun facts, and a carbon calculator. The poll and the calculator both collected and produced results without the user ever leaving the banner advertisement. Only when an individual clicked "learn more" was she taken to a micro-site landing page with additional content and data collection opportunities.

13-5g Search Engine Optimization

The largest category of online expenditures is for spots on search engines. Funds devoted to search engines constitute nearly 50 percent of digital advertising expenditures.[13] About 80 percent of all Web traffic begins at a search engine. Therefore, making sure that a company's name or brand becomes one of the first ones listed when a person performs a search will be a key marketing goal. **SEO**, or **search engine optimization**, is the process of increasing the probability of a particular company's Web site emerging from a search.

Optimization can be achieved in one of three ways. First, a paid search insertion comes up when certain products or information are sought. Companies can speed this process by registering with various search engines in order to have the site indexed and also by paying a higher placement fee for top positions. The placement of the ad on a search page depends on the price the company pays and the algorithm a search engine used to determine the advertisement's relevance to a particular search word or phrase.

> **Widgets:**
> Mini-applications embedded in a banner ad that permit a consumer access to some form of dynamic content provided by an external source other than the company where the ad resides.
>
> **Search Engine Optimization:**
> The process of increasing the probability of a particular company's Web site emerging from a search.

Second, a company can increase identification through the natural or organic emergence of the site. This method involves developing efficient and effective organic results that arise from a natural search process. Each search engine uses a slightly different set of algorithms to identify key phrases that match what was typed into the search box. To be listed first in an organic search requires time and effort. Normally, a new Web site will probably not emerge at the top of the search results. It takes time for the search engine to locate the site.

Some studies suggest that the impact of organic listings can be impressive. For sites that come up on the first page of a search or within the top ten, Web traffic increases nine fold. For second- and third-page listings, Web traffic increases six fold. In terms of sales, being a top ten listing has resulted in a 42 percent increase in sales the first month and a 100 percent increase the second month.[14]

The third optimization method, paid search ads, includes small text boxes that appear when a particular word is typed in or it can be paid link boxes at the top or side of a search result. Research suggests that these search ads have a strong positive impact on brand awareness, perception, and purchase intentions, even when consumers do not click the paid search ad.

Companies spend large amounts on search engine optimization. The typical click-through rate for online advertising remains around 0.2 percent; for search advertising it is around five percent. Although the early results are impressive, marketers should remember that search engine optimization represents a long-term investment. The effects do not occur quickly. Getting into the top ten listings of a search can take months or years. It requires optimizing content, programming, and finding the codes that will be picked up by search engines (see **Figure 13-15**).

Figure 13-15: This Twin Cities-based catering business uses a popular online service for building and maintaining commercial websites. The service has handy tools for maximizing SEO, including guides on best key words and tips for localizing searches.

13-6 MOBILE MARKETING

Over 70 percent of the U.S. population now owns a smartphone. Estimates suggest the figure will rise to almost 60 percent and tablet penetration will increase to 50 percent. Individuals now spend an average of two hours and 21 minutes per day using some type of mobile device. [15]

Mobile phones provide a device linking individuals to social networks, thereby allowing them to post comments, pictures, and videos and read the thoughts of others. People can check-in, tweet, and update their status anytime and anywhere. They can download deals from companies, read reviews, check prices, and share information. Further, a mobile device offers a method for shopping. Purchases can be made with a mobile phone. Product information can be obtained. Consumers are able to check store hours, get directions to a business, and compare prices. These activities can take place anywhere, including the retailer's store.

Companies can take advantage of mobile phones by sending text message ads to consumers. While these may be annoying, they can also be effective when created properly. A text message received around lunchtime or dinnertime from a restaurant offering a special deal might entice a consumer to visit the restaurant. Two keys to text message advertising include gaining the permission of the mobile phone owner and carefully timing when a message is sent.

In-app advertisements offer a popular new type of mobile advertising. Globally, almost 32 billion apps are downloaded to smartphones each year. Advertisers spend $2.9 billion on in-app advertising while consumers spend $26.1 billion buying apps. These apps vary from games to those that check weather, stocks, or recognize songs. This type of advertising becomes more effective when it relates to the app's content. For instance, weather-related products should be promoted on a weather app.

Mobile phones allow marketers to create location-based advertising campaigns. **Geo-targeting** is an approach that involves reaching customers where they are located based on their mobile device. Geo-targeting represents a unique and attrac-

In-app Advertising:
An advertisement embedded within a mobile app.

Geo-targeting:
A mobile marketing tactic that reaches customers where they are located based on their mobile device.

tive feature of mobile marketing. By downloading an app, a fast food restaurant can identify a person's location and show him how far he is from the nearest outlet and provide walking or driving directions to that unit. When someone checks in, software can instantly send a special promotion and information about the nearest locations. Marketing experts believe this location-based marketing approach will grow in use in the future. Businesses can harness the ability to drive consumers to retail outlets near where they are located, which can be an effective method to engage consumers with a brand on a one-to-one basis.

Creating successful geo-targeting campaigns requires two actions. First, consumers should be in control of the engagement. They opt-in for the app. Second, the brand should provide a discount or something of value to consumers. Campaigns that follow these principles routinely yield engagement and performance measures that are higher than any other type of digital advertising.

13-7 SOCIAL MEDIA

Social interaction remains the fundamental basis of social media. It is one consumer talking to another, or to many others. Skilled marketers realize the potential inherent in such exchanges (see **Figure 13-16**). The newness of this type of communication has meant that companies are still developing ideas regarding the best approaches to utilize. The primary methods currently being used are 1) content seeding, 2) real-time marketing, and 3) viral marketing.

Figure 13-16:
This Los Angeles-based singer | composer uses a variety of social media sites to communicate with her followers. She includes SoundCloud to provide free audio streaming of her latest songs.

13-7a   Content Seeding

People plant seeds into the ground believing that they will germinate and grow into a living plant that bears fruit or flowers. The same concept applies to social media marketing. **Content seeding** involves providing incentives for consumers to share content about a brand. The incentive does not have to be financial, although financial incentives tend to be the most frequently used. An incentive can be information, uniqueness, novelty, or anything that engages consumers with the brand and motivates them to share with others.

> **Content Seeding:**
> Providing incentives for consumers to share content about a brand.

Most people like to compete, especially if they feel they can win. When Microsoft launched a recent version of Windows, the company asked high schools to submit videos for a computer lab makeover. The "School Pride" campaign invited visitors to vote on the best video submission. To add intrigue and encourage sharing,

Microsoft used a social graph that allowed Web visitors to have friends go to the site and vote for the best entry, thereby increasing a school's chances of winning. The contest generated an increase of almost 75 percent in traffic to the Web site.[16]

One contest that generated a great deal of social buzz was created for Esurance. Rather than spending $4 million on a Super Bowl ad, the company purchased the first ad slot after the game at a cost $2.5 million. The ad announced that one lucky viewer would win the difference, about $1.5 million, who tweeted the hashtag #EsuranceSave30 within 36 hours of the ad airing. The ad created a tremendous burst of Twitter shares. Leo Burnett, Esurance's agency, reported the following statistics from the campaign: [17]

- 5.4 million tweets with the #EsuranceSave30 hashtag

- More than 200,000 entries within the first minutes of the television ad

- 2.6 billion social impressions on Twitter

- 332,000 views of an Esurance commercial that had been posted to YouTube

- 261,000 new followers on the official Esurance Twitter account

- A 12-fold spike in the visits to the Esurance Web site within the first hours of the television ad

Appealing to consumer altruism, such as a campaign to donate blood in the wake of a tragedy, offers an additional content seeding approach. Storms in the United States created shortages of blood for the Red Cross. The organization used the Internet to inspire individuals to share. The organization created a badge graphic announcing the shortage and encouraged individuals to share the badge on their social networks and with their friends.

13-7b Real-time Marketing

The idea of real-time marketing existed prior to the 2013 Super Bowl, but it was the infamous blackout during the game in the New Orleans Superdome that legitimized it as a feasible social media strategy. Oreo sent a message via Twitter that it is okay to dunk an Oreo cookie "in the dark." The message was placed on an image of an Oreo cookie, set in light, shadow and darkness. That message became a viral hit, being retweeted 15,000 times within the first 14 hours.

Real-time Marketing: The creation and execution of an instantaneous marketing message in response to or in conjunction with a live event.

Real-time marketing is the creation and execution of an instantaneous marketing message in response to or in conjunction with a live event. The success of Oreos led marketers for other brands to set up "war rooms" during major live events. These war rooms contain top marketing executives, creatives, digital technicians, and attorneys. The group seeks to strike instantly with an approved message when an opportunity occurs.

Effective real-time marketing does not occur on the fly, without any thought. The approach requires upfront strategic planning before assembling a war room and prior to any live event. While seeking to display human emotions and reactions to live events, those actions must be carefully planned to ensure they resonate with consumers (or businesses) and remain consistent with the brand's overall brand image and integrated marketing communications plan. The tone presented in a real-time marketing message becomes the key. It should correlate with the tone present in other company advertisements and other social media efforts. During these pre-planning sessions, company leaders discuss and sometimes even prepare messages and ads to be used for various situations that might occur during a live event. While it may seem the message was a quick reaction, it may have been discussed and designed weeks earlier.

Real-time marketing can be utilized in places other than live sporting events. During a snowstorm in the Northeast, Starbucks' marketing team put together a social media plan for Facebook and Twitter that focused on conversations about the anticipated blizzard. Snow-themed ads appeared on Facebook and Twitter with the creative focusing on an image of warm cup of java. The Twitter ads appeared when individuals clicked on #blizzard, #snowstorm, and other related hashtags.[18]

13-7c   Viral Marketing

> **Viral Marketing:**
> Preparing a marketing message to be passed from one consumer to another through digital venues or social media.

Preparing a marketing message to be passed from one consumer to another through digital venues or social media is **viral marketing**. It can be an e-mail, a video posted to a personal blog or on YouTube, or a posting on one of the social media platforms. It then evolves into a form of advocacy or word-of-mouth endorsement. The term "viral" derives from the image of a person being "infected" with the marketing message and then spreading it to friends, like a virus. The difference is that the individual voluntarily sends the message to others.

Viral marketing messages may include advertisements, hyperlinked promotions, online newsletters, streaming videos, and games. For instance, about a dozen videos were posted on YouTube of a man claiming to be the "world's fastest nudist." He streaks through various locations in New York City wearing only tennis shoes, tube socks, and a fanny pack positioned strategically in front. The links to the videos were e-mailed from individual to individual. They were posted on popular blogs such as The Huffington Post and Gawker. One appeared on CNN on Anderson Cooper 360. The campaign turned out to be a viral video campaign for Zappos.com, an online shoe and apparel store. The viral campaign highlighted that Zappos was selling clothes, because additional videos were posted that showed a van screeching up to the "fastest nudist" and several people jumping out wearing Zappos T-shirts. As the van leaves, the video shows the nudist dressed in pants and a shirt.[19]

Viral campaigns do not always succeed or yield positive results. Most brands would be thrilled to have three viral videos within one year, as Kmart did. The first YouTube video that went viral was "Ship My Pants," an advertisement created by Kmart. The video was viewed 20 million times. A short time later an advertisement posted to YouTube, "Big Gas Savings" based on a milder naughty double entendre, was viewed over six million times. Then "Show Your Joe" was a holiday ad that featured men playing Jingle Bells with their privates, viewed over 15 million times. Despite all three ads going viral and being viewed over 40 million times in total, sales fell 2.1 percent for the retailer.

Research regarding the impact of viral messages suggests that 61 percent of individuals exposed to a viral message or video had favorable opinions about the brand. Purchase intentions increased around five percent, but were greater if the viral message was recommended by a friend via social media rather than a company.[20]

Individuals should receive an incentive to pass the message along. A message with entertainment value is one type of incentive. Other incentives may be financial, such as free merchandise or a discount for messages passed along to friends that lead to purchases, logging onto a Web site, or registering for an e-newsletter. The incentive could also be found in the campaign's uniqueness. A personalized message has a greater chance of being passed along.

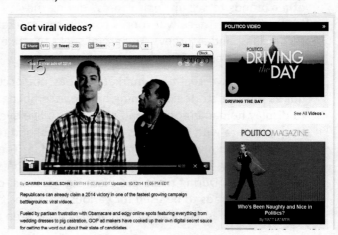

The many forms of digital marketing mean that viral marketing has lost some of its luster. Many consumers have lost enthusiasm and are less willing to re-send messages. The marketing team can take advantage of the ability to track the results of a viral campaign and analyze the results to determine whether such as program will be effective.

Summary

1. **Discuss current global Internet usage.** Globally, Internet penetration is at 39 percent. The highest penetration is North America with 84 percent of the population having access to the Internet. Australia and Europe are next, at 67 percent and 68 percent, respectively. Internet access is now available on smartphones and tablets as well as PCs and laptops. Internet usage varies based on the platform that is being used.

2. **Identify the benefits of digital marketing.** Internet marketing provides the benefits of sales, interactivity, multimedia capabilities, global reach, flexibility, cost efficiencies, real-time information, communication, and database warehousing.

3. **Discus the importance of e-commerce.** An e-commerce site has three primary components: a catalog, a shopping cart, and a payment system. Bricks-and-clicks operations must have a fourth component: a location finder. The catalog is a visual presentation of the merchandise to be sold. The shopping cart is some type of mechanism that allows a consumer to select merchandise and put it into a virtual shopping cart until he or she is finished making selections. For bricks-and-clicks operations, where individuals may want to locate or purchase from a bricks-and-mortar site, it is important to include a locator that will provide an address and a map to the facility. Although online purchases are growing at a rapid rate, many consumers are still not sure about making online purchases for two reasons: security issues and purchase behavior habits. Many consumers are afraid to use credit cards because of concerns that their credit card number will be stolen. Others are concerned about fraud and dishonest e-commerce Web sites that will take their money and never ship the merchandise or ship poor-quality merchandise. In terms of purchasing habits, consumers feel more comfortable purchasing products from retail outlets because that is the way they have always shopped. To encourage consumers and businesses to start making Internet purchases, a firm must provide some type of incentive. This is especially true for the long run. The incentives that can be used are financial incentives, convenience incentives, and value-added incentives.

4. **Identify and explain the various digital marketing strategies.** Digital marketing strategies include interactive marketing, content marketing, behavioral targeting, blogs and newsletters, email marketing, digital advertising, and search engine optimization. Interactive marketing involves a two-way communication to engage consumers with brands. Content marketing is the publishing of useful information to the Web to connect with consumers and businesses. Behavioral targeting uses Web analytics to send targeted messages to individuals. Blogs and newsletters can be used to engage individuals with a company and provide opportunities for interaction. Digital advertising can be through banner ads or search engines. SEO is the process of optimizing search marketing strategies to increase the chances an ad or organic search result appears.

5. **Explain how firms can use mobile marketing.** With 50 percent of consumers having smartphones or tablets, mobile marketing has increased in importance. Mobile marketing can reach consumers wherever they are located. Geo-targeting can be used to target individuals that are within a certain proximity of a business.

6. **Examine strategies that can be used in social media marketing.** Social media provides a mechanism for firms to interact with consumers and engage them with the brands. Content seeding involves using incentives or placing content in social media that encourages individuals to respond and become engaged. Real-time marketing looks for opportunities during live events to utilize social media to promote the brand. Viral marketing attempts to create unique content that is shared from one consumer to another through some digital means.

Key Terms

behavioral targeting	e-commerce	sponsored marketing
blogs	geo-targeting	viral marketing
bricks-and-clicks	interactive marketing	widgets
clicks-only firms	real-time marketing	
content marketing	search engine optimization	
content seeding	(SEO)	

Discussion Questions

1. Have you used the Internet to research a product before making a purchase? If so, how much time did you spend conducting online research? How did the information influence your decision? Where did you make the final purchase?

2. Access Nielsen/NetRatings. What information is available on the Web site? Report on at least three articles or pieces of information that interest you. Use a screen capture to place the content from the Web site in your document.

3. Section 13-4 describes three types of retail stores (bricks-and-mortar, bricks-and-clicks, and clicks-only). Discuss each type in terms of your personal shopping experiences. How much shopping do you do at each and what types of products do you buy in each? Talk to your parents and grandparents. Compare your responses to those of your relatives.

4. Figure 13.7 identifies reasons for shopping online. Re-order the list based on your personal reasons for shopping online. Explain why you placed them in the order that you did.

5. Pick one of the following product categories. Access five companies that operate in that particular industry. Compare and contrast each company in terms of the e-commerce components and incentives discussed in Section   13-4.

   a. Football equipment and fan memorabilia

   b. Cheerleading supplies and uniforms

   c. Dishes

   d. Jeans or another type of clothing

6. What are your thoughts about behavioral targeting? Does it influence your purchase decision or thoughts about a brand? Why or why not?

7. Pick one of the following product categories and access two companies that operate in that particular industry. Evaluate their Web sites based on the information provided in Section 13-5, Digital Marketing Strategies. Which strategies do you believe are being used? Provide support from the Web site and explain why you think the brand is using the strategy.

   a. Sports equipment and fan memorabilia

   b. Electronics such as radios, TVs, or stereos

   c. Household appliances such as electric mixers, toasters, or coffee makers

   d. Jeans or another type of clothing

   e. Shoes

8. Go to the Internet and locate a company-sponsored blog. Discuss how the blog is being used and the benefit you see for the blog. Provide a screen capture and URL of the blog you chose.

9. In your opinion is e-mail marketing effective? Why or why not? What type of e-mail marketing messages work with you?

10. How effective is digital advertising to you personally? Discuss at least two incidents where you clicked on an advertisement or accessed content through a digital advertisement. Explain why the digital ad worked.

11. Do you pay attention to search engine ads? Why or why not? Do you think SEO is important for companies? Why or why not?

12. What are your thoughts about mobile marketing? Discuss instances where mobile marketing has been effective with you and situations where it is not. What are the differences? How can a company use mobile marketing effectively to reach you?

13. What are your thoughts about geo-targeting? When would you be willing to accept geo-targeted ads? Would you download a brand's app that allows geo-targeting? Why or why not?

14. Identify the social media sites, such as Facebook, Twitter, Instagram, YouTube, etc. that you use. Discuss how much time you spend on each one and what type of activities you conduct with each.

15. For you personally, how effective is social media advertising? Give examples of good social media approaches being used by brands and poor approaches you have seen. Provide screen captures of your examples.

16. Have you ever received a viral marketing message or accessed a viral message on a blog or site such as YouTube? If so, discuss your reaction to it. Whether you have received a viral marketing message or not, what are your feelings about it? What are the pros and cons of a company using viral marketing messages?

Review Questions

(Answers are on Last Page of the Chapter)

True or False

1. The global Internet penetration rate is 39 percent.

2. A major benefit of the Internet is it has the capability of being interactive.

3. Online sales now account for about 10 percent of all retail sales.

4. Behavioral targeting consists of providing useful information and product-use solutions to potential customers.

5. Search engine optimization is the process of increasing the probability of a particular company's website emerging from a search.

6. Content seeding involves producing material that is useful to consumers or businesses and posted on a company's Web site.

7. Viral marketing takes place as one customer passes along a message to other potential buyers.

Multiple Choice

8. Which country boasts the highest level of Internet penetration?

    a. United States

    b. Switzerland

    c. France

    d. Spain

9. The category with the highest percentage of online sales is

    a. autos and parts

    b. apparel and accessories

    c. books, music, and videos

    d. computers and electronics

10. The development of marketing programs that create interaction between consumers and businesses is

    a. interactive marketing

    b. digital marketing

    c. e-mail marketing

    d. SEO

11. Of the three types of SEO results, the best is:

     a. paid search insertions

     b. organic search results

     c. paid search ads

12. Reaching customers where they are located based on their mobile devices is known as:

     a. search engine optimization

     b. interactive marketing

     c. geo-targeting

     d. behavioral targeting

13. All of the following are social media strategies, except:

     a. content seeding

     b. real-time marketing

     c. geo-targeting

     d. viral marketing

Blog

Clow-Lascu: *Marketing: Essentials 5e Blog*

CATEGORY ARCHIVES: CHAPTER13

Marketing for the Holidays (Chapter 13)

Posted on November 17, 2014 | Leave a comment

Thanksgiving and Christmas always brings increased advertising by brands and especially for retailers. This article in CMO Today should generate some interesting discussion because for the 2014 holidays the number one marketing method will be email.

CMO Today Article: You've Got Mail and More is Coming

Discussion Questions:

1. After reading the article, what are your thoughts about the use of email as the primary marketing tactic?
2. Look at the bar graph of the most used channels for 2014 holidays. Rank these channels in terms of influence on your holiday purchases. What is the most effective, what is second, etc. Justify your ranking.
3. Look at the graph of the popular social media marketing tactics. Identify the three that are most effective with you. Explain why.

What Is Happening Today?

Learn More! For videos and articles that relate to Chapter 13:

blogclowlascu.net/category/chapter13

Includes Discussion Questions with each Post!

Notes

1. Internet World Stats, www.internetworldstats.com, accessed September 16, 2014
2. How People Use the Internet, http://blog.dashburst.com/infographic/internet-usage-statstics, accessed September 15, 2014
3. Fred V. Vogelstein, "E-Commerce," *Fortune* 146, no. 13 (December 30, 2002): 166.
4. William Launder, "Marketers Seek Extra Edge to Go Viral," *Wall Street Journal*, http://online.wsj.com/article/SB10001424127887323980604579031391201753578, August 25, 2013.

5. Alan Mitchell, "Marketers Must Grasp the Net or Face Oblivion," *Marketing News* 22, no. 3 (February 18, 1999): 30–31.

6. March Cohen, "A Revolutionary Marketing Strategy: Answer Customers' Questions," *The New York Times*, www.nytimes.com/2013/02/28/business/smallbusiness, February 27, 2013.

7. Sarah Halzack, "Marketing Moves to the Blogosphere," *Washingtonpost.com* (www.washingtonpost.com/wp-dyn/content/article/2008/08/24/AR20080824051517), August 25, 2008.

8. Basil Katz, "Email Newsletters Aim for Inbox and Wallet," *Reuters* (www.reuters.com/articlePrint?articleId=USTRE5894XI20090910), September 10, 2009.

9. "Re-Marketing Helps Boost Online Shoppers' Baskets," *Data Strategy* 3, no. 7 (May 2007), p. 9.

10. Ingrid Lunden, "Nielsen: Internet Display Advertising Grew 32% in 2013," http://techcrunch.com/2014/01/27/nielsen-internet-display-advertising-grew-32-in-2103, January 27, 2014.

11. "Online Ad Spending Consolidates Among Search, Banners, Video," *eMarkter Digital Intelligence*, February 3, 2012, www.smarketer.com/articles/print.aspx?R=1008815.

12. Brian Morrissey, "Beefing Up Banner Ads," *Adweek* (www.adweek.com/aw/content_display/news/digital/e3if04360897e1103df4b92464543af6649), February 15, 2010.

13. "Problem Solved," *BtoB* 92, no. 15 (November 12, 2007), p. 21; "Online Ad Spending Consolidates Among Search, Banners, Video," *eMarkter Digital Intelligence*, February 3, 2012, www.smarketer.com/articles/print.aspx?R=1008815

14. "Problem Solved," *BtoB* 92, no. 15 (November 12, 2007), p. 21

15. "Multiscreen Campaign Importance Rises with Smart Device Use," *eMarketer*, November 25, 2013, www.emarketer.com/articles/print.aspx?R=1010413.

16. "5 Ways to Encourage Customers to Share Your Content," *Marketo White Paper*, www.marketo.com, 2013.

17. "Esurance Hands Out That $1.5 million, Releases Mind-Boggling Stats," *Adweek*, www.adweek.com/adfreak/esurance-hands-out-that-15-million," accessed February 10, 2104.

18. Christopher Heine, "Starbucks Pushes Snow Day on Facebok, Twitter," *Adweek*, www.adweek.com/news/technology/starbucks-pushes-snow-day-on-facebook-twitter," February 8, 2013.

19. Andrew Adam Newman, "A Campaign for Clothes by a Guy Not Wearing Any," *The New York Times* (www.nytimes.com/2009/10/29/business/media/29zappos.html), October 29, 2009.

20. Todd Wasserman, "So Your Ad Went Viral – Big Deal," http://mashable.com/2013/12/12/so-your-ad-went-viral-big-deal, December 12, 2013.

Cases

Case 18-1 Bluefly.com

In 1999, Bluefly.com was founded as an online retailer of designer brand clothing and the latest fashion trends. The headquarters is located in New York City in the heart of the fashion district. The company's fashion buyers are constantly searching for the newest fashions and accessories from more than 350 fashion designers. Everything sold by Bluefly.com is of the highest quality, but sold for at least 40 percent below other fashion retailers.

The name Bluefly.com was selected because the founders believed that because it was an online retailer, they would have to be hard to catch and always be nimble, fast, and ready to change directions on a dime. The "fly" appeared to be a perfect symbol of these objectives. The idea of "blue" came from the desire to convey the company has a "friendly personality." Because Bluefly.com has no brick-and-mortar stores, they had to develop ways of enticing consumers to browse and shop at their Web site. One of the primary incentives used was contests. They have designed several types of contests since their opening in 1999 and always have some type of promotion on their Web site. The goal of these promotions is to attract individuals to the Web site and to encourage them to make a purchase.

One contest held by Bluefly.com offered visitors an opportunity to win a $1,000 shopping spree or a much-sought after Hermès Birkin bag, similar to the one that was shown on HBO's Sex and the City. The handbag was valued at $20,000. To enter the contest, individuals had to supply their e-mail address, but they could enter the contest daily to improve their chances of winning. The idea was to get them to access the site on a regular basis. Although they may not make a purchase on the first visit, the founders of the company believed that if they kept coming back, they would make a purchase. The Hermès handbag promotion added more than 100,000 names to Bluefly.com's database. The financial benefit of using this methodology to acquire customers is that the average cost of acquisition for each new customer was only $23.07, compared with an average order of $154.

Another promotion offered by Bluefly.com was "30 Bags in 30 Days." It was a sweepstakes directed toward fashion-oriented consumers who had the opportunity to win accessories that even celebrities and socialites were waiting months to purchase. The promotion resulted in a 100 percent increase in visits to the Web site and a 62 percent increase in sales. Some customers asked Bluefly.com to send them a daily e-mail to remind them to register for the sweepstakes.

In addition to the contests, Bluefly.com uses one-time discounts for new customers, follow-up e-mails after a purchase, e-newsletters, and personalization of the Web software based on the person's past purchases and browsing behavior. The Web site is attractive and easy to navigate, and the checkout process is among the best. It encourages customers to purchase when they see a product they like because when the inventory is gone, they pull the product from their virtual store. Knowing a particular piece of clothing may not be available tomorrow encourages customers to make a purchase while they are on the Web site. Another tactic used by Bluefly.com is the development of a blog called flypaper, which was designed to keep their customers updated on fashion trends.

In advertising, Bluefly.com has taken a more controversial approach. Its primary target market is women ages 25 to 49 who are fashion conscious and have a desire to wear the latest fashion trends by fashion designers. But its ads often use naked or scantily clad females that one might expect for a beer commercial. For instance, a recent $3 million campaign featured a TV spot depicting a woman standing nude in front of her closet, which was full of clothes. Unable to find anything appropriate, she goes to the party completely naked. Some TV stations refused to show the ad, others allowed the ad but it had to be edited. In a print ad, a naked woman is shown boarding a train. Bluefly.com ran a contest asking Web browsers to supply the caption. Of the over 1,000 suggested, the winning caption, supplied by Julie Navarro, was "I think I forgot to turn off the stove—no wait, that's not it." Before answering the questions that follow, visit Bluefly.com at www.bluefly.com.

Questions

1. What has Bluefly.com done to attract customers to their Web site and to encourage them to make a purchase?

2. Examine the various digital strategies listed in Section 13-5. Discuss each one in terms of a potential strategy for Bluefly.com.

3. Because customers cannot try on the clothes before they are purchased, how can Bluefly.com assure customers to go ahead and make a purchase?

4. What is your opinion of their advertising approach?

5. Examine the three social media strategies discussed in Section 13-7. How can Bluefly.com use these to market its Web site?

6. What is your evaluation of the Bluefly.com's Web site and their overall business approach?

Sources: Bluefly.com Web site available at www.bluefly.com, accessed on April 30, 2007; Lorrie Grant, "Retailers Hope Shoppers Buy Blogs as the Place to Go," *USA Today* (August 25, 2005): Money 5b; Maye Dollarhide, "Bluefly Buzz Bags Shoppers," *Incentive 180*, no. 1 (January 2006): 10; David Sparrow, "Get 'Em to Bite," *Catalog Age* 20, no. 4 (April 2003): 35–36; Kenneth Hein and Diane Anderson, "Ads Au Natural a Wise Crack," *Brandweek* 46, no. 38 (October 24, 2005): 38.

Case 18-2 Selling Video Games

With two young children at home, Kyle and Aleecia Hendricks have seen firsthand the attraction of video games to kids. Not only their kids, but also almost every child they know plays video games and spends hours doing it. Wanting to start their own business, the Hendricks investigated the cost of opening a video game retail store. They soon found it was too expensive because of the capital needed for a building and the money needed for inventory. But in the process, Kyle did meet and have dinner with a representative of a video game distribution company. He suggested that the Hendricks should consider starting an online retail business (i.e., a clicks-only operation).

Before launching their online business, the Hendricks spent some time studying the habits of children. Although they had plenty of firsthand experience, they wanted to make sure that their experience (i.e., their children) was typical. Here are some of the facts that they learned about children, ages 5 to 18:

- Boys have an interest in sports, video games, music, cars, and girls.
- Mostly boys watch Japanese anime.
- Boys are crazy about superheroes, high-velocity fighting, and explosions.
- Boys need to be reached with a rich blend of print, broadcast, Internet, and event marketing.
- Boys are heavily involved in outdoor activities like skateboarding and indoor activities like playing video games and computer games and using the Internet.
- In terms of advertising, boys are picture-oriented, whereas girls tend to read the text.
- Girls (75 percent) say they love or like sports, compared with 85 percent for boys.
- Girls spend an average of 15 hours per week playing, watching, reading, talking, or thinking about sports, compared with 17 hours for boys.
- Girls play sports because they are interested in challenging themselves and being with friends, whereas boys play sports because they relish the competition.

Based on this preliminary information, the Hendricks decided to specialize in selling sports-related video games. Before launching their Web site, the Hendricks obtained two studies. One was a NeoPets Youth Study compiled by Advertising Age, and the other was a study by Taylor Research & Consulting Group.

Questions

1. In designing a website, should the Hendricks focus on girls, boys, children, or parents? Justify your choice.

2. Examine the digital marketing strategies discussed in Section 13-5. Discuss each one in terms of a potential strategy that the Hendricks could use.

3. From your discussion in Question 2, rank order your choices from the most desirable to the least desirable. Explain your ranking.

4. Should the Hendricks use SEO to increase visits to their Web site? Why or why not?

5. Examine the social media strategies discussed in Section 13-7. Discuss each one in terms of this Web site. If you could choose only one because of financial constraints, which would it be? Why?

6. In launching the Web site, what are the two primary strategies you would use? Explain why? (Assume in this response you have limited dollars to spend).

Sources: This case is based on Edmund O. Lawler, "Nonstop Action," *Advertising Age* 74, no. 7 (February 17, 2003): S-2; Rebecca Gardyn, "A League of Their Own," *American De*mographics 23, no. 3 (March 2001): 12–13.

Answers to Review Questions

Answers: 1) T 2) T, 3) T, 4) T, 5) F, 6) T, 7) F, 8) T, 9) a, 10) d, 11) a, 12) b, 13) c 14) c

Chapter 14

Promotions, Sponsorships, and Public Relations

Learning Objectives

After studying
this chapter,
you should be able to:

1. Discuss the reasons for a shift in marketing expenditures to promotions.

2. Identify the various forms of consumer promotions.

3. Identify the various types of coupons and distribution methods.

4. Explain the importance of in-store promotions in purchasing behavior.

5. Discuss the goals of trade promotions.

6. Identify the various types of trade promotions.

7. Discuss the issue of slotting fees.

8. Describe the current use of sponsorships.

9. Identify the role of public relations in integrated marketing communications (IMC).

Chapter Outline

Figure 14.1: Spring break resorts are a popular place for brands to promote products.

14-1 CHAPTER OVERVIEW

Ft. Lauderdale, Panama City, Daytona Beach, Key West, and Miami Beach are Florida hot spots for spring breakers. Other hot spots include Cancun, Mexico, Lake Havasu, Arizona, the Bahamas, and Las Vegas. In the past, almost all spring breakers went to Florida, but not so anymore. In fact, only 28 percent will stay in the United States; 72 percent will leave the country, with many going to Mexico.

College students out for spring break are not the only ones who will hit the beaches, hotels, and nightspots. Numerous companies will also be there. Arriving there ahead of the first spring break student and staying after the last one leaves, companies will spend an estimated $85 million on marketing to this crowd. Although various strategies will be used, a common theme is advertising, promotions, and giveaways.

Hawaiian Tropic will spend $300,000 marketing to spring break students. They will send ambassadors out to various beaches to spray Hawaiian Tropic sunblock on young, tanned bodies. They will give out thousands of free samples, thousands of coupons, and thousands of premiums like beverage coolers and sports bags. They will host autograph signings with their branded calendar reps, bikini parties, and block parties. Sunsilk will distribute one million sample packs of shampoo, conditioner, and hair cream at hotels. Through partnerships with various hotels, these samples will be placed in the hotel room next to the sink, not on the beach where it will get lost. The chances of the product being used increases greatly if it is available at the place where it would be used. In addition to the free samples, Sunsilk will give away gift cards valued at 2.2 million dollars.

Procter & Gamble will be giving away 1.6 million samples of Secret and Kuku Coco Butter deodorant and body spray. They will also distribute 800,000 postcards that look like VIP invitations and that can be used to gain admission to various block parties, nightspots, and other attractions.

Some hotels have realized the power of branded giveaways and developed partnerships with various companies. At these hotels, students will receive a survival pack with products such as Pepto-Bismol, Crest toothpaste, Tone body wash, and Bic razors. To further increase their exposure, Bic has spent money on billboards and Bic lounge areas on the beach where spring breakers can cool off under umbrellas, play interactive games, and register for a sweepstakes.

Why do companies flock to these spring break locations? Why do they give away millions of dollars worth of free stuff ? The hope is that students will adopt their brand. Companies know that the best method of gaining new customers is to get that customer to try a sample. If he or she likes the sample, the chance of making a future purchase is much greater. With all of the clutter in advertising, companies are always looking for new ways of reaching potential customers.[1]

Consumer and trade promotions are a critical component of the integrated marketing communications (IMC) effort. Over the past few years, dollars have been shifted from advertising to promotions. The next section of this chapter, Section 14-2, examines why this shift in spending has occurred.

Promotions can be divided into two types: consumer (or sales) promotions and trade promotions. Section 14-3 examines the major forms of consumer promotion with a focus on couponing—the most pervasive consumer promotion used. Not only are consumer promotions used to stimulate sales, they are also used to generate store traffic because the final decision to purchase a particular brand is often made inside the retail store. Section 14-4 examines in-store promotions that companies use to gain attention and to persuade consumers to make a purchase. The last section, Section 14-5, deals with trade promotions. While these tend not to be seen by most people, they are critical for pushing products through the channel and ensuring that products are on retail shelves so that consumers can purchase them.

14-2 PROMOTIONS

In recent years, firms have shifted more of their communications budgets from advertising to trade and consumer promotions. Trade promotions refer to offers made to channel members, whereas consumer promotions are offers given to end users or consumers. Approximately 82.5 percent of all consumer marketing dollars are now being spent on promotions, compared with 40 percent 15 years ago. Trade promotions account for the highest percentage of marketing expenditures, at 54 percent, with consumer promotions accounting for 28.5 percent. Only 17.5 percent of consumer marketing expenditures are now being spent on advertising. [2]

This shift toward greater use of promotions has occurred for several reasons. First, promotions normally have an immediate impact on sales, whereas advertising takes a longer period of time. The impact is not only immediate but is often quite dramatic in terms of increased sales.

A second reason for the shift to more promotions is increased brand proliferation and brand parity. Consumers and businesses have more choices today. Most buyers see little difference among firms and among various brands. For example, in choosing a restaurant, consumers may have some preferences, but they will patronize a number of different restaurants and will often switch just for variety. The same can be said for purchasing a new pair of jeans. Consumers may have a preference but often buy the brand that offers the best price, style, or fit. In most clothes closets, you will find several brands of jeans.

A third reason for the increase of promotions is greater consumer acceptance of promotions and, in some instances, consumers' demand for special deals. The airline industry still struggles financially as travelers have become accustomed to price wars and low fares. Many travelers postpone travel until prices are reduced. Most automobiles are purchased with some type of factory rebate. Pizza coupons arrive in the mail regularly, and it is not unusual for consumers to buy whichever brand has a coupon. Most grocery stores have a price offer on either Coke or Pepsi products, and many consumers purchase the brand that is on sale. Many clothes are purchased only when they are on sale. A view of any Wednesday or Sunday newspaper indicates how many promotions are being offered to consumers on a regular basis.

A fourth reason for the increase in promotions is the declining impact of advertising. With remote controls and digital video recorders, consumers are zapping out many commercials. Those they do watch, view, or hear are quickly forgotten as a result of the high number of commercials they are exposed to each day. Because it is easier to stimulate action with a promotion than with advertising, many companies are shifting dollars to promotions. There are, however, brand managers and marketing experts who believe such a shift may erode the brand equity that a firm has spent years in establishing. Recall from previous chapters that brand equity is primarily built on advertising, and an overreliance on promotions can erode brand image. Although advertising may not be as effective as in the past, it is still a critical component of the IMC package. Whatever promotions a company uses, they must be part of the company's IMC program and fit with the advertising that is being done.

14-3 *CONSUMER PROMOTIONS*

Consumer promotions are used to stimulate some type of activity on the part of a consumer or business. Most of these promotions are aimed at consumers, but the promotions can also be targeted to businesses if the business is the final user of the product. For example, an office supply store may offer a business a special promotion to either make an immediate purchase or place a larger order. If the business purchases the office supplies for its own consumption, then the promotion is a sales or consumer promotion. If, however, it is reselling the office supplies, then it is a trade promotion.

Companies can use ten primary types of consumer promotions (see **Figure 14-2**). It is important that the consumer promotions fit into the company's IMC effort and are part of the company's strategic thinking. If not, the message sent to consumers via a consumer promotion may contradict the firm's IMC effort. For instance, if a firm wants to project an image of offering superior quality, using coupons on a regular basis conveys a different message to buyers. Mentally, one would say, "If this product is of such high quality, why do they always offer coupons?" Although coupons can be used, other consumer promotion tools may do a better job of promoting the product while maintaining the higher image desired.

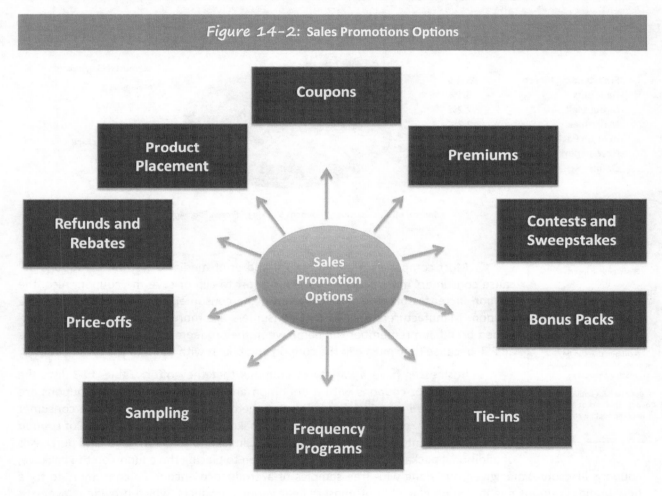

Figure 14-2: Sales Promotions Options

14-3a: Coupons

Coupons are an excellent strategy for stimulating sales, especially in the short run. The number of coupons has increased from 17 billion in 1970 to more than 329 billion today. Approximately 85 percent of American consumers redeem coupons, although most are not avid coupon clippers. Of 329 billion coupons distributed, only 2.9 billion, or 0.8 percent, are redeemed. This number is down from a 1.4 percent redemption rate in 2000. Only 18.5 percent of consumers use coupons on a regular basis, and 23.3 percent

Part Four: Marketing Communications

rarely or never use coupons. Consumers who are concerned with saving money are the most inclined to use coupons. But the demographic profile of coupon clippers is not what most would expect: 43 percent are men and 32 percent are from households with incomes from $40,000 to $75,000.[3]

Figure 14-3 identifies the various methods of distributing coupons and the percentage with which each is used. Manufacturers distribute approximately 80 percent of all coupons, and the primary method used is print media. Although magazines and newspapers themselves have coupons, 85.6 percent of all coupons are distributed via **freestanding inserts (FSI)**, which are sheets of coupons distributed in newspapers, primarily on Sunday and Wednesday. Approximately 6.1 percent of coupons are handed out at events or with samples of the product, 2.2 percent of coupons are distributed through direct mail, 2.1 percent more are distributed either in or on a product's package, 1.9 percent in newspapers, 2.2 percent are placed in magazines, and just 0.2 percent are Internet-based coupons.[4]

Figure 14-3: Coupon Distribution Methods

Freestanding Inserts	85.4%
Handouts	6.1%
Direct Mail	2.2%
Magazines	2.2%
In or on Package	2.1%
Newspapers	1.8%
Online	0.2%

Source: Michael Hartnett, "Coupons Still King," *Frozen Food Age 55,* no. 3 (October 2006): 41.

Coupons:
Sales promotion that offers customers some type of price reduction.

Freestanding Inserts (FSI):
Sheets of coupons distributed in newspapers, primarily on Sunday.

Instant Redemption Coupon:
A coupon that can be redeemed immediately while making a purchase.

Bounce-back Coupons:
Coupons that cannot be used until the next purchase.

Most companies prefer using FSI and print media to distribute coupons because consumers must make a conscious effort to clip or save the coupon. Also, the coupon increases brand awareness even if the consumer does not actually use the coupon. Manufacturers believe that consumers are more likely to purchase a couponed brand and remember the name when they redeem a coupon, especially if it is an FSI, because they must clip the coupon and take it with them to the retail outlet.

Businesses have a variety of coupons that they offer. Table 14-1 lists the different types of coupons with a definition and an example of each. Coupons are often distributed in retail stores by placing them on or near packages. The consumer can immediately redeem the coupon while making the purchase. This type of coupon is called an **instant redemption coupon** and can lead to trial purchases and purchases of additional packages of a product. In addition to placing the coupon on the package, coupons are sometimes given out along with free samples of a product to encourage consumers to try a new brand. Coupons might also be placed in dispensers near various products, which provide convenient access for customers. All of these methods are forms of instant redemption coupons because customers can use them immediately.

Bounce-back coupons are placed inside packages so that customers cannot redeem them at the time of the original purchase. This approach encourages repeat purchases because the coupon cannot be used until the next purchase. Another trend is to have coupons issued at the cash register during checkout. These are scanner-delivered coupons because they are triggered by an item being scanned, usually a com-

Table 14-1: Types of Coupons		
Type of Coupon	**Definition**	**Example**
Instant redemption coupons	Coupons that can be instantly redeemed	A coupon attached to a can of coffee for 50 cents off
Bounce-back coupons	Coupons that cannot be immediately used but must be used on the next trip to the store	A coupon inside a can of coffee for 50 cents off the next purchase
Scanner-delivered coupons	Coupons issued at the cash register during checkout	A 50-cent coupon for Folger's coffee issued after the shopper purchased a can of Maxwell House
Cross-ruffing coupons	A coupon placed on another product	A 50-cent coupon for Betty Crocker's cake icing placed on a Betty Crocker cake mix
Response-offer coupons	A coupon issued upon the request of a consumer	A $30 coupon issued to consumers who call a toll-free number after viewing a television advertisement
E-coupons (U-pons)	A coupon issued to the consumer via the Internet	A coupon for 50 cents off a can of Folger's coffee issued electronically

peting brand. **Scanner-delivered coupons** are designed to encourage brand switching during the next shopping trip.

Another type of coupon is the **cross-ruffing coupon**, which is the placement of a coupon for one product on another product. For example, a coupon for a French onion dip might be placed on a package of potato chips. To be successful, cross-ruffing coupons must be used with products that fit together logically and that are normally purchased and consumed simultaneously. Typically, a manufacturer uses cross-ruffing to encourage consumers to purchase another one of its products or brands. For example, General Mills might place a coupon on a Honey Nut Cheerios box for another cereal, such as Golden Grahams or Wheaties. This type of couponing tactic encourages consumers to purchase within the same brand or family of products.

On other occasions, a manufacturer might develop a cross-ruffing coupon program with another company. To boost sales of its Fruity Cheerios breakfast cereal, General Mills put coupons and advertisements on milk containers. The rationale for the coupon was that because cereal and milk are often purchased on the same shopping trip, a coupon on the milk will be another opportunity to reach consumers.[5]

Response-offer coupons are issued following a request by a consumer. Requests might come through a 1-800 number, the Internet, or mail. Coupons are then mailed to the consumer or sent by Internet to be printed by the consumer. The coupon can also be faxed, which is a common method in the business-to-business sector. Office supply companies and other vendors use response-offer coupons to invite business customers to make purchases or place orders. Firms also distribute coupons through their sales representatives, which allows for instant redemptions because the salesperson also takes the order.

Digital coupons are any electronically delivered coupons through the Internet or on a mobile phone. While many digital coupons are accessed through the Internet and printed at home, an increasing percentage are accessed through smartphones and scanned at retail checkout. The use of digital coupons continues to grow faster than any other form of coupon redemption. Most are delivered over

> **Scanner-delivered Coupons:**
> Coupons issued at the cash register during checkout.
>
> **Cross-ruffing Coupon:**
> A coupon for one product placed on another product.
>
> **Response-offer Coupons:**
> Coupons issued following a request by a consumer.
>
> **Digital coupons:**
> Electronically delivered coupons.

the Internet and printed by the consumer. Although e-coupons make up less than one percent of all coupons distributed, approximately 38 percent of all U.S. households have used some type of Internet coupon, with grocery products being the largest category.

A high percentage of digital coupons are from coupon sites such as coolsavings.com and valuepages.com. It is not surprising that individuals who use digital coupons tend to switch brands and purchase whichever brand offers the lowest price or best value.[6]

14-3b: Premiums

Premiums offer consumers some type of free merchandise for purchasing the product (see **Figure 14-4**). Cereal manufacturers have used prizes such as puzzles, games, and toys for years to entice consumers to purchase their brand of cereal. Banks have offered gifts, such as personal organizers, to small businesses that open an account with them. Premiums offer a major benefit not possible with coupons—customers pay full price for the product. If the premium is picked carefully, the premium can actually enhance a brand's equity. Unfortunately, premiums tend to be used by regular customers, rather than new customers. Premiums are not as effective as coupons in encouraging trial purchases.

Figure 14-4: Baseball stadiums entice children with fun birthday party packages that promise attractive premiums, such as visors with the team's name and logo.

If a firm wants to reward customers for their loyalty, offering premiums is one way of accomplishing this goal. Premiums can also be used to encourage customers to stock up, which would make promotional offers from competitors less attractive. If Hollywood Tanning Salon offers consumers two free tans with the purchase of ten tanning sessions, it accomplishes two major goals. First, it gets full price for the ten sessions. Second, it encourages current customers to stay with the salon rather than switch to another firm offering a coupon.

To be effective, premiums must be attractive to the customer. If a free gift is being offered, the gift must be an item that is desirable and that reinforces the firm's IMC effort (see **Figure 14-5**). A firm that is marketing upscale products may want to offer a personalized gift, such as an attaché case with the customer's name inscribed on it, as the premium. Such a strategy would be appropriate for a private golf course soliciting new members. Sometimes, premiums are used with another type of promotion, such as a coupon. This procedure of using two or more promotions in a single offer is called an overlay.

14-3c: Contests and Sweepstakes

Both contests and sweepstakes allow participants an opportunity to win prizes. The difference between contests and sweepstakes is what a participant must do to win. In a contest, participants might be required to perform an activity or to make a purchase to be eligible to win. In sweepstakes, participants do not need to make a purchase, and the winners are determined by a random drawing in which every entrant has an equal chance of being selected.

Whereas coupons appeal to price-conscious consumers, contests and sweepstakes appeal to individuals who enjoy higher levels of excitement and stimulation. Price-conscious consumers may not participate in contests and sweepstakes because they see the contests or sweepstakes as increasing the cost of the service.[7] To increase the effectiveness of a sweepstakes or contest, firms should emphasize the fun, fantasy, and stimulation aspect. Consumers enter contests and sweepstakes for the experience as well as the hope of winning.

Contests should be structured to provide participants with a challenge as well as excitement. It can be producing a recipe using a particular brand's product, an essay about American freedom for high school students, or a bikini contest at a local nightclub. Frito-Lay holds a contest each year that encourages consumers to submit their own advertisements for Doritos. The contest not only encourages consumers to submit ads, but individuals are asked to vote on their favorite. The contest creates consumer engagement, online chatter, and the winning ad is often among the best of the Super Bowl ads.

Figure 14-5: Cosmetics companies often offer customers a valuable free gift.

For a sweepstakes, consumers are not asked to perform some task. All they have to do to enter is fill out an entry form. In Monster.com's sweepstakes, individuals registered online. Prizes included $20,000 in cash, a Toyota Prius, a trip to Florida, or a donation to a charity (see **Figure 14-6**). A sweepstakes held by Jackson Hewitt Tax Service offered 500 prizes, such as cash and VIP opportunities at NASCAR races. Individuals could register at Jackson Hewitt locations or online.[8]

Figure 14-6: In Monster.com's sweepstakes, contestants could have won a trip to Florida.

Both contests and sweepstakes are effective means for building customer traffic or generating interest in a firm's products. Retailers use them at a grand opening or at other special events to encourage consumers to visit the store. Manufacturers use them to encourage consumers to purchase their products.

14-3d: Bonus Packs

Bonus packs are additional merchandise offered at the same price or slightly higher price. It might be four bars of soap packaged together and sold for the price of three individual packages. Two containers of potato chips might be packaged together and sold for 50 percent more than the price of one container. The manufacturer's objective in developing a bonus pack is to entice consumers to switch to its brand from a competing brand or to entice current consumers to stock up so a competing brand's promotion is not attractive (see **Figure 14-7**).

If the bonus pack contained 25 percent or more additional product, research has indicated consumers were more likely to switch, especially if they believed the manufacturer was incurring the cost of the extra product. If the consumer believed the manufacturer increased the price to add the bonus product, then they were less likely to

> **Bonus Packs:** Sales promotion that offers customers some type of discount for purchasing multiple items.

Figure 14-7: Cosmetics companies use bonus packs to attract consumers and to entice them to switch from a competing brand.

purchase the bonus pack. Almost 75 percent of all consumers believe that consumers will pay for the additional amount either directly or indirectly. Yet, 51 percent of consumers interviewed said they have purchased a bonus pack because they believed it was a good value, and 58 percent said they have tried a different brand to take advantage of a bonus pack promotion.[9]

14-3e: Tie-ins

Promotional **tie-ins** include two or more goods or services within the same promotional offer. The tie-ins can be either intra-company or intercompany. An **intracompany tie-in** involves two or more distinct products within the same company. For example, Mondelēz, which has brands such as Nabisco, Ritz, Oreos, and Newtons, could place a 20 percent discount coupon for Oreos on one of its Nabisco product's Post cereal boxes. An **intercompany tie-in** involves two different companies offering complementary products. The St. Louis Cardinals baseball team could provide a 50 percent off coupon to the nearby Gateway Arch with the purchase of an adult ticket to a Cardinals game (see **Figure 14-8**).

Tie-ins can be an excellent means of stimulating demand for a particular product. It works best if consumers are offered some type of promotional incentive for a high-demand item if the low-demand item is purchased. Another approach is to offer a combination ticket in which the consumer gets two products for a reduced price. For example, tourists can save $30 with a combination ticket that allows them into both Busch Gardens and Adventure Island.

Tie-ins:
Sales promotion of two or more goods or services within the same promotional offer.

Intracompany Tie-in:
A sales promotion involving two or more distinct products within the same company.

Intercompany Tie-in:
A sales promotion involving two different companies offering complementary products.

Figure 14-8: The Gateway Arch in St. Louis is not far from the St. Louis Cardinals baseball stadium. The Cardinals could provide an intercompany tie-in by offering a 50 percent off coupon to the Gateway Arch with the purchase of an adult ticket to a Cardinals game.

Intercompany tie-ins are more difficult to coordinate because two firms have to agree to the promotion. More lead time is needed because both companies will have to approve each detail of the joint promotion, and each company must feel it is benefiting from the joint promotion. A unique tie-in promotion was developed between DaimlerChrysler Jeep and JCPenney for Penney's 100th anniversary. Old Toledo Brands developed a special Jeep line of apparel that included denim jeans, denim jackets, sports shirts, T-shirts, cargo pants, vests, outerwear, and hats. The Jeep apparel line was featured on JCPenney's Web site and in four JCPenney catalogs—workwear, outdoor apparel, big and tall, and Christmas. In addition to the special Jeep apparel, DaimlerChrysler developed a Jeep Jeans Wrangler vehicle with DuPont Teflon-coated seat covers, roll bars, and a JCPenney's 100th anniversary logo. Both the Jeep apparel line and the JCPenney anniversary Jeep vehicle were promoted in a joint sweepstakes with ads appearing in point-of-purchase displays in JCPenney stores, in the JCPenney Christmas catalog, and on AOL, Yahoo!, and MSN Web sites. The grand prize was the first Jeep Jeans Wrangler vehicle to roll off the assembly line. First prize was two all-expenses-paid trips to Camp Jeep. Second-place prizes were his and her Jeep mountain bikes. Third-place prizes were 50 water- and stain-resistant Jeep denim jackets.[10]

14-3f: Frequency Programs

Most sales promotion programs are of short duration and focus on boosting sales immediately, brand switching, or repeat purchase behavior. Few focus on developing brand loyalty and enhancing brand equity, which is the goal of frequency programs.

Frequency programs, also called loyalty programs, are sales promotions aimed at current customers that are designed to build repeat purchase behavior and brand loyalty by rewarding customers for their patronage. Frequency programs have the following four characteristics:

1. They require multiple purchases over a period of time.

2. There is a formal method for accumulating points or credits for purchases.

3. There is a standardized redemption process.

4. Rewards come in the form of additional goods, services, discounts, or cash when a certain number of points are accumulated.[11]

The first and perhaps the most popular frequency program is the frequent-flier program used by airlines. American Airlines launched the first such program in 1981. The other airlines quickly countered with their versions so as not to be at a competitive disadvantage. At first, the idea seemed great. Airlines gave away free seats. Minimal additional costs were accrued because the seats they gave away would have been empty anyway. The frequent-flier programs turned out to be more popular than expected. More than 22 million travelers have enrolled in some type of frequent-flier program. On the average, each traveler has joined 2.26 programs resulting in more than 50 million members. It is estimated that 70 percent of all business travelers are in one or more frequent-flier clubs.[12]

Successful frequency or loyalty programs require a strong brand name, which is built on brand equity and brand awareness. If customers join a frequency program because of the rewards being offered, the frequency program will fail. To succeed, customers' rationale for joining must be to receive a reward for their loyalty to a specific brand. A major problem with the airlines is that passengers are members of multiple frequent-flier programs and that the frequent miles given do not develop loyalty, but the frequent-flier miles are necessary to maintain patronage.

Frequency Programs: Sales promotions offered to current customers and designed to build repeat purchase behavior.

A successful frequency program ties customers to a firm because the firm provides quality products and rewards them for their loyalty. A recent survey by FrequencyMarketing, Inc. of Milford, Ohio, found that 55 percent of Americans belong to at least one loyalty-type program. For households with incomes above $75,000, that participation jumps to 71 percent. From a business's perspective, the most interesting data are that 43 percent reported that membership in a frequency program led to more frequent purchases, and 16 percent reported that they purchased only one brand because of their membership. Once a customer joins a loyalty program, he or she tends to spend, on the average, 27 percent more with that company (see **Figure 14-9**).[13]

To obtain this type of success not only requires offering a quality product, but it also requires the right mix of rewards that match the firm's customer base. Probably the most successful frequency program is the American Express Membership Rewards program. Participants in this loyalty program spend four times more than a cardholder who is not enrolled. Original rewards included airline miles but now have expanded to more than 120 partners, such as hotels, merchandise, retailers, and movie tickets.[14]

14-3g: Sampling

Sampling is used primarily by food and beverage manufacturers but can also be used by almost any type of good or service (see **Figure 14-10**). An attorney can use sampling by offering a free initial consultation. A fitness center can offer a trial membership for a week. A business-to-business firm could offer the use of a new machine for 30 days or samples of its products. The goal of sampling is to encourage consumers or businesses to try a new product. Often, coupons or other consumer promotions are tied with sampling in an overlay to further increase the probability that a purchase is made.

Just before Thanksgiving, Sam's Club hosts its annual Holiday Taste of Sam's Club. It is an all-day sampling promotion. Visitors to Sam's can sample holiday dishes, such as citrus grilled pork loin, rosemary and garlic racks of lamb, prime rib, and the traditional turkey and dressing (see **Figure 14-11**). Wild Oats Market has a similar sampling promotion. The company offers samples of turkey, classic prime rib, classic vegetarian, and petite vegetarian dinners.[15] Gyms often allow consumers to try the machines before they commit to a membership. This is a form of sampling. According to a survey by Supermarket News, 42 percent of respondents said sampling and demonstrations of a product are the most effective promotional tool.[16] When consumers can sample a product, it reduces purchase risk and allows them to make a personal evaluation of the product. While sampling is an expensive method of reaching consumers, it works. If the sample also includes a coupon or some other type of promotional offer, it is an effective means of generating a trial purchase.

Figure 14-9: Department stores like Macy's offer their best prices to customers who have a loyalty card.

Sampling:
Sales promotions that include the free delivery of an actual product or portion of a product.

Figure 14-10: Offering a sample is an important aspect of selling --especially in the food industry.

Figure 14-11: Just before Thanksgiving, Sam's Club hosts its annual Holiday Taste of Sam's Club. It is an all-day sampling promotion. Visitors to Sam's can sample holiday dishes.

14-3h: Price-offs

Price-offs involve a reduction in the listed retail price of a product (see **Figure 14-12**). Price-offs are used to attract consumers, to reduce purchase risk, and to stimulate demand. Price-offs have the greatest impact on price-sensitive consumers and, unfortunately, also with current customers who would usually be willing to pay full price. From a firm's perspective, price-offs are an excellent tool for boosting sales because the impact is almost instantaneous. The disadvantage is that, if used too frequently, customers come to expect the reduced price and are not willing to pay full price for the product.

Retailers such as Coyote Wild (see **Figure 14-13**) use price reductions to attract shoppers into the store and to encourage them to make specific purchases. In addition

Figure 14-12: Fifty-percent off sales are becoming more common in Europe; in the past, price-offs were strictly regulated by the government, and sales were only permitted twice a year.

to purchasing the item on sale, retailers hope shoppers will purchase other merchandise. Price-offs are common during Thanksgiving. Supermarkets often reduce the price of turkeys, sometimes below cost, in the hope that the shopper will purchase other items. In some cases, the price reduction is used to remain competitive and to meet the prices of a competitor. It is also used to discourage customers from taking advantage of a promotion by a competitor. For example, if a particular brand of cookies launches a promotional campaign that includes a sweepstakes and coupons, a competitor may use a price-off strategy to discourage consumers from switching brands.

> **Price-offs:**
> Sales promotion that offers a reduction of the retail price of a product.

One Year Anniversary Sale!

Save 15% Storewide

Up To 75% Off Select Items In Stock

Ask about our complimentary in-home design consultations.

coyote wild

3500 Lakeland Drive, Suite 517 • 601.664.7150

Figure 14-13:   This advertisement by Coyote Wild promotes its one-year anniversary sale of 15 percent off storewide and up to 75 percent off on selected items.

Source: Sample print advertisement courtesy of The Miles Agency and Alliance One Advertising, Inc.

> **Rebates and Refunds:** Sales promotions that are a cash reimbursement to a customer for the purchase of a product.

14-3i: Refunds and Rebates

Rather than use coupons to reduce the price of products, firms can use a rebate or refund. **Rebates and refunds** are cash reimbursements paid to consumers with some type of proof of purchase. Technically, a rebate refers to reimbursements for a durable good, whereas a refund refers to reimbursements for a soft good or service. However, the words are often used interchangeably today.

The primary objective of offering a refund or rebate is to reward individuals for the purchase of a product. Because the process involves mailing in proof-of-purchase documentation and waiting four to six weeks for the reimbursement, refunds and rebates are not as effective in stimulating a purchase. The exception, however, is in the automotive industry, where consumers expect to get a rebate. A recent study by JD Powers and Associates found that buyers expect to receive a discount of $3,000 or more on a new car. Among new car buyers, individuals who compared two or more models typically bought the less expensive model.[17] Because rebates have been overused in the industry, they are now expected by consumers and cannot be stopped unless all of the manufacturers are willing to discontinue the practice. Such a decision, however, would likely bring federal government action against the automobile industry for price fixing or price collusion.

Computer and electronics manufacturers often use rebates to stimulate sales. For instance, Toshiba recently offered a $200 rebate for its big-screen televisions and high-definition (HD) DVD players. Rebates are also used for business-to-business promotions. Brady Corporation, which is a manufacturer and marketer of complete solutions that identify and protect premises, products and people, offered $100 and $150 rebates to companies that purchased selected equipment from the company.[18]

14-3j: Product Placement

Product placement is a recent phenomenon that involves the placement of branded products in movies and television shows. Because of so much advertising clutter and the fact that many viewers tune out commercials, companies use product placement as a subtle way of advertising. The close-up of the product often lasts only a few seconds but is caught by most of the viewers. In an episode of the TV series Dirt on the FX station, a tabloid editor played by Courteney Cox leaves a Hollywood party. She challenges another character in the show to "Keep up with me if you can." The valet in the show delivers her car to her, a black Pontiac Solstice GXP convertible. The appearance of the Pontiac Solstice was no accident. It was a product placement by Pontiac. Similarly, Nissan has placed its vehicles on Desperate Housewives and Heroes. GMC had some of its vehicles featured in an opening sequence on Monday Night Football, and Toyota used its Tundra truck in a Sunday Night Football episode.[19]

Another version of product placement is **branded media**, which is a movie or show that contains a brand name or logo with a story line that intersects the brand's mission or current advertising campaign.

The Toyota Prius was a central part of the TV show The New Adventures of Old Christine and the environmentally conscious character she played on the show. The Prius automobile was been involved in a number of the show's plots and was even featured in a duel with a gas-guzzling Hummer. Similarly, the Toyota Prius was prominently featured in the Larry David show, Curb Your Enthusiasm; in fact, Larry David gave away, with great fanfare, a Prius hybrid used in the show for a charity event. The value of such exposure is difficult for advertisers to measure, but it certainly is effective. For both branded media and product placement, the goal is to get the branded product before the audience in such a way that it is credible and does not appear to be a commercial.[20]

> **Product Placement:** Sales promotion technique of placing branded goods or services in movies, on television shows, or in theatrical performances.
>
> **Branded Media:** A movie or show that contains a brand name or logo with a story line that intersects the brand's mission or current advertising campaign.

14-4 IN-STORE PROMOTIONS

Although shoppers might compile lists, written or mental, more than two-thirds of purchase decisions are made while in a retail store, and most shoppers walk out with twice the number of products they had planned on purchasing.[21] That means packaging, pricing, point-of-purchase displays, and in-store promotions, such as sampling and coupons, are critically important in swaying consumers to purchase a particular brand. Advertising and sales promotions may get consumers to a retail store, but once in the store, shoppers add items to their shopping lists and switch brands because of a shelf display, a point-of-purchase display, or product package.

Studies by the Point-of-Purchase Advertising Institute (POPAI) found that the cost of point-of-purchase displays per thousand impressions was about the same as for outdoor advertising, $6.50 per thousand. Compared with other media, point-of-purchase displays are an excellent means of reaching consumers. As illustrated in Figure 14-14, the cost per 1,000 impressions for newspapers is $19.00; for television, $16.00; for magazines, $10.00; and for radio, $7.00. The difference was that point-of-purchase displays generate anywhere from a two to 65 percent increase in sales, depending on the product category, the quality of the display, and the equity of the brand. The most effective point-of-purchase displays are those that highlight a brand and a theme and are consistent with the brand's IMC thrust (i.e., customers instantly recognize

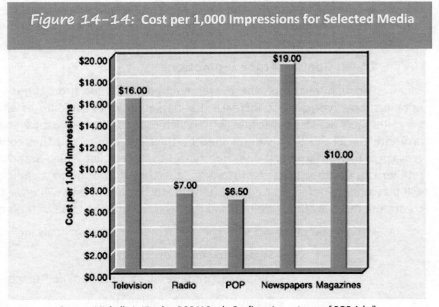

Figure 14-14: Cost per 1,000 Impressions for Selected Media

Source: Michelle L. Kirsche, POPAI Study Confirms Importance of POP Ads," *Drug Store News 26* (October 11, 2004): 4-5

the point-of-purchase display because they have seen advertising and other promotions with the same visuals, logo, graphics, or message).[22]

With so many purchase decisions made in the store, packaging becomes a critical piece of communication and is the last opportunity to convince a shopper to purchase a particular brand. The first task packaging has to accomplish is to attract the shopper's attention. That is not easy. Eye-tracking studies show consumers view only about 50 percent of the brands within in a product category.[23] The package must stand out and communicate the brand name and the most important assets quickly. Because consumers are walking down an aisle and scanning the shelves, brand equity and brand awareness are important. Brands and logos that consumers know are more likely to be seen, and brands that are valued by customers have a better chance of being selected.

Although packaging must attract attention, it must also protect the product and make it easy for retailers to stock. Odd-shaped packages may be attractive but a hassle for retailers to place on shelves. It is also important to make sure the packaging stays fresh. Although it is important to maintain some consistency so that shoppers can quickly recognize a brand, it is also important to change aspects of the package over time so that it will generate new interest. Just as ads can wear out over time, so can packaging design.

14-5 TRADE PROMOTIONS

Trade promotions are the expenditures or incentives used by manufacturers and other members of the marketing channel to help push their products through the channel. Trade promotions can be targeted toward retailers, distributors, wholesalers, brokers, or agents. The primary objective of trade promotions is to build relationships with other members of the marketing channel and to encourage them to sell the firm's products. When a retailer stocks a manufacturer's merchandise, consumers have the opportunity to buy the product. The same is true for distributors, wholesalers, brokers, or agents. It is a two-step process. The first step is convincing the channel member to stock the product; the second is to convince the channel member to push the product.

14-5a: Goals of Trade Promotions

For manufacturers, the overarching goal of trade promotions is to increase sales of their brand. Retailers, however, seek to increase the market share of their stores and to boost sales of a product category. Retailers are less concerned with which brand sells the most as long as the product line sells. They will promote the brand that is demanded by their customers and that contributes the most to the retailers' gross profit. For example, it does not matter to the retailer which brand of athletic shoes sells as long as the retailer can sell the shoes to customers, and they do not go to a competitor. To accomplish this, retailers will play one manufacturer against another to see which one will offer the best trade promotion and thus create the most profit for them when they sell the merchandise to their customers.

From a manufacturer's perspective, trade promotion goals include: [24]

- Stimulating initial distribution
- Obtaining prime retail locations or shelf space
- Supporting established brands
- Countering competitive actions

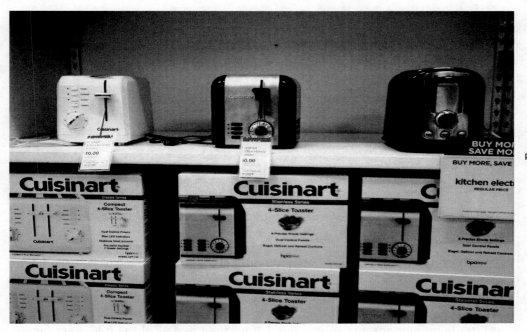

Figure 14-15: Manufacturers such Cuisinart rely on trade promotions to push their toasters through the distribution channel.

- Increasing order size
- Building retail inventories
- Reducing excess inventories of the manufacturer
- Enhancing channel relationships
- Enhancing the IMC program

Manufacturers such as Cuisinart (see Figure 14-15) must use trade promotions to ensure that their products are in retail stores and are pushed through the distribution channel by the various channel members.

When a company introduces a new product, enters a new territory, or uses a new channel outlet, trade promotions are needed to push that product through the channel. Without any type of incentive, channel members are reluctant to add a new product. The same is true for obtaining prime locations and shelf space inside a retail store. A typical discount store, for instance, sells more than 40,000 products. Not all can have the best locations. In choosing how to display products and brands, retailers want to maximize their revenue and profits. For a manufacturer to obtain prime space or even more space than it already has normally requires some trade promotion incentives. This is even true for established brands. When a competitor offers a retail chain a trade incentive for extra shelf space, a manufacturer may have to match the competitor's offer just to maintain its current space. Keep in mind that the retailer's goals are sales and profits. If one manufacturer offers a discount on its brand and that brand sells as well as the competitor, then it makes sense for the retailer to offer more space to the discounted brand because the retailer will make more money.

Trade promotions are used to increase order sizes, to build retail inventories, and to reduce a manufacturer's excess inventory. By offering special trade deals, retailers or other channel members can be enticed to increase the size of their order. This serves two purposes. First, it encourages retailers to push the manufacturer's brand because they have a high inventory, and, because of the trade incentive, they will probably earn more per item. Second, because of the higher retail inventory, it will reduce the amount of the product category retailers will order from the manufacturer's competitors.

Theoretically, trade promotions should enhance relationships with channel members and enhance the firm's IMC program. In reality, neither tends to happen. Retailers and other channel members tend to go with the vendor that offers the best trade promotions, and manufacturers and other channel members tend to use trade promotions to boost sales and prevent competitors from stealing market share, rather than use strategies related to a broader IMC effort. Much like sales promotions, trade promotions normally produce faster and more dramatic results. If sales are down, a trade promotion is often used to get back to the target level. If a competitor is encroaching on a firm's market share, trade promotion is used to counter the competitor's actions and to persuade channel members to stay loyal.

14-5b: Types of Trade Promotions

Companies can use a variety of trade promotions, such as: [25]

- Trade allowances
- Trade contests
- Trade incentives
- Cooperative advertising programs
- Trade shows

Choosing the correct trade promotion is an important decision. Each has its own set of advantages and disadvantages. The more a firm ties its trade promotion strategy to its IMC effort, the greater will be the impact of trade promotions, and, in the long run, the less the firm will have to spend on trade promotions. Rather than use trade promotions as a reactive tool, if planned as part of the IMC, they can become a proactive method of pushing products through the channel.

Trade Allowances

Trade allowances offer some type of financial incentive to channel members to motivate them to make a purchase. The most common trade allowances are off-invoice allowances, slotting fees, and exit fees. An **off-invoice allowance** is a financial discount or price-off on each pallet, case, or item ordered. These types of trade allowances are common during holiday seasons and promotional seasons and are used to encourage retailers to purchase large quantities of various items. For example, a manufacturer might offer a ten percent discount on fall apparel orders that are received by May 1. In addition to a specified date, manufacturers might also place a minimum order size as a further condition. Off-invoice allowances are also used to encourage retailers to stock up on a particular brand and to meet a competitor's marketing actions. From the manufacturer's viewpoint, the problems with trade allowances are (1) channel members failing to pass along allowances to the consumers, (2) forward buying, and (3) diversions.

When manufacturers provide a trade allowance to a retailer, they would like to see that price reduction passed on to consumers so it will stimulate sales of their brand. More than 50 percent of the time, however, retailers do not pass the savings on to the consumer. Instead, they charge consumers the same price and pocket the allowance.[26] A tactic that retailers sometimes use to accomplish this is **forward buying**, which occurs when a retailer purchases excess inventory of a product while it is on-deal to be sold later when it is off-deal. During a "sale period," the savings will be passed on to the consumer, but when the sale is over, the retailer still has merchandise left that was purchased at a lower price, thus generating extra profits. The primary difficulty for the manufacturer is that new orders are then delayed because the retailer has excess inventory and does not need to buy for some time, creating an erratic production schedule for the manufacturer.[27]

When manufacturers offer deals that are not offered nationwide, retailers sometimes engage in a practice called **diversion.** Diversion occurs when a retailer purchases a product on-deal in one location and ships it to another location where it is off-deal. A manufacturer may offer an off-invoice allowance of $5.00 per case for the product on the West Coast. A retailer like Wal-Mart or Target that normally purchases 50,000 cases a month may purchase an extra 50,000 or 100,000 cases on-deal and have them shipped to other parts of the country. This again allows the retailer to sell the merchandise at the regular retail price but earn higher margins because the merchandise was purchased at a lower price.

Trade Allowances:
Some type of financial incentive to channel members to motivate them to make a purchase.

Off-invoice Allowance:
A financial discount or price-off on each case that a member of the distribution channel orders.

Forward Buying:
When a retailer purchases excess inventory of a product while it is on-deal to be sold later when it is off-deal.

Diversion:
A situation in which a retailer purchases a product on-deal in one location and ships it to another location, where it is off-deal.

Every year, approximately 20,000 new products are introduced with only about 2,000 being successful.[28] Retailers must make a decision on which of these 20,000 items to stock before they know which will be successful and which will not. As a result, most retailers charge **slotting fees**, which are funds paid to retailers to stock new products. Retailers justify charging slotting fees because it costs them to add new products to their inventories and to stock the merchandise. If the product is not successful, the investment in initial inventory represents a loss, especially when the retailer has stocked a large number of stores. Also, adding a new product in the retail store means allocating shelf space to it. Because shelves are always filled with products, adding a new product means either getting rid of another brand or product or reducing the amount of shelf space allocated to other products. Regardless of which method is used, the retailer has both time and money invested when making the adjustment for the new product (see **Figure 14-16**).

Figure 14-16: To make room for new products, most retailers either have to reduce shelf space allocated to current products or delete a current product from their inventory.

> **Slotting Fees:**
> Fees that retailers charge to stock manufacturers' brands.

Retailers believe that charging slotting fees reduces the number of new products being introduced, which in turn will reduce the number of new product failures. Although retailers are slow to admit it, another reason for supporting slotting fees is that this practice adds to their bottom line. Because most retailers have such low operating margins and markups, slotting fees provide additional funds to support retail operations. It has been estimated that 20 to 40 percent of the net profits earned by retailers come from slotting fees and other trade promotions.[29]

Manufacturers allocate between $1 million and $2 million per product for slotting fees for a national rollout. As would be expected, manufacturers oppose these slotting fees and see them as a form of extortion. Because retailers control the channel and access to consumers, manufacturers have little choice but to pay the fees if they want their items on the store's shelves.

Slotting fees virtually prohibit small manufacturers from getting their products on store shelves because they cannot afford to pay millions of dollars to each large retail chain. Although some large retail operations have small vendor policies, getting merchandise on their shelves remains extremely challenging. If they are lucky enough to get shelf space, keeping it is another story. For example, one small manufacturer experienced a drop in sales from $500 per day to only $50 per day when its shelf space was reduced because a large, national manufacturer paid the store a large slotting fee to stock one of its new products.[30]

Instead of slotting fees, some retailers charge **exit fees**, which are fees paid to remove an item from a retailer's inventory. This approach is often used when a manufacturer wants to introduce a new size of a product or a new version, such as a three-liter bottle of Pepsi or the new Diet Vanilla Coke. Because Pepsi and Coke already have products on the retailer's shelves and have a strong brand name, adding a new version of their product is a much lower risk than adding an entirely new product. In these situations, retailers may ask for exit fees if the new version of the product fails or if one of the current versions must be removed from the inventory to make room for the new item.

Trade Contests

In a trade contest, rewards are given to brokers, retail salespeople, retail stores, wholesalers, agents, or other channel members for achieving a specific goal. The goal can be achieving the highest sales within a specified time period, or it can be for all channel members to reach a minimum target level. For example, a hardware manufacturer can run a contest among its distributors and offer a grand prize to the distributor with the highest sales, with second- and third-place prizes for runners up. An alternative strategy is to offer prizes to all distributors who reach a certain level, perhaps 100,000 cases or $500,000 in sales. With this latter approach, the prize level is set at a point that only a small number of distributors can reach.

Money or prizes awarded in trade contests are known as **spiff money**. The rewards can be cash or items such as luggage, a television, apparel, or a trip to an exotic place such as the Bahamas. Contests can be held at any level of the distribution channel. Most contests are within an organization and not between rivals. The difficulty of contests at the retail level is that individual buyers in large organizations are often prohibited from participating in vendor contests because they create conflicts of interest and may unfairly influence the buyers' purchase decisions. Although the goal of the contest is to influence a buyer to make purchases, the buying organization does not want someone making purchases for 2,000 stores based on the buyer winning some sales contest.

Recently, the National Frozen & Refrigerated Foods Association ran an ice cream and frozen dessert display contest. The grand prize of $1,200 was awarded to Harris Teeter store No. 157 in Matthews, North Carolina, for a trio of extensive case-top displays running the length of the store aisle. Each display ran for two to three weeks and carried a different theme, such as a 1950s display with a carhop and Elvis. In addition to the grand prize, the association awarded 12 regional first- and second-place prizes worth $500 and $300, respectively, as well as 25 third-place prizes of $200. The ultimate goal of the contest was to boost sales of ice cream and frozen dessert items. During the 12 weeks of the contest, frozen dessert sales were up 7.2 percent and ice cream sales were up 3.1 percent.[31]

Trade Incentives

Trade incentives are similar to trade allowances; however, instead of price discounts, they involve the retailer performing some type of function to receive the allowance. The most common trade incentive is the **cooperative merchandising agreement** (CMA), which is a formal agreement between the retailer and manufacturer to undertake a cooperative marketing effort. The agreement may involve advertisements produced by the retailer that features the manufacturer's brand. It may involve the retailer featuring the manufacturer's brand as a price leader in the store. It could involve the retailer emphasizing the manufacturer's brand in the display window, point-of-purchase display, or special shelf display.

The advantage of the CMA agreement over trade allowances is that the retailer agrees to perform some function in exchange for the price discount. As would be expected, CMAs are popular with manufacturers because they are receiving

Exit Fees:
Monies paid to remove an item from a retailer's inventory.

Spiff Money:
Monies or prizes awarded in trade contests.

Trade Incentives:
Some type of financial incentive that involves the retailer performing some type of function to receive a trade allowance.

Cooperative Merchandising Agreement (CMA):
A formal agreement between the retailer and manufacturer to undertake a cooperative marketing effort.

some tangible benefit in exchange for the price discount. With a CMA, the manufacturer knows that either all of the price discount or a specified portion will be passed on to consumers. Perhaps the most important benefit, however, is that it allows the manufacturer to incorporate the CMA into the firm's IMC effort.

A major benefit of a CMA for retailers is that it allows them to develop **calendar promotions**, which are promotional campaigns that retailers plan for their customers through manufacturer trade incentives. Through CMAs, retailers can schedule the time particular brands will be on sale. This allows them to alternate or rotate brands on sale such that, for their price-sensitive customers, at least one brand is always on sale (see **Figure 14-17**). Although this may not be desirable from the manufacturer's viewpoint, it is for retailers. As stated previously, retailers' interest is not in boosting the sales of a particular brand but of the entire product category. By always having a brand on sale, retailers tend to sell more of that product category. Instead of offering retailers price discounts, a manufacturer may offer a premium or bonus pack. For example, a manufacturer may offer a bonus pack of one case for each 20 that are purchased within the next 30 days. The bonus packs are free to the retailer and are awarded for either placing the order by a certain date, agreeing to a minimum-sized order, or both.

Figure 14-17: Because of CMAs, most grocery stores can keep at least one brand of soft drink on sale at all times.

Cooperative Advertising Programs

Most manufacturers have some type of **cooperative advertising program**, in which the manufacturer agrees to reimburse retailers or other channel members for a portion of their advertising costs for featuring the manufacturer's brands in an advertisement. To receive the reimbursement, the retailer must follow specific guidelines concerning the placement of the ad and its content. In almost all cases, no competing brands may appear in the ad, and in most cases, the manufacturer's brand must be prominently featured.

One of the most well-known co-op advertising programs is by Intel Corporation. Almost everyone has seen the Intel symbol and logo in computer ads by various computer manufacturers. Intel spends about $750 million a year to promote the "Intel inside" theme. Intel offers a six percent co-op fund to all PC makers who place the Intel logo on their computers. Furthermore, Intel allows a four percent fund accrual on the cost of print ads featuring the "Intel inside" logo and provides two percent for TV and radio ads that include the Intel video or audio tag. This accrued co-op money can be used to pay up to 66 percent of the cost of a print advertisement and 50 percent of the cost of a broadcast ad. Intel cuts any payment in half for any advertisement that features a third-party logo of any type to ensure it is the only co-op brand featured in an ad. Approximately 1,400 PC makers worldwide, including the top ten PC makers, take advantage of the Intel co-op advertising program.[32]

Co-op advertising programs benefit retailers because manufacturers pay a portion of the advertising costs. For most retailers, advertising national brands enhances the retailers' image and attracts custom-

Calendar Promotions:
Promotional campaigns that retailers plan for their customers through manufacturer trade incentives.

Cooperative Advertising Program:
An arrangement whereby a manufacturer agrees to reimburse retailers or other channel members that feature the manufacturer's brands in the ad for a portion of their advertising costs.

ers to the stores. Manufacturers benefit because they gain additional advertising exposure at a reduced cost. More important, almost all co-op advertising programs are tied to sales, which means advertising costs are directly related to retail sales. Furthermore, if retailers feature a particular manufacturer's brand in a store advertisement, they tend to encourage their in-store clerks and salespeople to push that particular brand. So the manufacturer not only benefits from the advertisement, but also from increased emphasis within the store.

Trade Shows

In the business-to-business market, trade show expenditures are $9.7 billion a year, ranking third behind advertising and sales promotions.[33] Trade shows offer the opportunity for retailers and manufacturers to interact. Manufacturers are able to locate new potential customers as well as to develop stronger relationships with current customers. Occasionally, a deal might be consummated, but usually, it is a time for sharing information. In addition, attendees will often request additional information or make contact with an exhibitor once they arrive back home from the trade show. A survey by American Business Media found that 77 percent of business executives gathered additional information from the exhibitor's Web site, 73 percent talked to one of the exhibitor's salespeople, and 40 percent called a toll-free number. The survey also found that more than 70 percent of the respondents to the survey purchased or recommended the good or service to someone else.[34]

Although U.S. companies and attendees make few deals during trade shows, it is a different situation with international customers. First, international attendees tend to be senior executives with the power to make purchase decisions, not the salespeople and purchasing agents who normally attend from U.S. companies. Second, international attendees spend more time at each vendor's booth and gather more information. Third, many international attendees want to consummate deals or at least discuss purchase arrangements.[35]

Trade promotions are critical elements of marketing, especially within the distribution channel. Table 14-2 reviews all of the various forms of trade promotions.

Table 14-2: Forms of Trade Promotions

Type of Trade Promotion	Definition
Off-invoice allowance	A financial discount or price-off on each case ordered
Slotting fees	Monies paid to retailers by channel members to manufacturers to motivate them to stock new products in the retail store
Exit fees	Monies paid to remove an item from a retailer's inventory
Trade contest	Rewards given to brokers, retail salespeople, retail stores, wholesalers, agents, or other channel members for achieving a specific goal
Cooperative Merchandising Agreement	A formal agreement between the retailer and manufacturer to undertake a cooperative marketing effort
Cooperative Advertising Program	The manufacturer agrees to reimburse retailers or other channel members for a portion of their advertising costs for featuring manufacturer's brands in the ad
Trade shows	Shows where manufacturers can display products and meet buyers

14-6 SPONSORSHIPS

Sponsorship marketing involves a company paying a fee to an event, person, or organization in exchange for a direct association with that event, person, or organization. In North America, companies spent $20.6 billion on sponsorships ranging from an event like a Little League baseball tournament or a local fall festival to the naming rights of a professional sports arena.[36] Figure 14-18 provides a breakdown of various types of sponsorships in North America. Notice sports constitute almost 70 percent of all sponsorships, totaling $14.35 billion.

> **Sponsorship Marketing:** Marketing that involves a company paying a fee that to an event, a person, or and organization in exchange for a direct association with that event, person or organization.

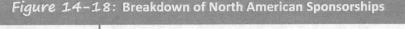

Figure 14-18: Breakdown of North American Sponsorships

Sports	69.6%
Entertainment	10.0%
Causes	8.9%
Arts	4.5%
Festivals & Fairs	4.1%
Other	2.8%

- Sports
- Entertainment
- Causes
- Arts
- Festivals & Fairs
- Other

Source: "North American Sponsorship Spending Forecast To Grow by 4.3% This Year,' www.marketingcharts.com/north-american-sponsorship-spending-forecast-to-grow-by-4-3-this-year-39118, January 13, 2014.

In choosing a sponsorship, it is important to match the audience profile with the company's target market. A firm whose primary customers are females should examine opportunities to sponsor events that involve females, such as a female softball team, the WNBA, or a beauty pageant. It is also important to make sure the image of the event matches the image the company wants to project. A tuxedo or formal gown retailer sponsoring a dance or beauty pageant is a better fit than sponsoring a rodeo or wrestling tournament.

One of the most effective sports sponsorships has been NASCAR, which has grown from primarily beer, auto parts, and tobacco sponsors in the 1970s to include a wide range of consumer products, business-to-business products, and Internet brands today. According to Performance Research, 72 percent of NASCAR fans buy products that support the sport, and 40 percent of the fans will switch their brand loyalty to NASCAR-related brands. The sport has seen a tremendous increase in attendance since 1990 to 75 million fans today, with women now making up 40 percent of the fans. Currently, 58 percent are between the ages of 18 and 44, 42 percent earn $50,000 or more per year, and 40 percent have children younger than age 18. In addition, the sport generates strong Nielsen TV ratings. A recent Daytona 500 race scored a Nielsen rating of 10, with a 24 percent market share.

Such lucrative ratings and fans' support cost sponsors money. The annual rate to endorse a top-notch driver has risen from $6,000 in 1963 to $3 million in 1987 to $15 million today. The price tag of a primary sponsorship slot on a race car ranges from $8 million to $15 million. In one year, it is estimated that the racing teams and the racetracks combined produced $558 million in sponsorships.[37]

Recently, companies have been paying big money for naming rights to ballparks and stadiums. Stadium deals topped $1.54 billion. Some of the stadiums, with the corresponding price tags, are: [38]

- Citigroup Financial, New York (MLB Mets), $400 million for 20 years
- American Airlines, Dallas (NBA Mavericks), $195 million, 30 years
- America West Arena, Phoenix (NBA Suns, NHL Coyotes), $26 million for 30 years
- Coors Field, Denver (MLB Rockies), $15 million, indefinite
- Delta Center, Salt Lake City (NBA Jazz), $25 million for 20 years
- Fleetcenter, Boston (NBA Celtics, NHL Bruins), $30 million for 15 years
- Minute Maid Park, Houston (MLB Astros), $100 million for 30 years
- Staples Center, Los Angeles (NBA Clippers, Lakers, NHL Kings), $116 million for 20 years

Some organizations have moved away from sports sponsorships and toward more cultural events, such as classical music groups, jazz bands, visual art exhibits, dance troupes, and theater performances. Cultural sponsorships are a good match for products that are sold to an upscale audience. Although sports sponsorships are aimed at men, cultural sponsorships appear to have a greater impact on women. According to Paul Fox, vice president of Brand Strategy at Young & Rubicam advertising agency, "preliminary results would suggest that among upscale females [social responsibility, cultural sponsorships] may be more of a driver of brand esteem, and it also impacts brand differentiation as well."

Accenture sponsored the exhibit "Manet/Velazquez: The French Taste for Spanish Paintings" at the Metropolitan Museum of Art in New York City. In addition to creating a brand tie with the museum, Accenture used the event to entertain upscale customers and prospects by holding a number of black-tie events. In addition, Accenture was able to showcase their technology expertise by building a Web site for the exhibit and an interactive map that compared the Manet/Velazquez exhibit with 38 American and French paintings.

As with the other marketing tools, the sponsorships should be integrated with the firm's advertising and IMC plan. The public should easily recognize the link between the person, group, or organization being sponsored and the company involved. It is also important to maximize the sponsorship through advertising, trade and consumer promotions, and public relations. Unless a sponsorship is surrounded by some kind of supporting marketing effort, the sponsorship may not be effective at accomplishing the firm's IMC objectives.

14-7 PUBLIC RELATIONS

The Public Relations department is responsible for overseeing publicity and communications with groups such as employees, stockholders, public interest groups, the government, and society as a whole. It is important that the PR department work closely with the marketing department and be involved in the company's IMC effort to ensure that every piece of communication produced by the company speaks with one voice. The key functions of the public relations department include:

• Monitoring internal and external publics

• Providing information to each public that reinforces the firm's IMC effort

• Promoting sponsorships, event-marketing efforts, cause-related marketing efforts and other image-building activities

• Reacting to any news or emergencies that occur that might have an impact on the firm and the IMC effort being conducted

Often, major PR efforts of a firm are handled by an external PR firm for the same reasons that a firm hires an external advertising agency. In some cases, the advertising agency handles the PR function, but usually a separate firm is hired. Because the work of the PR firm is different, it is important that the PR firm understand the IMC effort of the client and how it fits into the picture. Special events, activities, and news releases produced by the PR firm must strengthen the firm's IMC effort. PR departments monitor various internal and external constituencies, or stakeholders.

The PR department is also responsible for monitoring the actions and opinions of each group. The PR department should address any changes in attitudes, views, or concerns that develop.

One of the most important, and most difficult, tasks is the handling of negative publicity. A positive image that has taken years to build can be destroyed overnight. It is the PR department's responsibility to ensure that this does not happen. Crisis management and other techniques are used to help a firm cope with any circumstances that threaten the firm's image, regardless of the cause.

Many times a crisis contains the potential to improve the firm's position and image -- if handled properly. For example, PepsiCo encountered some negative publicity about hypodermic needles being found in its products. The management team was quick to respond with photographs and video that demonstrated how bottles and cans are turned upside down while empty before they are filled with any soft drink and how it would have been impossible to put a needle into a soft drink. Pepsi's quick and positive response eliminated negative publicity and at the same time demonstrated to consumers the safety of its products. Unfortunately, the reaction of Ford and Bridgestone to the faulty tires on the new Ford Explorers was not handled as well. Instead of immediately seeking to correct the problem, both denied a problem existed and tried to blame it on tires that were not inflated correctly by consumers. The public did not buy the excuse, and the outcry against both companies was so strong that it cost them sales, damaged their images, and cost the chief executive officer (CEO) of Ford his job.

Part Four: Marketing Communications

Crisis management involves either accepting the blame for an event and offering an apology, or refuting in a tactful manner those making the charges. Both Pepsi and Ford used the latter strategy. The public accepted Pepsi's explanation because it was supported by hard evidence but rejected Ford's explanation because they did not believe the entire problem was underinflated tires.

Instead of blaming drivers for not making sure the tires were inflated properly, Ford would have been wiser to accept the blame and have taken immediate steps to correct the problem. When 200 people in Belgium and France came down with nausea and dizziness from drinking Coke, CEO Douglas Ivester flew to Brussels and published a personal apology in Belgium newspapers for the problem. Coke set up special consumer hotlines and offered to pay the medical bills for anyone who got sick. Coke's investigation into the incident identified the cause of the illness as poor-quality carbon dioxide and a fungicide that was used to treat the wooden pallets. According to Ivester, when a crisis occurs, the strategy should be the following: (1) visible, (2) sympathetic, and (3) responsive.

Screenshot

Summary

1. Discuss the reasons for a shift in marketing expenditures to promotions. First, promotions normally have an immediate impact on sales, whereas advertising takes a longer period of time to produce an impact. Second, because of increased brand proliferation and brand parity, consumers and businesses have more choices today and see little difference among firms and among various brands. Third, there is consumer acceptance of promotions, and in some instances, there is a demand for special deals before purchases will be made. Fourth, there is a decline in the impact of advertising. With remote controls and digital video recorders, consumers are zapping out many commercials, and those they do watch, view, or hear are quickly forgotten as a result of the high number of commercials they are exposed to each day.

2. Identify the various forms of consumer promotions. Firms can use 10 different types of consumer promotions. They include coupons, premiums, contests and sweepstakes, bonus packs, tie-ins, frequency programs, sampling, price-offs, refunds and rebates, and product placement.

3. Identify the various types of coupons and distribution methods. The types of coupons are instant redemption coupons, bounce-back coupons, scanner-delivered coupons, cross-ruffing coupons, response-offer coupons, and e-coupons. Distribution methods include print media; FSI; direct mail; on-, in-, or near-package; and other methods, such as in-store, fax, Internet, scanner-delivered, and sampling. The most common is FSI, which makes up 85.60 percent of all coupons.

4. Explain the importance of in-store promotions in purchasing behavior. Shoppers make approximately two-thirds of all brand purchase decisions while in a retail store, and most shoppers walk out with twice the number of products they had planned on purchasing. This means that packaging, pricing, point-of-purchase displays, and in-store promotions, such as sampling and coupons, are critically important in swaying consumers to purchase a particular brand.

5. Discuss the goals of trade promotions. For manufacturers, the overarching goal of trade promotions is to increase sales of their brand. Retailers, however, seek to increase the market share of their stores and to boost sales of a product category. Retailers are less concerned with which brand sells the most as long as the product line sells. More specific goals of trade promotions include (1) stimulating initial distribution, (2) obtaining prime retail locations or shelf space, (3) supporting established brands, (4) countering competitive actions, (5) increasing order size, (6) building retail inventories, (7) reducing excess inventories of the manufacturer, (8) enhancing channel relationships, and (9) enhancing the IMC program.

6. Identify the various types of trade promotions. Companies have a variety of trade promotions that can be used, such as (1) trade allowances, (2) trade contests, (3) trade incentives, (4) cooperative advertising programs, and (5) trade shows. Choosing the correct trade promotion is an important decision. The more a firm ties its trade promotion strategy to its IMC effort, the greater will be the impact of trade promotions, and in the long run, the less the firm will have to spend on trade promotions. Rather than use trade promotions as a reactive tool, if planned as part of the IMC, they can become a proactive method of pushing products through the channel.

7. Discuss the issue of slotting fees. Because retailers must make decisions about which items to stock and which not to stock, most retailers charge a slotting fee for new products. Slotting fees are funds paid to retailers to stock new products. Retailers justify charging slotting fees because it costs them to add new products to their inventories and to stock the merchandise. If the product is not successful, the investment in initial inventory represents a loss, especially when the retailer has stocked a large number of stores. Also, adding a new product in the retail store means allocating shelf space to it. Because shelves are always filled with products, adding a new product means either deleting another brand or product or reducing the amount of shelf space allocated to other products. Slotting fees cost manufacturers between $1 million and $2 million per product. Retailers believe that, by charging slotting fees, they reduce the number of new products being introduced, which, in turn, reduces the number of new product failures. As would be expected, manufacturers oppose slotting fees and see them as a form of extortion. Because retailers control the channel and access to consumers, manufacturers have little choice but to pay the fees if they want their items on the store's shelves.

8. Describe the current use of sponsorships. Sponsorship marketing involves a company paying a fee to an event, person, or organization in exchange for a direct association with that event, person, or organization. Worldwide, companies spent $33.8 billion on sponsorships, ranging from an event like a Little League baseball tournament or a local fall festival to the naming rights to a professional sports arena. Most sponsorships are in the area of sports. Recently, companies have paid big money for naming rights to ballparks and stadiums. Stadium deals topped $1.4 billion in 2006. Beyond sports, some organizations sponsor cultural events, such as classical music groups, jazz bands, visual art exhibits, dance troupes, and theater performances.

  9. Identify the role of public relations in integrated marketing communications (IMC). The PR department is responsible for overseeing publicity and communications with groups such as employees, stockholders, public interest groups, the government, and society as a whole. It is important that the public relations department work closely with the marketing department and be involved in the company's IMC effort to ensure that every piece of communication produced by the company speaks with one voice. The key functions of the PR department include: (1) monitoring internal and external publics; (2) providing information to each public that reinforces the firm's IMC effort; (3) promoting sponsorships, event marketing efforts, cause-related marketing efforts, and other image-building activities; and (4) reacting to any news or emergencies that occurs that might affect the firm and IMC effort being conducted.

Key Terms

bonus packs	exit fees	refunds
bounce-back coupons	forward buying	response-offer coupons
branded media	freestanding inserts (FSI)	sampling
calendar promotions	frequency programs	scanner-delivered coupons
contests and sweepstakes	instant redemption coupon	slotting fees
cooperative advertising pro-gram	intercompany tie-in	spiff money
	intracompany tie-in	sponsorship marketing
cooperative merchandising agreement (CMA)	off-invoice allowance	tie-ins
	overlay	trade allowances
coupons	premiums	trade incentives
cross-ruffing coupon	price-offs	
diversion	product placement	
e-coupons	rebates	

Discussion Questions

1. Read the chapter-opening about spring break and the use of promotions. Have you had any personal experiences with promotions offered at spring break? What is your evaluation of the promotions presented in the opening and with any you experienced personally?

2. Go to the Internet and access three different resorts or vacation destinations. Discuss the promotions that each offer. Copy and paste the promotional offer into your document that you submit along with the URL of each Web site.

3. From the list of consumer promotions provided in Section 14-3, discuss each consumer promotion as it relates to your personal purchase behavior. Discuss things such as frequency of use, your attitude toward each, how these promotions affect your purchase behavior, and what types of offers have an impact on you.

4. Pick one of the consumer promotions identified in Section 14-3 that interests you. Use the Internet and an article database to locate more information about it. Write a summary of what you learn. How is it being used and what are the most successful strategies?

5. Pick one of the following types of products. Discuss how each of the consumer promotions presented in Section 14-3 (listed in Figure 14-2) could be used. Which ones would be most effective? Which ones would be least effective? Why?

a. Pizza

b. Hiking shoes

c. Dental services

d. Janitorial services for a business

e. Video game

6. List all of the loyalty or frequency programs that you participate in or have a card for. Which ones influence your purchase decisions? Why? Discuss why you joined each one. What frequency or loyalty programs are you a member of, but do not use ? Discuss why.

7. What is your opinion of product placements? Do they impact your purchase decisions? Why or why not? Do they have an effect on your image of the brands ? Why or why not? Identify at least four product placements you have seen on television or in a movie. How effective do you think each product placement is? Provide support for your answer.

8. The next time you are in a store, make a note of all of the promotions you see, especially point-of-purchase displays. Write a short report detailing the information. What promotions were the most effective? Why? Which promotions were not effective? Why?

9. In Section 14-4, it was stated that two-thirds of all product and brand purchases are not planned. What is your evaluation of this statistic? Talk to at least five other people about how closely they follow a shopping list and how many things they purchase that were not planned.

10. Pick one of the trade promotions listed in Section 14-5b. Find additional articles and information about the trade promotion selected. Write a short report of your findings.

11. What are your thoughts about sponsorships? Are they effective? Why or why not?

12. A new trend for universities and colleges is naming buildings and sports facilities after brands, that is, accepting naming rights from companies. Do you think this is right? Why or why not? Should public universities accept private money from companies in exchange for naming rights? Justify your answer.

Review Questions

(Answers are on Last Page of the Chapter)

True or False

1. About 85 percent of all coupons are distributed via FSI.

2. Coupons placed inside packages so that customers cannot redeem them at the time of the original purchase are called cross-ruffing coupons.

3. Response-offer coupons are issued following a request by a consumer.

4. The fastest growing method of coupon distribution is digital coupons.

5. The difference between contests and sweepstakes is that, in sweepstakes, participants may be required to perform an activity or to make a purchase to be eligible to win, whereas in a contest, participants do not need to make a purchase, and the winners are determined by a random drawing in which every entrant has an equal chance of being selected.

6. Four bars of soap might be packaged together and sold for the price of three individual packages in a bonus pack.

7. An example of an intracompany tie-in would be the St. Louis Cardinals baseball team providing a 50 percent off coupon to the nearby Gateway Arch with the purchase of an adult ticket to a Cardinals' baseball game.

8. Frequency programs are consumer promotions aimed at current customers that are designed to build repeat purchase behavior and brand loyalty by rewarding customers for their patronage.

9. Sponsorship marketing involves a company paying a fee to an event, person, or organization in exchange for a direct association with the event, person, or organization.

Multiple Choice

10. A reduction in the listed retail price of a product used to attract consumers, to reduce purchase risk, and to stimulate demand is known as a:

  a. rebate.

  b. price-off.

  c. promotional tie-in.

  d. none of the above.

11. A movie or show that contains a brand name or logo with a story line that intersects the brand's mission or current advertising campaign is known as

  a. trailer media.

  b. market media.

  c. cooperative media.

  d. branded media.

12. Expenditures or incentives used by manufacturers and other members of the marketing channel to help push their products through the channel are known as

  a. market promotions.

  b. rebate promotions.

  c. cooperative promotions.

  d. trade promotions.

Blog

Clow-Lascu: *Marketing: Essentials 5e Blog*

CATEGORY ARCHIVES: CHAPTER13

Marketing for the Holidays

Posted on November 17, 2014 | Leave a comment

Thanksgiving and Christmas always brings increased advertising by brands and especially for retailers. This article in CMO Today should generate some interesting discussion because for the 2014 holidays the number one marketing method will be email.

CMO Today Article: You've Got Mail and More is Coming

Discussion Questions:

1. After reading the article, what are your thoughts about the use of email as the primary marketing tactic?
2. Look at the bar graph of the most used channels for 2014 holidays. Rank these channels in terms of influence on your holiday purchases. What is the most effective, what is second, etc. Justify your ranking.
3. Look at the graph of the popular social media marketing tactics. Identify the three that are most effective with you. Explain why.

What Is Happening Today?

Learn More! For videos and articles that relate to Chapter 14:

blogclowlascu.net/category/chapter14

Includes Discussion Questions with each Post!

Notes

1. Amy Johannes, "Spring Breakaway," *Promo* 20, no. 3, (February 2007): 22–25; Sandra O'Laughlin, "Bic Heads South for Spring Break," *Brandweek* 46, no. 11 (March 14, 2005): 38; Laura Petrecca, "Spring-Break Pitches Check into Hotels," *USA Today* (March 20, 2006): Money 03b.

2. "Upward Bound," *Promo SourceBook* 2005 17 (2005): 11–13.

3. Jakki J. Mohr and George S. Low, "Escaping the Catch-22 of Trade Promotion Spending," *Marketing Management* 2 (1993): 30–39.

4. Kristen Cloud, "Report: Coupon Redemption Remains Strong, Digital Gains in Popularity," www.theshelbyreport.com/2014/01/17

5. Kathleen M. Joyce, "Fast Clip," available at www.promomagnews.com (April 2003): 35, 43–44.

6. Noreen O'Leary, "Dealing with Coupons," *Adweek* 46, no. 8 (February 21, 2005): 29.

7. Michael Hartnett, "Coupons Still King," *Frozen Food Age* 55, no. 3 (October 2006): 41; Joseph Gatti, "Coupon Distribution Up, But Web Dispersal Still Scanty," *Direct Marketing* (October 1, 2003): 1–2.

8. Stephanie Thompson, ''Cheerio Ads on Milk: Why Didn't You Think of That?'' *Advertising Age* 77, no. 36 (September 4, 2006): 4, 40.

9. Kristen Cloud, "Report: Coupon Redemption Remains Strong, Digital Gains in Popularity," www.theshelbyreport.com/2014/01/17.

10. Noreen O'Leary, ''Dealing with Coupons,'' *Adweek* 46, no. 8 (February 21, 2005): 29.

11. William C. LaFief and Brian T. Engelland, ''The Effects of Optimal Stimulation Level of Value Consciousness on Consumer Use of Coupons and Contests,'' *Midwest Marketing Association 1995 Proceedings*, (1995): 83–87.

12. ''Promo in Dex,'' *Promo* 20, no. 3 (February 2007): 11–13.

13. Larry J. Seibert, ''What Consumers Think About Bonus Pack Sales Promotions,'' *Marketing News* 31, no. 4 (February 7, 1997): 9.

14. Sandra Dolbow, ''Jeep Drives Penney's 100th,'' *Brandweek* 43, no. 23 (June 10, 2002): 12.

15. Patricia J. Daughtery, Richard J. Fox, and Frederick J. Stephenson, ''Frequency Marketing Programs: A Clarification with Strategic Marketing Implications,'' *Journal of Promotional Management* 2, no. 1 (1993): 5–26.

16. Ibid.

17. Libby Estell, ''Loyalty Lessons,'' Incentive 176, no. 11 (November 2002): 38–42.

18. ''News Watch,'' *Supermarket News* 54, no. 47 (November 20, 2006): 40–42.

19. Carol Angrisani, ''Theme Parks,'' *Supermarket News* 54, no. 40 (October 2, 2006): 45–46.

20. Joe Kohn, ''Studies: Rebates Are Strong Poison,'' *Automotive News* 77, no. 6000(September 2, 2002): 6.

21. ''Brady Corp. Offers 'Rebate Rally' Promotion,'' *Electrical Contracting Products* 10, no. 1 (January 2007): 10.

22. Jon Lafayette, ''Automakers, Advertisers Turn to Marketing Deals,'' *Automotive News* 81 (March 5, 2007): 38.

23. Marc Graser and T. L. Stanley, ''10 Favorite Product Placement Deals,'' *Advertising Age* 77, no. 51 (December 18, 2006): 35.

24. Deb Peth and John Moscicki, ''Adding High-Tech POP,'' *Convenience Store News* 42, no. 11 (September 18, 2006): 99.

25. ''POP Impact Quantified,'' *Frozen Food Age* 50, no. 2 (September 2001): 10; Michelle L. Kirsche, ''POPAI Study Confirms Importance of POP Ads,'' *Drug Store News* 26 (October 11, 2004): 4–5.

26. Peth and Moscicki, ''Adding High-Tech POP,'' 99.

27. Kenneth E. Clow and Donald Baack, *Integrated Advertising, Promotion, and Marketing Communications* (Upper Saddle River, N.J.: Prentice-Hall, 2002): 396–399.

28. Ibid., 378.

29. Philip Zerillo and Dawn Iacobucci, ''Trade Promotions: A Call for a More Rational Approach,'' *Business Horizons* 38, no. 4 (July/August 1995): 69–76.

30. Prakash L. Abad, ''Quantity Restrictions and the Reseller's Response to a Temporary Price Reduction or an Announced Price Increase,'' *Asia-Pacific Journal of Operational Management* 23, no. 1 (March 2006): 1–23.

31. Julie Gallagher, ''Introduction Incentives,'' *Supermarket News* 54, no. 43 (October 23, 2006): 65–67.

32. Jack J. Kasulis, ''Managing Trade Promotions in the Context of Market Power,'' *Journal of the Academy of Marketing Science* 27, no. 3 (Summer 1999): 320–332.

33. Martin Hoover, ''Supermarket 'Slotting' Leaves Small Firms Out,'' *Business Cour er: Serving the Cincinnati-Northern Kentucky Region* 16, no. 25 (October 8, 1999): 3–4.

34. David Wellman, ''Displays Power Adult Frozen Novelty Sales,'' *Frozen Food Age* 51, no. 4 (November 2002): 1–2.

35. Bradley Johnson, ''IBM Moves Back to Intel Co-op Deal,'' *Advertising Age* 68, no. 10 (March 10, 1997): 4; ''Intel Inside Program,'' Intel Web site available at www.intel.com/pressroom/intel_inside.htim, accessed on April 5, 2007.

36. Kelly Lanigan, ''B2B Media: Trends & Forecasts,'' *Expo* (November/December 2006): 62–70.

37. Ellie Booker, ''Studies Show Events' Importance,'' *B-to-B* 91, no. 9 (July 10, 2006): 15.

38. Matthew Flamm, ''Alien Influences,'' *Crain's New York Business* 15, no. 46 (November 15, 1999): 35–36.

Cases

Case 14-1 Ace Air Conditioning & Heating

Alfred (Ace) Zinkhan founded Ace Air Conditioning & Heating as a family business in 1984. He worked part-time repairing air conditioners and heating systems for the first five years until he was able to generate enough revenue to quit his job and devote full-time to the small business. Ace Air Conditioning & Heating now generates $1.5 million a year in gross income and employs four service technicians, a full-time secretary, and a part-time bookkeeper.

Ace started his business repairing only residential systems. Then, in 1995, after working on a large air conditioning system for a local business, he decided to offer his services to business customers as well.

The last component of his business was added in 2002, when a local contractor asked him to install some furnaces and air conditioners in new homes they were building. Ace found the work easier because the house was not yet completed. He did not have to crawl under structures or go into attics to locate vents and other components that needed repairing. He also found that the new construction was the most profitable. The contribution margins were higher, and the amount of time it took his employees to do the work was less.

Sitting down with his bookkeeper, Ace got a better picture of what he is currently facing. Increased competition in the area has cost him two large business clients and some residential customers he serviced in the past. This has resulted in 12 percent decline in revenues for this past year. The bookkeeper also provided him facts concerning the breakdown of his business in the three areas of residential, business, and new-construction customers, the average margins on each job, and the percentage of gross income each generates.

Based on the information provided in the table, Ace realizes that most of his income comes from business customers, yet residential customers make up almost two-thirds of his customers. In addition, the smallest component of his business is new construction, yet it generates the highest gross margins.

Type of Customer	Gross Revenue ($)	Gross Margin (%)	Percent of Total Customers (%)
Business	675,798	40	27
Residential	407,420	29	62
New construction	433,325	48	11

Because the level of competition has increased, Ace realizes he may need to use consumer promotions to entice new customers to use his services.

He also wonders if he needs to use promotions to in some way reward his current customers and to keep them from switching to a competitor. Last, he wonders: Can he use promotions to encourage some customers who are now using one of his competitors to switch to his company?

Questions

1. From the information given, which group or groups of customers should Ace Air Conditioning & Heating pursue?

2. What consumer promotions can he use to attract residential customers? Would the promotions be different for current customers versus new customers?

3. Should he use consumer promotions for his business customers and the new construction customers? Why or why not? If he should, which should he use?

4. Various manufacturers of heating and air conditions systems, such as Lennox, have approached Ace about cooperative advertising. They have offered to pay 50 to 70 percent of the cost of local advertising in exchange for him using their brand in the homes and businesses that he services. What are the pros and cons of such an arrangement?

5. Every year there is a home and garden show at the civic center in town. About 45,000 local home owners and businesspeople attend. There are usually about 200 exhibitors. The cost for a booth, materials and supplies would be $6,000. Should Ace participate in the show? What are the benefits? What are the disadvantages?

Case 14-2 Yonex

Yonex, originally Yoneyama Company, Ltd., was founded in Japan in 1946 by Minoru Yoneyama as a manufacturer of wooden floats for fishing nets. The business thrived until the introduction of plastic floats forced it out of business. At that time, Minoru Yoneyama vowed that his company would never again fail because it was left behind technologically.

Using his knowledge of wood crafting, the Yoneyama Company started building badminton racquets in 1957 under various brand names. In 1961, the first "Yoneyama" brand badminton racquet was produced, and two years later, Yoneyama Trading, Ltd., was established in Tokyo to distribute the Yoneyama racquets internationally.

The company's devotion to innovation attracted attention in 1969, when it introduced the first aluminum badminton racquet, the #700. Today, the Yonex badminton racquets are used by 80 percent of professional badminton players, and Yonex is the world's leading distributor of badminton racquets. Spurred by the success of its badminton racquets, Yoneyama entered the tennis racquet market in 1971. By 1973, the company's new logo "YY" and blue and green color combinations were common sights on both badminton courts as well as tennis courts. In 1978, Yoneyama introduced the first ultralight badminton racquet. Then in 1980, it introduced the world's first "isometric" tennis racquet and the superlight R-7. Very quickly, Yoneyama became a powerful force in the tennis racquet market.

To more effectively expand internationally, Yonex Corporation established subsidiaries in the United States, the United Kingdom, Germany, Canada, Taiwan, and Hong Kong. Yonex continues to produce the most technologically advanced tennis and badminton racquets, which are used by both amateur and professional players. The company has also moved into producing technologically advanced golf clubs and equipment.

To push the sale of its tennis racquets, Yonex signed tennis stars Anna Kournikova, Monica Seles, and Martina Hingis. With their signing, Yonex was ready to expand its market share in the tennis racquet market. Its goal was to be the market leader. It recognizes that coupons are not an effective method to promote its tennis racquet because the message conveyed to consumers would conflict with its image as a technological leader. In addition to reaching adults, Yonex would like to focus on the youth market because, if it can win them over, it will have them for a lifetime. With recent ads by the tennis industry targeting young people appearing on the Cartoon Network, TBS, and TNT, Yonex believes that now is the time to develop a major offensive. With tennis stars signed and advertising in place, the only piece of the puzzle left is the consumer and trade promotions that should be used.

Questions

1. Discuss each of the consumer promotion options listed in Section 15-3 in terms of its effectiveness for Yonex tennis racquets, considering the company's position in the market and the current image that it wants to maintain.

2. What trade promotions should Yonex use to encourage sporting goods stores to stock its tennis racquets and to push them over other brands?

3. What consumer promotional mix would you recommend for Yonex? Justify your position and discuss how you would use each consumer promotional element you picked.

Sources: Mike Troy, "Tennis Industry Courts Kids to Push Entry-less Sales at Mass," *Discount Store News* 36, no. 6 (March 17, 1997): 19; Terry Lefton, "Kournikova's Big Racket; Wizards Meet the MLB," *Brandweek* 41, no. 5 (January 31, 2000): 18; Yonex Web site available at www.yonex.co.uk, accessed on April 5, 2007.

Answers to Review Questions

Answers: 1) T, 2) F, 3) T, 4) T, 5) F, 6) T, 7) F, 8) T, 9) T, 10) b, 11) d, 12) d

Chapter 15

Personal Selling and Direct Response Marketing

Learning Objectives

After studying
this chapter,
you should be able to:

1. Explain the different types of personal selling.

2. Discuss the various buyer-seller relationships.

3. Identify the steps in the selling process and briefly describe each step.

4. Explain the concepts of data warehousing and database management.

5. Identify the steps in developing a customer relationship management program.

6 Explain the concept of direct response marketing and list the various methods of direct marketing.

Chapter Outline

15-1 Chapter Overview

15-2 Personal Selling

    15-2a Types of Personal Selling

    15-2b Buyer-Seller Relationships

    15-2c The Selling Process

15-3 Database Marketing

    15-3a Data Warehousing

    15-3b Data Mining

    15-3c Customer Relationship Management

15-4 Direct Response Marketing

Summary

Key Terms

Discussion Questions

Review Questions

Blog

Notes

Case 15-1: National South Bank

Case 15-2: FishUSA

15-1 CHAPTER OVERVIEW

Salespeople are essential in many transactions, especially for high-cost items like real estate. Instead of using a real estate agent, Jay and Marcie decided to explore some new houses on their own. Using the Yellow Pages, real estate ads in the newspaper, and the Internet, they located a new-construction community that offered new homes for sale and encouraged new home buyers to see what they had to offer. Arriving at their appointment, Jay and Marcie were shown a photo album of new homes that had just been built. Each was described in detail in terms of construction. The salesperson took great pride and stated several times that the company offered the best-quality built homes in the area. Before taking them on a tour of three new homes in the gated community that were almost ready for the market (see **Figure 15-1**), the salesperson pointed to

Figure 15-1: Successful realtors work closely with their clients to assure that all questions about a potential home, including those in construction phase, are addressed.

plaques that hung on the wall, framing awards the company had recently won for innovative home design. As Jay and Marcie toured the three new homes on display, they were impressed (see **Figure 15-2**). The homes were beautiful. The price was a little higher than they wanted to pay for a home, but, as the salesperson pointed out the quality construction, he reassured them that the higher cost was a small price to pay for the quality that they would be receiving .

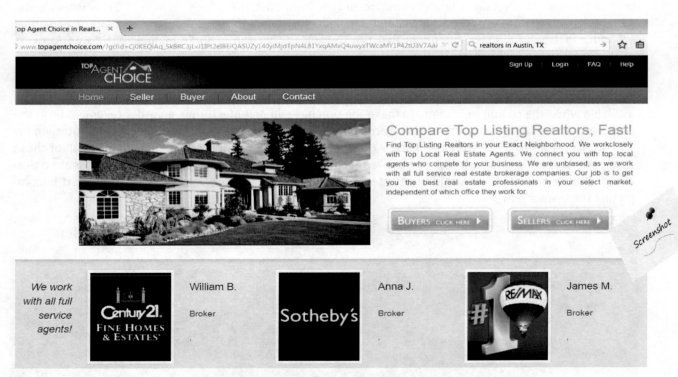

Figure 15-2: Online services, like this realtor rating Web site, provide consumers with a powerful tool for finding the right kind of salesperson for their important purchase.

Salespeople are also important when purchasing items at retail stores. They help customers locate merchandise, answer questions, and check out the products. Sales clerks at some retailers have to be hunted down, and they know little about the merchandise being sold, whereas, at other stores, the salespeople greet you as you walk in and are eager to assist you in finding just the right item.

Retail sales, however, are only part of the personal selling component of integrated marketing communications (IMC). Business-to-business sales make up a significant component of personal selling. Although consumer and retail sales are discussed in this chapter, the primary focus of the personal selling component of the chapter is on business-to-business selling. Section 15-2 discusses the various types of personal selling, buyer-seller relationships, and the selling process. Section 15-3 examines the role of databases in the IMC and how they are used to support personal selling, customer service, and direct marketing. The concepts of data warehousing and data mining are presented, along with a recent database customer service program called customer relationship management. Because of advances in technology, databases have become a central component of business operations. The last section of the chapter, Section 15-4, discusses direct marketing. Firms have various methods of direct response marketing that include mail, e-mail, catalogs, the Internet, and the telephone.

15-2   PERSONAL SELLING

Personal selling is an important component of IMC, especially for business-to-business transactions. Personal selling occurs in many situations, ranging from the sales clerk at a local store helping a customer locate a particular item to the field salesperson for Boeing talking to airline companies, the Pentagon, or governments of other nations about purchasing airplanes. Personal selling offers one major advantage not found in the other forms of marketing: two-way communication. The seller is able to interact with the buyer to provide relevant information and to answer any questions or objections the buyer may raise.

15-2a: Types of Personal Selling

Personal selling can be classified into three broad categories: order takers, order getters, and support personnel. Order takers process routine orders from customers (see Figure 15-3), whereas order getters actively generate potential leads and persuade customers to make a purchase. Support personnel are individuals who directly support or assist in the selling function in some manner but do not process orders or directly solicit orders.

Order takers can be seen in a variety of selling roles. In retailing, they operate the cash register, stock shelves, and answer basic questions from customers. Their role is to assist the customer and to be available when the customer is ready to make the purchase. In manufacturing, an order taker can be in the corporate office taking customer orders by telephone, fax, e-mail, or the Internet. For a distributor, an order taker may go to retail stores and stock the shelves with the distributor's merchandise. In all of these cases, the order taker does not take an active role in seeking customers or persuading them to make a purchase. The merchandise is presold or selected by the customer. The order taker's task is to assist in completing the transaction.

Figure 15-3: Order takers in this retailing operation process routine orders from customers.

Order getters, however, actively seek new customers and work to persuade customers to purchase more. In retail, a salesperson at a car dealer or a furniture store may be an order getter if part of his or her task is to persuade customers to make a purchase. In retail situations in which salespeople are paid a commission, they are likely to be order getters because the more customers they can convince to make a purchase, the more the salespeople can earn. These salespeople are also more likely to be involved in **cross-selling**, which involves the marketing of additional items with the purchase of a particular good or service. A salesperson at a clothing store may encourage a customer purchasing a new pair of pants to purchase a sweater to match it. A bank may encourage a customer opening a checking account to also open a safety deposit box or to apply for a home equity loan.

Most order getters work in the business-to-business area as **field salespeople**. A field salesperson is involved in going to a potential customer's place of business to solicit business. Field salespeople can be used in the consumer market, but this is limited primarily to insurance, Amway, and Avon, all of which use a direct marketing approach. Using salespeople in the business-to-business market is feasible because there are fewer buyers and each buyer tends to make a large volume purchase. Figure 15-4 highlights the primary differences between order takers and order getters.

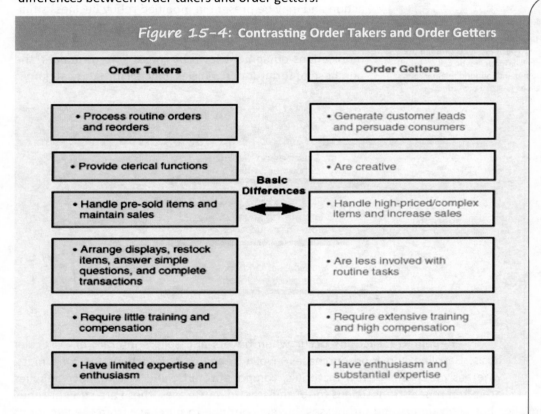

Figure 15-4: Contrasting Order Takers and Order Getters

Order Takers	Basic Differences	Order Getters
• Process routine orders and reorders		• Generate customer leads and persuade consumers
• Provide clerical functions		• Are creative
• Handle pre-sold items and maintain sales		• Handle high-priced/complex items and increase sales
• Arrange displays, restock items, answer simple questions, and complete transactions		• Are less involved with routine tasks
• Require little training and compensation		• Require extensive training and high compensation
• Have limited expertise and enthusiasm		• Have enthusiasm and substantial expertise

Order Takers: Salespeople who process routine orders from customers.

Order Getters: Salespeople who actively generate potential leads and persuade customers to make a purchase.

Cross-selling: The marketing of additional items with the purchase of a particular good or service.

Field Salesperson: A salesperson who is involved in going to a potential customer's place of business to solicit accounts.

Outbound Telemarketing: The process through which an order-getter salesperson calls prospects and attempts to persuade them to make a purchase.

Inbound Telemarketing: The process through which an order-taker salesperson handles incoming calls from customers and prospects.

Support Personnel: Individuals who directly support or assist in the selling function in some manner but do not process orders or directly solicit orders.

Missionary Salesperson: A sales support person whose task is to provide information about a good or service.

Many companies are now using telemarketing to sell their products. If the company is calling customers and attempting to persuade them to purchase the product, this is called **outbound telemarketing** and is done by an order getter. If the company is manning telephones that customers call with orders, then it is **inbound telemarketing** and is handled by order takers. Both are used in the business-to-business market and in the consumer market (see **Figure 15-5**).

The last category of salespeople is the **support personnel**. The most common support individual is the **missionary salesperson**, whose task is to provide information about a good or service. Pharmaceutical companies use missionary salespersons to distribute new drugs and provide doctors with information. The order getter makes the actual sales pitch. With highly technical products, sales engineers are used to discuss the technical aspects of the product and to answer questions a potential customer may have. Usually, this is done in conjunction with a salesperson, using a team approach.

Figure 15-5: Business-to-business vendors typically use a variety of salespeople to push products through the channel, including field salespeople who call on retail stores, and both outbound and inbound telemarketers to solicit orders as well as take orders.

15-2b: Buyer-Seller Relationships

Personal selling allows a buyer and a seller to interact. This two-way communication is called a **buyer-seller dyad** and is illustrated in Figure 15-6. Buyers have the opportunity to ask questions, and sellers have the opportunity to provide information. If the salesperson is able to meet a consumer (or business) need, a transaction is likely to occur.

The most basic type of buyer-seller dyad relationship is the **single transaction**, which occurs when the buyer and seller interact for the purpose of a single purchase. This situation may occur in new-buy situations in the business-to-business market and for expensive consumer products such as real estate. At the next level are **occasional transactions**, which require an infrequent buyer-seller interaction and may be present in modified rebuy business situations. Occasional transactions may occur in the purchase of equipment, vehicles, computing equipment, and telecommunications equipment for a business. For consumers, the purchase of furniture or vehicles may fall into this category.

Buyer-seller Dyad:
Two-way communication between a buyer and a seller.

Single Transaction:
Buyer and seller interacting for the purpose of a single transaction.

Occasional Transactions:
Transactions whereby buyer and seller interact infrequently in the process of making the transaction.

Repeat Transactions:
Buyer and seller interacting over multiple transactions.

Contractual Agreement:
A written agreement between the buyer and seller that states the terms of the interaction, costs, and length of the commitment.

Figure 15-6: Contrasting The Buyer - Seller Dyad

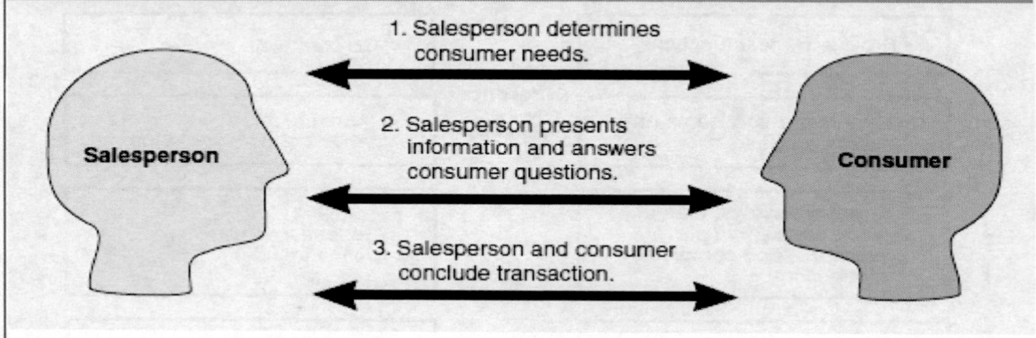

Salesperson

1. Salesperson determines consumer needs.

2. Salesperson presents information and answers consumer questions.

3. Salesperson and consumer conclude transaction.

Consumer

Repeat transactions occur when buyers and sellers interact on a regular basis. Gasoline and food purchases involve repeated transactions for consumers, whereas purchases of raw materials, component parts, and maintenance supplies are often repeat transactions for businesses. In most cases, these are straight rebuy business situations. For both consumers and businesses, buyers continue to purchase from the vendor as long as their needs are being met and a more attractive vendor does not come along.

For these first three types of buyer-seller dyad situations, transactions are made between the seller and buyer with little or no relationship between the two parties. They meet, they exchange information, and a transaction occurs. There is no commitment or loyalty from either side toward the other party. To ensure a greater commitment from buyers, sellers will often attempt to move the dyad to a higher level, the **contractual agreement**. With a contractual agreement, a written agreement between the buyer and seller is established that states the terms of the interaction, costs, and length of the commitment. With a contractual agreement both the buyer and seller benefit. Buyers are guaranteed a steady supply of a specific product at a predetermined price. Sellers benefit because the buying situation becomes a straight rebuy situation and does not require active selling. As long as they can meet the needs of the buyer, they are guaranteed a sale for the length of the contract and do not have to worry about a competitor taking their client away.

Whereas contractual agreements represent a more involved form of dyad relationship, they may or may not involve trust. **Trust relationships** in a buyer-seller dyad are based on a mutual respect and understanding of both parties and a commitment to work together. In many countries outside the United States, trust relationships are expected, and company executives are insulted at the suggestion the agreement should be solidified through a written contract (see **Figure 15-7**).

Figure 15-7: In many countries, a handshake is more valuable than a written contract.

At the next level is the electronic data interchange (EDI) relationship, which expands the trust relationship to include the sharing of data between the buying and selling firms. EDI relationships often are established between intermediaries within the distribution channel. They take place when the buyer and seller electronically share information about production, inventory, shipping, and purchasing. Such relationships involve a high level of trust because the seller has access to all of the buying firm's production information, and the seller ships the materials automatically. Most EDI relationships are with single-vendor sources, which sellers like because they know the customer is not making any purchases from a competitor, and as long as the customer is satisfied, they will keep the contract. Sellers also know that with EDI it is more difficult for the buyer to switch vendors because of the physical cost of hooking up with a new vendor.

> **Trust Relationships:** Buyer-seller dyads based on mutual respect and understanding of both parties and a commitment to work together.
>
> **Strategic Partnership:** Partnership in which the buyer and seller exchange information at the highest levels with the goal of collaboration.

At the highest level of the buyer-seller dyad interaction is the **strategic partnership**. With this approach, the buyer and seller share information at the highest levels. The goal of this relationship is to collaborate on plans to benefit both parties and the customers of the buying firm. In this type of relationship, the seller actively examines ways to modify its products to improve the position of the buying firm in the marketplace. Table 15-1 reviews these various levels of the buyer-seller dyad.

Table 15-1: Buyer-Seller Dyad Relationships	
Relationship	**Definition**
Single transactions	The buyer and seller interact for the purpose of a single transaction.
Occasional transactions	The buyer and seller interact infrequently.
Repeat transactions	The buyer and seller interact on a regular basis.
Contractual agreement	A written agreement between the buyer and seller states the terms of the interaction, costs, and length of the commitment.
Trust relationship	The buyer-seller dyad is based on mutual respect and an understanding of both parties, and a commitment to work together.
EDI	This trust relationship includes the sharing of data between the buying and selling firms.
Strategic partnership	The buyer and seller exchange information at the highest levels with the goal of collaboration.

Sources: Kenneth E. Clow and Donald Baack, *Integrated Advertising, Promotion, and Marketing Communication* (Upper Saddle River, N.J.: Prentice Hall, 2002), 454.

Personal selling, perhaps more than any of the other components of an IMC program, must be built on trust, honesty, and integrity. Regardless of the type of relationship between the buyer and seller, the buyer must have confidence that he or she is being given the correct and honest information. Yet this is not always the case. Because of the lack of skill, pressure from sales managers, the desire to earn more money, and the need to meet a sales quota, salespeople may be tempted to use unethical techniques ranging from putting pressure on a buyer to make a purchase immediately to telling outright lies. Although high-pressure techniques are not in the long-term best interest for a salesperson and the selling firm, lying and other forms of dishonesty are much worse.

It is important for salespeople to realize that receiving referrals, obtaining repeat business, and building a strong reputation are the keys to successful sales. Success is the result of salespeople being honest with buyers about their products, the products' attributes, and the benefits to the buyer. It is important for salespeople to believe in what they are selling. If they do not, it is impossible to present the product to potential buyers with passion and honesty.

Many salespeople are paid a commission on their sales to encourage them to concentrate on selling. Although a commission will certainly encourage a salesperson to push harder for sales, it can also be detrimental if unethical behaviors are used to obtain those sales.

15-2c: The Selling Process

The selling process consists of prospecting for leads, preparing a presales approach, determining customer wants, giving a sales presentation, answering questions and objections, closing the sale, and following up. These steps are summarized in Figure 15-8. Order getters are involved in all seven steps, and order takers are involved in four or five of the steps. Order takers do not prospect and often do not determine customer needs or follow up after the sale. They might only answer questions and close the sale.

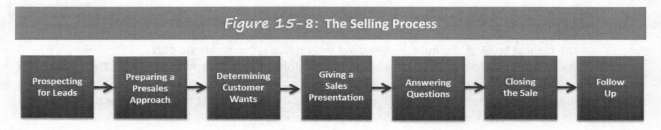

Figure 15-8: The Selling Process

| Prospecting for Leads | → | Preparing a Presales Approach | → | Determining Customer Wants | → | Giving a Sales Presentation | → | Answering Questions | → | Closing the Sale | → | Follow Up |

> **Prospects:**
> Potential customers of a firm.

Prospecting for Leads

The first step in the selling process is prospecting for leads. **Prospects** are potential customers who have a need for the product being sold and the ability to purchase the product.[1] For example, for a small electric motor manufacturer, prospects are all of the businesses that use small electric motors. They could be other manufacturers, they may be feed mills, they may be government organizations, or they could be distributors of electric supplies. Although all of these firms could be potential customers, salespeople for the small electric motor manufacturer would have to find some way of locating the businesses that would offer the best opportunity for making a sale. The goal of prospecting is to develop a list of viable companies, or consumers, that would be the most likely to make a purchase.

Often, developing a list of potential customers can be the most difficult task in prospecting. Salespeople have several options, and the best method will depend on factors such as the type of product being sold, the expertise of the company, and the competition they face. One of the best sources for new customers is the firm's current customers. Often, they can provide the names of decision makers, influencers, and purchasing agents. Having a name and a referral often allows the salesperson to bypass the gatekeepers and talk directly with individuals who would be involved in the purchase decision (see Figure 15-9).

Commercial and government databases can provide potential customers. Commercial sources such as CompuServe; Discloser, Inc.; Hoovers; and the Funk and Scott Index of Corporations and Industries

Figure 15-9: Having a name and a referral often allows the salesperson to bypass the gatekeepers and talk directly with individuals who would be involved in the purchase decision. Networking at trade shows can be an effective way to meet and greet decision-makers.

can be used. Government sources include the Census of Business, the Census of Manufacturers, and the Standard Industrial Classification Code. Also, many marketing research firms sell information about companies that can be used. For example, one New York–based research firm offers an online database of executives at 900,000 organizations in 172 countries. The company constantly updates the information and can provide information such as geographic location of the firm, names of company management personnel, job function, title, contact information, firm size and type, and organizational structure.[2]

A business can gather names and information from prospective buyers at trade shows. Most are excellent prospects because the primary reason they attend trade shows is to look at vendors and see what each vendor offers. Contacts can be obtained from advertising and Internet inquiries resulting from the business advertising its products and encouraging interested parties to make an inquiry. Names obtained through this method are almost always good prospects because the potential customers are making the contact and want more information.

For small businesses and consumer services, networking can be used to become acquainted with potential customers. Professional, social, and business organizations are common places for networking. An insurance agent could develop valuable contacts through networking at the chamber of commerce, Kiwanis, Rotary, or other meetings of civic organizations. Business-to-business salespeople often join professional or trade associations to meet potential prospects.

The least-productive method of prospecting is cold canvassing because the buyer knows little about the prospect and a lot of time is spent calling on prospects that have little or no interest. Because of the high cost of making a personal sales call, this method of prospecting is usually not cost effective. Instead of using a salesperson's time, some companies hire missionary salespeople to make cold calls; their task is not to make a sale but to leave information or a sample of the product. A salesperson would then call only on the ones the missionary salespeople identified as viable prospects.

The second part of prospecting is qualifying the leads. It is important to choose the prospects with the greatest potential or to rank them based on potential. Some questions, for instance, that a small electric motor manufacturer might ask include:

1. What size of electric motors does the company use, and how many does it purchase each year?

2. Who is the company's current supplier?

3. How satisfied is the customer with its current supplier?

4. Does the company purchase from one vendor or multiple vendors?

5. Does the company fit with our current customer base, and do we understand the prospect's business so we can develop a relationship with the prospect?

6. How difficult will it be to get past the gatekeeper and talk with the engineers, users, and decision makers?

7. What criteria will the prospect likely use in making a decision?

Part Four: Marketing Communications

Each potential customer can be classified into categories such as A, B, or C based on the responses to these questions. Although a salesperson may not have solid answers for each question, through research he or she can gather enough information to make an intelligent decision. For instance, suppose a salesperson finds that a prospect purchases a large volume of electric motors in the size the manufacturer produces and that the prospect tends to use a single source vendor. Because of the high sales volume, this prospect is attractive, but key information that is needed is: Who is the current supplier, and how satisfied is the prospect with its current vendor? If the company is very satisfied, this prospect may be classified in the B or C category. However, if the company is not completely satisfied with its current vendor, then this prospect would immediately be placed in the A category and be among the first sales calls the salesperson will make. The better a salesperson does in qualifying prospects, the more effective he or she will be in generating sales because the salesperson will spend more time calling on prospects with the highest probability of making a purchase.

Preparing a Presales Approach

In the presales approach, the salesperson gathers information about the potential customer to determine the best sales approach. Useful information would include:

- Current vendor(s)
- Prospect's customers
- Customer needs
- Critical product attributes and benefits desired
- Relative mixture of price, service, and product attributes desired
- Trade promotions used in the past and planned in the future
- Expectations about use of consumer promotions and advertising
- Risk factors in switching vendors

If the prospect's current vendor was not determined during the prospecting step, determining it during this step is essential. Successful salespeople know their competitors, the approaches they are likely to use, and the reasons the customer chose the competitor. Armed with information about the competing firm the prospect is currently using, the salesperson is able to emphasize his or her company's strengths that are perceived as weaknesses for the current vendor. For instance, a salesperson may know that a current vendor has to ship products 1,500 miles by rail to reach the customer. With a facility only 200 miles from the customer, the salesperson is able to emphasize the importance of on-time delivery and how the closeness of the facility will ensure a steady supply without ever revealing that he or she knows the situation the current vendor faces.

Having some knowledge of the prospect's customers will enhance the salesperson's ability to make an effective presentation. The salesperson would benefit from knowing which product attributes are most important to the prospect's customers and how the prospect will use the selling firm's products. For example, if you are selling dental supplies or equipment, it is important to understand the dentist's patient base. Does the dentist deal primarily with pediatrics or mature patients? How will your product or equipment benefit the patient? How will it improve the quality of dental care that the dentist will provide? Will the product make the dental practice more efficient or allow patients to be served faster? The more the salesperson understands about the dentist's practice and how the product will improve the dentist's practice, the more likely he or she will be to make a sale.[3]

In making a purchase decision, critical product attributes are evaluated from the perspective of the desired benefits. Knowing in advance what benefits are desired and what attributes the prospect will be examining allows the salesperson to have the correct information available. Closely tied with this knowledge is information about the relative mix of price, service, and product attributes. For some customers, price will be the critical purchase decision factor. For others, it will be a service component such as on-time delivery or the ability to handle large fluctuations in orders. Yet for others, it may be some product attribute such as the stress strength of a cable or sheet of aluminum. By knowing the emphasis the prospect is likely to put on the price, service, and product attributes, the salesperson is more likely to focus on the points of interest to the prospect and present the information in the correct manner.

For buyers, switching vendors is a risk, depending on the level of relationship they have with the current vendor. If it is only at the transaction level, then little risk is involved and switching is done relatively easily. However, if it is a trust relationship, contractual agreement, or EDI relationship, then switching becomes more difficult and is normally done only if the firm is unhappy with the current vendor. To make a switch otherwise would require a demonstration of some benefit that is significantly superior to the current vendor. Price sometimes can make a difference. For example, if another vendor can offer a component part for 70 cents less and the prospect purchases 300,000 of these parts a year, that would be a savings of $210,000. But making the switch still involves a risk. If the new vendor does not supply the parts in a timely manner, the cost of down time can quickly eat into the cost savings.

Determining Customer Wants

If a salesperson has done a good job in the presales approach, most of the information that is needed for the sales call has already been gathered. All that is needed during this step is confirmation of what the customer's needs are. The situation, however, is different for order takers. They do not make an initial contact with the customer and do not prospect or use a presales approach. Their first knowledge and contact with the customer occur when the customer makes the contact. Before launching into a sales pitch, the salesperson should first determine the customer's needs.

When shopping for a boat, many buyers may not know what features they want or need. An in-house salesperson should begin by asking individuals questions about how they will use the boat. Will it be for fishing, leisure boating, or pulling skiers? How much boating will they do? Will it be for just the two of them, or will they be using it for entertaining others? If others, how many others? From these questions, the salesperson can expand to presenting features such as engine size, engine type, and features of the models. By asking the right questions, the salesperson can determine the boat that will best meet the customer's needs and increase his or her chances of making a sale (see **Figure 15-10**).

Giving a Sales Presentation

After determining a prospect or current customers needs, the salesperson is in a position to make a sales presentation. The salesperson can use four basic sales approaches:

- Stimulus-response
- Need-satisfaction
- Problem-solution
- Mission-sharing

Figure 15-10: In selling a boat, the salesperson should first determine the customer's needs by asking the right questions.

Stimulus-response Sales Approach: Sometimes referred to as the canned sales approach, uses specific statements (stimuli) to solicit specific responses from customers.

Need-satisfaction Sales Approach: Sales approach aimed at discovering a customer's needs and then providing solutions that satisfy those needs.

Problem-solution Sales Approach: Sales approach that requires the salesperson to analyze the prospect's operation and offer a viable solution.

Mission-sharing Sales Approach: Sales approach that involves two organizations developing a common mission and then sharing resources to accomplish that mission.

The **stimulus-response sales approach**, sometimes referred to as the canned sales approach, uses specific statements (stimuli) to solicit specific responses from customers. Often, the salespeople memorize the stimulus statements (the pitch), and offer memorized or scripted responses to specific questions they are asked. For instance, salespeople may ask prospects if they feel they are paying too much for their car insurance. Most prospects will answer yes (the stimuli), and the salespeople will then explain how they can save the prospects money on car insurance. If, by chance, prospects say no, the salesperson has another question already scripted that will lead into the sales pitch. This sales approach is common for telemarketers, retail sales clerks, and new field salespeople.

The **need-satisfaction sales approach** is aimed at discovering a customer's needs and then providing solutions that satisfy those needs (see **Figure 15-11**). This approach requires the salesperson to be skillful and to ask the right questions. The major difference with this approach is that the salesperson does not have a canned list of responses and questions that are designed to lead to the sales pitch. It is an excellent approach for in-house salespeople or order takers who are responding to a prospect's inquiry. Retail sales clerks of complex items like computers will often use this approach. Order getters also use this approach to amplify or clarify information they gathered in the presales approach.

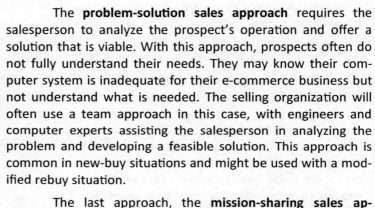

The **problem-solution sales approach** requires the salesperson to analyze the prospect's operation and offer a solution that is viable. With this approach, prospects often do not fully understand their needs. They may know their computer system is inadequate for their e-commerce business but not understand what is needed. The selling organization will often use a team approach in this case, with engineers and computer experts assisting the salesperson in analyzing the problem and developing a feasible solution. This approach is common in new-buy situations and might be used with a modified rebuy situation.

The last approach, the **mission-sharing sales approach**, involves two organizations developing a common mission and then sharing resources to accomplish that mission. This requires the strategic partnership relationship that was discussed previously. In some ways, such a partnership resembles a ''joint venture'' project. With the increased pressure of global competition, firms have seen the need to cooperate on a higher level. Buyers and sellers who enter into a strategic partnership relationship can use this sales approach to ensure that both the buyer and seller are benefiting from the relationship. The goal is to work together for the benefit of both firms. **Table 15-2** summarizes the four selling approaches.

Figure 15-11: This Salesperson for a pharmaceutical manufacturer is confident with her decision to deploy a need-satisfaction sales approach for her pitch to buyers at a regional hospital.

The primary factor in determining which approach is used is the form of a buyer-seller dyad. For transaction-type relationships, salespeople are likely to use the first two: stimulus-response and need-satisfaction. Occasional transactions will tend to use either the need-satisfaction or problem-solution. For repeat transactions and the other higher order types of dyad relationships, problem-solution presentations are the best. The mission-sharing approach is only used with the strategic partnership since higher level personnel are part of the sales process.

Table 15-2: Selling Approaches

Type of Selling Approach	Definition	Example
Stimulus-response approach	Sometimes referred to as the canned sales approach, this approach uses a specific canned sales presentation.	A telemarketer sells aluminum siding for a house, using statements (stimuli) to solicit specific responses from customers.
Need-satisfaction approach	This approach is aimed at discovering a customer's needs and then providing solutions that satisfy those needs.	A salesperson at an electronics store questions a customer about how he or she will be using a camera before offering a particular brand of digital camera with the features that best meet the customer's needs.
Problem-solution	This approach requires a salesperson to analyze the prospect's operation and offer a viable solution.	With the help of computer approach specialists, a salesperson examines the computing needs of a new e-commerce business and then offers a computing network that will meet all of the customer's needs.
Mission-sharing approach	This approach involves two organizations developing a common mission and then sharing resources to accomplish that mission.	A supplier of fiberglass partners with a manufacturer of racing boats to produce a higher quality fiberglass that will withstand the high speeds of boat racing.

Additional factors that determine the selling approach are the dollar value of the sale and the role of personal selling in the IMC plan. If the dollar value of the sale is high, there is a tendency to shift to a higher-level sales approach. The same is true for IMC plans in which personal selling is prominent.

Answering Questions

Few sales are closed immediately after the presentation. Prospects will have questions and doubts about making the purchase. Skillfully answering questions and addressing objections and doubts can make the difference between closing a sale and not closing a sale. The disadvantage of the stimulus-response sales approach is that, if prospects raise questions not in the script, salespeople often are not prepared to provide an answer. In fact, most salespeople using this approach skip this step and move directly from the sales presentation to the closing. With the need-satisfaction approach, the salesperson will attempt to relate his or her responses to the needs that were identified earlier in the sales presentation. If this can be done successfully, a sale will often occur. With the problem-solution approach and the mission-sharing approach, few questions and objections are raised if the selling team has done a good job in understanding the problem and developing a joint mission.

A salesperson has six different methods he or she can use to overcome objections. They include: [4]

- Direct answer method
- Non-dispute method
- Offset method
- Dispute method
- Comparative-item method
- Turn-around (boomerang) method

With the direct answer method, any objections or questions are met with direct responses. In the non-dispute method, the salesperson avoids or delays any direct answers, or passively accepts the objection without providing an answer or disputing the prospect's claim. With the offset method, the salesperson accepts the objection but offsets it with information about the product's benefits or attributes. Often, the salesperson will use a demonstration, a comparison, or a testimonial to offset the objection.

With the dispute method, the salesperson confronts the objection directly, indirectly, or with a demonstration that shows that the objection is not true or is not founded on correct facts. With the comparative-item method, the prospect is shown two or more products, and when the prospect objects to one, the salesperson will immediately switch to another product to which the objection cannot apply. When using the turn-around, or boomerang, method, the salesperson converts the objection into a reason to make a purchase. If the person says it is too expensive, the salesperson replies that the cost is the very reason it should be purchased.

Which method of handling questions and objections should be used depends on multiple factors, such as the buying situation, the personalities of both the buyer and seller, and the product being sold. Table 15-3 summarizes each of the methods of overcoming objections with an example of each.

Table 15-3: Overcoming Objections

Method	Definition	Example
Direct answer	Objections or questions are met with direct responses.	"We produce all of the sizes you need, and we will make sure they meet your specifications."
Nondispute	Objections or questions are avoided, or the salesperson delays any direct answers or passively accepts the objection without providing an answer or disputing the prospect's claim	"I understand your concern, and it is legitimate." Without responding to the concern, the salesperson goes on, "Let me show you the different sizes we offer."
Offset	The objections or questions are offset with information about the product's benefits or attributes.	"I understand your concern, but let me show you all of the sizes we offer and how we go about ensuring that your specifications are met."
Dispute	Objections or questions are confronted directly, indirectly, or by demonstrating that the objection is not true or not founded on correct facts.	"Somebody gave you incorrect information. We can supply every size you use in your business, and we can meet those specifications. I am confident that our product is stronger than what you are currently using."
Comparative-item	The prospect is shown two or more products and, when the prospect objects to one, the salesperson immediately switches to another product to which the objection cannot apply.	"Because this particular brand does not have the size you need to fit with your product, let me show you this other brand. It comes in the size you need and will meet your specifications."
Turn-around	The salesperson converts the objection into a reason to make a purchase.	"I understand you cannot afford it (boomerang) right now, but with what your competitors have just introduced, you cannot afford not to switch immediately. Any delay will cost you sales and future customers."

Sources: Sean Dwyer, John Hill, and Warren Martin, "An Empirical Investigation of Critical Success Factors in the Personal Selling Process for Homogenous Goods," *Journal of Personal Selling & Sales Management* 20, no. 3 (Summer 2000): 152–161.

Closing the Sale

Although closing the sale is the most important step, for many salespeople it is the most difficult step in the entire process, primarily because of the fear that the prospect will say no.

Closings can be classified into six different categories: [5]

- Straightforward close
- Presumptive close
- Arousal close
- Minor-decision close
- Single obstacle close
- Silent close

With the straightforward close, the salesperson asks for the order in a direct manner and, if necessary, summarizes the benefits for the prospect. With the presumptive close, the salesperson assumes the prospect is ready to buy and therefore asks a question in terms of how to write up the sale. A retail sales clerk may ask if the person would like to pay with cash, check, or credit card. A field salesperson may ask how soon the customer wants the product shipped and in what quantity. With the arousal close, the salesperson appeals to the prospect's emotions or creates a sense of urgency. Insurance agents often appeal to taking care of loved ones before it is too late.

With the minor-decision close, the salesperson seeks approval of small-decision questions through-out the presentation. Then, when the purchase question is asked, the prospect has already responded yes to several smaller-decision questions. If the prospect is almost ready to buy, but has just one objection, a salesperson can use the single obstacle close, which involves answering that one objection within the close. The last closing method is the silent close. With this close, the salesperson says nothing. The salesperson just waits and lets the prospect make the decision.

The best closing depends on a salesperson's personality and personal preference as well as the selling situation. Most salespeople tend to use a particular method more than the others but may use all six. Most likely, however, they have two or three they tend to use most of the time.

Following Up

Satisfied customers usually purchase again and in the business-to-business sector often develop a strong loyalty to a particular vendor. Unhappy customers, however, not only defect to a competitor, but also spread negative word-of-mouth communication about the firm. Because it is much more cost effective to retain an old customer than to obtain new ones, follow-up is a critical component of the selling process. The difficulty is that, for many salespeople, it is the least-attractive component of the sale, especially if the salesperson is paid a commission. The salesperson does not want to spend time at activities that do not generate sales.

15-3 DATABASES

Databases have become an important component of IMC programs. They can be used for a variety of purposes, ranging from providing information to salespeople and other company personnel to direct response marketing. Determining how the database will be used and who will be using it is crucial in the development process. The design of the database system and the type of data that will be collected are contingent on how the product is used and who will use it. Some typical applications for databases include: [6]

- Providing information about a firm's customers to internal personnel, such as the service call center, salespeople, and the marketing department
- Generating information about what customers purchase and why they make the purchase for the marketing department
- Providing purchase information and demographic information for direct response marketing programs

- Yielding information about the role of various members of the buying center for business-to-business transactions for field salespeople

- Tracking changes in purchasing behaviors and purchasing criteria used by customers for salespeople and the marketing department

- Storage of data about customers for a customer relationship management program

Service call centers need access to customer records when a customer calls. They need to be easily accessible and easy to understand. Customers expect a service call representative to know what they purchased and be able to answer questions about their account. Salespeople need the same information without waiting for a printout of a customer's purchase history or for an assistant in the firm to obtain the information. This is especially critical in preparing for a sales call and sometimes during a sales call. For a salesperson, direct access to customer information can make a difference.

Databases are important for marketing departments. Customer data help marketing personnel to understand what is being purchased and by whom. These data can be used to develop profiles of the firm's best customers and to determine the best target market for the various products sold by the firm. Databases are an important component of a direct response marketing campaign, which will be discussed in Section 15-4. They are also essential in tracking changes in purchase behavior, alerting marketing personnel to the need to either modify their product offering or alter their marketing communications material.

> **Data Warehousing:**
> The process of capturing and storing data within a single database that is accessible to internal personnel for a variety of internal purposes, such as marketing, sales, and customer service.

15-3a: Data Warehousing

Data warehousing is the process of capturing and storing data within a single database that is accessible to internal personnel for a variety of purposes, such as marketing, sales, and customer service. It also involves collecting data for decision making and sharing with vendors to improve inventory management. Building a data warehouse involves understanding who will use the data and how it will be used. Too often, companies develop a database only to find that they either have the wrong information, not enough information, or that the information cannot be accessed by the individuals who need it. Collecting the right information for a data warehouse is crucial.

Organizations have two sources of data: internal data and external data. Internal data come from sales transactions by customers. It also can be obtained from salespeople, service personnel, call center technicians, and others who have contact with customers (see **Figure 15-12**). To make a database viable, every person who has contact with customers should be able to access information as well as add information to a customer's record. Most companies do not collect enough information about their customers, and company personnel are not trained to contribute information about customers that may be of value to someone else at a later time.

Figure 15-12:
For managing internal data obtained from salespeople, many businesses use cloud-based customer relations database services like Salesforce.com.

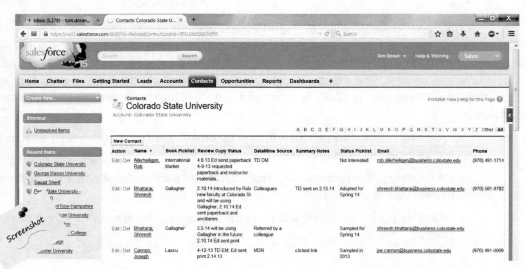
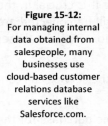

In most cases, internal data are insufficient to develop an optimal data warehouse. Secondary data, such as psychographics, lifestyle, attitudes, interests, media habits, hobbies, and brand purchases, can be collected from external commercial database services. These data can then be attached to a purchase history to create a stronger profile of each customer.

An important source of data is checkout scanners at retail stores. This technology makes it possible for nearly every business to track purchasing data on an individual basis. These data can be tied in with specific customers through frequency cards used for more efficient marketing programs. The data warehouse information can also be used by retail store managers, logistics staff, category managers, and business executives to make better decisions and to improve productivity of their operations. Some typical decisions that can be made through data warehouse technology include: [7]

- Site selection for retail stores

- Understanding of customer buying behaviors and preferences

- Product assortment decisions

- Inventory management and logistics

- Product pricing and promotional offers

- Vendor management

Data warehouses provide important information in site selection decisions. Once a potential site has been selected, commercial sources can be used to build a customer profile of the people who live in the surrounding area. The retailer can then use this information to locate an existing store with a similar customer profile. A model can be built that will project performance of the new store and provide information on how much to spend on marketing for the store launch and what consumer promotions would optimize the foot traffic at launch and create the growth desired.

In the past, retailers ordered the same product mix for all of the stores in their chain regardless of where the store was located. Data warehousing now makes it possible to modify the product mix and assortment for each individual store. Based on sales data, the mix of styles, colors, and sizes can be different for each store. This improves inventory management efficiency because smaller inventories of products are needed. Furthermore, by sharing this sales information with vendors, manufacturers can plan productions and modify shipments to meet the needs of each store. The results are fewer out-of-stock or overstocked situations and higher sales revenue.

These databases are now being used to determine optimal prices and promotions. Through analysis of sales information and trends, retailers are better able to make a decision on when to lower prices to stimulate demand. Sales models developed through the data can also indicate how much to reduce the prices. The same type of information can be used to optimize promotions. Which consumer promotions should be used, and how much should the price-off or coupon be? Models will predict the impact on sales; for instance, for a 25-cent-off coupon versus a 40-cent-off coupon.

To be effective, data warehousing has to be integrated with the other components of the IMC plan. One of the best examples of an integrated database system is the Education and Healthcare Division of Dell Computer Corporation. Dubbed the Integrated Generation Plan or the "Funnel Project," the integrated campaign features e-mail, direct mail, events, and a monthly electronic newsletter designed to drive prospects to Dell's Web site. In addition, Dell collects the names of small-business owners, schools, and hospitals through trade shows, telemarketing, e-mail, and direct mail. Using incentives, Dell is able to drive these contacts to the Dell Web site, where Dell collects more information about each person, such as job function and computing needs of the organization. With all of these data in one location, Dell is better able to reach these individuals. The best prospects are contacted by a salesperson from Dell, whereas other prospects are contacted through some type of direct marketing campaign. Information gathered into Dell's database helps Dell establish whether direct mail, direct e-mail, or a telemarketer would constitute the optimal approach. Having names, job titles, and other pertinent information allows Dell to customize the message to best fit each person's needs. With the database information, Dell's response rate in its direct marketing campaign is 3.4 percent for direct mail and 12 percent for targeted e-mail (see Figure 15-13), much higher than the industry average for direct response marketing campaigns.[8]

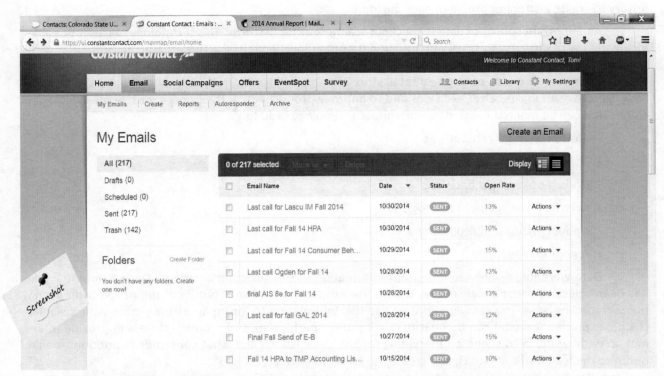

Figure 15-13: For targeted e-mail campaigns, the publisher of this textbook uses cloud-based services like Constant Contact and MailChimp to send publication announcements to course instructors. These services track data like open rates, click rates and e-mail bounces for each specific e-mail campaign.

15-3b: Data Mining

A major benefit of developing a data warehouse is the ability to perform data mining. Data mining involves computer analysis of customer data to determine patterns, profiles, or relationships for the purpose of customer profiling or predicting purchase behavior. Data mining is similar to mining in the last century panning for gold. Instead of using a pan and sifting through dirt, rocks, and minerals, computers sift through thousands and sometimes millions of records searching for patterns and relationships that might help marketers better understand customer purchase behavior. The most common use of data mining involves profiling of the firm's customers.[9]

Through developing profiles of current customers, the marketing team has a better idea of who is purchasing from the company and what they purchase. This information can be used to develop marketing programs aimed at prospects who meet the profile of the firm's best customers. It can also identify customers who may be in that second tier that the company should concentrate on because they match the profile of the firm's best customers but not the purchase history. Because the customers are already purchasing from the firm, it is easier to encourage them to increase their purchases than it is to seek entirely new customers. Even hospitals are using this technology as competition for patients increases. By augmenting internal patient data with information from consulting firms like Solucient and CPM Consulting Group, hospitals can create profiles of individuals who are likely to need health care or will be selecting a health care provider.[10] Marketing to this group is more cost effective than marketing to the entire general population.

Data mining will also suggest cross-selling opportunities that may exist with current customers. For example, Amazon.com collects data on every person who logs on to its site and makes a purchase. By mining purchase history and the material viewed, Amazon.com is able to determine a customer's preferences and, each time the person logs on, suggest new books or products that match the customer's interests (see **Figure 15-14**).

Another use of data mining is to develop models that predict future purchase behavior based on past purchase activities. Rodale Press used this type of modeling to develop an understanding of Staples, Inc.'s best catalog customers. Through data mining, Staples was able to identify current customers who fit the profile of its best catalog customers and would be inclined to purchase from a catalog. By mailing catalogs to only this portion of the list, Staples reduced mailing costs and increased response rates. According to Tom Rocco, vice president of Rodale Press publishing

Figure 15-14: Data mining allows companies to profile customer preferences.

company, "Response modeling is an important part of the mailing program for many of the companies that rent our lists. They can tighten their mail programs to target the most likely respondents." [11]

Developing relationships with customers is an important ingredient in building brand loyalty as well as encouraging repeat purchase behavior. Through tying marketing efforts to information gained through data mining, companies can maximize their database marketing effort. Database marketing refers to marketing programs developed through information gathered from databases and targeted to specific customer segments. The example about Rodale Press and Staples, Inc., is an illustration of a database-marketing program. **Figure 15-15** reviews the relationship between data warehousing, data mining, and database marketing.

Figure 15-15: Applying Database Marketing

Structuring the Data Warehouse → **Data Mining** → **Database Marketing**

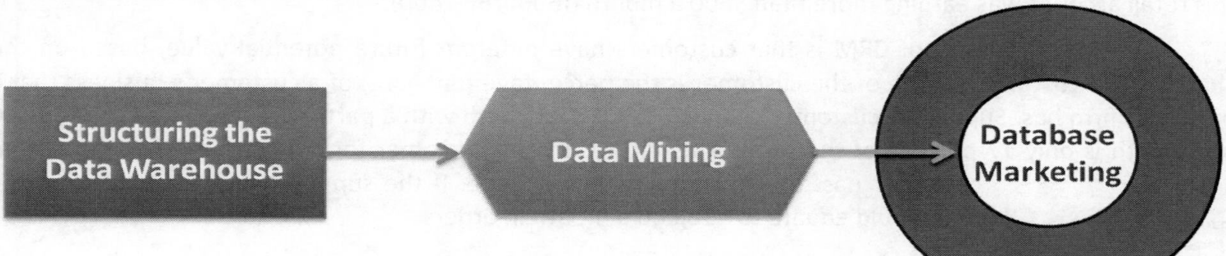

Company compiles, sorts and stores relevant customer information:

- Demographic | lifestyle characteristics
- Past purchase behavior
- Attitudes
- Desired product features
- Trends
- Other relevant customer info

Company:

- Reviews info in data warehouse to highlight marketing opportunities
- Derives customer profiles based on most meaningful factors
- Generates possible market segments with unique needs
- Desired product features
- Prioritizes market segments based on profit potential

Company pinpoints its marketing efforts to stimulate customer interest and to offer tailored approaches to its various customer groups.

15-3c: Customer Relationship Management

Customer relationship management (CRM) is designed to build long-term loyalty with customers through the use of a personal touch. CRM programs go beyond the development of a database for traditional direct marketing or personal selling techniques. They also encompass product modifications to meet the needs of each individual customer.

Developing a CRM program requires four steps: [12]

1. Identify the organization's customers.

2. Differentiate customers in terms of their needs and value to the organization.

3. Interact with customers in a cost-effective and efficient manner.

4. Customize the product offering to meet individual customer needs.

Customer relationship management is based on the two tenets of (1) lifetime value of a customer and (2) share of the customer. The lifetime value of a customer is a measure of the value of a customer over the typical life span of a firm's customers. The first step in calculating the lifetime value of a customer is to multiply the average amount of money a customer spends with each purchase or visit, the number of purchases per year, and the average life span of a customer. The second step involves subtracting the costs of acquiring and servicing the customer from the number calculated in the first step and adding the value of any new customers that were received through referrals. Lifetime value calculations are based on the idea that customers are not of equal value to a company, even customers who spend the same amount of money. Because of acquisition costs, servicing costs, or customer referrals customers can either gain or lose value.

In examining the lifetime value of its customers, a local janitorial service noticed that the cost of servicing a particular retail account was greater than what the janitorial service was earning from the account. Total direct and indirect costs were about $400 a month more than the income. But as the janitorial service began to count the number of referrals that were obtained because of television ads that featured the retail account, it realized that it had picked up 17 new accounts in just six months. The total net earnings of those 17 accounts were more than $6,000 per month. Thus, in terms of lifetime value to the firm, this retail account was earning more than $600 a month ([6000/6] – 400).

The second tenet of CRM is that customers have different future potential value, based on the **share of the customer**. Share of the customer is the percentage (or share) of a customer's business that a particular firm has. Suppose a customer spends $3,000 per month with a particular supplier. If that $3,000 per month is only 17 percent of the total expenditures by the customer for that particular product, that

> **Share of the Customer:** The percentage (or share) of a customer's business that a particular firm has.

customer has a high future potential value. If the supplier were the sole provider, that would equate to $18,000 a month in orders.

By combining the lifetime value of a customer with the share of the customer, a firm is able to rank-order its customers based on their value to the firm. At this point, the firm is ready for the third step in CRM: interacting with customers in a cost-effective and efficient manner. The best customers may receive weekly personal visits from salespeople or other company personnel, the second-tier customers may receive monthly visits with a phone contact between the personal visits, the third-tier customers may receive visits twice a year with phone contact on a monthly basis, and so forth. The marketing program that is designed should match the customers' value to the firm.

Integrated with the third step is customizing the product to meet the needs of the customer. The degree of customization will depend on the value of each customer. Customers of high value receive a higher degree of customization, whereas those of low value may not receive any type of customization. For example, Barnes and Noble uses CRM to maximize its revenue from its book buyers. A database tracks buyers' long-term purchasing behavior. If the customer buys a book in a store or through the Web site, a prompt may appear indicating that this particular customer has purchased all of the books written by a certain author except the latest one. The customer is then told about the new book. This process can even be proactive so that the customer is contacted by e-mail or some other means each time the author comes out with a new book. Mitchell's of Westport is a high-end clothing store that has created an effective CRM program. The company has customer data available to the sales staff on each customer's preferences, sizes, and previous purchases. High-ticket purchases are followed up with thank-you notes; customers are notified of sales and given invitations to special events when specific products are available. This personalization has resulted in a high level of loyalty to the store. Even customers who have moved to new cities return to the store to buy clothing.[13]

15-4 DIRECT RESPONSE MARKETING

Direct response marketing (or direct marketing) is the promotion of a product from the producer directly to the consumer or business user without the use of any type of channel members. More than $175 billion a year is spent on some type of direct response marketing. Sales from direct response marketing programs are estimated at $2.065 trillion, which is 10.3 percent of the U.S. gross domestic product.[14] Direct marketing programs allow a producer or manufacturer of a product to develop direct links with potential customers as well as current customers. According to research conducted by Direct Marketing, 62 percent of direct response marketing budgets are focused on prospecting for new customers, new contacts, or new business, whereas 38 percent is directed toward customer retention (see **Figure 15-16**).[15] Because channel members are bypassed, direct marketing normally allows a producer to earn greater profits or reduce the selling price. More important, it can help in developing a stronger brand loyalty with customers.

A key to a good direct marketing program is the quality of information contained within the firm's database. Not only should it have the basic demographic information, but psychographic and purchase behavior information should also be available. Using this information, a direct marketing program should begin by dividing each contact into one of three categories: buyers, inquirers, or prospects. Buyers are individuals who have purchased in the past, inquirers are individuals who have requested information, and prospects are individuals who fit the target profile but have not had any previous contact

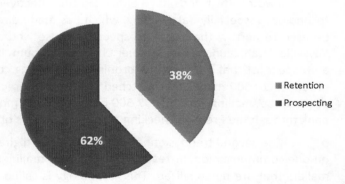

Figure 15-16 Focus of Direct Marketing Budget.
Source: Richard H. Levey, "Prospects Look Good," *Direct* 16 (December 1, 2004): 1–5.

with the firm. The direct marketing message that is designed will vary, depending on which group is being targeted.[16] **Figure 15-17** provides information on the usage rate of the various methods of direct marketing by firms.

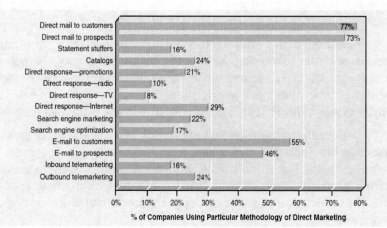

Figure 15-17: Direct Marketing Methods Used by Companies That Engage in Direct Marketing.
Source: Richard H. Levy "Prospects Looks Good" *Direct* 16 (December 1, 2004): 1-5

Direct mail is the most common form of direct marketing. Of the companies that engaged in direct response marketing, 77 percent mailed offers to customers and 73 percent mailed offers to prospects (see **Figure 15-17**). Direct mail can be used to generate leads, build interest, produce inquiries, and stimulate sales. A recent survey by *American Demographics* indicated that 77 percent of adults regularly read their direct mail and that 59 percent have read their direct mail during the past week. However, when it comes to reading every piece of direct mail, the percentages are much lower (9 percent). The most loyal group tends to be female (59 percent) and with household incomes of less than $30,000 (46 percent). Approximately 16 percent of the population will read direct-mail pieces related to products they would like to purchase or have considered purchasing. Again, this group tends to be female (61 percent), and almost one-third (28 percent) live in the Midwest.[17]

Direct mail offers marketers a major advantage: Its effects are measurable. The number of leads and orders can be easily tracked to direct-mail pieces, so a company can readily see how effective its direct-mail program is. Because of the relative ease of measuring results, direct mailing lends itself well to experimenting with different formats, colors, and designs to find the optimal mix.

Two recent trends have enhanced the effectiveness of direct-mail programs. The first is database technology, especially data mining, which has made direct mail more effective. Database information can be used to narrow the list of prospects to those who are most likely to respond. When Barnes Bank of Kaysville, Utah, launched its Premier Checking account, it hired Sharp Analytics of Salt Lake City to produce a prospect list that matched the profiles of qualifying customers for the Premier account. Sharp Analytics produced 10,000 names that matched the profile. Direct mailers were sent to each person. The total cost of the direct mailing was only $7,500 but resulted in more than $4 million in new money brought into the bank through the Premier Checking account as well as other bank products.[18]

The second trend is enhanced printing and digital technology that allows businesses to design one-on-one communication. Instead of running mass mailings that are impersonal, it is now possible to prepare mailers that are personalized. This technology is called digital direct-to-press. It is especially attractive in the business-to-business market because computers can be programmed to send a specific message to a printer. This gives the marketing team a high-quality one-of-a-kind piece to send to each potential customer, and each one can be adapted to the specific company being targeted. In the business-to-business sector, information about the firm's customers and the locations of its customers' offices can be included in the mailing. The digital direct-to-press can also be sent to homes but is usually not cost effective. Personalizing each direct-mail piece is much more expensive than running mass offers with only a personalized cover letter. It takes a great deal of expertise to design a computer program that produces personalized messages.

Although the Internet has become very popular with consumers, catalogs are still an effective means of direct marketing, being used by 24 percent of the companies that engage in direct marketing (see **Figure 15-17**). Consumers can view catalogs at their leisure, and because most catalogs are kept for a period of time, they have a long shelf life. Days and even weeks after receiving a catalog, a consumer or business may refer to it for a purchase. One of the attractive features of catalogs is the soft sales approach.

Because of the high cost of printing and mailing catalogs, most catalog retailers have gone to more selective distribution lists. Database information about customers and potential customers is used to develop a mailing list of individuals who are the most likely to purchase merchandise through the catalog. Rather than one large catalog, many companies offer small, specialty catalogs that focus on a particular line of products like outdoor clothing, children's clothing, hunting and fishing equipment, or kitchen merchandise.

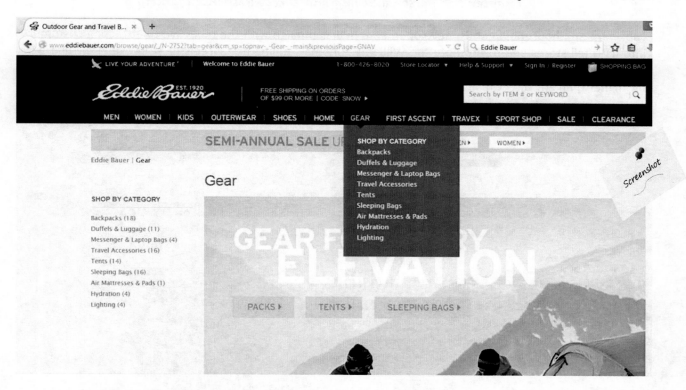

Over the past few years, there has been a strong move to wed catalogs with a firm's Internet Web site. Often, consumers and businesses will examine a catalog but make the purchase either on the Internet or by telephone. According to Harvey Kanter, vice president at cataloger Eddie Bauer, "There is no question that there is a crossover between the two channels. It's the richest customer to have. The catalog is not only a significant vehicle to drive its own business, but also for the customers to look and shop online. It's used as a tool in that regard. The Internet continues to grow as a percent of our direct business. We'll have over 50 percent penetration this year." [19] Many marketing experts believe that in the future, catalogs will take on a greater and greater role as a tool to drive customers to Web sites, where orders will be placed.

The Internet is still a relatively new channel for direct response marketing The Internet is a place for consumers and businesses to get information about products and specific brands. Although ordering capability may be in place, it was not the central thrust of the website. However, that is now changing with software such as Connectify Direct, NCR's Relationship Optimizer, and Prime Response Prime@Vantage, which allows a firm to create an interactive site. The software analyzes online purchases, click-streams, and other interactions to develop personalized messages. In addition, the online behavior of a customer can be combined with demographic and psychographic data from either an internal database or an external database firm. Using all of this information, the software can suggest specific products the consumer is most likely to purchase. All of this analysis can occur while the person is still online. For example, a person who is looking at computer games and has purchased a certain type of game in the past may receive an offer for a new game that has just been introduced.

Using this type of technology, marketers can directly market to consumers and businesses on specific Web sites, which is being done by 29 percent of the companies engaged in direct response marketing (see **Figure 15-17**). Marketers can also use the same technology with search engines. Direct marketing ads can be placed on a search engine, or, through the search engine optimization software just discussed, the ad can be the result of a specific search and click-throughs.

Many companies are developing e-mail direct response marketing campaigns. Notice from the survey conducted by Direct Marketing that e-mail campaigns are second only to direct mail. Direct marketing e-mails to customers are used by 55 percent of the firms, whereas 46 percent send e-mail direct offers to prospects (see **Figure 15-17**). E-mail makes it possible for the company to deliver customized messages or promotions to customers similar to those sent in the mail. Recently, Williams-Sonoma Inc., a retailer of cookware and household goods, developed an e-mail campaign with the objective of attracting customers into its retail stores and to promote the Williams-Sonoma's online bridal registry. Approximately five percent of the customers contacted by e-mail visited a local Williams-Sonoma store. This total was considerably higher than any direct-mail method the retailer had used before (see **Figure 15-18**).[20]

Figure 15-18: Retailers of cookware and household goods can benefit from e-mail campaigns.

Research by the Direct Marketing Association found that e-mail delivers the highest return on investment by a wide margin. For every dollar spent on e-mail marketing, sales are $40.56. In comparison, the return on investment (ROI) for online display advertising is $19.72, for direct mobile advertising $10.51, and for print catalogs $7.30.[21] One reason for this high return is the quality of databases and precise targeting of e-mails to prospective customers. It is also partly as a result of the newness of the medium. Over time, the ROI is expected to decline.

Telemarketing has been an important medium for direct marketing, although legislation has altered its viability. Both consumers and businesses have grown impatient with telemarketers calling them at inopportune times and selling merchandise that is of no interest. Both the Federal Trade Commission and the Federal Communications Commission worked together to establish a federal do-not-call list that blocks telemarketing calls. Although the law stops some telemarketers, it exempts charities, political candidates, and businesses that already have a relationship with a customer. For example, if you have a credit card with Texaco, then Texaco can call you about other products, even if you are on the no-call list. Although the law has reduced the number of telemarketing calls, this approach remains a viable method of direct marketing.

In the business-to-business sector, telemarketing is a viable tool for reaching prospects. Field salespeople can spend $1,000 to $2,000 a week just in traveling costs to see only ten prospects. Bonuses and commissions can cost a company from five to seven percent of the orders taken. Telemarketers, however, cost only $35,000 a year and can make 250 calls a week, with no additional traveling expenses or hefty commissions.[22]

Although the future of outbound telemarketing is uncertain, inbound telemarketing can be an important component of a direct marketing campaign. Inbound telemarketers are used to support direct marketing programs in other media, such as mail, e-mail, catalogs, or television. It is important for companies to post toll-free numbers prominently and frequently in all direct response marketing and promotional materials to make sure consumers know where to go to gather additional information and place orders.

The mass media may be a part of a direct response marketing campaign. Compared with the other forms of direct marketing, mass media direct response offers tend to be used less, primarily because of a lower response rate. When used, the most common forms of mass media direct response marketing are television, radio, magazines, and newspapers. Television offers the advantage of access to a mass audience and is an excellent choice for products with a general appeal to the masses. Radio does not have the reach of television but still can be used to convey direct marketing messages.

However, unless toll-free numbers and Web addresses are easy to remember and repeated frequently, consumers will have difficulty retaining the information, because in many cases, they are not in a situation in which they can write down the information. The print media, such as newspapers and magazines, are better for direct marketing programs. Viewers can study ads and write down information.

Summary

1. Explain the different types of personal selling. Personal selling can be classified into three broad categories: order takers, order getters, and support personnel. Order takers process routine orders from customers, whereas order getters actively generate potential leads and persuade customers to make a purchase. Support personnel are individuals who directly support or assist in the selling function in some manner but do not process orders or directly solicit orders. A field salesperson is an order getter who is involved in going to a potential customer's place of business to solicit business. If the company is calling customers and attempting to persuade them to purchase the product, this is called outbound telemarketing and is done by an order getter. If the company is manning telephones that customers call with orders, then it is inbound telemarketing, handled by order takers. A missionary salesperson, belonging to the last category of salespeople, provides information about a good or service.

2. Discuss the various buyer-seller relationships. The most basic type of buyer-seller dyad relationship is the single transaction, which occurs when the buyer and seller interact for the purpose of a single transaction. At the next level are occasional transactions that require an infrequent buyer-seller interaction and may be present in modified rebuy situations. Repeat transactions are at the third level and are characterized by buyers and sellers interacting on a regular basis. To ensure a greater commitment from buyers, sellers will often attempt to move the dyad to a higher level—the contractual agreement—which is a written agreement between the buyer and seller. Although contractual agreements are a stronger form of dyad relationship, they may or may not involve trust. Trust relationships are based on mutual respect and understanding of both parties and a commitment to work together. At the next level is the EDI relationship, which expands the trust relationship to include the sharing of data between the buying and selling firms. At the highest level of the buyer-seller dyad interaction is the strategic partnership. With this approach, the buyer and seller share information at the highest levels. The goal of this relationship is to collaborate on plans to benefit both parties and the customers of the buying firm.

3. Identify the steps in the selling process and briefly describe each step. The first step in the selling process is prospecting for leads. In this step, viable customers are identified and qualified. Step two is the presales approach, in which the buyer gathers as much information as possible about the potential customer. In step three, the buyer determines the customer's needs to prepare the best selling approach and the strategy involved in presenting the product in its best light. Step four involves giving the sales presentation. Various methods can be used, depending on the ability and style of salespeople as well as the selling situation. Step five is answering any objections or questions the customer may raise. Step six is closing the sale. Various types of closings can be used, depending on the situation. The last step is the follow-up to ensure that the customer is satisfied with the sale.

4. Explain the concepts of data warehousing and database management. Data warehousing is the process of collecting, sorting, and retrieving relevant information about a firm's customers and potential customers. Through a process known as data mining, a company can gather useful information about its customers that can be used for profiling its best customers, developing marketing programs, and predicting future purchase behavior.

5. Identify the steps in developing a customer relationship management program. CRM is a database application program designed to build long-term loyalty with customers through the use of a personal touch. The steps required to build a CRM program include (1) identifying the organization's customers, (2) differentiating customers in terms of their needs and value to the organization, (3) interacting with customers in a cost-effective and efficient manner, and (4) customizing the product offering to meet individual customer needs. CRM is based on the two tenets of (1) lifetime value of a customer and (2) share of the customer.

Part Four: Marketing Communications

6. *Explain the concept of direct marketing and list the various methods of direct marketing.* Direct marketing is the promotion of a product from the producer directly to the consumer or business user without the use of any type of channel members. The typical direct-marketing venues include mail, catalogs, mass media, the Internet, e-mail, and telemarketing.

Key Terms

buyer-seller dyad
contractual agreement
cross-selling
data warehousing
field salesperson
inbound telemarketing
mission-sharing sales approach
missionary salesperson

need-satisfaction sales approach
occasional transactions
order getters
order takers
outbound telemarketing
problem-solution sales approach
prospects

repeat transactions
share of the customer
single transaction
stimulus-response sales approach
strategic partnership
support personnel
trust relationships

Discussion Questions

1. Discuss a recent experience you had with a salesperson at a retail store. Was it a positive or negative experience? Which type of buyer-seller dyad was it?

2. Compare and contrast the various levels of buyer-seller relationships discussed in Section 15-2b in terms of your personal experience. Identify companies or salespeople you have interacted with for each type of relationship.

3. Pick a business that sells to another business, government, or institution. Discuss various ways a salesperson could prospect for new leads. What types of questions would be asked to qualify each lead?

4. For each of the following products and situations, which type of sales approach should be used? Justify your response.

    a. Selling kitchen appliances to a consumer in a retail store

    b. Selling car insurance to a consumer who stops at the office

    c. Selling liability insurance to a business on a cold call

    d. Selling accounting services to a large corporation

    e. Selling a new car to a consumer

    f. Selling a fleet of cars to a business for use by corporate personnel

5. Suppose you were in the process of purchasing a new vehicle. Look through the various methods of handling objections. Discuss each method in terms of how you would relate to a salesperson using that method with you in an effort to handle objections you had in purchasing the new vehicle. Which methods work, which methods do not? Why?

6. Suppose you now work as the account executive for an advertising agency. You have handled the objections of a potential client. Look through the closings. Discuss each close in terms of how you would get this client to agree to hire your advertising agency. Which close do you prefer? Why?

7. Using a database or the Internet, do some research on answering objections in the selling process. Write a short paper on what you find. Be sure to provide your sources of information.

8. Using a database or the Internet, do some research on closing a sale in the selling process. Write a short paper on what you find. Be sure to provide your sources of information.

9. Using a database such as EbscoHost or the Internet, do some research on data mining. What did you learn? Be sure to provide your sources of information.

10. Direct response marketing is an effective means of reaching consumers. Discuss each method of direct response marketing in terms of your personal experience. Which methods work with you, which do not? Why? What type of offer does it take for you to respond to a direct response marketing offer? Explain.

True or False

1. EDI provides speed and accuracy in buying and selling transactions; therefore, it is advisable that this system should be used with all potential buyers.

2. To meet sales quotas or to earn more money, it is okay for salespeople to use unethical techniques and to persuade the customer in aggressive ways to make an immediate purchase.

3. The least productive method of prospecting is cold canvassing because the buyer knows little about the prospect and a lot of time is spent on calling prospects with no interest.

4. With the presumptive close, the salesperson asks for an order in a direct manner and, if necessary, summarizes the benefits for the prospect.

5. Because it is more cost effective to retain current customers than to attract new ones, the follow-up is a critical component of the sales process.

6. Databases are important components of an IMC program and direct marketing campaign.

7. Data mining involves computer analysis of customer data to determine patterns, profiles, and relationships for the purpose of predicting purchase behavior.

8. Database marketing is a modern marketing program developed through information gathering from multisource databases and targeted to very broad customer segments.

Multiple Choice

9. Which category actively generates leads and solicits orders from prospects or customers?

    a. Order takers

    b. Order getters

    c. Support personnel

10. In which kind of buyer-seller relationship are the terms of interaction, cost, and length of commitment established in a written agreement?

    a. Occasional transaction

    b. Repeated transaction

    c. Contractual agreement

    d. Trust relationship

11. What information will be relevant to determine the best sales approach?

    a. Current vendors

    b. Critical product attributes

    c. Expectations about sales promotion and advertising

    d. All of the above

12. Which sales approach, sometimes referred to as the canned sales approach, applies specific statements to solicit responses from customers?

    a. Stimulus-response sales approach

    b. Need-satisfaction sales approach

    c. Problem-solution sales approach

    d. Mission-sharing sales approach

13. Which method is applied when the salesperson confronts the customer objection directly, indirectly, or by a demonstration that the objection is not true or not founded on correct facts?

    a. Direct answer method

   b. Offset method

   c. Dispute methods

   d. Turn-around method

14. In the context of closing the sale, which category refers to the salesperson's appeals to the customer's emotions or attempts at creating a sense of urgency?

   a. Presumptive close

   b. Arousal close

   c. Minor-decision close

   d. Single obstacle close

15. Direct marketing is focused on which customer category?

   a. Buyers

   b. Inquirers

   c. Prospects

   d. All of the above

Blog

Clow-Lascu: *Marketing: Essentials 5e Blog*

CATEGORY ARCHIVES: CHAPTER13

Marketing for the Holidays

Posted on November 17, 2014 | Leave a comment

Thanksgiving and Christmas always brings increased advertising by brands and especially for retailers. This article in CMO Today should generate some interesting discussion because for the 2014 holidays the number one marketing method will be email.

CMO Today Article: You've Got Mail and More is Coming

Discussion Questions:

1. After reading the article, what are your thoughts about the use of email as the primary marketing tactic?
2. Look at the bar graph of the most used channels for 2014 holidays. Rank these channels in terms of influence on your holiday purchases. What is the most effective, what is second, etc. Justify your ranking.
3. Look at the graph of the popular social media marketing tactics. Identify the three that are most effective with you. Explain why.

What Is Happening Today?

Learn More! For videos and articles that relate to Chapter 15:

blogclowlascu.net/category/chapter15

Includes Discussion Questions with each Post!

Notes

1.   Anthony J. Ubraniak, "Prospecting Systems That Work," American Salesman 48 (November 2003): 25–28.
2.   Victoria Ocken, "Making the Most of Online Databases," *Marketing News* 36, no. 20 (September 30, 2002): 17.
3.   Roger P. Lewis, "Strategic Selling," *Proofs* 87 (November 2004): 54.
4.   Sean Dwyer, John Hill, and Warren Martin, "An Empirical Investigation of Critical Success Factors in the Personal Selling Process for Homogenous Goods," *Journal of Personal Selling & Sales Management* 20, no. 3 (Summer 2000): 152–161.
5.   Sean Dwyer, John Hill, and Warren Martin, "An Empirical Investigation of Critical Success Factors in the Personal Selling Process for Homogenous Goods," *Journal of Personal Selling & Sales Management* 20, no. 3 (Summer 2000): 152–161.
6.   Kenneth E. Clow and Donald Baack, Integrated Advertising, *Promotion and Marketing Communications*, 3rd ed. (Upper Saddle River, N.J.: Prentice Hall, 2007): 350.
7.   Dan Ross, "What Is BI and What Do We Do with It?" *Retail Merchandiser* 47, no. 3 (March 2007): 25–26.
8.   Carol Krol, "Schools and Hospitals in Path of Dell's Funnel," *B to B* 87, no. 6 (June 10, 2002): 25.
9.   Dan Ross, "What Is BI and What Do We Do with It?" *Retail Merchandiser* 47, no. 3 (March 2007): 25–26.

10. Russell C. Coile, Jr., ''Competing in a Consumer Choice Market,'' *Journal of Healthcare Management* 46, no. 5 (September/October 2001): 297–300.

11. Eric Cohen, ''Database Marketing,'' *Target Marketing* 22, no. 4 (April 1999): 50.

12. ''A Crash Course in Customer Relationship Management,'' *Harvard Management Update* 5, no. 3 (March 2000): 3–4.

13. Mary McCaig, ''A Small Retailer Uses CRM to Make a Big Splash,'' *Apparel Industry* 1, no. 10 (October 2000): 30–34.

14. Ken Magill, ''Growth of DM Spending to Falter,'' *Direct* 18, no. 13 (November 1, 2006): 10.

15. Richard H. Levey, ''Prospects Look Good,'' *Direct* 16 (December 1, 2004): 1–5.

16. Kellee Harris, ''What Direct Marketers Know That You Don't,'' *Sporting Goods Business* 33, no. 15 (October 11, 2000): 12.

17. Sandra Yin, ''Mail Openers,'' *American Demographics* 23, no. 10 (October 2001): 20–21.

18. ''Direct Mail Campaign Helps Boost Bank's Revenues by $4 Million,'' *Bank Marketing* 39, no. 2 (March 2007): 40.

19. Andrea Lillo, ''Catalogs Feed Off Internet Growth'' *Home Textiles Today* 21, no. 15 (December 16, 2002): 1, 6.

20. Jeff Sweat and Rick Whiting, ''Instant Marketing,'' *Information Week* 746 (August 2, 1999): 34–37.

21. http://www.marketing-schools.org/types-of-marketing/catalog-marketing.html

22. Nicole Ridgway, ''Dialing for Dollars,'' *Forbes* 170, no. 11 (November 25, 2002): 226–227.

Cases

Case 15-1 National South Bank

National South Bank had been in business for more than ten years and had expanded to a total of 11 facilities in three different towns. It was a locally owned and managed facility that had built a solid reputation for service, especially with the business community. The retail side of the business, which was directed toward consumers, had done well, especially with the baby boomer generation.

National South was one of three locally owned banks, with total assets and facilities approximately equal to the other two locally owned banks combined. The difficulty National South faced was the large regional and national banks in the town. There were 18 of them, for a city with a population of 95,000 and a county population of slightly less than 160,000. Competition for customers was intense. But National South uncovered one area of town, on the north side, where the market seemed to be underserved. The area had grown rapidly during the previous five years, and a bank merger had reduced the number of facilities serving the north side. Eager to establish a presence in this area, National South built a large branch facility. It was now time to develop a marketing program for the branch's grand opening.

The first step National South took was to seek information from Claritas about the geodemographic makeup of the area. Using PRIZM, Claritas located the top market segments in the area that made up 90 percent of the population. These geodemographic groups are described in the accompanying table.

PRIZM Cluster Name	Size	Description	This PRIZM Cluster Is Most Likely to
Second city elite	30%	Upscale executive families Age group: 45+ Professional Household income: $67,800	Add a bathroom Own a laptop computer Own an Acura Read *Bon Appetit*
Upward bound	24%	Young, upscale, white-collar families Age group: Under 18, 35–54 Professional Household income: $62,100	Be brand loyal Buy a new station wagon Have 401(K) plan Watch *The Tonight Show* Read *Vogue*
Middleburg managers	16%	Mid-level, white-collar couples Age group: 35–44, 65+ Professional/white collar Household income: $42,000	Own a laptop computer Have a home equity loan Watch the QVC channel Read *PC Magazine* Jog or run
Small-town downtown	12%	Older renters and young Age group: 18–44 White collar/blue collar Household income: $22,800	Shop at Target Buy a VCR Have a school loan Watch MTV Read *Muscle and Fitness*
Southside city	8%	African American service workers Age group: 18–34 Blue collar/service Household income: $17,000	Be pro-wrestling fans Buy gospel music Own a Mazda Watch BET Read *GQ*

Source: http://cluster2.claritas.com

The second step for National South Bank was to hire a direct marketing firm to handle the opening of the branch facility. National South recognized that it was in a delicate situation because it already had three other facilities in the town. Although it wanted new customers for the branch, it wanted to attract customers from competing banks, not have its current customers transfer their accounts to the new branch. Although National South Bank was aware that some customers were likely to switch because the new location was more convenient for them, its objective was to ensure that the vast majority of customers were new. To attract these customers, the bank would have to offer some incentives. Some that were suggested included:

- Free checking for six months
- Free safety deposit box for one year
- Free online banking for six months
- A free gift such as a kitchen appliance, briefcase, or makeup kit
- Reduced introductory interest rate on a home equity loan

National South Bank recognized that it could not advertise these incentives on television or in the newspaper without upsetting its current customers, and it could not afford to offer these incentives to all of its current customers. By using a direct response marketing approach, National South felt that it could promote the new facility without many of its current customers knowing what incentives were being offered.

The direct marketing firm that was retained suggested that National South attempt a direct-mail campaign in the area surrounding the new facility, which could be followed up with a door hanger placed at each resident's home. Another suggestion was engaging in some tie-in partnerships with a few of the businesses in the area where they could place free direct response marketing pieces in the business and in the shoppers' bags as they checked out.

Questions

1. Which two market segments would you suggest that National South Bank attract?

2. What incentives would you offer to each market segment selected in question 1?

3. Design a direct-mail piece for National South Bank directed to one of the market segments.

4. Discuss a direct response marketing program for National South Bank that would include the market segments you indicated in question 1.

5. Do you think that National South Bank made the right decision in not offering free incentives in television and newspaper ads? Justify your answer.

6. How would you advertise this new branch facility without offending current customers at the other three facilities?

Sources: Interview with Graham Morris of Newcomer, Morris & Young, January 9, 2003; Claritas, Inc., available at: http://cluster2.claritas.com, February 18, 2003.

Case 15-2 FishDream

Recreation is a multibillion-dollar industry in the United States, and retail sales of sporting goods amount to $62 billion annually. Another $130 billion is spent on hunting, fishing, and wildlife watching, with $34 billion being spent by hunters, $41.8 billion on fishing, and $55 billion on wildlife viewing. The steady increase in annual expenditures attracts new firms into the industry, and, with the rise of Internet commerce, reaching consumers of recreational, hunting, and fishing supplies and equipment is easier now.

Because of the increasing demand for fishing supplies, FishDream was founded as an online fishing tackle shop. It started in one of the owners' garage and has expanded twice to larger facilities. The business is currently in Jacksonville, Florida where they operate a showroom and the online business. Unlike most online stores, FishDream stocks nearly all of the products they sell. This significantly decreases the time between a customer's order and the time the order arrives at the customer's address.

The store focuses solely on fishing supplies and equipment. It carries most of the top-quality national brands, such as G. Loomis, St. Croix, Cortland, Lamiglas, Pflueger, and Redington. Merchandise ranges from downriggers for offshore fishing, to tip-ups for ice fishing, to rods and reels for surf fishing. The company is constantly adding new products and looking for cutting-edge innovations. FishDream was founded on the belief that, to succeed, online retailers must follow the same business principles as a brick-and-mortar store. The guiding philosophy of the company is to provide quality customer service. Customer satisfaction is paramount. FishDream wants every customer to be completely satisfied with the product he or she purchases.

A special price offer from the manufacturer and an error in placing an order resulted in FishDream having an excessively large inventory of rods for fly-fishing. They desperately needed to sell most of them to make room for other merchandise. Management discussed four options to move these fishing rods. First, they could promote the rods on the Web site and offer a special price-off. Although this would stimulate sales, it would also reduce profits on the rods because of the price discount. Second, they could just hold the inventory until next year. The fear with this option was that newer rods would come out and make this year's rod harder to sell. They then might have to offer the rods at a steep discount, which would result in a loss on each one sold. It also meant they could not carry sufficient inventory of other products. The third option was to send an e-mail to everyone in the database. The problem with this option was that their database did not have enough information about individuals, so it would be impossible to identify who would be interested in fly-fishing rods. It would have to be sent to everyone in their database. Also, they probably had the e-mails of only about 15 percent of their customers. The last option was to just promote the fishing rods on the company's main page in hopes that enough individuals would see it and be willing to make a purchase at the regular retail price.

Questions

1. Of the four options, which one would you recommend? Why?

2. Based on the material presented in this chapter, outline how FishDream could develop a data warehouse that would provide better information about their customers.

3. Assuming FishDream develops a quality database of their online sales transactions and ties them in with customer information, how can they use the concept of data mining?

4. Can FishDream use CRM to develop stronger relationships with customers and to boost sales? If so, how?

5. Although most orders are placed online through the Web site, a significant number of customers like to place the order via the telephone. Therefore, FishDream has a number of inside salespeople working in their call center to handle these sales calls. Look through the material on personal selling and answer the following two questions:

a. What type of salespeople are FishDream's inside sales staff?

b. From the buyer-seller relationships discussed in Section 15-2b, which type would be the most common and which type of relationship should FishDream stress with their sales staff?

.

Source:

http://www.outsideonline.com/blog/outdoor-adventure/americans-spent-a-lot-of-money-on-hunting-fishing-and-wildlife-watching-in-2011.html

Answers to Review Questions

Answers: 1) T, 2) F, 3) T, 4) T, 5) F, 6) T, 7) F, 8) T, 9)T, 10) b, 11) d, 12) d

The Marketing Plan:

A Strategic Marketing Perspective

OVERVIEW

The marketing plan is an essential element of the company strategic plan, an effort to maintain a fit between company objectives and capabilities and the continuously changing company environment. The approach to the marketing plan presented here addresses this important aspect of planning. You should first focus on corporate planning and, subsequently, on the marketing strategy.

A-1 DEFINING THE COMPANY'S MISSION STATEMENT

Most organizations prominently articulate their mission statement. If your project involves creating a marketing plan for an existing business, check the company Web site to identify its mission statement. If you are creating your own new business, then articulate a mission statement that expresses the vision and principles of the company, a guide to what the company wants to accomplish in the marketplace. The mission should underscore the distinctive differentiating aspects of the business and the company's approach to its different stakeholders: consumers, employees, and society.

A-2 IDENTIFYING COMPANY GOALS AND OBJECTIVES

A company's objectives stem from its mission statement. Objectives can be expressed in many different terms, including profit, sales, market share, and return on investment (ROI). Company objectives may be to enter new international markets or to increase market share in the national market. Alternatively, they may involve focusing on research and development to bring cutting-edge technology to the marketplace. Objectives can also be expressed in terms of societal outcomes, such as increasing literacy or reducing world hunger, depending on the focus of the business.

As mentioned in Chapter 1, the ultimate organizational goal is creating profit for the company and wealth for its shareholders. In that sense, increasing productivity and production volume, maximizing consumption, and as a result, increasing sales constitute primary objectives for the company, which can be accomplished with the appropriate marketing strategies. In the process of achieving organizational goals, companies offer quality and value to consumers and businesses, leading to a higher level of customer satisfaction. They compete to offer a wide variety of goods and services and a maximum number of choices for consumers. As they compete, they lower prices that consumers pay for their products to gain market share. Based on your understanding of the company, what are the different goals and objectives it is pursuing? If working with a hypothetical company, you could think about the goals of competition in the process of identifying the goals and objectives of your company.

A-3 MANAGING THE BUSINESS PORTFOLIO

The third step in creating the marketing plan involves evaluating the different strategic business units of the company. At this stage, the company must identify the products that have great promise in the marketplace and need additional resources, the products that are performing well in a mature market, and those that are not, which must be divested. At this stage, establishing a strategic fit with the market is essential. The company may have the resources to support a particular strategic business unit, but if the unit does not fit with the company's long-term goals or if selling the unit would generate resources that could be invested to further the company's goals, the company may consider selling this particular business. Companies periodically review their different businesses and make decisions on whether to acquire new ones or divest those that might be unprofitable or that do not represent a good fit. In the analysis of the portfolio, you will benefit from using the growth-share matrix of the Boston Consulting Group and the product-market matrix introduced in Chapter 8 (especially Section 8-9). Place the different business units in the appropriate categories and comment on their position. Do they need additional resources? Are they performing optimally? Scrutinize them in terms of their market and financial performance and potential.

A-4 STRATEGIC BUSINESS UNIT PLANNING

A-4a Developing the Strategic Business Unit Mission

Each business unit must develop its own mission statement, focusing on the strategic fit between strategic business unit (SBU) resources and the company goals with regard to its target markets. The SBU mission statement should be more specific than the corporate mission statement, focusing on the brand or product itself.

A-4b Conducting the Strengths, Weaknesses, Opportunities, and Threats Analysis

An important step in the analysis process involves identifying the company's strengths, weaknesses, opportunities, and threats (SWOT). First, examine the microenvironment of marketing, addressing its strengths and weaknesses; more specifically, examine strengths and weaknesses related to the company, consumers, suppliers, intermediaries, other facilitators of marketing functions, and the competition (see Table A-1). Next, examine threats and opportunities in the sociodemographic and cultural environment, the economic and natural environments, the technological environment, and the political and legal environments (see Chapters 2 and 3 and Table A-2).

Microenvironment Strengths, Weaknesses, Opportunities, and Threats Analysis   TABLE A-1

Microenvironment	List of Strengths	List of Weaknesses
Company		
Consumers		
Suppliers		
Intermediaries		
Other facilitators		
Competition		

Macroenvironment Strengths, Weaknesses, Opportunities, and Threats Analysis   TABLE A-2

Macroenvironment	List of Threats	List of Opportunities
Sociodemographic and cultural		
Economic		
Natural		
Technological		
Political		
Legal		

A-5 THE MARKETING PLAN

The marketing plan will focus on the SBU you have selected and a good or service that you have proposed to analyze. It involves the following steps.

A-5a Identifying Marketing Objectives

Marketing objectives could be defined in terms of dollar sales, units sold, or in terms of market share. They can also be defined in terms of brand awareness or customer traffic, as would be the case for a retail operation.

A-5b Defining the Marketing Strategy

The marketing strategy involves identifying segments of consumers who are similar with regard to key traits and who would respond well to a product and related marketing mix (market segmentation); selecting the segments that the company can serve most efficiently and developing products tailored to each (market targeting); and offering the products to the market, communicating through the marketing mix the product traits and benefits that differentiate the product in the consumer's mind (market positioning).

At this stage, you should clearly identify the different market segments, select the segments that represent the best fit with the company goals and objectives, and design the strategies aimed to serve these segments more effectively than competitors. Refer to Chapter 6 in your analysis.

An important component of the marketing strategy is a competitive analysis. Identify and describe the products, markets, and strategies competitors are using and how your company or product is different. It is important to clearly identify the unique selling proposition or market that is being served.

A-5c Developing the Marketing Mix

After identifying the overall marketing strategy, you can proceed to develop the marketing mix—the four Ps of marketing (product, place, price, and promotion)—that the company can use to influence demand for its products:

- Product—Decide on design, features, brand name, packaging, and service components that will best meet the needs of the target market that has been identified. Refer to Chapters 8 and 9.

- Place—Decide on the types of channels used, market coverage, assortment, transportation and logistics, and inventory management that will be needed to move the product from production to the consumer or business customer. Refer to Chapters 10 and 11.

- Price—Decide on the price, discounts, and credit terms that will be used. Because of brand parity, pricing is an important decision variable in purchase decisions. Refer to Chapter 12.

- Promotion—Decide on advertising, personal selling, consumer promotion, public relations (PR), and publicity that the company should pursue. Although the nature of the product will have some impact on which method of promotion will be primary, it is also important to consider how competitors are promoting their product. Not only is it necessary to gain the attention of potential customers, it is also necessary to convince them concerning the superiority of the product being offered. Refer to Chapters 13 through 16.

A-5d Marketing Implementation

Suggest how marketing plans can be turned into marketing action programs to accomplish the marketing objectives. For example, the marketing objective may be to increase awareness of a new product among the selected target market. Implementation may involve developing a series of television and magazine ads that promote this new product. Furthermore, identify which television shows and which magazines would be the most effective in reaching the projected target market.

A-5e Marketing Control

Suggest the different procedures for evaluating the outcomes of the implemented marketing strategies and the corrective actions needed to ensure that the previously stated marketing objectives are met. For example, if the objective was to increase product awareness by 30 percent, the day-after recall (DAR) tests could be used to determine whether the objective has been reached. If not, the corrective action could be the purchase of additional television time or the development of a new advertising theme.

Careers in Marketing

Marketing is a popular major in most business schools and offers graduates a wide variety of career opportunities. The purpose of this appendix is to provide students with information about possible careers and marketing positions. Marketing positions can be organized into three categories: general marketing positions, positions in marketing communications, and sales positions.

B-1 GENERAL MARKETING POSITIONS

B-1a Marketing Management

Marketing managers are usually selected based on extensive work experience, especially in the case of larger firms. This advanced position requires major responsibility. However, with proper training in entry-level positions, graduates can quickly advance up the corporate ladder to the level of marketing manager.

B-1b Brand or Product Management

Brand or product managers are responsible for managing a brand or a particular product of a company throughout the brand or product life cycle (PLC). Typically, these managers are responsible for segmenting the market and targeting and positioning the brands or products for which they are responsible. In effect, this manager is responsible for the brand or product as a strategic business unit and is in charge of overseeing the development, pricing, promotion, and distribution of the product. Most university graduates are expected to work in sales or other areas of the company, acquiring valuable experience before advancing to brand or product management. For more information about managing brands and products, refer to B-1c Marketing Research

Students interested in a marketing research career will benefit from extensive training in statistical methods and behavioral sciences. For analysts focusing on consumer goods firms, it is especially useful to have a background in psychology and psychometric measurement. Individuals working for a marketing research firm would have the title of marketing analyst or marketing researcher. Individuals could also specialize in developing and maintaining a database (i.e., they would be involved in database marketing). For more information about the tasks of marketing researchers, refer to Chapter 7.

B-2 POSITIONS IN MARKETING COMMUNICATIONS

B-2a Account Management

Account executives typically work for an advertising agency and are in charge of managing the advertising firm's relationship with existing and potential clients. They usually have at least 3 years' experience in lower-level advertising positions or in sales. Account executives are responsible for the day-to-day activities related to a particular account or set of accounts.

Account supervisors are in charge of managing the relationship of the advertising firm to the client; they typically have more work experience than account executives.

Management supervisors are responsible for coordinating the tasks of different account executives and account supervisors with the goals and objectives of top management. Management supervisors tend to be more seasoned managers.

Creative directors are in charge of the creative staff, coordinating the tasks of creative groups, broadcast production, and studio work. These individuals are typically not business majors; they tend to major in the liberal arts areas—often in art or graphic design.

Traffic managers are responsible for coordinating the work that has to be done for a client. They often will choose creatives and other agency personnel who will work on an account. Because they know the completion date, they will work with a schedule to ensure all of the work is finished on time.

It should be mentioned that graduates with a goal of working for an advertising agency are often recruited for positions involving managing traffic (the management of the ad production at different stages) or print production.

The goal of most marketing majors going into advertising is to become account executives in 3 to 5 years after graduation. Often, they must accept lower-level jobs, such as account executive assistant, before they are placed in charge of an advertising account.

B-2b Media Management

Media planners are in charge of planning how often, where, and when advertisements will appear and in what media. These individuals tend to have a keen understanding of their client's business and are hired with some experience. Their goal is to match media with the ad's target market to ensure maximum effectiveness. Media buyers are in charge of actual space and time media purchases.

Media researchers are marketing researchers specializing in media. They research the effectiveness of particular media, trends in the media in general, and developments for individual media competitors.

B-2c Other Promotion-Related Positions

Numerous positions that do not center on advertising or media may appeal to marketing graduates. Direct marketing managers are in charge of a company's direct marketing efforts. For additional information on direct marketing, refer to Chapter 16.

Event marketing managers are in charge of marketing particular events. In one example, sports marketing managers could focus on marketing a particular competition, such as the World Cup. Online marketing managers typically have an advertising focus, a sales focus addressing online retailing, or both.

B-3 SALES POSITIONS

Most entry-level jobs for marketing degrees are in the area of sales. Many marketing graduates who decide to use sales as a stepping-stone to other careers find that sales positions are particularly challenging and attractive and choose to remain in sales for the rest of their career. In many areas, salaries and commissions are particularly attractive, as is the freedom to be in charge of one's own territory. Order takers process routine orders from customers. Retail staff tend to operate as order getters, unless they are able to persuade the consumer to buy and close the sale. Order getters actively generate potential leads and persuade customers to make a purchase. In industrial sales, order getters tend to have a degree in engineering and a master's degree in business administration. If they do not have a business degree, their companies are often likely to sponsor their best employee in the pursuit of this degree. Sales support personnel are individuals who directly support or assist in the selling function in some manner but do not process orders or directly solicit orders. Examples of sales support staff are customer service representatives, who handle the service hotline of the company. For more information about the opportunities in sales, refer to Chapter 16.

In addition to the marketing positions previously addressed, other types of positions fall in the realm of marketing. For example, graduates may elect to work for transportation and logistics companies or for a wholesaler. Chapter 10 contains additional information on the different types of opportunities. Graduates can also start out as assistants to buyers or purchasing agents, and then further advance to the position of buyer or purchasing agent for the company.

For information on careers in marketing, consult the following Web sites:

• American Marketing Association, www.marketingpower.com

• American Advertising Federation, www.aaf.org

• Marketing Jobs, www.marketingjobs.com

• Marketing and Sales Jobs, www.nationjob.com/marketing

Appendix C

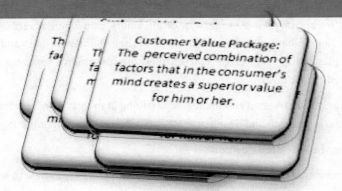

Customer Value Package:
The perceived combination of factors that in the consumer's mind creates a superior value for him or her.

Glossary of Key Terms

Note: All 547 glossary terms are available as e-Flash cards.

They are included in the self-scoring *Online Practice Quizzes.*

Check the *Booklist* tab at **www.textbookmedia.com** for more information.

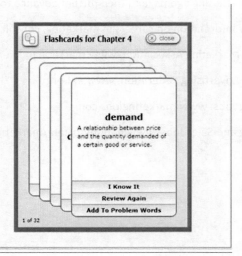

Acceleration Principle: An increase or decrease in consumer demand for a product that can create a drastic change in derived business demand.

Accessibility: The ability to communicate with and reach the target market.

Accessory Pricing: Pricing of accessories and other optional products sold with the main product.

Acculturation: The process of learning a new culture.

Achievers: Psychographic group of individuals who are goal-oriented, conservative, committed to career and family, and favor established, prestige products that demonstrate success to peers.

Actionability: The extent to which the target market segment is responsive to the marketing strategies used.

Administered Channel Arrangement: An arrangement between intermediaries such that a dominant member of the distribution channel in terms of size, expertise, or influence coordinates the tasks of each member in the channel.

Advertising Appeal: The design a creative will use to attract attention to and interest in an advertisement.

Advertising Effectiveness Research: Studies conducted to examine the effectiveness and appropriateness of advertisements aimed at individual markets.

Advertising: Any form of paid communication directed to an organization's customers or other stakeholders.

Affective Message Strategies: Messages designed to invoke feelings and emotions within the audience.

Agents: Intermediaries who represent buyers or sellers; they do not take possession of or title to the merchandise, and they work based on commission or fees.

AIDA: An acronym that stands for attention, interest, desire, and action.

All-Purpose Discount Stores: General merchandise discount stores that offer a wide variety of merchandise and limited depth.

Analogy Method: A method for estimation that relies on developments and findings in similar markets or where the product is in the same life cycle stage.

Aspirational Groups: Groups that individuals aspire to join in the future—for example, by virtue of education, employment, and training.

Assimilation: Adapting to and fully integrating into the new culture.

Associative Reference Groups: Groups that individuals belong to.

Atmospherics: The general atmosphere of the store created by its physical attributes, including lighting and music tempo, the fixtures and other displays, colors, and store layout.

Attitudes: Relatively enduring and consistent feelings (affective responses) about a good or service.

Attribute/Benefit Positioning: Positioning that communicates product attributes and benefits, differentiating each brand from the other company.

Attribution Theory: The process of deciding the cause of a service failure or poor service.

Audience: The individuals who observe a marketing communication and decode the message.

Augmented Product: A product enhanced by the addition of extra or unsolicited services or benefits, such as a warranty, repair services, maintenance, and other services that enhance product use to prompt a purchase.

Bait and Switch: A marketing tactic in which a retailer promotes a special deal on a particular product and then, when consumers arrive at the store, the retailer attempts to switch them to a higher-priced item.

Battle of the Brands: The conflict between manufacturers and resellers to promote their own brands.

Behavioral Targeting: The utilization of Web data to target individuals.

Beliefs: Associations between a good or service and attributes of that good or service.

Believers: Psychographic group of individuals who are conservative, conventional, and focus on tradition, family, religion, and community. They prefer established brands, favoring American products.

Benefit Segmentation: The process of identifying market segments based on important differences between the benefits sought by the target market from purchasing a particular product.

Bid Pricing: Pricing that involves competitive bidding for a contract, whereby a firm will price based on how it believes competitors will price, rather than based on demand or costs.

Big Emerging Markets (BEMs): Large countries with emerging markets that present the greatest potential for international trade and expansion.

Blogs: Online musings that cover a wide range of topics.

Blueprinting: The process of diagramming a service operation.

Bonus Packs: Sales promotion that offers customers some type of discount for purchasing multiple items.

Bounce-back Coupons: Coupons that cannot be used until the next purchase.

Brand Advertising: An advertisement designed to promote a particular brand with little or no information in the advertisement.

Brand Awareness Research: Research investigating how consumers' knowledge and recognition of a brand name affects their purchasing behavior.

Brand Character (or Trade Character): A character that personifies the brand.

Brand Equity (or Brand Franchise): Brands with high consumer awareness and loyalty.

Brand Extensions: The use of an existing brand name to introduce products in a new product category.

Brand Image: The consumer perception of the particular brand.

Brand Logo: A distinctive mark, sign, symbol, or graphic version of a company's name that is used to identify and promote the company's product.

Brand Mark: The part of a brand that can be seen but not spoken.

Brand Name: The part of a brand that can be spoken; it may include words, letters, or numbers.

Brand: A name, design, symbol, or a combination thereof that identifies the product or the seller and that is used to differentiate the product from competitors' offerings.

Branded Media: A movie or show that contains a brand name or logo with a story line that intersects the brand's mission or current advertising campaign.

Brand-Name Generation: The testing of brand names and logos.

Bricks-and-Clicks: Firms that operate both a bricks-and-mortar facility and an Internet e-commerce site.

Brokers: Intermediaries who bring buyers and sellers together; they do not take possession of or title to the merchandise, and they work based on commission or fees.

Bundling: Pricing of bundled products sold together.

Buyer Behavior Research: Research examining consumer brand preferences, brand attitudes, and brand-related behavior.

Buyer's Regret: A feeling of anxiety related to the consumer's loss of freedom to spend money on other products.

Buyer-Readiness Stage Segmentation: The process of segmenting the market based on individuals' stage of readiness to buy a product.

Buyer-seller Dyad: Two-way communication between a buyer and a seller.

Buying Center: Group of individuals who are involved in the purchase process.

By-Product Pricing: Pricing of by-products that are of low value to get rid of them.

Calendar Promotions: Promotional campaigns that retailers plan for their customers through manufacturer trade incentives.

Captive-Product Pricing: Pricing of products that must be used with the main product.

Cash Cows: Products with high market share and slow growth that generate large amounts of cash, in excess of the reinvestment required to maintain market share.

Catalog Retailers: Retailers selling products through mail catalogs.

Catalog Showrooms: Showrooms displaying the products of catalog retailers, offering high-turnover, brand-name goods at discount prices.

Causal (Experimental) Research: Research that examines cause-and-effect relationships.

Cause-related Marketing: A long-term partnership between a nonprofit organization and a corporation that is integrated into the corporation's marketing plan.

Central Business Districts: Business districts located in the commercial and cultural heart of the city, in the middle of busy downtowns, and close to movie theaters and banks.

Channel Captain: The dominant member of a channel of distribution.

Channel Length: The number of levels of distributors in a distribution channel.

Channel Performance and Coverage Studies: Studies investigating whether existing channels are appropriate for the marketing task at hand.

Channel Width: The number of independent intermediaries involved at a particular stage of distribution.

Channels of Distribution: The totality of organizations and individuals involved in the distribution process who take title to or assist in the transferring of title in the distribution process from the producer to the individual or organizational consumer.

Clicks-only Firms: Organizations that sell only over the Internet.

Co-Branding: Using the brands of two different companies on one single product.

Coercive Power: Power over channel members based on the ability of one or more intermediaries to remove privileges for noncompliance.

Cognitive Dissonance: An anxiety feeling of uncertainty about whether or not the consumer made the right purchase decision.

Cognitive Message Strategies: The presentation of rational arguments or pieces of information to consumers.

Combination Stores: Medium-sized retail stores that combine food and drug retailing.

Commercialization: Stage in the new product development process when the product is introduced to the market.

Commission Merchant: Agent who takes possession of goods on consignment from the local markets and then sells them at a central market location.

Community Shopping Centers: Shopping centers with fewer than 40 retailers, containing a department store, a supermarket, and several smaller specialty retailers.

Comparative Advertising: An advertisement that compares the featured brand with another brand, either named or implied.

Competitive Pricing Analyses: Pricing studies that determine the price the market will bear for the respective product category based on a survey of competitors' prices.

Competitive Product Studies: Studies that help in determining the overall product strategy for the product, the price that the market will bear for the respective product category, and the promotion that is appropriate in light of the competition.

Competitor Positioning: The process of comparing the firm's brand, directly or indirectly, with those of competitors.

Conative Message Strategies: Messages designed to elicit some type of audience behavior, such as a purchase or inquiry.

Concentrated Marketing: The process of selecting only one market segment and targeting it with one single brand.

Concept Development Research: Concept tests that evaluate the product or service offering and the related marketing mix in light of the different target markets.

Consequence: The degree of importance or danger of the outcome itself.

Consumer Segmentation Studies: Research conducted to identify market segment profiles.

Contact Methods: Methods used for approaching study respondents.

Content Analysis: Method that assesses the content of advertisements in a medium with verbal or visual content.

Content Marketing: Also known as branded content, content that is authentic and useful for businesses and/or consumers.

Content Seeding: Providing incentives for consumers to share content about a brand.

Continuous Innovations: Innovations that have no disruption on consumption patterns and involve only product alterations, such as new flavors or a new product that is an improvement over the old offering.

Contractual Agreement: A written agreement between the buyer and seller that states the terms of the interaction, costs, and length of the commitment.

Contractual Channel Arrangement: A contract between intermediaries that defines all the tasks that each channel member must perform with regard to production, delivery strategy and terms of sale, territorial rights, promotional support, the price policies of each intermediary, and contract length.

Controlled Test Marketing: Offering a new product to a group of stores and evaluating the market reaction to it.

Convenience Goods: Relatively inexpensive and frequently purchased products.

Convenience Sample: Sample composed of individuals who are easy to contact for the researcher.

Convenience Stores: Small retailers that are located in residential areas, are open long hours, and carry limited lines of high-turnover necessities.

Conventional Supermarkets: Self-service food retailers with annual sales of more than $2 million and with an area of less than 20,000 square feet.

Cooperative Advertising Program: An arrangement whereby a manufacturer agrees to reimburse retailers or other channel members that feature the manufacturer's brands in the ad for a portion of their advertising costs.

Cooperative Merchandising Agreement (CMA): A formal agreement between the retailer and manufacturer to undertake a cooperative marketing effort.

Core Product: The fundamental benefit, or problem solution, that consumers seek expected (or actual).

Cost Analyses: Methods used for projecting the cost of research.

Cost per thousand (CPM): The cost of reaching 1,000 members of a media vehicle's audience.

Cost-Based Pricing: Pricing strategy whereby the firm sets the price by calculating merchandise, service, and overhead costs and then adds an amount needed to cover the profit goal.

Coupons: Sales promotion that offers customers some type of price reduction.

Creatives: Individuals who actually design the advertisements.

Cross-ruffing Coupon: A coupon for one product placed on another product.

Cross-selling: The marketing of additional items with the purchase of a particular good or service.

Cues: Stimuli in the environment, such as products or advertisements, that create individual responses.

Cultural Values: Beliefs about a specific mode of conduct or desirable end state that guide the selection or evaluation of behavior.

Customary Pricing: Pricing strategy whereby a firm sets prices and attempts to maintain them over time.

Customer Lifetime Value (LTV): The estimated profitability of the customer over the course of his or her entire relationship with a company.

Customer Profit Potential: An estimate of the individual's contribution to a company's bottom line.

Customer Profit: Profit measure calculated as revenue minus costs for that particular customer.

Customer Relationship Management (CRM): A database application program designed to build long-term loyalty with customers through the use of a personal touch.

Customer Value Package: The perceived combination of factors that in the consumer's mind creates a superior value for him or her.

Data Collection Instruments: The instruments used to collect data, such as a questionnaire, a paper-and-pencil measure, or an electronic measurement device.

Data Mining: The process of compiling personal, pertinent, actionable information about the purchasing habits of current and potential consumers.

Data Warehousing: The process of capturing and storing data within a single database that is accessible to internal personnel for a variety of internal purposes, such as marketing, sales, and customer service.

Database Marketing: The collection, analysis, and use of large volumes of customer data to develop marketing programs and customer profiles.

Deceptive Pricing: Strategy used by sellers who state prices or price savings that may mislead consumers or that are not available to consumers.

Decider: The member of the buying center who makes the final decision.

Decline Stage: Stage in the product life cycle where products are rapidly losing ground to new technologies or product alternatives, and consequently, sales and profits are rapidly declining.

Decoding: The process of interpreting the meaning conveyed in a marketing message.

Degree of Product Newness: The extent to which a product or service is new to the market.

Delphi Method: A method of forecasting sales that involves asking a number of experts to estimate market performance, aggregating the results, and then sharing this information with the said experts; the process is repeated several times, until a consensus is reached.

Demand Curve: Curve that portrays the number of units bought for a particular price in a given time period.

Demand-Based Pricing: Pricing strategy that takes into consideration customers' perceptions of value, rather than the seller's cost, as the fundamental component of the pricing decision.

Demands: Wants backed by the ability to buy a respective good or service.

Demarketing: A company strategy aimed at reducing demand for its own products to benefit society.

Demographic Segmentation: The process of identifying market segments based on age, gender, race, income, education, occupation, social class, life cycle stage, and household size.

Demographics: Statistics that describe the population, such as age, gender, education, occupation, and income.

Depth Interviews: A qualitative research method involving extensive interviews aimed at discovering consumer motivations, feelings, and attitudes toward an issue of concern to the sponsor, using unstructured interrogation.

Derived Demand: Demand for a good or service that is generated from the demand for consumer goods and services.

Descriptive Research: All research methods observing or describing phenomena.

Differential Response: The extent to which market segments respond differently to marketing strategies.

Differentiated Marketing: A targeting strategy identifying market segments with different preferences for a particular product category and targeting each segment with different brands and different marketing strategies.

Digital coupons: Electronically delivered coupons.

Direct Channel of Distribution: A channel that has no intermediaries; the manufacturer sells directly to the final consumer.

Direct Response Marketing: The promotion of a product directly from the manufacturer or seller to the buyer without any intermediaries involved in the transaction.

Direct Selling: Selling that involves a salesperson, typically an independent distributor, contacting a consumer at a convenient location (e.g., his or her home or workplace), demonstrating the product's use and benefits, taking orders, and delivering the merchandise.

Direct-mail Retailing: Retailing using catalogs and other direct mail, instead of brick-and-mortar stores.

Dissociative Groups: Groups that individuals want to dissociate from through their behavior.

Distribution Centers: Computerized warehouses designed to move goods; they receive goods from different producers, take orders from buyers, and distribute them promptly.

Distribution Planning: The planning of the physical movement of products from the producer to individual or organizational consumers and the transfer of ownership and risk; it involves transportation, warehousing, and all the exchanges taking place at each channel level.

Distributors: Intermediaries whose task is to ensure the convenient, timely, and safe distribution of the product to consumers.

Diversification: Opportunity for expansion involving developing or acquiring new products for new markets.

Diversion: A situation in which a retailer purchases a product on-deal in one location and ships it to another location, where it is off-deal.

Dogs: Products with low market share and slow growth.

Drive (or Motive): A stimulus that encourages consumers to engage in an action to reduce the need.

Drive to Maturity: Stage of economic development in which modern technology is applied in all areas of the economy.

Dual Channel of Distribution: The use of two or more channels of distribution to appeal to different markets.

Dumping: Selling products below cost to get rid of excess inventory or to undermine competition.

Durable Goods: Tangible products that have a prolonged use.

Early Adopters: Consumers who purchase the product early in the life cycle and are opinion leaders in their communities.

Early Majority: Consumers who are more risk averse but enjoy the status of being among the first in their peer group to buy what will be a popular product.

E-Commerce: The selling of goods and services over the Internet.

Electronic Data Interchange (EDI): A trust relationship that includes the sharing of data between the buying and selling firm.

Emergency Goods: Goods purchased to address urgent needs.

Emerging Markets: Markets that are developing rapidly and have great potential.

Empathy: The caring, individualized attention the service firm provides to each customer.

Encoding: The process of transposing the objective or goal of a marketing communication concept into an actual marketing communication piece, such as an advertisement, brochure, or sign.

Ethics: Philosophical principles that serve as operational guidelines for both individuals and organizations concerning what is right and wrong.

Ethnography: The study of cultures.

Even Pricing: Setting selling prices at even numbers.

Exchanges and Transactions: Obtaining a desired good or service in exchange for some-thing else of value; involving at least two parties that mutually agree on the desirability of the traded items.

Exclusive Distribution: A strategy that has as a goal a high control of the intermediaries handling the product, and thus of the marketing strategy, by limiting them to just one or two per geographic area.

Exit Fees: Monies paid to remove an item from a retailer's inventory.

Expected (or Actual) Product: The basic physical product, including styling, features, brand name, and packaging, that delivers the benefits that consumers seek.

Experiencers: Psychographic group of individuals who are young, enthusiastic, and impulsive. They seek variety and excitement, and spend substantially on fashion, entertainment, and socializing.

Experiences: Personal experiences that consumers perceive as valuable because they fulfill consumer needs and wants.

Expert Power: Power over the other channel members based on experience and knowledge that a channel member possesses.

Exploratory Research: Research conducted early in the research process that helps further define a problem or identify additional problems that need to be investigated.

Extensive Problem Solving: Consumer decision making that involves going carefully through each of the steps of the consumer decision-making process.

External Secondary Data: Data collected by an entity not affiliated with the company.

Fad: A fashion that quickly becomes very popular and just as quickly disappears.

Family Branding (or Blanket Branding): Branding strategy whereby one brand name is used for more than one product.

Fashion: A current style.

Feedback: The response of the audience to the message.

Field Salesperson: A salesperson who is involved in going to a potential customer's place of business to solicit accounts.

Financial Risk: The amount of monetary loss the consumer incurs if the service fails.

Fixed Costs: Costs that do not vary with the amount of output.

Flexible Pricing: Pricing strategy that allows a firm to set prices based on negotiation with the customer, or based on customer buying power.

Focus Group Interviews: A qualitative research approach investigating a research question, using a moderator to guide discussion within a group of subjects recruited to meet certain characteristics.

Food Retailers: Retailers selling primarily food products.

Foreign Trade Zone (FTZ): Tax-free area in the United States that is not considered part of the United States in terms of import regulations and restrictions. Also called a free trade zone.

Forward Buying: When a retailer purchases excess inventory of a product while it is on-deal to be sold later when it is off-deal.

Freestanding Inserts (FSI): Sheets of coupons distributed in newspapers, primarily on Sunday.

Freight Forwarders: Specialized firms that collect shipments from different businesses, consolidate them for part of the distance, and deliver them to a destination, in what is typically a door-to-door service.

Frequency Programs: Sales promotions offered to current customers and designed to build repeat purchase behavior.

Full-Service Wholesalers: Independent intermediaries who provide a wide range of distribution tasks, such as product delivery, warehousing, sales force assistance, credit, research, planning, and installation and repair assistance, among others.

Functional Service Quality: The process whereby the service was performed.

Gap Theory: Method of measuring service quality that involves measuring the gap between expectations and customers evaluation of the service.

Gatekeeper: Individual who is responsible for the flow of information to the members of the buying center.

General Merchandise Discount Stores: Retailers that sell high volumes of merchandise, offer limited service, and charge lower prices.

Generation X: A segment of individuals born between 1965 and 1977, whose focus is on family and children, striving to balance family with work, and outsourcing household chores and babysitting.

Generation Y: A segment of individuals born between 1978 and 2002; they spend substantial amounts on clothing, automobiles, and college education; they live in rental apartments or with parents.

Generics: Products that emphasize the product, rather than the brand of the manufacturer or reseller.

Geographic Pricing: Pricing that accounts for the geographic location of the customers.

Geographic Segmentation: Market segmentation based on geographic location, such as country or region.

Geo-targeting: A mobile marketing tactic that reaches customers where they are located based on their mobile device.

Goods: Tangible products, such as cereals, automobiles, and clothing.

Green Marketing: The development and promotion of products that are environmentally safe.

Gross Domestic Product (GDP): The sum of all goods and services produced within the boundaries of a country.

Growth Stage: Stage in the product life cycle characterized by increasing competition, with new product variants offered to the market, as well as rapid product adoption by the target market.

Growth-share Matrix: Portfolio matrix developed by the Boston Consulting Group and one of the most popular bases for evaluating company product portfolios; it assumes that, to be successful, a company should have a portfolio of products with different growth rates and different market shares.

Heterogeneous Shopping Goods: Goods that vary significantly in terms of functions, physical characteristics, and quality, and that require a physical evaluation by the buyer.

Heuristics: Decision rules that individuals adopt to make a decision process more efficient.

High Mass Consumption: Stage of economic development in which leading sectors shift toward durable goods and an increased allocation to social welfare programs.

High-Income Countries: Highly industrialized countries that have well-developed industrial and service sectors and have a gross national income per capita of $12,676 and above.

High-Involvement Purchases: Purchases that have a high personal relevance.

Homogeneous Shopping Goods: Goods that vary little in terms of physical characteristics or functions.

Horizontal Integration: An acquisition or merger with an intermediary at the same level in the distribution channel.

Horizontal Marketing Systems (HMS): Intermediaries at the same level of the distribution channel pooling resources and achieving partial ownership of the system, achieving economies of scale, and playing on their individual strengths.

Hub-and-Spoke Distribution Centers: Distribution centers designed to speed up warehousing and delivery, by channeling operations to one center (hub) that is particularly well equipped to handle the distribution of products to their destination.

Hypermarkets: Very large retail stores in Europe that combine supermarket, discount, and warehouse retailing principles—similar to superstores in the U.S.

Ideas: Concepts that can be used to fulfill consumer needs and wants.

Impulse Goods: Goods bought without any earlier planning, such as candy, gum, and magazines.

In-app Advertising: An advertisement embedded within a mobile app.

Inbound Telemarketing: The process through which an order-taker salesperson handles incoming calls from customers and prospects.

Indirect Channel of Distribution: A channel that involves one or more intermediaries between the manufacturer and the consumer.

Industrialization: The use of machines and standardized operating procedures to increase the productivity and efficiency of a business.

Influencer: A member of the buying center who influences the decision but may not necessarily use the product.

Informative Advertising: An advertisement designed to provide the audience with some type of information.

Innovations: Dynamically Continuous Innovations that do not significantly alter consumer behavior but represent a change in the consumption pattern.

Innovators: Psychographic group of individuals who are successful, sophisticated, and receptive to new technologies.

Inseparability: The simultaneous production and consumption of a service.

Instant Redemption Coupon: A coupon that can be redeemed immediately while making a purchase.

Institutional Advertising: Advertising designed to build the corporate reputation or develop goodwill for the corporation.

Instrumental Values: Values related to processes whereby one can attain certain goals.

Intangibility: The lack of tangible assets of a service that can be seen, touched, smelled, heard, or tasted before a purchase.

Integrated Marketing Communications (IMC): The coordination and integration of all marketing communication tools, avenues, and sources within a company into a seamless program designed to maximize the communication impact on consumers, businesses, and other constituencies of an organization.

Intensive Distribution: A strategy that has as its purpose full market coverage, making the product available to all target consumers when and where consumers want it.

Interactive Marketing: The process of individualizing and personalizing everything—from the Web site content to the products being promoted.

Intercompany Tie-in: A sales promotion involving two different companies offering complementary products.

Intermediaries (or Middlemen or Channel Members): The organizations or individuals involved in the distribution process.

Intermodal Transportation: Transportation using two or more different transportation modes—a combination of truck, rail, air, and waterways.

Internal Secondary Data: Data previously collected by a company to address a problem not related to the current research question.

Internet or Digital Marketing: The promotion of products through the Internet.

Internet Retailing (or Interactive Home Shopping or Electronic Retailing): Selling through the Internet using Web sites to increase market penetration and market diversification.

Intracompany Tie-in: A sales promotion involving two or more distinct products within the same company.

Inventory: The amount of goods being stored.

Involvement: The level of mental and physical effort a consumer exerts in selecting a good or service.

Joint Demand: Demand for one product that is affected by the level of demand for another product.

Judgment Sample: A sample of individuals thought to be representative of the population.

Jury of Expert Opinion: An approach to sales forecasting based on the opinions of different experts.

Keiretsus: Japanese families of firms with interlocking stakes in one another.

Laggards: Consumers who are the last to adopt new products and who do so only in late maturity.

Late Majority: Consumers with limited means likely to adopt products only if the products are widely popular and the risk associated with buying them is minimal.

Law of Demand: Economic law whereby consumers are believed to purchase more products at a lower price than at a higher price.

Learning: Change in individual thought processes or behavior attributed to experience or new information.

Legitimate Power: Power over the other channel members by virtue of an intermediary's status or position in the firm.

Licensing: A process that involves a licensor, who shares the brand name, technology, and know-how with a licensee in return for royalties.

Lifestyles: Individuals' style of living as expressed through activities, interests, and opinions.

Limited Problem Solving: Consumer decision making that involves less problem solving. This type of decision making is used for products that are not especially visible, nor too expensive.

Limited-Service Wholesalers: Wholesalers who offer fewer services than full-service wholesalers, such as delivery and storage.

Line Extension: The process of extending the existing brand name by introducing new product offerings in an existing product category.

Logistics (or Physical Distribution): All the activities involved in the physical flow and storage of materials, semi-finished goods, and finished goods to customers in a manner that is efficient and cost effective.

Loss-Leader Pricing: Pricing whereby the firm advertises a product at a price that is significantly less than its usual price to create traffic in the stores for consumers to purchase higher-margin products.

Lower-Middle-Income Countries: Countries in this diverse group have a gross national income per capita of $1036 to $4,085 (U.S. dollars).

Low-Income Countries: Countries that are primarily agrarian and have low per capita income.

Low-Involvement Products: Products with limited personal relevance.

Loyalty Segmentation: The process of segmenting the market based on the degree of consumer loyalty to the brand.

Macroenvironment: Environment of the firm, which includes the socio-demographic and cultural environment, the economic and natural environment, the political environment, and the technological environment.

Makers: Psychographic group of individuals who are self-sufficient. They have the skill and energy to carry out projects, respect authority, and are unimpressed by material possessions.

Manufacturers' Agent (or Manufacturers' Representative): Representative who works as the company's sales representative, representing noncompeting manufacturers in a particular market, and is paid on a commission basis.

Manufacturers' Brands (or National Brands): Brands owned by a manufacturer.

Market Development: The process of developing new markets for the company's existing product or creating new product uses.

Market Orientation: A firm-wide focus on customer needs and on delivering high quality to consumers in the process of achieving company objectives.

Market Penetration: The process of increasing the usage rate of current customers and attracting competitors' customers to sell more products to present customers without changing the product.

Market Potential Studies: Studies conducted to evaluate the potential of a particular market.

Marketing Concept: A marketing philosophy that assumes a company can compete more effectively if it first researches consumers' generic needs, wants, and preferences, as well as good-or service-related attitudes and interests, and then delivers the goods and services more efficiently and effectively than competitors.

Marketing Decision Support Systems (MDSS): A coordinated collection of data, systems, tools, and techniques, complemented by supporting software and hardware designed for the gathering and interpretation of business and environmental data.

Marketing Era: Period from 1950 until the present, when the primary focus of marketing shifted to the needs of consumers and society.

Marketing Intelligence: Results obtained from monitoring developments in the firm's environment.

Marketing Research: The systematic design, collection, recording, analysis, interpretation, and reporting of information pertinent to a particular marketing decision facing a company.

Markets: All of the actual and potential consumers of a company's products.

Maturity Stage: Stage in the product life cycle characterized by a slow-down in sales growth as the product is adopted by most target consumers and by a leveling or decline in profits primarily as a result of intense price competition.

Measurability: The ability to estimate the size of a market segment.

Media Research: Studies that evaluate media availability and the appropriateness of the medium for a company's message.

Medium: The venue the source uses to send a marketing communication message to its intended audience.

Merchandise Mix: The product assortment and brands that the store carries.

Merchant Wholesalers: Independent intermediaries who take title to and possession of products distributed to resellers or organizational consumers.

Message: The completed marketing communication piece.

Microenvironment: Environment of the firm, which includes the company, its consumers, suppliers, distributors, and other facilitators of the marketing function and competition.

Micromarketing: A process that involves a microanalysis of the customer and customer-specific marketing.

Middle-Income Countries: Countries that are developing rapidly and have great potential.

Missionary Salesperson: A sales support person whose task is to provide information about a good or service.

Mission-sharing Sales Approach: Sales approach that involves two organizations developing a common mission and then sharing resources to accomplish that mission.

Modified Break-Even Analysis: Analysis that combines breakeven analysis with an evaluation of demand at various price levels, assuming that, as the price increases, demand will decrease in an elastic demand environment, where many product substitutes are available and competition is intense.

Modified Rebuy Situation: Occasional purchases or purchases for which the members of the buying center have limited experience.

Monopolistic Competition: Market that consists of many buyers and sellers and products that vary greatly in the same product category.

Morals: Personal beliefs or standards used to guide an individual's actions.

Multiattribute Segmentation: The process of segmenting the market by using multiple segmentation variables.

Multibranding: Using different brand names for products that the firm sells in the same product category.

Multichannel Distribution System (Hybrid Marketing Channel): The use of multiple (more than two) channels of distribution, thus offering customers multiple purchase and communication options.

Multichannel Marketing: The marketing of a product through two or more channels.

Multiple-Unit Pricing: Pricing whereby consumers get a discount to purchase a larger quantity with the purpose, ultimately, to increase sales volume.

Naturalistic Inquiry: An observational research approach that requires the use of natural rather than contrived settings because behaviors take substantial meaning from their context.

Needs: Basic human requirements: such as food and water.

Need-satisfaction Sales Approach: Sales approach aimed at discovering a customer's needs and then providing solutions that satisfy those needs.

Neighborhood Business Districts: Business districts that meet the needs of the neighborhood and that tend to be located on a main street of the neighborhood; typically, they have a supermarket, a drug store, and several smaller retailers.

Neighborhood Shopping Centers: Shopping centers that have between five and 15 retailers and that serve the neighborhood, providing convenience in the form of a supermarket, discount store, laundry service, and other smaller specialty stores.

Network Marketing (or Multilevel Marketing): An alternative distribution structure, using acquaintance networks for the purpose of distribution.

New Brands: New brands in new product categories for the firm.

New Buy Situation: Purchases made by a business for the first time or purchases for which no one in the organization has had previous experience.

No-Haggle Pricing: Pricing strategy that is aimed at consumers who are averse to negotiation, but who want, nevertheless, to have some sort of low-price guarantee.

Noise: Anything that interferes with the audience receiving the message.

Nondurable Goods: Tangible products that are consumed relatively quickly and purchased on a regular basis; they last less than two years.

Nonresponse: The inability or refusal by a respondent to participate in a study.

Observational Research (or Observation): A research approach whereby subjects are observed interacting with a product and reacting to other components of the marketing mix and the environment.

Occasion Segmentation: The process of segmenting based on the time or the occasion when the product should be purchased or consumed.

Occasional Transactions: Transactions whereby buyer and seller interact infrequently in the process of making the transaction.

Odd Pricing: Setting prices at below even dollar values.

Off-invoice Allowance: A financial discount or price-off on each case that a member of the distribution channel orders.

Off-Price Retailers: Retailers that sell brand-name and designer merchandise below regular retail.

Older Boomers: A segment of individuals born between 1946 and 1953, that spends money on upgrading the family home, on taking vacations, and on ensuring children's education and independence.

Oligopolistic Competition: Market that consists of few sellers who dominate the market.

Open-ended Questions: Questions with free-format responses that the respondent can address as he or she sees appropriate.

Opportunity Risk: The risk involved when consumers must choose one service over another.

Order Getters: Salespeople who actively generate potential leads and persuade customers to make a purchase.

Order Takers: Salespeople who process routine orders from customers.

Outbound Telemarketing: The process through which an order-getter salesperson calls prospects and attempts to persuade them to make a purchase.

Packaging: All the activities involved in designing the product container.

Patent: The grant of a property right to the inventor.

Penetration Pricing: Pricing strategy whereby firms initially price the product below the price of competitors to quickly penetrate the market at competitors' expense and acquire a large market share, and then gradually raise the price.

Perception: The manner in which people collect, organize, and interpret information from the world around them to create a meaningful image of reality.

Performance Risk: The chance that the service will not perform or provide the benefit for which it was purchased.

Perishability: The inability of a service to be inventoried or stored.

Personal Selling: A direct communication approach between the buyer and seller with the express purpose of selling a product.

Personality: An individual's unique psychological characteristics leading to specific response tendencies over time.

Persuasive Advertising: An advertisement designed to persuade viewers' thinking in some way.

Physical Risk: The probability that a service will actually cause physical harm to the customer.

Pioneer Advertising: An advertisement designed to build primary demand for a product.

Place: The physical movement of products from the producer to individual or organizational consumers and the transfer of ownership and risk; the third P of marketing.

Plant/Warehouse Location Study: A study that evaluates the appropriateness of plant or warehouse location to ensure that it is in accordance with the needs of the company.

Point-of-Sale (POS)-Based Projections: Market projections based on the use of store scanners in weekly and bi-weekly store audits.

Predatory Pricing: Pricing strategies used to eliminate small competitors and to deceive consumers.

Preference Goods: Convenience goods that become differentiated through branding and achieve some degree of brand loyalty.

Prestige Pricing: Strategy based on the premise that consumers will feel that products below a particular price will have inferior quality and will not convey a desired status and image.

Price Ceiling: The maximum amount that consumers are willing to pay for a product.

Price Confusion: Strategies to confuse consumers so that they do not quite understand the price that they ultimately have to pay.

Price Discounting: Strategy that involves reducing the price for purchasing larger quantities, responding to a promotion, paying cash, or responding earlier than a particular set time.

Price Discrimination: The practice of charging different prices to different buyers of the same merchandise.

Price Elasticity Studies: Studies examining the extent to which a particular market is price sensitive.

Price Elasticity: Buyer sensitivity to a change in price.

Price Fixing: Agreement among channel members at the same level in the channel of distribution to charge the same price to all customers.

Price Floor: The lowest price a company can charge to attain its profit goal.

Price Leadership: The tendency of one firm or a few firms to be the first to announce price changes, with the rest of the firms following.

Price/Quality Positioning: A strategy whereby products and services are positioned as offering the best value for the money.

Price: The amount of money necessary to purchase a product.; the second P of marketing.

Price-offs: Sales promotion that offers a reduction of the retail price of a product.

Primary Data: Data collected for the purpose of addressing the problem at hand.

Private Label Brands: Reseller (wholesaler or retailer) brands.

Private Warehouses: Warehouses that are owned or leased and operated by firms storing their own products.

Problem-solution Sales Approach: Sales approach that requires the salesperson to analyze the prospect's operation and offer a viable solution.

Product Advertising: Advertising designed to promote a firm's brand.

Product Class Positioning: A strategy used to differentiate a company as a leader in a product category as defined by the respective companies.

Product Concept: A marketing philosophy that assumes consumers prefer products that are of the highest quality and optimal performance.

Product Consistency: The extent to which the different product lines are related, use the same distribution channels, and have the same final consumers.

Product Depth: The number of different offerings for a product category.

Product Design: The aesthetic traits, style, and function of the product.

Product Development: The process of developing new products to appeal to the company's existing market.

Product Introduction Stage: Stage in the product life cycle when the product is available for purchase for the first time.

Product Length: The total number of brands in the product mix—all the brands the company sells.

Product Life Cycle (PLC): The performance of the product in terms of sales and profit over time.

Product Line Pricing: Pricing that involves creating price differences between the different items in the product line, such that specific price points are used to differentiate among the items in the line.

Product Line: The related brands the company offers in the same product category.

Product Mix: The complete assortment of the products that a company offers to its target consumers.

Product Packaging Design: Studies that evaluate consumers' reaction to a package, the extent to which the package adequately communicates information to the consumer, and the distribution implications of the package.

Product Placement: Sales promotion technique of placing branded goods or services in movies, on television shows, or in theatrical performances.

Product Portfolio: The totality of products the company manages as separate businesses.

Product Testing: Studies that estimate product preference and performance in a given market.

Product User Positioning: A positioning strategy that focuses on the product user, rather than on the product.

Product Width: The total number of product lines the company offers.

Product: Any offering that can satisfy consumer needs and wants; products include goods (tangible products), services, ideas, and experiences; the first P of marketing.

Production Concept: A marketing philosophy that assumes consumers prefer products that are easily accessible and inexpensive.

Production Era: Period between 1870 and 1930, when the primary focus of marketing was on producing the best products possible at the lowest price.

Product-market Matrix: A matrix used to identify future products and opportunities for companies.

Products: Any offering that can satisfy consumer needs and wants.

Profit Analyses: Studies that estimate product profit in specific markets.

Promotion: All forms of external communications directed toward consumers and businesses with an ultimate goal of developing customers; the forth P of marketing.

Promotional Pricing: Strategy that reduces prices temporarily to increase sales in the short run.

Prospects: Potential customers of a firm.

Psychographic Segmentation: The use of values, attitudes, interests, and other cultural variables to segment consumers.

Psychographics: Categorization of consumers according to lifestyles and personality.

Psychological Pricing: Setting prices to create a particular psychological effect.

Psychological Risk: The chance that the purchase of the service will not fit the individual's self-concept.

Public Relations (PR): A communication venue that addresses issues an organization faces and represents the organization to the public, media, and various stakeholders.

Public Warehouses: Independent facilities that provide storage rental and related services.

Publicity: A form of public relations produced by the news media but not paid for or sponsored by the business concern.

Puffery: When a firm makes an exaggerated claim about its goods or services, without making an overt attempt to deceive or mislead.

Pull Strategy: A strategy whereby the manufacturer first focuses on consumer demand through extensive promotion, expecting that consumers will request the brand through the channel.

Purchaser: The member of the buying center who makes the actual purchase.

Purchasing Agents: Agents with a long-term relationship with buyers who select, receive, and ship goods to buyers and are paid on a commission basis.

Pure Competition: Market that consists of many buyers and sellers, where no buyer or seller can control price or the market.

Pure Monopoly: Market that consists of only one seller.

Push Strategy: A strategy that focuses on intermediaries, providing the necessary incentives for them to cooperate in selling the product to the final consumer.

Qualitative Research: Research that involves a small number of respondents answering open-ended questions.

Quantitative Research: A structured type of research that involves either descriptive research approaches, such as survey research, or causal research approaches, such as experiments in which responses can be summarized or analyzed with numbers.

Question Marks (or Problem Children): Low market share and high-growth products that require more cash investment than they generate.

Rack Jobbers: Wholesalers that manage the store shelves carrying their products.

Radical Innovations (or Discontinuous Innovations): Innovations that create new industries or new standards of management, manufacturing, and servicing, and that represent fundamental changes for consumers, entailing departures from established consumption.

Random Probability Sample: A sample in which each individual selected for the study has a known and equal chance of being included in the study.

Reach: The number of people, households, or businesses in a target audience exposed to a media message at least once during a given time period.

Real-time Marketing: The creation and execution of an instantaneous marketing message in response to or in conjunction with a live event.

Rebates and Refunds: Sales promotions that are a cash reimbursement to a customer for the purchase of a product.

Reciprocity: The practice of one business making a purchase from another business that, in turn, patronizes the first business.

Reference Groups: Groups that serve as a point of reference for individuals in the process of shaping their attitude and behavior.

Reference Price: The price that consumers carry in their mind for a particular product or brand.

Referent Power: Power over the other channel members based on the close match in terms of values and objectives that members of the channel share.

Regional Shopping Centers: Shopping centers that consist of at least 100 stores that sell shopping goods to a geographically dispersed market.

Reinforcement: Learning achieved by strengthening the relationship between the cue and the response.

Relationship Marketing: The process of developing and nurturing relationships with all the parties participating in the transactions involving a company's products; the development of marketing strategies aimed at enhancing relationships in the channel.

Reliability: The ability of the service firm to perform the service provided in a dependable and accurate manner [service]; the extent to which data are likely to be free from random error and yield consistent results [scale].

Religion: A way of defining a society's relationship to the supernatural and, as a result, determining dominant values and attitudes.

Reorder Point: An inventory level at which new orders are placed.

Repeat Transactions: Buyer and seller interacting over multiple transactions.

Resale Price Maintenance: Manufacturers requiring retailers to charge a particular price for a product.

Research Approach: The method used to collect data.

Response: An attempt to satisfy an individual drive.

Response-offer Coupons: Coupons issued following a request by a consumer.

Responsiveness: The willingness of the firm's staff to help customers and to provide prompt service.

Retention: The ability of the firm to maintain a particular customer over time.

Reward Power: Power over the channel members based on an anticipation of special privileges, such as a financial reward for conducting a particular behavior.

Roles: The activities people are expected to perform according to individuals around them.

Rostow Model of Economic Development: A model of economic development in which each stage of development is a function of productivity, economic exchange, technological improvements, and income.

Routine Problem Solving: Consumer decision making whereby consumers engage in habitual purchase decisions involving products that they purchase frequently.

Sales Era: Period between 1930 and 1950, when the primary focus of marketing was on selling.

Sales Force Compensation, Quota, and Territory Studies: Different studies pertaining to personal selling activities; they are crucial in helping to determine the appropriate sales and incentive strategies for certain markets.

Sales Force Composite Estimates: Research studies in which sales forecasts are based on the personal observations and forecasts of the local sales force.

Sales Forecasts: Projected sales for a particular territory.

Sales Potential Studies: Studies forecasting optimal sales performance.

Sales Promotions: Incentives to encourage end users or consumers to purchase a product.

Sample Size: The number of study participants.

Sample: A segment of the population selected for the study and considered to be representative of the total population of interest.

Sampling Frame: The list from which sampling units are selected.

Sampling Procedure: The procedure used in the selection of sampling units.

Sampling Unit: The individuals or groups included in the study.

Sampling: Sales promotions that include the free delivery of an actual product or portion of a product.

Satisfaction: A match between consumer expectations and good or service performance.

Scanner-delivered Coupons: Coupons issued at the cash register during checkout.

Scrambled Merchandising: Scrambled merchandising involves retailers adding complementary product categories not included in the existing merchandise mix and more services to create one-stop shopping convenience for target consumers.

Search Engine Optimization: The process of increasing the probability of a particular company's Web site emerging from a search.

Secondary Business District: Shopping areas, consisting primarily of convenience and specialty stores, that form at the intersection between two important streets.

Secondary Data: Data collected to address a problem other than the problem at hand.

Segment Marketing: A process that involves identifying consumers who are similar with regard to key traits, such as product-related needs and wants, and who would respond well to a similar marketing mix.

Segmentation: The process of identifying consumers or markets that are similar with regard to key traits, such as product-related needs and wants, and that would respond well to a product and related marketing mix.

Selective Distortion: Consumers adapting information to fit their own existing knowledge.

Selective Distribution: A strategy whereby firms have some control over the marketing strategy by limiting distribution to a select group of resellers in each area, while, at the same time, the company can achieve a reasonable sales volume and profits.

Selective Exposure: The stimuli that consumers choose to pay attention to.

Selective Retention: Remembering only information about a good or service that supports personal knowledge or beliefs.

Selling Agent: Agent that holds an exclusive arrangement with the company, represents all its operations in a particular market, and acts as the sales or marketing department of the firm.

Semantic Differential Scale: Scale that is anchored by words with opposite meanings.

Service Distribution: The availability and accessibility of a service to consumers.

Service Failures: Instances in which a service is either not performed at all or is poorly performed.

Service Mix: The different types of services offered to retail customers.

Service Recovery: The process of attempting to regain a customer's confidence after a service failure.

Servicemark: Words, symbols, marks, and signs that are legally registered for a single company's use that identify and distinguish the source of a service.

Services: Intangible activities or benefits that individuals acquire but that do not result in ownership, such as an airplane trip, a massage, or the preparation of a will.

Share of the Customer: The percentage (or share) of a customer's business that a particular firm has.

Shopping Centers: Groups of stores that are planned, developed, and managed as one entity.

Shopping Goods: Goods that consumers perceive as higher risk but for which they are willing to spend a greater amount of purchase effort to find and evaluate.

Simulated Test Marketing: Test marketing that simulates purchase environments in that target consumers are observed in the product related decision-making process.

Single Transaction: Buyer and seller interacting for the purpose of a single transaction.

Situational Influences: Influences that are attributed to the purchase situation.

Skimming: Pricing strategy whereby the product is priced higher than that of competitors.

Slotting Fees: Fees that retailers charge to stock manufacturers' brands.

Social Class: Relatively permanent divisions within society that exist in a status hierarchy, with the members of each division sharing similar values, attitudes, interests, and opinions.

Social Risk: The probability that a service will not meet with approval from others who are significant to the consumer making the purchase.

Societal Marketing Concept: A marketing philosophy that assumes the company will have an advantage over competitors if it applies the marketing concept in a manner that maximizes society's well-being.

Sociodemographic and Cultural Environment: A component of the macroenvironment that comprises elements such as demographics, subcultures, cultural values, and all other elements in the environment related to consumers' backgrounds, values, attitudes, interests, and behaviors.

Source: The organization that originates a marketing communication message.

Specialty Goods: Goods that reach the ultimate in differentiation and brand loyalty in that only the chosen brand is acceptable to the consumer.

Spiff Money: Monies or prizes awarded in trade contests.

Sponsored Content: A brand sponsors the content of a blogger or related Web site.

Sponsorship Marketing: Marketing that involves a company paying a fee that to an event, a person, or and organization in exchange for a direct association with that event, person or organization.

Stability: The extent to which preferences are stable, rather than changing, in a market segment.

Staples: Goods that are bought routinely, such as milk, cheese, bread, and soap.

Stars: High-share, high-growth products that create profits but require additional investment.

Status: The esteem which society bestows upon a particular role.

Stimuli: Cues in the environment, such as products and advertisements, that create individual responses.

Stimulus-response Sales Approach: Sometimes referred to as the canned sales approach, uses specific statements (stimuli) to solicit specific responses from customers.

Stock Turnover: The number of times a year that the inventory on hand is sold.

Strategic Partnership: Partnership in which the buyer and seller exchange information at the highest levels with the goal of collaboration.

Strivers: Psychographic group of individuals who are trendy and fun loving. They are concerned about others' opinions and approval, and demonstrate to peers their ability to buy.

Studies of Premiums, Coupons, and Deals: Studies that determine the appropriateness and effectiveness of premiums, coupons, and deals for a given target market.

Style: A general form of popular expression that could last for a longer period of time or that could be cyclical in nature.

Subcultures: Groups of individuals with shared value systems based on ethnicity or common background.

Substantiality: The extent to which the market is large enough to warrant investment.

Supercenters: Stores that carry an extensive food selection and drug products, as well as nonfood items (which account for at least 25 percent of sales), combining supermarket, discount, and warehouse retailing principles.

Superstores: Large retailers, such as combination stores or hypermarkets, that sell food, drugs, and other products.

Support Personnel: Individuals who directly support or assist in the selling function in some manner but do not process orders or directly solicit orders.

Survey Research: Descriptive research that involves the administration of personal, telephone, or mail questionnaires.

Survivors: Psychographic group of individuals who are concerned with safety and security. They focus on meeting needs rather than fulfilling desires, are brand loyal, and purchase discounted products.

Takeoff: Economic development stage in which growth becomes the norm, income rises, and leading sectors emerge.

Tangibles: The service provider's physical facilities, equipment, and appearance of its employees.

Target Market: Consumers or markets that are similar in aspects relevant to the company.

Target Marketing: The process of focusing on those segments that the company can serve most effectively and designing products, services, and marketing programs with these segments in mind.

Technical Service Quality: The outcome of the service.

Television Home Shopping: Retailing through cable channels selling to consumers in their homes, through infomercials, and by direct-response advertising shown on broadcast and cable television.

Terminal Values: Values related to goals.

Test Marketing: Evaluating product performance in select markets that are representative of the target market before launching the product.

Thinkers: Psychographic group of individuals who are educated, conservative, and practical consumers who value knowledge and responsibility. They look for durability, functionality, and value.

Tie-ins: Sales promotion of two or more goods or services within the same promotional offer.

Time Series and Econometric Methods: Methods that use the data of past performance to predict future market demand.

Time-loss Risk: The amount of time the consumer lost as a result of the failure of the service.

Trade Allowances: Some type of financial incentive to channel members to motivate them to make a purchase.

Trade Incentives: Some type of financial incentive that involves the retailer performing some type of function to receive a trade allowance.

Trade Promotions: Incentives directed toward channel members to encourage them to purchase, stock, or push a product through the channel.

Trademark: Words, symbols, marks, and signs that are legally registered for a single company's use.

Trading Companies: Complex marketing systems that specialize in providing intermediary service and reducing risk through extensive information channels and financial assistance.

Traditional Society: Economic development stage in which the economy is dominated by agriculture, minimal productivity, and low growth in per capita output.

Transitional Society: Economic development stage in which there is increased productivity in agriculture; manufacturing begins to emerge.

Trust Relationships: Buyer-seller dyads based on mutual respect and understanding of both parties and a commitment to work together.

Uncertainty: The probability that a particular outcome or consequence will occur.

Undifferentiated Marketing: A targeting strategy aiming the product at the market using a single strategy, regardless of the number of segments.

Unit Pricing: Pricing that allows consumers to compare among prices for different brands and for different package sizes of the different brands.

Upper-Middle-Income Countries: Countries with rapidly developing economies, and especially in urban areas, an infrastructure that is on par with that of developed countries. According to the World Bank, countries considered upper-middle-income countries have a gross national income per capita of $3,466 to $12,615 (U.S. dollars).

Usage Rate Segmentation: The process of segmenting markets based on the extent to which consumers are nonusers, occasional users, medium users, or heavy users of a product.

Use or Applications Positioning: The process of marketing a precise product application that differentiates it in consumers' minds from other products that have a more general use.

User Status Segmentation: The process of determining consumer status—as users of competitors' products, ex-users, potential users, first-time users, or regular users.

User: An individual member of the buying center who actually uses the product or is responsible for the product being used.

Validity: The extent to which data collected are free from bias.

Value Chain (or Supply Chain): The chain of activities performed in the process of developing, producing, marketing, delivering, and servicing a product for the benefit of the customer.

Value Delivery Chain: The participants involved in the value chain.

Value: The overall price given the quality of the product; perceived as important for the first purchase decision.

Value-based Philosophy: A philosophy that focuses on customers, ensuring that their needs are addressed in a manner that delivers a product of high quality and value, leading to consumer satisfaction.

Values: Important elements of culture defined as enduring beliefs about a specific mode of conduct or desirable end state.

Variability: The unwanted or random levels of service quality customers receive when they patronize a service.

Variable Costs: Costs, such as raw materials, packaging, and shipping costs, that vary with the amount of output.

Variable Pricing: Strategy of changing prices in response to changes in cost or demand.

Vending Machines: An interactive mode of retailing convenience goods.

Vertical Integration: The acquisition or merger with an intermediary in the channel that is either a supplier or a buyer.

Vertical Marketing Systems (VMS): Intermediary marketing systems that consist of manufacturers, wholesalers, and retailers in the same channel who have partial VMS ownership acting as a unified whole.

Viral Marketing: Preparing a marketing message to be passed from one consumer to another through digital venues or social media.

Wants: Needs that are directed at a particular product—for example, to meet the need for transportation, consumers may purchase an automobile or a bus ride.

Warehouse Clubs (or Wholesale Clubs): Stores that require members to pay an annual fee and that operate in low-overhead, warehouse-type facilities, offering limited lines of brand-name and dealer-brand groceries, apparel, appliances, and other goods at a substantial discount.

Warehousing: The marketing function whereby goods are stored, identified, and sorted in the process of transfer to an intermediary in the distribution channel or to the final consumer.

Wholesalers and Distributors: Intermediaries that purchase goods from a manufacturer for resale to other members of the channel.

Wholesaling: All the activities involved in buying and handling the goods intended for sale to resellers or other organizational users.

Widgets: Mini-applications embedded in a banner ad that permit a consumer access to some form of dynamic content provided by an external source other than the company where the ad resides.

Younger Boomers: A segment of individuals born between 1954 and 1964, whose focus is on family and home, who pay a large proportion of their income for mortgages, furnishings, pets, and children's toys.

Zoomers: A special subcategory of boomers whose lifestyles resemble those of individuals who are 20 years younger, who perform daily exercise, calculate daily nutritional and caloric needs, orchestrate a social support system, have a positive self-concept and a passion for living to the fullest, and acquire the resources necessary to live an adventurous life.

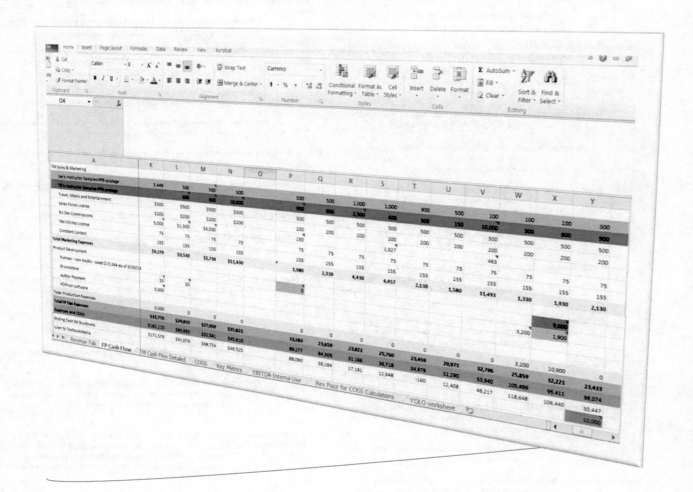

Communications Budget

Integrated Marketing Communications Budget

Developing a communication budget is difficult. It is challenging to identify the benefits and effectiveness of the various communication methods. Although the previous discussion provides companies with an idea of the relative amounts to be spent on each type of marketing communication, it does not provide much help in terms of determining the overall budget. For this task, firms use a variety of methods, such as:

- Objective and task
- Percentage of sales
- Historical
- Comparative parity
- Executive judgment
- All you can afford

Companies using the **objective-and-task method** first identify communication goals, such as target audience reach, awareness, comprehension, or even sales. Research is conducted to determine the cost of achieving the respective goals. Then the necessary sum is allocated based on the estimated cost to achieve each objective. This method is the most popular one used by multinational corporations in the process of deciding on their advertising budgets because it takes into consideration firms' strategies. Most marketing experts also see it as the best method because the budget is built on what it costs to achieve an objective.

The **percent-of-sales method** determines the total budget allocated to communication based on past or projected sales. This method is difficult to adopt for firms entering new markets or introducing a new product because no past sales data are available. The problem with this method is that it causes advertising expenditures to decline as sales decline; at this point, the company should increase advertising spending, not reduce it. This method is appropriate for stable markets where sales do not fluctuate considerably or where sales are slowly increasing and for firms with a long presence in a particular market. This method is used by almost half of the companies in stable international markets, with firms in Brazil and Hong Kong using it the most.

Firms using the **historical method** base the communication budget on past expenditures, usually giving more weight to recent expenditures. The percent-of-sales method often uses the historical method as a first step, if the percentage allocated to advertising is based on past, rather than on projected, sales. This method is not recommended for firms in an unstable economic, political, or competitive environment or where sales show wide fluctuation. It is based on the premise that past marketing expenditures have been sufficient to accomplish the firm's goals and that future expenditures should continue at the same level.

The **competitive-parity method** uses competitors' level of communication spending as benchmarks for a firm's own advertising expenditure. This approach is used in highly competitive markets to ensure that established firms maintain their market share. In the automobile industry, soft drink industry, and many other mature industries, firms spend about the same amount of money on marketing as their competitors. For firms entering a new market or a new industry, the method will indicate how much will have to be spent to be competitive. If a new soft drink company wants to compete on the same level as Coke and Pepsi, it will have to spend about the same amount, or more, to gain recognition. For brands that are not well established, this may be a dangerous strategy. The pay-off to reach the break-even point may take so long that a new brand can never be profitable. The more serious problem with this approach is that it suggests that a firm's goals and strategies are identical with those of competitors, which, most likely, is not the case.

In the **executive-judgment method**, executive opinion is used in determining the communication budget. This is based on the philosophy that executives know the industry, know what is happening with the com-petition, and most importantly, know the future strategic direction of the firm. The danger is that, unless these executives have a marketing background, the budget may not be grounded on a solid marketing foundation.

The last method is used by many small and medium-sized enterprises competing in markets with the large budget Fortune 500 corporations. The **all-you-can-afford method** best suits the financial limitations of these firms. Unfortunately, this approach completely ignores strategic issues and the competition. More seriously, when tough economic times hit, the marketing dollars are usually cut first. When this situation occurs, it creates a downward spiral that gains momentum over time. As communication budgets are cut, demand falls, causing another reduction in the communication budget, which, in turn, further reduces demand. In time, the company declares bankruptcy and wonders what happened to its customers.

Subject Index

Page numbers in italics indicate illustrations and captions, and *t* indicates tables.

Index of Companies,

Organizations,

and Products

Page numbers in italics indicate illustrations and captions, and *t* indicates tables.